THE COMPLETE WORKS OF
ST TERESA OF JESUS, III

Other titles in the *Classics of Spiritual Writing* series:

The Complete Works of St Teresa of Jesus, I,
trans. and ed. E. Allison Peers

The Complete Works of St Teresa of Jesus, III,
trans. and ed. E. Allison Peers

The Confessions of St Augustine,
trans. F. J. Sheed

The Rule of St Benedict,
trans. and ed. Abbot Justin
McCann, O.S.B.

THIS EDITION (SEVENTH IMPRESSION) FIRST PUBLISHED 1972
SHEED & WARD LTD,
33 MAIDEN LANE,
LONDON WC2E 7LA

© SHEED & WARD LTD

NIHIL OBSTAT: CANON GEORGE SMITH, D.D., PH.D., CENSOR
IMPRIMATUR: E. MORROGH BERNARD, V.G.
WESTMINSTER, 6 FEBRUARY 1946

PRINTED IN GREAT BRITAIN BY
REDWOOD PRESS LIMITED
TROWBRIDGE, WILTSHIRE

THE COMPLETE WORKS OF ST TERESA OF JESUS

VOLUME III

TRANSLATED AND EDITED BY

E. ALLISON PEERS

FROM THE CRITICAL EDITION OF

P. SILVERIO DE SANTA TERESA, C.D.

SHEED AND WARD – LONDON

CONTENTS OF VOLUME III

BOOK OF THE FOUNDATIONS

PAGE

INTRODUCTION xi

PROLOGUE xxi

CHAPTER I.—Of the ways in which this and the other foundations came
to be projected 1

CHAPTER II.—How our Father General came to Ávila and what resulted
from his visit 4

CHAPTER III.—How the negotiations began for the foundation of the
convent of Saint Joseph at Medina del Campo 7

CHAPTER IV.—Describes certain favours bestowed by the Lord on the nuns
in these convents and gives advice to prioresses as to their treatment of
them 15

CHAPTER V.—Gives certain counsels on matters concerning prayer and
revelations. This is very profitable for those engaged in occupations
belonging to the active life 19

CHAPTER VI.—Gives warning of the harm which may come to spiritual
people through their not knowing when the spirit is to be resisted. Treats
of the soul's desires to communicate. Deception which may arise here.
There are important things in this chapter for those who govern these
houses 26

CHAPTER VII.—How to treat nuns suffering from melancholy. This
chapter is necessary for superiors 36

CHAPTER VIII.—Gives certain advice concerning revelations and visions 40

CHAPTER IX.—Describes how she left Medina del Campo to make the
foundation of Saint Joseph at Malagón 44

CHAPTER X.—Describes the foundation of a house at Valladolid. This
convent is entitled the Conception of Our Lady of Carmel . . 46

CHAPTER XI.—Continues the subject already begun concerning Doña
Casilda de Padilla and how she achieved her holy desires to enter the
religious life 53

CHAPTER XII.—Describes the life and death of a nun whom Our Lord
brought to this same house, Beatriz de la Encarnación, who
lived so perfectly and died in such a way that it is right a memorial should be made
of her 57

CHAPTER XIII.—Describes how the first house for friars of the Primitive
Rule of the Discalced Carmelites was founded, in the year 1568, and
by whom 61

CHAPTER XIV.—Continues to describe the foundation of the first house PAGE for Discalced Carmelite friars. Says something of the life which they led, and of the benefits that Our Lord began to bestow upon them there, to the honour and glory of God 65

CHAPTER XV.—Describes the foundation of the convent of the glorious Saint Joseph in the city of Toledo, which took place in the year 1569 . 69

CHAPTER XVI.—Describes certain things which happened in this convent of Saint Joseph, Toledo, to the honour and glory of God. . . 76

CHAPTER XVII.—Describes the foundation of the monastery and the convent of Pastrana, which took place in the same year, 1570—I mean 1569 79

CHAPTER XVIII.—Describes the foundation of the convent of Saint Joseph, Salamanca, which took place in the year 1570. Gives certain important counsels to prioresses 86

CHAPTER XIX.—Continues to describe the foundation of the convent of Saint Joseph in the city of Salamanca 92

CHAPTER XX.—Describes the foundation of the convent of Our Lady of the Annunciation, Alba de Tormes, in the year 1571 . . 97

CHAPTER XXI.—Describes the foundation of the glorious Saint Joseph of Carmel, Segovia. This foundation was made on Saint Joseph's Day in the year 1574 104

CHAPTER XXII.—Describes the foundation of the glorious Saint Joseph of the Saviour in the town of Beas, made on Saint Matthias' Day in the 108 year 1575.

CHAPTER XXIII.—Describes the foundation of the convent of the glorious Saint Joseph of Carmel in the city of Seville. The first Mass was said here on the Feast of the Most Holy Trinity in the year 1575 . . 116

CHAPTER XXIV.—Continues to describe the foundation of Saint Joseph of Carmel in the city of Seville 122

CHAPTER XXV.—Continues to describe the foundation of the glorious Saint Joseph in Seville and of what happened when it had a house of its own 129

CHAPTER XXVI.—Continues to describe the same foundation of the convent of Saint Joseph in the city of Seville. Gives some information about the first nun who entered the house which is very noteworthy . 134

CHAPTER XXVII.—Describes the foundation made in the town of Caravaca. The Most Holy Sacrament was reserved here on New Year's Day in the same year, 1576. The dedication of the house is to the glorious Saint Joseph 140

CHAPTER XXVIII.—The foundation of Villanueva de la Jara . . 149

CHAPTER XXIX.—Describes the foundation of Saint Joseph of Our Lady of the Street, in Palencia, on the Feast of King David in the year 1580 . 165

CHAPTER XXX.—Describes the foundation of the convent of the Most Holy Trinity, in the city of Soria. This foundation was made in the year 1581. The first Mass was said on the Feast of our Father Saint Eliseus. 177

CONTENTS

CHAPTER XXXI.—This chapter begins to describe the foundation of the PAGE glorious Saint Joseph of Saint Anne in the city of Burgos. The first Mass was said here on the nineteenth day of April, in the Octave of Easter, 1582 183

MINOR PROSE WORKS

INTRODUCTION 207

CONSTITUTIONS WHICH THE MOTHER TERESA OF JESUS GAVE TO THE DISCALCED CARMELITE NUNS

Of the order to be observed in things spiritual . . . 219
On what days the Lord is to be received 220
Of things temporal 221
Of fasts 222
Of enclosure 223
Of the receiving of novices 224
Of the humble offices 225
Of sick nuns 226
Of the departed 228
Of the obligations of each nun in her office . . . 228
Of the Chapter for grave faults 231
Of slight faults 232
Of faults of medium gravity 233
Of grave faults 233
Of graver faults 234
Of the gravest faults 236

METHOD FOR THE VISITATION OF CONVENTS OF DISCALCED CARMELITE NUNS 239

MAXIMS of the Mother Teresa of Jesus, written for her nuns . . 256

ANSWER of Saint Teresa of Jesus to a spiritual challenge . . . 261

JUDGMENT given by Saint Teresa upon various writings on the words " Seek thyself in Me." 266

THOUGHTS AND MAXIMS of Saint Teresa of Jesus . . . 269

POEMS

TRANSLATOR'S INTRODUCTION 271

I.—I live, yet no true life I know. . . . (" Vivo sin vivir en mí. . . . ") . 277

II.—I am Thine, and born for Thee. . . . ("Vuestra soy, para Vos nací. . . .") 279

III.—I gave myself to Love Divine. . . . (" Yo toda me entregué y dí. . . . ") 282

IV.—God, if Thy love so great and high. . . . ("Si el amor que me tenéis. . . .") 282

V.—Happy the heart where love has come to birth. . . . (" Dichoso el corazón enamorado. . . . ") 283

VI.—O Loveliness, that dost exceed. . . . (" ¡ Oh Hermosura que ecedéis. . . . !") 283

CONTENTS

PAGE

VII.—Ah, my God, without Thee. . . . (" ¡ Cuán triste es, Dios mío . . .! ")   284

VIII.—Soul, thou must seek thyself in Me. . . . (" Alma, buscarte has en Mí. . . .")   287

IX.—Let nothing disturb thee. . . . (" Nada te turbe. . . .")   .   .   288

X.—Let us journey on to Heaven. . . . (" Caminemos para el cielo. . . .")   288

XI.—" Oh, shepherds, ye who watch your flocks. . . ." (" ¡ Ah, pastores que veláis . . .! ")   290

XII.—This day, to save our souls from death. . . . (" Hoy nos viene a redimir. . . .")   291

XIII.—" Since love has given us. . . . " (" Pues el amor. . . .")   .   292

XIV.—" My shepherd-boy, go, see who's calling. . . . " (" Mi gallejo, mira quién llama. . . .")   293

XV.—See, His blood He's shedding. . . . (" Vertiendo está sangre. . . .")   294

XVI.—Look, Gil, and see. . . . (" Este Niño viene llorando. . . .")   .   295

XVII.—See, it has stopped. . . . (" Pues que la estrella. . . .")   .   .   296

XVIII.—O Cross, my joy and happiness! . . . (" Cruz, descanso sabroso de mi vida. . . .")   297

XIX.—Through the Cross both happiness. . . . (" En la cruz está la vida. . . .")   298

XX.—Let us journey on to Heaven. . . . ("Caminemos para el cielo. . . .")   299

XXI.—If suffering for the sake of love. . . . (" ¿ Si el padecer con amor. . . .?")   300

XXII.—Since the world and all its friends. . . . (" Hoy ha vencido un guerrero. . . .")   301

XXIII.—O thou gentle lover. . . . (" O gran amadora. . . .")   .   302

XXIV.—" Maiden, who brought thee here . . ?" (" ¿ Quién os trajo acá, doncella. . . .? ")   304

XXV.—My sister, you are giv'n this veil. . . . (" Hermana, porque veléis. . . .")   304

XXVI.—Let my rejoicing be in tears. . . . (" Sea mi gozo en el llanto. . . .")   305

XXVII.—Oh, blessèd is this happy maid. . . . (" Oh, dichosa tal zagala. . . .")   307

XXVIII.—Oh, what unprecedented grace! . . . ("¡ Oh qué bien tan sin segundo . . .!")   308

XXIX.—All ye who with our Master fight. . . . (" Todos los que militáis. . . .")   309

XXX.—Since while still in prison. . . . (" Pues que nuestro Esposo. . . . ")   310

XXXI.—Since Thou giv'st us, King of Heaven. . . . (" Pues nos dais vestido nuevo. . . .")   311

CONTENTS

APPENDIX

DOCUMENTS ILLUSTRATIVE OF THE LIFE, WORKS AND PAGE
VIRTUES OF SAINT TERESA . . . . .

I.—Statement of P. Pedro Ibáñez on the spirit of Saint Teresa . . 313

II.—Report made by the Master Fray Domingo Báñez on the spirit of
Saint Teresa and on the autograph narrative of her life . . 333

III.—Address given by Saint Teresa to the nuns of the Convent of the
Incarnation, Ávila, when, in the year 1571, after having renounced the
Mitigated Rule, she went to that Convent as Superior . . 337

IV.—Virtues of our Mother Saint Teresa according to a report made by her
cousin the Venerable Mother María de San Jerónimo . . 338

V.—The last acts of the life of Saint Teresa. By the Venerable Ana de San
Bartolomé 352

VI.—Extracts from depositions taken from Sister Teresa de Jesús, the Saint's
niece. Ávila, 1596. 362

VII.—Letter from the Master Fray Luis de León to the Mother Prioress Ana
de Jesús and the Discalced Carmelite Nuns of the Convent at Madrid . 368

SELECT BIBLIOGRAPHY 379

INDICES

1. Subject-Index to the Works of St. Teresa 388
2. Index to the principal figures of speech and illustrations used by St. Teresa 393
3. Index to the Scriptural quotations and references made by St. Teresa . 398
4. Index to persons 400
5. Index to places 407

BOOK OF THE FOUNDATIONS

INTRODUCTION

St. Teresa's Divine fervour could not for long be contained within the narrow walls of St. Joseph's, Ávila. The love which seeks not its own cannot fail to communicate itself to others and both the saintly lives of those twelve nuns of hers and the ineffable peace which they enjoyed were destined to make themselves felt throughout the country.

Down to the present we have been following the course of St. Teresa's purely spiritual life, starting from her earliest years in the house of the austere Don Alonso de Cepeda and the boarding-school of Our Lady of Grace. We have witnessed the development of that generous heart, with its innate and intense love, and of that strong and vigorous character, which could never be satisfied by the casual, unambitious progress of so many a Christian. In her own inimitable way she opens her spiritual treasury to us in her *Life*, and still more widely and freely in the *Way of perfection* and the *Interior Castle*, the last of which, in particular, is a book written in letters of gold.

But Teresa of Ávila is not one of those saints whom we can fully understand by making an exact and detailed study of their interior lives: there are other points of view from which we must regard her if we are to appreciate her personality as a whole. So varied and so outstanding were her natural gifts, so manifold, extensive and continuous were her social relationships, that her character has countless delicate shades which baffle every effort of the investigator who seeks to classify and define them. Even were we entirely to disregard the part played by the supernatural in St. Teresa's life and personality, there is such inexhaustible wealth in them for the student of psychology that he finds the immortal Foundress one of the most interesting individuals who have ever lived.

The task of founding a series of Reformed convents, upon which she entered, with heroic intrepidity and apostolic zeal, undaunted by the formidable obstacles which a woman of such keen intelligence cannot have failed to foresee, at the mature age of fifty-two, gave her a magnificent opportunity to develop natural gifts which had hitherto lain dormant within her. Her valiant and vigorous personality had to face disapproval, unpopularity, jealousy, ridicule, disdain. She had to cope with physical trials which it is difficult for us now even to picture. She had to encourage and fortify her own companions while herself finding life none too easy. How well she did all this we learn from the faithful Julián de Ávila, who followed her wherever she went with unfailing loyalty. These, he writes of a trying journey from Beas to Seville,

These, and many other trials which presented themselves, we bore with the greatest joy, for the holy Mother encouraged us every one with her profitable and delightful conversation. Sometimes she would speak of the weightiest subjects; at other times she would say things for our entertainment; sometimes, again, she would make up verses, and very good ones, for she was most skilful at this, although she did it only when she found her material ready to hand. Given though she was, therefore, to prayer, it did not hinder our spiritual intercourse with her from being friendly and beneficial both to the soul and to the body.[1]

Close intimacy, then, and healthy fun were the rule in those motley little groups which travelled about Spain under the leadership of Mother Teresa. As she once told Ana de San Bartolomé, she disliked "gloomy people", and wanted to see no gloom in any of her own companions. At the same time she never allowed them to forget that they were on their Father's business. As they journeyed, writes M. Ana, "she would start conversations about God, and men who were accustomed to swear and quarrel on the road would prefer listening to them to any worldly pleasure: this I actually heard from their own mouths".[2] Not only did she teach her muleteers to moderate their language in her presence but she induced them to adapt their habits to the needs of her nomadic community. With the aid of strips of canvas she contrived to secure enclosure for her nuns and nobody was allowed to speak to them. As far as possible, the time-table of each day's journey was adjusted to that of convent life, with regard to prayer, self-examination, recitation of the Divine office and other acts prescribed by the Rule. While the nuns were engaged in these pious exercises the animated and talkative little group of drivers and muleteers would keep respectful silence, until the Mother gave the order which permitted conversation again and which they would receive with unconcealed satisfaction. It is to Ana de San Bartolomé, again, that we owe these details of the journeys:

---

[1] *Vida de Santa Teresa*, p. 285.   [2] P. Silverio, II, 301.

The order of proceedings was this. First of all, each day, they would hear Mass and communicate, and, however hurried they were, this was never omitted. There was always holy water and a little bell which, at the appointed hours, we rang for silence. And everyone knew that, as soon as it rang, they must all be quiet. There was a clock, to give us the hours for prayer; and, when the bell rang at the end of a period of prayer or silence, it was wonderful to see how delighted the men were at being able to speak again; and the Saint was always careful at these times to give them something to eat, as a reward for being so good in keeping silence.[1]

A longer account of these same journeys, written by P. Gracián,[2] who also frequently took part in them, describes the scenes at the inns or other lodgings where the travellers would spend their nights.

Generally she would be accompanied by three of us friars and by some laymen. Before we reached the inn, she would send one of her companions ahead of the rest to see about the rooms, asking preferably for large rooms, to take two or three persons each, so that they could all be near together. And he would have to tell the people to get everything ready so that the nuns should not need to ask for anything and the innkeepers should not have to go to their room. . . . They always went out veiled, and, if there was time, the first thing we did each day was to go to Mass, when the holy Mother would communicate. They would shut the door of their room at the inn and one of them would act as portress with as much circumspection as though they were in the convent. . . . When the rooms had no doors, the Mother would order us (i.e., the friars and laymen) to stand outside the entrance and see that nobody came near. In some places we could get no private room at all and then we would fetch some frieze blankets from the carriages so that they could have their privacy just the same. In the inns, on the roads and in the carriages the nuns always had their little bell and rang at the proper times for silence and prayer and the recitation of the Offices, just as if they were in their own convent. It was extraordinary to see how particular the Mother was about the provision of necessaries for those who accompanied her: she seemed to think of nothing else—she might have been going about on mules all her life.

<hr/>

[1] P. Silverio, II, 301.   [2] P. Silverio, V, xi–xii.

St. Teresa needed all her ingenuity to prevent her companions from getting fatigued by their journeys and abandoning her instead of following her happily and good-humouredly as they always did. Discomforts were numerous. There was snow and rain; there were icy winds and scorching suns; there were bad meals and dreadful roads. Inns in those days lacked not only comfort but cleanliness—a terrible mortification for St. Teresa— while nights spent in them were punctuated by noisy quarrels and fights often accompanied by bloodshed. María de San José describes a typical episode which occurred on a journey from Beas to Seville. It was Whitsuntide. They had reached an inn on the near side of Córdoba. St. Teresa was taken ill, with an alarmingly high temperature. The only room available "had, I think", narrates the writer, "previously been inhabited by pigs, and the ceiling was so low that we could hardly stand upright." The place was crawling with vermin: "we did what we could to improve matters"—but that was obviously not much. But most trying of all for the sick woman were the shouting and swearing of the men and the noise of the dancers and their musical instruments, which could be quelled "neither by en- treaties nor by gifts." In the end, they had to take her on in the blazing midday sun; and that night, rather than risk enduring a second inn like the first, they camped out in the fields.[1]

But all their experiences were not as disagreeable as these. What with the beauties of the landscape and the interior favours which they were so often granted, they found many consolations even during the journeys themselves. That very journey to Seville just referred to had its compensating moments. As the little procession sallied forth from Beas in mid-May, when the lovely Andalusian countryside is at its best, the Mother Foundress, familiar only with the endless dead levels of Castile and La Mancha, must have been lost in wonder. First came the mar- vellous panorama discernible from the Úbeda hills, with the blue- mantled Sierra Morena dominating the horizon. Then, as the sun grew stronger and the hour of the *siesta* drew near, the party halted in a shady, flower-strewn wood, near a tiny stream, in which innumerable birds poured out their songs of praise. St. Teresa, unable any longer to remain with her companions, went away a stone's throw from them to rejoice alone in all this beauty. "On the first day," María de San José tells us, "we reached a lovely piece of woodland, and we could hardly drag our holy Mother away from it, for all the various flowers and the

[1] *Libro de recreaciones*, p. 102. [Cit. P. Silverio, V, xiv. A second and not dissimilar episode follows.]

thousands of singing-birds seemed to be losing themselves in giving praise to God."[1]

The earliest journeys of the Mother Foundress were uneventful and tranquil. People gazed curiously and not always approvingly at the strange-looking little party and were shy of approaching it. Sometimes they spoke slightingly of it and Julián de Ávila, ever-loyal, would then be quick to defend St. Teresa from any such detraction. "It is like speaking ill of one who drinks great draughts of water," he writes, "through not knowing what it is to be thirsty."[2] But soon things altered. The fame of the Saint's virtues and good works spread far and wide and people no longer stood aloof but flocked to see her till the unwelcome publicity caused her more embarrassment than the earlier coldness and detraction. People of all ages and all social classes spoke of her with admiration. With well-born ladies like Doña Luisa de la Cerda and Doña María de Mendoza she could more than hold her own, her temperamental affability and courtesy mingling with an unaffected simplicity and bluntness which made her no less acceptable to the common people. It is difficult to imagine how pleasant a surprise it must have been to those simple, devout people of the sixteenth century when, instead of the unapproachable figure of mystery and marvel which they had supposed the great Carmelite Reformer to be, they found an ordinary plain-spoken, smiling woman, for all the world (as it seemed) like one of themselves. The pseudo-mystics of the day were notorious, with their ashen-pale countenances, their hands showing the marks of the stigmata, their fierce contortions and their periodical swoons. Nothing like that here! When Mother Teresa met a group of villagers, her talk with them would be of market prices and the progress of the crops. We have some animated descriptions of the effects which she produced upon humble people. Her popularity, once she became known, would have no limits. On one occasion, Julián de Ávila tells us, the entire village of Beas came out to meet her and some villagers on horseback rode on ahead of the rest and led her back in procession. A journey which she made from Malagón to Villanueva de la Jara is described by Ana de San Bartolomé as a succession of boisterous welcomes as she went from one village to another, the streets of which were so crowded that there was no room to turn. In villages of La Mancha and Andalusia, stories of her visits are still current—exaggerated, embroidered and deformed, no doubt, but clearly testifying to the remarkable impression which she had made nearly four centuries earlier. The people of Spain recognized that she epitomized to perfection characteristic Spanish

[1] *Op. cit., loc. cit.*   [2] *Vida de Santa Teresa,* p. 270.

virtues and they showed their appreciation of the fact in their own traditional and hearty way.

All this and more we may gather from a number of contemporary writers but we shall learn most from a narrative more interesting than any of these—that of St. Teresa herself. P. García de Toledo, as we have seen, had ordered her to write the account of her first foundation—St. Joseph's, Ávila: the hardest and most trying, just because it was the first—and, as at that time she had apparently not thought of making any more, she intercalated the five chapters which describe the experiment in the latter part of her autobiography. When in 1567 she made her second foundation at Medina del Campo, she wrote nothing about the trials which she had had to endure before completing it, nor about any of her later experiences of the same kind down to the year 1570, when one day, after Communion, she learned from the Lord that it was His will she should write an account of all her foundations one after another.[1] She did not set to work on this, however, until the instruction was confirmed by the authority of one of her confessors, who assured her of the genuineness of what she had heard. It was in August 1573, when she was making arrangements for a projected foundation at Salamanca, that her confessor there, P. Jerónimo Ripalda, instructed her to write a history of all her foundations down to that time, as she herself tells us in her preface.

Before leaving Salamanca for her Segovian foundation she had completed nine chapters.[2] After that time, to judge from her own statement in Chapter XXVII, she had apparently very little leisure for writing more and not a great deal of inclination. P. Gracián, however, took up the matter with her, told her she must finish the book, and, when she pleaded lack of time and physical weariness, said she could do the work little by little, or in any way she liked ("poco a poco, u como pudiese"). This disposed of her objections, and, as a result, twenty-seven chapters were written by November 14, 1576.[3]

At this time St. Teresa was at Toledo, and, both in health and in energy (to quote her own words), "better, I think, than I

---

[1] *Relations*, IX (Vol. I, p. 339, above.)

[2] The Bollandists (*Acta S. Teresiae a Jesu*, p. 345) and La Fuente (*Escritos de Santa Teresa*, I, 176) affirm, without citing evidence, that she wrote twenty chapters at Salamanca. They omit to notice, however, that in her account of the Valladolid foundation (Chap. X) she refers to events which happened later than 1573 and that in Chap. XIII she gives the number of foundations of the Reform as ten, which number was not attained till 1575.

[3] [See penultimate paragraph (p. 148) of that chapter.]

have been for years."[1] It was apparently in July 1576 that
Gracián had laid this task upon her, for she tells her brother about
it on the twenty-fourth of that month, and asks him, as he is in
Ávila, to get and send her the manuscript of the part of the
Foundations which she has already written, together with some
other papers that she will need in order to write the rest.[2] She
did not begin writing, however, until October, for on the fifth
of that month she wrote to Gracián: "Now I shall begin the
matter of the foundations."[3] The account of the Alba foundation[4]
had apparently already been written, as it is one of the papers
which she asks her brother to bring her; further, she speaks in it
of Don Francisco de Velázquez as though he were still alive,
whereas actually he had died in 1574. But the writing of the
remaining chapters in hardly more than five weeks was a considerable feat to one whose other occupations were so numerous
and exacting.

Between 1576 and 1580 the persecution of the Discalced
Reform by the friars of the Observance interrupted the series
of foundations and it is probable that each of the accounts
of the last four of these (1580–2) was written at the time
when the foundation was made. Of the last of all—that
of Burgos—this was certainly the case, as we may infer from
its length and from internal evidence:[5] external proof is to
be found in a deposition by Don Antonio Aguiar in the
Canonization Process.[6]

Such, so far as we can trace it, is the history of this particularly
charming book, with its simple, fresh and animated narrative,
its ingenuous regard for the exact truth and its no less ingenuous
admission of occasional inaccuracies. If it were perfect from
the literary point of view it would be less attractive than it is,
but at least we can say that its author's excuses for her presumed
sins of omission and commission are uncalled-for. Only rarely
does she omit any fact of importance and never does she give
a single detail which her readers could spare—indeed, as we read
her delightfully human narrative we are disposed to wish that
she had lingered over each foundation longer than she did.

The General Introduction has described how, in 1592, by order
of King Philip II, P. Doria asked the Valladolid professor, Don
Francisco Sobrino, for the autograph of the *Foundations,* so that

---

[1] Letter to Don Lorenzo de Cepeda (July 24, 1576).
[2] *Ibid.*
[3] Letter to P. Gracián (October 5, 1576).
[4] Chap. XX.
[5] Cf. pp. 191, n. 2, 204, n. 3, below.
[6] [Cit. P. Silverio, V, xxi–xxii.]

it might be sent to the new royal library of El Escorial. On
August 18, the manuscript was duly delivered to Don García
de Loaysa, later Primate of Spain, who in turn presented it to
Fray Diego de Yepes, Prior of the Escorial Hieronymites. In
many respects it is similar to the autograph of the *Life*, and,
like it, has marginal additions, glosses and a few emendations
in the hand of P. Gracián: these occur chiefly in the first seven
chapters. Later, P. Báñez scored out a great many of the glosses
and emendations, and restored the original readings, much as
P. Ribera did with the *Interior Castle*.[1] Most of the emendations
which P. Báñez left, such as those in Chapter V, were adopted
by the editors as though they had been made by the author.

St. Teresa herself gave the book no title, though on the first
page of the autograph one of the Escorial librarians has written:
"Original Book of the Foundations of her Reform made in Spain
by the glorious Virgin, Saint Teresa of Jesus, written by her
hand. . . ." But the division into chapters is hers, as are the
summaries of each chapter, save that of Chapter XII, which is
from the pen of the nun who wrote the titles to the Escorial
manuscript of the *Way of perfection*.[2] After completing what we
may call the "second period" of her work with the account of the
foundation at Caravaca (Chapter XXVII), she wrote the
accounts of the remaining four in separate *cuadernos*. On the last
sheet appears an account, in her hand, of the transference of the
jurisdiction of St. Joseph's, Ávila from the Ordinary to the
Carmelite Order, which took place in 1577.

The autograph is in a perfect state of preservation; several
of its chapters show signs of having been frequently read. The
hand is still clear, but has lost some of its original firmness, and
in the last chapters there are clear signs of weakness and age.
The fact that there are more slips of the pen and similar errors
in this than in her other autographs may be due to the haste with
which parts of the book were written.

A number of early copies are still extant. One of the first
was made by Don Pedro Manso, nephew of the Saint's confessor
Dr. Manso, who helped her in the last of her foundations and made
the famous remark that she was worse to argue with than any
number of theologians. A second copy, made for the Valladolid
Carmelites by Dr. Sobrino before he parted with the autograph
in 1592, was lost in the disturbances of 1835. A sixteenth-century
copy, already referred to as containing some of the Relations,[3]
is in the possession of the Discalced Carmelite nuns of Toledo.
The Royal Academy of History has a copy, prepared, with a

[1] Cf. Vol. II, pp. 194–5, above.   [2] Vol. II p. xvii, above.
[3] Vol. I, p. 304, above.

view to a new edition, by order of P. Ribera (but not actually made by him): this, like various other copies, omits the story of Casilda de Padilla, which occupies Chapter XI and part of Chapter X, no doubt by command from authority, which probably considered the Saint's frankness concerning a member of an aristocratic family undesirable. As will be easily understood, many of the convents referred to in the *Foundations* wished to have copies of the book before it became available in printed form and we know of the earlier existence of a great many more which have long been lost.

Most critics have explained the omission of the *Foundations* from the *editio princeps* of St. Teresa's *Works* by the fact that many of the persons mentioned in the book were still living. This was still true, however, when the first edition of the *Foundations* appeared in Brussels in 1610 and it seems more probable that responsibility for the omission is to be attributed to Fray Luis de León. Its publication in 1610 was largely due to M. Ana de Jesús, who was tireless in promoting the publication of St. Teresa's works in France and the Low Countries. She was aided by P. Gracián, who at that time lived in Flanders, though he had some scruples about it, as he explained in a letter to his sister, "on account of some foolish things (*boberías*) which she says about me concerning the foundation at Seville."[1]

The edition is entitled: *Book of the Foundations of the Discalced Carmelite Sisters, written by the Mother Foundress Teresa of Jesus.* It suppresses the Padilla story: as the lady was not only still alive but had passed from the Carmelite to the Franciscan Order, it would not be solely on her account that the story of her youthful determination to become a Carmelite nun was omitted. Only in mid-eighteenth century was it allowed to appear.

Both this edition and that of 1623, published at Saragossa, contain numerous variants and errata—the latter has even more than the former. In 1645 the Superiors of the Discalced arranged for P. Antonio de la Madre de Dios to set about preparing a dependable edition from the autograph. The results of this work, in which P. Antonio had the collaboration of two Hieronymites from El Escorial, appeared in the edition of St. Teresa's works published in 1661. Though better than any previous edition of the *Foundations*, this retained most of the additions and emendations made by P. Gracián and not deleted by P. Báñez, and no succeeding edition has been much better, that of La Fuente not excepted. [P. Silverio was the first to give St. Teresa's text as nearly as possible in the state in which she left it, relegating

---

[1] Cit. P. Silverio, V, xlii. She uses the same playful word to him about the writings in her letter to him of October 5, 1576 (p. xvii, above).

the whole of Gracián's emendations to footnotes. This, wherever they are of a kind which it is possible to adopt in a translation, has also been done in the pages which follow. P. Silverio adds ample historical notes, which have here been abbreviated even more than his notes to St. Teresa's writings. Few readers of this translation, other than those able to read Spanish with ease, will require anything beyond these comparatively brief indications.]

BOOK OF THE FOUNDATIONS OF SAINT TERESA OF JESUS, WRITTEN BY HERSELF[1]

PROLOGUE

JESUS

I have found by experience, quite apart from what I have read in many places, how great a blessing it is for a soul not to swerve from obedience. Herein, I believe, consists progress in virtue and the gradual acquisition of humility, while it also affords us security against doubts (which it is well for us mortals to have while we are living this life) as to whether we are straying from the road to Heaven. Herein is to be found tranquillity, which is so greatly prized by souls desirous of pleasing God. For if they have truly resigned themselves to this holy obedience, and surrendered their understanding to it, and are willing to follow no other opinion than their confessor's (and, if they are monks or nuns, their superior's), the devil ceases to attack them by continually unsettling them, for he sees that he is losing rather than gaining. Our unruly impulses, too, so fond of getting their own way, and even of mastering the reason where it is a question of things which can give us pleasure, come to an end, and we remember that we have resolutely surrendered our wills to the will of God, by subjecting ourselves to him whom we obey in His place. Since His Majesty, of His goodness, has given me light to recognize the greatness of the treasure hidden in this precious virtue, I have striven, however feebly and imperfectly, to possess it, though I am often discouraged in the task by the lack of virtue which I find in myself, for I realize that, for some of the things which I am commanded to do, I need more of it. May the Divine Majesty supply what is lacking for this work which I am now beginning.

In the year 1562, when I was in the Convent of Saint Joseph, at Ávila, which had been founded in that very year, I was commanded by the Dominican Father Fray García de Toledo,[2] who at the time was my confessor, to write an account of the foundation of that convent, and also of many other things, as anyone who reads the book, if it is ever published, will see. It is now eleven years later, and I am in Salamanca, in this year

---

[1] The title is not original.   [2] Cf. Vol. I, p. 3, above.

1573, and my confessor, the Father Rector of the Company, Master Ripalda by name,[1] has seen this book which describes my first foundation, and has thought that it would be a service to Our Lord if I were to write about seven other religious houses which, by the goodness of Our Lord, have been founded since that time, and also about the beginnings of the monasteries of the Discalced Fathers of the Primitive Rule. So he has commanded me to do this.[2] I have so much to do—letter-writing and other occupations which I am bound to undertake because they are done in obedience to my superior's orders—that I thought at first it would be an impossibility. But while I was commending myself to God, somewhat depressed because I was of so little use and so weak in health that, even without this new command, I often thought my constitution would never endure the work I had to do, the Lord said to me: "Daughter, obedience gives strength."

May it please His Majesty to make this true, and may He grant me grace to enable me to relate, to His glory, the favours which He has bestowed upon this Order through these foundations. It may be taken for granted that everything will be related quite truthfully, without any exaggeration, to the best of my knowledge, exactly as it happened. For even in a matter of the smallest importance I would not lie for anything on this earth; and if I were to do so in a thing which I am writing so that Our Lord may be praised, it would weigh heavily on my conscience and I should think I was not only wasting time but deceiving my readers as to the things of God, and in that case, instead of being praised on their account, He would be offended. To lie, therefore, would be to betray Him. May it please His Majesty not to forsake me, lest I do this. Each of the foundations will be mentioned, and I shall try, if I can, to write briefly; for my style is so heavy that even against my will I fear I shall be unable to avoid wearying others and myself. But my daughters, to whom this will be given when my days are ended, will be able to bear with it out of their love for me.

As I am seeking no kind of advantage for myself, and have no reason to do so, since I seek His praise and glory (and it will be seen that there are many occasions for this), may it please Our Lord that my readers be very far from attributing any such thing to me, for to do so would be contrary to the truth. Let

---

[1] Cf. Vol. I, pp. 6, 320, above.

[2] St. Teresa is clearly trying to link up this first chapter with Chaps. XXXII to XXXVI of her *Life*, which would more properly come here but were no doubt given the place they actually have because she had then no intention of making any other foundations than St. Joseph's, Ávila. In the 1623 edition of her works, these chapters were printed at the beginning of the *Foundations*.

them beg His Majesty to forgive me for having made so little use of all these favours. You have much more reason, daughters, to complain of me in this regard than to thank me for what I have done. Let us all give thinks to the Divine Goodness, my daughters, for all the favours He has granted us. For His love, I beg every reader for one Ave Maria, to help me out of purgatory and toward the vision of Jesus Christ, Our Lord, Who liveth and reigneth with the Father and the Holy Spirit for evermore. Amen.

As I have a poor memory, I expect many very important things will be omitted, and others will be put in which might well be left out: just as might be expected, in fact, of one with my witlessness and stupidity and also with so little quiet time for writing. I am also bidden, if the occasion presents itself, to say something about prayer and about the mistakes which those who practise it may make, with the result that they fail to press onward. In everything I submit to the doctrine of my Mother, the Holy Roman Church,[1] and I have resolved that before this reaches your hands, my sisters and daughters, it shall be seen by learned and spiritual men. I begin in the name of the Lord, invoking the aid of His glorious Mother, whose habit, though unworthily, I wear, and of my glorious Father and lord Saint Joseph, in whose house I am, for this convent of Discalced nuns is named after him and I have been continually helped by his prayers.

In the year 1573, on the day of Saint Louis, King of France, being the twenty-fourth day of August.

PRAISED BE GOD!

---

[1] The word " Roman " was added by St. Teresa in the margin, as also in the introduction and the epilogue to the *Interior Castle* (Vol. II, pp. 200, 351, above). Was this due to the suggestion of some theologian who read the two manuscripts?

HERE BEGINNETH THE FOUNDATION OF SAINT JOSEPH OF THE CARMEL OF MEDINA DEL CAMPO

CHAPTER I

Of the ways in which this and the other foundations came to be projected.

I was still in the house of Saint Joseph of Ávila five years after its foundation, and, as I now believe, those were the most restful years of my life, the calm and quiet of which my soul often sorely misses. During this time there entered it, as religious, several girls who were quite young and whom the world seemed already to have claimed for its own, to judge by their showiness and curiosity. But the Lord very quickly freed them from these vanities, drew them into His household and endowed them with a perfection that quite confounded me. Our numbers rose to thirteen, which is the figure I had resolved we would not exceed.[1]

I was very happy among such holy and pure souls, whose only care was to serve and praise Our Lord. His Majesty sent us whatever we needed without our asking for it, and when we lacked anything, which was very seldom, they would rejoice all the more. I would praise Our Lord when I saw so many sublime virtues, and especially when I found how little the nuns cared about anything save His service. I, who was superior[2] there, never remember giving a thought to our needs, for I was convinced that the Lord would not fail those who had no other anxiety than how to please Him. And if occasionally there was not sufficient sustenance for us all, I had only to say that what there was must go to those who most needed it and each would think she had no such need, so that everything was all right until God sent enough for us all.

Then there was the virtue of obedience, to which I am most devoted, though I knew nothing of how to practise it until these servants of God showed me so clearly that I could not have remained ignorant if there had been any virtue in me at all. In this connection I could tell of many things which I observed

---

[1] As we have already seen (Vol. I, p. 260, n. 2, above) St. Teresa later increased the number. [P. Silverio, V, 7, n., gives the names of the first nuns, with the dates of their professions.] There were at first no lay sisters and the nuns took it in turns to do the housework and cooking.

[2] The Spanish word is not *superiora*, but *mayor* (" senior ", " elder "): this was the word commonly used among the Carmelites, and in some other religious Orders, to designate the superior of a community.

in that convent. One of them occurs to me now, which is this. One day, in the refectory, they gave us portions of cucumber, and mine was a very small one and rotten inside. I called a sister quietly—one of the most intelligent and gifted we had—and, in order to test her obedience, told her to go to her little garden—we each had a garden—and plant the cucumber there. She asked me if she was to plant it upright or sideways. I told her sideways. So she went and planted it, without its ever occurring to her that it could not possibly do anything but shrivel up. The fact that she was acting under obedience blinded[1] her natural reason and made her believe that she was doing quite a normal thing.[2]

By chance, again, I gave a nun six or seven things to do which were inconsistent with one another; and she said nothing, but set to work, thinking it would be possible for her to perform them all. There was a well in the convent, the water in which, according to the report of those who had tested it, was very bad, and it was so deep that it seemed impossible that the water would ever flow. I sent for workmen to see what they could do about it and they laughed at me and said I was trying to throw money away. I asked the sisters what they thought about it. "Try it," said one. "Our Lord will have to find us someone to bring us water and give us food; and it will be much cheaper for His Majesty to get it here, from this house, so He will not fail to do it." I noted the great faith and confidence with which she said this and was convinced she was right; and against the advice of the expert, who knew all about water, I had the work done. And the Lord was pleased, so that we got a flow of water which was quite sufficient for us, and good to drink, and we have it still.[3]

I do not relate this because I think it a miracle—I could tell of other such things too—but to illustrate the faith which these sisters had, for everything happened just as I say, and my primary intention is not to praise the nuns in these convents, for so far, by the goodness of the Lord, they have all walked in this way. It would be a very long business to write about these things, and many others, though it would not be unprofitable, for sometimes such descriptions encourage those who come after them to imitate them. However, if the Lord wills that they should be known, the superiors can order the prioresses to write about them.

---

[1] P. Gracián altered *cegó* [" blinded "] to *captivó* [" took prisoner "] and added, after " reason ", " in the service of Christ."

[2] The nun referred to here was María Bautista (Ocampo), the Saint's niece, later Prioress of the Discalced community at Valladolid.

[3] The well is in existence to this day, though it is now no longer used except for the garden. It is known as the " Samaritan woman's well " or " María Bautista's well ". Tradition says that it was María Bautista who gave the advice quoted in the text and that the Bishop of Ávila, Don Álvaro de Mendoza, came himself and tried the water before it was generally used.

This miserable sinner, then, was living[1] among these angelic souls—and they seemed to me to be nothing less, for they concealed none of their faults from me, however interior, while the Lord granted them an abundance of favours, lofty desires and detachment. Their consolation was solitude; and they used to assure me that they never tired of being alone: the thought that anyone might come to see them, even their brothers or sisters, was a torment to them. The sister who had the most opportunities of remaining alone in a hermitage counted herself the happiest. When I reflected on the great worth of these souls and the more than woman-like courage which God was giving them to suffer and to serve Him, I would often think that it must be with some great aim in view that the Lord was giving them these riches, though what has since happened never entered my mind, for at that time such a thing seemed impossible because there was no basis for imagining it. As time went on, my desires to do something for the good of some soul grew greater and greater, and I often felt like one who has a large amount of treasure in her charge and would like everyone to enjoy it but whose hands are tied so that she cannot distribute it. In just this way it seemed to me that my soul was bound; for the favours which the Lord granted it during those years were very great and they all seemed to be ill spent upon me. But I served the Lord with my poor prayers; and I always persuaded the sisters to do the same and to be zealous for the good of souls and the increase of His Church. Thus all who had to do with them were invariably edified, and in this my great desires found satisfaction.

After four years, or, I think, a little more, it chanced that there came to see me a Franciscan friar, called Fray Alonso Maldonado, a great servant of God, who had the same desires as I for the good of souls—only he was able to put his into practice, for which reason I greatly envied him. He had only a little while previously returned from the Indies.[2] He began to tell me about the many millions of souls perishing there for lack of teaching, and, before going away, he gave us a sermon and a talk inciting us to penitence. I was so distressed at the way all these souls were being lost that I could not contain myself. I went to one of the hermitages,[3] weeping sorely, and called upon Our Lord, beseeching Him to find me a means of gaining some soul for His service when so many were being carried away by the devil. I begged

---

[1] Gracián alters this to: "I was living, then."

[2] Alonso Maldonado, a very eloquent preacher, had been Commissary-General of the Western Indies.

[3] St. Teresa had had some hermitages built in the garden of St. Joseph's, to give the nuns opportunity for solitude. Cf. *Life*, Chap. XXXVIII (Vol. I, p. 270, n. 2, above).

Him that my prayers might be of some avail, since I had nothing else to give. How I envied those who could spend their lives ministering to others for the love of Our Lord, even though they might suffer a thousand deaths! Whenever I read in the lives of saints of how they converted souls, I seem to feel much more devout, tender and envious of them than when I read of all the martyrdoms that they suffered. This is an inclination given me by Our Lord; and I think He prizes one soul which by His mercy, and through our diligence and prayer, we may have gained for Him, more than all the other services we can render Him.

While suffering this terrible distress, I was praying one night when Our Lord appeared to me in His usual way, and said to me very lovingly, as if He wished to bring me comfort: "Wait a little, daughter, and thou shalt see great things." These words remained so firmly fixed in my heart that I could not forget them. However much I thought about them, I could not discover what they meant, or see any possible way of imagining it; nevertheless I was greatly comforted and completely persuaded that the words would prove true. But there never occurred to my imagination any method by which they could become so.

In this way went by, I should say, another six months, after which there happened the event that I shall now describe.

CHAPTER II

How our Father General came to Ávila and what resulted from his visit.

Our Generals always reside in Rome and none of them had ever visited Spain,[1] so it seemed quite impossible that one should do so. But nothing is impossible if Our Lord wills it, and His Majesty ordained that what had never happened before should happen now. I believe, when I heard of it, I was troubled; because, as has already been said with regard to the foundation of Saint Joseph's, that house was not subject to the friars, for the reason then given.[2] I was afraid of two things: first, that the General might be angry with me, and, if he did not know how these things had happened, his anger would be justified; secondly, that he might make me go back to the Convent of the Incarna-

---

[1] By Spain must here be meant Castile, for a number of Generals are known to have visited Catalonia and Aragon [which were, of course, the parts of the Peninsula most easily accessible from Italy].

[2] Cf. *Life*, Chaps. XXXII, XXXIII (Vol. I, pp. 224, 231–2, above).

tion, which belongs to the Mitigated Rule, and, for many reasons which there is no need to enumerate, that would have been a disappointment to me. It will suffice to mention one of these reasons—namely, that I could not have kept the Primitive Rule at all strictly, for there were more than one hundred and fifty nuns in the convent and there is always more concord and tranquillity where numbers are few. Our Lord arranged everything better than I had expected; for the General is such a servant of His, and so discreet and learned, that he regarded the work as good, and, for the rest, showed me not the least displeasure. His name is Fray Juan Bautista Rubeo de Revena,[1] a most outstanding person in the Order, and very rightly so.

When he reached Ávila, I arranged for him to come to Saint Joseph's and the Bishop was pleased that he should be shown all the respect which was paid to his own person. I told him my story quite truthfully and simply, for, whatever the consequences, I am always inclined to deal in that way with prelates, as they are in the place of God, and also with confessors, for otherwise I should not think my soul was safe. And so I told him about my soul, and about almost the whole of my life, wicked as it has been. He comforted me greatly and assured me that he would not order me to leave.

He was glad when he saw our way of life; for it gave him a picture, however imperfect, of our Order as it had been in its early days; and he was able to observe how we were keeping the Primitive Rule in all its strictness—there was not another house in the whole Order where this was kept[2]: the Mitigated Rule is followed everywhere. And being willing, as he was, that we should continue what we had begun, he gave me complete patents for the foundation of more houses,[3] and also added

---

[1] Fra Giovanni Battista Rossi (the surname is here latinized as Rubeo) (1507-1578) was born at Ravenna, entered the Carmelite Order at seventeen, studied at Siena and Padua and became a Professor at the University of Rome. He was elected General of the Order in 1564. Philip II of Spain, who was interested in the reform of the Orders, obtained from Pius V a Brief (dated February 24, 1566) ordering P. Rubeo to visit that country. He arrived on May 13 and was received by the King in June. He then went south, held a Provincial Chapter at Seville in September, went on to Lisbon in November and in February 1567 started from Salamanca on a visitation of the Province of Castile. He came to Ávila on April 11, 1567, stayed a month and held a Provincial Chapter, at which P. Alonso González was named Provincial of Castile and P. Ángel de Salazar Prior of the house at Ávila. He finally visited Valencia and Barcelona, leaving Spain in the late summer.

[2] There were, in fact, at least two others: the monastery of Mount Olivet, near Genoa, and that of Our Lady of Hope, at Onda, near Castellón de la Plana.

[3] The first, dated in Ávila, April 27, 1567, authorizes the foundation of new houses, to be subject to the jurisdiction of the Order, not more than twenty-five nuns to live in the same house: two may be transferred to each from the Incarnation. The second, dated in Madrid, May 16, 1567, limits the new foundations to Old and New Castile.

censures, so that no Provincial should be able to stop me. I did not ask for these, but he realized from my manner of prayer that I had fervent desires to help souls come nearer to God.

I did not seek these things[1] for myself; it seemed to me foolish to do so, for I saw clearly that a poor woman[2] such as I, entirely without influence, could do nothing. But when these desires come to the soul it is impossible to drive them away. Faith and the love of pleasing God make possible what according to natural reason is not so; and thus, when I found how desirous our most reverend General was that more religious houses should be founded, I thought I saw them already built. Remembering the words which Our Lord had addressed to me, I now began to foresee a start being made with things I had not previously been able to envisage at all. I was very sorry when I saw our Father General returning to Rome; I had conceived a great love for him and felt very much deserted when he left. He showed me very real and genuine kindness: whenever he could be free he would come here to talk of spiritual things, and, as he was one to whom the Lord must have granted great favours, it made us very happy to hear him on this subject. But, before he left, the Bishop, Don Álvaro de Mendoza, who is very fond of helping those whom he sees trying to serve God in greater perfection, obtained a licence for the foundation in his diocese of a few monasteries for Discalced friars of the Primitive Rule. Others also asked him for the same thing. He would have liked to give it them, but he found that there was opposition in the Order, and so, lest he should set the province at variance, he refrained for the time being.

After some days, I began to think how necessary it was, if convents for women were to be founded, that there should be friars following the same Rule, and, seeing how few there were in this province—it even seemed to me that they were dying out—I commended the matter earnestly to Our Lord, and wrote a letter to our Father General, begging him as well as I could to grant this permission, explaining the reasons why it would be a great service to God, suggesting that the inconveniences which it might cause were not sufficient to hinder so good a work and representing to him what a service it would be to Our Lady, to whom he was most devoted. It must have been she who brought it about, for this letter of mine reached him when he was in

---

[1] [*Lit.*: " means "; but that word was evidently an afterthought, for] it has been written by St. Teresa between the lines of her manuscript. [The reference is to the " these " (i.e. patents and censures) just above.]

[2] [*Lit.*: *mujercilla*, " little woman ", the diminutive suffix having a depreciatory force.]

Valencia,[1] from which city he sent me a licence for the foundation of two monasteries, as might have been expected of one who desired the strictest observance of the Rule in the Order. Lest there should be opposition, he sent the licence to the then Provincial and also to his predecessor, whom it was extremely difficult to convince. But seeing that the most important thing had been done, I was hopeful that the Lord would perform the rest; and in the end, with the help of the Bishop, who took a real and personal interest in the matter, they both gave their consent.

Though I was now relieved at having obtained the licences, my anxiety only grew greater, for, as far as I knew, there was not a friar in the province to put them into effect, nor any secular person who would make the necessary beginning. So I besought Our Lord continually that He would raise up at least one such person. Further, I had no house, or any means of obtaining one. Here was a poor Discalced nun, without help from anywhere, except from the Lord, loaded with patents and good wishes but devoid of all possibility of making them effective. But I was not devoid either of courage or of hope: as the Lord had given me the one thing, He would give the other as well. Everything seemed to me quite possible now and so I set to work.

Oh, greatness of God! How dost Thou show forth Thy power in giving such boldness to a mere ant! It is not Thou that art to blame, my Lord, if those who love Thee do no great deeds; it is our weak-mindedness and cowardice. It is because we never make firm resolutions but are filled with a thousand fears and scruples arising from human prudence, that Thou, my God, workest not Thy marvels and wonders. Who loves more than Thou to give, if Thou hast anyone that will receive, or to accept services performed at our own cost? May Thy Majesty grant me to have rendered Thee some service and to care about nothing save returning to Thee some part of all I have received. Amen.

CHAPTER III

How the negotiations began for the foundation of the convent of Saint Joseph at Medina del Campo.

Occupied as I was with all these anxieties, I determined to seek the help of the Fathers of the Company, who were thought

---

[1] Actually the General was in Barcelona: he had gone there at the end of July 1567 and stayed for six weeks. The patent for the foundation of two reformed monasteries is dated from Barcelona, August 14, 1567.

a great deal of in that place—that is, in Medina. As I said in writing of my first foundation, I had for many years been in touch with them on spiritual matters, and they had done me so much good that I am always particularly devoted to them.[1] I wrote to the Rector there, and told him what our Father General had commanded me: he happened for a great many years to have been my confessor, as I have said, though I did not then give his name, which was Baltasar Álvarez;[2] he is now Provincial. He and the others said they would do what they could in the matter and they did a great deal to obtain the consent of the town, and of the prelate, which is always difficult when a monastery is to be founded in poverty. So the negotiations took some days.[3]

In order to further them a cleric went there, who was a great servant of God, greatly detached from all worldly things and much given to prayer. He was chaplain in the convent where I was living and the Lord had given him the same desires as He had given me, and so he has helped me greatly, as will be seen later: his name was Julián de Ávila.[4] I now had the licence, but I had neither a house nor so much as a farthing for buying one. And as for credit to go upon, how could a gadabout[5] like myself have any unless the Lord gave it? However, the Lord provided, for a girl of excellent character, for whom there had been no room at Saint Joseph's, knowing that another house was being founded, came to ask to be received into it.[6] She had a little money—very little, not enough for buying a house but only for renting one and for helping us to make the journey to Medina; so we found a house and rented it. Without any other support than this, we left Ávila—two nuns from Saint Joseph's[7] and myself, and four from the Incarnation[8] (the convent of the Miti-

---

[1] [Cf. *Life*, Chap. XXIII: Vol. I, p. 152, above.] The College of the Society of Jesus at Medina del Campo had been founded fourteen years previously, in 1553.

[2] Cf. *Life*, Chap. XXIV [Vol. I, p. 155, above]. When St. Teresa went to Medina, in the summer of 1567, he was Rector and Novice-master; in 1573, when this chapter was being written, he was acting as Provincial during the absence of P. Gil González Dávila, who was in Rome for the election of a new General.

[3] Documents show that the negotiations covered approximately the month of July 1567. The prelate mentioned was the Bishop of Salamanca.

[4] He was a man of forty, and a native of Ávila: his sister, María de San José, was one of the earliest nuns to enter St. Joseph's and he himself was its first chaplain. He accompanied St. Teresa in the journeys connected with her first eleven foundations, after which she used her own Discalced friars for this purpose. P. Gerardo de San Juan de la Cruz published an extensive *Vida del Maestro Julián de Ávila* in 1915.

[5] [*Romera*: *lit.* "female pilgrim". But, just as pilgrimages in Spain are often quite frankly only outings, or excursions, made with a pious purpose, so the meaning here seems to be a wandering or roving woman.]

[6] This was Isabel Fontecha, in religion Isabel de Jesús.

[7] María Bautista, St. Teresa's niece, and Ana de los Ángeles.

[8] St. Teresa's cousins, Inés de Jesús and Ana de la Encarnación, Isabel de la Cruz and Teresa de la Columna [P. Silverio, V, 20, n. 6, gives some later biographical details concerning the last two.]

gated Rule, where I had lived before Saint Joseph's was founded),
with our Father Chaplain Julián de Ávila.

When this became known in the city there was a great deal
of uncharitable talk. Some said I was mad; others, that this folly
would soon come to an end. The Bishop, as he has since told
me, thought it the height of folly, although at the time he did
not tell me this, or do anything else to upset me, for he was very
fond of me and would not cause me distress. My friends had told
me so repeatedly, but I took little notice of them, for what they
were dubious about seemed to me so easy that I could not persuade myself it could fail to turn out well. Before ever we left
Ávila, I had written to a Father of our Order, called Fray
Antonio de Heredia.[1] asking him to buy me a house. He was
at that time Prior of a monastery of our Order there, called Saint
Anne's. He took up the matter with a lady who was very much
devoted to him[2] and who had a house in an excellent situation,
though the whole of it, except for one room, was in a very
dilapidated state. She was good enough to promise to sell it to
him and they arranged it without her asking him for a deposit
or any other security than his word: had she done otherwise
we should have been helpless, but the Lord was preparing the
way for us. The house was almost falling down: so much was
there to be done to it that while it was being repaired we had to
hire another.

Our first night found us on the outskirts of Arévalo, but tired
out after the bad time we had had getting there. A clerical
friend, who had found us a lodging in the house of some devout
women, came to meet us, and told me privately that we should
never get the house at all: it was near an Augustinian monastery[3]
and the monks were opposed to our going there, so we should be
forced into a lawsuit. But oh, God! What little power has the
strongest opposition when Thou, Lord, art pleased to bestow
courage. This new difficulty seemed rather to stimulate me, for
I thought that, if the devil was beginning to trouble us already, the
convent must certainly be going to have work to do for the Lord.
However, I asked our friend to say nothing about it lest he should
frighten the two nuns from the Incarnation[4]—the others would

[1] Antonio de Heredia (1510–1601) and St. John of the Cross (1542–1591) were
the first Discalced friars. The former was Prior successively of Toledo (1561),
Ávila (1565) and Medina (1567) before embracing the Reform as described below.
[2] Her name was Doña María Suárez de Fuente el Sol.
[3] It was called Our Lady of Grace and stood opposite the hospital where St. John
of the Cross spent part of his boyhood. Neither monastery nor hospital is still
standing.
[4] [P. Silverio assumes that Isabel de la Cruz and Teresa de la Columna are meant
and that the stauncher two were the author's cousins]. The clerical friend referred
to was one Alfonso Esteban. It appears that he brought a letter for P. Julián from

have endured any trial for my sake. One of the two was Sub-Prioress there at the time and they had tried to prevent her from leaving.[1] Both had well-connected relatives, who had been opposed to their coming, for they all thought it ridiculous and I saw afterwards that they had ample justification for this. But, when the Lord is pleased that I should found one of these houses, my mind seems unable to find any contrary argument sufficiently weighty to make me desist from the task until it has been accomplished. And then all the difficulties come to my mind at once, as will be seen later.

Having reached our lodging, I found that there was a Dominican friar in the place, a very great servant of God, who during the time I was at Saint Joseph's had been my confessor. As I said a great deal about his virtue when I was speaking of that foundation,[2] I will do no more now than give his name: Maestro Fray Domingo Bañes. He is a man of great learning and discretion, and I allowed myself to be entirely guided by his opinion, which was that the work I had planned was not so difficult; for the more one gets to know of God the easier His work becomes, and it all seemed to him quite practicable because of certain favours which he knew His Majesty was granting me and because of what he had seen at the time of the foundation of Saint Joseph's. It was a great comfort to me to see him; for, once I had his opinion, I thought, everything would go well. So, when he arrived, I told him in the strictest confidence what was happening. He thought it should be possible for us to settle the difficulty with the Augustinians very quickly; but, not knowing what to do with all these nuns, I found it hard to endure the slightest delay. So we all passed that night in great anxiety, for the matter had at once been disclosed to all the nuns who were in the lodging.

In the morning came the Prior of our Order, Fray Antonio. He said the house which he had made an agreement to buy was quite large enough for us and had a porch which might be made into a little church if we fitted it up with hangings. This we resolved to do: to me, at least, it seemed a very good idea, for

---

the owner of the house advising him not to leave Ávila until the Augustinians had been placated. St. Teresa, having got so far, decided to consult P. Báñez, who was at Arévalo, and took the matter less seriously. So St. Teresa sent her four Incarnation nuns for a few days to a village where the brother of Inés and Ana was the parish priest, and went on with the others, including P. Antonio, who (cf. text, below) had also come to meet them. They first went to Olmedo to visit the Bishop, Don Álvaro de Mendoza, who lent them a carriage for the remainder of the journey. All this took place on August 13-14, 1567.

[1] Isabel de la Cruz.
[2] *Life*, Chap. XXXIX (Vol. I, p. 280, above).

the most important thing for us was to get to work quickly, since we were away from our convents, and also because I was afraid of opposition, having been warned by the experience of my first foundation. So I was anxious that we should have taken possession before it became known that we had arrived; accordingly, we decided to do so at once. Our father Fray Domingo agreed to this also.

We arrived at Medina del Campo at midnight on the eve of the festival of Our Lady in August. In order not to disturb anyone, we alighted at the monastery of Saint Anne and went to the house on foot.[1] It was a great mercy on the part of the Lord that we met no one, for it was just at that time that they were shutting in the bulls which were to take part in the next day's bull-fight. We were so much absorbed in our task that we thought of nothing else; but the Lord, who always remembers those desirous of serving Him—and we certainly had no other aim than that—delivered us from all danger.

Having reached the house, we entered the courtyard. The walls seemed to me in a very tumbledown condition and by day they appeared worse still. The Lord must have been pleased that the blessed Father should have become blind or he would have seen that it was not fitting to put the Most Holy Sacrament in such a place. When I looked at the porch I saw that we should have to remove some of the earth from it; there were holes in the roof; and the walls were not plastered. The night was nearly over and we had only a few hangings[2]—I believe altogether there were three. These, in view of the length of the porch, were of no use at all. I did not know what to do, for I saw that it would not be seemly to put an altar there. But it was the Lord's will that it should be done at once, for by His providence the lady's steward had a great deal of tapestry belonging to her and also a blue damask bedspread, and she had said that we were to be given whatever we wanted, for she was very good to us.[3]

When I saw how well we were provided for, I praised the Lord, and the others all did the same. We did not know what to do for nails and it was not a time at which we could buy any. So

---

[1] " I went on in front," writes P. Julián de Ávila, " so as to get there first and warn the Carmelite Fathers; and by midnight I was hammering at the door: eventually they woke up and let me in." (*Vida de Santa Teresa*, Part III, Chap. VIII). Details of money spent by these Fathers on a lamp and oil " for the new convent ", and on supper for " the youths who came with the nuns " are still on record.

[2] *Reposteros*: large squares of cloth or other material, generally bearing the arms of their owner, used as coverings for the loads carried by mules, as hangings for balconies and as decorations for the interiors of houses.

[3] They had apparently met Doña María Suárez somewhere on their way to Medina and it was at St. Teresa's request that she had written a note to this effect to her steward which the little party probably delivered to him themselves.

we started to look round the walls; and at last, after some trouble, we collected a sufficient number. Then the hanging was begun, while we nuns set to work to clean the floor; and we all worked so quickly that, by daybreak, the altar was set up and the bell hung in a gallery, so that Mass was said immediately. There was no need for us to do more before taking possession. But we did not stop there; we had the Most Holy Sacrament reserved, and through the chinks of the door, which was opposite the altar, we were able to see the Mass—it was the only way we could do so.

So far I was very pleased, for it gives me the greatest joy when I see one more church in which there is reservation of the Most Holy Sacrament. But my joy was of short duration. For, when Mass had been offered, I went to look at the courtyard through a window and saw that its walls had partly fallen down, so that many days would be necessary before they could be repaired. Oh, God help me! What anguish filled my heart when I saw His Majesty turned out into the street, and in times so full of peril as these, on account of those Lutherans!

Together with these thoughts came others, concerning all the difficulties which might be put in our way by those who had spoken ill of us, for I clearly realized that they had done so with good reason.[1] It seemed to me impossible for us to go any farther with the work we had begun; for, just as previously everything had seemed easy to me, when I had reflected that it was being done for God's sake, so now temptation began to intensify its hold upon me as if I had never received any favours from Him at all. All I could think of was my own weakness and lack of power. What good result could I hope for when I was relying on anything so miserable as myself? If I had been alone, I believe I could have endured it better; but to think that my companions would have to return to their houses, after all the opposition they had encountered before leaving, was a terrible trial to me. I thought that, as the beginning of our enterprise had gone wrong, I must have been mistaken in supposing that the Lord would help us. To all this was added the fear that what I had learned in prayer might have been an illusion; and this was not the least of my distresses, but the greatest, for it caused me the most terrible fear that the devil might have been deceiving me. Oh, my God! What it is to see a soul whom Thou art pleased

---

[1] When St. Teresa's intention to found a convent of her Reform in Medina became known, a meeting of the city authorities and leading religious of the locality was held, at which the project was strongly criticized, one monk going to the length of comparing the Saint with Magdalena de la Cruz, the false nun of Córdoba who gave out that she was sinless but later confessed her frauds and did public penance. The good sense, however, of the majority of those present prevailed.

to allow to suffer! When I recall this affliction and other trials
that I have endured while making these foundations, I really do
not think that any of my physical trials, numerous though they
have been, are worthy of the least remembrance by comparison
with this.

Greatly as all these troubles oppressed me, I said nothing
about them to my companions, for I had no wish that they should
be more distressed than they were already. So I bore this trial
alone until the evening, when the Rector of the Company sent
one of the Fathers to see me, and he gave me great encouragement and comfort. I did not tell him all my troubles but only
the grief I felt at our finding ourselves in the street. I began to
discuss with him the question of searching for a house which we
could lease, at whatever cost, so that we could move there while
our repairs were being done here; and when I saw how many
people were coming to visit us, and that none of them had
observed our folly, I began to feel comforted. This was by the
mercy of God; had they done so, the Most Holy Sacrament
would certainly have been taken from us. I realize now how
foolish I was and how careless they were not to consume the Host;
but I thought that, if this were done, it would be all up with
us.[1]

But, try as we would, we could find no house to let anywhere,
and this caused me extreme distress both by night and by day.
For, although I always left men to keep guard over the Most
Holy Sacrament, I was afraid they might go to sleep; and so
I used to get up in the night, and look at it through the window,
for, when the moon was very bright, I could see it easily. During
all these days many people were visiting us, and not only did
they not think our foundation at all a bad one but it gave them
great devotion to see Our Lord once more in the porch; and His
Majesty, never weary of humbling Himself for our sakes, did not
seem to want to leave it.

At the end of a week, a merchant, who was living in a very
good house, saw what we needed and told us we could have the
upper part of his house and live there as if it were our own.[2]
It had a very large gilded hall, which he gave us for a church,
and a lady, called Doña Elena de Quiroga, a great servant of
God, who was living near the house we had bought, said that she
would help me so that I could at once begin to build a chapel
in which the Most Holy Sacrament might be placed and also try

---

[1] At that time St. Teresa considered the reservation of the Blessed Sacrament an
essential condition for a new foundation. It was not until 1570 (Chap. XIX,
p. 93, below) that she founded a convent without making this provision.

[2] Blas de Medina was the merchant's name.   Cf. Ribera, Book II, Chap. IX.

to find us accommodation so that we could be enclosed. Other people gave us abundant alms, so that we had more than enough to eat, but it was this lady who helped me most.[1]

With all this happening, I began to be easier in my mind; for we were completely enclosed where we were, and we began to say the Hours, while the good Prior[2] took up the matter of the house with all speed, and went to great trouble about it. He said that, in spite of everything, it would not be finished for two months; but it was so well done that we were able to stay there with reasonable comfort for several years. Since then Our Lord has gone on improving things for us.[3]

While I was there, I was continually preoccupied about monasteries for friars; and, having no friars, as I have said, I did not know what to do. So I resolved to discuss the matter in the strictest confidence with the Prior there, and see what advice he would give me. I did this: he was very glad when he heard of it and promised me that he would be the first to join us. I took that for a joke and told him so; for although, besides being a learned man, he was a good friar, given to recollection, very studious and fond of his cell, he did not seem to me to be at all the man for the beginning of an enterprise of this kind; he had not sufficient spirituality, nor could he have endured the necessary privations, being delicate in health and not accustomed to them. But he reassured me most earnestly and told me that for a long time the Lord had been calling him to a stricter life, that he had already resolved to go to the Carthusians and that they had assured him that they would receive him. None the less, though very glad to hear this of him, I was not quite satisfied: I asked him, therefore, to let us wait a while so that he might practise the things which he would have to promise to do. He did so; a year passed, during which time he experienced so many trials and persecutions from false witnesses that it seemed as if it was the Lord's intention to prove him. He himself bore it all so well, and made such steady progress, that I praised Our Lord, for it seemed to me that His Majesty was preparing him for this new life.

Shortly afterwards there happened to arrive a young Father who was studying in Salamanca. With him was a companion, who told me great things about the life which that Father was

---

[1] Doña Elena, who was a niece of Cardinal Quiroga, took the Discalced Carmelite habit on October 14, 1581, at Medina del Campo, where her daughter, Jerónima de la Encarnación, was already a nun. As Elena de Jesús, she eventually became Prioress of the Toledo convent and died in 1596.

[2] Antonio de Heredia.

[3] In 1570 the nuns bought several houses and some land, which made it possible for them to live more spaciously.

leading. His name is Fray Juan de la Cruz.[1] I praised Our Lord; and, when I spoke to the friar, I liked him very much; he told me that he too was preparing to go to the Carthusians.[2] I described to him what I had in view and begged him earnestly to wait until the Lord gave us a monastery, pointing out what a great blessing it would be, if he were destined for a higher life, that he should lead it within his own Order, and how much better service he would thus render to the Lord. He gave me his word to do this provided there were no long delay. When I saw that I had two friars to make a beginning with,[3] the thing seemed to me settled, although I was still not quite satisfied with the Prior. So for this reason, and also because I had as yet no place to begin in, I waited for some little time.

The nuns continued to win good opinions in the town, and aroused much devotion—I believe deservedly, for none of them had any other aim than to see how each could best serve Our Lord. In every detail they followed the same procedure as had been adopted at Saint Joseph's at Ávila, the Rule and Constitutions for all our convents being one and the same. The Lord began to call some to take the habit, and so numerous were the favours which He granted them that I was amazed.[4] May He be blessed for ever. Amen. For, in order to love, He seems only to wait to be loved Himself.

CHAPTER IV

Describes certain favours bestowed by the Lord on the nuns in these convents and gives advice to prioresses as to their treatment of them.

It has seemed well to me, before going farther (for I do not know how much more life or opportunity the Lord will grant me, and I seem to have a little time now), to give some counsels by which prioresses may learn how to guide their subjects to the greater profit of their souls, although in a way less to their

---

[1] [I.e. John of the Cross. This was, of course, the Saint of that name, for an outline of whose life see my edition of his *Complete Works*, I, xxv–xxix.] For " is ", St. Teresa originally had " was ", but made the change in the manuscript [for the young friar had not taken the name " de la Cruz " when she first met him].

[2] He had thought, it seems, of entering the Carthusian house of El Paular, in the province of Segovia.

[3] " A friar and a half ", she is reported to have said, and there has been some doubt as to exactly what she meant. [Cf. *S.S.M.*, I, 232, and my *Spirit of Flame*, London, 1943, pp. 18–19.]

[4] St. Teresa left M. Inés de Jesús as Prioress of the new house and M. Ana de la Encarnación as Sub-Prioress. The Convent is still much the same as when it was founded, the Saint's cell being used as a chapel.

liking. It should be observed that, when I was commanded to write of these foundations, seven, not counting the first, that of Saint Joseph of Ávila, which was written about at the time, but including the most recent, that of Alba de Tormes, had been established by the help of the Lord.[1] The reason why more were not made is that my superiors tied me down to work of another kind, as will be seen later.

Now, recalling the spiritual history of those years in these convents, I have realized the necessity for what I want to say. May it please Our Lord to enable me to succeed in meeting this necessity. As these things are not delusions there is no need for us to be alarmed; for, as I have said elsewhere, in certain brief works which I have written for the sisters,[2] if we walk with a pure conscience and in obedience, the Lord will never allow the devil to have such power over us as to deceive us in a way that can harm our souls: on the contrary, it is he who will suffer deception. And, as he knows this, I believe he does less harm than our imagination and evil humours, especially if we suffer from melancholy, for women have weak constitutions and the love of self that reigns in us is very subtle. People have come to me in great numbers, both men and women, to say nothing of nuns from these houses, and it has been quite clear to me that they often deceive themselves against their will. I really believe that the devil must intrude himself in order to mock us; but of all those whom, as I say, I have seen, I have never, through the goodness of the Lord, heard of any who have been forsaken by Him. Perhaps He is anxious to discipline them through these trials, so that experience may bring them gain.

Things to do with prayer and perfection have been so much neglected in the world, through our sins, that I shall have to explain myself in this way. For even when they do not see the dangers people are afraid to walk on this road. What would they be, then, if we were to tell them about some of the dangers? Although, it is true, there is danger in everything, and for every reason it is needful for us to walk in fear all our lives long and to beg the Lord to teach us and not to forsake us, yet, as I think I have already said, if there are any lives in which there is much less danger than in others, it is those of persons who think often of God and strive after perfection.

How often, my Lord, dost Thou deliver us from the dangers

---

[1] [This is correct (Alba de Tormes having been founded on January 25, 1571, and the next, that of Segovia, not until after she had begun to write, over three years later) if we leave out of account, as she is evidently doing, the houses founded for men.] During the three years' interval, as we shall see, St. Teresa had returned to Ávila as Prioress of the Incarnation.

[2] *Way of perfection*, Chap. XL. [Vol. II, pp. 172-6, above.]

into which we run, even though we escape them only to fight against Thee! How, then, can anyone believe that Thou wilt not deliver us when our sole aim is to please Thee and to make Thee our delight?[1] For myself, I can never believe this. It might be that, for His own secret reasons, God would permit things to turn out in some particular way, but what is good has never led to evil. Let this, then, encourage us to travel more determinedly along the road in order to please our Spouse the better and to find Him the sooner; let it never have the effect of persuading us to give up the journey. It must spur us on to go boldly forward over steep mountain roads like the road of this life; it must not make cowards of us as we go; for sooner or later, if we walk humbly, we shall by the mercy of God reach that city of Jerusalem, where all that we have suffered will be of little or no moment, by comparison with what we shall enjoy.

Now when these little dovecotes of the Virgin Our Lady began to be filled, His Divine Majesty began to show forth His greatness in these poor weak women, who none the less were strong in desire and in their detachment from all created things; for, if the soul walks with a pure conscience, it is this that most unites it with its Creator. It is hardly necessary to point this out, for, if one has genuine detachment, it is, I think, impossible to offend the Lord. For in that case, in all one's conversations and intercourse with others, one never leaves Him, and in the same way His Majesty seems to be unwilling tc withdraw from the soul. It is this that I see here at the present time and I can say it in all truth. Let those who come after us, and read this, fear, and if they do not see what I see now let them not blame the times for it, for the time is always propitious for God to grant His great favours to those who truly serve Him. Let them consider, therefore, if there is any fault in them and amend it.

I sometimes hear it said, with regard to the early history of the Orders, that the Lord granted these saintly precursors of ours greater favours because they were laying their foundations.[2] That is quite true. But they had always to remember that they were the foundations on which would be built up those who were to come. If we who are now alive do not fall away from the

---

[1] The words from the beginning of the paragraph down to this point are underlined in the autograph by Gracián, who has written in the margin, " Good argument and of great consolation".

[2] Here St. Teresa has obliterated one complete line and parts of two others and written, " That is quite true. But " above the obliterated part. Gracián also wrote something here, both in the text and in the margin, but it too has been crossed out and is indecipherable. There are various other changes made by Gracián in this paragraph, but, except where shown, they are not followed in the text and all are trivial.

standards of those who have gone before us, and[1] if those who
come after us do not fall away from our own, the building will
stand firmly for ever. Of what use is it to me that the saints of
past days should have been what they were if I, coming after
them, am so wicked that I leave their building a wreck through
my wicked habits? For it is clear that those who come after
think less of those who have preceded them long years since than
of those whom they see before them. A fine thing it is for me
to make capital out of not being one of the first, and yet not to
think what a difference there is between my life and virtues
and those of others to whom God granted such great favours!

O God, what crooked excuses we make and what manifest
delusions we harbour! I am not speaking of those who are
founding religious Orders, for, as God has chosen them for such
great work, He has given them more grace.[2] It grieves me, my
God, that I should be so wicked and do so little in Thy service, and
I well know that it is my own fault that Thou hast not granted
me the favours which Thou gavest to those who went before me.
I grieve over my life, Lord, when I compare it with theirs,
and I cannot say this without weeping. I see that I have wasted
what they gained with their labours and I have no grounds for
complaining of Thee. Nor has any of us any right to complain;
rather, if one of us sees her Order in any way decadent, she must
strive to become so firm a stone in it that by her means the
building will be raised up again; and in this the Lord will help
her.

Returning now to what I was saying—and I have wandered
a long way from it—the favours granted by the Lord in these
houses are so great that, while in each house there may be one
or two nuns whom God is now leading by the way of meditation,
all the rest attain to perfect contemplation, and some of them are
so far advanced that they attain to raptures.[3] Upon others the
Lord bestows His favours in a different way, and at the same time
He gives them revelations and visions which are clearly seen
to be the work of God. There is no house now in which one,
two or three of these may not be found. I know quite well that
this does not constitute sanctity, nor is it my intention to praise
such nuns as these alone: I say it rather to show that the counsels
I wish to give are not purposeless.

[1] The "and" is inserted by Gracián.
[2] This sentence is a marginal insertion in St. Teresa's hand.
[3] From the beginning of the paragraph down to this point the manuscript is very
hard to decipher, Gracián having crossed out a great many words and substituted his
own emendations, which read: "while the Lord leads them all by the way of meditation, some attain to perfect contemplation and others are so far advanced that they
attain to raptures." Most of the early copies and editions follow Gracián: in our
text, however, St. Teresa's own words are restored.

CHAPTER V

Gives certain counsels on matters concerning prayer and revelations.[1]
*This is very profitable for those engaged in occupations belonging
to the active life.*

It is not my belief, or my meaning, that what I am going to
say here is so accurate that it can be taken as an infallible rule,
for in such difficult matters to think that would be foolish. There
are many paths on this spiritual road, and I may say something
accurate about one of them, but those who are not following
that path will not understand it: that will be because they are
following another. If I fail to help anybody, the Lord will
take the will for the deed, for He knows that, though I have
not myself experienced all I describe,[2] I have observed it in
others.

The first thing I wish to discuss, as far as my limited understanding will allow, is the nature of the essence of perfect prayer.
For I have come across some people who believe that the whole
thing consists in thought; and thus, if they are able to think a
great deal about God, however much the effort may cost them,
they immediately imagine they are spiritually minded; while,
if they become distracted, and their efforts to think of good
things fail, they at once become greatly discouraged and suppose
themselves to be lost. Learned men will not have such ignorant
beliefs as this, although I have met a few who had, but, as far as
we women are concerned, it behoves us to be forewarned. I
do not mean that it is not a favour from the Lord if any of us
is able to be continually meditating upon His works;[3] and it is
good for us to try to do this. But it must be realized that not
everyone has by nature an imagination capable of meditating,
whereas all souls are capable of love.[4] I have written elsewhere
of what I believe to be the reasons for this wandering of the
imagination—not of all of them, for that would be impossible,
but of a few. And so I am not discussing that now; I am only
anxious to explain that the soul is not thought, nor is the will

---

[1] The words " and revelations " are crossed out in the text.
[2] Besides making two other trivial corrections in this paragraph, Gracián has
crossed out this clause and re-written it in the margin, substituting " may not
have " for " have not ".
[3] Gracián crosses out the phrase " if . . . works " and writes in the margin: " to
be able to keep the thought continually occupied in thinking of Him."
[4] Gracián [anticipating the final sentence of the paragraph] adds in the margin:
" in which, rather than in thinking, consists perfection."

controlled by thought[1]—it would be a great misfortune if it
were.[2] The soul's profit, then, consists not in thinking much
but in loving much.

How will this love be acquired? By our resolving to work
and to suffer and by our doing so whenever the occasion offers.[3]
It is very true that by thinking what we owe the Lord, and Who
He is, and what we are, a soul will be led to make such a resolution. To do this is a great merit and very fitting for beginners—
that is to say, of course, when there is no impediment in the shape
of things which concern obedience or the profit of our neighbours.[4]
If either of these two things stands in the way, we must renounce
for a time what we so much desire to give to God, which we feel
we are doing when we are alone, and thinking of Him and rejoicing in the favours which He bestows upon us. To give up
all this for either of these two reasons is to please Him and to work
for Him; for, as He said with His own mouth, "That which ye
have done for one of these little ones, ye do for Me."[5] And in
all that concerns obedience, He would not have one that loves
Him well take any other road than that which He Himself took,
obediens usque ad mortem.[6]

Now if this be true, what is the reason of the discontent which
we generally experience when for a great part of the day we have
not been withdrawn apart and absorbed in God, although we
may have been employing ourselves in these other matters?
There are two reasons, I think. One, the more important,
is a kind of self-love which insinuates itself here, and so subtly
that we do not realize that we are more anxious to give pleasure
to ourselves than to God. For, of course, when one has begun to
taste "how sweet the Lord is,"[7] one finds more pleasure in allowing the body to rest from its labours and the soul to receive His
gifts.[8]

Oh, the charity of those who truly love this Lord and are
aware of their own condition! How little rest will they be able
to take if they see that they can do anything to help even one soul

[1] Gracián substitutes: " nor is the will, even though it be controlled [more literally
here and in the text, " commanded "] by thought."

[2] " As has been said above," adds Gracián.

[3] Gracián emends thus: " And if you ask: ' How will this love be acquired? '
I answer: ' By a soul's resolving to work and to suffer for God and doing so whenever
the occasion offers' ."

[4] Gracián adds: " [and] to which we are bound by charity. For in such cases,
[if either, etc.]."

[5] St. Matthew xxv, 40.

[6] Philippians ii, 8: " He humbled himself, becoming obedient unto death, even
to the death of the cross."

[7] Psalm xxxiii, 9 [A.V., xxxiv, 8].

[8] The author here interrupts the thread of her argument and comes to her second
reason only ten paragraphs later (p. 25, below).

to make progress and love God better, or to give it some comfort or save it from some danger! How little real rest will they get out of any time that they may take to rest in! Even if they can do nothing for others by their actions, they can do a great deal by means of prayer, importuning the Lord for the many souls the thought of whose ruin causes them such grief. They lose their own comfort, and look upon it as well lost, because they are not thinking of their own pleasure but of how better to do the Lord's will. It is the same as regards obedience. It would be a terrible thing if God were to be telling us plainly to go about His business in some way and we would not do it but stood looking at Him because that gave us greater pleasure. A pretty way it is of advancing in the love of God to tie His hands by thinking that there is only one way in which He can benefit us!

I know some people[1] (apart, as I say, from what I have myself experienced) who have taught me this truth when I have been dreadfully worried at having so little time, and so have been sorry to see that they too were always full up with business and many other things, imposed upon them by obedience. And I would think to myself, and even tell them, that amid such a hurried life spiritual growth was not possible—and at that time they had certainly achieved very little. But, O Lord, how different are Thy ways from our clumsy[2] imaginings! When once a soul is resolved to love Thee and has resigned itself into Thy hands, Thou wilt have nothing of it save that it shall obey Thee and find out for itself how it may best serve Thee and desire to do so. It has no need to look for paths or to choose them, for its will is Thine. Thou, my Lord, takest upon Thyself the task of guiding it in the way which is the greatest benefit to it. And even though our superior[3] has no mind to our souls' profit but is satisfied with seeing that we do such work as is judged advantageous to the community, Thou, my God, hast a mind to our profit and dost dispose the soul and prepare things for it to do in such a way that, without knowing how, we find ourselves[4] so much more spiritual and so greatly benefited[5] that we[6] are astonished.

Only a few days ago I was speaking with someone to whom all this was applicable. For almost fifteen years he had been

---

[1] St. Teresa added here " by sight " [which seems a pointless phrase unless she means that she has actually talked with these people and not merely corresponded with them]. Gracián crossed out the words and added, "with whom I have had to do."

[2] Gracián has crossed out " clumsy."

[3] [*Lit.*: " the prelate "—a word often used by St. Teresa of the superiors of religious communities.] Gracián underlines these sentences and writes " Note this " in the margin.

[4] Gracián: "souls find themselves."

[5] Gracián adds in the margin: " obeying such orders with fidelity for God's sake."

[6] Gracián: "they ".

kept so busy by obedience in various offices and positions of authority that he could not remember in all that time having had a day to himself, though he did everything that he could to set aside certain periods in the day for prayer and to keep his conscience pure. He is one of the most amenable people to obedience that I have ever seen and he influences everyone he has to do with. And the Lord has amply recompensed him for it, so that, without knowing how, he has found himself in possession of that spiritual freedom, so much valued and desired by all, which belongs to the perfect, and in which is found all the happiness to be desired in this life. While wanting nothing, such persons possess all things. No earthly thing do they either fear or desire; no trials can disturb them; no pleasure can excite them: no one, in fact, can rob them of their peace, since it proceeds from God alone. And, as no one can rob them of God, only the fear of losing Him can cause them distress: about everything else in the world they feel as though it did not exist, for it can neither add to, nor subtract from, their joy. O happy obedience and happy the distraction it brings, which is so fruitful in achievement!

Nor is this person the only one of his kind: I have known many others. Some of them I had not seen for years—even for a great many years—and when I asked them what they had been doing they would say they had been spending all their time in occupations imposed upon them by obedience and charity. And yet I found them so far advanced in spiritual matters that I was astounded. So come, then, my daughters, let there be no disappointment when obedience keeps you busy in outward tasks. If it sends you to the kitchen, remember that the Lord walks among the pots and pans[1] and that He will help you in inward tasks and in outward ones too.

I remember a monk telling me that he had made a resolution, to which he attached great importance, never to refuse to do anything which his superior commanded him, however much labour it might cost him. One day when it was very late and he was so completely exhausted by his work that he could not longer keep on with it and was going off to rest, his superior met him and told him to take his spade and go and dig in the garden. He said nothing, although he was so weary that he could hardly stand, but took his spade, and, just as he was about to enter a passage leading to the garden (which I saw many years after being told about this, for I was able to found a house in the place), Our Lord appeared to him, bearing His Cross, and looking so tired

---

[1] [*Entre los pucheros anda el Señor*: perhaps the most celebrated phrase in the whole of St. Teresa's writings].

and fatigued that He made him realize very clearly how his own sufferings were nothing by comparison with His.[1]

I believe it is the devil who, seeing there is no path which leads more quickly to the highest perfection than that of obedience, suggests all these objections and difficulties under the guise of good. Let this be carefully noted and it will become quite clear that I am telling the truth. The highest perfection consists not in interior favours or in great raptures or in visions or in the spirit of prophecy, but in the bringing of our wills so closely into conformity with the will of God[2] that, as soon as we realize He wills anything, we desire it ourselves with all our might, and take the bitter with the sweet, knowing that to be His Majesty's will.[3] This, I think, is a most difficult thing—not so much the actual performance of it as the joy in doing something which brings our will wholly into opposition with our nature, as is certainly the case here. But, if our love is perfect, it has this quality of leading us to forget our own pleasure in order to please Him Whom we love. And that is indeed what happens. Immense as our trials may be, they become sweet to us if we know we are pleasing God. And so those who have reached this state love to be persecuted and dishonoured and wronged. This is very true; and it is so well known and so evident that there is no reason for me to insist upon it.

What I do want to make clear is the reason why, as I believe, obedience brings us the sooner to that happy state and is the best means of attaining it. It is because we are in no way masters of our own wills, and cannot employ them purely and sincerely in the service of God, until we submit them to reason, and the true way for us so to submit them is that of obedience. This cannot be done by means of reasoning;[4] for our nature and our love of self can argue so effectively that reasoning would never get us anywhere. Very often what seems to us the best of reasons for not doing a thing if we have no desire to do it seems ridiculous when we want to do it.

There is so much that might be said about this interior strife, and about the pains taken by the devil and the world and our

---

[1] P. Jerónimo de San José and P. Francisco de Santa María both apply this story to Francisco de la Concepción and say that the house referred to was that founded by the Discalced Carmelite friars at La Roda. But in 1573, when this chapter was written, St. Teresa had not been to La Roda: indeed, she went there only in 1580. The attribution, therefore, must be wrong. A more likely guess is Toledo.

[2] Gracián writes in the margin here: " Wherein consists perfection."

[3] This thought is developed in *Interior Castle*, V. iii.

[4] [*Lit.*: " by reasons ". Undoubtedly, I think, St. Teresa is intentionally using the same word as she has used just above. This habit is commented upon in Vol. I, p. xx, above]. In this and the preceding lines Gracián has made some changes, which Báñez has crossed through, restoring the author's text. There are several other examples of this proceeding in the chapter, but all are trivial.

sensuality to warp our reason, that we might go on writing about this for ever. But the question is what can be done about it. Just as in a troublesome dispute both sides get tired of arguing and put the matter into the hands of a judge, so our soul must have recourse to a judge, who will be either our superior or our confessor. We must resolve to give up arguing and searching for reasons, to trust the words of the Lord, Who says: "He that heareth you, heareth Me"[1] and to pay no further attention to our own wishes. Such great importance does the Lord attach to this submissiveness (and rightly so, for it makes Him Lord of the free will that He has given us) that if we practise it, now entirely annihilating our own desires, now winning only after a thousand battles, and thinking the judgment given in our case to be folly, we shall come, by means of this painful exercise, to resign ourselves entirely to doing what we are commanded. We shall do it in the end, whether it costs us pain or no, and the Lord, for His part, will help us so much that, just because we submit our will and reason to Him, He will make us masters of them. Then, being masters of ourselves, we shall be able to employ ourselves wholly in the service of God, making Him a complete surrender of our will so that He may unite it with His own, beseeching Him that the fire of His love may come down from Heaven and consume this sacrifice and giving up everything that may displease Him. For there will be nothing more left for us to do, since, at the cost of all this labour, we shall have laid our gifts on the altar, which, so far as in us lies, will have no more to do with the earth.

Clearly a person cannot give what he does not possess: he must have the thing first. And, believe me, there is no better way of acquiring this treasure than to dig and toil in order to get it from this mine of obedience. The more we dig, the more we shall find; and the more we submit to men, and have no other will than that of our superiors, the more completely we shall become masters of our wills and bring them into conformity with the will of God. Consider, then, sisters, if our renunciation of the pleasure of solitude is not well rewarded. I assure you that lack of solitude need not prevent you from preparing to attain this genuine union of which I have spoken and which consists in making our will one with the will of God. This is the union which I desire and should like to see in you all: I do not covet for you those delectable kinds of absorption which it is possible to experience and which are given the name of union. They may amount to union if the result of them is what I have described; but if such suspension leaves behind it little obedience,

[1] St. Luke x, 16.

and much self-will, it seems to me that it will be a union with love of self, not with the will of God. May His Majesty grant that I myself may act according to my belief.

The second reason which can account for this discontent is, I think, that, as solitude brings with it few opportunities for offending the Lord (the devils being with us everywhere, there must always be a few), the solitary soul seems to be purer; for, if it is afraid of offending Him, it is very greatly encouraged when it meets no stumbling-block. This certainly seems to me a more sufficient reason for desiring to have no intercourse with anyone than that of obtaining great favours and consolations from God.

It is here, my daughters, that love is to be found—not hidden away in corners but in the midst of occasions of sin; and believe me, although we may more often fail and commit small lapses, our gain will be incomparably the greater. Remember I am assuming all the time that we are acting in this way out of obedience or charity: if one of these motives is not involved, I do not hesitate to say that solitude is best. And, even if we are acting as I say, we may still have a desire for solitude, for that desire is ever present in souls which truly love God. The reason I say we gain more in the other way is that it makes us realize what we are and of how much our own virtue is capable. For if a person is always recollected, however holy he may think himself to be,[1] he does not know if he is patient and humble, and he has no means of knowing it. A man may be very strong, but how can he be sure he is if he has not proved himself in battle? Saint Peter thought he was strong enough, but look what happened to him when he was tempted: and then, after that fall of his, he rose again and, having lost all trust in himself, learned to place his trust in God, and eventually, as we know, became a martyr.

O God, if only we could understand what a plight we are in! Unless we understand this there is danger for us in everything. For that reason it is very good for us to be under the orders of others, so that we may appreciate our own lowliness. And I think it is a greater favour if the Lord sends us a single day of humble self-knowledge, even at the cost of many afflictions and trials, than many days of prayer. The more so because the true lover everywhere loves his Beloved, and continually remembers Him. It would be a bad business if we could practise prayer only by getting alone in corners. I know that I cannot be alone for many hours, but, O my Lord, how potent with Thee is a sigh issuing from the heart, a sigh of sorrow at the

[1] The words " think himself to " are inserted as an afterthought by the author.

thought, not only that we are in this exile, but that we have no opportunity to enjoy a solitude which might give us fruition of Thee![1]

This makes it clear that we are His slaves, sold through love of Him, and of our own free will, to the virtue of obedience, since it is through obedience that we have to some extent renounced the fruition of God Himself. But this is nothing, if we consider that it was by obedience that He came out of the bosom of the Father to be our slave. How, then, can we repay Him this favour? What service can we render Him for it? We must needs be careful, in doing good works, even those of obedience and charity, not to fail to have frequent inward recourse to our God. And, believe me, it is not length of time spent in prayer that brings a soul benefit: when we spend our time in good works, it is a great help to us and a better and quicker preparation for the enkindling of our love than many hours of meditation. Everything must come from the hand of God. May He be blessed for ever and ever.

CHAPTER VI

Gives warning of the harm which may come to spiritual people through their not knowing when the spirit is to be resisted. Treats of the soul's desires to communicate. Deception which may arise here. There are important things in this chapter for those who govern these houses.

I have been trying very hard to discover the source of a deep absorption which I have seen in certain persons to whom the Lord gives great joy in prayer and who leave nothing undone in order to prepare themselves for the reception of His favours. I am not now speaking of occasions when the soul is suspended and transported by His Majesty, for of this I have written a great deal elsewhere[2] and about a thing like that there is nothing that one can say, for if it is a genuine rapture we ourselves are powerless, whatever our efforts at resistance. It must be observed that in such a rapture the force which deprives us of our self-control lasts only a short time. But often it begins with a Prayer of Quiet, which resembles a spiritual sleep, and so absorbs the soul that, if we do not know how to proceed here, much time may be lost

---

[1] " Good comfort for those occupied in works of charity ", adds Gracián, in the margin of the autograph.

[2] Notably in *Life*, Chap. XX [Vol. I, pp. 119–30, above].

and our strength may become exhausted through our own fault and with little profit to ourselves.

I wish I knew how to explain myself here, but it is so difficult that I do not know if I shall be able to do so: I am quite sure, however, that souls who are deceived in this way will understand if they will only believe me. I know some, souls of great virtue, who have been in such a state for seven or eight hours and have believed it all to be rapture; and every virtuous practice affected them in such a way that they immediately relinquished control of themselves, because they thought that it was not right to resist the Lord. If they were to go on in that way, and to find no remedy, they would gradually lose their senses or die. What I understand to be the case here is that, when the Lord begins to comfort[1] the soul, our nature, being so fond of pleasure, abandons itself so completely to this pleasurable condition that it would not move, or lose what it has gained, for anything in the world. For in truth this pleasure is greater than any worldly pleasure, and may be bestowed upon a person of weak constitution, or upon one whose mind (or, to put it better, whose imagination) has no natural versatility, but who, once he has begun to study a subject, continues his study and never seeks distraction; in such a case this is what happens here, according to the person's nature, constitution or weakness. Many people, when they begin to think of anything—not necessarily of a thing having to do with God—remain absorbed in it and look at objects without noticing them: such people are temperamentally slow and seem to be so absent-minded that they forget what they are going to say. And, oh, if such persons should become melancholy! They will begin to nurse a thousand pleasant delusions.

Of this kind of temperament I shall say something later on; but what I have described may take place even in those who do not possess it, as also in persons who are worn out by penance. For, as I have said, when love begins to cause them sense-pleasure,[2] they allow themselves, as I have already said, to be carried completely away by it. In my opinion, their love would be much better if they did not allow themselves to be carried away, for at this stage in their prayer they are quite capable of offering resistance. For just as, in cases of physical debility, a faintness is felt which prevents the subject from speaking

[1] [*Regalar*. The real meaning of this ubiquitous word here is "show signs of affection for"; and "pet", "caress", "fondle", though hardly seemly in the context, would not, as far as the actual *sense* is concerned, be too strong. Cf. Translator's Preface (Vol. I, pp. xxi–xxii, above).]

[2] [*Lit.*, "pleasure in the sense."] Gracián substituted "sensible" for "in the sense" but Báñez restored the original reading. There are frequent examples of this emendation and restoration throughout the chapter, but no more that need be recorded.

or moving, so it is here, if we do not resist; for, if the physical constitution is weak, the power of the spirit constrains and subdues it.

I may be asked what difference there is between this and rapture, for the two things, at least in appearance, are the same. This is not an unreasonable thing to say, but it is incorrect. For rapture, or union of all the faculties, as I have said, lasts only a short time and leaves in the soul marked effects and an interior light, together with many other benefits: the understanding does not work at all—it is the Lord Who is at work in the will. In this state the position is very different. The body is captive, but the will, the memory and the understanding are not. Their operations, however, are irregular, and, if by chance they are occupied in a particular subject, they will keep on debating it among themselves all the time.

I find no advantage in this bodily weakness, for it is nothing else, except that it has sprung from a good beginning; it would be more to the point to use the time well rather than to spend so much of it in a state of absorption. Much more merit can be derived from a single act, and from the frequent arousing of the will to love God, than from the abandonment of it to this state of inertia. So I advise prioresses to make all possible efforts to prevent these long swoons, for in my opinion they do nothing but paralyse the faculties and senses and hinder them from fulfilling the commands of the soul; and in this way they deprive them of the advantage which, if they proceed with care, they generally gain. If a prioress finds that this is caused by weakness, she must dispense from fasts and disciplines (I refer to those which are not of obligation, and there may be times when she can forbid all such things with a clear conscience) and give such persons duties to do so as to distract them from thoughts of self.

And even when a soul is not subject to these swoons, such treatment is still necessary if the imagination is apt to get deeply absorbed,[1] even though it be on lofty subjects concerning prayer. For it sometimes happens that such a soul loses control of itself, especially if it has received some extraordinary favour from the Lord, or seen some vision. This may affect it in such a way that it believes itself always to be seeing the vision, whereas in fact it saw it only once. Anyone who finds herself thus absorbed for many days on end must try to change the subject of her meditation. Provided she is meditating on things concerning God, there is no disadvantage in turning from one subject to another, so long as they all have to do with Him. And she will sometimes derive as much joy from meditating on His creatures and on the

[1] [*Lit.*: " much employed "—but the context shows what is intended.]

power which He manifested in creating them as in thinking upon the Creator Himself.

O hapless human misery, which sin has brought to such a pass that even in what is good we need restraint and measure lest we should so ruin our health as to be unable to enjoy it! It is certainly a good thing for many people, especially those who are imaginative or weak in intelligence, to know this about themselves: it is very necessary for them to do so and they will serve Our Lord the better for it. And when anyone finds that her imagination is occupied with a mystery of the Passion, or with the glory of Heaven, or with anything of that kind, and for many days she is unable to think of anything else, anxious as she is to do so, or to throw off her absorption in it, let her realize that it is good for her to do what she can to distract herself. If she does not, she will come in time to realize what harm has ensued and that this has arisen from the causes I have mentioned—either from great physical weakness, or from the imagination, which is much worse. For when a madman gets an idea into his head he is not his own master and cannot distract himself or think of anything else, and no reasoning can persuade him to do so, because he is not master of his reason; and the same thing is true here, though this is a delectable madness. And, oh, if such a person has a melancholy temperament! It may then do her a great deal of harm. I cannot think of any way in which this absorption can be good. For the soul has a capacity for the fruition of God Himself; so why, as God is infinite, should it remain the captive of only one of His wonders or mysteries, except for some such reason as I have given, since there are so many of them with which it can busy itself? And the more of such things we wish to meditate upon, the more is revealed of His wonders.

I do not mean that in the course of a single hour, or even of a whole day, we should meditate on many things, for to do this might well be to derive profit from none. These things are so subtle that I should not like you to think I am saying anything which it is not in my mind to say or to mistake one thing for another. In fact the right understanding of this chapter is so important that, although it is a burden to me to write it, I do not regret doing so, and I should like anyone who does not understand it at first to read it many times, especially prioresses and novice-mistresses, who have to guide the sisters in prayer. For, if they are not careful at first, they will find later on that it takes them a long time to remedy this kind of weakness.

If I were to write down all that has come to my notice about this danger, you would see that I am doing well in laying so much stress on it. I will give just one example, from which you may deduce everything else.[1] In one of these convents of ours, there were a nun and a lay sister, both highly favoured in prayer and both mortified, humble and full of virtues and the recipients of many favours from the Lord, Who communicated to them some of His wonders. In particular, they were so detached and so absorbed in love for Him that, although we tried to observe them closely, they did not appear to be failing to respond to the favours bestowed on them by Our Lord, so far as any response is possible to our base nature. (I have dwelt at this length upon their virtue so that those who have less may have the greater misgivings.) They began to experience vehement impulses of desire for the Lord which they could not satisfy. They thought, however, that when they communicated these impulses calmed down, so they obtained permission from their confessors to communicate frequently; but the result was such an increase of distress that unless they communicated daily they thought they were about to die. Their confessors, one of whom was a very spiritual man, seeing such souls with such vehement desires, thought this remedy necessary for their trouble.

But it did not stop here. The yearnings of one of them became so strong that she had to communicate early each morning, in order, as she thought, to sustain her life; and they were not persons who would pretend anything, or tell a lie, for anything in the world. I was not there at the time but the Prioress wrote to me about what was happening, saying that she could do nothing with them and that there were some people who said that they ought to be given this help since there was no alternative to it. By the Lord's good pleasure, I realized at once what was happening, but until I got there I said nothing, for fear I might be mistaken; and it would not have been right for me to contradict those who approved what had been done until I could produce my reasons.

One of these confessors was so humble that, as soon as I arrived and spoke to him, he believed me. The other was less spiritual, and indeed by comparison with the first had hardly any spirituality at all: to persuade this latter was quite impossible. I did not mind this, however, as I was in no way bound to him. I started to talk to the nuns and to give them many reasons, sufficient, in my opinion, to prove to them that the idea that they would die without this particular help was pure imagination. But the notion was so deeply rooted in their minds that no

---

[1] According to P. Francisco de Santa María, this incident took place at Medina del Campo and the choir-nun referred to was a certain Alberta Bautista, who professed in 1569 and died in 1583, while the lay sister was called Inés de la Concepción. Daily communion, in St. Teresa's day, was very seldom allowed to the laity.

argument could eradicate it and it was useless to reason with them further. So, seeing that it was in vain, I told them that I had those very desires myself and yet I should stay away from Communion, so that they might realize that they ought not to communicate except when all the nuns did so together: we would all three die together, I said, for I thought that was better than that such a custom should be established in these convents where there were others who loved God as much as they did and who might wish to imitate them.

The harm which this habit of theirs had done them had got to such a pitch (the devil must have had something to do with it) that it really seemed as if, when they did not communicate, they had reached the point of death. I was very stern with them, for the more I realized how refractory they were being to obedience, because they thought they could not help themselves, the more convinced I was that it was a temptation. They spent the first day in great suffering; the next tried them less; and in this way they gradually got better, so that, when I went to Communion myself because I was ordered to do so (I would not have gone otherwise because of their great weakness), they bore it extremely well.

Soon afterwards, both they and all the other sisters realized that this had been a temptation to which they had been fortunate to put a stop while they could, for the same convent a little later had some difficult times with its superiors (it had nothing to do with these two nuns: I may say something about it later on)[1] and they would not have approved of such a custom or even tolerated it.

Oh, how many other things of this kind I could describe! I will describe only one: it happened, not in a convent of our Order, but in a Cistercian house.[2] There was a nun who was not less virtuous[3] than those I have referred to. By dint of much discipline and fasting she had become so weak that, whenever she communicated or had occasion to be enkindled in devotion, she would fall to the ground and remain there for eight or nine hours: both she and the other nuns thought it was a case of

---

[1] In 1571 there were two cases of friction between this Medina community and the Provincial of the Calced: no doubt the reference here is to these. The first was concerned with the disposal of the possessions of Isabel de los Angeles, the family and the Provincial holding one view and the novice herself another. The second arose from the election as Prioress of Teresa de Quesada, one of the Incarnation nuns who had come to Medina with St. Teresa (p. 8, above).

[2] This may have been the Cistercian convent of Olmedo, in the province of Valladolid, where St. Teresa often stayed when travelling in connection with her foundations.

[3] St. Teresa omits the word "less", presumably through an oversight. Gracián emended the whole passage but Báñez crossed out his emendations and supplied the missing word, which is adopted by all the editions.

rapture. This happened to her so often that, if she had not found relief, I think she would have come to great harm. The fame of her raptures spread through the whole town: for myself, I was sorry to hear of this, for the Lord was pleased to reveal to me what the matter was and I had misgivings as to what might come of it. Her confessor, who was a great friend of mine, came to tell me about it. I gave him my opinion—that she was wasting her time, for these fits could not possibly be raptures or anything else but the result of weakness.[1] I told him he must forbid her fasting and discipline and provide her with some distraction. She was obedient and did as he said. Soon she became stronger and stopped thinking about raptures. If she had really been experiencing them, this remedy could have done nothing to stop them until it was the will of God that they should cease. For the power of the spirit is so great that our own power is insufficient to resist it, and, as I have said, it produces notable effects in the soul. But this other experience leaves no more effect than if it had not happened, except for producing weariness in the body.

From this we must learn that anything which gets the better of us to such an extent that we think our reason is not free must be considered suspicious, for in that way we shall never gain freedom of spirit, one of the marks of which is that we can find God in all things even while we are thinking of them. Anything other than this is spiritual bondage, and, apart from the harm which it does to the body, it constrains the soul and retards its growth. It is as when we make a journey and get into a marsh or a bog from which we cannot escape. To some extent it is like this with the soul, which, if it wishes to advance, must not only walk but fly.

Oh, when people say, and believe, that they are absorbed in the Deity, and have no control of themselves, because of the suspension of their faculties, and can find no means of distraction, and add that this often happens to them, let them consider my advice: there is no need for them to be afraid, whether this lasts for a day, or for four days, or for eight days, for it is not surprising that such a condition should arise in a person with a weak constitution, and that it should continue for so long a time. I mean, of course, if it happens occasionally:[2] if it is frequent,

---

[1] Gracián makes the sentence end at " anything " but inserts above: " (she was) being weak and (wasting her time)." Báñez restores the original text in both places.

[2] [*Lit.*: " it is understood (that I mean) occasionally "—a characteristically Teresan compression.] These words were written by St. Teresa in the margin of the autograph and have not previously been included in any Spanish edition of the *Foundations*: some of the letters were cut off by the binder of the manuscript, and thus the sense was destroyed.

some remedy must be found. The good side of all this is that there is no question of fault or sin and it will lose us no merit; on the other hand, it has all the disadvantages I have referred to and a great many more. With regard to communions, the disadvantage will be considerable, if a soul's love leads it to disobey the confessor or the prioress. It is quite natural that it should feel lonely, but it must not feel excessively so, or its feelings may lead it to commit excesses. In this as in other respects, it is essential for such souls to be mortified and made to realize that it is better for them to sacrifice their own desires than to have their desired consolation.

Love of self, too, may interfere here. This has happened to me, for on several occasions when I have just communicated, and the Sacred Form has still been almost whole, I have seen others communicating and wished I had not already done so in order that I might do it again. At the time there would seem no reason to pay any attention to these feelings, but they came to me so often that I began to reflect about them, and I wondered if they had more to do with the love of God or with my own pleasure. For, when we go to Communion, we are generally conscious of devotion and joy, but these feelings were carrying me right away. Now, I argued, if I communicated in order to have God in my soul, I had Him there already; if I went to fulfil my obligation to receive Holy Communion, I had already fulfilled it; and if I went in order to receive the favours which are bestowed with the Most Holy Sacrament, I had already received them. In short, I came to see quite clearly that the only reason behind my feelings was a desire to experience once more a pleasure of sense.

I remember I was once staying in a place where there was a convent of our Order, and I made the acquaintance of a woman there whom the whole town described as a very great servant of God, as indeed she must have been. She used to communicate daily and had no confessor of her own but went now to one church to communicate and now to another. I observed this and felt I should have liked to see her obeying one person rather than communicating so often. She lived alone and seemed to me to do very much as she pleased; but as she was a good woman all that she did was good. I used sometimes to talk to her about her life, but she paid no heed to what I said, and rightly so, for she was far better than I, though in this respect I did not think I was wrong. When the saintly Fray Peter of Alcántara came to this town, I got him to talk to her and was not at all pleased with his account of the conversation. There may be nothing in this, for we are such miserable creatures that we are never very pleased except with those who choose to walk along our own road: and I believed that she had served the Lord better and done more penance in one year than I had in a great many. She was stricken by a mortal sickness—and this is the point I am coming to: she saw to it that Mass was said in her house daily and that she was given the Most Holy Sacrament.

During the course of her illness, a priest, a great servant of God, who used often to say Mass for her, thought it unsuitable that there should be Communion in her house every day. This must have been a temptation of the devil, for it happened on the last day of her life. When she saw that Mass was over and she was without the Lord, she was so annoyed and angry with the priest that he was greatly scandalized and came to tell me about it. I was very sorry, and even now I do not know if she was reconciled with him, for I believe she died immediately.

This led me to realize the harm which comes from having our own way in anything, especially in a matter of such importance. For it is right that anyone who so often approaches the Lord should be so conscious of his own unworthiness that he should not do so of his own free will. And what we lack before we can approach so great a Lord, which must needs be a great deal, can be supplied by obedience to those who command us. To this good woman there presented itself an opportunity for great humility, and perhaps by embracing it she would have gained more than if she had communicated; for she would have realized that the priest was not to blame, but that it had been ordained by the Lord, Who saw how miserable a sinner she was and how unworthy to receive Him in so poor a lodging. This happened to one person whose prudent confessors often forbade her to communicate, because she did so too frequently.[1] Though feeling the deprivation very deeply, she desired God's honour so much more than her own that she constantly praised Him for having inspired her confessor to watch over her, and to prevent His Majesty from entering so poor a lodging. By means of these reflections she obeyed with great tranquillity of soul, though at the same time with a devout and loving distress. She would never have disobeyed her orders for the whole world.

Believe me, any love of God (and I do not say that such a thing really is love but only that it seems so to us) which stirs the passions in such a way as to lead to the commission of some offence against Him, or troubles the peace of the loving soul so that it cannot listen to reason is clearly nothing else but self-

[1] " Good example and good soul," wrote Gracián in the margin of the autograph. St. Teresa is, in fact, writing of herself here.

interest. And the devil will not go to sleep over his task of causing us distress when he thinks he can do us the maximum of harm, as he did to that woman. The story certainly alarmed me greatly, though I did not think it would imperil her salvation, for the goodness of God is great; still, the temptation came at a very critical time.

I have spoken of it here so that prioresses may be on the alert, and sisters may fear and reflect and examine themselves as to the way in which they draw near to receive so great a favour. If they do this in order to please God they know quite well that He is better pleased with obedience than with sacrifice.[1] And if that is the case, and if I therefore earn more merit, why am I troubled about it? I do not mean that it is wrong for them to feel a humble distress, for they have not all attained to the perfection of feeling none whenever they simply do what they think most pleasing to God; but, once the will is completely detached from all self-interest, it is clear that it will harbour no regrets but will rather rejoice that an opportunity has arrived for it to please the Lord in a way which costs it so dear; and it will humble itself and be quite satisfied with spiritual communion.

But as in the early stages, and even more so later on, it is of His favour that the Lord bestows on us these great desires to approach Him (I am referring to the early stages because it is beginners who most need to consider this, and they are not so strong in the other aspects of perfection which I have mentioned), He allows us to experience deep emotion and distress when He inflicts this deprivation upon us; yet He also grants us a tranquillity of soul which will lead us to make acts of humility. If, however, we show any signs of trouble or passion, or argue with our superior or our confessor, we may be sure that this desire is a manifest temptation. Let no one, then, be determined to communicate when her confessor tells her not to do so. I should not envy any merit she might gain by doing so, for in these matters we must not be our own judges. The judge must be He who has the keys wherewith to bind or to loose. May the Lord be pleased to give us light, so that in matters of such importance we may know how to act, and may His help never fail us, lest our use of the favours which He gives us should lead us to displease Him.

[1] 1 Kings [A.V., 1 Samuel] xv, 22.

CHAPTER VII

How to treat nuns suffering from melancholy. This chapter is necessary for superiors.[1]

These sisters of mine at Saint Joseph's, in Salamanca, where I am living while writing this, have urged me to say something about the treatment of nuns who have a tendency to melancholy; for, however much we try not to admit such persons, melancholy is so subtle a thing that it remains latent when this is to its advantage, and so we are not always aware of it until it is past remedy. I am not sure, but I believe I said something about this in a little book[2] of mine: still, no great harm will be done if I say something about it here, provided the Lord is pleased to enable me to do so. It may be that I have spoken of it already: but I would do so a hundred times more if I thought I could say anything useful about it. This kind of temperament has so many methods of getting its own way that we must examine them all if we are to bear with it and control it and prevent it from harming others.

It must be observed that not all who are of a melancholy temperament will give us trouble. Persons of a humble and amenable disposition, though they suffer a great deal themselves, do no harm to others, especially if they are intelligent. And there are also various degrees of melancholy. In some people I really believe the devil uses it as a means of winning their souls, and, if they are not very careful, he will succeed. For, as the principal characteristic of this temperament is that it dominates and blinds the reason, what mischief will our passions not accomplish? To have no reason is to be mad, and some people who suffer from this affliction do go mad; in those of whom we are now speaking, however, the matter is not so serious. It would be much better if it were; for, to have to behave like a reasonable person to anyone who has lost her reason, and to have to treat her as such, is an intolerable trial. Those who are completely possessed by this malady are to be pitied, but they do no harm; the way to control them, if there be such a way, is to use fear.

Those in whom this serious malady has only begun (and, even if not rooted in them, it is of the same type and springs from

---

[1] [The noun (*perladas*) is feminine and the reference will therefore be to the prioresses mentioned in the preceding chapter.]

[2] [*Librico pequeño*: " tiny little book." On this, see Vol. i, p. xli, above.]

the same source) must be given the same remedy if no other methods suffice to cure them. The superiors must have recourse to the penances current in the Order and contrive to control the sufferers so that they may realize that they are never to act according to their own will. For, if they once find that their complaints and the desperate condition which the devil induces in them are occasionally effective, they are lost; and one person of this kind is sufficient to upset an entire convent. As the poor creature has no means of her own by which to defend herself against the wiles of the devil, the superior must use the greatest care in directing her, both inwardly and outwardly. The sufferer's reason being beclouded, it is essential that the superior's should be all the clearer, lest the devil begin to make use of her in order to bring her under his sway. This is a dangerous thing; for sometimes the melancholy temperament oppresses the reason sufficiently to dominate it altogether. In that case there is no more question of culpability than there would be in madmen, whatever the outrages they may perpetrate. Those, however, whose reason is not gone, but only slightly affected, have a certain degree of culpability; for at other times they are quite well. It is important that, at times when they are so affected, these latter should be allowed no liberties, lest when they are well they should be unable to keep themselves in check, this being a terrible trick of the devil. So, if we consider the matter, we shall see that their principal desire is to act according to their own will and to say whatever comes to their lips, remarking upon the faults of others so as to mask their own and delighting in whatever pleases them. They are, in fact, like persons who in themselves have no power of resistance. If their passions are not mortified, and each of them wants to do exactly as she pleases, what will the result be if no resistance is offered to them?

I repeat, as one who has seen and dealt with many persons afflicted in this way, that there is no other remedy for it than to use all the ways and means in our power to bring them under control. If words do not suffice, they must be punished; if trifling punishments are not enough, they must have severe ones; if one month's imprisonment is not sufficient, they must have four: there is no better way of benefiting their souls. For, as I have said and now repeat (and it is for their own good that they should understand it), they may once in a way be unable to control themselves, but they are not suffering from confirmed madness, which would free them from all culpability. As they suffer in this way only occasionally, and not all the time, their souls are in great danger, unless, as I say, they have so far lost their reason that they are forced to act and speak in a way which they would not if they could avoid it. It is a great mercy of God if those whom He visits with this malady are submissive to those who direct them, for therein lies their great hope of overcoming the peril of which I have spoken. If any such person reads this, let her realize, for the love of God, that it may perhaps affect her salvation.

I know some persons who have all but completely lost their reason, yet who are so humble and fearful of offending God that, though in secret they almost melt away in tears, they act only as they are commanded and endure their infirmity as others do. This is a greater martyrdom for them and for that reason they will have the greater glory; they are going through purgatory in this life so as not to have it in the next. But I repeat that those who do not willingly act in this way must be disciplined by their superiors and must not deceive themselves with indiscreet shows of piety lest they upset all the other sisters by their exaggerations.

In addition to the danger which has already been described, there is another and a very great one. So miserable is our nature that, when a person suffering in this way shows every sign of being in good health, all her companions, having no idea of the seriousness of her inward malady, will think that they too are afflicted by melancholy, and that their little ways may be put up with too. In point of fact it is the devil who puts this into their minds; and such havoc does he work among them that, when its extent comes to be realized, it will be difficult to set right. So important is this that we must never be careless about it; and, if a melancholy nun should resist her superior, she must on no account be excused but must pay for it as a nun would who was well. The same applies if she speaks ill to a sister, and so in all similar matters.

It seems unjust to punish one who is sick like one who is well when the former cannot help herself. But it seems equally so to bind and chastise madmen instead of allowing them to kill everybody. Believe me, I have tried both ways, and I think I have attempted every kind of remedy, and there is none but this. A prioress who out of the kindness of her heart has begun to allow such nuns freedom will eventually find it impossible to do anything with them, and there will be no curing them until great harm has been done to the rest. Madmen have to be bound and punished to prevent them from killing others, and, if it is right to do this (though it makes one very sorry for them,[1] as they cannot help themselves), how much more so is it to

---

[1] Gracián deleted this clause and substituted: " and a work of mercy ".

care for these melancholy nuns lest with the liberties they take they do harm to others! And often, as I have said, I really believe that the trouble comes from those who are used to freedom, have little humility and have been ill disciplined; and that this is more to blame than their temperament. I know it is so in some; for, when they have been brought before a person they are afraid of, I have seen them become docile, so I know that they can. Why, then, can they not become docile to please God? I am afraid, as I have said, that the devil takes advantage of this humour to win many souls.

We hear more of melancholy now than we used to, as that term is apt to be applied to every kind of self-will and desire for freedom. It has occurred to me, therefore, that it would be a good idea if in these houses of ours, and in all religious houses, we were never to take this word upon our lips, as it seems to encourage the granting of undue liberty. It should simply be described as a serious illness—and it is certainly serious enough—and be treated as such. Sometimes, in order to make this humour tractable, it is essential to correct it by means of medicine. This should be done in the infirmary and it should be understood that, when the sick nun returns to the community, she must be as humble as all the rest and as obedient as all the rest, and if she is not, no excuse must be made for her temperament: this is fitting both for the reasons I have given and for others to be given later. Without their realizing it, prioresses must treat these nuns very kindly, like true mothers, and seek possible means of curing them.

I seem to be contradicting myself, for so far I have said that they should be treated with severity. This I repeat, for they must not think that they can have their own way, nor must they be allowed to have it. The basis of their training must be their obligation to obey: the harm comes through their feeling themselves to be free. But the prioress is not obliged to order them to do anything in which she sees they are likely to disobey her because they have not sufficient strength to make the required effort. In all important matters she should lead them skilfully and lovingly, so that, if possible, they may be controlled by love, which is by far the best way: this she can generally do by showing that she is greatly attached to them, which she can make them realize by her acts and words. Superiors must know, too, that the best remedy which they can give such persons is to keep them busy with their duties so that they have no opportunity of imagining things, which is the cause of all their trouble. Though they may not perform these duties very well, any shortcomings in this respect should be put up with, for that is easier than having to put up with much greater ones when they are beyond cure. I believe this is the most effective remedy that can be applied. Superiors should also see that as a general rule they do not spend long periods in prayer, for as a rule their imagination is weak and overmuch prayer will do them great harm; besides, they will fancy things which neither they nor those who hear of them can possibly understand. Care should be taken that they eat fish only rarely; and they should not fast for as long as the rest.

It seems excessive to give so much advice about this one complaint, and none about any other, when our miserable lives are so full of grievous complaints—especially the lives of us weak women. There are two reasons for my doing so. First, such people think they are well, and will not realize that they are suffering from this complaint at all; and, as they are not obliged to stay in bed or to call a doctor, and have no fever, the prioress has to be their doctor; yet their complaint is more harmful to perfection than any which may force them to keep their beds and endanger their lives. The second reason is that when they are ill in other ways they either recover or die: from this, however, they rarely recover, nor do they die of it, but they completely lose their reason, and that is a death which kills others as well as themselves. Inwardly they suffer all the pains of death with their afflictions, fancies and scruples, and this will give them abundant merit, though they always refer to such things as temptations; if they could once come to realize that they all proceed from the same complaint, it would be a great relief to them, provided they attached no importance to it. I am indeed very sorry for them, as all of us who have to do with them must be when we realize that the Lord might afflict any of us with a like burden; we must therefore bear with them, as I have said, without their realizing it. May the Lord grant that my views are sound on what it is well to do in cases of this grievous malady.

CHAPTER VIII

Gives certain advice concerning revelations and visions.

Some people seem to be frightened at the very mention of visions or revelations. I do not know why they think a soul being led in this way by God is on such a dangerous path, nor what is the source of this alarm. I do not want here to discuss what visions are good and what are bad, or the signs which very learned people have given me by which the good may be distinguished from the bad. My subject is the course which anyone who finds herself receiving them will do best to pursue, for there are few confessors to whom she can go who will not make her afraid. Confessors are really less alarmed when they hear that the devil is harassing a soul with all kinds of temptation, with a spirit of blasphemy or with foolish and unseemly ideas, than they are scandalized at being told that a person has seen or heard some angel, or has had a vision of Jesus Christ crucified, Our Lord.

Nor will I now discuss when the revelations are of God, for that becomes clear from the great blessings which they bring to the soul. I am concerned with the forms assumed by the devil in order to deceive us when he takes the likeness of Christ Our Lord or of His saints. For my own part, I believe that His Majesty will not allow him, or give him the power, to deceive anyone with such appearances unless the person himself be to blame[1]: rather will the deceiver himself be deceived. I mean that for humble souls no deception is possible[2] and so there is no reason why they should be afraid: they must trust in the Lord and pay little heed to these things, except when they lead them to praise Him the more.

I know of a person whose confessors made her terribly depressed about such things; and yet, as she discovered later by the great results and good works which proceeded from them, they were of God. She found it very difficult, when she saw His figure in any vision, to make the sign of the Cross and expressions of contempt, as she had been ordered to do.[3] Later she consulted a very learned Dominican, Fray Domingo Báñez,[4] who told her that she was acting wrongly and that no one should ever do this. For, he said, wherever we see a representation of Our Lord it is right for us to reverence it, even if it has been painted by the devil himself; for he is a skilful painter, and, though trying to harm us, he is doing us a kindness if he paints us a crucifix or any other picture in so lifelike a way as to leave a deep impression upon our hearts. This argument seemed to me excellent; for, when we see a very fine picture, we always value it even if we know it has been painted by a wicked man, and we should never allow the identity of the painter to hinder our devotion. Just so the good or the evil is not in the vision, but in the person who sees it, and depends upon his profiting by it and upon his

[1] This clause is interlinear.
[2] This clause is marginal.
[3] Cf. *Life*, Chap. XXIX, *Interior Castle*, VI, ix (Vol. I, p. 189, Vol. II, p. 318, above).
[4] P. Báñez's name is written by St. Teresa in the margin.

humility. Where there is humility, no harm can possibly ensue, even though the vision come from the devil; and where there is no humility, there can be no profit, even if the vision come from God. For if what should engender humility in the soul, which knows it does not deserve such a favour, makes it proud, it becomes like the spider, which turns all its food into poison, instead of resembling the bee, which turns it into honey.

I will explain myself further. If Our Lord, of His goodness, is pleased to reveal Himself to a soul, so that it may know Him and love Him better, or to show it any of His secrets, or to grant it any special consolations and favours; and if the soul, which, as I have said, should be covered with confusion and recognize how little one so base has deserved this, at once considers itself a saint, and thinks that it has gained this favour because of some service which it has done, it is clear that the great good which it should derive from that favour will be turned into evil, as in the case of the spider. Let us now suppose that it is the devil who brings about these apparitions in order to incite the soul to pride. If the soul, thinking they are of God, humbles itself and recognizes how unworthy it is of so great a favour and strives to serve Him better; if, seeing itself rich, yet unworthy of eating the crumbs which fall from the table of those to whom it has heard God has granted these favours—I mean, unworthy of being the servant of any of them; if it humbles itself and begins to strive to do penance, to devote itself more earnestly to prayer and to be more careful not to offend this Lord Whom it believes to be the Giver of this favour, but to obey Him more perfectly: then I can assure it that the devil will not return, but will flee in disgrace and leave no evil in the soul.

If a person is told to do anything, or the future is prophesied to her, in a revelation, it is essential that she should discuss the matter with a discreet and learned confessor, and neither do nor believe anything but what that confessor tells her. She can consult the prioress about it so that a suitable confessor may be found for her. And let her take this warning: if she does not obey the confessor in what he says, and allow herself to be guided by him, she is possessed either of an evil spirit or of a terrible melancholy. For supposing the confessor should be wrong, she will still be doing right in not departing from what he tells her, even were it an angel of God who had been speaking to her; for His Majesty will give him light, or will ordain that what he says shall be justified. She cannot be in danger, then, if she obeys him, whereas by doing otherwise she may be incurring much danger and harm.

It should be remembered that the weakness of our nature is very great, especially in women, and that it shows itself most markedly in this way of prayer; so it is essential that we should not at once suppose every little imagining of ours to be a vision; if it is one, we may be sure that the fact will soon become clear. When a person is subject to melancholy much more caution is necessary; fancies of this kind have come to me and I have been quite alarmed to find how possible it is for people to think they see what they do not.

I was once visited by a confessor who was thought a great deal of, and who had been told by someone in confession that Our Lady often came to her, sat down on her bed and stayed talking with her for more than an hour, telling her about things that were going to happen and a great deal more. Many of these things were foolish, but one or two were to the point, and so she believed all the rest. I saw at once what was the matter, though I did not venture to say so, for we are living in a world in which we have to think of people's opinions of us if our words are to have any effect. I said, therefore, that it would be best for him to wait and see if the prophecies came true, to make enquiries about other effects produced by the vision and to find out what kind of life that person was living. In the end he discovered that the whole thing was foolishness.

I could say a great deal more about this, which would be useful in proving the point I am making—namely, that a soul should not believe things at once, but should wait awhile and be quite sure of their truth before communicating them to anyone, lest, without meaning to do so, it should deceive a confessor. For, if a man has no experience of these things, however learned he may be, his learning will not enable him to understand them. Not many years ago—quite recently, indeed— some most learned and spiritual men were greatly bewildered by things of this kind which someone reported to them. But eventually the man in question went and discussed them with a person who had had experience of favours granted by the Lord and who saw clearly that he was deluded and crazy. Although this was not discovered at the time, but kept a close secret, the Lord soon made it clearly known, though the person who had been consulted and had realized what was wrong suffered a great deal at first through not being believed.[1]

[1] This was apparently a personal experience, as the details coincide with those of a story told by M. Isabel de Santo Domingo about a certain Juan Manteca, of Ávila. St. Teresa, on being consulted, found that he was deluded. This incident took place in 1565 [which, however, is hardly a date that would be described in 1573 as " quite recent " (ha . . . harto poco tiempo). There must have been many such cases in these years].

For these and similar reasons, it is very important that each sister should discuss her method of prayer quite frankly with her prioress, who in her turn must be most careful to keep in mind the temperament of that sister and her progress in perfection, so that she may help the confessor to understand her case better, and may also choose a special confessor if the one the sister has is not capable of treating such cases. We must all take great care that things like these, even if they are clearly of God, or favours recognized as being miraculous, are not discussed with people outside the convent, or with confessors who are not prudent enough to keep silent about them; this is a more important point than may be realized. The sisters, too, should not discuss such things among themselves. The prioress must be prudent, and must tend always to praise those who are outstanding in humility, mortification and obedience, rather than those led by God along this most supernatural way of prayer, even though they also possess these other virtues. For if they are being led by the Spirit of the Lord, He will grant them humility, which will lead them to love being despised: thus they themselves will take no harm, and others will benefit. For, as they cannot attain thus far, since God gives these favours to whom He will, they would become discouraged unless they had these other virtues, which, though also given by God, can more readily be obtained by us and in the religious life are of great price. May His Majesty bestow them upon us, for, if we are diligent, watchful and prayerful, He will deny them to none of us, provided we strive to attain them and have confidence in His mercy.

CHAPTER IX

Describes how she left Medina del Campo to make the foundation of Saint Joseph at Malagón.

How far I have wandered from my subject! Still, it may be that some of these counsels will have been more useful than an account of the foundations. While I was at Saint Joseph's, in Medina del Campo, it comforted me very much to see how closely the sisters there were walking in the steps of those of Saint Joseph's in Ávila, in the faithful observance of their Rule, in sisterly love and in spirituality, and how Our Lord was providing their house with what was needed, both in the church and by the nuns themselves. The sisters whom they received year by year seemed to have been chosen by the Lord, and were such as befitted the foundation of this kind of building. To these early stages, I believe, is to be traced all future good; for those who come later walk in the path which they already find.

There was a lady in Toledo, a sister of the Duke of Medinaceli, in whose house I had been staying at the order of my superiors, as I have explained at greater length in writing of the foundation of Saint Joseph's.[1] While there she became particularly fond of me and this must have helped to encourage her to do as she did, for His Majesty often uses means which to us who are ignorant of the future seem of little value. When this lady heard that I had a licence to found convents, she began to urge on me the foundation of a house in a town called Malagón, which belonged to her. I was not at all anxious to act upon the suggestion, because it was so small a place, and I should have been forced to accept an endowment for its maintenance; and I was very much opposed to that.

I discussed the matter with learned men, and with my confessor,[2] and they all told me I was wrong, for the Holy Council[3] allowed us to possess endowments and so I ought not on this account to refrain from founding a convent in which, in my opinion, the Lord would be so well served. To their counsels were added the numerous importunities of this lady, so that I could not do other than accept the offer. The endowment she gave us was quite adequate—and I always like our convents either to be completely without money or else to have enough to make it needless for the nuns to beg the necessaries of life from anybody.

I did everything in my power to ensure that none of the sisters should possess anything of her own, but that they should all keep the Constitution in every respect as did these other convents of ours which had been founded in poverty. When all the deeds had been drawn up, I sent for certain sisters to come with me to make the foundation and we went with this lady to Malagón.[4] Here,

---

[1] Cf. *Life*, Chap. XXXIV (Vol. I, pp. 232-3, above). Doña Luisa de la Cerda asked St. Teresa to make a foundation at Malagón at a time when she was discussing with Don Bernardino de Mendoza, brother of the Bishop of Ávila, the possibility of founding a convent on land belonging to him at Río de Olmos, near Valladolid. Unable, however, to reject such a suggestion without careful thought, she left for the capital, with Ana de los Ángeles and Antonia del Espíritu Santo, at the beginning of November 1567, where she stayed with Doña Leonor de Mascareñas for a fortnight, going on to Alcalá de Henares, and, in February 1568, to Toledo. In Alcalá she was able to see and consult P. Domingo Báñez (see text below).

[2] I.e., P. Domingo Báñez.

[3] The Council of Trent (Session 25, *De Regularibus*, Cap. 3).

[4] Permission to make the foundation was granted by the Provincial, Fray Alonso González, in a patent signed at La Moraleja on March 24, 1568. The agreement with Doña Luisa was signed on March 30. Besides taking with her the two nuns referred to above, St. Teresa sent to the Incarnation, Ávila, for five more.

however, the house was not ready for our entry, so we stayed for more than a week in a room in the castle.[1]

On Palm Sunday, in the year 1568, a procession from the village came to receive us, and, wearing our veils and white mantles, we went to the parish church. Here a sermon was preached and the Most Holy Sacrament was then taken to our convent. All were greatly edified and I remained there for some days. On one of these days, after communicating, I was given to understand by Our Lord that He would be well served in that house.[2] I think I must have been there rather less than two months,[3] for the spirit soon moved me to go at once and found the house in Valladolid, for a reason which I shall now relate.

CHAPTER X

Describes the foundation of a house at Valladolid. This convent is entitled the Conception of Our Lady of Carmel.

Four or five months before the foundation of this convent of Saint Joseph at Malagón, I was talking with a young man, a person of some importance, who told me that, if I wanted to found a convent in Valladolid, he would give me a house which he had there, with a fine big garden in which there was a large vineyard: he would do this very gladly and grant me possession of it at once.[4] It was a most valuable gift, and I accepted it, though I had not quite decided to found my convent there because the house was almost a quarter of a league from the city. I thought, however, that, if we started there, we might move into the city later, and, as it was such a pleasure to him to give us the house, I was unwilling to decline his kind offer or to be an impediment to his devotion. About two months after this

[1] I.e., the Malagón residence of Doña Luisa, quite near the church referred to.

[2] After some years, on December 8, 1579, the community moved, with Doña Luisa's concurrence, to a quieter situation at the south of the town, where the Carmelite Convent still stands to-day. Of all St. Teresa's convents, it is the one which has changed least.

[3] Palm Sunday, in 1568, fell on April 11, and, in a letter written to Doña Luisa on May 18, St. Teresa says she is leaving Malagón on the following day. The Prioress of the new community was M. Ana de los Ángeles, and the novice-mistress, Isabel de Jesús, one of the nuns who had come from Ávila.

[4] This was Don Bernardino de Mendoza, referred to above (p. 45, n. 1). He had visited St. Joseph's, Ávila, and met St. Teresa there. It was on one of these visits that he first made his offer and he repeated it more pressingly when he saw the Saint at Olmedo, a town through which she had passed on her way to Medina. Don Bernardino died at Úbeda early in 1568 and St. Teresa heard of his death while at Alcalá de Henares.

he was attacked by a sudden illness which deprived him of the power of speech, so that he was unable to make a proper confession, though he made a great many signs to show that he was asking pardon of the Lord. Very shortly afterwards he died, a long way from the place where I was staying. The Lord told me that his salvation had been in great jeopardy, but that He had had compassion on him because of that service which he had done for His Mother by giving her a house for a convent of her Order; but He added that he would not be delivered from purgatory until the first Mass had been said there. The grievous afflictions of this soul were constantly in my mind; so, although I was anxious to make a foundation in Toledo, I gave up the idea for the time, and went with all possible haste to found the convent, as well as I could, at Valladolid.

It was impossible to do it as quickly as I had wished, for I was detained for a good many days[1] at Saint Joseph's in Ávila, where I was in charge, and after that at Saint Joseph's in Medina del Campo, through which city I passed on my way. While I was there, the Lord told me one day, in prayer, to make haste, as that soul was in great suffering; so, although I had made little preparation, I set to work and arrived at Valladolid on Saint Lawrence's day. When I saw the house, I was dreadfully distressed, for I knew that, unless we spent a great deal upon it, it would be foolish to have nuns there. It was a beautiful place, and the garden was delightful, but it was so near the river that it could not fail to be unhealthy.[2]

Tired as I was, I had to go to Mass at a house belonging to our Order, which I had seen on entering the city, and it was so far away that my sufferings were doubled. However, I said nothing to my companions[3] lest I should discourage them. Despite my weakness, I had some faith that the Lord, Who had told me what I have just narrated, would put matters right. With the utmost secrecy I engaged workmen and began to have fences made, as was necessary for our seclusion. With us was the priest whom I have mentioned, Julián de Ávila by name,[4] and also one of the two friars already referred to who wished to enter the Discalced Reform and was studying our way of life in these convents.[5] Julián de Ávila saw about getting a licence from the Ordinary, who had given us good hopes of this before I arrived. It could not be obtained very quickly and a Sunday

[1] From June 2 to 30, 1568. She was still Prioress of St. Joseph's, Ávila.
[2] The estate lay to the south of the city, on the bank of the river Pisuerga.
[3] There were three of these. One of them, Isabel de la Cruz, who came from the Incarnation, Ávila, became the first Prioress of the Valladolid foundation.
[4] [Cf. p. 8, above.]
[5] St. John of the Cross [cf. pp. 14-15, above].

passed before it reached us.[1] However, we were given leave to have Mass said in the place where we had decided to have our church and accordingly it was said for us there.

I was very far from thinking that what had been said to me about that soul would be fulfilled then; for, although I was told that it would happen at our first Mass, I thought that meant the Mass when the Most Holy Sacrament was placed in the church. When the priest was approaching us in the place where we were to communicate, holding the Most Holy Sacrament in his hands, and as I was preparing to receive it, I saw a vision of the young man in question, with a happy and resplendent countenance, standing beside the priest with his hands joined together, and thanking me for what I had done to enable his soul to be freed from purgatory and go to Heaven.[2] Actually, when I first heard that he was in the way of salvation, I had been expecting anything but that; indeed, I had been greatly distressed, as I thought that one who had lived as he had needed a very different kind of death, for, although he had had some good qualities, he had been deeply immersed in things of this world. It is true he had told my companions that he always had the thought of death before him. It is a striking thing that Our Lord should be so much pleased at whatever service is done to His Mother: great is His mercy. May He be praised and blessed for everything, Who thus rewards the lowliness of our works with eternal life and glory, and, little as there is of worth in them, makes them great.

When the day of the Assumption of Our Lady had arrived—that is, the fifteenth of August in the year 1568—we took possession of this convent. We were there only a short time, for nearly all of us fell very ill.[3] A lady living in the locality observed this: her name was Doña María de Mendoza, wife of the Comendador Cobos, mother of the Marquis of Camarasa, a most Christian lady, greatly given to charity, as the abundance of her alms made very clear.[4] Some time before, when I had been in contact with her, she had been very good to me, for she is the sister of the Bishop of Ávila, who was so helpful to us in the foundation of the

---

[1] There seems to be an inaccuracy here. If they reached Valladolid on August 10, the next Sunday was the festival of the Assumption itself—the day on which the convent was founded. It must, therefore, have been on one of the intervening days that the problem of hearing Mass arose.

[2] Don Bernardino's liberation is commemorated in one of Rubens' great paintings, which hangs in the picture-gallery at Antwerp.

[3] The illness of the nuns was no doubt due to the low and unhealthy situation of the convent.

[4] She was also, of course, sister of Don Bernardino. Her husband, Don Francisco de los Cobos, who, besides being Comendador Mayor of León, had been secretary to the Emperor Charles V, had died before the events here recorded.

first convent and in everything concerning the Order. As she is so kind, and as she saw that we could not stay there without great difficulty, both because it was a long way to send alms and also because it was unhealthy, she said that she would take the house from us and buy us another. She did so, and the house she gave us was a better one; she also gave us all that we have needed down to the present and will continue to do so for as long as she lives.

On the Feast of Saint Blasius[1] we entered the house and had a fine procession, which aroused great devotion in the people. This devotion they still retain, for the Lord performs many works of mercy in this house and He has brought souls to it whose sanctity will be described in due course, to the praise of the Lord, Who by such means is pleased to magnify His works and to grant graces to His creatures. One girl in particular came to us here who, young though she was, showed us what the world is by despising it. I have thought it well to say this here so as to put to confusion those who have a great love for the world and to give an example to girls to whom the Lord grants good desires and inspirations so that they may learn how to act upon them.[2]

There is a lady here called Doña María de Acuña, sister of the Count of Buendía.[3] She was married to the Governor[4] of Castile. He died while she was still quite young, leaving her with a son and two daughters. She began to live a life of such sanctity, and to bring up her children so virtuously, as to merit that Our Lord should desire to have them for Himself. I was wrong—she had three daughters. One, in early life, became a nun, and another, having no wish to marry, lived a life of great edification with her mother. The son, when quite young, began to understand the nature of the world and soon God gave him such a clear call to enter the religious life that nobody was able to prevent him from doing so. His mother was so delighted at this that she must have helped him a great deal by praying to Our Lord,

[1] February 3, 1569. The house into which they moved had been bought for them by Doña María and was much nearer the centre of the city, near the thoroughfare now known as Ronda de Santa Teresa. The original altar-piece, representing Christ bound to the Column and Doña María at His feet, is still preserved in the Valladolid convent. The cell used by St. Teresa is also intact. Among the treasures of the convent is the Valladolid autograph of the *Way of perfection*.

[2] From the old editions, down to that of 1752, the rest of this chapter is omitted [Cf. p. xix, above].

[3] St. Teresa had first written " Duke " but substituted " Count ", which is correct. The lady had married Don Juan de Padilla Manrique, Adelantado Mayor of Castile, in 1547. They had a son and *three* daughters; the husband died in 1563. The son became a Jesuit; of the daughters, Luisa became a Franciscan nun (leaving the Order later) and María took the Dominican habit at Valladolid. It was then that Casilda became the heiress, as related in the text.

[4] [*Adelantado*: the Governor of a province, who acted as Chief Justice in peace and as Captain-General in war.]

though she gave no indication of this on account of her kinsfolk. The fact is that, when the Lord desires a soul for Himself, creatures have little power to keep it back. So it was here. Though he was urged insistently not to take this step, and postponed it for three years, at the end of that time he joined the Company of Jesus.[1] The lady's confessor[2] told me how she had said to him that never in her life had such joy filled her heart as on the day when her son made his profession.

O Lord, what great favour dost Thou bestow on those to whom Thou givest parents with so true a love for their children that they wish them to have no rank, estate and riches, but only that blessedness which will know no end! It is a sad thing that the world is so unhappy and so blind that parents think their good name[3] consists in not allowing the memory of their having owned that dunghill which we call worldly possessions to fade, forgetting that, sooner or later, all these must come to an end. Everything finite, however long it lasts, will come to an end, and we must count it of little value. Parents who forget this try to preserve their vanities at the cost of their poor children, and are audacious enough to rob God of the souls which He desires for Himself and to deprive those souls themselves of a great blessing. For, even though it may not be one which will last for ever, it is an invitation from God to be with Him, and it is a great blessing to find oneself free from the annoyances and the restrictions of the world, which bear hardest upon those who have the greatest possessions. Open their eyes, my God, and show them what kind of love it is their obligation to have for their children, lest they should do them great harm and their children should complain of them before God at the Last Judgment, when, though perhaps unwillingly, they will learn what everything is really worth.

Now, when God, of His mercy, called from the world, at the age of about seventeen years, Don Antonio de Padilla, this young son of Doña María de Acuña, the eldest daughter, Doña Luisa de Padilla, became heir to the family estates, for the Count of Buendía had no children and Don Antonio was heir to his title and also to the Governorship of Castile. As it is no part of my purpose to do so, I shall say nothing here of all that he had to suffer from his kinsfolk before carrying his plan into execution. This will be well understood by all who know how important worldly people think it is to have descendants.

O Jesus Christ, Son of the Eternal Father, Our Lord, true King over all things! What didst Thou leave in the world for Thy descendants to inherit from Thee? What didst Thou ever have,

---

[1] This was on March 8, 1572.   [2] P. Jerónimo Ripalda, S.J.
[3] [*Honra*. Cf. Vol. 1, p. 14, n. 2, above.]

my Lord, save trials, pains and insults? Indeed Thou hadst
only a beam of wood to rest upon while drinking the bitter
draught of death. Those of us, then, my God, who desire to be
Thy true children and not to renounce their inheritance must
never flee from suffering. Thy crest is five wounds. So, my children, let that too be our device if we are to inherit His kingdom.
Not by ease nor by comfort nor by honour nor by wealth can we
gain that which He purchased for us by so much blood. O you
who come of illustrious lineage, for the love of God open your
eyes. Behold the true knights of Jesus Christ and the princes of
His Church, Saint Peter and Saint Paul: never did these travel
by the road you are taking. Can you be imagining that a new
road is to be built for you? Do not think that for a moment.
See, the Lord is beginning to show you the true road by means
of people as young as those of whom we are now speaking.

I have several times seen and spoken with this Don Antonio.
He wished he had had far more possessions so as to have had more
to leave. Blessed youth and blessed maiden, who have merited
so much of God that, at an age when the world is apt to exercise
a complete sway over those who live in it, they have trampled
it beneath their feet. Blessed be He Who granted them this great
blessing.

When the eldest sister inherited the estates, she set no more
store by them than her brother had done, for from childhood
she had been so devoted to prayer, in which the Lord gives us the
light of true understanding, that she valued them as little as her
brother had done. God bless me! What trials, torments and lawsuits would many people have endured in order to succeed
to this inheritance! Some would even have risked their lives
and reputations for it. And yet these young people had no light
trials to suffer before they were allowed to give it up. The world
is like that, and unless we are blind we soon discover how capricious
it is. In order to be free from her inheritance, however, this girl
renounced it with the greatest good will in favour of her sister,
who was ten or eleven years of age, and was the only remaining
heir.[1] Her kinsfolk, fearing that the miserable remembrance
of these vanities might fade, arranged a marriage for this child
with one of her uncles, a brother of her father, and obtained
from the Sovereign Pontiff a dispensation for her betrothal.

It was not the Lord's will that the daughter of such a mother,
who had such a brother and sister, should suffer from deception
any more than they. So the events happened which I shall now
describe. At first the child was delighted with her worldly gar-

[1] [Actually there were two sisters still left: St. Teresa again falls into the mistake
which she has already once corrected.]

ments and adornments, which, being such as befitted her position, might well have attracted her while still so young. But she had not been betrothed for two months when, although at the time she did not realize this, the Lord began to give her light. She had been spending a very happy day with her betrothed, whom she loved with an intensity rare in a child of her age, when suddenly she became very sad, for she realized that the day was over and that all other days would come to an end in the same way. O greatness of God, which turned into hatred the happiness caused her by delight in things which must perish! She began to feel so sad that she could not hide the fact from her betrothed; and she had no idea why she was sad or what to say to him, though he kept asking her what was the matter.

About this time he had to make an unavoidable journey to a place a long way off; and, as she was very fond of him, she was very sorry about this. But the Lord then revealed to her the reason for her distress—that her soul was inclining towards that which would never end—and she began to realize that her brother and sister had taken the safest course when they had left her amid the world's perils. This thought, on the one hand, and, on the other, the belief that there was no help for it (for, until she enquired about it, she was not told that her betrothal need not hinder her from becoming a nun) continued to trouble her, as, above all, did the love she had for her betrothed, which prevented her from making any definite decision. So she continued to suffer great distress.

As the Lord desired her for Himself, He gradually freed her from human love and increased her desire to renounce everything. She was now moved only by a desire for salvation and for the discovery of the best means to that end. She thought that, if she became more absorbed in worldly things, she would forget to strive after what is eternal—such wisdom did God inspire in her at so early an age so that she might seek to gain that which never ends. Happy soul, to escape while still so young from the blindness in which many who are old end their days! As soon as she found that her will was free, she resolved to employ it wholly in God. Until then she had said nothing of all this but she now began to discuss it with her sister. The latter, to whom it seemed mere childishness, tried to dissuade her, and gave her several reasons for remaining in the world, saying that she could marry and still be saved. "Why, then," asked the child, "did you leave the world yourself?" Several days passed, and her desire continued to increase, though she dared say nothing to her mother; yet the very cause of this conflict may well have been her mother's devout prayers.

CHAPTER XI

Continues the subject already begun concerning Doña Casilda de Padilla and how she achieved her holy desires to enter the religious life.

About this time it happened that the habit[1] was to be given to a lay sister in this convent of the Conception.[2] I may say something about her vocation later. The two girls were of different stations, for this nun had been a peasant-girl; yet, because of the great favours which God bestowed on her, she merits that some memorial should be made of her, to His Majesty's praise. When Doña Casilda (for so this beloved of the Lord was called) came with her grandmother, the mother of her betrothed, to witness the clothing of that nun, she was greatly attracted by this convent, thinking that, being few in number and poor, the nuns could render the Lord better service. However, she had not yet determined to leave her betrothed, and it was this difficulty, as I have said, which kept her back more than any other.

She remembered that, before her betrothal, she had been accustomed to spend short periods in prayer, for her good and saintly mother had brought up the girls and their brother to do this. From the age of seven they had been in the habit of occasionally visiting an oratory with her and she had taught them how to meditate on the Passion of the Lord and had made them go frequently to confession; and so she lived to see the happy outcome of her desires that they might belong to God. She has herself told me that she used often to offer them to Him and beseech Him to take them out of the world, for she had already lost her illusions as to the value which should be set upon it. I sometimes think how grateful they will be to their mother when they find themselves with the fruition of eternal joys which she was the means of procuring for them, and also of the additional joy which she will have when she sees them, and of how the contrary will be true of parents who have not brought up their children as children of God (and they are more His than theirs) when such parents meet their children in hell, uttering curses in agonies of despair.

But I must return to what I was saying. When this girl found that she now disliked even the saying of the rosary, she grew very

[1] St. Teresa first wrote " profession " and then altered it to " habit ". Actually this sister took the habit on July 2, 1572 and was professed on August 6, 1573.

[2] The girl was known in religion as Sister Estefanía de los Apóstoles (1549-1617). Her reputation for saintliness and austerity of life penetrated as far as to the Court of Philip II and Philip III, and many edifying stories are told of her.

much afraid that she would become worse and worse, and thought it was quite clear that, if she came to this house, she would make certain of her salvation. She therefore made a definite decision to do so. One morning she came here with her mother and sister, who, when they entered the convent, had no idea that she was going to do what she did. Once she found herself inside, no one could turn her out. When she asked them to leave her there she wept so sorely and spoke so earnestly that everyone was astonished. Her mother, though inwardly glad, was afraid of her kinsfolk, and was anxious that she should not remain lest it should be said that this was due to her own persuasion. The Prioress[1] agreed with her, thinking that she was only a child and that she ought to test her vocation. This happened in the morning; and they had to remain there until the evening, when they sent for the child's confessor and for Father-Master Fray Domingo, a Dominican, who was my own confessor, and of whom I spoke at the beginning of this book. I was not, however, there myself.[2] This Father at once realized that the spirit of the Lord was at work in her and gave her great encouragement, for which he had to put up with a great deal from her kinsfolk. He promised to help her to return to the convent on some other day. This is how all people who claim to be serving God ought to act when they see that a soul has been called by Him: they should not think so much of human prudence.

After a great deal of persuasion, she left the convent for the time being, so that her mother should not be blamed, but her desires now grew more and more. Her mother began to break the news privately to her kinsfolk but they kept it secret lest it should come to the ears of her betrothed. They said it was mere childishness, and she must wait until she was of age, for she was not quite twelve years old. To this she replied by asking why, if they thought her old enough to be married, and given over to the world, she should not be old enough to give herself to God. From the things she said it was evident that it was not she who was speaking at all.

Soon it became impossible to keep the secret any longer and it had to be broken to the bridegroom. When she learned that this had been done, she felt she could not bear to wait and see him; so on the Feast of the Conception, when in the house of her

---

[1] M. María Bautista, a niece of St. Teresa.

[2] P. Báñez was at that time Regent of the Dominican College at Valladolid. [St. Teresa was Prioress of the Incarnation at that time. If this chapter of the *Foundations* was written in 1573 (p. xvi, above) the adventures of Doña Casilda must have begun in December 1572, and her final entry into religion have taken place in the year following. P. Silverio, however, dates the occurrences a year later: if that date is correct, Chapter XI must have been written late in, or after, the year 1574. Cf. p. xvii, above.]

grandmother, who was also to be her mother-in-law and knew nothing about this, she begged to be allowed to go into the country with her governess, for a little recreation. Her grandmother, to please her, agreed, and sent her out in a carriage with her servants. To one of these she gave some money and asked him to go to the door of this convent with some bundles of faggots, and wait for her there. Then she made the carriage take a route which led her past this house. When she reached the door, she told the other servant to go to the turn and ask for a jug of water, without saying for whóm it was. Then she got down very quickly from the carriage. They said they would bring the water to her, but that was not what she wanted. The faggots were there already and she told her servants to tell the people in the convent to come to the door and take them in. She stood close by them; and, when they opened the door, slipped inside, and threw her arms around the statue of Our Lady, weeping and begging the Prioress not to turn her away. The servants shouted and knocked at the door, but she went to the grille to speak to them and told them that she would never come out again and that they could go and tell her mother. The women who had come with her cried out at this but she took little notice of them. When her grandmother was told the news she decided to go to the convent at once.

But neither she, nor an uncle, nor her bridegroom, who came and talked with her at the grille and did their utmost to dissuade her, did anything, all the time they were with her, but increase her distress and leave her more resolute than ever. After making a great lamentation her betrothed said to her that she could serve God better by giving alms; but she answered that he could do that himself. To all the other arguments he put before her she replied that her principal duty was to work out her own salvation, and that she knew she was weak and could not do this amid all the world's temptations. Further, there was nothing in her conduct for him to complain of, for she had left him only for God, and in this she was doing him no wrong. When she saw that no argument could convince him she got up and left him.

He made no impression upon her; in fact, she was very much displeased with him. For the temptations and disturbances contrived by the devil rather help than hinder the soul on whom God has bestowed the light of the truth. On behalf of such a soul His Majesty Himself does battle, and in this case it became quite clear that it was not the girl who was speaking at all.

When the bridegroom and her kinsfolk saw how little they could accomplish by trying to persuade her to leave the convent willingly, they endeavoured to do so by force, and so obtained a Royal Order by which they could take her from the convent and set her free. During the whole of this period, which lasted from the Feast of the Conception to Holy Innocents' Day, when they took her away, she remained in the convent, and, though not given the habit, observed all the rules of the Order just as if she were wearing it and was extremely happy. On the day when they fetched her away, they took her to the house of a gentleman where she was called for by the officers of justice. On the way there she wept sorely, asking why she was being tormented when this could be of no service to them. While she was there, numerous efforts were made to persuade her, by religious as well as by others; for some thought her conduct was childish and others were anxious that she should enjoy the benefit of her rank. I should have to write at great length to relate the discussions which took place and the way in which she emerged from them all. The things she said left everyone astounded.

When they saw that their words were of no avail, they took her to her mother's house, with the intention of keeping her there for some time. Her mother was already tired of all these disturbances and gave her no encouragement; indeed, she seemed to be opposed to her. It may be that she was acting in this way in order to test her further; so at least she told me later, and she is so saintly a woman that one cannot but believe what she says. But the child did not realize this. Her confessor was also completely opposed to her, so that her only help was in God and in one of her mother's maids in whom she used to confide. She suffered many trials and troubles until she reached the age of twelve, when she found that, as they could not alter her desire to become a nun, they were thinking of letting her enter the convent where her sister was and in which there was less austerity.[1]

When she discovered this, she determined, by whatever means she could, to further her own happiness by carrying out her original plan. So one day, when she was in a church, where she had gone with her mother to hear Mass, and her mother went to a confessional to make her confession, she asked her governess to go to one of the Fathers and beg him to say a Mass for her. When she saw that she had gone, she stuck her overshoes up her sleeves, caught up her skirt and ran with the greatest possible haste to this convent, which was a long way away. Her governess, not finding her, went after her, and, as she was approaching the convent, called to a man to stop her. Later the man said he had found himself unable to stir, and so had let her go. The girl entered by the outer door of the convent, shut it behind her and began to cry out. By the time her governess arrived, she was already in the convent, where they gave her the

[1] The Dominican house in Valladolid, where her sister María was.

habit at once. Thus were fulfilled the good beginnings which the
Lord had wrought in her. Very soon His Majesty began to reward
her with spiritual favours and she to serve Him with the greatest
happiness, the deepest humility and the most complete detachment.[1]

May He be blessed for ever, Who can make one for so long
a lover of rich dresses happy in poor garments of frieze. These,
however, could not hide her beauty, for the Lord had given her
natural as well as spiritual graces, and both in temperament
and in intelligence she was so attractive that she moved all the
nuns to praise His Majesty. May He grant that there may be
many who will thus answer His call.

CHAPTER XII

*Describes the life and death of a nun whom Our Lord brought to this
same house, Beatriz de la Encarnación, who lived so perfectly and
died in such a way that it is right a memorial should be made of
her.*[2]

There entered this convent as a nun a lady named Doña
Beatriz Oñez; she was related in some way to Doña Casilda
and came to us some years before her.[3] Her spirituality filled
all the nuns with amazement when they saw the great virtues
which the Lord was bestowing on her. The nuns and the
Prioress[4] affirmed that all her life long they never found anything in her which could be considered an imperfection. They
never saw her change countenance for any reason whatsoever;

[1] Doña Casilda took the name of Casilda Juliana de la Concepción [the reference
being, no doubt, to the fact that it was on the Feast of the Immaculate Conception
that she first entered the Convent]. She did not profess until January 13, 1577.
In 1581 she was given papal licence to migrate to the Franciscan Order and she was
then [at the age of barely twenty-one] made Abbess of the Convent in the village
of Santa Gadea del Cid, near Burgos, this being a house of the Mitigated Rule
connected with the Padilla family. Later she was joined there by her ex-Dominican
sister María and in 1589 the community moved to Burgos. [Beyond that point
we need not follow her history.] It may be added that their uncle who was to have
married her, Don Martín de Padilla, consoled himself with her sister Luisa, who
for this purpose abandoned her Franciscan vocation. After his death she re-entered
the religious life, this time as a Discalced Carmelite (1607) and became Luisa de la
Cruz.
[2] This chapter-heading is in the handwriting of the same nun who wrote
the headings in the Escorial manuscript of the *Way of perfection* (Vol. II, p. xvii,
above).
[3] Beatriz de la Encarnación, as she was called in religion, professed on September
17, 1570, and died on May 5, 1573.
[4] M. María Bautista.

and her modesty and cheerfulness were clear signs of the joy
that she had within her soul. She would be silent without seem-
ing in the least depressed; and, though she loved silence, she
practised it in such a way as to excite no particular notice. She
was never known to utter a word for which she could be reproved;
and showed no signs of obstinacy, or ever excused herself,
although, in order to test her, the Prioress would sometimes
blame her for what she had not done, according to our custom
in these houses, as an exercise in mortification. She never made
any complaint about anything whatsoever or about any of her
sisters; nor, whatever the duties she had to do, did she, by look
or by word, cause displeasure to any of them, or give reason
to think that there was any imperfection in her. Nor was
occasion ever found to accuse her in the Chapter of any kind
of fault, though correctors frequently draw attention to very
trifling ones. In every respect both her inward and her outward demeanour were remarkable; this was because her mind
was ever dwelling upon eternity and the end for which God
has created us. The praises of God and the most heartfelt thanks
to Him were ever in her mouth: her life, in short, was one perpetual prayer.

With regard to obedience she never went astray but always
attended to the orders given her with promptness, perfection
and cheerfulness. So extreme was the charity which she bore
to her neighbour that she used to say she would allow herself
to be cut into a thousand pieces for anyone's sake, if this would
save him from losing his soul and bring him fruition of her
Brother—for so she used to call Our Lord—Jesus Christ. In all
her trials, grievous as these were, in her terrible illness which
I shall describe later, and in her severest pains, she bore everything with the most extreme goodwill and happiness as if they
were great consolations and delights. Our Lord must have
richly endowed her spirit, for otherwise the cheerfulness with
which she bore these things would not have been possible.

It chanced that in this city of Valladolid a number of persons
were to be burned for serious crimes. She must have known
that they were not going to their deaths as well prepared as
they should have been, and this caused her the very greatest
distress. So she went with this sore trouble to Our Lord and
besought Him most fervently for the salvation of those souls,
telling Him that she would suffer in exchange for what they
had merited (or so that she might herself win merit enough to
obtain their salvation—I do not remember her exact words),
and that, for the rest of her life, He might give her as many
trials and afflictions as she could bear. On that very night her

first bout of fever began and she suffered continually until she died. The criminals, however, went to their deaths well, so it seems that God heard her prayer.

She then developed an intestinal abscess, which caused her such terrible pain that she needed all the favours God had shown to her soul in order to bear it patiently. As this abscess was internal, none of the medicines which they gave her could touch it until the Lord was pleased that it should open and discharge of its own accord, so that she became somewhat better. Her desire to suffer was not easily satisfied; thus, on a festival of the Cross, after she had listened to a sermon, this desire increased so much that she flung herself on her bed in a flood of tears, and, when they asked her what was the matter, begged them to pray to God that He would give her many trials and she would then be happy.

She talked with the Prioress about everything that concerned the interior life; and this brought her comfort. Throughout her illness she never caused anyone the least trouble nor did anything beyond what the infirmarian told her, even in so small a matter as the drinking of a little water. It is very usual for souls given to prayer to desire trials when they have none, but it is given to few, while suffering these trials, to do so and rejoice. While she was in the throes of her illness, which lasted only for a short time, and was suffering exceedingly from the pain, an abscess formed in her throat, which prevented her from swallowing. In the presence of some of the sisters, she said to the Prioress, who was dutifully comforting her and encouraging her to bear these sufferings, that she had no pain and would not change places with any of the sisters who were in good health. She had the Lord, for Whom she was suffering, always before her eyes, and she would do all she could not to speak of her pain lest anyone should realize how severe it was. So, except when it was causing her great distress, she complained of it very little.

She thought there was no one on earth more wicked than she, and so, in every way that could be seen, she had a deep humility. When discussing other people's virtues, she was extremely happy. In matters of mortification she was austere in the extreme. She was so clever at withdrawing secretly from every kind of recreation that only those who were watching her closely would realize what she was doing. She seemed not to be living or having any intercourse with creatures at all, so little store did she set by any of them; and however things went with her she bore them with a tranquillity which was seen never to falter. So unfailing was this that a sister once told her she was like certain very honourable people who, if they were starving, would rather die than let anyone see they were hungry; for the sisters could not believe that she did not feel certain things, though she never gave the appearance of doing so.

Whatever tasks or duties she had to perform were done with such a singleness of aim that she never lost merit on account of any of them. " The smallest thing is beyond price," she used to say to the sisters, " if it is done for the love of God. We ought not to turn our eyes anywhere, sisters, save for that one end, and in order to please Him." She never interfered in things which were not her concern, and so never found fault with anyone but herself. She was so grieved if anyone spoke well of her that she took care not to speak well of anyone else in her presence, in order not to distress her. She never sought her own pleasure, either by going into the garden or by means of anything else created; for it would be dreadful, she said, to seek relief from the pains which Our Lord was giving her; and so she never asked for anything but accepted whatever was given her. She used also to say that it would be a cross to her to find pleasure in anything but God. As a matter of fact, when I asked the nuns in her house about her, there was not one who had ever observed in her anything which seemed not to belong to a soul of great perfection.

When her time came and Our Lord was pleased to take her from this life, her pains increased, and she had so many sufferings to bear that the sisters would sometimes go to see her in order to praise Our Lord for the joy with which she bore them. The chaplain who was confessor in that convent had a particular desire to be present at her death; for, having heard her confessions, he looked upon her as a saint. The Lord was pleased to grant him this desire. While she was still fully conscious, and after she had received Extreme Unction, they sent for him so that, if it became necessary, he could absolve her that night and help her to die. A little before nine o'clock, when all the sisters were with her, and he was there also, all her pain was taken from her, and about a quarter of an hour later she died. She lifted up her eyes in the greatest peace and on her face there was seen a kind of joy; she seemed to be looking at something which caused her great happiness, for she smiled twice. All the sisters who were there, and the priest himself, were conscious of such spiritual joy and gladness that they can only say they thought they were in Heaven. So with this joy which I am describing, and with her eyes fixed upon Heaven, she died, looking like an angel; and we may indeed believe, both because of our faith and because of her life, that God took her to her rest as a reward for her many desires to suffer for Him.

The chaplain affirms, and has repeated to many people, that at the time the body was laid in its grave he was conscious of a very strong and sweet fragrance which was being emitted from it. The sacristan also affirms that in not one of all the candles which were burning during the last rites, and at the funeral, was there any diminution of the wax. All this may be believed of the mercy of God. When I was speaking of these matters with a confessor of hers, belonging to the Company of Jesus, who had confessed her and directed her soul for many years, he said that there was nothing remarkable in this, and that it did not surprise him, for he knew that Our Lord often communed with her.

May it please His Majesty, my daughters, to teach us how to profit by a companionship as good as hers and by many others which Our Lord gives us in these houses. It may be that I shall say something about them, so that those of you who are a little lukewarm may endeavour to imitate them and that we may all praise the Lord, Who thus allows His greatness to shine forth in a few weak women.

CHAPTER XIII

Describes how the first house for friars of the Primitive Rule of the Discalced Carmelites was founded, in the year 1568, and by whom.

Before starting for the Valladolid foundation, I had arranged with Fray Antonio de Jesús, who at that time was Prior of Saint Anne's, in Medina, a house belonging to the Order of Carmel, and with Fray John of the Cross, as I have already said, that, if a monastery of the Primitive Discalced Rule could be founded, they should be the first to enter it. As I had not the means for founding such a house, I could only commend the matter to Our Lord, for, as I have said, I was already satisfied with these Fathers. During the year which had passed since I had first discussed the subject with Fray Antonio de Jesús, the Lord had exercised him in trials, which he had borne with great perfection. Fray John of the Cross needed no testing, for, though he was living among the Calced fathers of the Observance,[1] he had always led a life of great perfection and religious zeal. Our Lord, Who had given me the chief thing—namely, friars to begin the work—was pleased to provide everything else.

[1] [*Lit.*: " of the Cloth " (*del Paño*). This term is often used to distinguish the Carmelites of the " Observance ", who kept the Mitigated Rule, from the Discalced, who wore sackcloth or a coarse frieze.]

A gentleman of Ávila, Don Rafael by name,[1] whom I had not previously known, came to hear (I forget how) that we were anxious to found a monastery for Discalced friars. He came to me with the offer of a house which he had in a little village,[2] of very few inhabitants—less than twenty, I think, though I do not now remember.[3] He kept a house there for a bailiff, who used it for the grain[4] which he collected as rents. Although I saw what kind of place it would be, I praised Our Lord and gave him the warmest thanks. He told me it was on the road to Medina del Campo, a town through which I had to pass on my way to the Valladolid foundation, so it would be on my direct route, and I should be able to see it. I told him I would look at it, and I did so. I left Ávila in June,[5] with a single nun for my companion,[6] and also with Father Julián Dávila, the priest I have mentioned, chaplain of Saint Joseph's, Ávila, who helped me on these journeys.

Although we set out early in the morning, we were unfamiliar with the road and so went astray; and, as little is known of the place, we could find no one to direct us. We travelled all that day in the greatest discomfort, for the sun was very strong. When we thought we were near the village, we found we had as far again still to go. I always remember the fatigue of that long roundabout journey. We arrived only a little before nightfall. When we entered the house, we found it in such a condition that we dared not spend the night there, so dirty was it and so numerous were the harvesters who were about. It had a fair-sized porch, a room divided into two, with a loft above it, and a little kitchen: that is all there was of the building which was to be our monastery. I thought that the porch might be made into a church, that the loft would do quite well for the choir and that the friars could sleep in the room below. But my companion, though a much better person than I am and a great lover of penance, could not bear the thought of my founding a monastery there. "Mother," she said, "I am certain that no

---

[1] Rafael Mejía was a leading citizen of Ávila, who made this offer in June 1568 when St. Teresa was staying in Ávila after making her foundation at Malagón.

[2] "The village was called Duruelo," writes Gracián in the margin of the autograph. It was eight and a half leagues from Ávila.

[3] Twenty was in fact the approximate number of families in the village, not of individual inhabitants. Some years later the village grew smaller still, and, except for a few houses, disappeared.

[4] [Lit.: "for the bread (pan)." In some parts of Spain the country-people pay their rents in wheat, or other grain, instead of in money. The room or building where such grain is stored is called a panera ("granary").]

[5] [Actually on the last day of June.]

[6] Antonia del Espíritu Santo, one of the first four nuns to take the habit at St. Joseph's, Ávila [Vol. I, p. 249, above]. She went with St. Teresa on her journeys to Medina del Campo, Malagón, Valladolid and Toledo.

one, however good and spiritual, could endure this. You must not consider it." The Father who was travelling with me,[1] though he thought as she did, made no objection when I told him what was in my mind. We went and spent the night in the church, but so great was our fatigue that we would not spend it in vigil.

When we reached Medina, I at once spoke with Fray Antonio, told him what had happened, and said that, if he had the courage to stay there for some time, he might be sure that God would soon help him: the great thing was to make a start. I think I foresaw then what the Lord has now done, as definitely, one might say, as I see it now, and indeed much more so than I have seen it until quite recently; though, by the goodness of God, at the time of my writing this, there are ten monasteries for Discalced friars.[2] I told him he might be sure that, if they saw we were proposing to take a fine, large house, neither the last Provincial nor the present one[3] would give us leave to begin, and, as I said at first, we could only do it with his consent. Besides, we had no alternative; and in a little hamlet and a house of that kind no one would take any notice of them. The courage which God had given him was greater than mine; and he said that he would be willing to live, not only there, but in a pig-sty. Fray John of the Cross agreed with him.

It now remained for us to get the consent of the two Fathers already mentioned, for it was on this condition that our Father General had given us the licence. I hoped in Our Lord that we should get it, and so I left Fray Antonio to see about doing all that he could as to collecting things for the house and set off with Fray John of the Cross to make the foundation at Valladolid which I have already described. As we were there for some days while the workmen were putting the house straight, and were not enclosed, there was an opportunity to tell Fray John of the Cross all about our way of life, so that he might have an exact knowledge of everything, both of the mortification we practise and of the sisterly way in which we live and the recreation which we take in common. All this is characterized

---

[1] P. Julián de Ávila. [The surname is sometimes spelt Davila, as in the text just above.]

[2] These were at Duruelo, Pastrana, Mancera, Alcalá de Henares, Altomira, La Roda, Granada, La Peñuela, Seville and Almodóvar del Campo. The last of these was founded in 1575 [which fixes a *terminus ab quo* for the date at which this chapter was written. Cf. p. xvii, above].

[3] Fray Alonso González and Fray Ángel de Salazar, who are named in the patent issued by the General on August 14, 1567, as the persons to whom the authority to recognize these houses was given. The former was elected Provincial in April 1567, and was succeeded by the latter on September 23 of the same year. P. Salazar was also Provincial from 1570 to 1576 and from 1580 to 1583.

by such moderation that it serves to bring out the sisters' faults, and gives us a little relief from the severity of the Rule. He was so good a man that I, at least, could have learned much more from him than he from me. I did not do so, however, but merely showed him the way in which the sisters live.

It pleased God that the Provincial of our Order, Fray Alonso González, whose approval I had to obtain, should be there also. He was an old man, very well disposed and quite devoid of guile. In asking for his approval I talked to him a great deal about the matter and told him that if he hindered so good a work he would have to answer to God for it. As His Majesty was pleased that the foundation should be made, He made him well disposed to the idea, and he became quite easy to deal with. Doña María de Mendoza also arrived, with the Bishop of Ávila, her brother, who has always been our helper and patron, and they obtained his final approval, together with that of the former Provincial, Fray Ángel de Salazar, who I had been afraid would make a lot of difficulties.[1] But about this time there occurred a certain urgent matter for which the assistance of Doña María de Mendoza was needed, and that, I believe, helped us a great deal. Still, even had this not happened, Our Lord would have put it into his heart to consent, as He did into that of the Father General, who at first was very far from doing so.

God help me, how many things have I seen in the course of these foundations, which seemed impossible, and how easy has it been for His Majesty to overcome them! How ashamed I am, after all I have seen, not to be better! For now that I come to write of it, I am amazed and desire Our Lord to make everybody realize how little—almost nothing, indeed,—we creatures have done in making these foundations. Everything has been ordained by the Lord, and from such humble beginnings that only His Majesty could have raised them to the state they are in now. May He be blessed for ever. Amen.

---

[1] Fray Ángel, who had been very helpful with the foundations for Discalced nuns, showed signs of being difficult over the foundations for friars. The records of the Reform show that Doña María actually asked P. Salazar to authorize the Duruelo foundation in return for the help she had given him.

CHAPTER XIV

Continues to describe the foundation of the first house for Discalced Carmelite friars. Says something of the life which they led, and of the benefits that Our Lord began to bestow upon them there, to the honour and glory of God.

As I now had the approval of these two authorities, I thought I needed nothing further. We arranged that Fray John of the Cross should go to the house and get it ready so that somehow or other the friars might go in, while I myself hurried the foundation on as much as I could, for I was very much afraid we might meet with some obstacle. So this was done. Fray Antonio had already collected some of the things they would need, and we helped him as far as we could, though that was not much. He came to Valladolid to have a talk with me, and was very happy; and he told me what he had collected, which was little enough. The only articles with which he was well provided were clocks, of which he had five: I thought that very amusing. He said that he would not go there without making provision for keeping regular hours. But I believe he had not even anything to sleep on.

We took a little time getting the house ready, as there was no money and they had wanted to do a great deal to it. When it was completed, Fray Antonio, with great goodwill, renounced his priorship and made a vow to observe the Primitive Rule; for, although they told him that he ought to test his vocation for it first, he would not do so but went off to his little house with the greatest joy in the world; Fray John was there already.

Fray Antonio has told me that when he came in sight of the hamlet he felt a very great inward joy, thinking that he had now done with the world for good, by renouncing it entirely and burying himself in that solitary retreat. Neither of them considered the house at all bad: in fact, they thought themselves extremely fortunate.

O God, how little have buildings and outward comforts to do with the inward life of the soul! For love of Him I beg you, my sisters and fathers, never to be other than very modest in this matter of large and sumptuous houses. Let us bear in mind our true founders, those holy Fathers from whom we are descended, for we know it was the road of poverty and humility which they took that led them to the fruition of God.

I have really seen greater spirituality, and even inward joy, in places where there has seemed to be no kind of physical comfort at all than later on, when there has been a large house and comfort in abundance. However large the house may be, of what benefit is that to us? We can make use only of a single cell—what do we gain by its being very large and well built? What, indeed? We have not to spend all our time looking at the walls. If we remember that this house is not to be our home for ever, but only for the short period of our life, whatever the length of that may be, everything will become acceptable to us; and we shall realize that, the less we have here, the greater will be our fruition in eternity, where the mansions we shall inhabit will correspond to the love with which we have imitated the life of our good Jesus. If we say that these are the beginnings of a restoration of the Rule of the Virgin, His Mother and Our Lady and Patroness, let us not wrong her, or our holy fathers of past days, by failing to live as they did. Since our weakness prevents us from doing this in every respect, we should be particularly careful about things which have nothing to do with the sustaining of life; for, as these two Fathers showed, we have only to undertake a little pleasant toil, and, if we resolve to endure that, our difficulties will be over, for we shall have but a light affliction and it will all come at the beginning.

On the first or second Sunday of Advent in the year 1568[1] (I do not remember which of these Sundays it was) the first Mass was said in that little Bethlehem of a porch—for I do not think it was any better than that. During the following Lent, I passed the place on my way to our foundation at Toledo. I arrived in the morning: Fray Antonio de Jesús was sweeping out the church porch with that happy expression which never leaves him. "How is this, Father?" I said to him. "Whatever has become of your dignity?"[2] And he answered in these words, which showed me how very happy he was: "I curse the time when I had any." Then I went into the little church and was amazed to see what spirituality the Lord had inspired there. And I was not alone in this, for two merchants, who were friends of mine, and had come as far as this with me from Medina, did nothing but weep. There were so many crosses about and so many skulls!

I have never forgotten one little wooden cross, above the holy water, on which was stuck a piece of paper with a picture of Christ: it seemed to inspire greater devotion than if it had been a crucifix of the finest workmanship. The choir was in the loft, the centre of which was quite high, so that they could say the Hours, but they had to stoop very low in order to enter far enough

---

[1] It was the first: November 28, 1568. [See *St. John of the Cross*, I, xxvi.]
[2] [*Honra*. Cf. Vol. I, p. 14, n. 2, above.]

to hear Mass. They had turned the two corners next to the church into two little hermitages; as the place was very cold these were filled with hay, and they could only sit or lie in them, for the roof almost came down on their heads. The hermitages had two little windows overlooking the altar, and two stones for pillows, and above these[1] their crosses and skulls. I gather that, after finishing Matins, they did not go back to their cells until Prime, but remained here in prayer, and they would pray so earnestly that sometimes, when the hour for Prime came, their habits would be covered with snow without their having noticed it. They said their Hours with another Father, who was of the Observance;[2] he had come to stay with them, but, as he was very infirm, he did not change his habit. They also had another friar, a young man not in orders.[3]

They used to go out and preach in many places in the district which were without instruction, and for that reason, too, I was glad that the house had been founded there, for they told me that there was no monastery near, nor any means of getting one, which was a great pity. In this short time they had gained such a good reputation that, when I heard of it, it made me extremely happy. They went out to preach, as I say, as far as a league and a half or two leagues, bare-footed (for at that time they had not the hemp sandals which they were ordered to wear later)[4] and through all the cold and snow. When they had preached and heard confessions and had returned to their monastery for a meal it would be very late. But this was very little trouble to them, so happy were they.

Of food they had quite enough, for the villages in the district would provide them with more than they needed, and certain gentlemen who lived in these villages would come to them for confession and offer them better houses and sites. One of these was Don Luis, Lord of the Five Towns.[5] This gentleman had built a church for a picture of Our Lady, which was certainly fully worthy of being held in veneration. His father had sent it from Flanders, by a merchant, to his mother or grandmother— I forget which. He was so fond of it that he kept it for many

---

[1] [*Lit.*: "and there"; but I take this to mean above the pillows.]

[2] [*Paño*: and so frequently where this word occurs in the text. Cf. p. 61, n. 1, above.]

[3] The Father referred to was Fray José de Cristo, another Carmelite from Medina del Campo. Little more is heard of him, and he is thought either to have died or to have left the Reform. Of the infirm Father, nothing further is known.

[4] Cf. St. Teresa's letter to P. Mariano, December 12, 1576. Gracián's Constitutions (1575) allow hemp sandals, and in the Alcalá Constitutions of 1581, approved by St. John of the Cross, their use is made obligatory. Since 1876, leather-soled sandals have been worn.

[5] Don Luis de Toledo. The "five towns" were Salmoral, Noharros, San Miguel, Montalvo and Gallegos.

years, and later had it brought to him on his deathbed. It is a large piece—in all my life I have never seen a finer one and other people say the same thing. When, at that gentleman's request, Fray Antonio de Jesús went to the place and saw the picture, he was so much attracted by it, and rightly so, that he agreed to transfer the monastery there. The place is called Mancera.[1] Although they had no well-water, and seemed to have no means of getting any, this gentleman provided them with a monastery suitable to their profession and gave them ornaments for it. He did it all very well.

I do not want to omit the story of how the Lord gave them water, which was considered to be miraculous. One day, after supper, Fray Antonio, who was Prior, was in the cloisters with his friars, talking about their need of water. The Prior got up, took a staff which he generally carried in his hand and with one part of it made what I think was the sign of the Cross—though I am not quite sure if it was a cross: anyhow, he pointed to a place with the stick and said: "Now dig here." They had dug only a very little way when so much water gushed out that it is difficult now to stop it even for the purpose of cleaning the well; it is excellent drinking water; they have used it for everything, and, as I say, it is inexhaustible. Afterwards they marked out a garden and tried to find water there and made a water-wheel and spent a great deal upon it; but even to this day they have been unable to find any.

Well, when I saw that little house, which so recently it had been impossible to live in, filled with such spirituality that, wherever I looked, I seemed to find cause for edification, and when I learned of their way of life, their mortification and prayer and the good example they gave (for a gentleman and his wife, whom I knew, came there from a neighbouring village to see me and could not say enough about their sanctity and the great good they were doing in those villages), I could not give Our Lord sufficient thanks, so great was my inward joy, for I thought I had seen a beginning made to the great profit of our Order and the service of Our Lord. May it please His Majesty to carry it on as it is going now and that thought of mine will then be turned into reality. The merchants who had accompanied me told me they would not have missed coming for the whole world. What a thing virtue is, for that poverty was more pleasing to them than all the riches they themselves possessed and brought their souls satisfaction and comfort.

When these Fathers and I had talked over a number of things, I urged them specially, being weak and wicked myself, not to

---

[1] Mancera was about four miles from Duruelo.

practise such severity in matters of penance, as to which they were very strict. As it had cost me so many desires and prayers to obtain men from the Lord who would make a beginning, and as I saw what a good beginning they had made, I was afraid that the devil might be trying to bring their work to an end before my hopes could be fulfilled. Imperfect and wanting in faith as I am, I did not reflect that this was the work of God and that it was for His Majesty to carry it farther. They, having what I lacked, paid small heed to my requests that they would give up their practices, and so I went away as happy as could be, though I did not give God the praises due to Him for such great grace. May it please His Majesty of His goodness that I may be worthy to serve Him and so repay some part of all I owe Him. Amen. For I saw quite well that this was a much greater grace than He had given me in enabling me to found houses for nuns.

CHAPTER XV

Describes the foundation of the convent of the glorious Saint Joseph in the city of Toledo, which took place in the year 1569.

In the city of Toledo there lived an honourable man and servant of God, who was a merchant. He had never wanted to marry but led the life of a devout Catholic and was a very truthful and good-living man. He was amassing wealth by lawful trade with the intention of using his money in a way that would be very pleasing to the Lord. This man, who was called Martín Ramírez, fell mortally ill. A father of the Company of Jesus, Pablo Hernández by name,[1] who had heard my confessions there when I was arranging for the Malagón foundation, learned of his illness, and, being very anxious that one of our monasteries should be founded in that city, went to see him. He told him how great a service such a foundation would render to Our Lord, and how he could establish chaplaincies and appoint chaplains, who could live in that monastery, and how certain festivals could be celebrated there, together with other observances which he had had it in mind to establish in one of the parishes of the city.

He was already so ill that he saw there would be no time to arrange this, so he left it in the hands of a brother of his, named Alonso Álvarez Ramírez. God then took him to Himself. He had done well to make this arrangement, for this Alonso Álvarez

---

[1] Cf. *Relations*, IV (Vol. I, p. 320, n. 9, above).

is a most discreet and God-fearing man, strictly truthful, generous with his alms and very much open to reason. I can say this about him with all sincerity, as I have had a good deal to do with him and can speak as an eye-witness.

When Martín Ramírez died,[1] I was still busy with the Valladolid foundation, and it was there that I heard from Father Pablo Hernández, of the Company, and from Alonso Álvarez himself. They gave me an account of what was happening and told me to come quickly if I wanted to accept this foundation, so I left there soon after the house was ready.[2] I reached Toledo on the eve of the festival of Our Lady of the Incarnation[3] and went to the house of Doña Luisa, in which I had stayed several times: she was the foundress of Malagón. I was received with great joy, as she has a great affection for me. I took as companions two nuns from Saint Joseph's, Ávila,[4] who were great servants of God. We were given a room at once, as usual, and there we stayed in as great seclusion as if we had been in a convent.

I began at once to discuss the question with Alonso Álvarez and a son-in-law of his, named Diego Ortiz, who, though a very good man and a theologian,[5] was more decided in his opinions than Alonso Álvarez and was not so amenable to reason. They began by proposing many conditions to me which I did not think it fitting to accept. While we were discussing the arrangements we were looking for a house to let of which we could have immediate possession, but although we looked everywhere we could find nothing suitable nor could I persuade the Governor to give me a licence (for there was no Archbishop at this time[6]), though the lady who was our hostess did everything possible for us. There was also a gentleman, Don Pedro Manrique by name,[7] who was a Canon of the Cathedral and a son of the Governor[8] of Castile. He was a great servant of God—or rather is, for he is still alive, and, though in very poor health, entered the Company of Jesus some years after the foundation of this house, and is

[1] October 31, 1568.
[2] St. Teresa received these letters at Valladolid in December 1568 and left on February 21, 1569.
[3] March 24, 1569.
[4] Isabel de San Pablo and Isabel de Santo Domingo. St. Teresa had passed through Ávila on her way to Toledo. Julián de Ávila being ill, they were accompanied by Gonzalo de Aranda (Vol. I, pp. 249, 256, above).
[5] He was for many years Professor of Theology in Toledo University.
[6] The Archbishop at that time was the celebrated Dominican Fray Bartolomé de Carranza but he was in a prison of the Inquisition. In that sense there was, as St. Teresa says, "no Archbishop."
[7] Don Pedro Manrique was the uncle of the Casilda de Padilla referred to in Chapters X, XI. He joined the Society of Jesus only in 1573 and died four years later.
[8] [Adelantado. Cf. p. 49, n. 4, above.]

still with them. He was an important person in the city, for he is a
very intelligent and worthy man. In spite of all this, I could not
get them to give me this licence: as soon as I had partially persuaded the Governor,[1] I met with opposition from the Council.[2]
Furthermore, Alonso Álvarez and I were unable to reach an
agreement, on account of his giving so much freedom to his son-in-
law. In the end, we had to break off the negotiations altogether.

I did not know what to do, for it was solely for this purpose
that I had come and I knew there would be a great deal of talk
if I went away without making the foundation. Still, I was
more distressed at not getting the licence than at anything else,
for I believed that, once we had a house, Our Lord would provide,
as He has done elsewhere. So I determined to approach the
Governor and, going to a church near his house, sent to beg
him to be good enough to come and speak to me. More than two
months had now passed since we had begun work on this matter
and each day things grew worse. When I saw him, I told him
that it was hard that there should be women anxious to live in
such austerity and perfection, and strictly enclosed, while those
who had never done any such thing themselves but were living a
comfortable life should try to hinder work which was of such
service to Our Lord. I told him all this and a good deal more,
speaking with a resoluteness with which I was inspired by the
Lord. This touched his heart and before I left him he gave me
the licence.

When I left him I was very pleased; for, though I had nothing
as yet, I felt I had everything. I must have had about three or
four ducats, with which I bought two paintings[3] (as I had nothing
in the way of a picture to put behind the altar), two mattresses
and a blanket. Now that I had broken off negotiations with
Alonso Álvarez, there was no possible way of getting a house.
But a merchant of the city, a friend of mine, who would never
marry but spent his time in good work among prisoners, and
in many other worthy deeds, had told me not to worry about it,
for he would find me a house. His name was Alonso de Ávila.
But he fell ill. A few days earlier there had come to the city a
Franciscan friar, a very holy man, called Fray Martín de la Cruz.
He stayed for some days, and, when he went away, sent me a
young penitent of his called Andrada.[4] This youth was not at all

[1] [*Gobernador.*] The Ecclesiastical Governor of Toledo, Don Gómez Tello Girón.
[2] The Council which administered the temporal possessions of the Archbishops
of Toledo.
[3] These are still preserved by the Discalced Carmelite nuns at Toledo, together
with a manuscript biography of Alonso de Ávila, who is mentioned in the text below.
[4] Apart from the facts that later he became well-to-do, married and was blessed
with many children, some of whose descendants were still living when Francisco

rich—indeed, he was very poor—but Fray Martín had asked him to do whatever I told him. He came to me one day in church when I was at Mass and told me what the holy friar had said to him, adding that I could rely upon his doing anything he could for me, although he could help us only by personal service. I thanked him, but I was very much amused, and my companions were still more so, to see what help the holy man had sent us, for his dress was not that of a person with whom Discalced nuns should have anything to do.

However, when I found myself with the licence, but without anyone to help me, and had no idea what to do or to whom to commend the task of looking for a house which we could hire, I remembered this young man whom Fray Martín de la Cruz had sent me and spoke about him to my companions. They had a good laugh at me and told me not to rely on a person like that or the result would be that our project would come to everybody's knowledge. But I would not listen to them, for, as he had been sent by that servant of God, I was confident that there must be something he could do and that there was some mystery about it. So I sent for him, told him what was going on, charged him to observe the strictest secrecy, and asked him to look for a house for me, promising to give him security for the rent. The security would come from the good Alonso de Ávila, who, as I have said, had fallen ill. The young man thought this would be quite easy and said he would look for a house. On the morning of the very next day, when I was at Mass in the church of the Company of Jesus, he came and spoke to me, and said that he had found a house and had brought the keys with him, so that, as it was quite near, we could go to see it. We did so; and it proved to be such a good house that we stayed in it for almost a year.[1]

Often, when I think of this foundation, the ways of God amaze me. For nearly three months—or at least for more·than two: I cannot remember exactly—rich people had been going all over Toledo looking for a house, and they could no more find one than if there had not been a single house in the city. And then there comes along this young man, not in the least rich, but very poor, and the Lord is pleased for him to find a house immediately. On the other hand, when we might have made the foundation without any trouble, if we could have come to an arrangement with Alonso Álvarez, it was not His will that we should, but quite the contrary, for He wanted us to take trouble over the foundation and to have the house founded in poverty.

de Santa María wrote his *Historia de la Reforma*, nothing is known of this young man who gave such great help to St. Teresa.

[1] I.e., from May 14, 1569, down to the end of May or the beginning of June, 1570.

As we were pleased with the house, I gave orders at once for it to be taken possession of before anything could be done in it, so that we should have no further hindrance. Very soon afterwards, Andrada came to tell me that the house would be vacated that very day and we could send in our furniture. I told him there was not much to send, as we had nothing but two mattresses and a blanket. He must have been astounded; and my companions were annoyed at my telling him this, and asked me how I could have done such a thing, for now that he had seen we were so poor he would not give us any further help. Of that I took no notice, and it seemed to make little difference to him, for He Who had given him that goodwill would surely continue it in him until His work was completed. And so it fell out; for what with helping to get the house ready and finding workmen for us I do not believe we ourselves worked harder than he did. We borrowed the articles which were necessary for having Mass said, and at dusk we went with one of the workmen to take possession of the house; we took with us a little bell, of the kind used at the Elevation, for we had no other. I was full of misgivings. We spent all that night preparing the house. The only place for the church was a room which had to be entered from a little house adjacent to it. This was occupied by some women, but its owner had granted us the use of it when she let us our own.

Just before dawn, when we had everything ready (we had not dared to say anything to the women in case they gave away our secret), we began to undo the door, which was in the partition-wall, and led into a very small courtyard. The women, who were in bed, heard the noise and got up in terror. We had as much as we could do to quiet them. It was now time for Mass and this was said at once. Although they strongly objected, they did us no harm, and, when they saw the purpose of it all, the Lord calmed them.[1]

Afterwards I realized how badly we had arranged all this, but at the time we were, by God's grace, so absorbed in His work that the inconveniences never occurred to us. When the owner of the house heard that it had been made into a church, there was some trouble, for she was the wife of a man of property and she made a tremendous commotion about it. But when she saw that, if we liked the house, we would buy it from her at a good price, the Lord was pleased to calm her down as well.

[1] The house was situated in the Plazuela de Barrio Nuevo, near the church of Nuestra Señora del Tránsito. The first Mass was said in it by P. Juan de la Magdalena, Prior of the Calced Carmelites of Toledo, and was attended by Doña Luisa de la Cerda and a good part of her household. The Calced Carmelites were extremely sympathetic to the new foundation, furnishing its sacristy and saying Mass for the nuns daily.

Then, too, when the members of the Council heard that the convent for which they had never been willing to give a licence was duly founded, they were very angry, and went to see a dignitary of the Church to whom, in confidence, I had communicated our plans, and told him what they proposed to do. As the Governor had had to go away after giving me the licence, he was not in the city, so they went to report to the person I have mentioned, amazed that a mere woman could have had the audacity to found a convent against their will. His reply was that he knew nothing of the matter and he pacified them as well as he could, saying that the same thing had been done elsewhere, and that it would not have been done without sufficient reason.

Some days later, we were served with an order prohibiting us from having Mass said until we could show our authority for what we had done. I answered very meekly that I would follow their instructions, though I had no obligation to obey them in the matter, and I asked Don Pedro Manrique, the gentleman whom I have mentioned, to go and speak to them and to show them our authority. As the foundation had already been made, he was able to satisfy them; had it been otherwise, we should have had trouble.[1]

For some days we had nothing for our beds except the mattresses and the blanket and on that first day we had not so much as a scrap of brushwood to broil a sardine on. Then someone, I do not know who, was moved by Our Lord to leave a bundle of wood in the church, which was of some help to us. At night it was rather cold, and we felt this, although, as well as the blanket, we had the frieze capes which we wear over our habits; these, which we often find useful, we spread over ourselves. It will seem incredible that we should have been staying in the house of that lady who was so much attached to me, and yet should have gone into the convent in such poverty. I do not know why it was, unless God wished us to prove the blessedness of this virtue by experience. I did not ask her for anything, as I dislike worrying people, and she may not perhaps have thought of it; in any case she could never give us as much as I owe her already.

It was all a great blessing to us, for such was the inward comfort and joy which we felt that I often think how much good the Lord has stored up in the virtues. Our lack of necessaries seemed to me a pleasant subject for contemplation, but it lasted only a short time, for Alonso Álvarez himself and others soon began to provide us with more than we wanted, and it is a fact

---

[1] According to Ribera (II, xiv), the nuns were supported, not only by Don Pedro Manrique, but also by P. Vicente Barrón, at that time a Counsellor of the Holy Office, and St. Teresa's confessor in Toledo.

that my distress then was such that I felt exactly as if I had previously had a great many golden trinkets and had been robbed of them and left in poverty. I was really sorry when our poverty drew to a close, and so were my companions. When I saw them looking sad I asked them what was wrong with them. "What do you suppose can be the matter, Mother?" they answered. "We do not seem to be poor any longer."[1]

From that time forward the desire for great poverty increased in me and I felt sufficiently mistress of myself to despise temporal blessings, a lack of which increases inward blessings and undoubtedly brings with it satisfaction and tranquillity. During the time when I had been discussing the foundation with Alonso Álvarez, there were many people who considered I was wrong, and who told me so, for they thought his family neither illustrious nor well born, though quite good for what it was, as I have said, and they considered I ought not to find any lack of comfort in a place as important as Toledo. I did not take much notice of this, for, glory be to God, I have always attached more value to virtue than to descent; but they had said so much to the Governor about this that he gave me the licence on condition that I made the foundation as I had done elsewhere.

I did not know what to do, for, when the convent was founded, discussions on the subject began once more. As the foundation was now made, I took the middle course of giving them the chancel, but allowing them no rights in the convent itself; and this holds good still. There was already somebody, an important person, who wanted to have the chancel, and there were so many opinions on the subject that I did not know what to decide. Our Lord was pleased to give me light on the subject: once, for example, He reminded me how little importance rank and position would have before the Judgment Seat of God. He rebuked me severely for having listened to those who were talking to me in this way, for these were not matters which should trouble those of us who had long since learned to despise the world.[2]

These and other considerations made me feel very much ashamed of myself and I resolved to settle the matter under dispute by giving them the chancel. I have never regretted this, for it has become clear to us how little opportunity we ourselves should have had of buying a house, whereas by their help we bought the house where we are now, which is one of the good

---

[1] When things grew better, St. Teresa sent to Ávila for more nuns from the Incarnation and four were given her, of whom only one, Doña Juana Yera (Juana del Espíritu Santo) was able to stand the austerities of the new life: the remainder returned to Ávila. Two sisters from Malagón, Ana de Jesús and Isabel de San José, also joined this community.

[2] On this, see *Relations*, VIII (Vol. I, p. 338, above).

houses of Toledo, and cost twelve thousand ducats. And as we have so many Masses said and celebrate so many festivals in it, it is a great joy to the nuns as well as to the people. If I had considered the vain opinions of the world, it would have been impossible, as far as we can see, for us to have such a comfortable place, besides which we should have been offending one who did us this charity with so good a will.[1]

CHAPTER XVI

Describes certain things which happened in this convent of Saint Joseph, Toledo, to the honour and glory of God.

I have thought it well to say something of the way in which some of the nuns laboured in the service of Our Lord, in order that those who come after them may ever strive to imitate these good beginnings. Before the house was bought, we received a nun here called Ana de la Madre de Dios; she was forty years of age and had spent her whole life in the Lord's service. And although her life and her household had been full of comforts, for she was living alone and had some property, she preferred to embrace a life of poverty and submission in the Order, and so came to speak to me about it. She had very poor health; but when I saw a soul so good and so full of resolution, her coming seemed to me a good beginning for the foundation and so I accepted her. And it pleased God to give her much better health in her life of austerity and submission than she had enjoyed in the midst of freedom and comfort.

What aroused my devotion, and why I am writing of this now is that, before making her profession, she gave all she possessed to the Order—and she was very rich—as an alms to the house. I was troubled about this and would not agree to it, telling her that she might perhaps repent of it, or that we might not allow her to make her profession, and so it would

---

[1] There was a great deal of trouble before an agreement could finally be reached, connected chiefly with the new chapel which was to be erected, and the patronage of which Don Martín Ramírez had willed to his niece, Doña Francisca, and her legitimate heirs, his original intention having been to found a church in which Masses would be said for his soul. Don Diego Ortiz, Doña Francisca's husband, proved quite inflexible on this point, but fortunately Don Martín's executors were reasonable, and, on May 18, 1570, a deed was drawn up by which Mother Teresa was granted a sum of money for the purchase of some houses, she in her turn undertaking to build within ten years a chapel in which Don Martín and his family would be buried. The houses were at once bought, and a chapel, dedicated to St. Joseph, was built, which in 1591 was enlarged to its present size. It is of no artistic merit but contains several fine paintings by El Greco.

be an extreme step for her to take. True, if what I suggested should happen, we should return to her what she had given us, but I wanted to put the case to her at its very worst: first, lest it should be a source of temptation to her; secondly, in order the better to test her spirituality. She replied that, if this should happen, she would go and beg for the love of God, and I could not dissuade her from her purpose. She had a very happy life with us and enjoyed excellent health.[1]

Strict mortification and obedience were practised in this convent: in fact, when I was there, the Superior had to be careful what she said, as the nuns always did as they were told at once, even if she spoke carelessly. On one occasion they were all looking at a pond in the garden and the Prioress said to them, of a nun who was standing close by: "What would she do if I told her to throw herself in?" She had hardly spoken when the sister was in the water, with the result that she had to go and change her habit. On another occasion, when I was there, the nuns were going to confession, and while one of them was waiting for another, who was in the confessional, she went up to speak to the Superior. The latter asked her[2] what she was thinking of. Was that the proper way to collect her thoughts before confession? She should put her head in a well which was in the garden and think over her sins there. The sister thought she really meant that she was to throw herself into the well and went to obey so quickly that, if they had not gone after her at once, she would have done so, thinking that she was rendering God the greatest service in the world. Many similar examples of the nuns' great mortification might be quoted: such a pitch did it reach that some learned men had to be asked to explain to them when and how they must obey, and to restrain them in this; for some of the things they were doing were exaggerated, and, had it not been for their good intentions, they would have been acting, not so much meritoriously as wrongly. And these things occurred not only in this convent (though it happens that I have been speaking only of this one) but in all of them. I wish I had had nothing to do with them, for then I could describe some of them, in order that Our Lord might be praised in His servants.

It happened, while I was there, that one of the sisters became

---

[1] Ana de la Madre de Dios, in the world Ana de Palma, had first met St. Teresa at Doña Luisa de la Cerda's, and, on losing her husband, had joined the Discalced Carmelites. She made her profession on November 15, 1570. Francisco de Santa María (*Historia de la Reforma*, Vol. I, Book II, Chap. XXV) says that her generosity in making gifts to the community moved St. Teresa to exclaim: " Daughter, don't bring me anything more, or I shall turn both it and you out of the house." Later, she helped to found the Discalced Convent at Cuerva and died in 1610.

[2] This is the author's own correction for her original: " to the Prioress. I asked her, etc."

mortally ill. When she had received the Sacrament and been given Extreme Unction, her joy and happiness were so great that we felt able to ask her to commend us to God in Heaven, and to the saints to whom we have devotion, just as if she were in the next world already. A little while before she died I went in to sit with her, having previously gone into the presence of the Most Holy Sacrament to beseech the Lord to grant her a good death. As I went in, I saw His Majesty at the head of her bed, with His arms half extended as though He were protecting her. He told me that I might be certain He would protect all the nuns who died in these convents and that they need have no fear of temptations in the hour of death. I was greatly comforted and recollected. After a little, I went up to her and spoke to her, and she said to me: "O Mother, what great things I am going to see!" And so she died like an angel.[1]

In some of our nuns who have died since then I have noticed a kind of tranquillity and calm; it seemed as though they were being granted rapture or quiet in prayer, and they showed no sign of having any temptation whatsoever. I trust, therefore, in the goodness of God, that He will help us on our deathbeds through the merits of His Son, and of His glorious Mother, whose habit we wear. So let us strive, daughters, to become true Carmelites, for our day's work will soon be over. If we knew what affliction comes to many people at the hour of death, and the subtleties and deceptions with which the devil tempts them, we should think this help of great value.

One thing occurs to me here, which I want to tell you, for I knew the person concerned—indeed, he was related in some way to some relatives of mine. He was a great gambler, but he had also a certain amount of learning, of which the devil made use to try to deceive him, by making him believe that amendment at the hour of death was of no value. This became such a fixed idea with him that nothing whatever could persuade him to make his confession; all arguments were useless, yet the poor man was extremely distressed at his wicked life, of which he had fully repented. But he would ask of what use it was for him to confess when he knew that he was condemned already. His confessor, a Dominican friar, who was a learned man, did nothing but argue with him, but the devil taught him such subtleties that it was all in vain. He continued in this way for some days; his confessor did not know what to do, but both he and others must have commended him earnestly to the Lord, for He had mercy on him.

[1] The historians of the Reform state that the sister referred to here is Petronila de San Andrés, the fourth professed nun of the Toledo foundation, who died in 1576.

When his complaint, which was a pain in the side, became much worse, the confessor returned and must have thought out more arguments to put before him; but he would have achieved very little if the Lord had not had compassion on him and softened his heart. As soon as the confessor began to talk to him and to put forward these arguments, he sat up in bed as if he had not been ill at all, and said: "So you say that my confession may be of some avail? Well, then, I will make it." He sent for a scrivener or notary (I forget which) and made a most solemn oath never to gamble again and to amend his life. He asked them to witness this, made a very good confession and received the Sacraments with such devotion that, as far as we can tell according to our Faith, he was saved. May it please Our Lord, sisters, that we may live as true daughters of the Virgin and hold fast to our profession, so that Our Lord may give us the grace which He has promised us. Amen.

CHAPTER XVII

Describes the foundation of the monastery and the convent of Pastrana, which took place in the same year, 1570—I mean 1569.

About a fortnight after the Toledo house had been founded occurred the vigil of the Feast of Pentecost.[1] I had got the little church ready, put up the curtains and other things—and there was a great deal of this to be done. (As I have said, we were almost a year in that house). We had completed all the arrangements, but these days of continual consultations with the workmen had worn me out. On that morning, as we were sitting down to our meal in the refectory, I felt so relieved when I saw that there was no more to be done, and that I could spend some time in the joy of communion with Our Lord during that festival, that I could scarcely eat, such happiness was in my soul.

I was not, however, destined to enjoy this relief for long, for, while I was still there, they came to tell me that a servant had come from the Princess of Éboli, wife of Ruy Gómez de Silva. I went out and learned that she had sent him for me: there had been an arrangement between us for some time that I should found a religious house in Pastrana, but I had not supposed that it would be so soon. It troubled me, because the Toledo convent had been so recently founded, and had met with so much opposition, that it was very dangerous to leave it. So I decided at once

_____
[1] May 28, 1569.

not to go and told the servant so. He replied that that would be awkward, as the Princess was already there, and had gone solely for that purpose, and that if I did not go she would be offended. None the less, I had not the slightest intention of going, so I told him to stay and have a meal and said I would write to the Princess before he left. He was a very honest fellow, and, though at first he took it ill, he quite understood when I told him my reasons.

The nuns had just arrived to take up residence in the convent and none of us saw how I could possibly leave so soon. I therefore went into the presence of the Most Holy Sacrament to beg the Lord to show me how to write in such terms as not to cause the Princess annoyance, for we were in a very bad way, the Reform for friars having just begun, and from every standpoint it would be useful to have Ruy Gómez on our side, as he had such influence with the King and with everyone else.[1] I am not sure if I thought of this at the time but I remember quite well that I did not want to displease the Princess. While I was reasoning like this, a message came to me from Our Lord, telling me to go without fail, for there was far more afoot than that foundation, and to take with me the Rule and Constitutions.

When I learned this, although I still realized that there were good reasons for not going, I dared not do otherwise than follow my usual custom in such circumstances—namely, to be guided by my confessor. So I sent for him, without telling him what I had been told in prayer—for I am always better satisfied if I leave this out: I beseech the Lord to give my confessors light according to what they are capable by nature of understanding, and, when His Majesty wishes a thing to be done, He puts it into their hearts. This has often happened to me, and it did so now, for, when my confessor[2] had considered the whole matter, he thought I ought to go, and I therefore resolved to do so.

I left Toledo on the day after the Feast of Pentecost.[3] The

---

[1] Ruy Gómez de Silva was, in fact, at that time, one of the most influential people in the country. A Portuguese by nationality, he had come to Spain as a child with the Empress Isabel, consort of Charles V, and been brought up with Philip II, who had a warm and unfailing affection for him. He died in 1573. His wife, Doña Ana de Mendoza y la Cerda, was descended from some of the noblest families in Spain. Her great physical beauty, however, was accompanied by less admirable traits of character—she was capricious, haughty and domineering, as even St. Teresa's generous and charitable treatment of the subject makes clear, and she caused the Saint no little trouble, both over her foundations and over the *Life* (Vol. I, pp. 6-7, above).

[2] P. Vicente Barrón.

[3] May 30, 1569. With St. Teresa went Isabel de San Pablo and a nun of the Incarnation—Doña Antonia del Águila. From Madrid onward she had also with her a friend of Doña Leonor, Doña Antonia Brances, who took the habit at Pastrana as Beatriz del Sacremento.

road took us through Madrid, and my companions and I went to spend the night in a convent of Franciscan nuns, with the lady who had founded it and was living in it. Her name was Doña Leonor de Mascareñas[1]: she had been governess to the King and was a great servant of Our Lord. I had stayed here on other occasions when I had chanced to be passing that way, and she had always been extremely kind to me.

This lady told me that she was delighted I had come at such a time, for there was a hermit there who was very anxious to make my acquaintance, as he and his companions, she thought, were living a life very similar to that of our Rule. As I had only two friars, the idea struck me that it would be a great thing if this could be managed, and I therefore begged her to arrange for us to have a talk together. He was living in a room which this lady had given him, with another friar, a young man called Fray Juan de la Miseria,[2] a great servant of God, and very simple in worldly matters. While we were talking together, he happened to tell me that he wanted to go to Rome.

Before I go on, I will say what I know about this Father. His name was Mariano de San Benito[3]: he was Italian by nationality, a doctor and a man of great skill and ability. He had been in the service of the Queen of Poland, had had the oversight of her entire household and had never been inclined to marry. He held a Commandery in the Order of Saint John and Our Lord had called him to forsake everything in order the better to procure his own salvation. He had suffered a number of trials, for it had been alleged against him that he had been concerned in a man's death, and for two years he was in prison, where he refused to engage an advocate or anyone else to defend him, but trusted in God and in His justice alone. There were witnesses who said he had asked them to kill this man; but what happened to the old men in the story of Saint Susanna also happened here. Each of them was asked where he was at the time: one replied that he was sitting

---

[1] Cf. p. 45, above.

[2] Fray Juan de la Miseria was an Italian who first came to Spain on a pilgrimage to Santiago de Compostela, remained there as a sculptor and afterwards became a hermit, in company with P. Mariano, whom he had known in Italy. Later he studied and practised the art of painting and he was painting some pictures for Doña Leonor while staying in her house.

[3] Mariano Azaro was a well-born and well-to-do Italian, some details of whose biography are given in the text. The Queen whom he had served was Catherine of Austria, consort of Sigismund II, King of Poland, A Knight of the Order of St. John of Jerusalem, and a skilled mathematician and engineer, he had fought for Philip II against the French and taken part in the battle of St. Quintin. Later Philip II employed him on the canalization of the Tagus and the Guadalquivir, and it was while engaged on this work that he met P. Mateo de la Fuente and decided to become a hermit. In 1568, Philip II summoned him to help in a scheme for using the Tagus to irrigate the country around Aranjuez. He was on his way back to his hermitage when he met St. Teresa.

on a bed and another that he was at a window. In the end they had to confess that they had made up the story. He assured me that it had cost him a great deal of money to get those witnesses set free instead of having them punished, and that the very man who had given him all this trouble had fallen into his power, so that he could have laid an information against him, but that he had made every possible effort to see that he was done no harm.

These and other virtues (for he is a pure and chaste man and dislikes having to do with women) must have won him grace from Our Lord to realize the nature of the world and to strive to withdraw from it. So he began to consider what Order he would enter, and, after investigating first one and then another, found them all, so he told me, unsuitable for a man of his type. Then he learned that near Seville there were some hermits living together in a Desert,[1] which they called El Tardón, and that they had as their Superior a very saintly man, called Father Mateo.[2] Each hermit had his own cell and they lived separately, not saying the Divine Office, but meeting in an oratory for Mass. They had no money, nor would they receive alms; each maintained himself by the labour of his hands and each took his meals alone in conditions of extreme poverty. When I heard of this, it seemed to me a picture of the life of our holy fathers. He had been living in this way for eight years. When the Holy Council of Trent was held, and hermits were commanded to make their submission to the Orders, he wanted to go to Rome and ask permission that he and his companions might be left as they were, and he was thinking of doing this when I spoke to him.

When he described to me the way in which they lived, I showed him our Primitive Rule and told him that in our Order he could keep all his observances with less trouble, for they were the same as our own, and in particular he could live by the labour of his hands, which was the thing that most attracted him, for he told me that the world was ruined by greed and that it was this fact that brought religious Orders into contempt. I agreed with him there, and we soon found we were of the same mind both in this and in everything else, so that, when I told him why I thought he could be of great service to God in this habit of ours, he replied that he would consider it that very night. I saw that he had almost

---

[1] [The Desert (*desierto*) is a religious community for solitaries, the members of which live either in cells within the precincts or in hermitages outside. Cf. *S.S.M*, II, 282.]

[2] P. Mateo de la Fuente, born about 1524, at Alminuete, in the province of Toledo, graduated at Salamanca University and then entered upon a hermit's life in the Sierra Morena. Later, on the advice of Juan de Ávila, his spiritual director, he went, with several companions, to a hermitage called El Tardón, in the province of Córdoba. (Previously the place had been called El Cardón, from the abundance of thistles (*cardo*) there.)

resolved to join us and understood now the meaning of what I
had been told in prayer—that there was something more afoot
than the foundation of the convent. It gave me the greatest
pleasure, for I thought it would be a great service to the Lord if
he entered the Order. His Majesty, Who had willed that he
should do so, inclined him in that direction on that same night,
and on the next day he called upon me with his mind quite made
up, amazed to find that he had so quickly changed his opinion,
especially (as he still says sometimes even to-day) at the suggestion
of a woman, as if it were she who was the cause and not the
Lord, Who alone can change the heart.

Wondrous are His judgments. This man, who had gone
for so many years without being able to make a resolution about
joining an Order (for he was not in one then, had taken no
vows and was under no obligation beyond that of living a retired
life), had now been suddenly moved by God and had learned
from Him how great a service he could render Him in this Order
and that His Majesty needed him for the carrying on and further-
ance of what had been begun. He has been a great help to us, and
it is already causing him many trials, and will cause him more
before everything is settled, so far as one can judge from the
opposition with which this Primitive Rule is now meeting. But,
with his skill, ability and goodness of life, he has influence with
many people who help and protect us.

He told me that at Pastrana, which was the very place I
was going to, Ruy Gómez had given him a good hermitage, and
a place where a group of hermits could settle, and that he would
make this over to our Order and take the habit there. I thanked
him and gave great praise to Our Lord, for, though our most
reverend Father General had sent me licences to found two
monasteries, I had founded only one.[1] So I sent a message
from the place where I was to the two Fathers already mentioned,
the present Provincial and his predecessor,[2] begging them
earnestly to give me leave, as the foundation could not be made
without their consent. I also wrote to the Bishop of Ávila, Don
Álvaro de Mendoza, who was a great help to us, asking him
to do what he could with them.

It pleased God that they should consent. They must have
thought that in so secluded a place the monastery could do them
little harm. Fray Mariano gave me his word that as soon as the
licence arrived he would go there, which made me extremely
happy. I found the Princess and Prince Ruy Gómez at Pastrana
and they gave me a very warm welcome. They allotted us a

---

[1] Duruelo.
[2] Alonso González and Ángel de Salazar.

lodging to ourselves, where we stayed longer than I had expected; for the house was so small that the Princess had had a large part of it pulled down and rebuilt: its outer walls had not been demolished but a great many alterations had been made in it.

I must have been there three months,[1] during which time there were many trials to be borne, as the Princess wanted me to do certain things which were not fitting in our Order, and I determined that, rather than do them, I would go away without making the foundation. The Prince, Ruy Gómez, with the commonsense which he had to a very marked degree, saw reason, and persuaded his wife to modify her demands. I, too, gave way in certain respects, as I was more anxious that the monastery should be founded than the convent, realizing how important it was, as has since become clear.

And now came the hermits I have spoken of, Mariano and his companion; and, as they brought the licence with them, the Prince and Princess were good enough to allow the hermitage which they had given him to be used by Discalced friars. I sent for the first of my friars, the Father Fray Antonio de Jesús, who was at Mancera, so that he might begin the foundation of the monastery. I had habits and mantles prepared for them and did all that I could to get them to take the habit at once.

Meanwhile I had sent to the convent at Medina del Campo for more nuns, for I had only two with me. There was a Father who had been there for some time, neither very old nor yet quite young, and an excellent preacher: his name was Fray Baltasar de Jesús.[2] When he heard that the monastery was being founded, he came with the nuns, meaning to become a Discalced friar himself. He did so as soon as he had arrived, and, when he told me of his decision, I praised God. He gave the habit to Father Mariano and his companion, and made them lay brothers, for Father Mariano did not wish to be ordained priest, but to enter the Order as the least of all the friars, and from this I could not dissuade him. Later, by the command of our most reverend

---

[1] Actually, she was there for less than two months, leaving on July 21.

[2] The nuns who came were Isabel de San Jerónimo and Ana de Jesús; with them came Jerónima de San Agustín from the Incarnation, Ávila. They were accompanied by P. Baltasar Nieto, an eloquent preacher, who at that time was with the Calced friars at Medina and had for some time been wanting to pass over to the Reform. St. Teresa and her companions made habits for the three friars from some frieze given her by the Prince and on July 9, 1569 they took the habit in the Palace oratory, P. Baltasar assuming the name "de Jesús". P. Antonio de Jesús arrived on July 13 and the Blessed Sacrament was then reserved in the monastery. P. Baltasar became Prior in 1570. The Pastrana house, where P. Gracián later spent his novitiate, became the most important Reformed house in Spain, and for some two centuries most of the Chapters-General were held there. The friars were expelled from the house in 1836 and in 1855 the Alcantarine Franciscans entered it and have had it ever since.

Father General, he took priest's orders.[1] When both monasteries had been founded and the Father Fray Antonio de Jesús had come, novices began to enter it (it will be seen later what some of them were like) and to serve Our Lord in all sincerity. But this, if it be His will, will be described by one who can write of it better than I, for I myself am unable to do the theme justice.[2]

With regard to the nuns, their convent was highly favoured by the Prince and Princess, the latter being most careful to look after them and treat them well, until the death of the Prince Ruy Gómez. Then, either through the wiles of the devil, or perhaps because the Lord allowed it (His Majesty knows which), the Princess, overcome with grief at his death, entered the convent as a nun herself.[3] In the state of distress she was in, the restrictions imposed by the enclosure, to which she was not accustomed, could not have pleased her, and, on account of the Holy Council, the Prioress could not give her all the freedom she desired. So she became displeased with her, and with all the nuns, to such an extent that, even after she had put off the habit and returned to her own house, she continued to be annoyed with them. The poor nuns were so upset about it that I tried, by making applications to the superiors of the Order and in every other possible way, to get the convent moved and to have them taken to Segovia, where a convent was being founded just then, as will be related in due course. They went there, leaving behind everything that the Princess had given them,[4] and taking with them certain nuns whom she had ordered them to admit though they had brought nothing with them. The beds and the small articles which the nuns themselves had brought with them they took away, leaving the people in the place very sorry. But I myself, when I saw that they were at peace, was the happiest person in the world, for I had it on excellent authority that they were in no way to blame for the Princess' displeasure; on the contrary, they treated her, while she wore the habit, exactly as they had done before. The sole reason for her displeasure was the one I have given, and the lady's own distress; a servant whom she brought with her is

[1] This was in Lent 1574.
[2] Here a word has been crossed out: it seems to be " always."
[3] After her return to Toledo, St. Teresa sent to Pastrana, as Prioress, M. Isabel de Santo Domingo, who had been Prioress at Toledo. It is she who is referred to by that title in the text above. The story goes that, on hearing that the Princess had taken the Carmelite habit in Madrid and was on her way to Pastrana, she exclaimed: " The Princess a nun! That will be the end of this house! "
[4] Before leaving for Toledo, St. Teresa, with her customary foresight, had instructed the nuns to make a complete inventory of everything the Princess gave them, and the Prioress saw to it that this continued to be done. This was fortunate, as the nuns had hardly reached Segovia when the Princess attempted to bring a lawsuit against them.

believed to have been wholly to blame for it. In short, the Lord permitted it. He must have seen that this was not a good place for the convent, for His judgments are deep and transcend the understanding of us all. For my own part, I should not have ventured to act as I did by relying solely on my own understanding; but I followed the opinion of persons of learning and sanctity.[1]

CHAPTER XVIII

Describes the foundation of the convent of Saint Joseph, Salamanca, which took place in the year 1570. Gives certain important counsels to prioresses.

When these two foundations had been made, I returned to the city of Toledo, where I stayed for some months until the house to which I have referred was purchased and left in complete order. While I was busy with this, I received a letter from a Rector of the Society of Jesus at Salamanca,[2] saying that a house of our Order would be very useful there, and giving me reasons for this belief. As the city is very poor,[3] I had not previously considered making a foundation there on a basis of poverty. But, when I considered that Ávila is equally poor and that God never fails us—nor do I think He will fail anyone who serves Him—I resolved to make the foundation, providing for it as reasonably well as I could, and accepting only a few nuns, who would help by working with their own hands. Going from Toledo to Ávila, I wrote to get the licence from the then Bishop,[4] who was so good about it that, when the Father Rector had told him of this Order and showed him what a service it could render to God, he granted it at once.

It seemed to me that, once I had the licence of the Ordinary,

---

[1] She consulted PP. Ángel de Salazar, Pedro Fernández, Domingo Báñez and Hernando del Castillo. The last-named, a close friend of the Prince and Princess, made a journey to Pastrana to remonstrate with the distinguished novice. The nuns reached Segovia in the Holy Week of 1574.

[2] P. Martín Gutiérrez. Cf. *Relaciones*, XV (Vol. I, p. 340, above).

[3] Neither now nor then could Salamanca, or the country around it, be correctly described as " poor "; but it was a University city, without any important industry, and hence, no doubt, with few wealthy citizens. There were also a great many religious houses established there already. It is in this sense that we must understand St. Teresa's reference.

[4] Don Pedro González de Mendoza, son of the fourth Duke del Infantado, was one of the most learned members of the Council of Trent. He became Bishop of Salamanca in 1560 and died in 1574. He was, of course, well acquainted with the Discalced Reform, having granted the licence for the Medina house in 1567.

the convent was as good as founded, so easy would everything be. And so I succeeded at once in renting a house, which I got through a lady whom I knew.[1] It was a difficult matter, as this was not the letting season, and the house was in the possession of some students. However, by the time there were people ready to go into it, they had given it up. They did not know for what purpose it was to be let to us—I took the greatest care of that: nobody knew anything about it until we had taken possession of it, for by this time I have some experience of what the devil will do to upset one of these convents. Although in this case God did not allow him to trouble us at the outset, as it was His will that the foundation should be made, the trials and the opposition which we have encountered subsequently have been so severe that even now, as I write this, though several years have passed since the foundation was made, things have not entirely settled down. So I believe great service is being rendered to God in it, since the devil finds it so intolerable.

When the licence had been obtained and the house made over to us, I set out for the place, relying on the mercy of God, for there was no one there who could help me in any way in the provision of many things that would be necessary before the house could be furnished. For greater secrecy, I took only one nun as companion,[2] and did not bring the rest to the house until we had possession; for I was warned by what had happened to me at Medina del Campo, where I found myself in great difficulties; this time, if any obstacles presented themselves, I should have to wrestle with them alone, apart from the single nun who was essential to me. We arrived on the eve of All Saints', after having covered a large part of the road during the previous night; it had been bitterly cold and in the place where we slept I had been extremely unwell.

I say nothing, in describing these foundations, of the sore trials which we endured on the roads, what with the cold, the sun and the snow. There were times when it did not stop snowing the whole day long; others when we lost our way; and others when we had to contend with numerous indispositions and fevers. As a rule, glory be to God, my health is poor, but I used to be very conscious that Our Lord was giving me strength. For it sometimes happened that, when I was occupied in a

[1] Probably Doña Beatriz Yáñez de Ovalle, wife of a cousin of Doña Juana de Ahumada's husband, Don Juan de Ovalle.

[2] M. María del Santísimo Sacramento, whom St. Teresa had taken from the Incarnation, Ávila, and made Prioress at Malagón. After spending some years at the Salamanca convent, she was transferred to Alba de Tormes, where she died in 1589. The word "companion" in the Spanish is feminine. One record says that P. Julián de Ávila went with the two nuns; another, that they took two friars of the Observance, F. Juan Mayllo and P. Francisco de Ledesma.

foundation, I would find myself in such suffering and pain that it caused me great anguish. I would feel that I could not even remain in my cell without lying down, and so I would turn to Our Lord and complain to His Majesty, asking Him how He expected me to do what I could not. Then, though the suffering continued, His Majesty would give me strength, and the fervour and the anxiety for the work with which He inspired me seemed to make me forget myself.

So far as I remember at the moment, no fear of trials ever kept me from making a foundation, though I particularly disliked journeys, especially long ones; but once I had started they troubled me very little, as I realized in Whose service they were being made, and remembered that the Lord would be praised in that house and that the Most Holy Sacrament would be reserved there. It is a special consolation to me to see one church more when I remember how many are being destroyed by the Lutherans. I cannot think of any trials, however severe, that we need dread, when they are the means of bringing such blessing to Christendom; and, though many of us do not think of this, it ought to be a great consolation to us that Jesus Christ, true God and true Man, should dwell in so many places, as He does, in the Most Holy Sacrament. For my own part I am certainly very much comforted when I am in choir and look at these pure souls, busy in the praises of God, and I cannot help feeling so, too, with regard to many other things, such as obedience, seeing how happy enclosure and solitude make the sisters and how glad they are when occasions for mortification present themselves. The more grace the Lord gives to prioresses for testing them in this, the happier I find them; and prioresses often grow wearier of testing them than do they of obeying, for in that respect their desires are never satisfied.

Though I may be digressing from the subject of the foundation which I began to describe, some ideas occurred to me here on the question of mortification, and perhaps, daughters, they will be useful to prioresses, so I will put them down now in case I forget them. Differing as they do in talents and virtues, superiors like to direct their nuns in their own way. A prioress who is extremely mortified will think any command which she gives for the subduing of the will easy, and so it would be for her, yet others may perhaps find it very troublesome. This we must carefully consider and we must not command others to do what would be hard for ourselves. Discretion is an important factor in government and in these houses of ours it is most necessary—I would even say more necessary than in others— since here greater care has to be taken about the inward life of the nuns as well as about the outward. Other prioresses, who are women of great spirituality, would be glad if the nuns' only duty were the recitation of prayers. In short, the Lord leads us all by different roads. But superiors must realize that they have been given their position, not so that they may choose a road for their daughters which is to their own liking, but in order that they may guide them along the road of the Rule and Constitution of the Order, even if they have to force themselves to do so and would prefer to act otherwise.

I was once in one of our houses with a prioress who was very fond of penance and made all the nuns lead penitential lives. She would discipline the whole community at once by ordering the recitation of the seven penitential Psalms, together with prayers and other things of the same kind. That is what happens if a prioress becomes absorbed in prayer: she keeps the entire community reciting prayers, even outside the stated hours—after Matins, indeed, when it would be better for the nuns to go to sleep. If, on the other hand, as I say, she is fond of mortification, there has to be continual activity in that direction, and these little lambs of the Virgin have to bear it all silently, just as if they were real lambs. I must admit that this arouses devotion in me as well as shame and at times leads me into sore temptation. For although when all the sisters are absorbed in God they do not think of this, I am afraid for their health, and should prefer that they kept the Rule, which gives them quite enough to do, and that any other requirements were imposed gently. This question of mortification, in particular, is of the greatest importance, and, for the love of Our Lord, I should like superiors to think about it with care. Discretion in such matters is very important and it is equally so for them to recognize where talents lie; if they are not very careful about this, instead of helping the nuns they will do them a great deal of harm and make them unsettled.

They must reflect that mortification of this kind is not of obligation: and that is the very first thing they must remember. Necessary though mortification is for winning the soul freedom and high perfection, this cannot be done in a short time: they must therefore help each soul little by little according to the mental and spiritual gifts which God has given them. You might think that no mental gifts are necessary for this, but you would be mistaken; for there are some who have to go through a great deal before they can understand what is meant by perfection or even by the spirit of our Rule, yet these may eventually become the holiest of all. They may not know when they can rightly excuse themselves, and when not, and they may be

doubtful about other trifling things which, once they understand them, they will do easily; but they have never properly
understood them, nor, which is worse, do they consider them
as having anything to do with perfection.

In one of our houses there is a nun who, so far as I can gather,
is one of the greatest servants of God in any of them. She is
very spiritual and receives many favours from His Majesty, and
is given to penance and to great humility; yet there are a few
things in the Constitutions which she cannot understand. When
we accuse each other of faults in chapter, she thinks this shows
a lack of charity, and asks how one can possibly say things about
other sisters. And she makes other remarks of this kind, saying,
for example, that she might be speaking against sisters who are
great servants of God. Yet I can see that in other respects she
is much better than those who understand the Constitutions
quite well. A prioress must not think that she can understand
souls immediately: let her leave this to God, Who alone can
understand them, and let her try to guide each soul in the way
by which His Majesty is leading it, always assuming that there
is no failure in obedience or in the observance of the most essential
points of the Rule and Constitution. That virgin who was
among the eleven thousand, and who went and hid herself, was
none the less for that reason a saint and a martyr: she may, in
fact, have suffered more than the rest, by going alone later on
to offer herself for martyrdom.[1]

I now return to the subject of mortification. In order to
mortify a nun, the prioress orders her to do something which,
though small in itself, is a heavy task for her. She does it, but
it upsets her very much and is such a source of temptation to
her that it would be better if she had not been ordered to do it.
As soon as the prioress sees this, she should realize that no effort
of this kind will make her perfect; she would do better to dissemble, and direct her gradually until the Lord has finished
His work in her, lest what is done in order to make her a better
nun (though even without that kind of perfection she might be
a very good one) should have the result of disturbing her rest
and afflicting her spirit, which is a most terrible thing. If she
sees others doing these things, she will gradually do them too,
as we have seen; and even if she does not, that particular virtue

---

[1] The Roman Martyrology (October 21) tells how in the fourth century A.D.
eleven thousand young maidens met their deaths near Cologne, at the hands of
the Huns, in defence of their virginity. One of them, however, Cordula by name,
was afraid and hid herself, but later on recovered her courage, gave herself up and
was martyred with the rest. The best known of these girl martyrs was St. Ursula.
The devotion to the " Eleven thousand Virgins " was very popular in Spain in St.
Teresa's day.

is not necessary for her salvation. I know a nun of this type, whose life has been one of great virtue, and who has served Our Lord in many ways and for a great number of years. She has certain imperfections and feelings which often she cannot restrain, and, recognizing this to be so, she tells me her troubles. I believe God allows her to fall into these faults without her committing sin (for there is no sin in them) so that she may become humble and learn from them that she is not altogether perfect. So there are some who will endure great mortifications, and, the greater the mortifications they are ordered to do, the greater the pleasure they will take in them, because the Lord has given them strength of soul to surrender their own wills. Others, however, will be unable to endure even the smallest mortifications; they will be like a child laden with two bushels of wheat; not only can he not carry them but he will break down under the load and fall to the ground. Forgive me, then, my daughters (I am speaking to prioresses): it is the things I have noticed in certain persons that have made me spend so long on this.

I will give you another piece of advice, which is very important: even in order to test obedience, you should never give any kind of command the fulfilment of which would lead a person into so much as a venial sin. I have known commands given which would have led to mortal sin had they been obeyed. Those to whom they were given would perhaps have been saved by pleading their innocence, but this would not apply to a prioress, who has only to command in order to be obeyed immediately. When the sisters hear and read about the saints of the desert and the things they did, they think everything they are ordered to do must be good, or at least that it will be right for them to do it. But nuns must also be warned that, even under orders, they must not do anything which would be a mortal sin apart from such orders, with the exception of things like absence from Mass or abstention from the fasts of the Church, which the prioress might have reasons for ordering. It would be wrong, for example, to throw oneself into a well or do anything of that kind, for no sister ought to suppose that God will work a miracle for her as He sometimes did for the saints. There are quite enough ways of practising perfect obedience without that.

I should recommend any such way provided it is free from these dangers. Once a sister at Malagón asked leave to take the discipline, and the Prioress, who must have been receiving the same request from others, answered : "Don't worry me." Then, as the nun became importunate, she said: "Get along with you and don't worry me." The nun, with great simplicity, began to walk up and down;[1] after she had been doing this for some hours, a sister asked her why she was walking about so much and she repeated the Prioress' command. At this point the bell rang for Matins, and when the Prioress asked why the sister was not there the other nun told her what had happened.

It is necessary, then, as I have said elsewhere, for prioresses to be wary with souls whom they have found to be obedient and to consider well what they are doing. A certain nun once brought her Prioress a very large worm, asking her to look and see what a fine specimen it was. The Prioress laughingly said: "Go and eat it, then." So she went away and with great care started to fry it. The cook asked her what she was doing and she said that she was going to eat it, which she was in fact about to do. Thus the Prioress' very careless remark might have done her a great deal of harm. Still, I much prefer obedience to be carried to excess, for I have a particular devotion to that virtue, and so I have done all in my power that others should have it. But it would have been of little use if the Lord through His exceeding great mercy had not given them all grace and inclination for it. May it please His Majesty to increase it in us all. Amen.

CHAPTER XIX

Continues to describe the foundation of the convent of Saint Joseph in the city of Salamanca.

I have been making a long digression. When I recall anything which the Lord has been pleased for me to learn by experience, it worries me if I cannot discuss it. For it may possibly do some good, as I believe it will. You, daughters, must always consult persons of learning, for they will show you the way of perfection with sincerity and discretion. If superiors wish to do their work well, it is very necessary for them to have learned men as their confessors; otherwise, though believing themselves to be acting in a holy way, they will commit many flagrant errors; they should also see that their nuns have learned men as confessors.

At noon, on the eve of All Saints' Day, in the year already mentioned, we reached the city of Salamanca. I sent from my

---

[1] [The untranslatable point of this anecdote is that the colloquial Spanish phrase here rendered " Get along with you " means, if taken literally, " Go for a walk." The corresponding English phrase would be " Run away."]

lodging for a good man who lived there and to whom I had commended the task of arranging for the house to be vacated for me. His name was Nicolás Gutiérrez[1] and he was a great servant of God. By his good life he had won from His Majesty great peace and joy in trials, of which he had had many, for he had seen great prosperity and had become very poor, but had borne his poverty with as much joy as his wealth. To make this foundation he laboured hard with great devotion and good will. When he came, he told me that the house had not yet been vacated, for he had not been able to get the students to leave it. I explained to him how important it was that we should have it at once before it became known that I was in the place, for, as I have said, I was always afraid that we might meet some disturbance. So he went to the owner of the house and pressed the matter so hard that it was vacated that same evening. It was almost nightfall when we went in.

This was the first foundation I made without having the Most Holy Sacrament reserved, for I never considered that I was taking possession of a house at all unless this was done. I now found that it was not essential, which was a great comfort to me because the students had left the house quite unprepared. As they were not very tidy people, the place was in such a state that we had to work hard at it all that night. Early on the next morning the first Mass was said there and I sent for more nuns, who would have to come from Medina del Campo.[2] On the night of All Saints' Day my companion and I were alone. There is one thing I must tell you, sisters: I feel like laughing when I remember the fears of my companion, whose name was María del Sacramento: she was an older nun than I and a great servant of God.

The house was very large and roomy,[3] with a great many attics, and my companion could not get the students out of her mind, for she thought that, as they had been so annoyed at having to leave the house, one of them might still be hiding

[1] Nicolás Gutiérrez and his wife Ana de la Fuente had no less than six daughters who were nuns in the Convent of the Incarnation, Ávila, and all of whom afterwards joined the Reform. These were Ana María de Jesús, Isabel de Jesús, Juliana de la Magdalena, Jerónima de San Agustín, Juana Bautista and María de San Pedro.

[2] Ana de la Encarnación and María de Cristo came from Medina and Jerónima de Jesús from Valladolid. Soon afterwards, two novices, Ana de Jesús and Juana de Jesús, came from Ávila, together with María de San Francisco, who had taken the habit at Toledo, on the foundation of the Reformed convent there, and, later, had gone back to Ávila with St. Teresa.

[3] The house, which still stands, is in the Plaza de Santa Teresa and is in the possession of the Siervas de San José, a community of sisters who devote themselves to the education of poor children. It is, in fact, quite a large house, with a fairsized central *patio*. On the façade are emblazoned the arms of the Ovalles, and of several other families related to them.

there. They could very well have done so, for there was plenty of opportunity. We shut ourselves up in a room, where the straw was, for this was the first thing that I had got in for the foundation of the house, as if we had some straw we should not be without a bed. That night we slept on the straw, with two or three blankets which had been lent us. On the next day, some nuns who lived near, and who, we had feared, would not be at all pleased at our coming, lent us some bed-clothes for the companions who were to join us, and also sent us alms. They came from the convent of Saint Elizabeth, and all the time we were in that house they did us numerous kind actions and gave us alms.[1]

When my companion found herself shut up in the room, she seemed to be a little calmer about the students, though she did nothing all the time but look about her fearfully, first in one direction and then in another. The devil must have helped in this by putting thoughts of danger into her mind in order to upset me, for, with my weak heart, very little is enough to do this. "What are you looking for?" I asked her. "Nobody can possibly get in here." "Mother," she replied, "I am wondering what you would do all alone if I were to die here." If this were to happen, I thought, it would certainly be a dreadful thing; and it made me reflect for a moment, and even frightened me a little; for, though I am not afraid of dead bodies, the sight of them always affects my heart, even when I am not alone. And the tolling of the bells (for, as I have said, it was the vigil of All Souls) gave the devil an opportunity to make us waste our time upon these childish thoughts; when he finds that he cannot frighten us in one way, he looks for other means of doing so. So I said to her: "Well, sister, I shall consider what is to be done if the occasion arises: now let me go to sleep." As we had had two bad nights, sleep soon drove away our fears. On the next day more nuns arrived, and they then vanished entirely.

The community remained in this house for about three years— I am not sure it was not four, for my memory is not very reliable here, as I myself was sent to the Convent of the Incarnation at Ávila.[2] I should never from choice have left a convent until it was clean and well-kept and arranged to my taste, nor have I ever done so. In this respect, God has shown me great favour; for I have always liked to be in the forefront of work, and I would provide even the smallest things for the comfort and convenience of the nuns, just as if I had to live in that house all my

[1] According to historians of the Reform, this charitable community, which is still in existence, supplied the new foundation with both food and garments.

[2] The Dominican P. Pedro Fernández, Apostolic Visitor to the Order of Carmel, appointed St. Teresa Prioress of the Incarnation in 1571: she took up her office on October 6 of that year.

life; so I was very glad when everything was done. It worried me a good deal to see what the sisters were suffering here—not for want of sustenance, for, as the house was a long way from any place where alms were obtainable, I had been very careful to provide for this, but because of their health, for the place was very damp and cold. This being due to its size, nothing could be done about it; the worst thing was that the Most Holy Sacrament was not reserved, which, in a community strictly enclosed, is a great discouragement. They did not take it as such, however, but bore it so gladly that one could not but praise the Lord; some of them told me that they thought it an imperfection to want another house, and that, if they had had the Most Holy Sacrament, they would have been quite happy there.

When the Superior of the Order saw the perfection of their life and learned what a bad time they were having, he was moved with pity for them and sent for me from the Incarnation.[1] They had already arranged with a gentleman in that city to give them another house, but it was in such a condition that more than a thousand ducats had to be spent before they could go in. It was part of an entailed estate, and its owner was agreeable to our taking possession of it, and walling it in, even without having the King's licence to do so. I got Father Julián de Ávila, who, as I have said, has been with me and helped me in making these foundations, to come with me and look at the house, so that we could report what would have to be done, for I have learned a good deal in these matters from experience.

We went there in August; and, though we made all possible haste, we were kept waiting till Michaelmas, which is the period when houses are let there. Our house was a long way from being finished; but, as we had not renewed the lease of our original house for a further year, it had been let to another tenant, who was anxious to get us out quickly. The whitewashing of the church was almost finished. The gentleman who had sold us the house was not there. Some people who wished us well said we were making a mistake in going in so quickly; but, when a thing has to be done urgently, it is useless to take people's advice unless they give help as well.

We went in on Michaelmas Eve, a little before dawn. It had already been announced that the Holy Sacrament would be reserved in the house on Michaelmas Day and that there would be a sermon.[2] On the evening before we went in, Our Lord

[1] This was in August 1573.
[2] The sermon was preached by the famous ascetic writer Fray Diego de Estella [S.S.M., II, 219-49]. "For this reason," remarked Ana de Jesús, "we knew that the greater part of this city would come to our ceremony." [P. Silverio, V, 159, n.1.]

was pleased to send a heavy rainstorm, so that it was difficult for us to take the things that we needed. The chapel had been re-built, but the roof was so badly made that most of it let in the rain. I assure you, daughters, I was very conscious of my imperfections that day. As the ceremony had been announced, I did not know what to do, and I was terribly upset, and said to Our Lord, as if complaining, that He must either not tell me to do these things or help us in our need. Nicolás Gutiérrez, good man, with his customary equanimity, told me, as quietly as if nothing had happened, not to be distressed, for God would put everything right. And so He did, for on Michaelmas Day, when it was time for the people to come, the sun began to shine; and this made me feel very devout and I realized how much better that good man had done to trust Our Lord than had I to be so troubled.

There was a large congregation, and we had music, and the Most Holy Sacrament was reserved with great solemnity; and, as the house was in a good situation, people got to hear about it and began to esteem it highly. In particular we were helped a great deal by the Countess of Monterrey, Doña María Pimentel.[1] and a lady called Doña Mariana, whose husband was Mayor of the city. But on the very next day, as if to temper our joy at having the Most Holy Sacrament with us, we were visited by the gentleman who owned the house, and he was so angry that I did not know what to do with him. The devil would not let him listen to reason—for we had fulfilled the whole of our part of the agreement with him. But it was useless for us to try to tell him that. After several people had spoken to him he became a little calmer, but afterwards he changed his mind. So I resolved to let him have his house again—and then he did not want that either: what he wanted was immediate payment for it. His wife, to whom the house really belonged, had wanted to sell it so as to give the money to her two daughters, and it was on this account that the licence to do so had been applied for, the money being deposited with someone of his own choice.

And in fact, though this happened more than three years ago, the purchase has not been completed, and I do not know if the convent will remain in that house (for which reason I have mentioned it here), or, if not, where it will go.[2] What I do

---

[1] The Count and Countess of Monterrey were close friends of St. Teresa and had obtained the permission of her superiors for her to stay with them on her return from the foundation at Alba de Tormes. After spending a few days in their palace (which dates from 1530 and is still standing) she returned to Ávila.

[2] The contract, which is dated October 6, 1573, stipulates that Mother Teresa shall pay the sum of 2,580 *ducados* within two years, and, during that period an annual

know is that in none of the other convents which the Lord has founded according to this Primitive Rule down to the present have the nuns suffered anything like such great trials as here. Our nuns here, by the mercy of God, are very good, and bear everything joyfully. May it please His Majesty to grant them greater progress, for it matters little whether we have a good house or not—indeed, it is a great pleasure for us to find ourselves in a house from which we may at any time be turned out, when we remember that the Lord of the world had no house at all. It has happened on several occasions that we have been in a house which was not our own, as will be seen in the history of these foundations; and it is a fact that I have never seen a nun in the least distressed about it. May it please His Divine Majesty, by His infinite goodness and mercy, that there may be a place for us in the eternal mansions. Amen. Amen.

CHAPTER XX

Describes the foundation of the convent of Our Lady of the Annunciation, Alba de Tormes, in the year 1571.

Less than two months had passed since All Saints' Day, on which we had taken possession of our house at Salamanca, when I received a message from the steward of the Duke of Alba and his wife, begging me to make a foundation in their town. I had no great desire to do so, because it was so small a place that we should need revenue for the house, and my own preference was for not making a foundation where that was the case.[1] But my confessor, Father-Master Fray Domingo Báñez, of whom I spoke at the beginning of the history of these foundations, happened to be at Salamanca,[2] and he reproved me,

---

rent of 15,010 *maravedis*. But as the estate was entailed, and no royal faculty had been given for the sale (p. 95, above), the contract was declared null and void, and, on September 19, 1580, the nuns were given notice to leave the house, which they did, according to a document in the possession of the community, on June 22, 1582. No doubt the delay was due to the difficulty of finding another house, for St. Teresa had petitioned the Bishop for permission to leave the house, on account of its unhealthiness, as long previously as September 12, 1579.

[1] Francisco de Velázquez and his wife had in fact tried to persuade St. Teresa, through her brother-in-law Juan de Ovalle, to make a foundation at Alba de Tormes as long previously as July 1569. But Alba had only 770 inhabitants, which made a settled income essential, and in addition they had apparently laid down conditions to which St. Teresa could not agree.

[2] P. Báñez was at Salamanca from October 1570 to March 1571, for what reason is not known. It will be recalled that he had given the Saint similar advice with regard to the Malagón foundation (Chapter IX: p. 45, above).

saying that, as the Council permitted religious houses to have revenues, it would be wrong to refrain from making a foundation for that reason. He added that I did not understand the situation, and that money was no obstacle to poverty and great perfection on the part of the nuns. Before writing any more, I will say who the foundress was and how the Lord moved her to found this convent.

The foundress of the Convent of the Annunciation of Our Lady in Alba de Tormes was Teresa de Layz, a daughter of noble parents very well descended and of pure Christian blood. As they were not as wealthy as they were well descended, they had settled in a village called Tordillos, two leagues from the said town of Alba.[1] It is a great pity there should be so much vanity in the world that people prefer putting up with the lack of instruction and many other things which help to give light to souls and which are not found in the isolation of small villages, to abating a single tittle of what they think so-called honour demands of them. They had already had four daughters when Teresa de Layz came to be born and they were greatly distressed to find that she was a girl as well.

It is certainly a matter for deep regret that mortals, not knowing what is best for them, and being wholly ignorant of the judgments of God, do not realize what great blessings can come from having daughters or what great harm can come from having sons, and, unwilling, apparently, to leave the matter to Him Who understands everything and is the Creator of us all, worry themselves to death about what ought to make them glad. Their faith being dormant, such people do not think ahead or remember that it is God who ordains it so and leave everything in His hands. And, besides being too blind to do this, they are so ignorant that they are unable to realize how little they can gain by worrying about it. God help me! How differently shall we look upon our ignorances on that day when the truth of all things will become known. And how many fathers will find themselves going to hell because they have had sons, and how many mothers, through the help of their daughters, will find themselves going to Heaven!

To return to what I was saying, things reached such a pass that these people troubled very little about the life of their infant daughter, and, on the third day after her birth, they left her alone and nobody gave a thought to her from morning till night. One good thing they had done, however, was to have her baptized by a priest as soon as she was born. On the night of that third day, the woman who looked after her came in, found what

[1] Tordillos, at that time, had only sixty inhabitants.

had happened and ran to see if she was dead, and with her
went several other people who were paying a visit to the mother
and who witnessed what I shall now describe. The woman
began to cry, and took the child in her arms, and said to her:
"Why, my poor little child, anyone would think you were not
a Christian!" meaning that they had treated her very cruelly.
The child raised its head and said: "But I am." After that she
never spoke again until the age when children normally begin
to do so. Those who heard her were astonished, and her mother
became quite fond of her, and from that time onward looked
after her well; in fact she used often to say that she hoped she
would live until she had seen what God would make of this
child. She brought her up very well and taught her many
virtuous habits.

When the time arrived at which her parents wanted to marry
her, she had no desire to marry and refused to do so. But she
found that her suitor was Francisco de Velázquez, now her
husband, and co-founder with her of this convent. She had
never seen him in her life; but, as soon as they mentioned his
name to her, she decided that she would marry, if it was to be
with him. For the Lord saw that this would be well if they
were to do the good work which they have now done for the
service of His Majesty. Besides being a virtuous and a wealthy
man, he is so fond of his wife that he does everything to please
her, and he does well to do so, for the Lord has most amply
provided him with all that can be expected in a wife. Apart
from the great care with which she manages his house, she is
so good that, when he took her to Alba, his native place, and
the Duke's chamberlains assigned a room in the same house
to a young gentleman, she was so distressed that she began to
dislike the place, for she was so young and good-looking that
the devil had begun to instil evil thoughts into the young man,
and if she had not been so good there might have been trouble.

When she found that this was the case, she said nothing of
it to her husband but asked him to take her away. He did so,
and took her to Salamanca, where they lived very happily and
with great worldly prosperity, as his position was such that
everyone was very anxious to please him and so he was well
treated.[1] They had only one trouble, that Our Lord had given
them no children; and Doña Teresa practised numerous devotions and prayers that children might be given her and besought
the Lord for nothing else, so that when she died she would leave

---

[1] Don Francisco was, from 1541 to 1566, a finance officer in the University of
Salamanca. He then took a similar position in the household of the Duke of Alba,
which he held till his death in 1574. His wife died in 1583.

behind her others who would praise His Majesty. For she thought it hard that her death should end everything and that there should be no one to praise Him after she had gone. She told me herself that she never gave Him any other reason for this desire of hers, and she is so truthful, Christian and virtuous a woman, as I have said, that when I see the good things she does they often make me praise Our Lord. She is a soul wholly desirous of blessing Him and never fails to use her time well.

Many years passed and she still had this desire, which she commended to Saint Andrew, who, in cases like this, she was told, was a good advocate. One night, after she had finished her many other devotions, and had gone to bed, she heard a voice saying: "Do not wish for children or you will send yourself to damnation." She was very much astonished and afraid, but in spite of what she had heard the desire did not leave her, for, as her motive was so good, she wondered why it should send her to damnation. So she continued praying to Our Lord, and in particular making a special prayer to Saint Andrew. Once, when she was feeling this desire very strongly (she does not know if she was awake or asleep, but in any case the event proved that the vision was a good one), she thought she was in a house in the courtyard of which, beneath the gallery, there was a well. She saw a green meadow there, carpeted with white flowers, and so beautiful that she cannot describe what it looked like. Near the well Saint Andrew appeared to her, a fine, venerable figure, whom it was a great delight to her to behold. And he said to her: "These are different children from those thou desirest." She would have been glad if the great joy which the sight of him there gave her had been never-ending, but it lasted no longer. She was quite clear, without anyone telling her so, that the saint was Saint Andrew, and also that it was the will of Our Lord that she should found a convent. From this it is evident that the vision was intellectual as well as imaginary and that it could not have been either a fancy of her own or an illusion sent by the devil.

That it was no fancy was clear from the striking effect it had produced on her. From that time onward she never again desired children: so convinced was she in her heart that it was the will of God for her to have none that she neither asked for them nor wished for them any more. Instead she began to think what she could do to accomplish the Lord's will. It is also evident that the vision did not come from the devil, not only from its results, for nothing that comes from him can accomplish anything good, but also because the convent has since been founded and great service is rendered in it to Our

Lord. Another reason why it could not have come from the devil is that the convent was not founded till more than six years afterwards and the devil has no foreknowledge of the future.

Astounded by this vision, she proposed to her husband that, as it was not God's will for them to have children, they might found a convent. Being so good a man and so fond of her, he was delighted at the idea, and they began to discuss where they should make the foundation. She was anxious to have it in her native village; but to that he made some sound objections to convince her that the place would not be a good one.

While he was discussing it with her, the Duchess of Alba sent for him, and, when he came, asked him to return to Alba and take up a position and office which she would give him in her household. When he had heard what she wanted him to do, and she had explained the situation to him, he accepted, though the post was a greatly inferior one to his post in Salamanca. His wife, on hearing of it, was greatly distressed, for, as I have said, she detested the place. But, when he assured her that no guests would be received in their house, she became somewhat more reconciled to it, though still rather worried, because she was much happier in Salamanca. He bought a house and sent for her; she came in great distress, which increased when she saw the house, for, though it was quite a spacious one and in an excellent situation, it had not many rooms, so all that night she was very much worried. On the next morning, however, when she went into the courtyard, she saw, on that very side of it, the well where she had seen Saint Andrew, and everything else was there before her eyes, exactly as she had seen it—I mean the place itself, not the saint nor the meadow nor the flowers, though she had, and still has, the picture of it quite clearly before her.

When she saw this, she was greatly moved and determined to found a convent there; and then there came to her a feeling of great comfort and tranquillity, and she no longer had any desire to go elsewhere. They set to work to buy a number of the adjoining houses until they had ample space. She thought a great deal as to the Order to which the house should belong, for she was anxious that there should be few nuns in it and that they should be very strictly enclosed. When she discussed the matter with two monks, belonging to different Orders, and very good and learned men, they both told her that it would be better for her to take up some other good work, because as a rule nuns are discontented people. They also gave her many other reasons, for, as the devil disliked the idea, he was anxious to put obstacles in her way, and so he persuaded her that the reasons which they had given her were good ones. As they were so insistent that the idea was not good, and the devil was even more intent upon putting obstacles in her way, she began to be afraid and worried; so she determined not to proceed further. She told her husband this, and it seemed to them both that as so many people had told them the idea was not a good one and their intention was to serve Our Lord they ought to abandon it. So they decided to marry a nephew of hers, the son of a favourite sister, and a very virtuous young man, to one of her husband's nieces, to give them a large part of their property, and to apply the rest to the good of their own souls. They were both convinced that this was the best thing to do and had quite decided to do it.

But, as Our Lord had ordained otherwise, their decision had little effect. Within a fortnight, their nephew fell very ill and after a short time Our Lord took him to Himself. To her this was an extreme grief, for she thought that his death had been caused by their determination to abandon what God had willed them to do in order to give their nephew the money, and this made her very much afraid. She remembered what had happened to the prophet Jonas, when he would not obey God, and she even thought that God had been punishing her by taking her dearly-loved nephew from her. From that day forward she resolved to let nothing hinder her from founding the convent, and her husband was in the same mind, though they did not know how to make their plan effective. Apparently what they eventually did was put into her heart by God, though the people to whom she spoke of it and described the kind of convent she wanted, laughed at her, for they thought she would never find the things she was looking for. One of these was her confessor, a friar of the Order of Saint Francis, a man of learning and distinction. This made her very disconsolate.

At about that time, this friar happened to go to a certain place[1] where they told him about these monasteries of Our Lady of Carmel which were just then being founded. He learned a great deal about them and then returned to this lady and told her he had at last found a way for her to establish a convent of the kind she desired. He told her what had happened and suggested that she should try to talk it over with me. This she did. We had considerable trouble in coming to an agreement, for when I have founded a religious house upon the basis of an endowment, I have always insisted that it must be a suffi-

---

[1] Probably to El Pedroso, where St. Peter of Alcántara had founded a Discalced monastery in 1557 [*S.S.M.*, II, 105]. The friars would be able to give him a full and favourable account of St. Teresa's Discalced foundations.

ciently large one, so that the nuns shall in no way be dependent on their relatives, or on anyone else, but that all necessary food and clothing, together with medical treatment, shall be provided for them in the house, as many difficulties arise when these necessaries are lacking. I have never lacked the courage and confidence to found religious houses without any endowment, on a basis of poverty: I have founded many such and I am certain that God will not fail them. But I have no belief in the foundation of a house with an endowment that is inadequate; I think it better that it should not be founded at all.

Eventually these people came to see reason and gave me a sum which would be sufficient for all the nuns we thought of receiving. And they also won my esteem by giving up their own house to us and going to live in a very poor one. The Most Holy Sacrament was reserved, and the foundation was made, on the Feast of the Conversion of Saint Paul, in the year 1571, to the honour and glory of God.[1] I believe great service is done to His Majesty in that house. May He be pleased ever to further its welfare.

I began to give some particulars of a few of the sisters in these convents, thinking that, when this book came to be read, those who are now there would not still be alive, and that thus their successors would be encouraged to continue the good beginnings which they had made. But later it occurred to me that there would be others who could do this better, and in great detail, and without the misgivings which I have had while doing it, for it has sometimes occurred to me that it may be thought I am writing from interested motives. I have therefore omitted numerous things which those who have seen and known them cannot fail to regard as miraculous, because they are supernatural. Of these I have desired to say nothing, nor will I say anything about the things which it has been clear Our Lord has done in answer to their prayers. In giving the years in which these foundations have been made I have some suspicion that I may sometimes be mistaken, although I have made every effort to recall the exact dates. This is not of great importance, for corrections can be made later, and I am speaking as well as my memory will allow me to do, so if there should be occasional errors it will not make much difference.

[1] The foundation deed was signed on the preceding day, January 24, 1571, by Francisco Velázquez and Teresa de Jesús. The latter's brother-in-law, Juan de Ovalle, signed for Teresa Laíz, who was unable to write. When St. Teresa left, in mid-February, the community was composed of the Prioress, Juana del Espíritu Santo; the Sub-Prioress, María del Santísimo Sacramento; and three other nuns, Guiomar de Jesús, Tomasína Bautista and María de San Francisco. It was in this convent, which has suffered little from violence, and even during the War of Independence was treated with notable respect, that St. Teresa died (October 4, 1582).

CHAPTER XXI

Describes the foundation of the glorious Saint Joseph of Carmel, Segovia. This foundation was made on Saint Joseph's Day in the year 1574.[1]

I have already related how, after I had founded the convents at Salamanca and Alba, and before the Salamanca convent had a house of its own, Father-Master Pedro Fernández, then Apostolic Commissary, ordered me to go for three years to the Convent of the Incarnation, at Ávila, and that later, seeing the necessitous condition of the Salamanca house, he told me to go back there and move them to a house of their own.[2] One day, when I was in prayer there, I was told by Our Lord to go and make a foundation at Segovia. To me this seemed an impossibility, for I could not go without being sent for, and I had understood from the Apostolic Commissary, Fray Pedro Fernández, that he did not want me to make any further foundations. I saw, too, that, as the three years for which I was to stay at the Incarnation were not over, he had good reason for not wanting this. While I was thinking the matter over, the Lord told me to speak to him about it and said that He would arrange it for me.

Being in Salamanca at the time, I wrote to him, saying that, as he already knew, I had been instructed by our most reverend General not to fail to make a foundation anywhere if I found an opportunity of doing so; that both the city and the Bishop of Segovia had agreed to accept one of our foundations; that I would make such a foundation if ordered to do so; and that I was telling him this to relieve my conscience, and, whatever the commands he might give me, I should feel happy and safe. These were approximately the words I used, and I added that I thought such a foundation would be a service rendered to God. It was clear that His Majesty desired it, for the Commissary told me at once to make the foundation and gave me a licence for doing so; this simply astounded me, in view of what I had heard him say on the matter. While still at Salamanca, I arranged to have a house taken for us on a lease; for, since my experiences at Toledo and Valladolid, I had decided that, for many reasons, it was better to take possession first and then to look for a house

---

[1] The MS. had originally 1573, which, by the addition of a stroke to the Roman numerals, was corrected to 1574.

[2] P. Gracián adds a marginal note here: " She came in the year 73, about St. James' tide [*por Santiago:* i.e., in late July or early August], and stayed until Christmas 74." It was often customary in Spain, at this time, to refer to the New Year as beginning at Christmas.

of our own. The chief reason for this was that I had not a farthing to buy a house with; and I knew that, once the convent was founded, the Lord would provide for it. Also, a more convenient site could then be chosen.

There was a widowed lady at Segovia called Doña Ana de Jimena,[1] whose husband had inherited an entailed property. She had been to see me once at Ávila: she was a very great servant of God and had always had a vocation for the cloister. So, when our house was founded, she entered it, together with a daughter of hers, who led a very good life, and the Lord recompensed her for the unhappiness which she had experienced as a wife and a widow by giving her a double happiness in religion. Both mother and daughter had always lived very recollected lives and served God well.

This saintly lady took a house and provided us with all that she saw we needed, both for the church and for ourselves, so that gave me but little trouble. But it seemed that no foundation could be made without our having trouble of some kind, and during the six months that I was there I was ill the whole time. I had gone there with a troublesome fever, a distaste for everything and much aridity and great darkness of soul. These, and physical ailments of many kinds, oppressed me greatly for some three months of this time.

On Saint Joseph's Day we reserved the Most Holy Sacrament; and, though I had the permission both of the Bishop[2] and of the city, I would not enter the house until the previous night, when I did so secretly. A long time had passed since the licence had been given; and, as I was in the Incarnation and had a Superior other than our Father General,[3] I had not been able to make the foundation. The licence of the Bishop, who had been in the city when he was asked for it, had been a verbal one, given to a gentleman, Andrés de Jimena, who had requested it on our behalf. He did not think it necessary to have it in writing, and this did not seem to me of any importance. But I was mistaken; for, when it was brought to the notice of the Vicar-General that the convent had been founded, he came at once in a great rage, and refused to allow Mass to be said there any longer. He also tried to imprison the priest who had said it—a Discalced friar[4] who

---

[1] In religion Ana de Jesús. She professed on July 2, 1575, was Prioress of this convent for some years, later held positions of authority elsewhere and died, at the age of eighty, in 1623. [This is not the Venerable Anne of Jesus (Ana de Lobera) who was so greatly esteemed by St. Teresa, St. John of the Cross and Luis de León, and on whom see *Life of the Venerable Anne of Jesus*, London, 1932].

[2] This was the famous Canonist Don Diego de Covarrubias y Leiva, a great supporter of the Discalced Carmelite Reform. He died in 1577.

[3] I.e., Fray Pedro Fernández.

[4] St. John of the Cross. The other members of the party, besides those named in the text, were Isabel de Jesús, a professed nun from the Salamanca house but a

was travelling with Father Julián de Ávila, and another servant of God, Antonio de Gaytán by name, who was accompanying me.[1]

This Don Antonio, when called by Our Lord some years previously, had been a gentleman living at Alba and greatly involved in the affairs of the world. But he had trampled his worldly interests beneath his feet and was now interested solely in doing Our Lord the greatest service. As mention will have to be made of him in accounts of later foundations, for he has helped me a great deal and worked hard on my behalf, I have just explained here who he is; if I were to describe all his virtues it would be a long time before I came to an end. What most concerned us was his great mortification, for not even the servants who accompanied us were so useful to us in our needs. He is a man of great prayer, and God has granted him such graces that things which would have been an annoyance to others were a pleasure to him and seemed to him quite light; and so it is with all his work in the matter of these foundations. It seems clear, then, that both he and Father Julián de Ávila were called to do this by God, though Father Julián has been helping me since my very first foundation. It must have been for the sake of these companions that Our Lord was pleased to prosper all I did. During our journeys they would speak of God and instruct those who accompanied us, and whom they met on their journeys, so that they continued to serve His Majesty in every way.

It is well, my daughters, that those of you who read of these foundations should know how much you owe to these men. For they laboured so hard and so disinterestedly to obtain this blessing which you enjoy of living in one of our houses, that you should commend them to Our Lord, so that they may derive some benefit from your prayers. If you realized what bad nights and days they endured, and what hardships attended their journeys, you would do this very willingly.

The Vicar-General would not leave our church without stationing an officer of the law at the door—I do not know why. The result of this was to cause those who were there some alarm. I was never greatly troubled myself as to what would happen after we had taken possession; it was before we went in that I used to be afraid. I sent for some people, relatives of one of the sisters whom I had with me as a companion,[2] and who were

---

native of Segovia and sister of Andrés de Jimena, and another nun who came from Segovia, María de Jesús.

[1] Don Antonio Gaytán accompanied St. Teresa on three of her foundation-journeys (Segovia, Beas and Seville). One of his daughters became a Discalced Carmelite nun in 1585.

[2] Isabel de Jesús. Cf. p. 105, n 4., above.

important people in the town, so that they should talk to the Vicar-General and tell him that I had a licence from the Bishop. He knew that perfectly well, as he afterwards told me, but he thought we should have informed him beforehand, which I think would have made things much worse. In the end, they persuaded him to let us remain in the convent, but he removed the Most Holy Sacrament. That did not trouble us. We stayed there for some months until we had bought a house, a proceeding which involved us in numerous lawsuits. We had had considerable trouble of this kind with the Franciscans over another house, not far away, which we had purchased. Our trouble about this one was with the Mercedarians and with the Chapter, which had a rent-charge on the house of its own.

O Jesus, what a trouble it is to have to strive against the opinions of many people! When I thought everything was at last settled, it all began again, for it was not enough to give them what they asked: they at once found some fresh obstacle. When I write of it like this it seems nothing, but it was very hard to endure.

A nephew of the Bishop, who was Prior and Canon of that church,[1] did all he could for us, as did a very great servant of God, a licentiate named Herrera. At last, after we had paid out a great deal of money, everything was arranged. We had still not concluded the lawsuit with the Mercedarians and we had to go into our new house with extreme secrecy. When they found us there, two or three days before Michaelmas, they thought it well to come to a final arrangement with us. The greatest distress which these difficulties caused me was that only seven or eight days were wanting before I completed my three years at the Incarnation and for the end of that period I had perforce to be there.

It was Our Lord's will that everything should be concluded so well that nothing remained in dispute, and two or three days later I went back to the Incarnation.[2] May His Name be blessed for ever, Who has ever granted me so many favours, and may all His creatures praise Him. Amen.

[1] Don Juan de Orozco y Covarrubias de Leiva, Prior of the Chapter of Segovia Cathedral, and later Bishop of Guadix and Baza.
[2] She left Segovia on September 30, 1574.

CHAPTER XXII

Describes the foundation of the glorious Saint Joseph of the Saviour in the town of Beas, made on Saint Matthias' Day in the year 1575.[1]

During the time I have been speaking of, when I had been sent from the Incarnation to Salamanca,[2] and was still there, there came a messenger from the town of Beas, bringing letters for me from a lady of that place, the parish priest and other persons, which requested me to go there and found a convent: they already had a house which could be used for it, so that I had only to go and make the foundation.

I asked the messenger for some further particulars. He spoke very well of the district, and rightly so, for it is a delightful part and has a pleasant climate. But, considering how many leagues lay between Beas and Salamanca,[3] I thought it folly to go there, especially as I could only go with a mandate from the Apostolic Commissary, who, as I have said, was opposed to my making more foundations, or at least was not anxious for me to do so. I thought, therefore, of replying that I could not go, and of saying nothing further. But afterwards it occurred to me that as the Commissary was in Salamanca at the time, it would not be right for me to do that without asking his opinion, in view of the instruction given me by our most reverend Father General not to refrain from making any possible foundation.

After reading the letters, he sent me a message that he thought it would be a pity to discourage them, for he was edified by their devotion; and so I had better write to them saying that provision would be made for the foundation when they had a licence from their Order. He added that I might be certain a licence would not be given, for he had heard things from other sources about the Knights of Santiago,[4] and there were people who had spent years in trying to obtain permissions from them. Still, he said, I ought not to send an unfavourable answer. I sometimes think of this, and realize how, when Our Lord wills a thing, even if

---

[1] As in the heading to the last chapter, and in several other places in this chapter, the date originally written was one year earlier and has been altered.

[2] Cf. p. 104, above.

[3] [Beas de Segura is situated on a tributary of the Guadalimar, in what is now the province of Jaén—a fertile spot in the mountain wastes of the Sierra Morena. It has close associations with St. John of the Cross.] St. Teresa's mandate for foundations extended only throughout Castile but in those days Beas was on the borders of the kingdom of Toledo, so she apparently felt justified in not declining the invitation on that score. (Cf. p. 123, below.)

[4] Cf. p. 112, below.

we do not desire it, we come unwittingly to be the instruments by which it is done. This is what happened here in the case of Father-Master Fray Pedro Fernández, the Commissary. Once the licence was obtained, he could not himself refuse permission, and accordingly the house was founded, in the following manner.

This convent, dedicated to the Blessed Saint Joseph, in the town of Beas, was founded on Saint Matthias' Day in the year 1575. To the honour and glory of God it began as follows. There lived in this town a gentleman called Sancho Rodríguez de Sandoval, a man of noble descent, who had great temporal wealth. He had married a lady called Doña Catalina Godínez. Among other children whom Our Lord gave them were two daughters, the founders of this convent, the elder named Doña Catalina Godínez and the younger Doña María de Sandoval. The elder was about fourteen years old[1] when Our Lord called her to serve Him. Until that age she was a long way from leaving the world: in fact, she had such a high opinion of herself that she thought all the offers of marriage which her father brought her very poor ones. One day she was in the room adjoining that of her father, who had not yet got up, when she chanced to read on a crucifix which was there the title placed over the Cross. Suddenly, as she read it, the Lord wrought a complete change in her. She had been thinking about a marriage that was being arranged for her, which was an exceedingly good one, and saying to herself: "How little it takes to please my father provided I marry the heir to some estate! But my intention is for my descendants to trace their rise from me." She had no inclination to be married, for she thought it demeaning to be subject to anyone, and she had no idea whence this pride came. The Lord knew how it could be cured. Blessed be His mercy!

As she read the title over the Cross, it seemed that a light came into her soul, to show her the truth, just as though the sun were entering a dark room. Thus illumined, she fixed her eyes on the Lord, shedding His blood on the Cross, and thought how ill treated He had been, and yet how very humble He was, and how different was the road that she was taking in her pride. She must have been there for some time when the Lord suspended her faculties, and gave her a full and true knowledge of her misery and a desire that all should realize it. He gave her such a great desire to suffer for God's sake that she longed to endure all that the martyrs had done, and at the same time conceived so deep a humility and self-detestation that, had it not been that such a thing would have offended God, she would have desired to be an utterly lost woman so that all might hate her; thus she began to

---

[1] Actually she had turned fifteen.

hate herself and to have vehement longings for penance, which
later she was able to fulfil. She immediately made a vow of
chastity and poverty, and was now so anxious to be subjected
to others that she would have rejoiced to have been taken away
as a captive to the country of the Moors. All these virtues have
been so lasting in her that it is clear they were a supernatural
favour from Our Lord, as will be shown later so that all may
praise Him.

Blessed be Thou, My God, for ever and ever, Who in a single
moment dost cause a soul to melt and then create it anew! What
is this, Lord? I should like to repeat the Apostles' question here,
when Thou didst heal the blind man and they asked if his parents
had sinned.[1] Who, I ask, had deserved so sovereign a favour?
Not she, for I have already described the thoughts from which
Thou didst deliver her when granting her that favour. Great
are Thy judgments, Lord. Thou knowest what Thou doest
and I do not know what I am saying, for Thy works and judgments are incomprehensible. Be Thou for ever glorified, Who
canst do greater things yet. What would become of me if this
were not so? Perhaps her mother had some part in it, for she
was so good a Christian that Thou mightest, in Thy goodness
and mercy, have been pleased for her to see such great virtue in
her daughters while she lived. I sometimes think Thou grantest
such favours as these to those who love Thee and art so good
as to grant them children who shall serve Thee.

While she was making these vows, such a loud noise was heard
in the room overhead that it seemed as if the whole place were
capsizing. The source of all the noise appeared to be a corner
of the room, and just above the place where she was sitting
she heard a loud roaring, which went on for some time. Her father,
who, as I have said, had not yet got up, became so alarmed that
he began to tremble, and, putting on some clothes and catching
up his sword, rushed into her room as though out of his mind
and asked fearfully what was the matter. She replied that she
had seen nothing. He looked into the room beyond, and, seeing
nothing there either, told her to go to her mother; and he asked
her mother not to leave her alone, telling her what he had heard.

This gives a very good idea of what the devil must feel when he
sees a soul which he had believed to be already won escaping
from him. As he is so great an enemy of our welfare, I am not
surprised that, when he sees the merciful Lord granting so many
favours at once, he should be alarmed and should show such clear
signs of his chagrin, especially if he realizes that the wealth which
they bring to that soul is likely to lose him various others which he

[1] St. John ix, 2.

had considered as his own. For I am convinced that Our Lord never grants so great a favour without benefiting others through it as well as the recipient. Though she never spoke about this, she had the greatest desire to enter the religious life and often begged her parents to allow her to do so, but they would never consent.

At the end of three years, during which time she had often asked their permission, she saw that they would never give in, so on Saint Joseph's Day[1] she dressed very plainly, telling no one but her mother, who would readily have consented to her becoming a nun, what her intention was. She dared not tell her father, but went to church, believing that, once she had been seen in that dress in the town, they would not hinder her purpose. And so it turned out. During the next three years she set apart hours for prayer, and mortified herself in every possible way, which the Lord taught her to do. She would even go into an open courtyard, moisten her face and then disfigure it by exposing it to the sun, so that offers of marriage, with which she was still being importuned, should cease.

She disliked ordering people about, but, as she had the oversight of her father's household, she could not avoid giving orders to the women. However, she would stay up until they were asleep, and then go and kiss their feet, for she was troubled at being served by those who were better than herself. As her father and mother kept her busy all day, she would spend the whole night, when she might have been asleep, in prayer, and she spent so much time in this way and took so little sleep that, had it not been supernatural, it would have seemed impossible. Her penances and disciplines were numerous; but, having no director, she spoke about them to no one. Among other things she went through the whole of one Lent wearing her father's coat of mail next to her flesh. She would go to out-of-the-way places in order to pray, when the devil would play strange tricks upon her. Often she would begin her prayers at ten o'clock in the evening and would not cease from them until it was day.

In these practices she spent nearly four years, when the Lord was pleased that she should serve Him in other and better ways and sent her most grievous and painful sicknesses, such as continual fever, dropsy and heart trouble, as well as a cancer in the breast, which had to be removed. These illnesses lasted in all for nearly seventeen years, during which time there were few days when she was well. After God had been granting her this favour for five years her father died. Her sister, who was fourteen years of age, had also begun to dress plainly a year after she herself

<hr />

[1] March 19, 1558.

had done so, though she, too, had been fond of finery; she also began to practise prayer. Her mother helped both of them in their good habits and desires, and agreed to their engaging in a most virtuous practice, though one quite foreign to their rank—namely, the instruction of little girls in sewing and reading, not for any profit to themselves, but only so as to teach them habits of prayer and the rudiments of the Faith. This did much good, for a great many children came to them, and, while still very young, learned good habits which may be seen in them even to this day. But this did not last long, for the devil, angry at their good works, persuaded their parents that they were demeaning themselves by allowing their daughters to be taught free of charge. This, together with the illnesses from which they were now beginning to suffer, made them give up this occupation.

Five years after their father's death, their mother died also,[1] and, as Doña Catalina had always felt called to become a nun, and would have done so before had she been able to gain her parents' consent, she now determined to enter the religious life immediately. There was no convent at Beas, and her relatives suggested that, as they had adequate means for doing so, she and her sister should found one in their native place, which would be to the greater service of Our Lord. As Beas is a place belonging to the Commandery of Santiago, a licence for this was necessary from the Council of the Orders, and she started to do all she could to obtain one.

This was so difficult that four years passed—years of great labour and expense—and no result was obtained until a petition had been presented to the King himself. As the difficulties were so great, her relatives told her that it was folly and she would have to abandon the idea; and, as she was almost always in bed, on account of the serious illnesses which have been described, they said no convent would receive her as a nun. She replied that if Our Lord restored her health within a month they must understand this to mean that the foundation was His will and in that case she herself would go to the capital to obtain the necessary permission.[2] At the time she said this, she had not left her bed for over six months, and had hardly been able to stir from it for eight. For eight years she had suffered from a continual fever, together with consumption and dropsy; she also had a burning fire in the liver, which was so violent that the heat could be felt through the bedclothes and burned her nightgown. This seems incredible, but I heard it from the physician who was attending her at the time, and it completely astounded me. She also had rheumatic gout and sciatica.

[1] The father died in 1560; the mother, in 1565.   [2] December 1573.

On the eve of the Feast of Saint Sebastian,[1] which was a Saturday, Our Lord restored her to such perfect health that she could see no way of concealing the fact so that the miracle might not become known. Her own testimony is that, when Our Lord was about to cure her, she felt an inward trembling which made her sister think that she was about to die, and she then became aware of an extraordinary change in herself, and felt so much better that she was conscious of a change in her soul also. She was the better pleased to be well again because she could now resume the negotiations about the convent. She had not minded suffering; for, from the time when God first called her, He inspired her with such hatred of herself that nothing of that kind was of great moment to her. She says her desire to suffer was so vehement that she besought God from the bottom of her heart to test her as to this in every possible way.

His Majesty did not fail to fulfil this desire for her: in eight years she was bled more than five hundred times, as well as being scarified and cupped so often that the marks could still be seen on her body. Sometimes they treated her wounds with salt, for one of the physicians said that this was a good thing for drawing out the poison which caused the pain in her side, and this they did to her more than twenty times. The most remarkable thing is that, when they told her that one of these remedies was to be used, she longed for the hour of the operation to come, and had no fear: indeed, she encouraged the physicians to use the cauteries, which they often did in treating her cancer and on other occasions when it was necessary. She says that the reason she wished for this was to see if her desires to be a martyr were genuine.

When she found herself suddenly cured, she discussed with her confessor and the physician the possibility of her being moved to some other town, so that it might be said that the change of climate had done it. But they refused to do this; in fact, the physicians made her recovery public, for they had looked on her as incurable, since the haemorrhage from the mouth had been so foul that they said it came from the lungs. She remained in bed for three days more, not daring to get up lest her recovery should become known; but as it could no more be concealed than her sickness had been, this ruse was of little effect.

She told me that, while she was praying to Our Lord one day in the preceding August, she had begged Him either to take from her the great desire which she had to be a nun and found a convent, or to give her the means of accomplishing her desire, and that she received an assurance of the greatest certainty

[1] January 19, 1574.

that she would be well in time to go to Madrid during Lent in order to obtain the licence. She says, too, that, though her illness at that time was much more trying than usual, she never lost hope that the Lord would grant her this favour. Twice they gave her Extreme Unction (and on one of these occasions she seemed so near her end that the physician said there was not time to send for the oil, as she would die before it came); yet she never lost her trust in the Lord that she would die a nun. (I do not mean that she was given Extreme Unction twice between August and Saint Sebastian's Day: it was earlier than that.) When her brothers, sisters and other relatives saw the favour which the Lord had granted her and the miracle which He had performed in restoring her so suddenly to health, they dared not place obstacles in the way of her journey, although they thought it foolish. She was in the capital for three months and in the end the licence was not given her. But, when she presented a petition to the King, and he learned that it was in favour of the Discalced Carmelite nuns, he ordered it to be given her at once.

When the time came for the foundation of the convent to be made, it became clear that she had brought it before God from the fact that, though it was so far away and there was so little money for its endowment, the authorities were willing to accept it. What His Majesty wills can never fail to be done. So the nuns came at the beginning of Lent in the year 1575.[1] They were received in the village with great solemnity and rejoicing, and there was a procession. In general, great satisfaction was felt at their coming: even the children made it evident that it was an act done in Our Lord's service. The convent was called Saint Joseph of the Saviour and was founded in that same Lent, on Saint Matthias' Day.

On the same day, the two sisters, to their great joy, took the habit.[2] Doña Catalina's health continued to improve. Her humility, obedience and longing to be despised are a clear indication of the genuineness of her desires to serve Our Lord. May He be glorified for ever and ever.

This sister told me, among other things, that, almost twenty years previously, she had gone to bed one night with a desire to find the most perfect religious Order in the world, so that she might become a nun in it. She began to dream and thought she was travelling along a very strait and narrow road, in the greatest danger of falling down what seemed to be steep precipices. Then she saw a Discalced friar, who said to her: "Come

---

[1] The records of the Convent give the day as February 16, but P. Francisco de Santa María favours February 18 or 21 [which P. Silverio thinks more likely].

[2] Catalina was thirty-six years old at the time; her sister, María, twenty-nine.

with me, sister," and took her to a house where there were a great many nuns and which was lit only by lighted candles which they held in their hands. (While I was at Beas, it was visited by a lay friar of the Order, called Fray Juan de la Miseria,[1] and when she saw him, she said it was he whom she had seen that night. She asked these nuns what their Order was, but they were all silent, raising their veils, however, and showing their cheerful, smiling faces. She assures me that these were the faces of the very sisters whom she saw at Beas, and that the Prioress took her by the hand and said: "Daughter, I want you here," and showed her the Constitutions and Rule. And when she awoke from this dream she felt as happy as if she had been in Heaven and wrote down what she remembered of the Rule. A long time passed before she spoke of it to a confessor or to anyone, and nobody could tell her anything about this Order.

Then there came a Father of the Company of Jesus,[2] who knew her wishes; and she showed him the paper and told him that if she could find that Order she would be happy, for she would enter it at once. He knew about these convents of ours, and told her that the Rule was that of the Order of Our Lady of Carmel. He did not say it as clearly as that, however, nor in such a way that she took it all in; he merely told her that it was the Rule of the convents which I was founding. So she contrived to send a messenger to me, as has been related.

At the time when they brought her the reply, she was so unwell that her confessor told her she must stay quietly where she was, for in such a state she would be sent away even if she were already in the convent, so she would certainly not be received from outside. This greatly distressed her and she turned to Our Lord with deep yearnings and said to Him: "My Lord and my God, I know by faith that Thou art One Who can do all things; let these desires be taken from me, then, Life of my soul, or give me the means to carry them into effect." This she said with the greatest confidence, begging Our Lady, by the grief which she felt when she saw her Son dead in her arms, to intercede for her. She heard a voice within herself, saying: "Believe and hope, for I am He that can do all things. Thou shalt have health; for, if He has had power to preserve thee through so many mortal illnesses, and to let none of them produce its effect upon thee,

---

[1] See Chapter XVII [p. 81, above].

[2] P. Bartolomé Bustamante, a noted theologian and humanist, who before entering the Society of Jesus had been secretary to Cardinal Pardo de Tavera. Besides other things he was a competent architect and designed the Hospital de Afuera, in Toledo, which was begun by the Cardinal and continued by his nephew Arias Pardo, who married, and was survived by, Doña Luisa de la Cerda. This makes it clear how P. Bustamante knew so much about the Discalced Carmelites.

it will be easier still for Him to take them away." These words, she said, were spoken with such power and confidence that she could not doubt that her desire would be fulfilled, though until the Lord restored her to health, as we have said, her infirmities became much more oppressive. Certainly what happened to her seems incredible. I am so wicked that, had I not been told it by the physician, and by members of her household, and by other people, it would not have been difficult for me to think that there was some exaggeration in it.

Although still delicate, she is now strong enough to observe the Rule and her health is quite good. She is always happy, and in every respect, as I have said, has such humility that she makes us all praise Our Lord. Both sisters made an unconditional gift to the Order of such property as they had, adding that, should they not themselves be received as nuns, they would require no compensation. She is quite detached from her relatives and her native place—indeed, she is always very anxious to be sent far away from her home, and earnestly importunes her superiors about this, though her obedience is so complete that she stays where she is with some degree of contentment. It was also out of obedience that she took the veil, for she had intended to be a lay sister and would not consider becoming a choir nun until I wrote to her giving her many reasons why she should, and finally reproving her for holding to her own opinion in face of the will of the Father Provincial. This, I told her with some severity, was not the way to win greater merit, and I put other points to her of the same kind. She is best pleased when spoken to in that way and what I said decided her, though very much against her own will. I know of nothing about this soul that is not pleasing to God and she is equally so to all her sisters. May it be His Majesty's will to keep her in His hand and to increase in her the virtues and grace which He has given her, to His greater service and honour. Amen.

CHAPTER XXIII

Describes the foundation of the convent of the glorious Saint Joseph of Carmel in the city of Seville. The first Mass was said here on the Feast of the Most Holy Trinity in the year 1575.

While I was in this town of Beas, waiting for the licence to come from the Council of the Orders for the foundation at Caravaca, I was visited there by a father of our Discalced Order, called Fray Jeronimo de la Madre de Dios (Gracián),[1] who had taken our habit a few years previously when living at Alcalá. He was a man of great learning, understanding and modesty; and to these qualities had been united such great virtues, for his whole life long, that it seemed as if Our Lady had chosen him for the welfare of this Primitive Order when he was in Alcalá; for he had wanted to become a religious, though he had had no idea of taking our habit. On account of the favour which he had won from the King and of his great ability his parents had had different plans for him, but he had no such ideas himself. At the very beginning of his studies, his father had wanted to put him to read law. But, though quite young, he was so much distressed at this that by dint of tears he persuaded his father to allow him to study theology. When he had taken his Master's degree he applied for admission to the Company of Jesus, and they accepted him, but for some reason told him to wait for a few days.[2] He tells me himself that the life of comfort he was leading was sheer torment to him, for he did not think it the proper road to Heaven; he always observed hours of prayer and he was recollected and modest in the extreme.

At that time, a great friend of his, called Fray Juan de Jesús,[3] who also held a Master's degree, entered our Order as a friar in the monastery of Pastrana. I am not sure if he first became interested in us through a letter which he had from this friar about the greatness and antiquity of our Order, or whether there was some other cause, but he took great pleasure in reading everything he could about it and in looking up the authorities quoted in the books that he read. Often, he says, he had scruples about neglecting his other studies because he could not forgo these— he even devoted to them the hours which he had for recreation. O wisdom and power of God! How little we can do to escape His will! Our Lord saw well how necessary such a person was for this work which His Majesty had begun. I often praise Him for helping us in this; for, however earnestly I had longed to ask His Majesty for a person who would organize everything for our Order in these early stages, I could never have asked for so excel-

---

[1] [See *S.S.M.*, II, 151-89]. Born at Valladolid in 1545, he had studied, and taken a brilliant degree, at the University of Alcalá. After his ordination to the priesthood, he had joined St. Teresa's Reform and was professed on April 25, 1573.

[2] He had been under the influence of the Society of Jesus since childhood. After graduating as Master he began to discuss his vocation with P. Gil González: of this period in his life he gives an account in *Peregrinación de Anastasio*, Diálogo IX.

[3] P. Juan de Roca was a native of Sanahuja, in the province of Lérida. He first met P. Gracián at the University of Alcalá, where the two became close friends. He took the habit at Pastrana on January 1, 1572. Greatly esteemed by St. Teresa for his virtue, learning and devotion to the Primitive Rule, he held several important offices in the Reform, and died in 1614, at the age of 71.

lent a person as He gave us in this friar. May He be blessed for ever.

When requested to go to Pastrana with the Prioress of the convent of our Order there, which had not then been transferred,[1] to arrange about the reception of a nun, he had no idea whatever of taking our habit. What means His Divine Majesty can employ! If he had determined to go and take the habit direct from Alcalá, he might well have found so many people opposing this course that he would never have taken it at all. But the Virgin, Our Lady, to whom he is extremely devoted, was anxious to reward him by bestowing her habit upon him, and so I think she became the intermediary by which God granted him this favour. It was through this glorious Virgin that he took the habit and became so devoted to the Order. She would not allow one so anxious to serve her to be without the means of carrying his desire into effect, for it is her custom to help those who desire her for their Protectress.[2]

As a boy in Madrid he used often to go to an image of Our Lady to which he was specially devoted: where it was I do not remember. He used to call her his Beloved and this was the image which he most commonly visited. She must have persuaded her Son to bestow on him the purity in which he has always lived. He says that he sometimes thought he saw her eyes full of tears because of the many offences committed against her Son. This inspired him with a fervent desire for the salvation of souls and made him very sad when he saw offences being committed against God. So greatly is he moved by this desire for the good of souls that any trouble seems light to him if he thinks it can in any way help them. This I have found by experience in the many trials that he has suffered.

When the Virgin brought him to Pastrana he came under a misconception, for he thought he was there to obtain the habit for a nun, whereas God's purpose in bringing him was to give him the habit for himself. Oh, the secrets of God! How continually He is preparing us to receive His favours, when we ourselves have no desire for them, and how He was rewarding this man for the good works which he had done, for the good example which he had always set, and for his great desire to serve His glorious Mother! His Majesty will always recompense this desire with great rewards.

Having arrived at Pastrana, he went to speak to the Prioress

[1] I.e., to Segovia. See p. 85, above. The Prioress was Isabel de Santo Domingo; the nun, Bárbara del Espíritu Santo, whose family Gracián knew well and whom he had been instrumental in leading into the Reform.
[2] All this is confirmed by Gracián in his *Peregrinación de Anastasio*, Diálogo I.

about the reception of this nun, and it seems that he also asked her to intercede with Our Lord that he might also take the habit himself. She liked his manner—and indeed it is so pleasant that, through the grace which Our Lord has given him, most people who meet him love him at once and so he is greatly loved by all who are under his jurisdiction, both friars and nuns. He never overlooks a fault, for he is extremely particular about the progress of the Order, but his reproofs are so gently and pleasantly conveyed that no one ever seems able to complain of him.

When this Prioress saw him, she felt about him as everyone else does: she became extremely desirous that he should enter the Order, and spoke about this to the sisters, telling them to reflect how important this was for them, for there were very few—hardly any, indeed—like him, and so they must all pray to Our Lord not to let him go without taking the habit. This Prioress is a very great servant of God and I believe His Majesty would have listened to her prayer alone. How much more, then, to the prayers of all those good souls who were there! All the nuns took the matter very much to heart, and besought His Majesty continually, with fasting, discipline and prayer; and so He was pleased to do us this favour. When Father Gracián went to the monastery of the Discalced friars and found there such strictness of observance and such readiness to serve Our Lord, and, above all, discovered that this was the Order of His glorious Mother, whom he so much desired to serve, his heart began to move him not to return to the world. The devil, however, suggested numerous obstacles to him—in particular, the grief which this would cause his parents, who were very fond of him and had quite counted on his being able to help them to provide for their sons and daughters, of whom there were a great number.[1] He, however, cast this care upon God, for Whom he was forsaking everything, and determined to become a subject of the Virgin and to take her habit. So they gave it him, to the great joy of all, especially of the nuns and the Prioress, who rendered great praise to Our Lord, thinking that His Majesty had granted them this favour in answer to their prayers.

He spent his year of preparation as humbly as one of the youngest novices. On one occasion his virtue was tested in a special way. During the absence of the Prior his place was taken by a friar who was very young, quite devoid of learning, and most deficient both in the ability and the prudence necessary for government; nor had he any experience, for it was not long

[1] There had been twenty in all, of whom only thirteen survived their infancy. Cf. *Peregrinación de Anastasio*, Diálogo I.

since he had entered the Order.[1] He carried severity to excess both in the way he ruled them and in the mortifications to which he made them submit. Whenever I think of it I am amazed that they were able to endure it, especially such persons as these: they certainly needed the spirituality given them by God to enable them to do so. Eventually it was discovered that this friar was of a melancholy disposition, and difficult to get on with anywhere, even when he was under authority. How much worse it must have been to submit to his rule! For, though he is a good religious, his temperament gets the better of him. God sometimes allows the mistake to be made of putting persons of this kind in authority so that they may perfect those whom He loves in the virtue of obedience.

This must have been the case here, for Fray Jerónimo de la Madre de Dios was given the clearest light by God in matters of obedience, so that he might teach his subjects, as one who had made such a good beginning in practising obedience himself. And, in order that he might not lack all the experience so necessary to us, he was attacked, during the three months preceding his profession, by the most severe temptations. Like the good captain of the Virgin's children that he was to become, he defended himself against them so well that, when the devil urged him with the greatest force to renounce the habit, he defended himself by promising never to abandon it and to take the vows. He gave me a work which he had written while struggling with these severe temptations: it filled me with devotion and showed clearly what courage the Lord was giving him.

It may seem an improper thing that he should have spoken to me in such great detail about his soul. Our Lord may have wished him to do this so that I might write of it here, to the end that He may be praised in His creatures, for I know that he has made such revelations neither to his confessor nor to anyone else. Occasionally there were reasons for this, for he thought that, as I was so much older than he, and also because of what he had heard about me, I ought to have some experience in such matters. He told me these things in the course of conversations about other subjects, together with other things of which I should have a great deal more to say were it not unsuitable for me to write of them.

---

[1] When P. Gracián took the habit, the Prior at Pastrana was P. Baltasar de Jesús, who, having to be away for some time on the business of the Order, left as novice-master a certain P. Ángel de San Gabriel. This seems to be the person referred to in the text. Things grew so bad, for the reasons here stated, that, in the spring of 1572, St. John of the Cross had to go to Pastrana and depose the novice-master, after which order and peace returned to the community.

I have certainly restrained myself a great deal here, for otherwise, if this should ever reach his hands, he might be troubled about it. But, if he ever sees it at all, he will not do so for a very long time, and so I have not been able, nor has it seemed to me right, to refrain from making mention of one who has done so much for the revival of the Primitive Rule. For, although he was not the first person to begin the movement, he came into it most opportunely and if I had not had such great trust in the mercy of God I should sometimes have regretted that it had been begun. I am speaking now of the monasteries, for the convents, by the goodness of God, have until now always prospered. The monasteries did not do badly but they had in them the germs of rapid decay; since, having no province of their own, they were governed by the Calced Fathers. Those who might have governed them, such as Fray Antonio de Jesús, who began the Reform, were not granted the authority to do so, nor did our most reverend Father General give them any Constitutions. In each house they did as they thought well. Until Constitutions were sent them, and while they followed their own rules as to government, there was a great deal of trouble, because some held one opinion and some another. There were times when this worried me dreadfully.

Our Lord saved this situation by means of the Father-Master Fray Jerónimo de la Madre de Dios, for he was made Apostolic Commissary and given rule and authority over both the friars and the nuns of the Discalced.[1] He compiled Constitutions for the friars (for we already had ours from our most reverend Father General, and he had therefore not to compile them for the nuns, but only for the friars) by virtue of the Apostolic authority which he had and with the great ability which the Lord has given him and to which I have already referred. The first time he made a visitation of the friars[2] he did everything so ably and sensibly that it seemed that he was indeed being helped by the Divine Majesty, and that Our Lady had chosen him to be the salvation of her Order. I earnestly intercede with her Son, that He may ever help him and give him grace to advance greatly in His service. Amen.

[1] P.M. Francisco Vargas, Apostolic Commissary for the reform of the Calced Carmelites in Andalusia, met P. Gracián in Granada and delegated to him the commission which he held from the Holy See. This was privately arranged but the Calced Carmelites found out about it and complained to the General of the Order, who secured from Gregory XIII a revocation of the faculties given. Philip II took the side of the Reform and worked through the Nuncio Ormaneto in the opposite direction.

[2] This was in the year 1575.

CHAPTER XXIV

Continues to describe the foundation of Saint Joseph of Carmel in the city of Seville.

When, as I have related, the Father-Master Fray Jerónimo Gracián came to see me at Beas,[1] we had never met, though I had been most anxious that we should. We had, however, exchanged several letters. I was simply delighted when I heard he was there, for the good accounts I had been given of him had made me extremely anxious to see him. But when I began to talk to him I was happier still, for he pleased me so much that it seemed to me as if those who had praised him to me hardly knew him at all.

I was greatly worried at the time, but when I saw him the Lord seemed to show me all the good that was to come to us through him, and during those days I was so exceedingly comforted and happy that I was really quite astonished at myself. At that time his commission did not extend beyond Andalusia, but, while he was at Beas, the Nuncio sent for him and gave him a commission to rule both the friars and the nuns of the Discalced Reform in the Province of Castile. This caused me such rejoicing of spirit that I was never tired of giving thanks to Our Lord during those days, and I wanted to do nothing else.

At this time the licence for making a foundation at Caravaca was brought, but it was not what I wanted for my purpose, and they had therefore to send to the capital again, for I wrote to the foundresses that the foundation could not possibly be made unless certain details omitted in the licence were inserted, and it was therefore necessary to apply to the capital once more.[2] I was very sorry to have to wait so long and I was anxious to return to Castile; but as Fray Jerónimo, who had authority over that house, being Commissary of the whole province of Castile,[3] was at Beas, I could do nothing without his agreeing to it, and I therefore communicated with him.

---

[1] As a result of Philip II's intervention, P. Gracián had been sent for by the Nuncio, and, on his way from Seville to Madrid, visited Beas in order to make the acquaintance of St. Teresa.

[2] Caravaca belonged to the Council of Orders, which meant that the project had to be submitted to the Council. The Saint, however, insisted that the new convent, if founded, must be under Carmelite jurisdiction, and was not prepared to make the foundation on any other condition.

[3] Actually he was then Commissary only for Andalusia. [Perhaps this was what St. Teresa had intended to write.]

He thought that, if once I went, the Caravaca foundation would never be made, and also that it would be a great service to God to make a foundation at Seville, which he believed would be very easy, as he had been asked to do it by several people who were able and willing to provide a house at once. The Archbishop of Seville,[1] he said, was very well disposed to the Order, so he thought we should be doing him a great service. It was accordingly arranged that the Prioress and the nuns whom I was to have taken to Caravaca should go to Seville. For several reasons I had always flatly refused to make any foundation of the Reform in Andalusia, and if I had known, when I went to Beas, that it was in the province of Andalusia, I should certainly not have gone there. The mistake I made was that, although the district itself is not in Andalusia (it is about four or five leagues, I think, from the boundary), it is in the Andalusian province.[2] When I saw that my superior was resolved on this foundation, I gave in at once, for Our Lord has granted me the favour of believing that my superiors are right in everything. Nevertheless, I had been determined to make another foundation, and had reasons for doing this, as well as very grave ones for not going to Seville.

When a beginning had been made with the preparations for the journey, for the heat was now starting in earnest, the Apostolic Commissary, Father Gracián, went to the Nuncio, who had sent for him, and we set off for Seville with my good companions, Father Julián de Ávila, Antonio Gaytán and a Discalced friar.[3] We went in covered carriages, which has always been our way of travelling. When we reached our inn, we would take whatever room they had, good or bad, and one of the sisters would go to the door of the room to get anything that we wanted: even our travelling companions never entered it.

Despite all our haste, we reached Seville only on the Thursday before the feast of the Most Holy Trinity,[4] having suffered from the severest heat on the way. Though we did not travel during the siesta hours, I can assure you, sisters, that, when the sun beat down on the carriages with all its might, going into them was like entering purgatory. Sometimes by thinking of hell, and

[1] This was Don Cristóbal de Rojas y Sandoval, son of the Marquis of Denia. He had attended the Council of Trent as Bishop of Oviedo and later was translated successively to Córdoba and (in 1571) to Seville. He died in 1580.

[2] In civil affairs it was dependent upon the Chancellery of Castile, yet it was in the diocese of Cartagena, which at that time took in an appreciable part of Andalusia. Further details are given in Ribera.

[3] She left Beas, on May 18, 1575, with María de San José, Isabel de San Francisco, María del Espíritu Santo, Isabel de San Jerónimo, Leonor de San Gabriel and Ana de San Alberto. The last-named afterwards went to Caravaca as Prioress. The Discalced friar referred to in the text was P. Gregorio Nacianceno, to whom P. Gracián had recently given the habit at Beas.

[4] May 26, 1575.

sometimes by remembering that we were doing and suffering something for God, the sisters bore the journey with great contentment and joy. So courageous were the six souls who were with me that I think I would have ventured into the country of the Turks in their company, and I believe they would have had the fortitude—or rather, Our Lord would have given it them—to suffer for Him, for that was the only thing they expressed a wish for or talked about and they were well practised in prayer and mortification. For, as they would have to live so far away, I had seen to it that those whom I thought most suitable were chosen. All this trouble was necessary, on account of the trials they had to endure, some of which—the worst of them—I will not describe, as to do so might affect certain other people.

One day, before the Feast of the Holy Spirit, God sent them a most heavy trial by allowing me to fall ill with a very high fever. I believe it was their cries to God for me which prevented it from going farther, for never in my whole life have I had a fever like this which did not get much worse. It was of such a kind that I seemed to have fallen into a lethargy, so completely helpless was I. They threw water over my face, but the sun made it so warm that it refreshed me very little.

I must not forget to tell you how bad the inn was where we found ourselves at this time of need. They gave us a little room roofed like a shed and without a window, into which the sun streamed whenever the door was opened. You must remember that the heat there is not like our Castilian heat but is much more trying. They made me lie down on a bed, but it was so full of ups and downs that I would rather have lain on the floor: I cannot think how I endured it—it seemed to be full of sharp stones. What a troublesome thing illness is! It is easy enough to bear anything if one is well. In the end I thought it best to get up, so that we could go on our way, for I preferred to endure the sun in the open air than in that little room.

Oh, whatever will become of the poor souls who are in hell and will never get out of it? For if a person does no more than pass from one trial to another there seems to be some relief even in the very change. Sometimes I have had a very severe pain in one part of the body, and, though changing my position gave me an equally severe pain in another part, it was a relief to do so. The same was true here. I was not at all distressed, as far as I remember, to find myself unwell: the sisters suffered far more than I. It was the Lord's pleasure that the illness in its worst form should last for no more than that day.

A little while—perhaps two days—earlier, another thing happened to us which put us in a rather difficult position. We were crossing the Guadalquivir in a boat. When it came to taking the carriages across in the ferry, they could not do so by means of the rope directly but had to make turns in the river. They used the rope in making the turns, so it was of some help to them. It chanced, however, that, whether because those who were holding it let go of it or for some other reason, the boat went off with the carriage but without either rope or oars. I was much sorrier for the distress of the boatman than alarmed at the danger. We began to pray and everyone else shouted loudly.

A gentleman, watching us from a neighbouring castle, was moved with pity for us and sent us help. We had not then lost the rope and our brethren were holding on to it with all their might. The current, however, was so strong that it threw some of them down. I shall never forget the boatman's little son, who made me feel very devout. He might have been about ten or eleven years old, and his distress when he saw his father in this trouble made me praise Our Lord. But His Majesty always has compassion on our trials, and so He had here. By chance, the boat struck a sandbank, in a place where there was little water, and so they were able to help us. We should have found it very hard to strike the right road again, as it was now night, if someone had not come from the castle to show us the way. I did not mean to describe these things, which are of no great importance, for I had already said enough of these mischances which befell us on our journeys. But I have been urged to say a great deal more about this.

On the last day[1] of the festival of the Holy Spirit there befell us what for me was a worse trial than those I have described. We travelled very quickly so as to reach Córdoba early in the morning and hear Mass without being seen. We were directed to go to a church across the bridge if we wanted to be quite alone. Just as we were about to cross, we found that a licence was necessary for carriages to do so and this could be given us only by the Governor.[2] It took us more than two hours to get it, as nobody was up, and a great many people came to find out who we were. We did not mind this, for, as the carriage was quite closed, they could not see us. When at last the licence came, the carriages could not get through the gate at the end of the bridge, and they had to saw us a way through, or something of the kind,[3] and this took a long time. At last we reached

---

[1] It would seem more likely that it was the first day of this festival.
[2] [Corregidor.]
[3] According to P. Julián de Ávila, they had to saw off the projecting ends of the axles.

the church, where Father Julián de Ávila was to say Mass, and, as it was dedicated to the Holy Spirit, we found it full of people. This, of course, we had not known. There was a solemn festival service and a sermon.

When I saw this I was very much distressed and thought it would be better for us to go away without hearing Mass than to be in the midst of such a tumult. But Father Julián de Ávila did not think so; and, as he was a theologian, we had to defer to his opinion; our other companions might perhaps have deferred to mine, which would have been a mistake, though I am not sure that I should have trusted my opinion alone. We alighted near the church: nobody could see our faces, for we always covered them with large veils; but their seeing us in the white frieze mantles which we wear, and our hemp-soled shoes, was enough to cause a commotion, and a commotion there was. This was a great shock for me, and for all of us, and it must have taken away my fever altogether.

Just as we were entering the church, a kindly man came up to me and tried to keep the people away from us. I begged him earnestly to take us to one of the chapels. He did so, and closed the door, and did not leave us until he had led us out of the church again. A few days later he came to Seville and said to a Father of our Order that he thought God must have bestowed a favour upon him for that kindness which he had done us, for he had come into a large estate of which he had had no expecta-tion. I assure you, daughters, that, though you may perhaps think all this was nothing, it was one of the worst experiences I have ever been through in my life; there was such an uproar among the people that you would have thought the church had been invaded by bulls. So I did not wait for the hour at which we were to have left the place; there was nowhere for us to have our siesta, but we stopped for it under a bridge.[1]

When we reached the house in Seville which Fray Mariano had taken for us on being advised of our journey,[2] I thought the whole thing was done, for, as I have said, the Archbishop was very well disposed to the Discalced Carmelites and had written to me several times in terms of great affection. This was not enough, however, to prevent me from suffering a great deal, for so God willed it. The Archbishop is very much opposed to the founding of convents in poverty and has reasons for being so. And that was what hindered us (or, it might be more

---

[1] The Roman Bridge, restored by the Moors and improved by Philip II. It connects the Campo de la Verdad, on the left bank of the Guadalquivir, where the church was, with the city.

[2] This house was situated in the Calle de las Armas—afterwards re-named after Alfonso XII. No trace of it now remains.

correct to say, helped us) in the making of this foundation. If he had been told about our intentions before we set out on our journey I am sure he would never have agreed to our coming. The Father Commissary and Fray Mariano (who was also delighted at my visit to Seville) had been so sure that they were doing the Archbishop a very great service in bringing me that they had said nothing to him beforehand; and, as I say, if they had told him, they might have been committing a great error in the belief that they were doing right. For, in making my other foundations, the first thing I had done was to try to get a licence from the Ordinary, as the Holy Council directs.

In this case we had not only taken it for granted, but as I say, had thought we were being of great service, as indeed we were, and this he afterwards realized. The Lord was pleased that none of our foundations should be made without my enduring great suffering, sometimes in one way and sometimes in another.

As soon as we reached the house, which, as I say, they had leased for us, I meant to take possession of it at once, as I usually did, so that we might say the Divine Office there. But Fray Mariano, who was awaiting us, began to put us off. He was unwilling to tell me the whole story for fear of distressing me. But, as the reasons he gave for delay were insufficient, I realized what the obstacle must be—namely, that we had been given no licence. Then he asked me to allow the convent to be founded on an endowment, or something of the kind—I do not remember exactly what his suggestion was. In the end, he told me that the Archbishop disliked giving licences to religious houses for women and that he had not given one since his appointment (he had been many years in Seville and Córdoba and he is a great servant of God) and that in particular he would not give a licence for any convent founded in poverty.

This was equivalent to saying that it would be impossible to found the convent at all. In the first place, even had it been possible, I should have been very sorry to found such a house in the city of Seville, for I have only allowed my foundations to have an endowment in small places, where this is essential if a foundation is to be made at all, as there is no other way of providing for one. In the second place, we had only about a farthing over from the expenses of the journey, and we had brought nothing whatever with us, except the clothes we had on and a few tunics and hoods and the proper coverings which we needed in the carriages. In fact, when those who had come with us were ready to return, we had to borrow money for them. Antonio Gaytán had a friend there who lent us some of this and Fray Mariano begged some more for the preparation of the house. We had, of course, no house of our own. The thing therefore seemed impossible.

After what must have been a great deal of insistence on the part of this Father, we were allowed to have Mass said on Trinity Sunday.[1] That was our first Mass; and an order was sent us that no bell must be rung, or even installed in the house, though actually we had installed one already. This went on for more than a fortnight, and I know that, had it not been for the Father Commissary and Fray Mariano, I should have decided, with very little regret, to take my nuns back to Beas and to go on from there to make the foundation at Caravaca. I had a great deal more to contend with during this time—my memory is so bad that I cannot remember how long it lasted, but I think for over a month. It would have been less trouble had we gone at once, as the establishment of the convent was already becoming known. Father Mariano would not let me write to the Archbishop, but gradually he overcame his opposition, with the aid of letters which the Father Commissary received from Madrid.

For my own part, I had few scruples, for my mind was set at rest by the fact that we had had Mass said with the Archbishop's permission and that we always said the Divine Office in choir. He kept on sending people to visit me and said he would come himself very soon. He sent one of his own chaplains to say the first Mass. I now began to see quite clearly that this was doing us no harm beyond distressing me. The reason for my distress, however, was not my own sufferings or those of my nuns, but the distress of the Father Commissary, who was very much troubled because it was he who had ordered me to come. He would have been terribly upset if there had been any disaster, and there were reasons enough why there might have been.

And now the Calced Fathers also came to enquire why this foundation had been made. I showed them the patents which I had received from our most reverend Father General. This mollified them, though I do not think it would have succeeded in doing so had they known of the actions of the Archbishop.[2] Nobody, however, was aware of this and everyone believed that

<hr/>

[1] May 29, 1575.

[2] In a letter (No. 74) dated June 18, 1575, St. Teresa reports this visit to the General (P. Rubeo) in these words: "Some [of the Calced Fathers] have been to see me. I like them, especially the Prior [P. Miguel de Ulloa]. It was an extremely fortunate occurrence. He came to see the patents on the authority of which I had made my foundations, etc."

the foundation had given him great satisfaction and pleasure. At last it pleased God that he should come to visit us, and I then told him of the trouble he was causing. Eventually he told me I could do just what I liked, and as I liked, and from that time forward he was helpful and kind to us on every possible occasion.

CHAPTER XXV

Continues to describe the foundation of the glorious Saint Joseph in Seville and of what happened when it had a house of its own.

No one would have thought that, in a wealthy city like Seville, where there were so many rich people, there would have been less help given us in making a foundation than in any of the other places where I had made one. But I obtained so much less help that I sometimes thought there was no use in our having a convent there at all. I do not know if it was due to the climate of those parts, where I have always heard it said that God gives the devils more power to tempt us,[1] but they certainly harassed me, and I have never found myself as cowardly in my whole life as I was here. I really did not know myself. True, I did not lose my habitual confidence in Our Lord, but my feelings were so different from what they have generally been since I began these activities that I was sure the Lord was to some extent withdrawing His hand from me and doing nothing for me, so as to make me see that if I had previously been courageous it was due to no strength of my own.

I stayed there from the date already mentioned[2] until just before Lent. I had no thought of buying a house, nor the means to do so, nor was there anyone who would stand surety for us as there had been elsewhere. Those who had said so much to the Apostolic Visitor about entering the Order, and had begged him to bring some nuns there, must afterwards have decided that the conditions under which we lived were too severe and supposed that they would be unable to bear them. Only a single nun, of whom I shall speak later, joined us.[3] The time now came when I was ordered to leave Andalusia, as there was work for me to do in Castile.[4] I was very much distressed at

[1] [Both St. Teresa and St. John of the Cross have left on record their characteristically Castilian dislike of the Andalusians.]
[2] May 26, 1575.
[3] Beatriz de la Madre de Dios, referred to in the next chapter.
[4] She had been ordered to take up her residence in some Castilian convent. [Cf. Vol. I, p. xxxii, above.]

the thought of leaving the nuns without a house, though I knew quite well that I should be of no use there, for God would not grant the favour which He bestows upon me here of enabling me to find people to help us in these activities.

It pleased God that about this time a brother of mine, Lorenzo de Cepeda by name, should come from the Indies, after having lived there for over thirty-four years. To him it seemed even worse than to me that the nuns should be in Seville without a house of their own. So he helped us a great deal, and in particular was instrumental in obtaining the house where they now live.[1] I was myself already laying the matter earnestly before Our Lord, beseeching Him not to let me leave them without a house, and I made the sisters beg this of Him also and of the glorious Saint Joseph. We had many processions and often prayed to Our Lady. In view of this, and of my brother's determination to help us, I began to negotiate about the purchase of several houses; and it seemed as if we were about to reach an arrangement when everything came to a full stop.

One day when I was in prayer, begging God to give my nuns a house, since they were His brides and were so anxious to please Him, He said to me: "I have heard you; let Me alone." I was as happy about this as if I already had the house, and very soon I did have it. His Majesty saved us from buying one which everybody liked because it was on a good site but which was old and in a bad condition, and the site alone was being sold for only a little less than the house which we now have. The thing was settled, and nothing remained but the drawing-up of the agreement. But I was not at all pleased, for it seemed to me that this was not in accordance with those last words that I had heard in prayer. Those words, as far as I could see, meant that we were to be given a good house; and it proved to be God's pleasure that this should be done, for the very person who was selling us the house, despite the profit he was making, discovered some difficulty about the signing of the agreement when everything else was completed. We were able, therefore, to get out of the arrangements without doing anyone wrong, and this was a great favour on the part of Our Lord, for, if our nuns had gone into the house, they would never, in all their lives, have finished the necessary work on it, and, as they had small means for the purpose, they would have found it a great burden.

Almost as soon as we came to Seville, we had a great deal of help from a servant of God, who, knowing that we had no one

---

[1] Cf. *Relations*, XLVI [Vol. I, p. 358, above].

to say Mass for us, came and said it daily, though his house was a long way off and the heat of the sun was terrific. His name was García Álvarez;[1] he was a very good man and much esteemed in the city for his good deeds, for he occupied himself with nothing else. Had he been wealthy, we should have wanted for nothing. Knowing the house well, he thought it would be very foolish for us to give so much for it, and, hoping to make us give up the idea, would tell us this every day. Then he and my brother went to see the house where we are now, and they thought so well of it, and very rightly so, that in two or three days the agreement was all ready.[2] Our Lord evidently meant us to have it.

We had no little trouble in moving into it, for the tenants would not go out, and the Franciscan friars, who lived near,[3] came to see us at once and urged us on no account to move there. Had the agreement not been duly completed, I should have praised God that the contract could still be broken, for we saw ourselves risking a payment of six thousand ducats, which was the price of the house, without being able to get possession of it. The Prioress[4] did not agree, but praised God that the contract could not be broken: His Majesty gave her much more faith and courage in everything concerning that house than He gave me—indeed, she has much more in every respect, for she is a great deal better than I.

For more than a month we were worried in this way, after which it pleased God that the Prioress and I, with two other nuns, should move into the house. We went in at night, so that the friars should not be aware of it until we had taken possession, which we did in great fear. Those who accompanied us said they thought every shadow they saw was a friar. At dawn, good García Álvarez, who went in with us, said the first Mass in the house, and after that we were no longer afraid.

[1] [St. Teresa writes the name "Garcialvarez"]. Little is known of this cleric beyond what is found here and in the *Libro de recreaciones* of María de San José. He was the first chaplain and confessor of the community, a man of little experience and learning whose zeal often outran his discretion. Eventually the Prioress prevailed upon the Apostolic Visitor, P. Pedro Fernández, to sanction her getting rid of him, much to his own disgust and to the relief of the community and of St. Teresa.
[2] The sureties were Don Lorenzo de Cepeda, a certain Pablo Matías (the father of one of the Discalced nuns) and Doña Juana Gómez de Chaves, the mother of the Sister Beatrice to be described in the next chapter. The agreement was signed on April 5, 1576.
[3] The Franciscan house had been founded in 1249 and stood in what is now the great Plaza de San Fernando.
[4] María de San José (Salazar: 1548-1603), whom St. Teresa had singled out for this position at Beas. She was one of her best beloved daughters and more than sixty of the Saint's letters to her are still extant. She was professed at Malagón in 1571. After several terms as Prioress at Seville, she made an impc..an foundation at Lisbon in 1585.

O Jesus! How often have I been frightened when taking possession of these houses! If it is possible to feel such fear when one is doing nothing wrong, but acting in the service of God, what must be the fear of those who are about to do wrong and strive against God and their neighbour? I cannot think what they can possibly gain by doing this or what pleasure they can expect to experience when there is such fear to outweigh it.

My brother was not there just then, for he had gone into hiding on account of a mistake made in the agreement, which had been drawn up in a great hurry, a mistake which was very prejudicial to the convent.[1] As he had stood surety for us, they would have taken him to prison, and this would have troubled us very much, when he had only just come from abroad. We were worried enough as it was, as there was considerable difficulty until he had assigned some property to us as security. Later, the matter was brought to a satisfactory conclusion, though, as if we had not had enough to put up with, we now became involved in a lawsuit, which lasted for some time. We shut ourselves up in some rooms on the ground floor, and my brother was there all day with the workmen. He provided us with food, as he had done for some time previously; for, as it was a private house that we were in, and not everyone knew that it was a convent, we received few alms, except from a saintly old man who was Prior in a Carthusian monastery at Las Cuevas,[2] and a very great servant of God. He came from Ávila and belonged to the Pantoja family. From the time of our arrival God gave him such great love for us that I think it will continue, and he will help us in every way, all his life long. It is right, sisters, that, if you read this, you should commend him to God, with others, whether alive or dead, who have been of such help to us. It is for that reason that I record this here: we owe a great deal to this saintly man.

All this, so far as I remember, lasted for more than a month, but I have a bad memory for dates and I might therefore be wrong: you must always understand my dates to be approximate —they are of no great importance. During this month my brother worked hard in making some of the rooms into a church

[1] He had taken advantage of a privilege then current and gone into sanctuary. The irregularity was over a tax called the *alcabala*, which the vendors of the house expected the community to pay. As they would not do so, an attempt was made to arrest the principal guarantor. In the end, there was a lawsuit, which the community lost. Cf. Letter 94 (May 9, 1576), written to P. Mariano.

[2] The Carthusian monastery of Santa María de las Cuevas stands in the northern part of Seville's suburb of Triana, one of the largest and finest buildings which the Carthusians possess in Spain. The Prior at this time was a saintly old man called Fernando Pantoja—an Avilan of noble birth, who had been received into the Order in that same monastery fifty-eight years before.

for us, and in getting everything ready, so there was nothing for us to do.

When it was finished, I wanted the Most Holy Sacrament to be reserved without any commotion, for I greatly dislike giving unnecessary trouble. I said this to Father García Álvarez and he discussed it with the Prior of Las Cuevas, who could not have taken more trouble about our affairs if they had been their own. Their opinion was that, as the existence of the convent was known in Seville, it would be improper to make the reservation except with due solemnity and in the presence of the Archbishop. Between them all they arranged for the Most Holy Sacrament to be brought, with great solemnity, from a parish church; and the Archbishop ordered the clergy and several confraternities to be present and the streets to be decorated.

Good García Álvarez decorated our cloister, which, as I have said, served as a passage, and he also decorated the church most beautifully, and set up some very fine altars and put several good ideas into execution. One of these last was a device to give us a supply of orange-flower water, which we had not asked for, or even wanted, though in the event it gave us great delight. It made us very happy to think that our festival should have been organized with such solemnity, with decorated streets, music and minstrels. The saintly Prior of Las Cuevas told me he had never seen such a festival in Seville and considered it to be manifestly the work of God. He himself walked in the procession, a thing he was not accustomed to do, and the Archbishop reserved the Most Holy Sacrament. So you see, daughters, these poor Discalced nuns were honoured by everybody, though a little earlier it had seemed as if, for all the water in the river, there would not be enough for them. The number of people who came was astonishing.[1]

One thing which happened was worthy of note, according to all who saw it. After a great many salvos of artillery had been fired and rockets had been let off, and when the procession was over and it was nearly night, the people got the idea of letting off more guns, and a little powder caught fire, I do not know how, so that it was a great wonder the person it belonged to was not killed. A huge flame leapt up to the top of the cloister, the arches of which were covered with silk hangings which they

[1] St. Teresa had wanted the foundation to be made quietly and informally but both P. Pantoja and García Álvarez favoured a public ceremony so that the Reform might become known in this important and wealthy city. After the procession St. Teresa kneeled to the Archbishop and asked for his blessing, which he gave her, but, to her surprise and confusion, he then kneeled to her in his turn and asked for hers. The Saint described this episode in a letter to M. Ana de Jesús. The house was vacated in 1586 for one in a quieter position, in the street now called after St. Teresa.

thought would have been set on fire. But they did not take the least harm: they were crimson and yellow hangings. What I consider most astonishing is that the stonework of the arches below the hangings was blackened with smoke, and yet the hangings above were not touched: it was just as if the fire had not reached them.

Everybody was amazed to see this and the nuns praised the Lord that they would not have to buy any more hangings. The devil must have been so angry at the solemnity with which the festival had been kept, and at the sight of still another house of God, that he wanted to have his revenge in some way and His Majesty would not allow it. May He be blessed for ever and ever. Amen.

CHAPTER XXVI

Continues to describe the same foundation of the convent of Saint Joseph in the city of Seville. Gives some information about the first nun who entered the house, which is very noteworthy.

You can well imagine, my daughters, what joy we had that day. My own joy, I can tell you, was very great, especially when I saw that I was leaving the sisters in such a good house, so well situated, and that the convent was well known and the nuns in it would be able to pay the greater part of its expenses, so that, with those who came to make up their numbers, however little these might bring, they would be able to live in it free of debt. What pleased me most of all was that I had shared their trials. As it was now possible for me to get some rest, I went away. This festival was held on the Sunday before Pentecost in the year 1576. On the following Monday[1] I left Seville, as the summer heat was beginning, and I wanted to avoid travelling during the festival and to get to Malagón in time for it, for I was very anxious to stop there for a day or two. It was for this reason that I made such haste.

It was not the Lord's pleasure that I should hear Mass in the church even once. The happiness of the nuns was greatly marred by my departure, which they felt very deeply. We had lived together for a whole year, and had suffered a great many trials, the most serious of which, as I say, I shall not set down here: apart from the first foundation, at Ávila, which cannot be compared with this, I do not think any foundation has caused me so many trials—most of them interior ones. May it please

[1] June 4, 1576.

His Divine Majesty that He may always be served in this house, as I hope He will be, for in that case nothing else matters. His Majesty has begun to attract good souls to the house. As to those in it whom I took there with me, five of them in all, I have already told you how good they were. That is only a part of what can be said of them, and it is the least important part. Of the first nun who entered this house, however, I will say something, as this will give you pleasure.

She was the daughter of most Christian parents: her father came from the hill-country. When she was still very young, about seven years old, an aunt of hers begged her mother to allow her to have the child, as she had no children of her own. She took her home and evidently treated her with kindness and showed her a proper love. There were some women, however, who must have hoped, before the child came, that they would inherit the aunt's property; but it became clear to them that she was growing fond of her niece, and so it seemed likely that she would leave her the greater part of it. So they agreed to commit a diabolical act which would make this impossible: they accused the child of having tried to murder her aunt and given one of them a few pence with which to buy corrosive sublimate. They told the aunt this, and, as there were three of them and they all said the same thing, she at once believed them, and the child's mother, who is a most virtuous woman, did so too.

The mother took the child home, thinking that she was being brought up to be a very bad woman. Beatriz de la Madre de Dios[1] told me that for more than a year she was whipped every day, and tortured, and forced to sleep on the floor, so that she should confess to this wicked deed. When the child said that she had not done it, and did not even know what corrosive sublimate was, the mother thought that this was still worse and that she was determined to conceal what she had done. The poor mother became distressed when she saw that the child was concealing it in so hardened a way, thinking that she would never amend. It is an extraordinary thing that she did not confess to a crime she had not committed in order to bring this ill-treatment to an end, but she was innocent and God enabled her always to speak the truth. And, as His Majesty defends those who do no wrong, He sent two of those women so much trouble that they seemed to be frenzied with grief, and they sent privately for the child and her aunt and begged their for-

---

[1] Beatriz was the daughter of Alfonso Gómez Ibero and Juana Gómez, of Triana: she took her surname of Chaves from her maternal grandmother. St. Teresa herself gave her the habit and she was professed on September 29, 1576. Her mother made her profession on November 10, 1577 as Juana de la Cruz.

giveness. When they found they were at the point of death, they retracted their words, as did the third woman, who died in childbirth. So in the end all three died in torment as a reward for what they had made that innocent child suffer.

I know this, not only from the child herself, but also from her mother, who, when she saw her a nun, was grieved at the cruel way in which she had treated her, and described it to me, together with various other things: the child had certainly suffered like a martyr. As the mother had no other children and was an extremely good Christian, God had permitted her to treat her daughter in this cruel way, intensely fond of her though she was. She is a most truthful and Christian woman.

When the child was a little more than twelve years old, she read a book about the life of Saint Anne. This inspired her with a great devotion to the saints of Mount Carmel, for the book said that the mother of Saint Anne (who, I believe, was called Merenciana) used often to visit them. Hence the devotion which she conceived to this Order of Our Lady grew so strong that she made a vow to become a nun of the Order and to live in chastity. When she was able, she would often spend periods in solitude and prayer. In this respect God and Our Lady granted her great and very special favours. She would have liked to become a nun at once, but dared not do so because of her father and mother, besides which she did not know where to find this Order, which is a striking fact, for there was a convent of the Mitigated Rule in Seville,[1] and yet she had never heard of the Order until she learned of our house many years later.

When she reached an age for marriage, her parents discussed together with whom they should marry her. She was still quite a girl; but they had no other children, for, though she had had brothers and sisters, they had all died, and she alone, whom they loved least, remained to them. At the time of the incident to which I have referred, she still had one brother, who had taken her part, saying that they ought not to believe such a story. When they had decided upon a husband for her, they spoke to her about it, thinking that she would not oppose them; but she told them that she had made a vow not to marry and that on no account would she ever marry, even if they were to kill her.

Either through blindness sent them by the devil or by the permission of God so that she should be a martyr, they took it into their heads that she had done some evil deed and that it was for this reason that she had refused to marry. As they had already betrothed her, and realized that this would be an affront to her

---

[1] A Sevillian lady, Doña Inés Farfán, founded this convent, which was situated near the Puerta de la Macarena, and was known as the Convent of the Incarnation.

suitor, they beat her and inflicted such treatment on her (even throttling her and trying to strangle her) that it was only by good luck that they did not kill her. But God, Who needed her for other purposes, spared her life. She has told me that she reached a point at which she would feel hardly anything, for she remembered the sufferings of Saint Agnes, which the Lord recalled to her, and rejoiced at being able to bear something for Him, and offered up her sufferings to Him continually. They thought she would die, for she was in bed for three months, unable to move.

It seems a very striking thing that a girl who never left her mother's side, and whose father, as I have heard, was a most sensible man, could have been thought so ill of, for she was always devout and modest, and so fond of giving alms that she gave away all she could get. But when Our Lord wishes to grant anyone the grace to suffer, He has many ways of doing so. For some years He continued to reveal to the parents their daughter's virtue, so that whenever she wanted money for alms they would give it her and instead of persecuting her they would show her kindnesses. But so strong was her desire to be a nun that everything became a trial to her, and, as she told me, she continued to be very much distressed and afflicted.

Thirteen or fourteen years before Father Gracián went to Seville, when no one knew anything of the Discalced Carmelites, she happened to be with her father and mother and two women who were their neighbours when there entered a friar of our Order, dressed in frieze, according to their present custom, and with bare feet. They say that he had an open and venerable countenance, but he was so old that his long beard looked as if it were made of silver. He came quite near her and began to speak a few words in a language which neither she nor anyone else could understand. When he had finished speaking, he made the sign of the Cross over her three times and said: "Beatriz, God make thee strong." Then he went away. While he was there, nobody moved, so astonished were they at the sight. The father asked her who he was, but she herself had supposed that it must be someone he knew. They then got up quickly to look for him but never saw him again. The incident made the girl very happy, and all the others were astonished, saying that it was God's doing, and as a result of it they held her in high regard, as has been said. All these years passed—fourteen, I believe—and she continued to serve Our Lord, praying Him to fulfil her desire.

She was greatly troubled at the time when Father-Master Fray Jerónimo Gracián came to Seville. One day she went to hear a sermon in one of the churches of Triana, where her father was living, without knowing who the preacher was. It was Father-Master Gracián. When she saw him in his habit, with his bare feet, going to receive the blessing, she at once remembered the friar whom she had seen before, for the habit was the same, though the face and the age were different, for Father Gracián was not then thirty. She tells me that she almost fainted, so great was her delight; for, although she had heard that a monastery had been founded in Triana, she did not know it was one of ours.[1] From that day forward she tried to go to Father Gracián for confession; it was God's will, however, that this should cost her a great deal of trouble, for she went a dozen times or more and he would never hear her confession. For she was young—she cannot have been quite twenty-seven at that time—and good-looking, and he was careful to have nothing to do with people of that kind, being very prudent.

One day, when she was in church weeping, for she was also very modest in this respect, a woman asked her what ailed her. She told her that she had been trying for a very long time to get a word with that Father, who was hearing confessions at the moment, and had been unable to do so. The woman took her to him and asked him to hear her confession, and so she was able to make a general confession to him. When he saw a soul so well endowed by God, it was a great comfort to him, and he comforted her in his turn by telling her that it was possible some Discalced nuns might be coming, and, if so, he would get them to receive her at once. This duly happened; and the first thing he ordered me to do was to receive her before anyone else, for he was satisfied with her soul, and told her so. When we came, she was very anxious that her parents should not hear of it, or there would be no opportunity for her to enter the convent. And so, on the very day of the Feast of the Most Holy Trinity, she left the women behind who used to go to the church with her, for her mother did not go there for confession—the Discalced Carmelite monastery, where she always made her confession and gave liberal alms on behalf of herself and her parents, being a long way away. She had arranged with a very good servant of God to take her to the convent and she told the women who were to have gone with her that this servant of God was very well known in Seville and did many good works: she would be back quite soon, she said. So saying, she left them. She took her habit and mantle of frieze—I cannot think how she could get along with them, but such was her joy that it made everything

[1] It was founded by P. Gracián on January 6, 1574, with the title of Nuestra Señora de los Remedios. Among its famous novices were P. Nicolás Doria and P. Gregorio Nacianceno (p. 123, above).

seem light. Her sole fear was that somebody might accost her and notice how heavily laden she was, for she was walking very differently from usual. But oh, what the love of God can do! She no longer thought of her own reputation and her only anxiety was that no one should thwart her desire. We opened the door to her at once; and I then sent to tell her mother about it. She came like one beside herself; but said that she realized what a favour God was granting her daughter, and, though greatly distressed, she bore her trouble, not by protesting that she would never speak to the girl again, as some mothers do, but with great composure. She gave us liberal alms.

The bride of Jesus Christ now began to enjoy the happiness which she had so greatly desired. She was so humble and so fond of doing anything there was to be done that we found it difficult to take the broom from her. Though she had lived in such luxury at home, her only recreation now was in work. Such was her happiness that she soon began to grow quite plump. This made her parents delighted to see her there.

The time now drew near for her profession.[1] Some two or three months before the date, in order that she should not have so much fruition without suffering, she was attacked by severe temptations—not that she ever drew back from her resolve to become professed but that it now seemed to her a very difficult thing. She forgot all the years of suffering through which she had gained the blessing she now had and the devil tormented her so much that she was powerless. Making the greatest effort, however, she vanquished him, and in the very midst of her torments resolved to make her profession. Our Lord, Who needed no further proof of her fortitude, visited her three days before her profession, gave her very special consolation and put the devil to flight. So comforted was she that during those three days she seemed to be beside herself with joy, and very rightly so, for it was a great favour that had been granted her.

A few days after she entered the convent, her father died and her mother took the habit in the same convent and gave it, as alms, all her possessions. Both mother and daughter are living in the greatest happiness, edifying all the nuns and serving Him Who has bestowed upon them so great a favour.

Before a year had passed, another girl came to us in the same way, against her parents' will.[2] It is thus that the Lord builds

---

[1] In a letter to María de San José written on June 18, 1576 (No. 97), St. Teresa observes that the best way to quell Sister Beatriz's temptations and sufferings will be to profess her.

[2] This is believed to have been Bernarda de San José, daughter of Pablo Matías (p. 131, above), who was taken without dowry, no doubt on account of the good offices which her father had rendered to the Order.

His house with souls so anxious to serve Him that no severity or strictness of enclosure can deter them from doing so. May He be blessed for ever and ever and for ever and ever be praised. Amen.

CHAPTER XXVII

Describes the foundation made in the town of Caravaca. The Most Holy Sacrament was reserved here on New Year's Day in the same year, 1576. The dedication of the house is to the glorious Saint Joseph.

When I was in Saint Joseph's, Ávila, about to set off for the foundation of Beas already described, and only the final preparations had still to be made, there came a special messenger, sent from Caravaca by a lady called Doña Catalina.[1] It appeared that, after hearing a sermon preached by a father of the Company of Jesus,[2] three girls had come to her house, determined never to leave it until a convent had been founded in the place. They must have done this by arrangement with the lady, for it was she who helped them in the matter of the foundation. They were daughters of some of the most important people in that town. The father of one, a very great servant of God and a man of great prudence, was called Rodrigo de Moya. Among them they had sufficient money for a foundation of this kind. They knew about the work which Our Lord has done in the foundation of these houses, of which they had heard from the Company of Jesus, which has always looked upon it with favour and helped it.

When I thought of the desire and fervour of those souls, who had sent a messenger from so far to enquire about the Order of Our Lady, I felt great devotion and conceived a desire to help them in their good intention. Learning that the place was near Beas, I took more nuns with me than I generally did, for, to judge by the letters, it seemed that we should not fail to come to an arrangement, so I thought I would go on there after completing the foundation at Beas. But, as I have said in speaking of the Seville foundation, the Lord had disposed otherwise; so my plans were of little effect. They had obtained a licence from the Council

---

[1] A blank space occurs in the manuscript here, as though St. Teresa had forgotten the lady's surname and intended to insert it later. She was Doña Catalina de Otálora, widow of a wealthy and influential gentleman named Muñoz, who had been a member of the Royal Council of Castile and of the Council of the Indies. According to Julián de Ávila, she took four girls into her house, but the names of only three of them are known and one of them had left before Gaytán and Ávila arrived at Caravaca.

[2] P. Leiva. The Society of Jesus had established itself at Caravaca in 1570.

of the Orders but this was of such a kind that, although I had fully intended to go there, I gave up the idea.[1]

The truth is that, when I learned at Beas where the place was situated, how far it was off the beaten track, how bad the road was, and how troublesome it would be, and how annoying to the superiors, to go and visit the nuns, I had very little desire to go and make the foundation. But as I had raised these people's hopes, I asked Father Julián de Ávila and Antonio Gaytán to go there and see what the place was like, and, if they thought well, to break off the negotiations. They found that the project was in a very unsatisfactory state; and that this was the fault, not of the girls who wished to become nuns, but of Doña Catalina, who had been the chief mover in the business. She had given the girls a room to themselves, however, so that they were already living in solitude.

The nuns were so much in earnest, especially two of them— I mean, these girls who were to become nuns—that they had no difficulty in persuading Father Julián and Antonio Gaytán. So, before these two returned, the agreement was drawn up[2] and they went away leaving the girls very happy. They thought so well of them, and of the district in general, that they kept on referring to this, though they also complained of the badness of the road.[3] When I saw that everything had been arranged and there was nothing to do but get the licence, I sent good Antonio Gaytán back there, and out of love for me he willingly put up with all this trouble. He and Father Julián were very anxious for the foundation to be made, and it is they whom we really have to thank for it, for, if they had not gone there and arranged it, I should have been very loth to proceed any farther.

I gave him what he needed[4] so that he could go and install the turn and the grilles in the house in which the foundation was to be begun; here the nuns would remain until they had found a suitable house of their own. So he stayed there, for a good many days, with Rodrigo de Moya, who, as I have said, was the father of one of these girls and let them have a part of his house with the greatest pleasure. It took him a good many days to do this.

When they had brought the licence and I was about to leave for Caravaca, I found that the licence provided that the house should be subject to the Commanders of the Order and that the

[1] Caravaca belonged to the Commandery of Santiago and the convent, if founded, was to be placed under its jurisdiction. This, as we saw in the case of Beas (p. 112, above), was an unwelcome condition to St. Teresa.
[2] March 10, 1575.
[3] The two joined St. Teresa at Beas, where she was at that time.
[4] I.e., the money necessary for the journey.

nuns were to promise them obedience. This I could not sanction, as the house was to belong to the Order of Our Lady of Carmel, so they applied for a fresh licence. But as in the case of Beas they could find no way of getting it. The King, however, when I wrote to him, was very kind to me and ordered a new licence to be issued,[1] for our present King, Don Philip, is very well disposed to religious who are known to keep their Rule, and will always help them. When he had heard of our life in these houses of ours, and of the way we kept the Primitive Rule, he gave us every kind of assistance. And so I beg you earnestly, daughters, always to offer special prayers for His Majesty, as we do now.

As it was necessary to make a fresh application for a licence, I left for Seville,[2] by order of the Father Provincial, who was then, as he is now, the Master Fray Jerónimo Gracián de la Madre de Dios, as I have said. The poor girls continued to live in enclosure until the following New Year's Day: they had sent to Ávila in the preceding February. The licence was now quickly obtained, but, as I was so far away and in a good deal of trouble myself, I could not give them any assistance. I was very sorry for them. They wrote to me frequently in great distress and I could not bear to keep them waiting any longer.

I could not possibly go myself, both because I was so far away and because my foundation was not concluded; so Fray Jerónimo Gracián, who, as has been said, was Apostolic Visitor, decided that the nuns who were intended for the foundation there and had remained at Saint Joseph's, Malagón, should go, although I could not accompany them. I saw to it that the nun appointed Prioress was one who, I was confident, would fill that office very well, so much better is she than I.[3] Taking with them all they needed, they set off with two of our Discalced Fathers,[4] for Father Julián de Ávila and Antonio Gaytán had returned, some days before, to their own part of the country, and I did not want them to go back there, as the distance was so great and the weather so bad, for it was now the end of December.

On reaching Caravaca,[5] the nuns were received in the village

---

[1] This licence bears the date June 9, 1575.

[2] May 18, 1575.

[3] María de San José, as she tells us herself in her *Libro de recreaciones*, had been chosen by St. Teresa as Prioress for Caravaca. But the Saint changed her mind and kept M. María for the Seville foundation, sending to Caravaca M. Ana de San Alberto, one of the first nuns to be professed at Malagón (1569). She left Seville for Malagón, and then, with Bárbara del Espíritu Santo, Ana de la Encarnación, Juana de San Jerónimo and Catalina de la Asunción, proceeded to Caravaca.

[4] One of these was almost certainly P. Ambrosio de San Pedro, Sub-Prior at the Carmelite monastery of Almodóvar del Campo. No information exists as to the identity of the second.

[5] On December 18, 1575, according to Ribera (Book III, Chapter VII).

with great joy, especially by the girls who had been living in enclosure there. They founded the convent and the Most Holy Sacrament was reserved there on the festival of the Name of Jesus in the year 1576.[1] Two of the girls took the habit at once. The other was of a very melancholy temperament, which had been intensified by her enclosure, and even more so by the strictness and penitence of her life. So it was arranged to send her home with one of her sisters.[2]

Behold the judgments of God, my daughters, and consider the obligation to serve Him incurred by those of us whom He has allowed to persevere until we have made our profession and to remain for ever in the house of God as daughters of the Virgin. His Majesty made use of this girl's good will and employed her property for the establishment of this convent; yet, when the time came for her to enjoy what she had so much desired, her fortitude failed her and her temperament got the better of her. Too often, daughters, we lay the blame for our changeableness and imperfections upon our temperament.

May it please His Majesty to give us an abundance of His grace, for, if we have this, nothing will impede us from advancing continually in His service. May He also protect and help us all, so that the good beginning which He has been pleased to implant in such wretched women as ourselves may not be lost through our own weakness. In His name, my sisters and daughters, I beg you always to pray to Our Lord for this; and let everyone who joins us in the future act as though this Primitive Rule of the Order of the Virgin, Our Lady, were beginning with her and never in any way consent to its mitigation. Remember that small things open the door to very great ones and that the world may gradually intrude without your noticing it. Remember that what you enjoy in peace has been gained by toil and poverty. If you examine the matter carefully, you will see that the majority of these houses have been founded not so much by man as by the mighty hand of God, and that, if we do not stand in His way, His Majesty loves to further the work He is doing. Where do you think a poor woman like myself, subject to others and without a farthing of her own or anyone to help her, found the means to perform such great works? This brother of mine, who helped me in the Seville foundation, had certain means, besides the courage and good will necessary for helping us, but at that time he was in the Indies.

Behold, my daughters, behold the hand of God. It cannot have been because I was of illustrious descent that He did me

---

[1] January 1, 1576.
[2] This girl soon recovered and was professed on July 1, 1578, as Francisca de la Madre de Dios.

this honour. However you look at it, you will see it was His
work. It is not right that we should do anything to detract from
it, even though we were to forfeit life, honour and peace—still
less as we have all these together here, for life means living in such
a way as to have no fear of death or of anything that may happen
during our lifetime, and having that continual joy which all of
you now possess, and a prosperity which can never be greater,
because we do not fear poverty but rather desire it. Is there anything, then, comparable with the inward and outward peace
which is always yours? You have it in your power to live and die
in that peace, just as you have seen nuns die in these houses of
ours. If, then, you beseech God continually to further His work,
and have no trust in yourselves, He will not deny you His compassion, provided you have confidence in Him and courageous
hearts, for this His Majesty loves greatly. Have no fear that He
will ever fail you. Never refuse to receive those who come to you
and want to be nuns on the ground that they have no worldly
possessions, provided that they have virtues, that you are satisfied
with their desires and abilities, and that they come not merely
to find a home for themselves but to serve God in greater perfection. If you receive such persons as these, God will provide for
you and will give you in double measure anything you may lose
through receiving them.

I have a great deal of experience in this matter. His Majesty
well knows that, so far as I can remember, I have never failed
to receive anyone because she lacked means, provided I have been
satisfied with everything else about her. The many nuns who have
been received by me for God's sake alone can testify to this, as
you yourselves know. And I can assure you that it has given me
less pleasure to receive those who brought a great deal with
them than those whom I took for God's sake alone: indeed, I had
misgivings about the former, whereas those who were poor
comforted my spirit and made me so happy that I would weep
for joy. That is the truth.[1]

Now if, when our houses were not yet bought and our foundations not yet made, He gave us so much help with them, why,
now that we have places to live in, should He not still do so?
Take my advice, daughters, or you will lose exactly where you
think you are gaining. When an applicant with money presents
herself, and she has no obligation to give this money to others,
who perhaps are not in need of it, it is well that she should give
it to you as alms: I confess I should think it showed a great

---

[1] Examination of the early registers of the Convents of the Discalced Reform
shows that many nuns without dowries, or with only extremely modest ones, were in
fact received during St. Teresa's lifetime.

failure in love on her part if she did not. But see to it that any such applicant acts on the advice of learned men, to the greater service of God, for it would be very wrong of us to expect to be given the property of any applicant except to that end. We gain much more—I mean, we gain in perfection—by her fulfilling her duty to God than by receiving anything she may bring. For we have none of us any other aim, and God grant that we never may have, save that His Majesty may be served in and through everything.

And although I am a miserable and wicked woman, I say this to His honour and glory, and that you may rejoice in the way these houses of His have been founded. Never in making the arrangements for their foundation, or in any matter which presented itself in relation to them, even if I thought I should not succeed except by deviating from this intention: never in any respect, with regard to these foundations, have I done, or would I do, anything which I believed in the least degree contrary to the Lord's will, according to the advice of my confessors, who, since I have been working in this way, have, as you know, been most learned men and servants of God. Indeed, so far as I remember, it has never occurred to my mind to act otherwise.

Perhaps I am deceiving myself: I may have done many wrong things without being aware of the fact and my imperfections must be innumerable. This Our Lord, Who is the true judge, knows. I am speaking only so far as I understand myself, and I can see very clearly that this did not come from me but from the will of God that the work should be done: because it was His own work, He helped me and granted me His grace. I say this, my daughters, so that you may realize that you have the greater obligations to Him and may know that, right down to this day, the foundations have been made without wrong being done to anyone. Blessed be He Who has done all this and awakened charity in the people who have helped us. May it please His Majesty ever to protect us and give us grace that we may not be ungrateful for all these favours. Amen.

Well, daughters, you have seen that we had some trials to bear, though I believe those I have described are only the least of them: if I were to describe them in detail, it would be very wearisome. I mean, for example, the state of the roads, the floods, the snowstorms, the losing of our way, and, above all, again and again, the ill health which has troubled me. Once—I forget if I have said this—on our first day's journey from Malagón to Beas, I happened to be ill with a fever and so many other complaints that, when I thought of the long distance we still had to go and found myself in this condition, I remembered our father Elias, when he was fleeing from Jezabel, and those words of his: "Lord, how can I suffer this? See Thou to it." And in fact, when His Majesty saw how weak I was, He suddenly took the fever and the other illnesses away from me. When looking back at this, I have thought that it happened because a priest, who was a servant of God, came to see me, and this may perhaps have been the reason, but in any case I was suddenly delivered from both my outward and my inward sufferings. And, once I was well, I bore all bodily trials with joy.

Then there were other things which were no small trials to me, such as having to put up with people of so many different temperaments in each place we visited, and leaving my sisters and daughters when I went from one place to another. I love them so much that I assure you that was not the least of my crosses, particularly when I thought I might never see them again and saw how sorry they were and how they wept. For, though they are detached from everything else, God has not granted them detachment in this, perhaps in order that it may be the greater torment to me. Nor am I detached from them, though I have always done my utmost not to show this, and indeed have rebuked them for their attachment. But this did little good, for their love for me is very deep and there are many ways in which it can be seen how true it is.

You have also heard that these foundations were made, not only with a licence from our most reverend Father General but under an express command subsequently given. And not only so, but he wrote to me about every house that we founded, saying it gave him the keenest pleasure that the foundations in question were being made. Really the greatest relief that I had in all my trials was to see what joy this gave him, for I felt that in affording it to him I was serving Our Lord, as he was my superior, and, quite apart from this, I have a great love for him. Either His Majesty was pleased at last to grant me some peace, or the devil was angry because so many houses were being founded for the service of Our Lord. It is quite certain that this was not the will of our Father General; for, when I begged him not to order me to make more foundations, he wrote saying that he would not do so because he wanted me to make as many as I have hairs on my head, and this was not many years since. Before I left Seville, a decree, issued in the Definitory, was brought me from a Chapter General, which, I think, should have considered the way in which the Order had increased.[1] This required me, not only to make no more foundations, but on no account

---

[1] This Chapter-General was held at Piacenza in May and June 1575 under the presidency of P. Rubeo.

to leave whatever house I should choose to live in—in other words, it sent me to prison.[1] For there is no nun whom the Provincial may not, for reasons necessary to the good of the Order, send from one place to another—I mean, from one convent to another. And the worst thing was that our Father General was displeased with me, without the least reason, because of information given him by people who were annoyed with me. It was this which caused me distress. At the same time two other things were said about me, which amounted to very grave accusations.

I tell you this, sisters, so that you may see how merciful Our Lord is and how His Majesty never forsakes those who desire to serve Him. Not only did this not distress me, but it made me so unexpectedly happy that I could not control myself; I am not at all surprised now at what King David did when he danced before the Ark of the Lord. I had no desire that they should do anything else than what they were doing, and my joy was so great that I did not know how to conceal it. I have no idea why this was so, for I have not felt like this at other times when I have found myself sorely slandered and oppressed. One at least of the things which they brought against me was most serious. The prohibition from making further foundations, would, but for the displeasure of the most reverend General, have been a great relief to me. To end my life in peace was a thing I had often desired. But this never occurred to the people who brought about the prohibition: they believed they were causing me the greatest distress in the world, though they may perhaps have had good intentions as well.

Sometimes, too, I was happy because of all the opposition and evil-speaking which I met with while going about making these foundations. Sometimes my adversaries' intentions were good and sometimes they had other motives for opposing me. But in no trial that befell me can I remember ever having felt so great a joy as this. I confess that at any other time any one of the three trials that came upon me all at once would have been a great trouble to me. I believe the chief reason for my rejoicing was my belief that, as I was being treated in this way by creatures, I must have been pleasing the Creator. For I know that he who takes pleasure in things of the earth, or in the praise of men, is making a great mistake, quite apart from the little gain that he can derive from them. People say one thing to-day and another

---

[1] The order was sent to the Castilian Provincial, P. Ángel de Salazar, who communicated it to St. Teresa through the Prior of the Calced Carmelites at Seville, Fray Miguel de Ulloa. P. Gracián, however, used his authority as Apostolic Commissary to sanction her remaining at Seville. Cf. Letter 91, written to P. Rubeo, at the beginning of February, 1576.

to-morrow; first they speak well of a thing and then ill. Blessed be Thou, my Lord and God, Who art unchangeable for ever and ever. Amen. He who serves Thee to the end will live endlessly in Thy eternity.

As I said when I began, I started to write about these foundations at the command of Father-Master Ripalda, of the Company of Jesus, at that time Rector of the College at Salamanca and my confessor. Of some of the foundations I wrote when I was in the convent of the glorious Saint Joseph there, in the year 1573. I then stopped writing on account of my numerous occupations, and I was unwilling to begin again, because he was no longer my confessor and we were in different parts of the country, and also because it was a great trial and labour to me to write, though I look upon the time as well spent because it has all been done under obedience. I had quite determined not to go on writing when I was ordered to complete this account of my foundations by the Father Apostolic Commissary, who is now Fray Jerónimo Gracián de la Madre de Dios. I told him what little opportunity I had for writing, and other things which occurred to me, speaking to him as one who, though obedient, is very wicked; I also told him how tired it made me, and I had reasons enough for being tired already. None the less, he ordered me to finish this account, little by little, as I was able. This I have done, submitting myself in every respect to those who understand these matters, so that they may suppress any part of it which they find amiss. For it is very likely that what seems to me the best part will seem to them bad. This work has been completed to-day, on the eve of Saint Eugenius, the fourteenth day of the month of November in the year 1576, in the convent of Saint Joseph, Toledo, where I am now living by order of the Father Apostolic Commissary, Master Fray Jerónimo Gracián de la Madre de Dios, whom we now have as Superior of the Discalced Carmelite friars and nuns of the Primitive Rule. He is also Visitor of the Carmelites of the Mitigation in Andalusia, to the glory and honour of Our Lord Jesus Christ, Who reigns and shall reign for ever. Amen.

For the love of Our Lord I beg the brethren and sisters who read this to commend me to Our Lord, that He may have compassion on me and deliver me from the pains of purgatory, and, if I have merited it, permit me to rejoice in Him. As you are not to see this for as long as I live, let me derive some profit after my death from the fatigue which the writing of it has caused me and from the great desire which I have had to succeed in saying something which may comfort you if it is thought well that you shall read it.

CHAPTER XXVIII

The foundation of Villanueva de la Jara.

After the Seville convent had been founded, my foundations came to an end for more than four years.[1] The reason for this was the very sudden beginning of the great persecutions which both friars and nuns of the Discalced Reform had to endure: though they had had many such already, none of them were so severe as these last, which almost brought the Reform to an end. It became clear how angry the devil was at this excellent beginning which Our Lord had made, and which, as it prospered so greatly, was clearly His work. The Discalced friars, and more especially their leaders, suffered greatly from the gross calumnies and opposition which came from nearly[2] all the Fathers of the Mitigation.[3]

These Fathers spoke against us to our most reverend Father General, who, though he was a most saintly man, and had given us the permission to found all these houses (except that of Saint Joseph, Ávila, which was the first of them, and was founded by a licence from the Pope), was so much worked upon that he did his utmost to prevent the Discalced Reform from making any further progress, though he was always well disposed towards our convents. Because I would have nothing to do with this, they made him very much displeased with me, and this was the greatest trial that I have had to bear while making these foundations, though I have had to bear a great many. For to give up assisting the progress of a work which I saw so clearly was for the service of Our Lord and the advancement of our Order was a thing which had been forbidden me by the very learned men who acted as my confessors and advisers, yet it would have been a terrible sacrifice[4] for me to oppose what I knew to be the will of my Superior, for, apart from my obligation to obey him, I had a most tender love for him, as was most certainly his due. But the truth is that, even had I wished to please him in this, I could not have done so, because the Order had Apostolic Visitors whom I was bound to obey.

[1] I.e., from January 1, 1576 (Caravaca) to February 21, 1580 (Villanueva de la Jara).
[2] The word " nearly " has been inserted by the author above the line, as though it were an afterthought.
[3] [For a brief outline of the events here referred to, see *S.S.M.*, I, 144, 234-7. Longer and fuller accounts will be found in the standard biographies of St. Teresa and St. John of the Cross. The chronology of the period can be traced in the biographical outline (Vol. I, pp. xxvii–xxxvi, above)].
[4] [*Lit.*, " it would have been a death."]

There died a saintly Nuncio,[1] who was very well disposed
to everything virtuous and therefore had a high esteem for the
Discalced friars. He was succeeded, however, by one whom God
seemed to have sent to try us by suffering. He was related in
some way to the Pope and must have been a servant of God,
but he began by showing very marked favour to the Calced
Friars; and the information which they gave him about us persuaded him that it would be right not to allow our early efforts
to proceed any farther. This policy he started to carry out with the
greatest severity, condemning, imprisoning and exiling those
who he thought might resist him.[2]

Those who suffered most were Fray Antonio de Jesús, who
founded the first monastery of Discalced friars, and Fray Jerónimo
Gracián, whom the previous Nuncio had appointed Apostolic
Visitor to the friars of the Mitigation: with them, and with Father
Mariano de San Benito, his displeasure was great. In writing
of the earlier foundations I have described these Fathers. On
others, who were among the most reverend of them, he also
inflicted penances, though less rigorously. Upon these Fathers
he laid many strict injunctions to have no more to do with any of
our business.

It was quite evident that all this came from God, and that His
Majesty was allowing it for the sake of some greater good, in
order that the virtue of these Fathers should become more
clearly manifest, as has in fact happened. This Nuncio appointed
a superior from among the Mitigated friars to visit our convents
and monasteries;[3] and, if he had found in them what he expected,
our troubles would have been great. As it was, we had to suffer

---

[1] Niccolo Ormaneto, who died in Madrid on June 18, 1577, always a good friend to
the Discalced Reform. His successor, Filippo Sega (Vol. I, pp. xxxiii, xxxiv, above) had
been prejudiced against the Reform by a relative, Cardinal Buoncompagni, though
on his arrival in Spain he examined the questions at issue with scrupulous care.
From Spain he passed to Portugal, and, later, served in Germany and France. He
died at Rome in 1596.

[2] P. Antonio de Jesús and P. Gabriel de la Asunción were imprisoned in the
Franciscan house of San Bernardino, in Madrid, and afterwards at La Roda, in
the province of Albacete. P. Mariano, who was known to have influence with the
King, was sent to Pastrana. P. Gracián was kept in the power of the Calced Friars
in Madrid. All these events took place in October-November 1578. During the
night of December 3-4, St. John of the Cross and his companion Fray Germán de
Santo Matía were kidnapped at Ávila and taken as prisoners to Toledo and La
Moraleja respectively. It is on record that Sega described St. Teresa to P. Juan
de Jesús (Roca), who was a prisoner in Madrid, as a " restless, gadabout, disobedient
and contumacious woman, who invented wicked doctrines and called them devotion,
transgressed the rules of enclosure, in opposition to the Council of Trent and to her
superiors, and taught others, against the commands of St. Paul, who had forbidden
women to teach." (*Reforma de los Descalzos*, Vol. I, Book IV, Chapter XXX.)

[3] On October 16, 1578, Sega put the Discalced under the jurisdiction of the Calced
Provincials of Castile and Andalusia, Fray Juan Gutiérrez de la Magdalena and
Fray Diego de Cárdenas, respectively.

very dearly, as will be narrated by one who can write of it better than I. All I am doing is to touch upon it, so that any nuns who come after us may know how great are their obligations to advance in perfection since they are now enjoying what in the past has cost us so dear. Some of the friars suffered a great deal during this period from serious accusations, which grieved me much more than anything I suffered myself; my own sufferings, indeed, brought me great pleasure. I seemed to be the cause of all their afflictions; if they had thrown me into the sea, as happened to Jonas, the storm would have ceased.

Praise be to God, Who prospers the truth. This He did here; for, when our Catholic King Don Philip learned what was happening, and was told about the lives and religious observances of the Discalced, he took our cause into his own hands and helped us by refusing to allow the Nuncio to be our sole judge, and assigning to him four assessors, weighty persons, three of them members of religious Orders, who were to examine our case carefully.[1] One of these was the Father-Master Fray Pedro Fernández, a person of most saintly life, great learning and understanding. He had been Apostolic Commissary and Visitor to the Calced Fathers of the Province of Castile and we Discalced were also subject to him. He was well informed about both Calced and Discalced and we all desired our way of life to be known. So, when I learned that the King had appointed him, I considered the matter as good as settled, as, by the mercy of God, it has been. May His Majesty grant this to redound to His honour and glory. Though there were many lords of the realm and bishops who hastened to tell the Nuncio the truth, all their efforts would have profited but little had not God made use of the King.

We are all under a great obligation, sisters, to commend him ceaselessly in our prayers to Our Lord, together with those who have helped His cause and that of the Virgin Our Lady, and I exhort you earnestly to do this. You will see now, sisters, how much opportunity there was for making foundations. We all occupied ourselves zealously in prayer and penance, beseeching God to prosper those we already had if they were to be for His service.

During the early period of these great trials, which from this brief description of them you may think to have been light, but which, when endured for so long, were very heavy, I had

---

[1] The good offices of the Count of Tendilla and the sympathy of the King with the Reform were responsible for the appointment of these assessors at the beginning of 1579. They were the Royal Chaplain and Almoner-in-Chief, Don Luis Manrique; an Augustinian, Fray Lorenzo de Villavicencio; and two Dominicans, Fray Hernando del Castillo and Fray Pedro Fernández. Their first act was to remove the Discalced from the jurisdiction of the two Provincials mentioned above, and give them as Superior the learned, prudent and sympathetic P. Ángel de Salazar.

received in Toledo, where I had come from the Seville foundation in the year 1576, letters brought by a cleric of Villanueva de la Jara from the municipality of that town. They concerned the possibility of our receiving into a convent nine women who some years ago had entered a hermitage of the glorious Saint Anne, which was in that town, with a small house adjoining it. They were living here in such recollectedness and sanctity that all the people were anxious to see their desires to be nuns fulfilled. There was also a letter from a Doctor, who is the parish priest there; his name is Agustín de Ervias and he is a man of learning and great virtue: it was his virtue which made him do all that he could to help in this holy work.[1]

To me it seemed quite unsuitable to arrange for the foundation of a convent here, for the following reasons. First, because there were so many applicants for admission and I thought it would be very difficult for them to accustom themselves to our way of life now that they were used to their own. Secondly, because there was hardly any means of subsistence for them, and there are scarcely more than a thousand inhabitants in the town, which would thus be of little help to persons living on alms; true, the municipality had offered to maintain them, but as a permanent arrangement that seemed to me hardly practicable. Thirdly, because they had no house. Fourthly, because they would be a long way from our other convents. Fifthly, because, although I was told they were very good, I had not seen them, and so I could not be sure if they had the qualities which we expect of those who enter our convents. I determined, therefore, to decline the suggestion altogether.

Before doing this I wanted to discuss it with my confessor, Doctor Velázquez, a Canon and Professor in Toledo, a most learned and virtuous man, now Bishop of Osma;[2] for it is my invariable custom never to act on my own opinion but always to be guided by such persons as he. When he had the letters and grasped the position, he told me not to decline, but to make a favourable answer; for, if God had united many hearts in one and the same purpose, it was evident that this would be for His service. I did as he said, neither accepting the suggestion entirely nor declining it. Time went on. They continued to urge the plan upon me and to find persons who would persuade me to accept; and this has been going on until this present year, 1580. All the time it seemed to me that it would be foolish to accept the sugges-

---

[1] This sincere admirer of St. Teresa and her Reform had been a Canon of Cuenca, but his preference for a cure of souls had impelled him to effect an exchange of positions with the parish priest of Villanueva de la Jara, Don Juan de Rojas.
[2] See *Relations*, VI (Vol. I, pp. 334-7, above).

tion; but, whenever I wrote to them, I could never bring myself to break off the matter entirely.

It so happened that Fray Antonio de Jesús arrived, to complete his term of exile,[1] at the monastery of Our Lady of Succour, which is three leagues from this town of Villanueva. He used to go and preach there; and the Prior of the monastery, who just now is Fray Gabriel de la Asunción,[2] a very prudent man and a servant of God, would also often go to the same place. They were both friends of Doctor Ervias and it was in this way that they made the acquaintance of these saintly sisters. Attracted by their virtue, and persuaded by the people and by the Doctor, they began to take a personal interest in this question and started to write me the most earnest and persuasive letters. When I was at Saint Joseph's, in Malagón, which is twenty-six leagues or more from Villanueva, the Father Prior himself came to speak to me about the matter, telling me what it would be possible to do and adding that, when the convent was founded, Doctor Ervias would contribute to its endowment three hundred ducats a year from the income of his benefice and that an application for approval of this would be made to Rome.

This seemed to me a very unstable arrangement, for I thought it might fall through after the foundation had been made, though otherwise, together with the little which the sisters had, the money would be quite sufficient. So I gave the Father Prior a great many reasons, which, in my opinion, should have been enough to convince him that it would be unsuitable to make the foundation. I told him that he and Fray Antonio ought to reconsider the matter very carefully, and that I left it to their consciences. With what I had said to them I thought that would be enough to keep the matter from going any farther.

After he had gone, I reflected on his anxiety that the foundation should be made and it occurred to me that he might persuade our present Superior, Fray Ángel de Salazar, to accept the convent. So I wrote to the Superior myself, in great haste, begging him not to give his permission and telling him my reasons for asking this. To judge from what he wrote to me later he had had no wish to give it if the idea did not seem to me a good one.

About six weeks had passed, or perhaps rather more, when, just as I was thinking that the affair was over, a messenger

---

[1] I.e., at the order of the Nuncio (p. 150, n. 1, above).

[2] P. Gabriel was a native of Pastrana who had won the esteem of the Prince and Princess of Éboli and had been present, in 1569, at the ceremony in their oratory when Fray Mariano and Fray Juan de la Miseria received the habit. He himself professed in 1570, and, after spending some time as Rector of the College at Alcalá de Henares, became, in 1576, Prior at La Roda, where he was also Catalina de Cardona's director. He died in 1584, at the early age of forty.

arrived with letters from the municipality, in which they bound themselves to provide without fail whatever might be necessary and also promised that Doctor Ervias would do what I have described. He brought urgent letters, too, from these two reverend Fathers. I was very much afraid of receiving so many sisters, for I thought they might form a faction, and oppose others who came there, as sometimes happens. Further, I could see no certain means of making provision for their maintenance, for, though offers had been made, it would be impossible to enforce their fulfilment. I found myself, therefore, in a state of great confusion. Since then I have realized that this was the work of the devil; for, though the Lord had given me courage, I felt so weak-hearted that I seemed to have no trust in God. But in the end those blessed souls were all stronger than I.

One day, after Communion, I had been commending the matter to God, as I used often to do, for the reason I had previously sent favourable answers to the letters was that I feared I might be hindering the profit of certain souls, my desire always being to further any means by which Our Lord may be praised and more people may be brought to serve Him. His Majesty reproved me severely, asking me what treasures I had had at my disposal when making the foundations already in existence. I was not to hesitate to accept this house, He said, for it would be greatly to His service and to the profit of souls.

So powerful are the words of God that not only does the understanding comprehend them but they give it light to understand the truth and dispose the will for putting it into execution. So it was with me: not only was I now glad to accept the convent but I realized I had been mistaken in delaying for so long by paying heed to human arguments, when I had such abundant opportunity of seeing what His Majesty has done for this holy Order.

Once I had decided to accept this foundation, it seemed to me that I should have to go there myself with the nuns who were to live there. Many reasons suggested themselves to me for this, though I was greatly disinclined to do it, for I had been very unwell when I came to Malagón[1] and was so still. But, thinking it would be a service to Our Lord if I went, I wrote to the Superior telling him to order me to do what he thought best. He sent me the licence for the foundation and an injunction to be present at it and take with me such nuns as I considered advisable. This made me very anxious because they would have to live with those who were there already. Commending the matter earnestly to Our Lord, I took two nuns from the convent of Saint Joseph in Toledo, one of whom would be Prioress,

[1] November 25, 1579.

together with two from Malagón, one of them to be Sub-Prioress.[1] As so many prayers had been made to His Majesty, this choice proved to be a good one, which seemed to me important, for, when foundations are made with our own nuns alone, they all get on well together.

Fray Antonio de Jesús and the Father Prior, Fray Gabriel de la Asunción, came to fetch us. Everything necessary was obtained from the people in the town and we left Malagón on the Saturday before Lent, February 13, 1580. God was pleased to give us fine weather and to make me so well in health that I felt as if I had never been ill. This amazed me, and I realized how important it is that we should not think of our own weak constitutions, when we realize we are serving the Lord. Whatever the opposition we may encounter, He has the power to make the weak strong and the infirm well. And if He should not do this, it will be the better for our souls if we suffer, and forget ourselves, but fix our eyes on His honour and glory. What is the use to us of life and health if we cannot throw them away for so great a King and Lord? Believe me, sisters, you will never go wrong if you do this.

I confess that my wickedness and weakness have often caused me many doubts and fears, but I can remember no occasion, since the Lord gave me the habit of a Discalced nun, nor even for some years before that, when, of His sheer compassion, He did not grant me grace to vanquish these temptations and to fling myself into whatever I believed to be most truly conducive to His service, however difficult it might be. I see quite clearly that my own part in the matter was small. But God wants no more from us than resolution—He will do everything Himself. May He be for ever blessed and praised. Amen.

We were to go to the monastery of Our Lady of Succour, which has already been mentioned as being three leagues from Villanueva. There we halted, as had been arranged, to advise them of our coming. I felt it right to obey these Fathers, with whom we came, in everything. The house stands in a very pleasant though a deserted and lonely place; and, when we approached it, the friars came out in due order to receive their Prior. As they advanced, bare-footed, in their poor frieze mantles, they inspired us with great devotion and I myself was very much touched by the sight: it was as if we were back in the great days of our holy Fathers. In that lonely field they seemed like fragrant white flowers, and in God's sight I believe they are,

[1] From Toledo she took María de los Mártires (for Prioress—not Ana de la Madre de Dios, as Ribera says) and Constanza de la Cruz; from Malagón, M. Ana de San Agustín and Elvira de San Ángelo, the latter as Sub-Prioress. The twenty-eight leagues' journey from Malagón to Villanueva de la Jara was a triumphal progress, so well known in that district had St. Teresa become.

for in my opinion very real service is rendered to Him there. They went into the church singing the Te Deum in tones of subdued reverence. The church has an underground entrance, which looks like a cave, and represents the cave of our father Elias. I entered with such inward joy that even if I had been a much longer time on the journey I should have thought it well spent, though I was very much grieved that the saintly woman through whom Our Lord founded this house was now dead: I did not deserve to see her but I had been very anxious to do so.[1]

It will not, I think, be a waste of time if I say something here of her life[2] and of how it came to please Our Lord that this monastery should be founded here, for I understand that many souls in the neighbourhood have found it of great benefit. When you think of this holy woman's penitent life, my sisters, you will realize how backward we are and will make fresh efforts to serve Our Lord. For there is no reason why we should be behind her, as we are not descended from such refined and noble people. Though this may be of no importance, I mention it because she had lived a life of luxury, in accordance with her rank: she was descended from the ducal family of Cardona and was thus known as Doña Catalina de Cardona. Later, she wrote to me several times, and signed her letters with the simple words "The Sinner."

Her life, before the Lord showed her such great favours, will be described by her biographers, who will relate in great detail the many things that there are to be said of it. But in case they should not come to your notice, I will repeat here what has been told me by certain people who knew her and whose testimony is worthy of credence.

Even while she lived among great men and people of high rank, this saintly woman was always very much concerned with her soul and practised penance. So great was the growth of her desire for such a life and for a place to live where she could have fruition of God alone and occupy herself in doing penance, that no one could hinder it. She would speak about this to her confessors and they would refuse her their consent; for the world is now so set upon discretion that it almost forgets the great favours granted by God to the holy men and women who serve Him in the deserts[3]; so I am not at all surprised that they thought this

---

[1] The monastery of Nuestra Señora del Socorro, referred to at length by Francisco de Santa María in his *Reforma de los Descalzos* (Vol. I, Book IV, Chapters XVII, XVIII), was founded in April 1572 by Catalina de Cardona, in a lonely district between Vala de Rey and La Roda.

[2] Cf. *Relations*, XXIII (Vol. I, p. 345, above).

[3] [Cf. p. 82, n. 1, above].

foolish. But, as His Majesty does not fail to further true desires and to see that they are carried out, He ordained it that she should go for confession to a Franciscan Father, Fray Francisco de Torres. I know this friar very well and believe him to be a holy man: for many years he has been living in the most fervent penitence and prayer and has suffered many persecutions. He must have known well what favours God grants to those who strive to receive them: he told her, therefore, not to draw back but to follow the vocation which His Majesty was giving her. I do not know if those were his words, but that was their meaning, and she put it into practice immediately.

She went to see a hermit who lived at Alcalá[1] and begged him to go with her, and to say nothing about it to anyone. They reached the place where this monastery stands, and she found there a little cave so small that she could hardly get into it. Here he left her. What love she must have had! She cared nothing about having any food or about the perils which she might encounter or about the scandal that would ensue when she did not return. How inebriated must that holy soul have been with the love of God! How absorbed in the desire that none should keep her from rejoicing in her Spouse! How determined to love the world no more, since she fled in this way from all its pleasures!

Let us reflect carefully upon this, sisters, and realize how she conquered everything at once. For, though you are doing no less than she did in entering this holy Order and offering your wills to God and making a profession of continual enclosure, I am not sure if some of us do not lose these early fervours and, in certain respects, become subject once more to self-love. May His Divine Majesty grant that this be not so, and that, as we are imitating this saintly woman in our desire to flee from the world, we may be far removed from it inwardly.

I have heard a great deal about the strict austerity of her life, only the smallest part of which can be known. Since she remained in that solitary place for so many years, and had such burning desires to do penance, and there was no one to restrain her, she must have inflicted terrible discipline upon her body. I will repeat what certain people, including the nuns of Saint Joseph's, Toledo, heard from her own mouth when she went to see them. She spoke to them as frankly as if they had been her own sisters, and she did the same to other people, for her humility must have been as great as her simplicity. As she was one who knew

---

[1] P. Piña, a priest who lived as a hermit on the Monte de la Vera Cruz, near Alcalá de Henares. His meeting with Doña Catalina took place at Estremera, a village belonging to the Prince of Éboli. With the two went Don Martín Alonso, who had been the Prince's chaplain.

that she had nothing of her own, she was very far from being vainglorious and rejoiced to speak of the favours which God was granting her, so that they might lead to the praise and glorification of His name. This is a dangerous practice for those who have not attained to her state, for at the very least they may seem to be indulging in self-praise. But from this accusation her frankness and holy simplicity must have saved her, for I never heard anyone make it.

She told them that she had spent eight years in that cave and for days on end had lived on plants and roots from the fields, for, after she had eaten three loaves left by the man who took her there, she had nothing else until one day she was visited by a shepherd boy. After that he used to supply her with bread and flour, with which she would make cakes,[1] baking them on a fire. Of these, which formed the whole of her meals, she partook every third day. This is quite true, for the friars who lived there are witnesses to it. Some time after this they found her very wasted. Occasionally they would persuade her to eat a sardine or something else of the kind, when she went on a journey in connection with her plan of founding a monastery, but she found that doing so did her more harm than good. Wine, so far as I know, she never drank at all. For discipline she wore a heavy chain, often for as long as an hour and a half or two hours on end. Her hair-shirts were very rough, as I was told by a woman who, when returning from a pilgrimage, had stayed with her one night, and, while pretending to be asleep, had seen her take off her hair-shirt, which was soaked with blood, and wash it. She suffered still more, as she used to tell the nuns I have mentioned, from evil spirits, which would appear to her in the form of huge mastiffs and leap on her shoulders, and on other occasions in the form of serpents; yet she was not in the least afraid of them.

After founding the monastery, she still went to her cave and slept there, leaving it only for the Divine Offices. Before going, she would attend Mass at the Mercedarian monastery, a quarter of a league distant, and sometimes she would go there on her knees. Her dress was of kersey (and her tunic, of frieze[2]), and was made in such a way that people thought she was a man.[3] When the years during which she lived in this solitude were over, the Lord was pleased to make her doings known, and she then began to arouse such devotion in people that she could not keep

[1] [*Tortillas.* In Spain this word now means "omelettes", but in some Spanish-American countries it still designates flour or meal cakes as in sixteenth-century Spain].

[2] The bracketed words, evidently an afterthought, were inserted by the author between the lines of her text.

[3] [Cf. p. 160, n. 1, below].

them away from her. She spoke to them all with great charity and love. As time went on, still greater numbers of people came to see her, and to be able to speak to her was considered no small thing. This tired her so much that she said it was killing her. There was one day when the whole country was full of carriages. Soon after the friars had come to live there, there would be nothing for it but that they must lift her up so that she could give the people her blessing; it was only in this way that she could get rid of them. When she had been in the cave for eight years (it was larger now, for all the people coming to see her had made it so) she had a very serious illness, so that it was thought she would die. All this took place in that cave.

She began to be anxious that a house for friars should be founded there as well, and she had this in mind for some time, though she could not decide to what Order it should belong. One day, when she was praying before a crucifix which she always had with her, Our Lord showed her a white mantle, which she understood to be that of the Discalced Carmelites. She had never previously heard that such friars existed. At that time only two of our monasteries had been founded—those of Mancera and Pastrana. She must have found out about them subsequently. When she heard of the Pastrana monastery (she had once been very friendly with the Princess of Éboli, wife of Prince Ruy Gómez, to whom Pastrana belonged), she set out to find a way of founding this monastery of her own, which she was so anxious to see.

It was there, in the monastery of Pastrana, in the church of Saint Peter (for that is its name), that she took the habit of Our Lady[1]; not, however, with the intention of becoming a nun and making her profession, for she had never any inclination to be a nun, as the Lord was leading her by another way, and she thought that if she were under obedience her desires for austerity and solitude might be forbidden her. In the presence of all the friars, then, she received the habit of Our Lady of Carmel.

Among those present was Father Mariano, of whom I have spoken in writing of these foundations: he told me with his own lips that he had been granted a suspension or rapture which took him out of himself, and that, while he was in that state, he saw many friars and nuns lying dead. Some of them had been beheaded; others had had their legs and arms cut off, and had thus been martyred. That was the meaning of this vision. He is not a man to say what he has not seen, neither is he accustomed

---

[1] This was on May 6, 1571. P. Baltasar de Jesús gave her the habit and the Prince and Princess of Éboli were present. Though she wore the Carmelite habit entire, her affection for the life of a hermit was so great that she never became a nun.

to experience these suspensions of the spirit, for God is not leading him by that road. Pray to God, sisters, that this may be true and that we in our day may merit so great a blessing and be numbered among the martyrs.

While at Pastrana, the saintly Cardona began to seek means for the founding of her monastery, and in order to get these she returned to the capital, which previously she had been so glad to leave.[1] To return must have been no light torment to her, and she encountered no little evil-speaking, as well as other trials, for on leaving her house she could never avoid the people, and this was so wherever she went. Some cut off pieces from her habit and some from her mantle. She then went to Toledo, where she stayed with our nuns.[2] They have all assured me that there was such a fragrance about her, like that of relics, that it clung even to her habit and her girdle, which, as they had taken them from her and given her fresh ones, she left behind. The fragrance was so sweet that it moved them to praise Our Lord. And the nearer they came to her, the sweeter it was, though her dress was of such a kind that, in that heat, which was very severe, one would have expected its odour to be offensive. (I know they would not say anything that was not entirely true.) So it inspired them with great devotion.

In the capital and elsewhere she was given the means for founding her monastery, and when she had obtained the licence it was duly begun. The church was built where her cave had been and they made another cave for her quite near it, in which there was a substantial tomb.[3] Here she lived, night and day, for nearly all the remainder of her life. She lived only a short time after the monastery had been founded there—about five and a half years—and, considering the austerity of her life, it seems a miracle that she lived as long as that. She died, I think, in the

[1] Her fame had spread so far that Princess Juana, sister of Philip II, wrote to the Prince of Éboli and to P. Mariano, asking them to bring her to Court, which they did, not without some contretemps, caused chiefly by the fact that she wore a friar's cowl. The Nuncio (Ormaneto), it seems, was scandalized at seeing "a Discalced Carmelite friar in a carriage with some ladies, scattering blessings as he went, like a bishop." He was placated by the explanation given him but was not apparently reconciled either to the blessings or to the cowl. (*Reforma de los Descalzos*, Vol. I, Book IV, Chapter XIV.)

[2] This stay was made on her way back from the capital to La Roda. It would be largely from the nuns of Toledo, though partly also, no doubt, from those of Villanueva, that St. Teresa gleaned all this biographical material.

[3] This idea came from P. Mariano, who found some suitable ground and had a cave prepared, twelve feet long by four wide. Eight feet of the length of the cave, however, were, at the hermit's wish, taken up by the "tomb" (*sepulcro*), which consisted of a carved representation of the dead Christ surrounded by His Mother and other faithful watchers. The hermit's cell, therefore, was only four feet square. A subterranean passage was constructed between the cave and the church, no doubt chiefly to ensure a more complete privacy.

year 1577.[1] Her funeral ceremonies were conducted with the greatest solemnity, for a gentleman named Juan de León,[2] who was most devoted to her, was very insistent on this. Her tomb lies, at present, in a chapel dedicated to Our Lady, to whom she had an extreme devotion, and it will remain there until a larger church can be built than the one they now have, which shall be worthy of containing her blessed body.

Great devotion exists in this monastery on account of her; it seems to have found continual expression there, and in the whole district, especially in those who view her retreat and the cave in which she lived before resolving to found the monastery.

I have been told, by those who know, that she felt so exhausted and distressed at the sight of all the people who came to visit her that she wanted to go to some other place where she would be unknown. She sent for the hermit who had brought her there to take her away but he had died. Our Lord, Whose will it was that this house should be built there for Our Lady, gave her no opportunity of going away, for, as I have said, I know He is well served there. The friars are amply fitted for the life and it is clear that they like seclusion. This is especially true of the Prior, whom God rescued from a life of great luxury so that he might take this habit: He has amply rewarded him in the spirituality of his friars.

We received great kindness there. They gave us some of the things they had in the church for the house we were about to found: and, as this saintly woman had been beloved by so many important persons, the church was well provided with ornaments. I felt very happy at being there, though I also felt a shame, which still persists, when I realized that she who had endured such severe penance was a woman like myself, more delicately nurtured, to judge from her position, and less of a sinner than I— in this respect there can be no comparison between us—yet I received from Our Lord much greater favours, and, considering the seriousness of my sins, it is a very great mercy that I am not already in hell. The one thing which brought me comfort was my desire to imitate her, if I could, though the comfort was not great, for my whole life has been spent in desires: it is in my deeds that I fail. May I be aided by the compassion of God, in which I have always put my trust through His Most Holy Son and the Virgin Our Lady, whose habit, through the goodness of the Lord, I wear.

One day, after communicating in that holy church, I became deeply recollected, and my faculties were suspended, so that I

---

[1] The date was May 11, 1577.
[2] St. Teresa writes "Fray" (Juan de León) which P. Gracián altered to "Don". The person in question was apparently not a friar, or even a priest.

was carried out of myself. While in that condition I had an intellectual vision of this saintly woman, as a glorified body, accompanied by angels. She told me not to grow weary but to strive to carry forward the work of making these foundations. I gathered, though she did not say so, that she was helping me before God. She also told me something else which there is no need to write down here. I was very much cheered and felt eager to go on with the work, and I hope, in the goodness of the Lord, that with such good help as these prayers will bring me I may be able in some degree to serve Him. You see by this, my sisters, that these trials of hers are now over and that the glory which she is enjoying will be everlasting. And now, for the love of the Lord, let us strive to follow this sister of ours. By hating ourselves, as she hated herself, we shall finish our course, for everything passes quickly and comes to an end.

We arrived at Villanueva de la Jara on the first Sunday of Lent, which was the eve of the Feast of Saint Peter's Chair and Saint Barbatian's day, in the year 1580.[1] On that same day, at the hour of High Mass, the Most Holy Sacrament was brought into the church of the glorious Saint Anne. The whole municipality, and several other people, including Doctor Ervias, came out to receive us, and we alighted at the church of the town, which was a long way from that of Saint Anne. So great was the people's joy that it made me very happy to see what pleasure it gave them to receive the Order of the most holy Virgin Our Lady. We could hear the bells ringing from a great distance. When we had entered the church, they began the Te Deum, one verse being taken by the choir, accompanied by the organ, and the next by the organ alone. When this was over, they brought the Most Holy Sacrament on a portable platform and on another a statue of Our Lady, with crosses and banners. The procession continued with great solemnity. We, in our white mantles and with veiled faces, walked in the middle of the procession next to the Most Holy Sacrament. Following us came our Discalced friars from the monastery, of whom there were a great many. The Franciscans (for there is a Franciscan house in the town) were also there, as well as a Dominican friar who happened to be in the place, and, although he was the only one, I was very pleased to see that habit there. As the route was a long one, many altars had been erected. At several points the procession stopped, and recited something about our Order, which moved us to great devotion, as it also did to see that all were praising the great God Whom we had present with us, and that for His sake so much notice was taken of us seven poor Discalced nuns who

[1] February 21, 1580.

were there. None the less, when I thought of this, it filled me with confusion: I remembered that I was one of them, and that, if I had had my deserts, they would all have turned against me.

I have given this long account of the honour paid here to the Virgin's habit so that you may praise Our Lord and beseech Him to make use of this foundation, for it affords me more pleasure when a foundation is made in face of great persecution and many trials and I derive a greater satisfaction from describing it to you. And, in fact, these sisters who were there had been suffering trials for almost six years—at least for more than the five and a half years which have passed since they entered this house of the glorious Saint Anne. I say nothing of the poverty and trials which they suffered in the gaining of their daily bread, for they would never ask alms, lest it should be thought that they were there in order to be fed by others. Nor do I speak of the lives of great penance which they lived, eating little and fasting often, sleeping in poor beds and living in a very small house, which was a great trial in view of the strictness with which they always observed their enclosure.

Their greatest trial, they told me, was their burning desire to wear the habit, which was a source of torment to them by night and by day: they began to think that they would never see a habit. Their whole prayer was that God would grant them this favour, and this prayer they commonly offered up with tears.[1] When they saw any obstacle arising, they would become greatly distressed and increase their penances. They gave up some of their food so that out of their earnings they might pay the messengers whom they sent me and make what return they could in their poverty to those who might be of some help to them. I myself, since knowing them and observing their saintliness, have been quite sure that their prayers and tears must have won them admission into the Order; and so I have considered that the Order possesses a greater treasure in having such souls than if it had a large income, and I hope that the house will make great progress.

When we entered the house, they were all standing at the inner door, each one in her distinctive garments. They were dressed as they had been when they first came to the house, for they had never wanted to dress like religious women living in the world,[2]

---

[1] According to the Convent records, the nine *beatas* took the habit on St. Matthias' Day (February 24), 1580, three of them as lay sisters. Their names in religion were María de Jesús, María de la Asunción, Lucía de Santa Ana, Ángela de la Trinidad, Inés de la Encarnación, Ana de la Madre de Dios, Catalina de San Alberto, Catalina de San Ángelo and Elvira de San José. The sermon was preached by P. Antonio de Jesús.

[2] [Sp., *beatas*. Cf. Vol. I, p. 241, above.]

but preferred to wait for the habit; the dress they were wearing, however, was very modest. It was quite clear from this how little they thought about themselves; they were so shabbily clad, and almost all of them were so thin, that it was evident they had been living a life of great penitence.

They received us with abundant tears of great joy, which were clearly not feigned. Their great virtue was evident from their happiness, their humility and their obedience to the Prioress and to all those who came to make the foundation, whom they could not do enough to please. Their sole fear was that, when the nuns saw the poverty and smallness of the house, they might go away again. None of them had ever assumed authority over the rest, but each, with deep sisterly love, had laboured as best she could. Two of them, the two eldest, did any business concerning the house that was necessary; the others never spoke with anyone or had any desire to do so. There was no house key, but only a bolt on the door, and none of them ever presumed to answer the door except the eldest. They slept very little, so as to earn their daily bread and to lose no time for prayer, on which they spent a great many hours: on festivals they would pray the whole day long.

As manuals of prayer they used the books of Fray Luis de Granada and Fray Peter of Alcántara. The greater part of their time was spent in the recitation of the Divine Offices, though only one of them read well and the remainder could read only a little, and their breviaries were not all of the same kind. Some of them were of the old Roman variety and had been given them by clergy who no longer used them. Others they had got as best they could. As they read so badly they would spend many hours on them. They did not recite the Office where anyone from outside could hear them. God will have accepted their intention and labour, but they can have said very little that was correct. When Fray Antonio de Jesús took over their direction, he allowed them to recite nothing but the Office of Our Lady. They had their oven in which they baked their bread, and they did everything in a methodical way, just as if they had been under orders.

All this made me praise Our Lord; and the more I had to do with them, the more pleased I was that I had come. Whatever trials I might have had to suffer, I should never, I think, have shirked coming to comfort these souls. Those of my companions who remained there told me that, for the first few days, they felt some repugnance at having to do so, but, once they got to know them and appreciate their virtue, they were very glad to stay with them and came to love them very dearly. A great deal can be accomplished by sanctity and virtue. And in fact these nuns were so good that, however many the difficulties and trials they might encounter, they would bear them all with the help of the Lord, as their desire is to suffer in His service; and any sister who does not feel this desire must not consider herself a true Discalced nun, for our desires must be directed, not towards rest but towards suffering, so that we may in some measure imitate our true Spouse. May it please His Majesty to give us grace for this. Amen.

This hermitage of Saint Anne began as follows. There lived here, in Villanueva de la Jara, the place under consideration, a cleric who was a native of Zamora and who had been a friar of Our Lady of Carmel. He was devoted to the glorious Saint Anne. His name was Diego de Guadalajara. He established this hermitage near his house so as to have somewhere to hear Mass. So deep was his devotion that he went to Rome and obtained a bull, with many indulgences, for this church or hermitage. He was a virtuous and a recollected man. When about to die, he made a will bequeathing us this house and all its contents for use as a convent of Our Lady of Carmel; if that were not practicable, a chaplain was to live in it and say a number of Masses each week, provided that, once the convent was established, there should be no further obligation for these Masses to be said.

For more than twenty years, therefore, the place was served by a chaplain. The property was in a bad state, for, although these girls went to live in the house, nothing but the house was theirs. The chaplain lived in another building belonging to the same foundation, which he will now give up to us with the rest— there is not a great deal of it. But so great is God's mercy that He will not fail to help a house dedicated to the glorious mother of Our Lady. May it please His Majesty ever to be served in it and may all creatures praise Him for ever and ever. Amen.

CHAPTER XXIX

Describes the foundation of Saint Joseph of Our Lady of the Street, in Palencia, on the Feast of King David in the year 1580.

When I had returned from the foundation of Villanueva de la Jara, my superior ordered me to go to Valladolid: this was at the request of the Bishop of Palencia, Don Álvaro de Mendoza,[1]

---

[1] Don Álvaro de Mendoza (cf. Vol. I, p. 232, above) came to Palencia as Bishop on February 9, 1578, nearly eight months after his appointment to the see and more than two years after its last occupant had died.

who accepted and helped the first of our convents—Saint Joseph's, Ávila—and always helps us in anything to do with this Order. He had left the diocese of Ávila on being translated to Palencia, where Our Lord put it into his heart to have another convent of this holy Order founded. When I reached Valladolid, I contracted such a serious illness that they thought I should die.[1] I was so listless and so mistrustful of my own powers that, although importuned by the Prioress of our Valladolid convent,[2] who was very anxious for this foundation to be made, I could not persuade myself to undertake it nor had I the means requisite for doing so. For the convent would have to be founded in poverty, and they told me the place was so poor that its maintenance would be impossible.

The foundation, together with the Burgos foundation, had been under discussion for more than a year, and previously I had been less disinclined to make it. But, when I went to Valladolid for this express purpose, I found that the project had many inconveniences. I am not sure whether this discovery was due to the great trouble and weakness caused by my illness, or whether the devil wanted to hinder the good that was afterwards done. The fact is, I am as amazed as I am distressed— and I often complain to Our Lord about this—to see how the poor soul has to share in the frailty of the body: it really seems as if it has to observe the same laws and participate in its needs and in things which cause it suffering.[3]

This, I think, is one of the great trials and miseries of life, when we have not much spirituality with which to control it. It is a trial to be ill and suffer great pains, but I think nothing of it if my soul is awake, for it will then be praising God and reflecting that these things come from His hand. But it is a terrible thing to be suffering on the one hand and yet achieving nothing on the other, especially if a soul is conscious of fervent desires to know neither inward nor outward rest, but to spend itself wholly in the service of its great God. In such a case it has no other remedy than patience, knowledge of its wretchedness and a resignation to the will of God, so that He may use it for whatever He pleases and as He pleases. I was in this state then: though still convalescent, I was suffering from such weakness that I had lost even the confidence which God had been wont to give me when I was about to begin a foundation. I felt that everything was impossible: it would have been a great

---

[1] This was a recurrence of an illness which she had had some six months earlier at Toledo. [See Vol. I, p. xxxv, above.]

[2] Her own niece, M. María Bautista.

[3] [I read *padecer* (" suffer ") for the *parecer* (" appear ") of the editions, which seems to make no sense.]

help had I been able to find anyone to encourage me; but some only increased my fears, while others, though they gave me some hope, were powerless to overcome my weakness.

It was just then that there happened to arrive a Father of the Company, called Master Ripalda:[1] he was a great servant of God and at one time he used to hear my confessions. I told him what a state I was in and said that I should like to put him in the place of God and ask him to give me his opinion about it. He began to encourage me a great deal and said that this cowardice was the effect of old age. But I was quite sure this was not so, for I am now older still and yet it has all left me. He cannot really have believed it himself, but said it to reprove me lest I should think my condition was of God. The foundations of Palencia and Burgos then continued side by side. I had no means for making either, but that was no disadvantage, for I generally began with less than nothing. He told me I must on no account abandon the idea: the same thing had been said to me previously at Toledo by a Provincial of the Society, Baltasar Álvarez by name,[2] but at that time I had been in good health.

This advice was not sufficient to make me decide to proceed; for, though I was influenced by it a good deal, I could not bring myself to make a definite resolution. I was held back either by the devil or, as I have suggested, by my illness, though I was now a great deal better. The Valladolid Prioress gave me all the help she could, for she was very anxious for the foundation to be made at Palencia; but she was also very much afraid when she saw how lukewarm I was. We need to be truly on fire or neither people nor servants of God will be able to help us; from this it will be seen that as a rule it is not I who am responsible for these foundations, but that they are the work of Him Who is Almighty.

One day, when I had just communicated, and was immersed in these doubts and irresolute about proceeding with either of the foundations, I had begged Our Lord to give me light so that in all things I might do His will, for my lukewarmness was not of such a kind that this desire ever left me. Our Lord said to me, in a tone of reproach: "What dost thou fear? When have I ever failed thee? I am the same now as I have always been. Do not give up either of these two foundations." O great God! How different are Thy words from the words of men! My courage and resolution now returned, and the whole world

---

[1] Cf. Vol. I, pp. 6, 320, above.
[2] To St. Teresa's great grief, P. Álvarez died in this same year 1580. The news of his death reached her when she was at Medina del Campo, on her way to Valladolid to see the Bishop.

would not have been sufficient to put any obstacles in my way. So I set to work at once on the matter and Our Lord began to provide me with the means.

I took two nuns so as to be able to buy the house: although they told me it would not be possible to live on alms in Palencia, I took no notice whatever of this warning, for I saw clearly that it would be impossible just then to obtain an endowment for it, and, as God had said that it was to be founded, His Majesty would provide the means. So, though I was not yet quite well again, and despite the severity of the weather, I determined to go. I left Valladolid on Holy Innocents' Day in the year I have mentioned,[1] a gentleman at Palencia having given us a house from the beginning of the New Year until midsummer. It was a house which he had on a lease and he had gone to live elsewhere.

I wrote to a Canon in the same city:[2] I did not know him but a friend of his had told me that he was a servant of God and I was convinced that he would be a great help to us, because the Lord Himself (and this has happened with regard to my other foundations) chooses someone to help Him everywhere— His Majesty well knows how little I can do myself. I sent to the Canon to beg him to get the house vacated for me with as much secrecy as he could, for there was someone still living there. He was not, however, to tell that person for what purpose it was needed; for, although several important people had shown good will in the matter, and the Bishop was very well disposed to us, I saw that it would be safer if no one knew.

Canon Reinoso (for that was the name of the person to whom I wrote) did this for us so well that not only was the house vacated but beds were provided for us there and other comforts in great abundance; and we had need of them, for the cold was intense and the previous day had been a very trying one, with a fog so thick that we could hardly see one another. We really had very little rest until everything was prepared for the saying of Mass on the next day, but we were in the house before anyone knew about it. This practice I have found it convenient to observe in making these foundations, for, if one begins asking people's opinions, the devil upsets everything: he cannot, of course, accomplish his aim but he does disturb people. So it was done; and early in the morning, when it was scarcely dawn, a priest whom we had with us, called Porras, a great servant of God, said Mass, as did another friend of the Valladolid nuns named

[1] December 28, 1580.
[2] She had actually written to this Canon, Don Jerónimo Reinoso, a native of Valladolid, before leaving that city. Four of her letters to him are extant.

Agustín de Vitoria,[1] who had lent me money for the furnishing of the house and had been a great comfort on the way.

Including myself, there were five nuns,[2] and a lay sister who has been with me for some time as my companion:[3] she is so great a servant of God and so discreet that she can help me more than others who are choir-nuns. That night we slept little, although, as I say, the journey had been tiring because of the rain.

I was very glad that the foundation had been made on the day on which there is a commemoration of King David[4], for I have a great devotion to him. On that same morning I at once sent a message to the most illustrious Bishop, who did not yet know that I was coming on that day. With the great kindness which he has always shown us, he came to see us immediately. He told us he would give us all the bread we needed, and instructed his steward to provide a great many things for us. This Order is so much indebted to him that any of its members who may read the story of these foundations must in duty bound commend him to Our Lord, whether he be living or dead, and I ask you, of your charity, to do this. Such great and widespread pleasure was shown by the people as to be quite remarkable and there was no one who showed any disapproval. The fact that the Bishop was known to have desired our coming was a great help to us, for he is much loved, but the people as a whole are the best and noblest I have seen and every day I rejoice more and more that I made the foundation there.

As the house we were in was not our own, we at once began to discuss buying another; for, although this one was for sale, it was in a very bad situation; and I thought the help I should have from the nuns who were coming to us would serve as a basis for negotiations. Little as this was in itself, it was a good deal for that place; though, if God had not given us the good friends He did, it would all have been to no purpose. Good Canon Reinoso brought with him a friend, Canon Salinas, a very kind

[1] Vitoria was a wealthy, pious and charitable citizen of Valladolid who had befriended the Discalced Carmelites in that city and whose daughter María was professed as a Carmelite there, in 1585, as María de San Agustín.

[2] St. Teresa took with her a cousin, Inés de Jesús, who had professed at the Incarnation, Ávila, Catalina del Espíritu Santo, María de San Bernardo and Juana de San Francisco; she also had with her Vitoria, Porras and P. Gracián. Soon after reaching Palencia, she sent to Salamanca for Isabel de Jesús and Beatriz de Jesús, who became Prioress and Sub-Prioress respectively.

[3] Ana de San Bartolomé, who had gone with St. Teresa on her travels since her accident on Christmas Eve, 1577, when she had fallen on the staircase at St. Joseph's, Ávila, and broken an arm. A good deal of biographical material is available in Spanish concerning this remarkable woman, who, on May 6, 1917, was beatified by Benedict XV.

[4] December 29, 1580.

and understanding man; between them, they took up the affair
as zealously as if it were their own—I think I might even say
more so—and they have always shown a great interest in this
house.

There is a house in the town, used as a hermitage, and visited
by people who have a deep devotion to Our Lady, called Our
Lady of the Street. In all the district and town great devotion
is felt for it and it is frequented by many people. It seemed to
His Lordship, and to us all, that it would be a good thing if
we were near that church. There was no house attached to it,
but there were two quite near, which, if we bought them, would
be sufficient for us if we had the church as well. The church
would have to be made over to us by the Chapter and a confraternity connected with it, and negotiations about this were
set in train. The Chapter at once made us a present of it, and,
although a good deal had to be done before an understanding
was reached with the confraternity, this was also achieved in
due course, for, as I have said, they are very good people in that
town, as good as any I have seen in my life.

When the owners of the houses saw that we were anxious to
buy them, they very properly put up their price. I thought it
well to go and inspect them and they seemed to me so poor
that I would not look at them, nor would those who accompanied us. Later it became clear that the devil was taking a
large hand in this, because of his annoyance at our coming.
The two Canons concerned thought the houses too far from the
Cathedral, as they were, though situated in the most densely
populated part of the city. In the end we all decided that they
would not be suitable for us and we should have to look elsewhere. This the two Canons began to do with such care and
diligence that I praised Our Lord and refrained from taking
no step that seemed to them advisable. At last they found a
house they liked which belonged to a person called Tamayo.
Some parts of it seemed very suitable for us, and near it was
the house of a prominent gentleman of the city, Suero de Vega
by name,[1] who is very well disposed to us and was most anxious
that we should go there, as were other people in the district.

The house in question was not large enough, but with it they
gave us another, though this was not of such a kind that we
could make use of the two together. When I had heard all that
they had to say about it, I was anxious for the purchase to be

---

[1] Suero de Vega, son of Juan de Vega, President of the Royal Council, was known in
Palencia as " Father of the poor ". Gracián has a good deal to say about him, both
in the *Peregrinación de Anastasio*, Diálogo XIII, and in his notes to Ribera's account
of this Palencian foundation. A son of Suero's took the habit of the Carmelite Reform
as Juan de la Madre de Dios.

made, but the Canons would not agree to this unless I saw it first. I had not wanted to go about the town so much, and I trusted them sufficiently to make it unnecessary. But eventually I went, and I also visited the houses near the church of Our Lady—not, however, with the intention of taking them, but merely so that the owner of the other house should not think we had no choice but to take his. As I have said, they looked to me, and to my companions, very poor, though we were astonished now that they could have appeared so to us. Thereupon we went to the second house, with our minds made up that none but this would suit us; we found many difficulties, but we ignored them, although they would have been very hard to overcome, for, in order to make a church, we should have had to take all the best living-rooms, and even then it would not have been a good one.

It is strange how one can make up one's mind to do a thing beforehand. The experience certainly taught me to have little confidence in myself, though in this case I was not the only one to be mistaken. When we left, we were quite decided in our own minds that no other house would suit us and were prepared to give what had been asked for it, which was a great deal, and to write about it to the owner, who was not in the city but lived quite near.

It will seem irrelevant for me to have spent so much time in discussing the purchase of the house until it becomes clear what the devil's object must have been in trying to prevent us from going to the house of Our Lady: whenever I think of it, I feel afraid.

As I have said, we all left the second house determined to take it, but on the next day, during Mass, I began to feel very much concerned as to whether I had done right, and was so restless about it that I could hardly remain quiet till Mass was over. I went up to receive the Most Holy Sacrament, and, as I took it, I heard the words: "That is the house for thee," in such a way that I felt completely decided to purchase, not the house I now had in mind, but the house of Our Lady. Then I began to think how difficult the change of plan would be now that the negotiations had been carried so far and those who had so carefully considered the matter had such a decided preference. But the Lord answered me: "They do not realize how much offence is done to Me there: this will be a great reparation." The idea passed through my mind that these words might be a delusion, yet I did not believe they were, for in the effect they produced on me I clearly recognized the working of the Spirit of God. Then He said to me at once: "It is I."

I now became quite calm and was no longer worried, as I had been previously, though I did not know how I could undo what had been done and correct the very bad impression I had given about that house; for I had spoken strongly to my sisters about its unsuitability and I should not have liked them on any account to go there without seeing it. However, I did not worry so much about this, for I knew they would approve anything I did: I was more concerned about the wishes of other people. I thought they would consider me vain and changeable for altering my opinion so quickly, and that is a thing which I greatly dislike. But none of these reflections was sufficient to make me give up the house of Our Lady, nor did I now think any longer of its disadvantages; for, if our going there could prevent the commission of a single venial sin, everything else would be of little account, and any of the nuns, I think, would have agreed with me, had they known what I knew.

The means I adopted were these. I was making my confessions at that time to Canon Reinoso, one of the two clerics who were helping me. I had never previously spoken to him of any spiritual experience of this kind, for no occasion of doing so had presented itself. But, as I have always been accustomed in these matters to do what my confessor advises, so that I may be travelling by the safest road, I resolved to tell him about this experience under the seal of secrecy, although I should never have decided without the deepest distress to refrain from doing what I had understood to be the Lord's will. None the less, I should have ended by doing whatever he ordered me, for I trusted in Our Lord that He would do what I had known Him do before, and change my confessor's opinion so that he would do what He willed.

I first told him on how many occasions Our Lord had been accustomed to teach me in this way, and how many things had already happened by which I had learned that His Spirit was at work in me. I then related to him what had now taken place, adding that I would follow his opinion, however much it hurt me to do so. He is a most prudent and saintly man, and, young as he is,[1] gives good advice in everything. Although he saw that a change of plan would occasion some remark, his decision was not that I should depart from what I had understood to be God's will. I suggested to him that we ought to wait for the messenger, and he agreed with me: in making this suggestion I was trusting God to find a way out of the difficulty. And so He did; for the owner of the house, who had been promised what he wanted and had asked of us, now demanded three

[1] He was thirty-five years old at the time, thirty years younger than St. Teresa.

hundred ducats more, which seemed ridiculous, for he was being paid too much already. We saw that this was the work of God, for the owner was anxious to sell the house and obviously he was not acting in his own interests by asking more after a sum had been agreed upon.

This made the problem a great deal easier. We now told him that we should be unable to do business with him, though this did not settle everything, for it was clear that for the sake of three hundred ducats we ought not to give up a house which seemed suitable for a convent. I told my confessor not to trouble about my reputation if he himself thought the house should be given up, but merely to tell his companions that I had determined to buy the house of Our Lady, whether it cost much or little, and whether it was in a bad condition or in a good one. His companion hasan extremely quick mind; and, though nothing was said to him, I think he must have guessed what had happened when he saw how suddenly I had changed my plans. So he never pressed me on the subject further.

Since then we have all seen what a great mistake we should have made in buying the other house: and we are amazed now when we consider how much greater are the advantages of the one we have. The chief advantage in our having taken it, which is very evident, is that Our Lord and His glorious Mother are well served in it and that numerous occasions of sin have been averted, for a great many nightly vigils used to be kept there, and, as it was only a hermitage, many things might have been done, the cessation of which would trouble the devil, while we on our part are glad to be able in some degree to serve our Mother and Lady and Patroness. We made a very great mistake in not having bought the house earlier: we ought never to have looked any farther. It is clear now that the devil was blinding us, and in a great many respects too, for the house has numerous advantages which we should never have found elsewhere, and the townspeople, who had been anxious that we should take it, were simply delighted when we did so: even those who had wanted us to go to the other house thought our choice an excellent one later on.

Blessed for ever and ever be He Who gave me light in this matter, as He does whenever I manage to do anything well, for every day I grow more astonished at the little ability I have for anything. It must not be supposed that this is humility; it is just that I see the thing more clearly every day. It seems to be Our Lord's will that both I and everyone else shall recognize that it is His Majesty alone who does these things, and that, just as He gave sight to the blind man by putting clay on his eyes, so His will is that a person as blind as I should not act blindly. There were various ways, as I have said, in which we acted very blindly indeed here, and, whenever I remember them, I feel like praising Our Lord yet again, though I am unfit to do so and I do not know how He bears with me. Blessed be His mercy. Amen.

These saintly friends of the Virgin now made great haste to conclude the purchase of the houses, and I think they got them very cheaply. They worked extremely hard, for in each of our foundations God is pleased to grant merit to those who help us: it is only I who do nothing, as I have said on other occasions, and as I should like never to stop saying, for it is the truth. The work they did in getting the house ready for us, in advancing the money for it (for I had none) and in standing surety for us was most valuable. In other places, until I have discovered someone who will stand as our surety, and that for a smaller sum than was needed here, I have found myself in great trouble; and not without cause, for, apart from my trust in Our Lord, I have not a farthing. But His Majesty has always been so gracious to me that no one has ever lost anything by trusting me, nor has ever failed to be repaid in full. I look upon that as a very great sign of the Lord's favour.

As the owners of the house were not satisfied with my two friends as sureties, the latter went in search of the Bishop's steward, whose name was Prudencio (I am not quite sure if I am right about that: they tell me now that that was his name, but, as we always spoke of him as the steward, I never heard it).[1] He has been so kind to us that we have been very much in his debt and still are. He asked them where they were going: they replied that they were looking for him to see if he would sign the bond. He laughed and said: "So you are coming like this to get me to stand security for all that money, are you?" And he signed the bond on the spot, without even dismounting from his mule, which is a thing worth remembering in these times.

I should be sorry to be backward in praising all the kindness which I found in Palencia, both in the people as a whole and in individuals.[2] Their attitude seemed to me quite like that of the primitive Church, and it is not a very common attitude in the world to-day. They knew that we had no money, and that

---

[1] His full name was Prudencio de Armentia. Besides being the Bishop's steward, he was a Canon of the Cathedral. Three of the other Canons, Martín Alonso de Salinas, Jerónimo Reinoso and Juan Rodríguez de Santa Cruz, joined him as co-sureties.

[2] The community remained in their first house until 1591 and then moved to the site of their present convent in the Calle de la Virreina.

they would have to provide us with food, and yet not only did they not forbid us to settle among them, but they said that in sending us God was granting them the very greatest of favours. And if the matter is looked at in the proper light, they were telling the truth, for, even had we done no more than give them another church for the Most Holy Sacrament to be reserved in, that is a great deal.

May He be blessed for ever. Amen. It is becoming clearer and clearer that He is'pleased to be here and that in the past there must have been improper conduct going on which goes on no longer. For many people used to keep vigils in the hermit-age; and, as it was lonely, they did not all come for reasons of devotion; but in this respect things are improving. The image of Our Lady had been put in a most unseemly place. The Bishop, Don Álvaro de Mendoza, has now, on his own initiative, built a chapel for it, and gradually many other things are being done to the honour and glory of this glorious Virgin and her Son. May He be for ever praised. Amen. Amen.

When the house was at last ready and the time had arrived for the nuns to enter it, the Bishop was anxious that they should do so with great solemnity, and so this was done on a day within the octave of the Feast of the Most Holy Sacrament.[1] The Bishop came himself from Valladolid, and the Chapter and the Orders came also. Nearly the whole town was present and there was a great deal of music. We all went in procession, from the house where we were staying, wearing our white mantles and with faces veiled, to a parish church near the house of Our Lady. There her image was awaiting us and we took the Most Holy Sacrament thence and reserved it in our church in due order and with great solemnity: the ceremony caused much devotion. There were also some nuns who had come for the foundation at Soria; they all had candles in their hands. I think the Lord was greatly praised there on that day. May it please Him to be for ever praised by all creatures. Amen. Amen.

While I was in Palencia it pleased God to bring about the separation between the Discalced and Calced Orders and to give each of them a province of its own, which was all that we desired for our peace and quietness. On the petition of our Catholic King, Don Philip, a brief conferring amplest powers to this effect was obtained from Rome, and His Majesty helped us a great deal in bringing the matter to a conclusion, as he had

---

[1] The ceremony took place on June 1, 1581. Besides the Bishop, the Chapter and representatives of the religious Orders, there were present the civic authorities of Palencia. St. Teresa, followed by her nuns, walked in the procession between the Bishop and Canon Reinoso. Among the Carmelite friars who attended were P. Nicolás Doria and P. Juan de Jesús (Roca).

helped us at the beginning. A Chapter was held at Alcalá by order of a reverend Father, Fray Juan de las Cuevas, who at that time was Prior at Talavera. He belongs to the Order of Saint Dominic and was nominated by His Majesty and appointed at Rome. He is a most holy and prudent man, as he has need to be for a task like this. The King bore the cost of it and at his command the whole University helped us. The Chapter was held in the Discalced College of Saint Cyril which we have there, in great peace and concord. It elected as Provincial Father-Master Fray Jerónimo Gracián de la Madre de Dios.[1]

As these Fathers will write elsewhere of what happened, there is no reason why I should describe it here. I have mentioned it because it was while we were labouring over this foundation that Our Lord accomplished a work which was of great moment to the honour and glory of His glorious Mother, since the Order is hers and she is our Lady and Patroness. This proved to be one of the most joyful and satisfying experiences that I could ever have in this life, and I had been suffering trials, persecutions and afflictions for more than five-and-twenty years: it would take a long time to recount them all; only Our Lord can know of them. And when I saw that they were all at an end, only those who know the trials we had endured can understand what joy filled my heart and how I longed that the whole world should praise Our Lord and that we should pray to Him for this holy King of ours, Don Philip, through whose mediation God brought everything to such a good end, for the devil had used such crafts that, had it not been for the King, all our work would have come to nothing.

Now, Calced and Discalced alike, we are all at peace, and no one hinders us in Our Lord's service. Therefore, my brothers and sisters, make haste to serve His Majesty, Who has so abundantly answered our prayers. Let those who are now with us consider the favours He has granted us, of which they have been witnesses, and also the trials and anxieties from which He has delivered us. And as for those who are to come after us, and who will find everything made plain for them, let them, for the love of Our Lord, allow no practice which makes for perfection to fall into abeyance. Let it never be said of them, as is said of some other Orders, that they do nothing but laud their beginnings. It is we who are the beginners now; but let

---

[1] [For the chronology of these events, see Outline of the life of St. Teresa, Vol. I, pp. xxvii-xxxvi, above.] Some delay was occasioned in the execution of the Brief of June 22, 1580, by the death of P. Pedro Fernández, to whom this work had been entrusted by the Pope. In January 1581, P. Juan de las Cuevas, Dominican Prior at Talavera de la Reina, was appointed in P. Fernández's place and the separation was effected on March 3.

them continually strive to be beginners too, in the sense of growing better and better all the time. Let them keep watch over the most trifling things and realize that the devil is always boring little holes through which in time great faults may enter. Let them never say: "This does not matter. We are being too particular about this." Oh, my daughters, everything matters if it is not helping us to make progress.

For the love of Our Lord I beg them to remember how quickly everything comes to an end, and how gracious Our Lord has been to us in bringing us to this Order, and how severely anyone will be punished who countenances any relaxation of this Rule. Fix your eyes always on the race from which we have sprung—the race of those holy prophets. How many saints we have in Heaven who wore this habit! Let us, with a holy boldness, and with the help of God, dare to be like them. The battle, my sisters, will last but a short time, and the end is eternal. Let us set aside things which in themselves are nothing for others which will bring us to that end which is no end, so that we may love and serve Him better, for He will live for ever and ever. Amen. Amen.

Thanks be given to God.

CHAPTER XXX

Describes the foundation of the convent of the Most Holy Trinity, in the city of Soria. This foundation was made in the year 1581. The first Mass was said on the Feast of our Father Saint Eliseus.

When I was in Palencia, working on the foundation there which has already been described, I was brought a letter from the Bishop of Osma, Doctor Velázquez. I had first got into touch with him when he was Canon and Professor at Toledo Cathedral, at a time when I was troubled by various fears, for I knew he was a most learned man and a servant of God, so I begged him very earnestly to take an interest in me and to hear my confession.[1] Busy as he was, he realized my need, and, when I asked him to do this for the love of Our Lord, he so readily acceded to my request that I was astounded. He became my confessor and director for the whole time I was in Toledo, which was a considerable period. I described my spiritual life to him with all frankness, as I am accustomed to do; and he helped

---

[1] For St. Teresa's earlier relations with Dr. Velázquez, who went to Osma as Bishop in 1578, see Vol. I, pp. 334–7, above.

me so much that from that time onwards I began to have fewer misgivings. There was, as a matter of fact, another reason for this, which it would not be suitable to describe here. But he really benefited me a great deal, for he reassured me by quoting Holy Scripture, which is the way that most helps me, when I am sure that a person understands what he is quoting, and that he leads a good life; and I was quite sure that he did both.

He wrote me this letter from Soria, where he was living at that time. It said that a lady who was a penitent of his there had discussed with him the foundation of a convent of our nuns. He approved of the idea and had told her that he would get me to go there and make the foundation and that I must not fail him. If I thought it was an expedient thing to do I was to let him know and he would then send for me. I was delighted at this; for, apart from the fact that the foundation would be useful, I was anxious to discuss certain spiritual matters with him and to see him, for, on account of the great spiritual help he had given me, I had become greatly attached to him.

The name of the lady who provided the foundation is Doña Beatriz de Beamonte y Navarra. She is descended from the royal house of Navarre and is the daughter of Don Francés de Beamonte, a man of high and illustrious lineage.[1] She had been married for some years and had no children and for a long time she had been anxious to found a convent. When she discussed the idea with the Bishop he told her about this Discalced Order of Our Lady and she thought the idea such a good one that she pressed him to carry it out as soon as possible.

She is a person of a very gentle disposition and of great generosity, and she leads a life of penitence; in short, she is a great servant of God. She had a good house in Soria, well built and excellently situated, which she said she would give us, together with all we needed to make the foundation; and this she did, by providing us with securities at five per cent, bringing in an income of five hundred ducats yearly.[2] The Bishop offered to give us an excellent church, with a vaulted roof, belonging to the neighbouring parish, which has been of great use to us,

---

[1] Besides providing so liberally for the Soria foundation, Doña Beatriz de Beamonte also helped the foundation made at Pamplona in 1583, which latter house she then entered as Beatriz de Cristo, living there till her death in 1600.

[2] [The securities are described by St. Teresa as *juros*. The dividends on these were guaranteed by the State, which as a rule gave the securities to the holder, in return for the gift of a sum of money. Thus Isabel the Catholic once offered an annual income in perpetuity of 1,000 *maravedis* in exchange for a gift of 10,000. In the phrase " de a xxv el millar ", here rendered " at five per cent," the " xxv " is explained by La Fuente (I, 453) as being an editorial misinterpretation for " 20,000 "—i.e. the capital value of the securities on redemption would be twenty times the income.]

a covered way connecting it with our convent. He was able to do this quite easily, as it was a poor church, and there are a great many in the town, so he transferred the parish elsewhere. He gave me an account of all this in a letter. I discussed it with the Father Provincial, who was there at the time, and both he and all our friends thought I should send a letter by messenger asking for someone to come and fetch me, as the Palencia foundation was now made. I was delighted to do this, for the reasons already given.

I began to get together the nuns whom I was to take there with me: there were seven of them, for the lady had wanted more rather than fewer, and a lay sister and my companion and myself.[1] A messenger came in a coach expressly to fetch us; I had said that I would bring two Discalced Fathers with me, so I took Fray Nicolás de Jesús María,[2] a native of Genoa and a man of great distinction and perfection. He had taken the habit at the age of over forty, I believe (at least, he is over forty now and it is not long since he entered the Order)[3], but he has made such progress in so short a time that it is evident Our Lord chose him to help the Order in those troublesome persecutions, for, of all the others who might have helped us, some were exiled and the rest were in prison. As he held no office (because, as I say, he has been so short a time in the Order) they took less notice of him, or God ordained it that he should give me this help.

He is so discreet that, when he was at the Calced monastery in Madrid, he dissembled his purpose as though he were there on other business, and they never knew that he was working on our behalf and so allowed him to remain.[4] We wrote to each other frequently, for at that time I was at the convent of Saint Joseph, in Ávila; and we used to discuss the best methods of procedure, which was a comfort to him. That I should be taken so much notice of—for want, as we say, of a better[5]—will

---

[1] The seven nuns were: Catalina de Cristo (Prioress), Beatriz de Jesús (Sub-Prioress), María de Cristo, Juana Bautista, María de Jesús, María de San José-Catalina del Espíritu Santo. The lay sister was María Bautista; St. Teresa's personal companion, Ana de San Bartolomé. With them went P. Nicolás Doria and a lay brother, Fray Eliseo de la Madre de Dios [together, apparently (see p. 182, below), with Canon Ribera, of Palencia].

[2] P. Nicolás Doria was an Italian, born of a noble Genoese family in 1539, who spent his early life in business. His extraordinary business capacity brought him to the notice of King Philip II and of Don Cristóbal de Rojas, Archbishop of Seville, and he might have had a distinguished worldly career, but, conceiving a vocation for the religious life, he entered the Discalced Carmelite Reform in 1577. For his subsequent history, see S.S.M., II., 155–8.

[3] Actually he took the habit when he was two months from his thirty-eighth birthday.

[4] This refers to the period when P. Gracián was kept in the Calced Carmelite house in Madrid by order of the Papal Nuncio.

[5] The popular Spanish saying alluded to may be rendered: " For want of a better man they made my husband Mayor."

show what straits the Order was in during that period. For the whole of this time I had experience of his perfection and discretion, and so he is one of the persons in this Order whom I greatly love in the Lord, and of whom I have a very high opinion. He, then, and a lay companion went with us.

I had little trouble on this journey, for the Bishop's messenger showed great regard for our comfort and helped us to find good lodgings. When we entered the diocese of Osma we found that the Bishop was so much loved that, to get good accommodation, we had only to say we were on his business. The weather helped us; the distances we covered each day were not long; and so we had little trouble on the way and enjoyed the journey; and when I heard the good things that were said about the sanctity of the Bishop, I was delighted. We arrived at Burgo de Osma on the Wednesday in the octave of the Feast of the Most Holy Sacrament.[1] We communicated there on the Thursday, which was the octave-day, and the day after our arrival. As we could not reach Soria in a single day, we also dined there. We spent that night in a church, as there seemed to be no other lodging, and it was not at all bad. On the next day we heard Mass there and reached Soria at about five o'clock in the afternoon. The saintly Bishop was at one of the windows of his house when we passed and from it gave us his blessing: this was no small comfort to me, for the blessing of a prelate and a holy man is greatly to be esteemed.

The lady who was to be our foundress was awaiting us at the door of her house, which was the place where the convent was to be founded. We did not think it was a good time to go in, as there were many people about. And there was nothing unusual in that; for, wherever we go, the world is so fond of novelties that the number of people would be a great trial to us if our faces were not veiled: as we wear our veils, however, we can put up with it. The lady had prepared a very fine, large room, where Mass was to be said, for the covered way into the church which the Bishop was to give us had still to be made.[2] On the next day, Mass was said: it was the Feast of our Father Saint Eliseus.[3]

---

[1] May 31, 1581. Tradition says that the party stayed at the Bishop's Palace.

[2] In the contract by which Doña Beatriz ceded her house to the Discalced community is a clause reserving for herself and her servants two rooms to be connected with the church by a covered way, which would be used both by them and by the community independently of each other. The Convent remains to this day, with very few modifications. Doña Beatriz's rooms can still be seen, together with the small window, about eighteen inches square, by which she was allowed on occasions to communicate with the nuns. Part of the covered way, however, has disappeared.

[3] There is some uncertainty here as to dates. The party reached Soria on June 2, 1581, and, as the feast of St. Eliseus fell (according to the Carmelite Calendar, into

The lady had provided everything that we could need and she left us in that room, where we remained quietly until the covered way was completed. This was done by the Feast of the Transfiguration.[1] On that day the first Mass was said in the church with great solemnity and before a large congregation. The preacher was a Father of the Company of Jesus,[2] for the Bishop had gone to Burgo de Osma: he never allows a day, or an hour, to pass without working. Yet he was not well at that time and had lost the sight of one of his eyes. This was a great distress to me, for I felt very sad that his sight, which was so profitable in Our Lord's service, should be lost. But God's judgments are His own. He must have permitted this so that His servant might have more merit and prove his resignation to His will, for he worked ceaselessly just as he had done in the past. He told me that it was no more of an affliction to him than if it had happened to his neighbour, and that he sometimes thought it would not trouble him if he lost the sight of the other eye as well, for in that case he would retire to a hermitage and serve God there without having any other obligation. Before he was made a bishop he had always considered this to be his vocation: he used sometimes to talk to me about it, and had almost decided to give up everything and go.

This I could not bear, for I thought that he would be of great help to the Church of God, and so I was anxious that he should be what he now is, though on the day when they offered him the see, and he sent to tell me about it, I was greatly perturbed, thinking it would be such a grievous burden to him, and was unable to enjoy any peace of mind or to do anything about it but go into the choir and commend him to Our Lord. His Majesty at once set my mind at rest, telling me that he would be of great service to Him, and it seems that this is proving true. Not only has he this eye trouble, as well as other very grievous trials, and his continual work, but he fasts four days in the week and does other penances; his food, too, is very unattractive. When he pays visits, he goes on foot, a thing which his servants cannot bear and about which they have complained

---

which it was introduced in 1399) on June 14, the author would seem to be mistaken. The Bollandists think that some votive Mass of St. Eliseus may have been said on June 3. The Parisian Carmelites (*Oeuvres*, etc., IV, 166) believe that the festival itself was at that time kept in Spain on June 4, but in the one document they cite in support of this view the figure 1 might easily have been omitted. A possible explanation is that the phrase [*luego otro día*] translated "on the next day" means, as elsewhere in St. Teresa, "on a subsequent day": cf. p. 119, n. 1, below. The first Prioress was M. Catalina de Cristo, foundress of the Discalced Convents of Pamplona (1583) and Barcelona (1588).

[1] August 6, 1581.
[2] P. Francisco Carrera, according to Ribera.

to me. His servants have to be virtuous people or they are not allowed in his house. He has little confidence in the entrusting of serious business to vicars-general—or, I believe, any kind of business: he prefers it all to go through his own hands. During his first two years here, he had to suffer the most severe persecutions from false witnesses, at which I was amazed, for he is upright and sincere in all his judgments. By this time these persecutions were already coming to an end, though people still made accusations against him in court and wherever else they thought they could do him harm. But his good work throughout the diocese is already becoming known and so these accusations have little force, and he has borne them all so perfectly that he has confounded his enemies and done good to those who he knew were doing him wrong. Much as he has to do, he never fails to find time for prayer[1].

I seem to be growing absorbed in my eulogy of this holy man (though what I have said is not much); but I want it to be known that it is to him that we owe the foundation of the Most Holy Trinity in Soria, and the knowledge of this will be a happiness to those who are to live there. Nothing has been lost by this digression, which those who are now there know to be true. Though he did not provide us with the endowment, he gave us the church, and, as I say, it was he who encouraged this lady to help us: she, as I have said, was not lacking in Christian spirit, virtue and penitence.

When the passage into the church was completed and everything prepared which we needed for our enclosure, it became necessary for me to go to the convent of Saint Joseph in Ávila.[2] As soon as I knew of this, I set out, in the terrible heat, by a road which was very bad for carriages. With me went a prebendary from Palencia, Ribera by name, who had been of the greatest help to me in the making of the passage and in all other ways, for Father Nicolás de Jesús María had left as soon as the agreement for the foundation had been drawn up, as he was badly needed elsewhere. At the time we were going to Soria, Ribera had some business to do there, so he went with us. From that time forward God gave him such a desire to help us that we may commend him to His Majesty with the other benefactors of the Order.

[1] The chief cause of the trouble seems to have been his disciplinary zeal. In 1583 he was translated to Santiago de Compostela, where attacks on him were also made, and soon afterwards, by royal permission, he retired on a small pension. He died in 1587.

[2] St. Teresa left Soria for Ávila, with B. Ana de San Bartolomé and Canon Ribera, on August 16, 1581. At Osma she met P. Diego de Yepes (cf. Yepes, Book II, Chap. XXXIII). On September 10, she was elected Prioress of St. Joseph's, Ávila.

I had no wish for anyone else to travel with me and the nun who was accompanying me: he is so careful that he was quite sufficient, and the less the commotion we make, the better I get on with these journeys. But this time I paid dearly for the comfort which I had experienced on the last one; for, though the young man who went with us knew the road as far as Segovia, it was not the carriage road that he knew, so he took us into parts where we often had to alight, and the carriage went along steep precipices till it almost hung in the air. If we took guides with us, they would direct us for as far as they knew the road to be good, and then, before we came to a bad part, they would leave us and say they had now some business to do elsewhere. Before reaching our inn, as we were not at all sure of the country, we had to endure a great deal of sun and often to risk the overturning of the carriage. I was sorry for our companion, for, although they would tell us that we were on the right road, we had often to retrace our steps. But he was so grounded in virtue that I do not think I ever saw him annoyed, which amazed me and led me to praise Our Lord, for upon a man who is grounded in virtue occasions of sin have little effect. I praise the Lord, Who was pleased to bring us safely out of that journey.

On Saint Bartholomew's Eve,[1] we arrived at Saint Joseph's, Segovia, where the nuns were growing concerned at our not having appeared; for on account of the road being so bad we were extremely late. They were very good to us there, for God never sends me trouble without at once recompensing me for it. So I rested there for a week or more: but the foundation had been made with so little difficulty that it is not worth mentioning—there was really no trouble at all. I came away very pleased, for the place seemed to me to be one where I hope, in the mercy of God, the community will render Him great service, as it is doing at present. May He be blessed and praised for all eternity. Amen. *Deo gratias.*

CHAPTER XXXI

This chapter begins to describe the foundation of the glorious Saint Joseph of Saint Anne in the city of Burgos. The first Mass was said here on the nineteenth day of April, in the Octave of Easter, 1582.

More than six years previously, some very religious people in the Company of Jesus, who had been long in the Company

[1] August 23, 1581.

and were both learned and spiritual, had told me that it would
be a great service to Our Lord if a house of this sacred Order
were founded at Burgos.[1] For this they gave me various reasons
which led me to have the same desire. But the many troubles
of the Order and my other foundations had given me no opportunity of accomplishing it.

In the year 1580, when I was at Valladolid, the Archbishop
of Burgos, who at that time had just succeeded to his see, passed
that way.[2] He had previously been Bishop of the Canary
Islands and was on his way thence. I have already said how
much this Order has been helped by the Bishop of Palencia,
Don Álvaro de Mendoza, who was the first person to sanction
the convent of Saint Joseph at Ávila, when he was Bishop there,
and since then has always been very kind to us and treats the
affairs of this Order as if they were his own, particularly when
I approach him about them. I spoke to this Bishop about it and
he said that he would be very pleased to put the matter to the
Archbishop; for, as he thinks great service is done to Our Lord in
these houses, he is very glad when another foundation is made.

The Archbishop would not enter Valladolid, but stayed at
the monastery of Saint Jerome, where the Bishop of Palencia
gave him a splendid reception, went to dine with him and
presented him with a girdle, or performed some ceremony or
other which had to be done by a Bishop.[3] He then asked him to
give me permission to found this convent. The Archbishop
said he would give it with great pleasure, for he had wanted
such a house in the Canaries, and had tried to get one founded,
for he was aware how much Our Lord is served in them, as
there was one in the place he came from and he knew about
me quite well. So the Bishop told me that, as the Archbishop
had been so delighted at the idea, I was not to wait for the
licence, and that, as the Council does not insist that the licence
must be in writing, but merely speaks of consent, this could be
taken as given.[4]

[1] It was in 1577 that a Jesuit Father had made St. Teresa this proposal.

[2] The Archbishop's name was Don Cristóbal Vela. He was the son of the first
Viceroy of Peru, at whose side five of St. Teresa's brothers had fought, in the celebrated battle of Iñaquito, against Gonzalo Pizarro. His uncle, Don Francisco Vela
Núñez, was her godfather. Documentary evidence exists that he was aware of
these facts, which makes his unsympathetic attitude to St. Teresa in this matter the
more surprising.

[3] The reference is to the pallium—a vestment, resembling a scarf, which the Pope
bestows on metropolitans and some archbishops. This was given to the new Archbishop of Burgos by Don Álvaro de Mendoza in the church of the Hieronymite Fathers,
formerly known as Nuestra Señora del Prado.

[4] The words of instruction issued by the Council of Trent (Session XXV: De
reformatione Regularium) are: " Nec de caetero similia loca erigantur sine Episcopi,
in cuius dioecesi erigenda sunt, licentia prius obtenta."

When speaking of the previous foundation at Palencia, I have said how much I disliked the idea of making a foundation at this time, for I had been so ill that it was thought I should not recover and I was still not completely well again. Such things, however, do not generally affect my work when I see that it is for the service of God, so I cannot understand the reason for the great disinclination which I felt at that time. If it be said that it was due to the poor prospects of the work, the answer is that the prospects of previous foundations had been poorer. Personally, now that I have seen what has happened, I believe it was the work of the devil; so at least it has generally been, for, whenever I am about to have trouble in making a founda- tion, Our Lord, Who knows what a miserable creature I am, always helps me in word and in deed. I have sometimes reflected how, in making certain foundations where I have had no trouble, His Majesty has given me no warnings at all. It has been so in this case: knowing what I should have to endure, He began to encourage me from the beginning. May He be praised for everything. It happened here as in the Palencia foundation which I have already described: the two foundations were arranged at the same time. He asked me, as if reprovingly, what I was afraid of. When had He failed me? "I am still the same," He said. "Do not omit to make these two foundations." As I said in giving an account of the last foundation, these words encouraged me greatly, and I need not go into this again here. All my sloth at once left me, which shows that it was not due to illness or old age. I began, then, to arrange both foundations together, as has been said.

It seemed better to make the Palencia foundation first, as the city was nearer, and because the weather was so severe and Burgos so cold, and also because it would please the good Bishop of Palencia. This, therefore, was done, as has been said. While I was there, the offer was made for the Soria foundation, and, as everything was finished at Palencia, I thought it would be better to go straight to Soria, first of all, and then on to Burgos.[1] The Bishop of Palencia thought it would be well to give the Archbishop an account of what was happening, and I begged him to do this for me. And so, after I had gone to Soria, he sent a Canon, Juan Alonso by name, to the Archbishop, for that express purpose. The Archbishop wrote to me very affection- ately to say how anxious he was for me to come; he also had a talk with the Canon and wrote to his Lordship, leaving the

---

[1] [The original Spanish text has " to go first and then on to Soria ". But this seems to be a slip on the part of the author, and P. Silverio corrects it in a footnote to read as in the text above.]

matter to him. What he did, he said, was prompted by his knowledge of Burgos: it would be necessary for me to go there by general consent.

So the Bishop decided that I should go there, and, in the first place, discuss the matter with the civic authorities. If they refused permission his hands would not be tied so that he would be unable to give it me himself. He had been at Ávila when the first convent was founded there and remembered the great disturbance and opposition it had stirred up. He was anxious to forestall this here and he thought it would be unsuitable to found a convent without an endowment or without the consent of the city. He knew I did not approve of this condition and it was for that reason, he said, that he spoke of it.

Having decided that I should go there, the Bishop very rightly considered the matter settled and sent to tell me to do so. But to me it seemed that the Archbishop was somewhat wanting in courage, and I wrote to thank him for the kindness he was doing me, but adding that it seemed to me worse to go without the city's consent than without telling them about it, because it would involve his Lordship in fresh trouble. I must have realized how little help I should get from him if I were to meet with any opposition: in any case I thought it a difficult matter on account of the contrary opinions which are usually to be found on such occasions. So I wrote to the Bishop of Palencia, begging him, as there was so little of the summer left and my complaints were so troublesome in a cold climate, to let the matter rest for the time being. I cast no aspersions on the Archbishop, because the Bishop was very much disappointed at the difficulties which the latter was making, after having been so well-disposed to me at first. As they are friends I was anxious not to cause ill-will between them. So I went from Soria to Ávila, little thinking that I should have to come back so soon; for various reasons a visit from me to the house of Saint Joseph at Ávila was very necessary.[1]

Now in this city of Burgos there lived a saintly widow, Catalina de Tolosa,[2] a native of Vizcaya, of whose virtues, both as to penance and as to prayer, almsgiving and charity I could speak at great length, as well as of her great intelligence and worth.

---

[1] It appears that Julián de Ávila had been permitting the nuns at St. Joseph's certain relaxations from the Rule, which St. Teresa went to rectify.

[2] This lady had married a wealthy Burgalese merchant, Sebastián Maláiz. Of her two sons and six daughters all, except one daughter who died young, joined the Discalced Carmelite Reform. Besides the four daughters mentioned in the text, a fifth entered the Burgos convent in 1586. The elder son, as Fray Sebastián de Jesús, became Provincial of Old Castile and Definitor-General; the second lectured in Arts and Theology in the Discalced Carmelite College at Salamanca. In 1587 the mother herself entered the Palencia convent as Catalina del Espíritu Santo.

She had sent two of her daughters as nuns to the Convent of the Conception belonging to our Order in Valladolid. This, I believe, was four years ago. She sent two other daughters to Palencia, after waiting for the foundation to be made there, and brought them there before I left the convent after its foundation.

All these four girls have turned out to be worthy children of such a mother: they are just like angels. She gave them good dowries and everything else in great abundance, for she is so rich that she does everything very handsomely, as she is able to do. When she came to Palencia, we thought it so certain we should get the Archbishop's licence that there seemed no reason for delay. So I asked her to find me a house to let, so that we might take possession, to install the grilles and turns and enter the cost to me—for it never entered my head that she would provide the money herself: I thought she would lend it me. But she was so anxious for the foundation to be made that it grieved her very much that the project should be allowed to rest; so, after I had left for Ávila, as I have said, never supposing that anything further could be done about the matter for the time being, she refused to let it drop, and, thinking that she had only to get the city's permission, began to seek this without telling me about it.

She had two neighbours, persons of importance and great servants of God, who were also very anxious to have the foundation. They were a mother and a daughter: the mother was a certain Doña María Manrique—she had a son who was a city councillor,[1] Don Alonso de Santo Domingo Manrique; the daughter's name was Doña Catalina. The two ladies discussed the matter with Don Alonso and suggested his asking the consent of the City Council. He spoke to Catalina de Tolosa, asking her what means of livelihood he was to say we had, as the Council would not give its consent if we had none. She said that she would bind herself (as she did) to provide us with a house if we needed one, and would also supply us with food. She then presented a petition signed with her name. Don Alonso went to work so skilfully that he obtained the consent of all the councillors and then got the Archbishop's, by taking him their written permission.[2] As soon as she had set the matter in motion, she wrote to me to say that she was arranging it. I did not take it seriously, knowing how hard it is to obtain permission for

[1] [*Regidor*.]
[2] Don Antonio brought up the matter to the Council, of which, as *procurador mayor*, he was a very influential member, on November 4, 1581. The Council deputed him, with a *regidor* named Hernán Ruiz de Castro, to consult the Archbishop. When the latter demurred, on financial grounds, Doña Catalina at once (November 7) sent a memorandum to the Council, offering the Reform a house and subsistence.

religious houses to be founded in poverty, and, as I did not know that she was committing herself to such obligations as I have described, and it never entered my head that she would do so, I thought there was much more still to be done.

However, one day within the octave of Saint Martin, when I had been commending the matter to Our Lord, I began to wonder what I could do about it if the licence were granted. For I thought that, with all my ailments, I could not myself stand the journey to Burgos, when it was so cold, as the cold always makes them worse: it would be rash for me to make so long a journey when I had hardly returned from one so trying as that from Soria which I have described. Furthermore, the Father Provincial[1] would not let me go, for he thought that the Prioress of Palencia[2] would do quite well, since there would be nothing left to be done and everything would be plain sailing. I was thinking over this, quite determined not to go, when the Lord addressed these words to me, which showed me that the licence had now been granted: "Make no account of the cold, for I am true heat. The devil is making every effort to hinder this foundation. Do thou make every effort in its favour, and go in person without fail, for it will bring thee great advantage."

This made me change my mind; my nature sometimes rebels when there are difficult things to be done, but my determination to suffer for this great God never wavers, so I ask Him not to pay any heed to these feelings of weakness but to command me to do what He pleases, and, with His help, I shall not fail to do it. There was snow on the ground just then and it was very cold. What caused me most misgivings was my poor health: had I been well, I do not think I should have troubled in the least. And it proved to be my health that troubled me all the time while I was making this foundation. There was very little cold, or at any rate I felt it very little, certainly no more so than when I was in Toledo. The Lord has amply fulfilled His word with regard to this.

A few days passed before I received the licence, together with letters from Catalina de Tolosa and her friend Doña Catalina.[3] They said there was great urgency. For they were afraid something untoward might happen, as the Victorine Order[4] had just come to make a foundation and the Calced Carmelites had been there for a long time endeavouring to make one too. Then

[1] Fray Jerónimo Gracián.
[2] M. Inés de Jesús.
[3] November 29, 1581.
[4] The Minims of St. Francis of Paula used to be known in Spain as *Victorianos* or *Vitorinos* from the attribution of the conquest of Málaga by Ferdinand the Catholic (1487) to the prayers of their founder, who at that time was trying to establish the Order in Spain.

there had come the Basilean monks, and this was another great obstacle.[1] The fact that so many other Orders had arrived at the same time as ourselves would have to be taken into consideration, though the amount of charity in the city was also a reason for giving thanks to Our Lord: although it no longer enjoyed its former prosperity, the city gave them its permission very gladly. I had always heard its charitableness praised, but I had not thought it would go as far as this. Some people helped one Order; others, another. But the Archbishop, after weighing all the disadvantages that might ensue, forbade our foundation, thinking that it would be harmful to the communities already living in poverty there, as they would be unable to maintain themselves. The latter may possibly have approached him on their own account or the devil may have suggested the idea in order to prevent the bestowal of great blessings by God in places where there are many monasteries, for He is mighty enough to maintain many as easily as few.

It was for this reason that these saintly ladies impressed on me the urgency of the matter: if I had been free to do as I liked, and had had no business to attend to, I should have set out immediately. For, when I saw them all working so diligently for the foundation, I reflected that I was the more bound not to allow the opportunity to slip through any negligence of mine. The words I had heard showed me that there was a great deal of opposition, though whence or from whom it came I could not then discover, for Catalina de Tolosa had already written to me to say that she would certainly be able to give me the house she was living in, the city was quite agreeable and so was the Archbishop. So I could not imagine whence this opposition which the devils were about to raise would come, though I had no doubt that the words I had heard were from God.

But His Majesty gives more light to superiors; for, when I wrote to the Father Provincial about my going for the purpose of which he already knew, he made no objection, but asked me if I had a written licence from the Archbishop. I wrote to Burgos to this effect and they replied that he had been told the city's consent had been asked for and had given his own approval. This, together with all he had said about the matter, seemed to leave no room for doubt.

The Father Provincial was anxious to go with us to make the foundation.[2] This was partly because he was free at the time,

---

[1] Neither the Calced Carmelites nor the Order of St. Basil actually made a foundation in Burgos.

[2] P. Gracián was accompanied by P. Pedro de la Purificación, a close and faithful friend of his, and by a lay brother, whose name has not come down to us. P. Pedro remained with St. Teresa after the Provincial had left for Valladolid (p. 196, below).

having been preaching during Advent, and having to go for a visitation to Soria: he had not seen the convent there since it had been founded, and Burgos would not be far out of his way. And partly he was anxious to go so that he might look after my health on the journey, because the weather was so severe, and I was so old and ill, and they apparently think my life of some importance. It was certainly by God's ordinance that he went, for the roads were frequently flooded, and so bad that he and his companions had to go on ahead to find the best paths for us, and help to drag the carriages out of the bogs: it was especially bad between Palencia and Burgos—in fact, it was very rash of us to set out when we did at all. True, Our Lord had told me that we could safely go, and that I was not to fear, for He would be with us. But I did not tell the Father Provincial this at the time, though it was a comfort to me in the great difficulties and dangers which we met, especially at the ford near Burgos known as the Pontoons.[1] Here, in many places, the water had risen so high that it had submerged these pontoons to such an extent that they could not be seen; and we could not find any way of going on, for there was water everywhere, and on either side it was very deep. In fact, it is very rash of anyone to travel that way, especially with carriages, for, if they heeled slightly, all would be lost: one of them, indeed, we actually saw in danger.

Before reaching this place we had taken a guide whom we had found at an inn and who knew the best way through, but it was certainly a very dangerous one. Then there was the question of lodgings. We could not cover our usual days' mileages on account of the bad roads, for it was quite usual for the carriages to sink into the mud and the animals would then have to be taken out of one of the carriages to drag out another. The Fathers who went with us had a very bad time, for we happened to have drivers who were young and rather careless. The fact that the Father Provincial was with us helped us a great deal, for he saw to everything, and he is of such a placid temperament that nothing seems to upset him. So he made our troubles seem light, though he could do nothing about the Pontoons, which gave him a real fright. For, when I saw that we were entering a regular sea of water,[2] with no sign of a path or a boat, even I was not without fear, despite all the strength Our Lord had given me. What, then, must have been my companions' state of mind? There were eight of us altogether: two who were to return with me and five who were to remain at

[1] The exact position of this ford is unknown: some think it was near the Malatos bridge; others put it farther down the river—which was, of course, the Arlanzón.
[2] [Lit., " a world of water ".]

Burgos, four choir nuns and one lay sister.[1] I believe I have not yet said who the Father Provincial was. It was Fray Jerónimo Gracián de la Madre de Dios, whom I have mentioned elsewhere. I was suffering from a troublesome sore throat which I had contracted on the road to Valladolid; I still had a temperature and eating caused me the greatest pain. This detracted from my enjoyment of the pleasanter parts of the journey. I am still suffering from this sore throat, though it is the end of June:[2] it is not nearly as troublesome as it was, but is still extremely painful. The nuns were all quite happy; and, once the danger was passed, they enjoyed talking about it. It is a great thing to suffer under obedience, especially for those who practise it as consistently as these nuns.

Despite the badness of this road, we reached Burgos, after making our way through the deep water which we encountered before entering the city. Our Father was anxious that, in order to commend our task to Christ, we should first of all pay a visit to the Holy Crucifix,[3] and stay there till nightfall, for it was early when we arrived, on the Friday after the Feast of the Conversion of Saint Paul, the twenty-sixth of January. We had determined to make the foundation at once and I had brought a great many letters from Canon Salinas (I have spoken of him in connection with the Palencia foundation, and he has taken just as much trouble here) and from other important people, urging their relatives and friends to help us in this undertaking.

They did so, and on the very next day the civic authorities came to see me in a body. They did not in the least repent of what they had said but were delighted I had come and told me to let them know how they could help me. If we had had any fear, it was about the city, but now we found that everything there was plain sailing. No one knew of our arrival (for the rain was too heavy for us to go to the house of the good Catalina de Tolosa) and we had thought of informing the Archbishop first of all, so that the first Mass might be said at once, for this is my practice almost everywhere. But we refrained on account of the weather.

---

[1] They were: Tomasina Bautista, the first Prioress of the house; Inés de la Cruz; Catalina de Jesús; Catalina de la Asunción (daughter of Catalina de Tolosa); and María Bautista (the lay sister). The two who were to return with St. Teresa were her niece Teresita and Ana de San Bartolomé.

[2] "July" appears in the manuscript, amended to "June".

[3] The famous crucifix in question was venerated in the Church of the Augustinian Fathers. At the time of the Napoleonic invasion it was taken to the Cathedral and can now be seen in the Capilla del Santo Cristo, where it is the object of devotional visits from high and low. Cf. Letter 404, to Doña Catalina de Tolosa, January 16, 1582.

Thanks to that saintly woman, we spent that night very comfortably, but it cost me a great deal of suffering. For she had lit a huge fire so that we might dry our wet clothes, and, although there was a chimney in the room, it made me feel so ill that on the next day I was unable to raise my head. So to those who came to see me I could only speak lying down: I spoke to them through a barred window over which we drew a curtain. As it was a day on which there was essential business to be done, this was a great trial to me.

Early the next morning the Father Provincial went to ask the most reverend Archbishop for his blessing, for we thought nothing more than this remained to be done. But he found him quite changed, and annoyed at my having come without a licence from him, just as though he had never ordered me to do so or had had anything to do with the matter. So he spoke with great annoyance to the Father Provincial about my coming. When at last he admitted that he had told me to do so, he said that he had meant me to come alone to discuss the matter with him: it was quite a different matter to bring all these nuns and Heaven knew how much I had distressed him! It was not of the least use for us to tell him that the matter had been arranged with the city just as he had asked; that no more business remained to be done before the foundation was made; and that the Bishop of Palencia had told me, when I had asked him if it was all right for me to come, that there was no reason to consult the Archbishop, as he had already said how much he desired this. That was how matters stood; but it was God's will that the foundation should be made, as the Archbishop himself said later, for, if we had definitely told him we were coming, he would have forbidden us to do so. In the end he dismissed the Father Provincial and told him that, unless we had an income and a house of our own, he would never give his consent and we might as well go back again. The roads, of course, were charming, and it was such nice weather!

O my Lord, how true it is that as soon as a person renders Thee some service he is rewarded with great trials! And what a priceless reward they are for those of us who truly love Thee, if only we recognize their value at the time! Just then we were not at all anxious for such a reward, for it seemed to make it impossible for us to go on, especially as the Archbishop had also said that our income and the purchase money for the house were not to be provided out of any dowries brought by the nuns. We had not been thinking of such a stipulation at a time like this and it became quite clear that we were helpless. But I did not myself believe that we were, for all the time I was sure that everything was for the best, and that, though the devil was trying to hinder our work, God would carry it into effect. The Father Provincial, too, came back in quite a cheerful mood, and was not in the least put out. God saw to this and kept him from being annoyed with me because I had not obtained the licence in writing as he had told me to do.

Meanwhile, several of the friends to whom Canon Salinas had written, as I have related, had been to see me; they had come to visit us at once, with their kinsfolk. They suggested that the Archbishop might be asked to give us permission for Mass to be said in the house so that we should not have to walk through the streets. There was a great deal of mud in the town; it seemed inexpedient that we should go out in our bare feet; and there was quite a good room in the house, which had served the Company of Jesus as a church when they had come to Burgos, and which they had used for more than ten years.[1] In view of this it seemed to us not at all unsuitable that we should take possession of this room until we had a house of our own. But we were never able to persuade the Archbishop to allow us to hear Mass there, though two Canons went to beg him to do so. What we did persuade him to allow us was that, once we had an assured income, we might make our foundation there until we had bought a house. For this purpose we were to provide sureties for the purchase of a house and we were not to leave the house we were in. The sureties were found at once, for Canon Salinas' friends offered to provide them, and Catalina de Tolosa said that she would give the necessary money for the foundation.

During all these discussions as to ways and means, more than three weeks must have gone by. We were unable to hear Mass except on festivals at very early hours and I still had a high temperature and was very unwell. But Catalina de Tolosa was most kind to us and took great care of me, and gave us our meals in the room where we lived alone, for the whole of that month, just as if she had been our mother. The Father Provincial and his companions were staying in the house of a friend of his, called Doctor Manso,[2] who had been at college with him, and was a Canon-Preacher in the Cathedral. It worried him dreadfully to find that he was having to stay so long but he did not see how he could leave us.

---

[1] The Society of Jesus came to Burgos in 1550, and in 1565 established themselves in the Colegio del Cardinal Mendoza. Doña Catalina lived in the Society's earlier residence (Huerto del Rey) and it was here that she received St. Teresa and her companions.

[2] Dr. Pedro Manso de Zúñiga was a native of Canillas, near Nájera. For some time he was St. Teresa's confessor and remained a staunch supporter of her Reform, himself founding a monastery and a convent.

When sureties had been arranged and an income secured to us, the Archbishop told us to communicate with the Vicar-General and the matter would then be settled. But the devil must have paid a visit to the Vicar-General as well, for, after he had had a long period for consideration, and we were thinking that now at last there could be no further delay, almost a month having been spent in trying to make the Archbishop happy about what we were doing, the Vicar-General sent me a memorandum to say that the licence would not be granted until we had a house of our own, and that the Archbishop was not now willing for us to make the foundation in the house we were in because it was damp and the street it was situated in was very noisy. And with regard to the security for the property, there were all sorts of complications and other obstacles—as if the discussion of the matter had only just begun! But there was nothing more to be said, for it was essential that the house should have the Archbishop's approval.

When the Father Provincial heard of this, he was greatly upset, as we all were, for obviously one needs time for the purchase of a site for a convent and it worried him to see us having to go out of the house to Mass; for, though the church was not far away,[1] and we heard Mass in a chapel where no one saw us, it caused the greatest distress to his Reverence and to ourselves that it should be necessary. It was then, I think, that he decided we should have to leave. I could not bear to do this when I remembered that the Lord had told me to accomplish this work for His sake, and I was so sure that it could be done that the difficulties worried me hardly at all. My only regret was for the Father Provincial: I was dreadfully sorry that he had come with us, for I had no idea how much his friends would do for us, as I shall afterwards relate. While I was so distressed, as were my companions also (though I did not trouble about them but only about the Father Provincial), Our Lord spoke to me at a time when I was not in prayer and said to me: "Now, Teresa, hold thou fast." Upon this I begged the Father Provincial more resolutely than ever to go away and leave us, and His Majesty must have urged him to do so, for Lent was near and he was obliged to go off to preach.

He and his friends gave orders that some rooms should be allotted to us in the Hospital of the Conception,[2] where the Most

[1] The parish church of St. Giles (San Gil), built at the end of the fourteenth century. The chapel is traditionally said to have been the Capilla de la Buena Mañana, so called from the Masses said there on certain days at dawn. There is no evidence, however, for the supposition.

[2] This hospital had been built in 1561 and was occupied by the Confraternity of the Conception on December 8, 1562.

Holy Sacrament was reserved and Mass was said daily. This gave him some satisfaction but it cost him no small trouble to get it done for us. For there was one good room, which had been taken by a widow who lived here, and not only would she not lend it to us, though she was not going into it herself for six months, but she was annoyed at our having been given rooms on the attic floor of the building, one of which communicated with her own. She was not satisfied at its being locked from the outside but she had it nailed up on her own side as well. Further, the brethren thought we should be wanting to get the entire hospital, an idea for which there were no grounds whatever, but it must have been God's will for us to win greater merit. They made the Father Provincial and myself promise, before a notary, that if we were ordered to leave we would do so at once.[1]

To me this was the hardest thing of all, for I was afraid that it would enable the widow, who was rich and had relatives in the place, to turn us out whenever she felt so inclined. But the Father Provincial, who was wiser than I, wanted us to do all they asked so that we might go in quickly. They gave us only two rooms and a kitchen. But in charge of the hospital was a great servant of God, Hernando de Matanzas,[2] who gave two more rooms for a parlour and was very kind to us, as he is to everyone, for he does a great deal for the poor. We also received much kindness from Francisco de Cuevas:[3] he is the postmaster here and he has a great deal to do with this hospital. He has always taken every opportunity of helping us.

I have named our early benefactors, so that the nuns who are in that convent now and those who come after them may remember them in their prayers, as it is right they should. This service, more than any other, is due to our founders, and though it was not my original intention, nor did it ever enter my head, that Catalina de Tolosa should be our founder, her good life won this honour for her from Our Lord, who ordained things in such a way that it could not be denied her. Apart from her having paid for the house when we had no means of doing so, it is impossible to describe what all the Archbishop's devious methods

---

[1] The agreement in question appears to be no longer extant.

[2] Don Hernando, a *regidor* of the city whose brother had been Mayor, appears to have been an *ex-officio* member of the Hospital board.

[3] Don Francisco, a Knight of Santiago, and husband of the Toledan authoress Luisa Sigea de Velasco, was left a widower in 1560; about this time he was appointed postmaster (*correo mayor*) of Burgos and given some kind of appointment in the Hospital of the Conception. A sixteenth-century *correo mayor* was a rather more important person than a postmaster is to-day: his jurisdiction often extended over a wide district.

cost her. It was the greatest affliction to her to think that the foundation might not be made and she was never weary of doing us kindnesses.

This hospital was a long way from her house but she very gladly came to visit us almost every day, and sent us all we needed, despite the fact that people never stopped saying things to her about us, and, had she not been the brave woman she is, that alone would have been enough to put her off the whole thing. It caused me great distress to see what she was suffering; for though as a rule she concealed it there were times when it was impossible to hide. This was especially so when they appealed to her conscience, for she has so tender a conscience that, in spite of all the temptations which some people have caused her, I never heard her say a word which could offend God. They would tell her she was going to hell and ask her how she could do what she was doing when she had children of her own. But she did it all with the approval of learned men: whatever her own wishes, not for anything in the world would I have agreed to her doing what she ought not, even had the foundation of a thousand convents been prevented thereby, still less when it was a question of only one. But as the project we were discussing was a secret one, I am not surprised that everybody took such an interest in it. She is a very discreet person and she answered people most discreetly and bore what they said in such a way that it really seemed as if God was teaching her how to please some and to put up with others and giving her all the necessary courage. How much more courage for doing great things have servants of God than people of noble descent who do not serve Him! I do not mean by this that she was not of quite pure descent, for she comes from a very noble house.

To go back to what I was saying, when the Father Provincial had seen us installed in a place where we could hear Mass and yet observe the rule of enclosure, he was anxious to go on to Valladolid, where he had to preach. But he was greatly troubled to see no vestige of hope that the Archbishop would give us his licence; and, though I always assured him that there were good grounds for such hope, he could not believe it. He certainly had strong reasons for his misgivings, which there is no point in setting down here; and, if he had little hope, his friends had less, and caused him great discouragement. I was more at ease when I saw him go, for, as I have said, my greatest distress proceeded from the fact that he was distressed too. He left us instructions that we were to look for a house which we could have for our own; and this was very difficult, for down to that time we had found no house for sale. Our friends were the more concerned about us, especially the two friends of the Father Provincial, and they were all agreed that, until we had a house, not a word should be said to the Archbishop. He was always saying that he yielded to none in his desire for this foundation to be made, and I believe this was so, for he is such a good Christian that he would never say anything but the truth. The fact did not betray itself, however, in his actions, for he asked things of us which seemed to be beyond our power. This was the devil's plan to prevent the foundation from being made. But, O Lord, how evident it is that Thou art mighty! For Thou didst use the very means by which the devil sought to hinder our plans so that they might prosper the more. Blessed be Thou for ever!

From the eve of Saint Matthias—the day we had gone into the hospital—until the eve of Saint Joseph[1] we continued to look at houses, one after another. They had many disadvantages and not one of those which were for sale was suitable for us to buy. I had been told of one house which belonged to a gentle-man who had been trying for some time past to sell it. Although so many Orders were looking for a house, it pleased God that this one should suit none of them: they are all surprised at this now and some have even repented of their judgment. One or two people had spoken to me about it, but so many of them thought it unsuitable that I had taken it as being so and quite forgotten it.

One day I was talking to a licentiate in medicine named Aguiar, who, as I have said, was a friend of our Father[2] and had been going to great trouble over searching for a house for us. He was telling me that he had looked at some and that in the whole city he could find nothing; and, to judge from what people were saying, it seemed impossible that anything would be obtainable. Then I remembered this house, which, as I say, we had given up thinking of, and it occurred to me that, even if it were as bad as they had said, we might make use of it at this time of need and sell it again later. So I asked Aguiar if he would be kind enough to look at it for me.

This did not seem to him a bad plan. He had not seen the house, and, though it was a rough, stormy day, he was good enough to go there at once. The person living in it was unwilling for it to be sold and refused to show it him. But he liked its situation and what he could see of it very much and so we deter-mined to start negotiations for buying it. The gentleman to whom

---

[1] I.e. from February 23 to March 18, 1582.
[2] Antonio Aguiar had been a fellow-student of Gracián's at Alcalá de Henares.

it belonged[1] was away, but he had given authority to sell it to
a cleric, a servant of God in whom His Majesty implanted
the desire to sell it to us and to treat us very fairly over it.[2]

It was arranged that I should go to see it. I was so extremely
pleased with it that, if I had been asked twice as much as I
understood they wanted for it, I should have thought it a bargain.
And that is not saying much, for two years previously its owner
had been offered that sum for the house and had refused to
take it. On the very next day the cleric came here with the
licentiate, who, when he saw that his companion was pleased
with it, wanted the deal to be concluded immediately. I had told
some friends about this and they had said that if I paid the sum
asked I should be giving five hundred ducats too much. I told
him this, but he thought it would be cheap even if I gave what
was asked, and I thought the same and felt sure that it would
be a mistake to hesitate any longer, though, as the money belonged to the Order, I had some scruples about it. This meeting
took place on the eve of the Feast of our glorious Father Saint
Joseph, before Mass; I told them we would meet again after Mass
and decide the matter.

The licentiate is a man of great intelligence: he saw quite well
that, if the thing became known, we should either have to pay
a great deal more for the house or should be unable to buy it at all.
So he got to work quickly and made the cleric promise to come
back after Mass. We nuns went and commended the matter to
God, Who said to me: "Art thou hesitating on account of
money?" meaning that the house was quite suitable for us. The
sisters had prayed earnestly to Saint Joseph that they might
have a house by the day of his festival, and, though they never
thought that they would get one so quickly, their prayers were
answered. Everyone impressed on me the importance of con-
cluding the purchase, and this was done, for the licentiate had
met a notary at the door,[3] which seemed a Divine dispensation,
and he came with him to me and said we must settle the matter
now. So he procured a witness, and, after he had shut the door
of the room so that nobody might know about it (for that was his
great fear), the sale was definitely made, on the eve of the Feast
of the glorious Saint Joseph,[4] as I have said, through the efficiency
and intelligence of this good friend.

[1] Only his name—Manuel Franco—is known.
[2] The new property—consisting of two houses and some adjacent ground—was
on the road to the Carthusian Monastery, and stood on the left bank of the Arlanzón,
above the hospital and church of St. Luke. To-day it is an Augustinian convent.
[3] By name Juan Ortega de la Torre Frías.
[4] The agreement was actually drafted on March 12, 1582, and confirmed four days
later.

No one thought we should get the house so cheaply, so, as soon as the news got round, purchasers began to present themselves, and said that the cleric who had made the bargain had simply given the house away, and the sale ought to be cancelled, for it was sheer robbery. The good cleric had to go through a great deal on account of this. The owners of the house were at once told about the matter: as I have said, both the owner and his wife were persons of rank and importance. They were so delighted that their house was to become a convent that they gave their approval to the sale for that reason alone, though actually by this time they could have done nothing else. On a subsequent date[1] the agreement was drawn up and one-third of the purchase money was paid, exactly as the cleric had required, for with regard to some of the details they drove a hard bargain. In order to get the house, however, we put up with everything.

It will seem irrelevant for me to have spent so long in describing the purchase of this house, but the fact is that those who studied the matter in detail thought it nothing less than a miracle, both because of the price and because of the blindness of all the religious who had looked at the house and passed it over. People who saw it now were as astonished as if it had not been in Burgos all this time and blamed the other religious and said they had been foolish. There had also been people looking for a house which was wanted for another convent, and houses were also needed for two more communities: one of these had been only recently founded and the other had been transferred from elsewhere because its house had been burned down. Then there was another wealthy person who was proposing to found a monastery and had recently looked at this house and not considered it further. All these very much regretted what they had done.

There was now such a talk in the city that we saw clearly how right the good licentiate had been about keeping our purchase secret and going to such pains in order to do so. We can truly say that, under God, it was he who gave us the house. It is a great advantage in every way to be intelligent. His extreme intelligence, together with the friendliness to us which God had inspired in him, was responsible for bringing the affair to a successful conclusion. For more than a month he continued to help us and to arrange for the furnishing of the house, which was done excellently and at small cost. It really seemed as if Our

---

[1] This phrase is the Spanish *lu:go otro día* (cf. p. 180. n. 3, above) which would normally be translated "on the next day," but which St. Teresa uses in the sense of "subsequently". Documentary evidence makes it clear that four days elapsed between the two events named. On March 16, 1582, before the same notary, St. Teresa conferred full powers for dealing with the property on P. Pedro de la Purificación and Don Antonio Aguiar.

Lord had been keeping the house for Himself, for almost every-thing necessary appeared to have been done in it already. The fact is that, when I saw it, and found that everything was as if it had been done purposely for us, it seemed to me like a dream that we should have it ready so quickly. Our Lord richly re-warded us for what we had gone through by bringing us into this paradise of delight, for what with the garden, the views and the water, it seemed nothing less. May He be blessed for ever. Amen.

The Archbishop heard of it at once and was greatly delighted that we had been so successful: he thought that it had all been due to his own obstinacy, and he was quite right. I wrote to him that I was glad he was pleased and I would make haste to get the house ready so that I might be completely in his good graces. Having told him this, I moved in as soon as I could, for I had been informed that they were trying to keep us in the hospital until some agreement or other had been completed. So, although a tenant who was living in the house had not gone, and it gave us a good deal of trouble to turn him out,[1] we got into one room. Then I was told that the Archbishop was very much annoyed at this. I pacified him as well as I could, for, even when angry, he is a good man, and his anger is soon over. He was also annoyed because he learned that we had grilles and turns, for this gave him the idea that I was trying to be quite independent of his jurisdiction. I wrote to him that I had no such wish, and that houses for people who lead recollected lives always have these, and that I had not ventured to put up so much as a cross lest he should disapprove, which was the truth. Despite all the good will he showed us, there was no way of getting him to grant us his licence.

He came to see the house, was very pleased with it and treated us most graciously, but not to the extent of granting us the licence, although he gave us more hope that he would do so. He said some agreement or other must be drawn up with Catalina de Tolosa. We were all very much afraid that he would never give us the licence, but Doctor Manso, that other friend of the Father Provincial of whom I have spoken, was also a great friend of the Archbishop, and waited till he found a suitable moment to remind him of the matter and urge its importance upon him. It had caused him great distress to see us wandering about as we had had to do; for even in this house, though it had a chapel which had been used by its previous owners for no other purpose than the saying of Mass, he would never allow us to have Mass said, so every Sunday and holy day we had to go out and hear

---

[1] A certain Jerónimo del Pino, nephew of the Augustinian P. Cristóbal de Santotis, who persuaded him to defer to St. Teresa's wishes.

Mass in a church. It was a good thing that we had one near,[1] but between the date on which we went into our house and that on which the foundation was made about a month elapsed, and all learned men said that that was quite sufficient reason for giving us this permission. The Archbishop is also a very learned man, and he saw that things were like this, so there seems to have been no other reason for his action except Our Lord's will that we should suffer. I myself bore this better than the rest, but there was one nun who would tremble with the distress it caused her to find herself out in the street.

We had no lack of trouble to endure before the agreement was drawn up, for first of all they said they would be satisfied with sureties, and then they wanted to have the money; and they worried us in many other ways. This was the fault not so much of the Archbishop as of a Vicar-General who fought bitterly against us, and if God had not in due course converted him and made him another man, I think the matter would never have ended. And oh, the suffering that this caused Catalina de Tolosa! It is indescribable. She bore everything with a patience which amazed me and was never tired of making provision for us. She gave us everything we needed for setting up house—beds and many other things—for her own house was well provided, and, numerous as were the things we needed, it seemed unlikely that we should lack any of them, even if she had to go short herself. Other ladies who have founded convents for us have given much more, but there is not one whose work for us has cost her one-tenth as much. Had it not been for her children, she would have given everything she had; and so anxious was she to see the convent finished that everything she did for that purpose seemed to her but light.

When I saw how much delay there was, I wrote to the Bishop of Palencia, begging him to write once more to the Archbishop, with whom he was very much displeased. For whatever the Archbishop did to us the Bishop regarded as done to himself; and what amazed us was that the Archbishop never imagined that he was doing us any wrong. I begged the Bishop to write to him again, telling him that we now had a house and that everything he required had been done, and entreating him to give us his sanction. The Bishop sent me an open letter to forward to him, but it was of such a kind that, had we done so, we should have ruined everything; so Doctor Manso, who was my confessor

---

[1] The church and hospital of St. Luke (San Lucas) were only a few yards from the Carmelites' new property. Both belonged to the Cathedral Chapter, which in 1612 disposed of them to a community of Augustinian nuns, who were living in the city.

and counsellor, would not allow it to be sent on. The letter was quite respectful, but there were certain truths in it which, in view of the Archbishop's nature, would have been quite sufficient to displease him—and he was already displeased at certain things about which the Bishop had written to him, though they had been great friends. He remarked to me that, just as people who were not friends had become so through the death of Our Lord, so on my account the Lord had made two who had been friends enemies. I told him that that would show him what sort of person I was; for I had been particularly careful, as I thought, to prevent them from being displeased with each other.

Once again, using the best arguments I could, I besought the Bishop to write another letter to the Archbishop, this time a very friendly one, showing him what a service he would be rendering to God. He did what I asked him: it cost him no small effort, but, when he saw that he would be rendering a service to God and a kindness to us (for he has always been consistently kind to me), he made this great effort; and he wrote to me that all he had done for the Order was nothing by comparison with that letter. In the end, combined with the evidence of Doctor Manso, it had the effect of persuading him to give us the licence: this he sent by Hernando de Matanzas, who derived no small pleasure from bringing it. It was a day on which the sisters were much more depressed than they had ever been before and good Catalina de Tolosa was quite inconsolable. It seemed as if the Lord wanted to oppress us most at the very moment when He was about to give us pleasure: even I, who had never until then lost confidence, had on the previous night had none whatever. May His name be blessed and praised for ever and ever. Amen.[1]

Doctor Manso had now a licence to say Mass on some early date[2] and to reserve the Most Holy Sacrament. He said our first Mass, and the Father Prior of Saint Paul's,[3] a Dominican monastery to which this Order has owed a great deal, as it has also to the Company of Jesus, sang the High Mass, to the accompaniment of most solemn music played by minstrels[4] who came without having to be asked. All our friends were very pleased,

---

[1] The Archbishop's licence, still extant, is dated April 15, 1582. It may be added that a number of spirited exchanges in conversation between the Saint and the Archbishop are on record [Cf. P. Silverio, V, 319, n. 4, 322, n. 1].

[2] [otro día. Cf. p. 199, n. 1, above.] The day was April 19, 1582.

[3] The Dominican house of St. Paul (San Pablo) was very near the Carmelite convent. The Prior, Fray Juan de Arcediano, was a man of great authority in his Order; among other things he was four times Rector of the College of St. Gregory, in Valladolid.

[4] The word *ministriles* here denotes players, chiefly of wind instruments, who performed at solemn ecclesiastical or civic functions.

and so was almost the whole city, for they had been very sorry to see the plight we had been in and thought the Archbishop was acting very wrongly. Sometimes I would regret the things I heard being said about him more than those that were happening to us. So great was the joy of good Catalina de Tolosa and of the sisters that it aroused my devotion, and I said to God: "Lord, what more do these Thy servants desire but to serve Thee and to see themselves placed by Thee in a cloister which they shall never leave?"

Only those who have experienced it will believe what pleasure we get from these foundations when we find ourselves at last in a cloister which can be entered by no one from the world. For, however much we may love those in the world, our love is not enough to deprive us of our great happiness when we find ourselves alone. It is as when a great many fish are taken from the river in a net: they cannot live unless they are put back in the river. Even so it is with souls accustomed to live in the streams of the waters of their Spouse: if they are drawn out of them by nets, which are the things of the world, they can have no true life until they find themselves back again. This I always observe in all these sisters and I have discovered it to be so by experience. Nuns who find themselves desirous of going out among worldly people, or of having a great deal to do with them, may well fear that they have not found the living water of which the Lord spoke to the woman of Samaria, and that the Spouse has hidden Himself from them; and they are right to fear this, since they are not content to remain with Him. I am afraid this springs from two sources: either they have not entered the religious life for His sake alone or else after entering it they have not realized how great a favour God has shown them in choosing them for Himself and freeing them from being subject to some man, who often brings a woman's life to an end—and God grant he may not also ruin her soul.

O Very Man and Very God, my Spouse! Is this a favour to be regarded lightly? Let us praise Him, my sisters, for having granted it to us, and let us not be weary of praising so great a King and Lord, Who has prepared for us a kingdom that has no end, in exchange for a few brief trials set amid a thousand joys, trials which will be over to-morrow. May He be blessed for ever. Amen. Amen.

Some little time after the house was founded, the Father Provincial and I thought that there were some difficulties about the endowment with which Catalina de Tolosa had provided it, and that these might lead to a lawsuit, which would cause her a certain amount of worry. We were anxious to trust in God rather than to be the occasion of giving her any trouble. For this and certain other reasons, all of them approved by the Father Provincial, we appeared before a notary, renounced the property she had given us and returned her all the legal documents. This was done with great secrecy, lest the Archbishop should hear of it and be offended, though in reality the sole party to suffer by it was this house. Yet when it becomes known that a house is founded in poverty there is no reason for fear, because everybody helps it; whereas, when the house is known to have money of its own, there is a risk that it may sometimes have to go without food. A means of helping us after the death of Catalina de Tolosa was found; for two of her daughters, who were to make their profession this year in our Palencia convent,[1] had renounced their property in her favour when they made their profession, and this renunciation she made them exchange for another in favour of this house. Another of her daughters,[2] who wished to take the habit here, left us her lawful share in the property of her father and mother, which is as much as was coming in from the endowment; the only drawback is that the house is not yet able to enjoy it. But I have always held that the nuns will lack nothing, because the Lord, Who provides for other houses dependent upon alms, will arouse people to provide for us or will Himself find means for its maintenance. Though no convent has been founded as this was, I have on various occasions besought the Lord, Whose will it was that it should be founded, to provide for its relief and supply what is necessary for it.

I did not want to leave the house until I saw if any nuns were entering it. But one day, after Communion, when I was thinking of all this, the Lord said to me: "Why dost thou doubt? This is all over now: thou canst quite well go." By this He meant that the nuns would lack nothing necessary. It happened in such a way that I never troubled about it again; I felt just as though I had been leaving them an excellent income. I began at once to get ready to go, for I realized that I was doing nothing more than enjoy myself in this house,[3] where I am very well off, whereas elsewhere I might have more troubles but I should be of greater use. The Archbishop and the Bishop of Palencia remained good friends. The Archbishop soon began to be very kind to us and gave the habit to a daughter of Catalina de

---

[1] I.e., in 1582. The two daughters professed on April 22 of that year as María de San José and Isabel de Jesús.

[2] Elena de Jesús, who took the habit in 1582, but, on account of her youth, was professed only on June 25, 1586. The mother, as we have seen (p. 186, n. 2, above), took the habit in 1587.

[3] This and several other phrases show that the Saint wrote this chapter before leaving Burgos.

Tolosa[1] and to another nun who entered the house shortly afterwards.[2] Until now there has been no lack of persons to help us and Our Lord will not allow His brides to suffer if they serve Him as it is their duty to do. To this end may His Majesty, by His great mercy and goodness, grant them grace.[3]

JESUS

I have thought it well to describe here how the nuns of Saint Joseph's, Ávila, which was the first of our convents to be founded, and the foundation of which is described elsewhere, and not in this book, came under the jurisdiction of the Order, though the house was founded under obedience to the Ordinary.

At the time of its foundation, the Bishop was Don Álvaro de Mendoza, now Bishop of Palencia, and all the time he was in Ávila he was extremely helpful to the nuns. When the convent was placed under his obedience, I gathered from Our Lord that it was expedient that this should be done, and the advisability of the course became clear later. For, during the whole period of the differences within the Order, we had great help from him and on many other occasions which presented themselves his friendliness became evident. He never allowed our nuns to be visited by a secular priest nor did he intervene in this convent except when I asked him to do so. Seventeen years or so—I forget the exact number[4]—passed in this way and I had no wish to transfer the jurisdiction.

At the end of this time, the Bishop of Ávila was translated to the see of Palencia. I was at the Toledo convent just then, and Our Lord told me that it would be well for the nuns of Saint Joseph's to transfer their obedience to the Order, and that I was to see to this, for otherwise the house would soon become lax. I had understood that it was right for us to be under the jurisdiction of the Ordinary, so there seemed to be a contradiction here, and I did not know what to do.[5] I consulted my confessor, the present Bishop of Osma, who is a very learned man.[6] He told me that there was no contradiction: that at the time what I did

---

[1] On the day after the foundation was made—April 20, 1582.
[2] The other nun was Doña Beatriz de Arceo y Cuevasrubias, a young widow, who took the habit in May, 1582, and professed, as Beatriz de Jesús, a year later.
[3] St. Teresa left Burgos on July 26, 1582, when she set out, with B. Ana and Teresita, for Ávila, where Teresita was to be professed. When they arrived at Medina del Campo, however, the Provincial, Fray Antonio de Jesús, sent her to Alba de Tormes, where, on October 4, 1582, she died.
[4] Actually fifteen years, from 1562 to 1577.
[5] Cf. *Life*, Chap. XXXIII (Vol. I, pp. 231-2, above).
[6] Dr. Velázquez: cf. p. 152, above.

must have been necessary but that now there was a better way. In a great many respects it has become clear that this is so and that my confessor had seen that it would be better for the convent to be united with the others than to remain alone.

He made me go to Ávila to see to the matter. I found that the Bishop was of a very different opinion and did not agree with us in the least. But, when I told him some of the reasons for thinking that harm might come to the nuns, he began to consider them, for he was greatly attached to the nuns and is a man of great intelligence. God helped me by putting into his mind other and weightier reasons than those I had given him and he decided to do as we suggested. Although several of his clergy came and told him it was inexpedient, their arguments were unavailing.

It was necessary to ask the opinions of the nuns themselves. Some of them found the change very trying, but so great was their affection for me that they accepted the reasons I gave them, especially the argument that we no longer had the Bishop, to whom the Order was so much indebted and of whom I was so fond, and that they would not have me any longer either. This argument carried great weight with them, and so a very important matter was decided. It has been clear to everyone how much the house would have lost had we done otherwise. Blessed be the Lord, Who devotes so much care to all that concerns His servants. May He be blessed for ever. Amen.

MINOR PROSE WORKS

INTRODUCTION

Constitutions Given to Her Nuns

In the Brief of February 7, 1562, issued at the time of the foundation of the Discalced Convent of St. Joseph, Ávila, St. Teresa was authorized to draw up "statutes and ordinances, lawful, honest and not contrary to Canon Law, and after making and ordering them, wholly or partially to improve, remodel, change, revoke or entirely abrogate them, according to the character of the times, and in the same way to draw up new ones."[1] The Brief confirms such constitutions and ordinances in advance, gives them apostolic authority, prescribes their observance and forbids any other authority to issue judgments, interpretations or definitions in any way contradicting them. The faculties given by this Brief were confirmed by another Brief from the same Pope (Pius IV) issued on July 17, 1565.

Armed with this authority, St. Teresa drew up the constitutions by which the then recently founded convent of St. Joseph, Ávila, was to be governed, and of the nature of which she gives some idea in Chapter XXXVI of her *Life*.[2] For some time, it would seem, after her first foundation was made, the nuns were content to follow their Mother Foundress's verbal instructions, but from the very beginning of her Reform St. Teresa was in touch with such wise counsellors as PP. Báñez, Daza and Baltasar Álvarez, on the subject of its organization, and in April 1567 we find her taking advantage of the visit to Ávila of the General of the Order to show him her written Constitutions, and to ask him, if he thought well, to give them his approval. That he did so we know from Fray Ángel de Salazar, at that time Provincial of the Calced Carmelites of Castile, who accompanied the General on his visit, and testified to that effect in 1595. Further, in Chapter XXIII of the *Foundations*, St. Teresa writes that, when Gracián was appointed Apostolic Commissary, he gave Constitutions to the Discalced friars, the Discalced nuns

---

[1] " . . . quaecumque statuta et Ordinationes licita et honesta, et juri Canonico non contraria, condendi, et postquam condita et ordinata fuerint, illa in toto vel in parte juxta temporum qualitatem in melius mutandi, reformandi, alterandi et etiam in totum tollendi, eaque abrogandi, ac alia similiter condendi, licentiam et liberam facultatem impertimur." (*Cit.* P. Silverio, II, 155.)

[2] Cf. Vol. I, p. 259, above.

already having had theirs from the Father General. There are also many references to the nuns' Constitutions in St. Teresa's letters.

It is doubtful if the autograph of the primitive Constitutions of St. Teresa is still in existence: if it is, its whereabouts are unknown. In the eighteenth century a detailed description of an alleged autograph was given, but, if this existed, it seems to have disappeared, with many other documents, from the Archives of the Discalced Carmelite Monastery of San Hermenegildo, Madrid, during the disturbances of the year 1835.[1] It must be allowed that there is some doubt as to whether the San Hermenegildo manuscript was in fact the autograph at all: P. Andrés de la Encarnación, whose judgment can generally be trusted, gives reasons, based upon internal evidence, for suspecting that it was not.[2] No autograph was known, at the beginning of the seventeenth century, by P. Jerónimo de San José, who made various fruitless efforts to find it, but could discover nothing but copies. These he reproduced, with annotations, in his *Historia del Carmen Descalzo*: save for occasional verbal variants, they are practically identical with one another. The title which they bear is: "Constitutions for the sisters of the Order of Our Lady of Mount Carmel of the Primitive Rule, without relaxation, given by the Most Reverend General of the said Order, Fray Juan Bautista Rubeo, in the year 1568."

Naturally a large number of copies of these Constitutions were made for the continually increasing number of Reformed convents: they were, however, always subject to such modifications as might be dictated by experience. It was not till 1581, the date of the Constitutions issued from Alcalá de Henares and printed in the same year at Salamanca, that anything of the kind was published. Half a century later, in 1637, as has just been said, P. Jerónimo de San José published St. Teresa's primitive Constitutions in order that they might not pass into oblivion.

One of the best-known copies of these Constitutions is preserved in the Discalced Carmelite convent known as the Convent of the Picture ("Convento de la Imagen") at Alcalá de Henares. This foundation was the work of M. María de Jesús, of whom the Saint writes in terms of such high praise in Chapter XXXV of her *Life*. In the year 1567, when passing through Madrid on her way to make the Malagón foundation, she was asked by her friend Doña Leonor de Mascareñas to make a détour, visit M. María's convent at Alcalá and organize the life of the com-

---

[1] *Año Teresiano*, VII, 159–60; National Library of Spain, MS. 12,703.
[2] *Memorias historiales*, O 93.

munity. As the Constitutions drawn up for St. Joseph's and her other foundations had just been approved by the General of the Order, it seems probable that she used these in organizing the Alcalá community and left it the copy referred to for its future use. Ribera, who visited the Convent of the Picture in 1585, tells us that there was a copy of the Constitutions there at that time; and eleven years later, Cardinal Alberto, Archbishop of Toledo, issued a decree ordering the community in question, which is and had always been dependent upon the Ordinary, to observe the Constitutions of St. Teresa. They do in fact keep them in their original form—i.e., without the modifications made in 1581. The only fundamental difference between this and other copies of the primitive Constitutions is that it omits the last section, "Of the gravest faults", which is found in the rest.[1]

In the year 1751 a copy of the Madrid manuscript of the Constitutions was made for the Archives of the Portuguese Congregation, and this copy, attested as genuine and correct by the Archivist of San Hermenegildo, is still extant. Except as to a few words, probably slips made by the amanuensis, this copy differs hardly at all from that reproduced by Fray Jerónimo de San José, and, in spite of these discrepancies, it resembles it much more nearly than the copy of Alcalá. It bears every sign of fidelity, even following St. Teresa's curious spellings of Latin. We have accordingly used it as a basis for our text in this edition.

The plan of the *Constitutions* is so methodical and their directions are so terse and clear that it is unnecessary to analyse them in detail. It will be observed at once that they abolish the modifications introduced into the Rule by Eugenius IV in 1432, dispensing from abstinence on several days of the week and limiting the yearly fast formerly observed on all week-days between Holy Cross Day and Easter to three days a week. It reveals St. Teresa's preference for the making of foundations without any endowment—and its instructions as to the dress of the nuns and the furnishing of their convents form an eloquent illustration of St. Teresa's love of poverty, while its insistence on silence, solitude, and other aids to recollectedness are a clear revelation of her spirituality. All the regulations concerning the enclosure, the admission of novices and the conditions under which the nuns may communicate with persons in the world,

---

[1] Cf. pp. 236–8, below. [David Lewis (*The Book of the Foundations*, etc., London, 1913) translates La Fuente's transcription of the Constitutions given to the Convent of the Picture.]

indicate a natural shrewdness combined with a wisdom mellowed by experience. In short, the *Constitutions* of St. Teresa are a pattern of religious observance, at once gentle and austere in their discipline and an effective means of leading souls to the highest degree of religious perfection. Founded as they are upon the firm bases of prayer, seclusion and penance, they form a commentary on the Rule of St. Albert, and at the same time, as it were, a protective covering to prevent its being relaxed or broken.

St. Teresa's ideas are, of course, strongly influenced by her experiences in the Convent of the Incarnation, where, before the foundation of St. Joseph's, she had spent the whole of her life as a religious. The nuns of the Observance had no Constitutions of their own but seem to have conformed in a general way, and *mutatis mutandis*, to those of the friars: the Seville community, however, still preserves a manuscript copy of a document entitled "Constitutions, in old Spanish, of the Calced Carmelite nuns before the time of St. Teresa," and described as an adaptation to women's communities of the rules observed by men. A comparison of these with the Teresan *Constitutions* translated below will show that, despite the greater austerity of the latter, the two had much in common.

After Gregory XIII had decreed the separation of the Calced and the Discalced in 1580, a Chapter of the Reform met at Alcalá de Henares on March 3, 1581, which discussed, among other things, the drawing up of Constitutions for friars and nuns. On the latter point St. Teresa made special representations to P. Gracián and P. Juan de las Cuevas (the Dominican Prior entrusted with the execution of the papal Brief) and arranged for all her Reformed communities to send memorials to the Chapter describing their life as it then was and the innovations which they deemed necessary to the Reform. As these memorials were submitted to her, before they went farther, for emendation and approval, they have a certain unity. St. Teresa, writing to Gracián (as Provincial) on February 21, 1581, stresses the importance of having the Reformed Constitutions printed for general distribution, "because, when they are in writing, there are prioresses who, without realizing what they are doing, add to them or subtract from them just as they please."

Gracián had the good sense to make St. Teresa's wishes his own and they were punctiliously respected by the Chapter. The Constitutions, both for friars and for nuns, were debated from March 7 to 13 and finally approved. Those for nuns were substantially the same as those drawn up by St. Teresa and authorized by Rubeo in 1567, and, except in a few places, they are couched in her own characteristic style. They consist of twenty chapters, preceded by the Rule of St. Albert and by two letters addressed respectively to St. Teresa and to the nuns of the Reform. By December they were ready for publication.

To study the Constitutions of Alcalá in any detail would be to overstep the limits laid down for these brief introductory notes, our concern being with the document originally drawn up by St. Teresa. In the footnotes to our translation, however, will be indicated the principal divergences between the text we follow and the others already referred to, and occasional references will be found to the 1581 Constitutions also.

METHOD FOR THE VISITATION OF CONVENTS

With the exception of St. Joseph's, Ávila, which, for reasons already given,[1] was until 1577 under the jurisdiction of the Ordinary, all St. Teresa's convents were subject to the Order and therefore received annual canonical visits from the Provincial. It is to a request made to St. Teresa by P. Jerónimo Gracián, the first Provincial of the Discalced Carmelites, that we owe the existence of this attractive opuscule. Anxious that his visits should be of the greatest possible profit to the recently founded communities, the young Provincial asked her to draw up for him some instructions based on her knowledge and experience. To the Saint, the request was a command, and its fruit was this highly practical little treatise—concise and robust in its expression and noteworthy, like all its author's work, for its insight into human nature.

The autograph, together with others already mentioned, is preserved in the library of the Escorial. Clearly written and free from erasures and corrections, it is, unlike most of St. Teresa's original manuscripts, divided into paragraphs. A few notes, apparently of no great importance, were written in the margins by Gracián, but most of these disappeared when the manuscript was cut by the binders. The condition of the manuscript, and especially of its early pages, suggests that it was very frequently consulted, no doubt by Gracián himself. For, he affirms, "I used it as a guide, during the whole of the time that I held the office (of visitor)."[2]

The exact date at which the treatise was composed is unknown, and among those who have investigated the subject there is considerable disagreement. Our own belief is that it was written in August or September, 1576, a short time before

[1] Cf. Vol. I, pp. 231–2, above.
[2] Jerónimo de San José: *Historia del Carmen Descalzo*, V, 876.

the author resumed the history of her foundations. At the conclusion of this opuscule she says: "I am now going to begin the last part of the history of my foundations," and suggests that her instructions for visitors might form part of this work when it was completed. The foundations here referred to are not, as most critics have believed, the last of all—i.e., those she made in 1581 and 1582—but those of Segovia, Beas, Seville and Caravaca, with the descriptions of the foundation of which she had intended to conclude her history. On October 31, 1576, she wrote to Gracián, from Toledo, that the book was nearly finished and that he would enjoy reading it. That the *Method for the visitation of convents* was already completed at that date is suggested by an earlier letter which St. Teresa received from Gracián and in which he says: "The *Manner of visiting the Discalced nuns* is as though (you had been) taught by God. May He be blessed for everything."

Like the Constitutions given by Gracián to the Discalced friars, this little treatise originated in conversations which that Father had with St. Teresa at the time of the foundation of the convent at Seville. It would seem that, though she liked his ease of manner and the discretion which he displayed in visiting the communities she had founded, she thought him inclined to be too expansive and frank and also a little too credulous as to what was told him. It will be observed that a considerable part of this opuscule appears to be directed towards the correction of these defects.

The treatise was not published until 1613, when it was printed in Madrid, with a preface, by Fray Alonso de Jesús María, at that time General of the Reform. The edition is an extremely rare one. In 1883 it was published by Don Francisco Herrero Bayona, in a photolithographic edition, with the *Way of perfection*. These are the two most noteworthy editions.

MAXIMS OF ST. TERESA TO HER NUNS

Since Don Teutonio de Braganza published his edition of the *Way of perfection* at Évora in 1583, nearly all later editions of that work, down to the present day, have included a collection of sixty-nine spiritual maxims by St. Teresa. These are devout sayings, couched in a more concise and concentrated style than we usually find in her works: practical, as well as spiritual, they deal for the most part with silence, humility, brotherly love, detachment, mortification, obedience and other similar matters.

Two years after they had appeared in the Évora volume under the simple title "Maxims of the Mother Teresa of Jesus",

Gracián reprinted them in his edition of the same work (Salamanca, 1585), adding to the title the words "to her nuns" and putting a number of masculine words into the feminine gender. Luis de León, save here and there, followed the Salamancan edition.

We cannot tell if St. Teresa wrote these counsels in a notebook as they came to her mind, or if they were collected by her daughters in religion, and, to ensure their perpetuation, given to Don Teutonio. In her correspondence she refers to copies of the *Way of perfection* and of the *Life of Saint Albert* which she was sending to the Portuguese prelate, but makes no mention whatever of these *Maxims*. Some light may perhaps be thrown on the question by Fray Alonso de los Ángeles, who, in evidence given at Salamanca in 1591 in connection with the Beatification process, states that a selection of certain *Maxims* by St. Teresa which had since been printed was made some thirteen or fourteen years previously by P. Jerónimo Gracián. Although other *Maxims* said to be by St. Teresa were published after the date of this evidence, none but those which we owe to the good Bishop had appeared in 1591 and it would therefore seem as if P. Alonso must have been referring to these. It seems entirely probable that Gracián, through whose hands passed all St. Teresa's writings, saw these *Maxims* at the time of the Sevilian foundation: the selection might even have been made by the two of them in collaboration.

Thirty of the *Maxims*, in the author's hand, have been preserved by the Discalced Carmelite nuns oŕ St. Anne, Madrid: these were published in facsimile by Don Francisco Herrero Bayona in 1881. Three years later, a similar edition of nine further maxims, together with some other Teresan autographs, was published in Madrid: no indication is given, however, as to where these originals are to be found. The sixty-first maxim, and a number of others, exist in the curious, but not uncommon, form of a manuscript consisting of letters cut from other Teresan autographs and pasted on a sheet of paper.

The *Maxims* are here published as in Gracián's edition, variants being recorded in footnotes.[1]

ANSWER OF SAINT TERESA TO A SPIRITUAL CHALLENGE

According to P. Antonio de San José, who in 1771 published this opuscule (as later editors have also done) in an edition of

[1] [Apart from the differences in gender already referred to, the Évora and Salamanca editions are so nearly similar that the variants cannot be shown in translation. The few exceptions will be found in the footnotes.]

St. Teresa's *Letters*, the autograph manuscript of it was preserved at that time by the Discalced Carmelite nuns of Burgos, complete except for one page, which was to be found in their convent of Guadalajara. This autograph, P. Antonio adds, bears on its first page the following inscription: "This was written by our Mother Teresa after she had founded the first Convent of Discalced nuns at Ávila, her superiors having sent her as Prioress to the Convent of the Incarnation, where she had been a religious. And she exercised the nuns of that holy [i.e., the Discalced] house in these holy challenges, of which we have had these ten sheets."

The autograph is no longer to be found at Burgos; and, as P. Antonio's statement is confirmed by similar evidence of about the same date, it is to be presumed that the manuscript was lost when the convent was sacked and burned by the French in 1808. The Guadalajara Convent of St. Joseph, however, still has the last page, which contains the final lines attributed by the author to herself. There is no doubt whatever as to the authenticity of this page of the autograph.

It would appear that the opuscule was written at the Convent of the Incarnation, where, as has been seen, St. Teresa was Prioress from 1571 to 1574. Apart from the inscription said to have been on the autograph, there is evidence for this in the fact that the nuns whose names figure in it come from that Convent. Isabel de la Cruz, for example, the third to be mentioned, was Sub-Prioress there when, in 1567, St. Teresa took her to help in the Reformed foundation at Medina; in the following year, she became Prioress of the Discalced house at Valladolid, and, when St. Teresa was sent as Prioress to the Incarnation, she brought her back to hold her former office: eventually she succeeded the Saint as Prioress. These data make it clear that the *Answer* was written between 1571 and 1574, and decisive confirmatory evidence can be found in the reference to the author made by Antonia del Águila: she is "our Mother Prioress, Teresa of Jesus."

It is believed that the "challenge" to which this opuscule is an "answer" was written by the Discalced Carmelite friars of Pastrana, a house established in 1569 (*Foundations*, Chapter XVII) in the hermitage presented by the Prince and Princess of Éboli. This monastery was, from its very foundation, exemplary for its austerity of life—a rival, indeed, in that respect, of Duruelo. The reference in the *Answer* to the challenger being at the time in certain "caves", whence he was to sally forth to the field of this world, was believed by P. Antonio de San José to indicate Gracián, who, after taking the habit at Pastrana in

April 1572, lived for long periods in the famous caves of the Cerro de San Pedro. P. Antonio states, too, that in the Burgos Convent there was a spiritual treatise written by Gracián and addressed to St. Teresa the title of which refers to a "challenge" issued by "Anastasio"—the name which Gracián later used for himself in his writings. This treatise is no longer extant, but it will be seen that the evidence points to a date in the latter half of 1572 for both the challenge and the answer.[1] If the "knight-errant" mentioned in the *Answer* is, as seems probable, St. John of the Cross, this date receives further support, since it was in 1572, between May and September, that he went to the Incarnation as Confessor.[2]

The argument of the opuscule is a curious one and there are reasons for thinking that there was a particular intention behind it. About 1571 there was a novice-master at Pastrana, Fray Ángel de San Gabriel by name, who was greatly enamoured of strange and exaggerated penances and mortifications and became a law unto himself in the imposing of them, so that St. John of the Cross had to return precipitately to Pastrana from Alcalá de Henares in order to undo some of the harm which he had been causing. The whole matter was reported to the Mother Foundress, who supported St. John of the Cross, but took the precaution of submitting it to P. Báñez, and received from him a letter, dated April 23, 1572, which condemns Fray Ángel and upholds the action taken against him. It was shortly after this that St. John of the Cross went to the Incarnation.

JUDGMENT GIVEN BY SAINT TERESA UPON VARIOUS WRITINGS

One day, towards the end of 1576, St. Teresa heard interiorly these words from the Lord: "Seek thyself in Me." She communicated them to her brother Don Lorenzo de Cepeda— not so much, probably, because she supposed he could explain them to her as because she thought it would do him good to meditate upon them. But evidently she found the words very obscure, since she asked for an explanation of them from three such spiritually minded men as Julián de Ávila, Francisco de Salcedo and St. John of the Cross. These three friends resolved to hold a number of meetings for the purpose of discussing the phrase and its implications; and the Bishop of Ávila, Don

---

[1] The custom according to which Carmelite communities sent spiritual challenges to one another has now practically ceased. Many of them, however, indulge in this practice among themselves. At St. Joseph's, Avila, for example, such challenges are held on Holy Cross Day (September 14), and in Advent and Lent.

[2] *St. John of the Cross*, I, xxvi.

Álvaro de Mendoza, who was also a highly spiritual person, decided that it would be advisable for each of them to set down his opinion in writing.

The sessions of this strange committee were held in the parlour of St. Joseph's, Ávila, and the nuns took part in the discussion. It had first been agreed that they should act as judges, until the Bishop decided instead to send the written commentaries to St. Teresa herself, who at that time was at Toledo. The Saint, in obedience to her good friend and patron, did as he instructed her, while protesting—in the introductory paragraph to her *Judgment*—that she would not have done so but for his command.

Adopting the light, ironical tone to be expected in a document of this type,[1] she first warns Francisco de Salcedo, that "saintly gentleman" so often mentioned in her *Life*, that she is afraid she will have to report him to the Inquisition. From a letter written to Lorenzo (*Letters*, 158, January 2, 1577), however, we gather that she liked Salcedo's answer, which was "just like him" (*harto por su humor respondió*) and that she thought he had been led astray by his excessive humility. Julián de Ávila, she thinks, "began well but finishes badly" and was unable to penetrate to the root of the matter under discussion. St. John of the Cross (as might have been expected of him) wrote at much greater length: his reply she finds excellent in quality and most suitable "for those who are thinking of following the Exercises practised in the Company of Jesus", but not entirely to the point. "God deliver me," she adds in the same light, and almost playful, tone which characterizes the whole opuscule, "from people who are so spiritual that they want to turn everything into perfect contemplation, come what may." Her brother Don Lorenzo she dismisses with affectionate summariness: "he has said more than he realizes," but "we forgive him the lack of humility"—of which he was apparently very conscious. "God grant," she adds in one of the most delightfully homely and realistic of all her metaphors, "that, as he has been so near the honey, some of it may stick to him." It appears, from the letter to Don Lorenzo just quoted, that answers were also submitted by a number of the nuns of St. Joseph's. "Some of the sisters' replies," she reports, "have made me laugh. Others are extremely good and have given me light on the meaning of the words." In the *Judgment*, however, as it has come down

---

[1] [Its Spanish title *Vejamen* . . . , here translated *Judgment*, recalls the burlesque ceremony held in Spanish universities before the conferring of a doctor's degree, when the candidate was banteringly eulogized and attacked by professors and fellow-students. The influence of this idea on St. Teresa will be obvious to the reader.]

to us, she neither criticizes nor even mentions the nuns' replies at all.

It is unfortunate that none of the replies pronounced upon should have been preserved, so that we could see them through our own eyes instead of only through those of St. Teresa. Don Lorenzo's alone, written largely in verse, is extant: it was first published by La Fuente from a manuscript in the Spanish National Library[1] [and again, from the original, by P. Silverio de Santa Teresa].[2] It may be added here that one of St. Teresa's poems (the eighth in this edition)[3] has a close connection with the subject of the *Judgment*.

St. Teresa refers in some detail to this opuscule in a letter written to M. María de San José, Prioress of the Discalced nuns in Seville, on March 2, 1577. "Here," she writes, "are the replies. . . . It was agreed that the question should be answered at St. Joseph's by those whose replies I am now sending, and that the nuns there should judge them. But the Bishop, who was there, ordered them to be sent to me to judge, though I had a headache too bad even to allow me to read them. Show them to Father Prior [i.e., Antonio de Jesús] and to P. Nicolás [Doria]. You will have to tell them what it is about, but do not let them read my judgment until they have seen the replies themselves. And send them back to me if you can, so that our Father [i.e., Gracián] may enjoy them."[4]

As St. Teresa had received all the answers to her question by January 2, 1577—and not only do we know that she could, on occasion, be a quick worker, but she tells us, at the end of her first paragraph, that she had had to do this hurriedly—it is not straining credulity to suppose that she had written her *Judgment* a few days later. I do not know why P. Grégoire de St. Joseph fixes the exact date of its composition at January 27, 1577[5] but it is fairly certain that it was written during that month of January, since by February 10 St. Teresa had heard that one of the writers had been annoyed by the bantering tone of her criticism. "You must know," she wrote to Lorenzo on that date (*Letters*, 168), that I guessed what the effect of my judgment would be. I thought you would not like it but it was quite impossible for me to criticize (what you wrote) seriously. If you looked (at what I wrote, you will have seen that) I did

[1] *Escritos de Santa Teresa*, I, 562.
[2] P. Silverio, VI, 534–5.
[3] See p. 287, below.
[4] *Letters*, 173.
[5] *Lettres de Sainte Thérèse de Jésus*, 2nd ed., II, 52. [P. Grégoire is followed by the Benedictines of Stanbrook (*Letters*, etc., II, 233).] P. Gerardo de San Juan de la Cruz (*Vida del M. Julián de Ávila*, p. 154) believes the date to have been some time in April [which seems definitely impossible].

not omit to praise a part of what you said. I could not have commented otherwise (than I did) on your reply (to my question) without telling a falsehood."[1]

The autograph of the *Judgment* has been preserved by the Discalced Carmelite nuns of Guadalajara with the exception of the part concerning Don Lorenzo de Cepeda, which has been lost. It was first published at Zaragoza, by Palafox, in 1657, in a volume of St. Teresa's letters issued under the authority of the superiors of the Order.

————

The briefer prose writings of which no mention is made in this introduction will be found to be sufficiently annotated in the footnotes to our text below.

[1] *Letters*, 168. The bracketed phrases, which have had to be supplied in order to complete the sense, provide a good illustration of St. Teresa's compressed style. Cf. Vol. I, pp. xvii–xix, above.

CONSTITUTIONS WHICH THE MOTHER TERESA OF JESUS GAVE TO THE DISCALCED CARMELITE NUNS[1]

OF THE ORDER TO BE OBSERVED IN THINGS SPIRITUAL.

Let Matins be said after nine o'clock, and not before, but not so long after as not to leave a quarter of an hour after they are over for a self-examination on the use made of the day. A bell shall be rung when the examination is to begin and a nun appointed by the mother prioress shall read in Spanish something about the mystery which is to be the subject of meditation on the following day. The time to be spent on this shall be such that at exactly eleven o'clock a bell will give the signal for the nuns to go to bed. This period of examination and prayer shall be observed by all the nuns together in choir. And after the offices have begun no sister shall leave the choir without permission.

In summer they are to rise at five and remain at prayer until six; in winter, at six and remain at prayer until seven. When prayer is over, the Hours are to be said at once as far as None, unless it be a solemn day or the feast of a saint to whom the sisters have a particular devotion, in which case they will leave None to be sung before Mass. On Sundays and festivals, Mass, Vespers and Matins are to be sung. On the first days of Easter and other days of great solemnity it shall be permissible to sing Lauds, especially on the day of the glorious Saint Joseph.[2]

The singing must never be in harmony but always in unison, and the voices must be even. As a rule everything, including the Mass, is to be said, and the Lord will be pleased to give us some time over for earning what we need.

Let it be seen that no one is absent from choir for any trifling cause. When the Hours are over, let all go to their duties. In summer, Mass shall be said at eight; in winter, at nine. Those who communicate shall remain for a short time in the choir.

---

[1] As has been said above (p. 209), we reproduce the Portugal copy (abbreviated P) in the text. References are made in the footnotes to the copy printed by Fray Jerónimo de San José (J) and to the copy in the Convent of the Picture (CP), Alcalá de Henares.

[2] CP has: " of Saint Albert." The 1581 Constitutions agree here with P. and J.

On What Days the Lord is to be Received.

There shall be Communion every Sunday and feast day, on all days of Our Lord and of Our Lady, of our Father Saint Albert and of Saint Joseph, and on whatever other days the confessor may think well, according to the devotion and spirituality of the sisters, by permission of the mother prioress. There shall also be Communion on the feast of the dedication of the house.

Shortly before dinner the bell shall be rung for the sisters' self-examination on what they have done down to that time; let them resolve to correct the most serious fault that they find in themselves and to that end say a Paternoster for obtaining God's grace. Let each nun, wherever she may be at the time, kneel down and make her brief examination. When two o'clock strikes, let Vespers be said, except during Lent, when they shall be said at eleven. After Vespers, when they are said at two, there shall be an hour's reading;[1] in Lent this hour shall begin at two. It is understood that, as soon as the clock strikes two, the bell will ring for Vespers. When the Vespers are of a feast this hour for reading shall begin after Compline.

Compline, in summer, shall be said at six o'clock; in winter, at five. At the stroke of eight, both in winter and in summer, the bell shall be rung for silence, which must be kept until after Prime on the next day. Let this rule be observed with great care. At other times no sister may speak to another without leave, except those who hold office and about things that are necessary. This leave the mother prioress will give when one sister wishes to speak to another about their Spouse in order to quicken their love for Him, or to comfort her if she is in some necessity or temptation. This does not apply to a simple question or answer, nor to a few words, which may be uttered without leave. One hour before Matins the bell will be rung for prayer. During this hour of prayer reading may be allowed, if they are minded to spend the hour after Vespers in prayer. Let them do this in so far as they find it a help to recollection.

Let the prioress see to it that there are good books, especially the Carthusian,[2] *Flos Sanctorum*,[3] *Contemptus mundi*,[4] *The Oratory*

---

[1] [By this term, here and elsewhere in St. Teresa, is understood the reading of spiritual books.]

[2] [The Spanish text makes this plural, presumably in error]. On "the Carthusian", see *Life*, Chap. XXXVIII (Vol. I, p. 270, n. 3, above).

[3] This is a general title covering a number of collections of Lives of Our Lord, the Blessed Virgin and the Saints which were then current.

[4] [The phonetic spelling *Contentus* is used in the text.] This was the title given at that time to the *Imitation of Christ*.

of Religious,[1] and the works of Fray Luis de Granada and Fray Peter of Alcántara, for sustenance like this is in its way as necessary for the soul as is food for the body. Each nun must spend the whole time during which she is not in the company of the Community, or occupied in its duties, in the cell or hermitage assigned her by the prioress—in whatever place, in short, is allotted to her for retirement. While there, except on festivals, she must have some occupation, and during this time of withdrawal she must fulfil the injunction of the Rule, and remain quite alone. No sister may enter another's cell, save by leave of the prioress, without committing a grave fault. There must be no workroom.[2]

OF THINGS TEMPORAL.

They must always live on alms, and have no income, and, for as long as they can do without it, there must be no begging. Nothing short of great necessity must drive them to ask for alms: they must provide for themselves, as Saint Paul did, by the work of their hands,[3] and the Lord will furnish them with what is needful. If they expect no more, and are content to have no comforts,[4] they will not lack enough to support life. If they strive with all their might to please the Lord, His Majesty will take care that they want nothing. They must earn their livelihood, not by fine work, but by spinning or sewing or other occupations which are not so highly skilled as to engage the attention and divert it from Our Lord. They must not work in gold or in silver. They must not hold out for any particular price for their workmanship, but be ready to take what is offered them. If they think this not good enough, let them give up the work.

The sisters must never possess any kind of private property: such a thing must not be allowed them, either in food or in clothing. Unless they hold office in the community, they may have no box, large or small, drawer or cupboard, nor any other private possession: everything they have must be in common. This is very necessary, for the devil uses small things gradually

---

[1] The *Oratorio de religiosos y ejercicio de virtuosos* was a highly esteemed work by Antonio de Guevara, Bishop of Mondoñedo, published at Valladolid in 1542, and frequently reprinted.

[2] That is to say, no room where the nuns could all do their work together. Cf. *Way of perfection*, Chap. IV (Vol. II, p. 18, above). The Constitutions in use at the Incarnation, Ávila, lay down that there shall be such a room, in which the nuns shall do their work together, under the supervision of the Prioress or her deputy, for fixed periods.

[3] Acts xx, 34.

[4] J. reads "and support themselves without comforts." With P agree both CP and the 1581 Constitutions.

to undermine our perfection in poverty. So if a sister is seen to be attached to anything the prioress must be very careful to take it away from her, whether it be a book or a cell or whatever else it may be.

OF FASTS.

Fasting must be observed, except on Sundays, from the Feast of the Exaltation of the Cross, in September, until Easter. No meat must ever be eaten, except in cases of necessity provided for by the Rule.

The habit shall be of frieze or coarse black woollen cloth,[1] and the smallest possible amount of material shall be used in the making of it. The sleeve shall be narrow and no wider at the bottom than at the top. There shall be no pleats in the habit, which must be circular, no longer behind than in front and reaching to the feet. The scapular shall be similarly made, and four inches shorter than the habit. The choir mantle shall be white and made of the same kind of frieze as the scapular, and the smallest possible amount of material must be used in the making of it, for regard must always be had to what is necessary and there must be no superfluity. The scapular must always be worn over the coifs. These must be of coarse linen and not pleated. Tunics must be of serge, and sheets also. Sandals must be hempen-soled, and for the sake of propriety stockings must be worn, these to be of hempen or other coarse cloth. Pillows must be of coarse linen; a finer linen may be used in cases of necessity.

The beds are to have no mattresses but only straw pallets: it has been proved by people who are weak and in poor health that mattresses can be dispensed with. No kind of curtain may be hung, except when necessary, and then matting made of esparto-grass must be used, or a portière curtain may be made from alfamar or coarse cloth, or anything of that kind provided it is of poor material. Each nun shall have a bed to herself. There must be no carpets, except in the church, and no cushions for reclining upon. All these rules have already been made for the Order and must be observed: they are specified because, when slackness creeps in, people sometimes forget what is demanded by the Order and is of obligation. Neither in the habits of the nuns nor on the beds must there be any colour— not even in so small a thing as a girdle. The use of sheepskin is forbidden: when a nun is ill, she can have a dressing-gown made of the same coarse cloth as the habit.

[1] [*De jerga o sayal negro. Sayal* is the word generally used by St. Teresa for this material, but *jerga* is preferred to it in the text of this paragraph.]

The hair must be cut short so that no time may be wasted in the combing of it. No mirrors are allowed or anything finely wrought; the rule must be a disregard of self in everything.[1]

OF ENCLOSURE.

No nun may be seen without a veil, save by her father, mother, brother or sisters, or except in circumstances which appear as reasonable as these and for some definite purpose. And then it must not be for recreation but only for seeing people who edify us and assist our exercises of prayer and afford us spiritual consolation: at any interview, except at one relating to affairs of the soul, a third person must always be present. The key of the grille and that of the porter's lodge must be kept by the prioress. When the physician comes, or the barber, or the confessor, or any other person whose presence is necessary, two nuns must always act as chaperones. And when any sick nun makes her confession, another nun must be present, standing in the background where she can see the confessor, but nobody except the sick nun herself must say more to him than the briefest word.

In houses where the Most Holy Sacrament is reserved in the choir, and there are chaplains and facilities in the convent for the adorning of the church, there must be no door leading to the church. In other cases, and where a door is essential, the key must be kept by the prioress, and the door must only be opened when two sisters are present and when it is unavoidable. Where these facilities exist and there is already a door leading to the church, it must be kept shut.[2]

The novices, like the professed nuns, may receive visitors; for in case they should be discontented it must be made clear that we do not want them except of their own free will, and so they must be given the chance of letting it be known if they do not wish to remain.

They must have nothing to do with matters of this world, nor talk about them, except when by so doing they can help others, or set them in the way of truth, or comfort them in some trial. If they find that their visitors are not trying to extract any profit from an interview, they must bring it quickly to an

---

[1] This does not, of course, refer to personal neatness and cleanliness, about which, as is known from many sources, St. Teresa was most particular.

[2] Before the Council of Trent, and for some time after it, nuns used to be permitted freely to go into their churches in order to attend to their cleaning, decoration, etc. In some of her convents, St. Teresa was obliged to allow this, but the practice was completely forbidden by the Constitutions of 1581, which provide that each house must have a sacristan, or a nun who would act as messenger (*mandadera*) for it, on whom would fall the duties referred to.

end, as has been said, for it is very important that our visitors should not waste their time, but go away better than they came, and that we too should be the better for their visits. Let the nun who acts as chaperone be very careful that this rule is observed: if it be not, it is her duty to tell the prioress about it; and, if she does not do so, she will incur the same penalty as the nun who breaks it. The chaperone must give such a nun two warnings, after which the punishment shall be nine days' imprisonment, and on the third of these days discipline in the refectory: this is a matter of great importance to the Order.

As far as possible, nuns should avoid talking to their relatives; for, apart from the difficulty they will have in shaking off the effect of what they say, it will be hard for them to refrain entirely from talking about worldly things with them.

When talking with anyone outside the convent, even with near relatives, they should observe great care; and, if these are not people who delight in speaking of the things of God, they should see them very seldom and bring their visits quickly to an end.

Of the Receiving of Novices.

Let great care be taken that those who are to be received be persons of prayer whose aim is complete perfection and contempt of the world. They should not be less than seventeen years of age.[1] If they are not detached from the world, they will find difficulty in enduring our practices here, and it is better to take this into consideration beforehand than to have to get rid of them later. Then they must have good health, and be intelligent and capable of reciting the Divine Office and of assisting in choir. Let no one be professed unless during the year of her novitiate she has been found to be of the right temperament and to have the other qualities necessary for keeping our rules. If she is deficient in any of these, she should not be taken, unless she serves the Lord so well, and is so useful for the house, that it becomes evident that she will not upset the place and that the Lord will be pleased to accede to her holy desires. Anyone who has not earnest desires, and does not feel herself to be called by the Lord to this state, must on no account be received. But if her personal qualities are satisfactory, she must not be refused because she has no alms to give the house: this has been our custom until now. If she wishes to give such alms to the house, and has the necessary means, and afterwards for any reason fails to do so, the case must not be taken to the courts, nor must

---

[1] This sentence is found in J. but not in CP.

she for that reason be refused profession. Great care must be taken that nothing is done out of self-interest, or gradually avarice will make itself felt, and we shall be paying more attention to the amount of a person's alms than to her goodness and other qualities: this must on no account happen, for it would be very wrong. The nuns must always bear in mind their profession of poverty, and poverty must characterize them in every respect; they must remember that their sustenance depends, not merely upon alms, but upon faith, perfection and trust in God alone. Let this Constitution be carefully considered and observed, as is expedient, and read to the sisters. When any sister is to be received, it must be with the consent of the majority of the community, as it must also when a sister is professed. The lay sisters to be received must be strong, and they must be known to have a desire to serve the Lord. They must remain for a year without taking the habit so that it may be seen if they are what they have been taken for, and so that they may themselves discover if they can stand the work. They must wear no veil over their faces, nor may they be given the black veil; they must not be professed until they have worn the habit for two years, unless their virtue is so great as to earn them earlier profession. Let them be treated with all charity and sisterly love, and supplied with food and clothing, like the rest.

OF THE HUMBLE OFFICES.[1]

The rota for sweeping the house must begin with the mother prioress, so that she may set a good example in everything. Let great care be taken that the sisters who act as wardrobe-keeper and storeroom-keeper provide for the nuns with charity, both as to their subsistence and in all other respects. As is laid down by the Rule, no more must be done for the prioress and the elder nuns than for the rest, but attention must be paid to the needs and the age of each—but chiefly to their needs, for sometimes the oldest nuns require least. Care should be taken that this rule is generally observed; for many reasons it is an expedient one. Let no sister discuss whether she has much or little to eat, or whether it is well or ill prepared. Let the prioress and the storeroom-keeper see to it that whatever the Lord gives is well prepared, so that they may be satisfied with what is provided for them, as they have nothing else. The sisters must be required to inform the mother prioress, and the novices, the novice-mistress, of their needs, both as to clothing and as to

[1] Thus P. and CP. J. has one title, "The Common Life", which embraces this section and the next.

food; and, if they require more than is usual, even though their need be not very great, they must first of all commend it to Our Lord, for our nature often demands more than it needs, and sometimes the devil encourages it in this, so as to make us afraid of penance and fasting.

OF SICK NUNS.

Sick nuns should be tended with the greatest love and indulgence and compassion, so far as this is in accordance with our vow of poverty, and they should praise Our Lord God when He makes good provision for them. If they lack things which the wealthy have for the relief of sickness, they must not become dissatisfied, for they came here with the resolve to forgo such things, and poverty implies doing without what perhaps we most need. The mother prioress must give close consideration to this: nuns who are in good health should go without necessaries rather than that sick nuns should be without certain comforts. The other sisters must visit those who are sick and cheer them. The sister appointed infirmarian must be one who has the skill and charity necessary for this office. During periods of illness nuns must try to practise the perfection they have acquired while in health: they must be patient, and, when their complaint is not serious, as little importunate as possible; they must be obedient to the infirmarian so that their illness may be profitable and beneficial to her and also edifying to the other sisters. Sick nuns must have linen and good beds—I mean, mattresses—and be carefully tended and treated with great charity.

The sisters must never be given set tasks[1] but each must work hard so that there may be food for all. They must pay careful heed to what the Rule ordains—that whoever would eat must also work—and remember the example of Saint Paul.[2] If of her own free will a sister ever wishes to undertake and finish a set task each day, she may do so, but in that case she is not to be given a penance if she fails to finish it.

Every day, when the sisters meet after supper or collation, the doorkeeper shall report what has been received that day as alms, together with the names of the donors, so that the sisters may all remember to beseech God to recompense them.

No fixed rule can be made as to the time of dinner, for that depends on what is given us by the Lord. When there is anything to eat, it shall be taken, in winter, at half-past eleven on a

---

[1] [The Spanish word is merely *tarea*, " task "]. The word was applied to a task set in advance, to be completed within a fixed period.
[2] 2 Thessalonians iii, 8-12.

fast-day appointed by the Church and at eleven when the fast is of the Order: in summer, the dinner-bell shall be rung at ten. If the Lord puts it into the mind of any sister to perform some act of mortification, let her first ask leave, and let not this good and devout practice fall into disuse, for it is not unprofitable, but it should be done quickly so as not to delay the reading. Except at dinner and supper, no sister may eat or drink without permission. When dinner is over, the mother prioress may allow all the nuns to talk of whatever they like, provided it be not outside the limits which a good religious ought to observe: they must all have their distaffs with them.

No kind of game is to be permitted, for the Lord will give grace to some so that they may give recreation to others. Provided this principle be observed, the time will always be well spent. Let them try not to annoy each other: both their fun and their talk must be in moderation. In the summer, at the conclusion of this hour during which they are all together, they may have an hour's sleep: anyone not wanting to sleep must keep silence.

After Compline and prayer, as described above, the mother prioress may again allow the sisters to talk, both in winter and in summer. They must have their work with them, as has been said, and the length of this period shall be wholly at the discretion of the mother prioress. No sister must embrace another, or touch her face or hands, and there must be no special friendships among them but each must have a general love for all the rest, as Christ often commanded his Apostles. This will be easy for them to do as they are so few in number. Let them strive to imitate their Spouse, Who gave His life for us. This habit of loving the whole community, and not merely individuals, is of great importance.

No sister may reprove another for the faults which she sees her commit: if they are serious, let her warn her of them in charity when they are alone together. If, after three such warnings, she does not amend, let her tell the mother prioress, but no other sister. As there are correctors whose special concern is with faults, all the others should take no notice of those they see, and not trouble about them, but concern themselves with their own. Let them not intervene when faults are committed in the course of their duties, unless they are serious ones, in which case they are bound to report them, as has been said. Let them be most careful not to excuse themselves, except when it is essential; this they will find a great help to progress.

The correctors must be very careful to observe faults that are committed, and, sometimes, on the prioress's command, they may reprove the culprits in public, even when this means that younger nuns will be reproving elder, so that they may be exercised in humility. They must never make any reply, even if they think they are not to blame. No sister may give or receive anything, or ask for anything, even from her parents, without the permission of the prioress, who must be shown everything given to the nuns as alms. Neither to the prioress nor to any of the sisters may the title "Doña" ever be used.[1]

Since everything must be done in conformity with our Rule, the punishment for faults and failures to do what has been said shall, for both graver and lighter faults, be the penalties provided at the end of these Constitutions. With regard to everything that has been laid down above, the mother prioress shall have the power to grant dispensations, in accordance with what is just, and with discretion and charity. She shall not have the power to make it incumbent upon them to consider their faults as mortal sin, but may impose corporal punishment upon them.

There shall be no decorations in the house, but only in the church; and nothing in it shall be finely carved—everything is to be made of rough wood. The house shall be small and the rooms low; it must answer all needs but contain nothing superfluous. Let it be as strong as possible, surrounded by a high fence, with a field in which hermitages can be made where the sisters may withdraw for prayer, in accordance with the practice of our holy Fathers.

Of the Departed.

The Sacraments must be administered as is commanded in the Ordinary. The funeral rites and burial of the dead are to be accompanied by a vigil and a sung Mass[2] and the year's mind shall also be kept with a vigil and a sung Mass. If possible, the Masses of Saint Gregory should be sung; if not, let them do whatever is practicable. Let the whole community recite an Office of the dead for nuns of their own convent, and for other nuns—that is, for any nuns of the Primitive Rule—let the Office of the dead be said and if possible[3] a Mass sung. For nuns of the Mitigation, let an office for the departed be said only.

Of the Obligations of each Nun in her Office.

It is the duty of the mother prioress to take great care that the Rule and Constitutions are observed in every way, to be

---

[1] This title, in St. Teresa's day, was reserved for well-born persons and was much coveted in the world.

[2] In J. and CP. the sentence ends here.

[3] This word, omitted in P., is supplied from J.

watchful over the observance in the house of the principles of
modesty and enclosure, and to ensure, with a mother's love,
that all duties are done and all needs provided for, both in
things spiritual and in things temporal. Let her strive to be
loved so that she may be obeyed. Let the prioress appoint as
portress and sacristan nuns whom she can trust, and whom,
when she thinks well, she can remove, so that there may never
be any excuse for a nun to feel that she has a right to an office.

s, except the sub-prioress,
key-bearers. They—or
able to read and keep

rioress to look after the
of the Offices shall be
Let great care be taken
ress, the sub-prioress will
be constantly with the
committed in choir and
nt.

accounts to the treasurer,
er must consult them in
iree keys for the convent
by the prioress and the

nd to all that has to do
ord is served there with
ist see that confessions
allow them, on pain of
l without leave, and in
erson appointed for the

r the senior portress, for
same person) to provide
bought for the house, if
speak gently and in an
ably to the sisters' needs
and receipts. When she
nd out for a particular
the price has been told
nust never allow a sister

to go to the turn without permission, and if anyone comes to
the grille she must call the sister whose duty it is to be present
at such interviews. She must tell nobody but the prioress of
anything that happens there, and give no letters to anyone but the
prioress, who must read them first. Nor must a message be given

to anyone until it has first been given to the prioress,[1] and no message must be sent out by anyone else on pain of grave sin.

The correctors must exercise great care as to noting the faults they may see—an important duty—and report them to the superior, as has been said.

The novice-mistress must be a person of great prudence, prayer and spirituality. She must be very careful to read the Constitutions to the novices and to teach them all they have to do as regards both ceremonial observances and mortification. She should attach more importance to inward than to outward observances. The novices will give her a daily account of the progress they are making in prayer, of how they are proceeding with the mystery on which they have to meditate and of what benefit they are deriving from it. She will instruct them as to how they are to carry out this exercise, and also how to act during periods of aridity, and show them how they must themselves gradually break in their wills, even in small matters. Let the holder of this office be sure that she is careless about nothing, for she is bringing up souls in which the Lord is to dwell. Let her treat them compassionately and lovingly, not marvelling at their faults, for their progress is bound to be gradual, and mortifying each of them, according to what she sees to be her powers of spiritual endurance. Let her attach more importance to their not failing in the virtues than to strictness of penance. The prioress should see that help is given to the novice-mistress in the teaching of the novices to read.

Once in each month let all the sisters report to the prioress what progress they have made in prayer and the way in which Our Lord is leading them. If they are not doing well, His Majesty will give her light to guide them. For them to do this is an act of humility and mortification and conducive to great progress. When the prioress sees that she has no one suitable to be novice-mistress, she must herself assume that office, so important is it, and take the work upon herself, appointing somebody to help her.

When nuns with duties to do have to omit the observance of any hour which they should devote to prayer, they must take some other hour, whichever is the freest for them—that is, when they have been unable to devote the whole of such an hour, or the greater part of it, to prayer.[2]

---

[1] " Until the prioress has first been told ", read CP., J. and the 1581 Constitutions.
[2] In CP, there follows here the paragraph beginning " The alms which the Lord gives . . .", which in our text is the last but one of the entire work.

Of the Chapter for Grave Faults.

The Chapter for grave faults shall be held once weekly. In it, according to the Rule, the sisters' faults are to be corrected in charity. The nuns attending it shall always be fasting. When the signal is given, and the nuns are all assembled in Chapter, the prioress or president shall give a sign and the sister who holds the office of lector shall then read these Constitutions and the Rule. The reader shall say: "Jube, Domine, benedicere," and the president shall answer: "Regularibus disciplinis nos instruere digneris, Magister Cœlestis," and they shall respond: "Amen." Then, if the mother prioress thinks well to make any brief remarks concerning either the reading or the correction of the sisters, she shall first of all say: "Benedicite", and the sisters shall prostrate themselves and answer "Dominus", remaining prostrate until bidden to rise. When they have risen they shall sit down again; and, the novices and lay sisters first, and afterwards the elder sisters, shall advance, two by two, into the middle of the Chapter House, and declare their faults and negligences to the president openly.[1] The lay sisters and the novices and those who have no seat nor voice in the Chapter shall be dismissed first of all. Only for two reasons shall the sisters speak in Chapter: either to give a simple account of their own and their sisters' sins or to answer any question which the president may put to them. And let anyone who is accused beware lest she accuse any other upon a mere suspicion that she may have of her: should anyone do this, she shall herself suffer the same punishment which belongs to the crime of which she has accused her. The same shall be done to any sister who accuses another of a fault for which she has already made satisfaction. But lest any vices or defects should be concealed, a sister shall be allowed to tell the mother prioress or the visitor of the house anything that she has seen or heard.

Any nun who accuses another falsely shall be punished similarly, and she shall also be obliged, as far as possible, to restore the reputation of the sister against whom she has spoken. The accused shall make no reply unless she is bidden to do so, and in the latter case she shall humbly say: "Benedicite"; if she replies impatiently, she shall be more severely punished, according to the president's discretion. This punishment shall be inflicted after her fit of passion is over.

Let the sisters be careful never in any way to divulge or make public the resolutions agreed upon at any Chapter or the secrets of its discussions. None of the punishments given or decisions

[1] "Kneeling", adds J.

announced by the mother in Chapter must be referred to outside it, in a grumbling spirit, by any sister, for this gives rise to discord and does away with a convent's peace, and divisions are formed and the duties of the elder sisters are encroached upon.

The mother prioress, or the president, with a zeal for charity or love of justice, and without dissimulation, may legitimately correct faults which are clearly revealed or confessed, according to what is here laid down.

The mother may lighten or abbreviate a penance due on account of any fault which has not been committed out of malice— at least on the first, second or third occasions of its commission. But if she finds any sisters sinning wilfully and maliciously, or out of bad habit, she must add to the penances laid down, and must neither excuse nor relax them without authority from the visitor. Those who habitually commit slight faults must be given penances appropriate to graver faults. Similarly, other penances must be increased if the sins to which they relate are habitual.

When faults have been heard or corrected, the psalms *Miserere mei* and *Deus misereatur* will be recited, as commanded in the Ordinary, and, the Chapter over, the president will say: "Sit nomen Domini benedictum," the community to answer: "Ex hoc nunc et usque in saeculum."

Of Slight Faults.

A slight fault is committed if, when the signal is given, any nun delays making proper speed or haste in preparing to come to choir in due order and with composure. If any nun comes in after the Office has begun, or reads or sings badly, or takes offence and does not immediately humble herself before all. If any nun is not ready with the passage she has to read at the appointed time. If any nun, out of negligence, has not the book from which she is to recite the Office. If any nun laughs in choir or makes another laugh. If any nuns arrive late for Divine service or for work. If any nun treats slightingly, or fails duly to observe, prostrations, genuflections or other ceremonies. If in choir, or in the dormitory, or in the cells, any nun makes a noise or disturbance. If any nun comes later than the appointed hour into Chapter or into the refectory or to her work. If any nun speaks or acts idly or has anything to do with idle matters. If she makes an unruly noise. If she treats carelessly any books, clothes or other things belonging to the convent, or breaks or loses anything which is used in the service of the house. If any nun eats or drinks without permission. Upon those who are accused, or accuse themselves, of these and similar things must be imposed and inflicted penances commensurate with the extent of their faults, in the shape of a prayer or prayers or of some act of humility, or of some special silence for having broken the silence of the Order, or of abstinence from some kind of food during some meal or refection.

OF FAULTS OF MEDIUM GRAVITY.

A fault of medium gravity is committed if any nun has not entered the choir by the end of the first psalm: when she enters late, she must prostrate herself until the mother prioress orders her to rise. If any nun presumes to sing or read in any other way than that in use. If any nun does not lower her eyes and attend to the Divine Office but betrays the levity of her mind. If any nun treats the altar ornaments with irreverence. If any nun does not come to the Chapter, or to her work, or to a sermon, or is not present at the common meal. If any nun knowingly neglects to fulfil a common order. If any nun is found guilty of negligence in the office assigned her. If any nun speaks in Chapter without permission. If a nun accused of anything makes a noise during the reading of the accusation. If any nun, out of revenge, presumes to accuse another of anything of which she has herself been accused on the same day. If any nun, in gesture or habit, is guilty of disorderly behaviour. If any nun swears or talks in a disorderly way, or, what is worse, makes a habit of doing so. If any nun quarrels with another, or makes any remark which will give offence to the sisters. If any nun is asked for pardon by one who has offended her and refuses to give it. If any nun enters the convent offices without permission. Let corrections of the above-mentioned and similar faults be made in chapter by means of a discipline, this to be administered by the president or by her to whom she appoints. The nun who has made an accusation is not to administer the penance, nor may the younger nuns administer it to the elders.

OF GRAVE FAULTS.

A grave fault is committed if any nun carries on immodest[1] conversation with any other. If any nun is found insulting another or uttering[2] maledictions or using disorderly language inconsistent

---

[1] *Inhonestamente* (" unseemly "), say CP. and P. J. has *inmodestamente* (" immodestly ") [P. Silverio adopts the reading of P.; I prefer J.]

[2] " Showing or uttering ", read CP. and P [The difference in the Spanish is only between *denostando* (J.) and *demostrando* (CP., P.).] J.'s correction seems justified by

with the religious life. If a nun has been angry with another. If any nun swears or speaks insultingly about any past fault of a sister for which she has made satisfaction, or about any natural defect, either of herself or of her parents. If any nun defends a fault, either her own or that of another. If any nun is found to have lied deliberately and falsely. If any nun makes a habit of not observing silence. If, at her work, or elsewhere, a nun is in the habit of relating news of the world. If any nun, without reason or permission, breaks the fasts of the Order, especially those instituted by the Church. If a nun takes anything from any of her sisters or from the community. If any nun exchanges or barters with another any cell or article of clothing given her for her use. If at the hour of rest, or at any other time, any nun enters another's cell without leave or without evident necessity. If any nun goes to the turn or parlour, or to any place where there are people from outside the convent, without special leave from the mother prioress. If a sister threatens the person of another in anger. If she raises her hand, or anything else, for the purpose of striking her, the penalty assigned to a grave fault shall be doubled for her. Those who ask forgiveness for faults of this kind, or who are not accused of them, shall be given two corrections in Chapter. They shall fast for two days on bread and water and take their meals at the very bottom of the tables, in the sight of the community, no table or place being laid for them. To those who have been accused of such faults shall be added a further correction and an additional day on bread and water.

Of Graver Faults.

A graver fault is committed if any nun dares to dispute in a captious spirit[1] and to make any discourteous remark to the mother prioress or to the president. If any nun maliciously strikes her sister, an act which will automatically involve her in excommunication and for which she must be shunned by all.[2] If any nun is found sowing discord among the sisters, or is accustomed to indulge in gossip or secret slander. If any nun, without leave from the mother prioress, or without a companion who can clearly hear what she says to act as witness, presumes to speak with persons outside the convent. If the nun accused of faults like these is convicted, let her at once prostrate herself,

---

the context. A similar divergence occurs at the word "insultingly" (denostando: demostrando) just below.

[1] J. omits this phrase, which is found, however, in both CP. and P.
[2] CP.: "withdrawn from all." J. and P. as in the text.

humbly ask forgiveness and bare her shoulders to receive the
sentence she has deserved, administered with a discipline, when
it seems good to the mother prioresss. When ordered to rise,
let her go to the cell which the mother prioress assigns her;
and let none venture to go near her or speak to her or send her
anything, so that she may realize she is set apart from the community and deprived of the society of the angels. While doing
penance she may not go to Communion or be appointed to any
office, nor may any duty be assigned to her under obedience or
any order entrusted to her. On the contrary, she shall be deprived of any office which she has held and shall have no voice
or seat in Chapter, save on the occasion of any accusation made
against her. She must be the last in order of all the nuns until
she has made full and complete satisfaction. In the refectory
she shall sit, not with the others, but in the middle of the room,
on the bare floor, clad in her mantle, and take bread and water,
unless by command of the mother prioress any other food be
given her out of compassion. Let the mother prioress behave
compassionately to her and send her some sister to comfort her.
If there is humility of heart in her, her sisters must help her,
and the whole community must give her help and encouragement, and the mother prioress must not object to her being
treated compassionately, sooner or later, to a greater or a lesser
extent, according as the nature of her offence may dictate. If
any nun should rebel openly against the mother prioress or
against her superior, or imagine or do anything against them
which is neither seemly nor lawful, let her do penance, over and
above that already described for forty days, and be deprived of
any voice and seat in the Chapter and of any office that she may
hold. And if this be done by means of conspiracy or malicious
agreement of the kind[1] made with persons in the world, causing
confusion and infamy among the sisters in the convent, let the
offenders be put in prison and be detained according to the
gravity of the ensuing scandal. And if as a result of this there
should be parties or divisions in the convent, both those who
cause them and those who abet them shall incur sentence of
excommunication and be imprisoned.

If any nun would hinder the mitigation or correction of
excesses, by charging the superiors with acting through dislike
or favour, or motives similar to these, let her be punished by
the penance aforementioned, which is assigned to those who
conspire against the mother prioress.

And if any nun dares to receive or give anyone letters, or to

[1] CP. comes to a sudden end here, except for adding the final paragraph (" As
to disciplines . . ."). J. agrees with P.

read them without leave from the mother prioress, or to send anything out of the convent or to keep for herself anything which is given her, that sister, whose excesses may cause scandal[1] in the world, shall, besides incurring the penances laid down in the Constitutions, at the canonical hours and at grace after meat, lie prostrate before the church door in view of the sisters as they pass.

OF THE GRAVEST FAULTS.

The gravest of faults is committed if a nun who does not fear to commit faults is incorrigible and refuses to do penance. If any nun apostasizes or goes outside the bounds of the community and thus incurs a sentence of excommunication. And it is the gravest of faults if any nun, instead of obeying an order given by her prelate or superior, is disobedient or openly rebellious, whether this order be given to her in particular or to all in general. It is the gravest of faults if any nun (and may God, Who is the fortress[2] of those that hope in Him, forbid this!) falls into the sin of sensuality and is convicted or seriously suspected of such a thing. If any nun has property, whether she confesses to having any or is found to have any on her death, in which latter case she will not be given ecclesiastical burial. If any nun lays violent hands on the mother prioress, or on any other sister, or reveals to others any crime committed by a sister or by the community, or betrays secrets of the community to persons in the world, or outside the convent, so that a nun from that convent may lose her reputation. If any nun seeks any kind of ambition or office, either for herself or for others, or does anything contrary to the Constitutions of the Order. Let such sisters be put in prison, or be condemned to fasting or abstinence in the place where they are, to a greater or a lesser degree, according to the extent and nature of their crime and at the discretion of the mother prioress or of the visitor of the sisters. Any such sister must at once be taken to the prison, under pain of rebellion, as the mother prioress commands. No sister in prison must be spoken to by any nun, save by those who act as her wardens, nor must they send her anything under pain of suffering the same penalty. And if a sister who is imprisoned escapes from her prison, the sister who is responsible for her, or to whom her escape is due, must, if found guilty of negligence, take her place in the same prison, and be given the punishment due to the sister who has escaped.

[1] P. omits "sister" and "may cause scandal", which are supplied from J.
[2] [Lit., "is in the fortress."]

In any convent where such things happen a prison must be set apart, and a nun imprisoned for such scandalous causes shall be set free only by the visitor. An apostate sister or a sister who commits sins of the flesh shall be imprisoned for life,[1] as shall those committing a crime for which the penalty in the world is death, and also those who will not be humble and recognize their faults, unless during their imprisonment they give proof of their patience and desire to amend, so that all who intercede for them consider that they deserve to be set free and the mother prioress and the visitor agree to this. It shall be understood that anyone imprisoned in this way loses all voice, both active and passive, in the Chapter and also her seat in it. She shall be forbidden all lawful acts[2] and all offices, and, if she is freed from prison, the privileges aforementioned shall not for that reason be restored to her, but only if this benefit be expressly conferred upon her. And if her seat in the Chapter be restored to her, she shall not necessarily regain her voice in its affairs; and, even if her active voice in its affairs be restored to her, she shall not necessarily regain her passive voice, unless, as has been said, it is expressly granted her. Any nun, however, who has fallen into any of the above-mentioned categories shall not be exonerated to the extent of becoming eligible for any office, nor shall she accompany the sisters to the turn, or anywhere else. A sister who has fallen into a sin of sensuality shall in no case, even though she repent and implore mercy and pardon, be received back into the community, save if some reasonable cause supervene and on the recommendation and advice of the visitor. If any nun be convicted before the prioress of having borne false witness against any other, or of having habitually slandered her, let her do her penance as follows. At the hour of dinner, without her mantle but wearing a scapular on the back and front of which have been sewn two tongue-shaped strips of red and white cloth, one of each on either side, let her sit on the floor, in the centre of the refectory, and take bread and water, as a symbol of punishment for her great sin of the tongue, and let her be taken thence to the prison, and if she be ever set free from prison let her have no voice or seat in the Chapter. And if the prioress (which God forbid) commit any of these faults, let her be at once deposed and severely punished. In every convent there shall be a copy of these Constitutions kept in a chest furnished with three keys, and also other copies, so that they may be read to all the sisters assembled together at such times as the mother prioress may order, and each

---

[1] [*Perpetuamente*]. This is the reading of J. P. has *perfectamente* [" perfectly "], presumably by a slip.

[2] " She shall be freed from all lawful arts ", reads P, unintelligibly.

of the sisters may have them firmly fixed in her memory, since it is in this way that, with the help of Our Lord, they will learn to make great progress. They should all take care to read them several times, for which reason there must be more copies of them in the convent than has already been said, so that any nun, when she wishes, may take a copy to her cell.

The alms which the Lord gives to the community in money shall always be immediately placed in the chest with the three keys, save when it amounts to less than nine or ten ducats, in which case it shall be given to the key-bearer appointed for the purpose by the prioress, and she shall give the bursar whatever the prioress tells her to spend; and each night, before the bell rings for silence, the bursar must render a detailed account of this to the prioress or to the said key-bearer. And, when the accounts have been rendered, let them all be entered in the convent book, which is examined by the visitor once a year.

DEO GRATIAS

As to disciplines to be taken, the Ordinary specifies the giving of some on days when the ferial office is said, and, during Lent and Advent, on every day when the ferial office is said; and, at other times, on Mondays, Wednesdays and Fridays,[1] when the ferial office is said on those days. On every Friday of the year the discipline is to be taken for the increase of the Faith, and for our benefactors, and for the souls in purgatory, and for captives, and for those who are in mortal sin: one Miserere, with prayers for the Church and for the objects mentioned. These disciplines each sister can give herself, in choir, after Matins. Other disciplines can be given with twigs, as commanded by the Ordinary. Let no one do more than this, or perform any penance, without permission.[2]

[1] P. adds "Tuesdays": but J., C.P., and the Constitutions of 1581 agree with the Ordinary of 1544 in giving three days only. This is the "Ordinary" referred to at the end of the paragraph.

[2] This paragraph seems out of place (Cf. p. 235, n. 1, above) but the fact that it is ound in all the copies suggests that it was in the autograph.

METHOD FOR THE VISITATION OF CONVENTS OF DISCALCED CARMELITE NUNS[1]

I confess, first of all, how imperfect I was, at the time when I began this work, as touching obedience; for, though I desire more than anything else to possess this virtue, it has caused me the greatest mortification and great repugnance also. May Our Lord grant that what I say may be to some purpose, for my sole trust is in His mercy and in the humility of him who has commanded me to write.[2] Because of this, God will do according to His almighty power without considering me.

Though it may seem inappropriate to begin with temporal things, I have thought it of the greatest importance to do so, in order that there may be greater progress in spiritual things, though this does not seem to be so in convents founded in poverty. But it is necessary to have order in everything and always to keep in mind questions of government and organization.

First, it may be laid down in advance that it is of the greatest importance for a superior to behave in such a way towards the nuns under his charge that, though on the one hand he will be kind to them and show them affection, he will make it equally clear that in fundamental matters he will be strict and never show any softness. I believe there is nothing in the world so bad for a superior as for those under him not to fear him and to think that they can treat him like an equal—and this is particularly bad for women. Once they see him to be so easily influenced that he will overlook their faults and modify his judgments so as not to cause them pain, it will be very difficult for him to govern them at all.

It is essential for them to realize that they have a superior who is unbending with regard to anything prejudicial to the Rule of their Order, and for the judge to be so upright in his justice as to convince them that he will never swerve from any course by which God is better served and perfection is increased, even were the world to perish. Up to a certain point he should be kind and affectionate to them, but only for so long as he sees no falling off in them. He must show himself merciful, and love

---

[1] The full title prefixed by an unknown hand to the original manuscript of this work is as follows: " Method for the visitation of convents of nuns, written by the holy Mother Teresa of Jesus, by the command of her Provincial Superior Fray Jerónimo Gracián de la Madre de Dios." This title, however, lacks precision, for, useful as the little treatise may be to nuns in general, it was actually written for her daughters alone.

[2] P. Jerónimo Gracián.

them like a father, for this will do a great deal to comfort them and keep them from leaving him; yet this other quality which I have mentioned is necessary as well. If he is to fail in either, it is incomparably better that he should fail in kindness than in severity.

For visitations are made only once a year, in order that the visitor may be able affectionately and gradually to correct and remedy faults; so, unless the nuns understand that at the end of each year any faults they commit will have to be redressed and punished, year after year will pass and the Rule and the Order will become so relaxed that, even if its amendment be desired, it will have become impossible. For, though it may be the prioress who is at fault, and the nuns may succeed in replacing her by another, they will themselves have become accustomed to laxity. Custom is a terrible thing in human nature; little by little and in trifling matters offences against order come to be committed which are irremediable, and a superior who fails to redress them in time will have a terrible account to render to God.

I think I am myself committing an offence against these communities of the Virgin Our Lady in writing of such things as these, since, by the goodness of the Lord, they are so far from requiring this severe treatment. But I am afraid that in time laxity may creep into our convents if these principles are forgotten: it is for that reason that I am speaking in this way, and also because, by the goodness of God, I see our convents making progress daily. And in some of these some flaw might perhaps develop if superiors have not acted with the severity which I recommend for the correction of trifles and for the removal of prioresses whom they may think to be unfit for their office.

It is particularly necessary to be ruthless about this, for there may be many saintly women who are not fitted to be prioresses, and any such must be removed quickly. For in houses where as much mortification and as many acts of humility are practised as in ours, no prioress will consider her removal an offence done to her: if she does so, she will make it clear that she is not fit for office, for one who is so imperfect as to wish to be a prioress cannot govern souls which strive so constantly after perfection.

The visitor must have God ever present with him, and bear in mind what favours He is showing to these houses, lest through anything he may do they become fewer in number. He must also put aside certain feelings of compassion which the devil very commonly turns to his own wicked ends. To do otherwise is the greatest cruelty that he can show the nuns under his jurisdiction.

It is impossible that all nuns who are elected prioresses can have the gifts necessary for that office, and whenever such a person is found wanting in them she must be removed during her first year. For in a single year she can do little harm; but, if she holds office for three, she may ruin the convent by allowing imperfections to become habitual. Of such extreme importance is it that this should be done that, however much it may distress the visitor, and even if he thinks the prioress to be a saint, and believes her errors to be unintentional, he must force himself not to allow her to retain her office. This I beg and entreat him to do, for the love of Our Lord; and when he sees that those who have to elect a prioress are under the sway of any prejudice or passion (which God forbid) he must annul the election and nominate prioresses from other convents so that the nuns may make a fresh election; for an election conducted in that way can never be successful.

I am not sure if what I have been discussing is a temporal or a spiritual matter. What I meant to say first of all is that the accounts of the convents must be examined with great care and attention and the visitor must not pass them over lightly. In particular it is of the greatest importance that in any house with a regular income the expenses should be adjusted to the income: the nuns must manage as best they can. For, glory be to God, all those which are endowed have enough to manage with quite well if they spend carefully. Unless this rule is observed, they will gradually get into debt and so become ruined, for if they should be in great need the superiors will think it unkind not to let them have the fruits of their own labour, or not to allow the relatives of each nun to provide for her, or not to sanction other arrangements of the kind which are quite common at the present time.[1] I would far rather see a community dissolved than come to this state. That is the reason I said that temporal conditions can have a harmful effect on spiritual conditions and are thus most important.

When a convent has been founded in poverty, the visitor must look carefully and be quite sure that it is contracting no debts; for if the nuns have faith and serve God they will lack nothing, provided they are not extravagant. He must find out, in both types of house, what allowance of food is given to the nuns, and how they are treated; with regard to sick nuns, he

---

[1] St. Teresa is here referring to abuses which were very common in certain convents —in the Convent of the Incarnation at Ávila, among others—and which she was anxious should not creep into her Reform. P. Gracián, or some other reviser, evidently taking the reference to be to the Discalced houses, altered " quite common " to " not common ", as though the author had made a slip. [In Spanish the difference between the two phrases is only one of two letters.]

must see that they are given sufficient of what is necessary for them, and this, if the prioress is courageous and diligent, the Lord never fails to provide, as we already know by experience.

In both types of convent he must observe what work is done, and reckon up what the nuns have earned by the labour of their own hands. This is doubly profitable: first, it encourages them and rewards those who do a great deal of work; secondly, in places where less attention is paid to manual labour, because the nuns have less need, they can be told how much is earned elsewhere; and, quite apart from its temporal advantages, such interest shown in their work is most profitable for them in every way. It is also a comfort to the nuns, when they are working, to know that the superior will hear of the results of what they do; for, though this is of no real importance, it is a great comfort to women who live in such strict enclosure to think that they will be pleasing the visitor when he comes down to the level of our weakness.

The visitor must also find out if too many presents have been given. This it is especially necessary to do in houses which have endowments, for in these more can be done in that way, and sometimes things which seem of but slight importance are sufficient to bring a convent to ruin. Prioresses who are extravagant may leave their nuns without food so as to be able to make gifts: there are a number of places in which this has been known to happen. For that reason it is necessary to consider what the community can do on its income and what alms it is able to give: a reasonable limit must be set to everything.

He must not allow the houses to be too large, and no debts must be incurred over their decoration or enlargement, save when really essential. To ensure this it will be necessary to order that no decoration is to be undertaken without notice of it being given to the superior, together with information as to the means available for doing it, so that he may give his permission or no according as he sees fit. This rule does not refer to small pieces of work, which can do no great harm; it is made because it is better not to have work done, even though this be to the detriment of the house, than to be worried all the time and to set a bad example by being in debt or not to have enough to eat.

It is very important that the visitor should always examine every part of the house to see if proper provision is made for seclusion. For it is well to remove occasions of sin and not to rely too much upon sanctity that is visible, however great it may be, for one never knows what the future will bring forth; and therefore, as I say, one should try to remove occasions of evil. In particular, it should be ascertained that the parlours have two grilles, one outside and one inside, through neither of which should it be possible to insert a hand. This is very important. The confessionals, which should also be looked to, must have nailed curtains: the window for Communion, too, must be a small one. The portress's lodge must have two bolts and the cloister door two keys, as the Acts prescribe: one key will be kept by the portress; the other, by the prioress. I know this is done at present, but I set it down here so that it may not be forgotten, for all these are things which it is necessary to look to continually, and the nuns must know that this is done lest they become careless.

It is also very important for the visitor to enquire about the chaplain and the priest who hears the nuns' confessions and to ascertain that there is not much communication between them, and nothing beyond what is necessary, and to make very special enquiries of the nuns about this and about the provision made for seclusion. And, if any nun has suffered temptations, he must listen to her very attentively, for, though she will often think her temptation to be other than it is, and will exaggerate in describing it, yet he may learn enough from her to enable him to discover the truth from the other nuns by laying upon them the obligation to tell him about it; and afterwards he will give them a severe rebuke for their wrong-doing so that they may be afraid to repeat it.

Severity with the nuns is also necessary when, through no fault of the prioress, one of them starts complaining about trifles, or exaggerates what she says. They must be made to realize how blind they are, so that they may not always be restless: when they find that they gain nothing by their complaints, but that the visitor sees through them, they will grow calm again. If the complaints are not serious, the visitor should always take the prioress's side, even though he may put right what is wrong, because if the nuns observe the simple rule of perfect obedience it will be a great aid to their tranquillity. Some of them might be tempted by the devil to think they know better than the prioress, and so be always on the look-out for unimportant things of this kind, which would be very bad for them. It is here that the visitor's discretion will come in: he will try to leave them in a better frame of mind, though, if they are melancholy by temperament, he will have more than enough to do. With melancholy nuns he must never be gentle, for if they think they can get their own way about anything they will never cease giving trouble and settle down quietly. So they must always realize that they are liable to be punished; and for this reason the visitor must take the side of the prioress.

If by any chance a nun tries to get herself transferred to another convent, she must be spoken to in such a way that both she and the others realize once and for all that this is impossible.[1] For no one who has not experienced it can realize what tremendous disadvantages there are in this and how, if nuns think it possible for them to leave their house for any urgent reasons they may like to put forward, the door is opened to temptations of the devil. And even when they are to be transferred they must not be told in advance or allowed to suppose that it was done at their own request: it must be effected indirectly. For a nun who is always wanting to change her convent will never settle down anywhere and will do a great deal of harm to the rest. The community must learn that such a nun will never be trusted by her superior in anything, and even if he had thought of transferring her elsewhere—I mean, for some necessary reason, such as the making of a foundation—he would not, for that very reason, do so. And it is right to act on that principle, for these temptations never come except to melancholy nuns or to nuns unfitted for doing work of much value. It might even perhaps be a good thing, before any nun has a chance to raise the question, for the visitor to have a talk with them all and show them how wrong it is and how concerned he would be if any of them had such a temptation. He could then explain the motives which prompt the desire to leave one's convent and tell them that none of them will be allowed to do so and that so far they are all needed where they are.

The visitor must find out if the prioress is making a special friend of any nun and doing more for her than for the rest: it is only this last consideration—the excessiveness of the friendship—that makes attention to this point necessary, for prioresses are always obliged to have more to do with the nuns who are more discreet and intelligent. And, as our nature prevents us from recognizing ourselves as what we really are, each of us thinks herself important, and thus the devil may be able to tempt some of the nuns in this way. For when no serious occasions of sin present themselves to us from without, he works us up about trifles concerning our community life, so that we may always be at war and our resistance may gain us merit. So the nuns may very well think that the prioress is ruled by this sister or by that. If any such friendship be excessive, the visitor must contrive to check it, for it is a great temptation to the weak; but it should not be completely ended, because, as I say, the people concerned may be such as to make these friendships

[1] Such transferences were much more common in St. Teresa's time than they are to-day.

necessary, though it is always well to lay great stress upon the inadvisability of special friendships of any kind. How this works out will soon be seen.

There are some nuns who think themselves so excessively perfect that everything they see appears to them wrong: it is always these nuns who have the most faults themselves, but they cannot see their own failings and so they throw all the blame on the poor prioress or on others, and worry the superior to death as he tries to put something right which is being done quite well as it is. It is necessary, then, as I have said, not to rely on the word of an individual nun when one is proposing to effect improvements, but to enquire of the rest; for in a convent where life is so strict it would be an intolerable thing if every superior, or the same superior at every visitation, were to issue new orders. This point is very important.[1] Except in serious matters, then, and, as I say, after obtaining reliable information from the other nuns, and from the prioress herself, as to what improvements they desire and why and how they desire them, no orders should be issued at all. For it is possible so to burden the community with such orders that they are unable to endure them and as a result they allow the important part of their Rule to slide.

The point on which the superior must strictly insist is the observance of the Constitutions; and where there is a prioress who takes upon herself the liberty of breaking these for some trifling reason, or does so habitually, thinking this or that rule to be of little importance, it must be realized that she will be doing the house great harm; and time will show that this is so, though it may not be evident at the moment. It is for this reason that religious houses, and even religious Orders, have in some places fallen into ruin: little heed is paid to trifling things and so they run into great error. The visitor must give all the nuns public warning that they are to tell him of any fault of this kind in the convent, and if he discovers such a fault he shall inflict upon any nun who has kept it from him a severe punishment. This will make prioresses afraid and they will proceed cautiously.

It is essential that, whether or no the prioresses are depressed by such things, the visitor should not temporize with them; they must realize that it will always be thus and that the chief reason their office is given them is that they may enforce the observance of the Rule and Constitutions—not that they may add to these, or subtract from them, out of their own heads—and that there must be someone to see that this is done and advise the superior.

[1] This sentence was written by St. Teresa in the margin of the autograph.

A prioress who does anything which she would be sorry for her superior to see cannot be considered to have properly fulfilled her duties; for, if I wish to keep something from one who is in the place of God, it is a sign that all is not being done as it should in His service. The superior, then, must observe if in their dealings with him the nuns are all being frank and truthful, and, if they are not, he must reprove them very severely, and see that he gets the truth from them, either by appealing to the prioress and other office-holders in the convent, or by employing some other method. For, without actually telling him falsehoods, they may be concealing certain things from him, and it is not right that, since he is the head, and they live under his rule, he should not know everything. For a body can do little good if it has no head, and a community is in exactly that position if it conceals from a visitor something which it is his duty to correct.

I conclude by saying this: for as long as the Constitutions are observed, everything will go smoothly. But if great care be not taken about this, and about the observance of the Rule, visitations will serve little purpose, for that is why they are held. If such trouble became habitual, which God forbid, the only remedy for it would be a change of prioress, perhaps even a transference of the whole community and the bringing into the convent of other nuns who are perfect in the observance of their Rule. This would amount to nothing more nor less than a re-founding of the convent, and the dispersal of the present members of the community among other houses, for one or two such nuns could do little harm in a community that was well organized.

It should be observed that there may be prioresses who will ask for liberty to do things which are contrary to the Constitution, and who may perhaps allege reasons for this which they think adequate because they know no better or want to make the superior think it necessary. And even if their proposals do not contravene the Constitution, they may be of such a kind that their acceptance would be dangerous; the visitor, not being there, does not realize how harmful they may be, and we are all apt to overrate the value of anything we desire. For that reason he will be wiser not to open the door to anything beyond what is in conformity with things as they are when he sees and knows by experience that these are going well: it is better to be certain than doubtful. In cases like these the visitor must be firm and not mind saying "No", but act with the freedom of which I spoke at first; and, in exercising his holy authority, not think of whether he is pleasing or displeasing nuns or prioresses: as time goes on, such an innovation might cause inconvenience, and the fact that it is something new is reason enough for not making a beginning.

With regard to permission for the reception of nuns, it is most important that the superior should not grant this before he has been given a full account of them, and, if he should be in a position to find out anything about them himself, he should do so. For some prioresses are so fond of receiving nuns that it takes very little to satisfy them. And when a prioress wants anything, and says she has made the necessary enquiries about it, those under her almost always accede to her wishes, and it might be that the prioress is influenced by friendship, kinship or other considerations, thinking that she is doing right, whereas she is really acting mistakenly.

It will be easier to remedy any errors made when receiving novices than when professing them. As to this last, the greatest care is necessary. During his visitation, the visitor must enquire if there are any novices and what they are like, so that, when the time comes for him to give his permission for them to be professed, he may know whether they are fit for profession or no. For it is possible that a prioress might be on good terms with a nun, or be fond of her, so that the other nuns would not dare to say what they thought about her, whereas they would tell the visitor. When possible, then, it would be more effective, if the day for the profession is near, to delay it until the superior has made his visitation, when, if he thought well, he could instruct the nuns to record their votes in secret, as at an election. It is so important that there should be nothing which can cause perpetual trouble and disturbance in the house that any pains taken in guarding against this will be well spent.

Great care must be observed as to the reception of lay sisters, for almost all prioresses like to have a large number of these and overload the houses with them, sometimes taking people who are able to do very little work. It is most important, therefore, that the visitor should not allow such admissions until he sees there is a real necessity for them. He must enquire about the lay sisters who are actually there, for, as no maximum number is fixed for them,[1] great harm may be done if admissions are not made with circumspection.

It should always be arranged that the number of nuns in a house remains below its maximum: a few places should be kept unfilled. For the opportunity may well present itself of taking some nun who will be very useful to the house and yet there will be no means of doing so, for to receive more than the maximum

[1] Though the primitive Constitutions say nothing about a maximum number, those of 1581 (see p. 210, above) fix the maximum at three for each convent.

number allowed must in no circumstances be permitted, as this would be paving the way to the ruin of convents and could not end otherwise. So it is better to prevent one house from benefiting than to do harm to all. If there is a convent which is not full, it may be allowable to transfer a nun to it from elsewhere, when her place in her own convent will be taken by another; if she had brought a dowry with her or alms had been given in her name, these should be returned to her, as she is going away for good and this is the only solution for that difficulty. If this cannot be done, the convent must cut its losses, but do not let a practice so harmful to all the nuns be begun. When the superior's leave is asked for the admission of a nun, he must be told what the total number of nuns is, so that he may decide if further admissions are expedient, for in so important a matter it is not right to rely upon the prioresses.

The visitor must also enquire if the prioresses give the nuns more to do than their obligation requires, both as to prayers and as to penances; for any prioress might impose whatever special duties she likes, and be so exacting about them as to overwork the nuns and ruin their health, and so make them unable to do what lies in their power. This does not refer to particular days on which a necessary addition may have to be made; but some prioresses are apt to be so indiscreet as almost to make a habit of this, and the nuns are afraid to protest, thinking that to do so would be taken as a sign of insufficient devotion, nor is it right that they should speak about it to anyone but the visitor.

He must listen to the choir offices, both sung and said, and find out if the pauses are being observed, and if all singing is done on a low tone, and if it is edifying and thus in keeping with our profession. For to sing on a high tone has two disadvantages: first, it sounds ill, as we do not sing in harmony; secondly, it conflicts with the modesty and spirituality of our way of life. If this be regarded as of little importance, the nuns will err through exaggeration and those who listen will derive no devotion from them. Let the voices be those of persons who practise mortification and not convey the impression that they are anxious to be well thought of by those who hear them. This is now quite a general fault, and there seems to be no remedy for it, so customary has it become. For this reason the point must be strongly emphasized.

It would be a very good thing if, when the visitor gives the prioress any important command, he were to charge one of the nuns under obedience, in the presence of the prioress, who is also under obedience, to write and tell him should she fail to accomplish it: it would be made clear to the prioress that the nun in question had no choice but to obey. This, in a way, would be equivalent to having the visitor always present and they would all be more careful and watchful lest they should commit any kind of offence.

Before a visitation begins, it will be well for the visitor to explain very seriously how wrong it is for a prioress to take a dislike to sisters who tell of any faults they may find in her. Although in describing these faults they may not be completely accurate, they are in conscience obliged to do their best; and, in a convent where mortification is aimed at, their doing so ought to please the prioress, since it helps her to carry out her duties better and to serve Our Lord. If, on the contrary, it makes her displeased with the nuns, this is a sure sign that she is not fit to rule them, and in such a case they will not dare to speak about her again, for they will think that, when the visitor goes, they will be left in a difficult position; and in this way laxity will become general. However saintly a prioress may be, the visitor must not allow her saintliness to prevent him from warning the nuns against this; for, our human nature being what it is, when the enemy has nothing else to seize upon he will put his finger upon this very thing and perhaps gain here what he is losing elsewhere.

It is most expedient that the visitor should observe strict secrecy about everything and that the prioress should not know who has spoken to him about her, for, as I have said, they are still living on earth, and, if it does nothing else, secrecy eliminates certain temptations, and at best can prevent great harm.

If the things said about the prioress are not important, they can be told her indirectly, without her knowing that they have been reported by the nuns: the oftener she can be made to think they are saying nothing about her at all, the better. But, when the things are important, it is more to the point to set them right than to consider her feelings.

The visitor must discover if any money enters the prioress's possession of which nothing is seen by the key-bearers. This is a matter of great moment, for she might receive money without thinking of it and she must never possess any save as directed by the Constitution. This precaution must also be observed in houses founded in poverty. I think I have spoken about this already, and the same will be true of other things I say: as the days pass, I forget them all, especially as I do not go back and reread what I have written.

It will be a great trial for the visitor to have to attend to all these trifles, but it would be a worse one if he found that, because he had neglected them, the nuns had not made progress. As I have said, however saintly a prioress may be, they must not be omitted. And in the government of women, the chief thing, as I said first of all, is for them to realize that they have a superior whom nothing on earth can move, but who himself observes, and makes others observe, all that his Rule requires, and punishes those who fail in this respect, and sees to it carefully that this is done in every house. They must be aware that he not only has to visit them every year but must know what they are doing every day. In such a case, perfection will gradually increase rather than diminish, for women, as a rule, have a sense of honour, but are also, as a rule, timid.

To act as has been said will be very helpful in keeping them from growing careless. Occasionally, when necessary, the rules should be not only repeated to the nuns, but also put into practice, for, if an example be made of one nun, they will all take warning by it. If at first the visitor finds little wrong, and, either out of compassion or from other motives, acts otherwise, he will be compelled later to be much more severe and these acts of compassion will prove to have been the worst kind of cruelty, for which he will have to render a strict account to God our Lord.

Some nuns are so simple that they consider it very wrong to speak of the faults of their prioress in matters which demand correction. They may think it a mean thing to do, but they must be reminded that it is expected of them, and also that, if they see that the prioress is acting contrarily to the Constitution or failing in any matter of moment, they should humbly point this out to her beforehand, for it may be that she is not aware of it. These same nuns may tell her that she may do a thing, and afterwards, if they are cross with her, may blame her for having done it. There is great ignorance as to the proper procedure at these visitations, and so it is necessary that the visitor should always advise the nuns and instruct them with discretion.

It is very important for the visitor to make enquiries about the conduct and influence of the confessor,[1] not merely of one or two of the nuns, but of all of them, and about the power which is given him. As he is not, and ought not to be, the vicar, and as the possibility that he may be is ruled out so that he may not have such influence, it is important that any communication which the nuns may have with him shall be extremely limited, and the less there is of it, the better. Great caution must be

[1] St. Teresa began to write " of the chaplain " and then altered the last word to " confessor."

exercised in giving him presents or showing him courtesies, unless these are quite small ones—occasionally such things are unavoidable. It would be better that he should be paid more than a chaplain normally receives than that he should be troubled about money, for there are many disadvantages in this.

It is also necessary for the visitor to warn prioresses not to be too generous and bountiful, but to remember that they are under an obligation to consider how they spend. Being only stewards, they must not spend money as if it were their own, but act reasonably and with great forethought and never be wasteful. Quite apart from their obligation not to set stumbling-blocks in the way of others, they are bound in conscience to do this, and also to keep watch over temporal things and to have nothing more of their own than any of the others have, except for things like the key of a writing-case or desk for keeping papers in—I mean letters. It is right that these should be kept private, especially if they contain instructions given by the superior, or things of that kind.

The visitor must inspect the nuns' habits and headgear and see if they are in conformity with the Constitution; and if (as may God forbid) there is ever anything in them which seems at all singular and not entirely edifying, he must have it burned in his presence. Such an incident will make the nuns afraid and they will at once amend their ways and remember it for the good of those who come after them.

He must also note their manner of talking, which should be simple, frank and devout, rather like that of hermits and people who live in retirement. They must use none of the new-fangled words—affectations, as I think people call them—which are current in a world always eager for new-fangled things. In all circumstances let them give preference to common expressions rather than to unusual ones.

As far as possible, lawsuits must be avoided and only be engaged in when there is no alternative. For what we lose in one way the Lord will give us in another. They must be encouraged to act with the greatest possible degree of perfection and it must be a rule that no nun shall bring a lawsuit, or defend herself in one, without first advising her superior and receiving a special authorization from him.

With regard to the admission of novices, the visitor is to admonish prioresses continually that they should pay more heed to their talents than to the dowries they bring with them, and never receive them from interested motives, but follow the principles laid down in the Constitutions, especially if there is anything wrong with their characters.

Those who come after us will have to carry on the work being done at present by the superior whom the Lord has given us,[1] from whom I have learned a great part of what I have said here, by being present at his visitations. In particular I have learned from him that a visitor must not be more intimate with one nun than with the rest, nor be alone with her, nor write to her, but must show equal affection to all the nuns, like a true father. For as soon as he becomes especially friendly with a nun in any convent, even though his friendship be like that of Saint Jerome for Saint Paula, he will no more be able to avoid being slandered than they were. And harm will be done, not only in that particular house but in all the houses, for the devil will at once see that the scandal gets about, for his own advantage; and because of our sins the world is so shameless about things like this that many disadvantages will ensue, as we are seeing at the present time.

For the same reason, the visitor will be thought less of, and the general affection which all the nuns will invariably have for him, if he is what he should be (an affection which they have for their visitor just now), will disappear, because they will think that he is bestowing all his affection in one quarter. It is a great advantage to him if he is much loved by them all. What has been said does not refer to occasions when showing affection is necessary but to circumstances in which the affection is notorious and excessive.

On entering the house—I am referring to religious houses—the visitor must see that he inspects the part of it that is enclosed. It is right that he should always do this, as well as looking over the whole of the house carefully, as has been said. When he goes through the part that is enclosed, he must always have his companion with him, as well as the prioress and some of the other nuns. And, even if he arrives early in the morning, he must on no account stay to dinner at the convent, however much he may be pressed to do so. He must inspect what he has come to see and then go immediately: if he has anything to say, it will be best for him to say it at the grille. For, although he may be acting in a perfectly honest and straightforward way, he is setting a precedent, and it may be that, in course of time, someone else will come to whom so much liberty ought not to be given and who nevertheless may want to take more. May it please the Lord not to permit this and may these things, which tend to edification, and all other things, be ever done as they are now. Amen, Amen.

The visitor must not allow overmuch food to be given him

[1] P. Jerónimo Gracián.

on the days when he is making his visitation, but only what is expedient, and, if he sees anything further provided, he must deliver a stern reproof. For it is unbecoming both to the profession of the visitor, which is poverty, and to that of the nuns, and it does them no good whatever, that they should eat more than is sufficient for them, nor is it conducive to that edification which is seemly in nuns.

At present I believe that, even if any excess of food were provided, there would hardly be any way of remedying it, for our present superior does not notice if he is given much or little and whether it is good or bad; and I am not sure that he would ever notice it unless he gave the matter very special attention. He is most anxious that whoever carries out the inspection should be alone—that is, without any male companion—because, if there should be any fault in the nuns, he does not want more than the one person to know of it. This is an admirable way of preventing any childish behaviour on the part of the nuns, if there should be any, from becoming known. At present, however—glory be to God!—little harm would be done in that way, for our superior looks on his nuns as a father might, and as such he keeps their secrets, and God reveals to him the gravity of anything that may happen because he is in His place. Anyone who is not like him would perhaps attach great importance to a mere nothing, and, not having the welfare of the nuns at heart, would not be careful to keep silence about it, so that the convent would end by losing its good name without cause. May Our Lord grant that superiors will always consider these things and act as he does.

It is unseemly for a visitor to show that he has a great affection for the prioress, or is on very good terms with her, at least in the presence of the community, for that will make the nuns afraid and they will not dare to tell him of her faults. Let him also bear in mind that they must be made to feel that he is not excusing her but is correcting anything in her that needs correction. For there is no discouragement which can affect a soul that is zealous for God and the Order. When she is troubled because she sees that the Order is declining, and, while waiting for the superior to come and put things right, observes that they are still in the same condition, she turns to God and resolves from that time forward to be silent, even if the whole world should be falling about her, for she sees how little is to be gained by speaking.

The poor nuns, when the visitor examines them, are heard only once, whereas a prioress has ample time to explain away her faults and to give explanations for them and palliate some of them and perhaps represent the poor creature who has accused her as being influenced by passion; for, though a prioress is not told the name of an accusing nun, she will have a fairly accurate idea of who the nun is, whereas the superior cannot be a witness of what has happened, and the evidence is given him in such a way that he cannot do other than believe it. So everything remains as it was. If he could be there for a few days and see for himself what was going on, he would learn the truth: prioresses never think they are not telling the truth, but such is our self-love that it is the rarest thing for us to blame ourselves or to understand ourselves either.

This has continually happened to me, and to prioresses who were very, very[1] great servants of God, and in whom I had such confidence that I thought it impossible for matters to be otherwise than as they had described them. Yet, after spending some days in the house, I would be amazed to find them very different indeed, and this in some important respect. The prioress would have told me that the accusations were dictated by ill-temper, yet I would find that they had been made by almost half the convent, and, as would afterwards become clear, it was the prioress who was not aware of her own faults. For my own part, I think that the devil, not having many opportunities of tempting the sisters, tempts prioresses to have opinions which in some ways conflict with their own, and it makes one praise Our Lord to see how they bear it all. So, personally, I make a point of never believing anyone till I have made full enquiries, so that I may explain to anyone who is in error how she comes to be so, for if the thing is not done in that way it is difficult to set it right. All this does not refer to serious matters, but serious matters can become more so if we do not act with caution.

I am amazed when I observe how cunning the devil is and see how he makes each of us imagine she is the most truthful person in the world. It is for this reason that I have said one cannot have entire confidence in a prioress or in any particular nun, and that on any important matter other nuns should be questioned with a view to the discovery of an effective remedy. May Our Lord always send us a prudent and saintly visitor, and, if He does this, His Majesty will not fail to give him light to act efficiently and to learn to know us, so that we shall all be excellently governed and souls will grow in perfection to the honour and glory of God.[2]

---

[1] [The repetition is found in the original Spanish and the word translated " very " is not the usual *muy*, but the stronger *harto*.]

[2] At the end of the opuscule proper, there is a blank page, after which comes the following address to Gracián.

I beseech Your Paternity, as a recompense for the mortification it has caused me to write this, to mortify yourself for my sake by writing certain instructions for visitors. If what I have written here has been at all to the point, your doing this will be an additional help and make it of greater service; for I am now going to begin the last part of the history of my foundations, and it could be inserted there and would be very profitable. At the same time, I am afraid there will never be another visitor as humble as he who has ordered me to write this and who will be willing to profit by it. But, as it is God's will, I could not do otherwise; for, if these houses are visited in the way that is usual in the Order, very little fruit will result from the visitations, and they might even do more harm than good. More things are requisite than those which I have described, but I do not understand them or cannot call them to mind. It is only at the beginning that such strict care will be necessary: once the nuns see what the visitation is to be like, there will be little more trouble about government.

Do what you can, my Father, to observe these counsels which I have set down, as Your Paternity is doing at present in these visitations. And all the rest Our Lord in His mercy, and through the merits of these sisters, will provide. For their intention throughout is to render Him effective service and to that end they are ready to receive instruction.[1]

---

[1] Though observations and maxims on the government of Discalced houses are to be found here and there in Gracián's writings, nothing is known of any treatise that he may have written in reply to this request of St. Teresa's and it seems unlikely that he did, in fact, accede to it.

MAXIMS OF THE MOTHER TERESA OF JESUS
WRITTEN FOR HER NUNS

1. Untilled soil, however fertile it may be, will bear thistles and thorns; and so it is with man's mind.
2. Always speak well of spiritual things, and of monks and nuns, priests and hermits.
3. When you are with many people, always say little.
4. Be modest in all you do and in all your intercourse with others.
5. Never be importunate, especially about things of little moment.
6. Speak to everyone with restrained cheerfulness.
7. Never make a mock of anything.
8. Never reprove anyone save discreetly, humbly and with a sense of your own shame.
9. Fall in with the mood of the person to whom you are speaking. Be happy with those who are happy and sad with those who are sad. In a word, be all things to all men so that you may gain all men.[1]
10. Never speak without thinking well of what you are going to say and commending it earnestly to Our Lord, lest you say anything displeasing to Him.
11. Never excuse yourself save when it is most probable that you are in the right.
12. Never speak of anything concerning yourself which is worthy of praise—such as your learning, virtues or descent—unless with the hope that some profit will come of it. If you do so speak, let it be with humility, and the remembrance that these are gifts from the hand of God.
13. Never exaggerate, but express your feelings with moderation.
14. Always introduce spiritual topics into all your talks and conversations: in this way you will avoid idle words and backbiting.
15. Never affirm anything unless you are sure it is true.
16. Never thrust yourself forward and give your opinion about anything unless you are asked for it, or charity requires that you should give it.
17. If anyone is speaking of spiritual matters, listen to him humbly, as a learner, and apply to yourself all the good things you hear.

[1] [1 Corinthians ix, 22.]

18. To your superior and confessor reveal all your temptations and imperfections and aversions, so that he may give you advice and help in overcoming them.

19. Do not stay outside your cell: leave it only for a good reason, and then, as you do so, ask God for grace not to offend Him.

20. Do not eat or drink, save at the proper times, and then give hearty thanks to God.

21. Do everything as though you really saw His Majesty before you; by acting thus a soul gains greatly.

22. Listen to ill of no one and speak ill of no one save of yourself: when you begin to like doing this, you are making good progress.

23. Address every action that you perform to God: offer it to Him and beg Him that it may be to His honour and glory.

24. When you are joyful, do not express your joy by laughing overmuch, but let it be humble, modest, pleasant and edifying.

25. Always think of yourself as everyone's servant; look for Christ Our Lord in everyone and you will then have respect and reverence for all.

26. Always be as ready to fulfil your vow of obedience as if Jesus Christ gave you each command through your prioress[1] or superior.

27. In all you do and at all times examine your conscience, and, having seen your faults, strive with Divine help to amend them: by following this course you will attain perfection.

28. Think not of the faults of others but of their[2] virtues and of your own faults.

29. Always cherish earnest desires to suffer for Christ in every respect and on every occasion.

30. Make fifty acts of self-oblation to God daily and make each with great fervour and desire for God.

31. Keep in mind all day the subject of your morning's meditation: be most diligent about this, for it is very profitable.

32. Treasure up the feelings which the Lord communicates to you and put into practice the desires which He gives you in prayer.

33. Always avoid being singular, as far as you can, for in community life this is a great evil.

34. Read the ordinances and rules of your Order very often and observe them faithfully.

---

[1] [*Lit.*, " prior ". This is one place where the masculine of the Évora edition has not been changed to the feminine.]

[2] [*Lit.*, " the ".]

35. Reflect upon the providence and wisdom of God in all created things and praise Him in them all.

36. Detach your heart from all things: seek God and you will find Him.

37. Never express outwardly any devotion which you do not feel, though you may rightly conceal devotion which you do feel.[1]

38. Do not express inward devotion except in cases of great necessity. "My secret to myself," say Saint Francis and Saint Bernard.

39. Whether your food be well or ill cooked, do not complain of it: remember the gall and the vinegar of Jesus Christ.

40. Speak to no one at table and do not raise your eyes to look at another.

41. Meditate upon the heavenly table, and upon its food, which is God, and upon the guests, who are the angels. Raise your eyes to that table and long to find yourself there.

42. In the presence of your superior, in whom you must see Jesus Christ, never speak except when necessary and speak with great reverence.

43. Never do anything which you could not do in the sight of all.

44. Never compare one person with another: comparisons are odious.

45. When reproved for anything, receive the reproof with both outward and inward humility, and pray to God for the person who has given it you.

46. If a superior orders you to do something, do not say that someone else ordered you to do the opposite, but realize that both of them acted with good intentions and obey the order given you.

47. Do not pander to your curiosity by talking or asking questions about things which do not concern you.

48. Keep in mind your past life, so that you may bewail it, and likewise your present lukewarmness, and the distance you have still to go before you reach Heaven: you will then live in fear, which is a source of great blessings.

49. Always do what those in your community bid you, if it is not contrary to obedience, and answer them with humility and gentleness.

[1] [" Which you do not feel " is literally " which there is not within "; " which you do feel " is not in the original.] All early editions have the maxim in this form. In that of 1635, and in later ones, for the second " devotion " was substituted " lack of devotion " (indevoción). The earlier reading seems better [both because of the sense and] because St. Teresa does not use the word indevoción. A copy of the Maxims preserved by the Discalced Carmelite nuns of Antequera, and dated 1604, reads indevoción and also has " Never seek " for " Never express."

50. Do not, except in cases of great need, ask for any special food or clothing.

51. Never fail to humble and mortify yourself in every way, until the end of your life.

52. Accustom yourself continually to make many acts of love, for they enkindle and melt the soul.

53. Make acts of all the other virtues.

54. Offer all things to the Eternal Father, in union with the merits of His Son Jesus Christ.

55. Be gentle to all and stern with yourself.

56. On festivals of the saints, think of their virtues and beg the Lord to bestow them on you.

57. Take great care over your nightly self-examination.

58. On days when you receive Communion, let your prayer consist in the realization that, miserable as you are, you will shortly be receiving God; at night, try to realize that you have received Him.

59. If you are a superior, reprove no one in anger, but only when your anger has passed, and your reproof will then be beneficial.

60. Strive greatly after perfection and devotion, and make use of both in all you do.

61. Constantly exercise yourself in the fear of the Lord, which brings the soul contrition and humility.

62. Consider how quickly people change and how little one can trust them, and so cling closely to God, Who never changes.

63. Try to discuss matters which concern your soul with a spiritual and learned confessor: confide in him and follow him in everything.

64. Whenever you receive Communion, ask God for some gift through the great compassion which He has shown in coming to your poor soul.

65. However many saints you may have as your intercessors, be especially devoted to Saint Joseph, who can obtain a great deal from God.

66. At times when you are sad and upset, do not abandon the good works of prayer and penance which you have been in the habit of doing. The devil will try to unsettle you and persuade you to abandon them, but rather than this you should do more of them than usual and you will see how quickly the Lord comes to your aid.

67. Do not speak of your temptations and imperfections to the members of your community who have made least progress, for if you do this you will harm both yourself and them;

speak about them, then, only to those who are nearest to perfection.

68. Remember that you have only one soul; that you have only one death to die; that you have only one life, which is short and has to be lived by you alone[1]; and that there is only one glory, which is eternal. If you do this, there will be many things about which you care nothing.

69. Let your desire be to see God; your fear, that you may lose Him; your sorrow, that you are not having fruition of Him; your joy, that He can bring you to Himself. Thus you will live in great peace.

---

[1] [*Lit.*, " that you have only one short life, which is individual (i.e., to yourself).] The Antequera copy has, after " life ", " one individual and one general account." In the *Maxims* as they used to be published with the *Constitutions* of the Convent of the Picture there is a reading almost identical with this.

ANSWER OF SAINT TERESA OF JESUS TO A SPIRITUAL CHALLENGE[1]

On seeing the cartel,[2] we thought that our strength was insufficient to permit of our entering the field against such valiant and doughty knights, since they would be certain of victory and would leave us completely despoiled of all we had, and perchance daunted into the bargain, and thus unable to do the little that is in our power. In view of this, no one—least of all Teresa of Jesus—took up the challenge. This is the whole truth and no invention.

We decided, however, to do as much as our strength permitted, and, after we have spent some days on these courtesies, we may, with the help and assistance of those who wish to take part in them, be able to sign the cartel.

The condition must be made that our challenger shall not turn his back, and hide in those caves of his,[3] but shall come out into the field of this world in which we live. It may be that, when he finds himself committed to perpetual war, prevented from ever laying down his arms, unable to relax, and deprived of even a moment in which he can rest in safety, he will become less bellicose. For there is a great deal of difference between the one kind of life and the other, and between words and deeds, and we ourselves know a little of the difference that there is between them.

Let him and his companions sally forth—let them sally forth, I say, from their delectable life: they may then soon be stumbling and falling and we shall be having to help them up again; for it is a terrible thing to be always in danger, and borne down with the weight of one's arms, and without any food. But perhaps, as our challenger[4] is so abundantly provided with this, he will send the help he has promised with all due speed. For if he gains his victory over us by hunger, he will gain little honour or advantage.

[1] For the text is used the MS. 6,615 (National Library of Spain) which has corrections not previously published in Spanish. It was collated with the autograph about the latter third of the eighteenth century.

[2] A number of words in this opuscule, such as " cartel ", " challenger ", " knight-errant ", are those commonly used in literary jousts and tournaments, which were much in vogue in St. Teresa's day, and long afterwards.

[3] [Cf. p. 214, above.]

[4] [Here, as above, the word translated " challenger " is *mantenedor*. But this word also has the meaning of " one who supplies (food, etc.) " and I think a rather clumsy transference of meaning is intended, especially as the " help " referred to just below is *mantenimiento* (" sustenance," " provisions ").]

To any knight or daughter of the Virgin who prays the Lord daily to be gracious to Sister Beatriz Juárez,[1] and to grant her not to speak ill-advisedly but to direct all her words to His glory, this sister will give two years of the merit she has gained by nursing most troublesome invalids.

Sister Ana de Vergas[2] says that if the said knights and brethren ask the Lord to rid her of an annoyance under which she is suffering and to grant her humility, she will give them all the merit that she gains thereby, if the Lord grants her any.

The Mother Sub-Prioress exhorts the said persons to ask the Lord to take away her self-will and says she will give them all she has merited in two years: her name is Isabel de la Cruz.[3]

Sister Sebastiana Gómez says that if any of the said persons will gaze on a crucifix three times a day, each of these times to represent one of the three hours for which the Lord hung on the Cross, and will obtain grace for her to conquer a great passion which is torturing her soul, she will pass on to them the merit she gains (if the Lord grants her any) for having conquered it.

Mother María de Tamayo will give any one of the said persons who will say a daily Paternoster and Ave Maria for her, so that the Lord may grant her patience and resignation to suffer her infirmities, the third part of the merits gained by her sufferings[4] on each day when they say the prayers. She is in a very serious condition and for a year or more has been unable to speak.

Sister Ana de la Miseria says that to any of the knights and daughters of the Virgin who will meditate upon the poverty in which Jesus Christ was born and died and will beg God to give her the poverty which she promised His Majesty, she will give all the merit that she may have in the Lord's eyes, despite the way in which she has failed Him in His service.[5]

Sister Isabel de Santángelo says that to any knight or daughter of the Virgin who will watch with the Lord for the three hours that He hung on the Cross before His death, and will obtain grace for her from His Majesty to keep her three vows in per-

---

[1] Beatriz Juárez left the Incarnation at some time subsequent to 1577, and, after spending some time in a newly founded Discalced house, and in the convent at Ocaña, was sent back to Ávila for reasons of health. She was greatly devoted to St. Teresa.

[2] Ana de Vergas was one of the signatories to the contract, concerning St. Teresa's dowry, made on October 31, 1536, between Don Alonso Sánchez de Cepeda and the nuns of the Incarnation.

[3] Cf. p. 214, above.

[4] [*Lit.*, "the third part of her sufferings"; but here, as elsewhere below, it seems to be the merits that are meant.]

[5] This paragraph, according to P. Antonio de San José, is not in the handwriting of the Saint.

fection, she will give a part of the spiritual trials that she has suffered.

Sister Beatriz Remón says that she will give one year of any merits she may gain to any brother, or daughter of the Virgin, who will beg daily that she may be given humility and obedience.

Sister María de la Cueva gives to any knight or daughter of the Virgin three years of her merits (and I know they are abundant, for she endures great interior trials) to anyone who will pray for faith and light and grace for her daily.

Sister María de San José will give a year of her merits to any of the said persons who will ask the Lord to give her humility and obedience.

Sister Catalina Álvarez says that she will give a year of her sufferings, and they have been many, to anyone who will ask the Lord to give her self-knowledge.

Sister Leonor de Contreras says that for any knight or sister who will ask Our Lady to obtain grace for her from her Son to serve Him and to persevere, she will say three Salves daily for the rest of her life; but such a person must pray for her in this way daily.

Sister Ana Sánchez says that for any knight or daughter of the Virgin who will beg the Lord daily to give her love for Him she will say three Ave Marias daily for him to Our Lady most pure.

Sister María Gutiérrez says that to any one of the said persons who will ask God to give her perfect love for Him and perseverance she will give a part of all her merits in the sight of the Lord.

Sister María Cimbrón[1] says that the said persons may have a share in all her sufferings if they will pray daily that she may be granted a good end: for a long time she has been unable to stir out of her bed and is in a very bad way.

Sister Inés Díaz says that for any one of the said persons who will ask daily that she may be given a share of the sorrow felt by the Virgin at the foot of the Cross she will say five Paternosters and Ave Marias.

Sister Juana de Jesús says that to any one of the said knights and sisters who will beg the Lord daily to grant her contrition for her sins, she will give a share in the many trials and offences which she has suffered on account of them, and these are certainly very numerous.

Sister Ana de Torres says that she will give the said persons all the merits that she may gain this year if they will beg Our

---

[1] In the contract mentioned above (p. 262, n. 2) this nun figures as Sub-Prioress of the Convent of the Incarnation.

Lord daily, by the torture which He suffered when they nailed Him to the Cross, to give her grace which will enable her to serve Him, and also obedience.

Sister Catalina de Velasco says that to any one of the said persons who will beg the Lord, by the pain which He felt when they nailed Him to the Cross, to give her grace so that she may not offend Him and our Order may continually increase, she will give the merit gained during the times which she spends with Our Lady daily; and these are really very numerous.

Sister Jerónima de la Cruz says that for any one of the said persons who will beg on her behalf for humility, patience and light to serve the Lord, she will say three Credos each day; and she will also give such persons a year of the trials that she has suffered. This petition must be made daily.

A knight-errant[1] says that, if the master of the field will obtain for him from the Lord the grace he needs to serve Him in all that obedience commands, he will give him all the merit that he may win this year through serving Him in obedience.[2]

Sister Estefanía Samaniego says that for any knight and daughters of the Virgin who will beg Our Lord to give her grace to serve Him, and not offend Him, and living faith and meekness, she will say the prayer of the Name of Jesus[3] daily and will give her a year's merits won by the infirmities and temptations which she has suffered.

Sister Antonia del Águila[4] says that if any knights and daughters of the Virgin will remember Our Lady's sorrows for a short time each day, and pray that the said sister may be given relief for a sore spiritual need, and also that long life may be granted to our Mother Prioress Teresa of Jesus, for the increase of our Order, she will give them a third part of her trials and infirmities for the whole of her life.

Teresa of Jesus says that if any knight of the Virgin will make a single daily act of firm resolution to suffer all his life long a superior who is very foolish, vicious, greedy and ill-disposed, she will give him half of her merits on each day that he does so,

[1] *Venturero*. Another technical term used in literary tourneys in the sense of "free-lance". P. Antonio de San José and P. Andrés de la Encarnación both opine that the reference here is to St. John of the Cross, who, at just about that time, had left his monastery to come to the Incarnation as confessor (p. 215, above). The suggestion seems a sound one and the word may be used in the sense of "transient", "temporary visitor."

[2] P. Antonio de San José states that neither this nor the next two paragraphs are in St. Teresa's hand.

[3] Thus the MS. The editions have: "the prayer, *O bone Jesus!*"

[4] The editions all have "N. de la Gila". Our reading is a correction found in the MS. Antonia del Águila, who came from an aristocratic Avilan family, accompanied St. Teresa on several of her foundations, though eventually poor health compelled her to return to the Incarnation.

both those received in Communion and those won through the many troubles which she has to bear—though, when all is said and done, there will be very little to give. He must meditate upon the humility which the Lord showed before His judges, and how He was obedient even to the death of the Cross. This agreement will be for six weeks.

JUDGMENT GIVEN BY SAINT TERESA UPON VARIOUS WRITINGS ON THE WORDS: "SEEK THYSELF IN ME."

I.H.S.

Were I not forced to do so by obedience, I should certainly not respond to this invitation or accept the task of acting as judge, and this for several reasons. These, however, would not include one put forward by my sisters here—namely that among the candidates is my brother, my love for whom might vitiate my judgment. For I have a great affection for all the candidates, since they have all helped me to bear my trials. By the time my brother arrived we had nearly drained the chalice, though he has drunk somewhat from it also, and, with the Lord's help, will yet drink more. May He give me grace not to say anything which merits denunciation by the Inquisition, in view of the state of my head after all the letters and business transactions which I have been engaged upon ever since last night. But obedience is capable of anything, so I will do what Your Lordship commands, whether well or ill. I wish I had had time to read the papers at my ease but I have found this impossible.

FROM FRANCISCO DE SALCEDO[1]

The words seem to have been spoken by the Spouse of our souls, Who says: "Seek thyself in Me." It is clear that Señor Francisco de Salcedo has gone wrong, for he insists very strongly that God is in all things, whereas the Spouse knows that He is in all things.

He also says a great deal about understanding and Union. Now it is well known that the understanding does not work in Union. If, then, it does not work, how can it seek anything? Those words of David: "I will hear that which God speaketh in me"[2] pleased me very much, for what he says about peace in the faculties is a thing to be highly esteemed—I understand the faculties to be meant by the "people."[3] But I have no intention

---

[1] In the autograph, all the cross-headings, except the one which follows this, have been cut off and have had to be supplied by the editor.

[2] Psalm lxxxiv, 9 [A.V. lxxxv, 8].

[3] [The reference is to the latter part of the text: " . . . for He will speak peace unto His people."]

of speaking well of a single thing that has been said, and so I say that it is not to the point, for the phrase does not tell us to *hear*, but to *seek*.

And the worst thing of all is that, unless the writer retracts, I shall have to denounce him to the Inquisition, which is close at hand. For at the very end of the paper in which he quotes things said by Saint Paul, and by the Holy Spirit, he says that he has put his signature to nonsense. Let him correct it at once: if he does not, he will see what happens.

From P. Julián de Ávila

He began well, but he finishes badly, and so he has not covered himself with glory. For he was asked to speak, not about created or uncreated light, and how they are united, but about our seeking ourselves in God. Nor did we ask him what are the feelings of a soul when it is so near its Creator, nor, if it is united with Him, whether or no he thinks there is any difference between them. For I do not believe anyone's understanding can settle these disputes: if it could, it would be easy to understand the difference that exists between Creator and creature. He also says: "When the soul is purified." I do not believe that either virtues or purifications are sufficient here, for this is a supernatural experience and it is given by God to whom He wills, and, if any preparation for it is possible, that preparation will come through love. However, I forgive him his errors, for he was not as lengthy as my Father Fray John of the Cross.

From P. John of the Cross

This Father in his reply gives some remarkably sound doctrine for those who are thinking of following the Exercises practised in the Company of Jesus, but it is not to our purpose. It would be a bad business for us if we could not seek God until we were dead to the world. Neither the Magdalen, nor the woman of Samaria, nor the Canaanitish woman was dead to the world when she found Him. He also says a great deal about our becoming one and the same thing with God in Union; but when this comes about, and God grants the soul this favour, He will not tell it to seek Him, for it will have found Him already.

God deliver me from people who are so spiritual that they want to turn everything into perfect contemplation, come what may. At the same time we are grateful for having been given so good an explanation of what we had not asked about. For this reason, it is well to speak ever of God; we shall derive benefit from a place where we are least expecting to find it.

From Señor Lorenzo de Cepeda, Her Brother

We are very grateful to Señor Lorenzo de Cepeda for his verses and reply.[1] If he has said more than he realizes, we forgive him the lack of humility which he shows in meddling with such lofty matters (as he says in his reply), for the sake of the refreshment which his verses have given us and his good advice (for which we did not ask him) about practising quiet in prayer—as though doing this were in our power! He knows, however, what trouble anyone who does this cannot fail to bring upon himself. God grant that, as he has been so near the honey, some of it may stick to him: he has greatly comforted me, although I can see that he has had ample reason for shame.

It is impossible to judge any one of these exercises to be better than another, for it is doing nobody an injustice to say that there are defects in them all. Your Lordship must order us all to amend; I must certainly[2] do so, for I have little humility and in that am not at all like my brother. All these gentlemen are so full of Divine grace[3] that they have erred through excess; for, as I have said, if anyone attains this favour of union of the soul with God, he has no longer to be told to seek God, for he already possesses Him. I kiss Your Lordship's hands many times for the honour which you have done me with your letter. In order not to weary Your Lordship further with these follies, I write no more now.

Your Lordship's unworthy servant and subject,

TERESA OF JESUS.

[1] [The reply was largely in verse. See p. 217, above.]
[2] Thus the MS. [*lit.*: I (*emphatic form*) must]. The editions have " I must perhaps."
[3] [*Lit.*: " so divine ", but the adjective can also mean " marvellous ", " extremely good ", and may be used ironically; or perhaps there is a play on the two senses of the word.]

THOUGHTS AND MAXIMS OF SAINT TERESA OF JESUS

Learn of me, for I am meek and humble.[1]

Saint Chrysostom: Perfect martyrdom is not accomplished by the shedding of blood alone. Martyrdom also consists in true abstinence from sins and in the practice and observance of the commandments of God. True patience in adversities also makes a person a martyr.[2]

It is union of our will with the will of God that gives our will its value, for it will then desire nothing save that which is the will of His Majesty.

To have this charity in perfection is glory.

On days when professions are made and habits given our ancient constitution prescribes that the sisters who have received the habit shall communicate.[3]

Remedies when we are persecuted and wronged.[4]

I must reflect that these things are done to God before they are done to me; for when the blow reaches me it has already been dealt to His Majesty by sin.

I must remember, too, that the true lover will already have made an agreement with her Spouse to be wholly His and to care nothing for herself; so, if He endures it, why should not we endure it as well? Our grief should be for the offence committed against His Majesty, since we ourselves are not wounded by it in our souls, but only in these bodies, which are but dust and have fully deserved to suffer.

To die and to suffer must be our desires.

[1] St. Matthew xi, 29. This and the three following " thoughts " were written by St. Teresa on a blank sheet of her breviary, which is in the possession of the Discalced Carmelite nuns of Medina del Campo.

[2] These ideas are found frequently in St. Chrysostom's homilies—e.g. *Contra Judaeos, In Psalm clvii, In Ascen. Domini*, etc.

[3] There is no extant autograph of these lines but it seems probable that they were originally written by St. Teresa.

[4] From MS. 12,763 (National Library of Spain), published, with some alterations, by Palafox in Vol. I of his edition of St. Teresa's letters. The autograph is not known.

No one is tempted above that which he is able to bear.[1]
Nothing happens save by the will of God. My Father, thou art the chariot of Israel and its guide, said Eliseus to Elias.[2]

Antiochus emitted such a stench on account of the many sins he had committed that he could neither endure his own company nor could those who accompanied him endure it.[3]

Confession is meant to enable us to tell our faults and sins, not our virtues, nor should we speak of such things as have to do with prayer, save with someone whom it is understood that we are to consult about them. This should be arranged by the prioress, and the nun should tell her what the matter is, so that she may see what it is best to do. For, as Cassian says, he who knows not of this remedy is like one who has never observed or learned that men can swim: if he sees people plunging into a river he will think that they must all be drowned.[4]

It was Our Lord's will that Joseph should relate his vision to his brethren, and that it should become known, even though it should cost him as dear as in fact it did.[5]

The soul is afraid when God is pleased to grant it a great favour: this must be understood as being reverence done to Him by the spirit, like that done by the four and twenty elders spoken of in Scripture.[6]

There are no sins but those which are known to be such; thus Our Lord did not allow that king to sin with Abraham's wife, because he thought she was not his wife but his sister.[7]

It is possible to recognize when the faculties are suspended, for certain things are brought before the soul which it is to commend to God. It is an angel who brings them, of whom the Scripture says that he was burning incense and offering prayers.[8]

[1] 1 Corinthians x, 13.
[2] 4 Kings [A.V., 2 Kings] ii, 12. These five " thoughts " are extant in autograph on a single sheet which was copied and certified by P. Andrés de la Encarnación in the eighteenth century. Many copies of the *Relations* include some of them.
[3] 2 Machabees ix, 10–12.
[4] *Collations*, VII, iv.
[5] Genesis xxxvii.
[6] Apocalypse iv, 10.
[7] Genesis xii.
[8] This paragraph is found in three manuscripts.

POEMS

TRANSLATOR'S INTRODUCTION[1]

For a considerable time, during the planning of this edition, I had thought of omitting the verses of St. Teresa from it altogether.

In the first place, except in rare flashes, she never achieved poetry—as, indeed, she tells us with the utmost frankness herself.

I know a person who, though no poet, composed some verses in a very short time, which were full of feeling and admirably descriptive of her pain: they did not come from her understanding. . . .[2]

There might be good reasons, it seemed to me, for translating verses illustrative of the author's spiritual experience, since, however halting or jingling they may be, they reveal a little more of her personality. It would be a pity, too, not to give a rendering of the lovely poem which, though she claims to have written it while "deeply absorbed in prayer,"[3] is evidently modelled upon certain poems in the secular *Cancioneros* of her day:

> O Loveliness, that dost exceed
> All other loveliness we know. . . .[4]

Even the artless carols (XI–XVII), featuring shepherds in the fields and at the Crib, who are first cousins to the characters of the sixteenth-century pastorals, are not unworthy of perpetuation, while the hymn (XXXI) chanted by the nuns as a prophylactic against the invasion of their rough frieze habits by vermin should certainly not be lost. But what was there to be gained by reproducing the lengthy and dreary doggerel in which the author invokes death (VII), the prosaic language which is wedded to unexceptionable sentiments in the verses with the refrain "Nuns of Carmel" (X, XX), the platitudinous panegyricizing of St. Hilarion and St. Catherine (XXII, XXIII)

---

[1][Some of the material used in this introduction is taken from the corresponding pages (VI, 1–lxiii) in P. Silverio; but, as the introduction itself, unlike the others in these volumes, is written from the standpoint of the translator, I have thought best to give it this title.]

[2] *Life*, Chapter XVI (Vol. I, pp. 97–8, above).

[3] See p. 283, n. 2, below.

[4] *Ibid*.

and the hortatory poems composed for the clothing or the profession of some Discalced sister (XXV–XXX)? It would surely
seem better to consign such productions to the oblivion which,
had they been written by a less famous hand, they would have
attained unaided.

Another reason for omitting these verses—or, at least, the
majority of them—was the fact that they have already been
admirably translated, in a volume quite easy of access, by the
Benedictines of Stanbrook, and, as has been explained in the preface, the translation of the Works as a whole was undertaken only
from a belief that there were certain definite services which a fresh
translation could render. Would it not suffice to refer would-be
readers of the poems to the Stanbrook translation?[1]

I was converted from this position after making a few tentative
experiments in the translation of those of the poems which,
from the literary standpoint, are the least estimable. Platitudinous
as were some of the sentiments, halting as was the rhythm,
imperfect as were the rhymes (even in a language as rich in
rhyme as Spanish), there was a directness, a virility, a power
which continually emerged, often at the most unexpected
moments. Most of the verses were doggerel, no doubt, but
beneath the inadequate expression there was a great personality
which could not be hidden. And, if I could convey the presence
of that personality with any degree of clearness, there might be
readers who would derive more help or inspiration from these
simple lines than from the profoundest and sublimest poetry.
After all, there are hymns which have comforted millions at times
of danger or in the hour of death and have become an integral
part of our national Christian heritage, and yet which from the
literary standpoint will not bear examination. Why should not
the rough verses of a Spanish Saint do as much as any of these?

Under the influence of such ideas I turned again to the Stanbrook versions and re-read them with some care. And I now
realized that, highly skilful as they are, they often convey a
somewhat different impression from that of their originals. As a
general rule (there are notable exceptions), they lengthen the
lines of St. Teresa's poems, so that what was sharp and staccato
becomes smooth and flowing, and for her rather blunt expressions
they substitute the conventional language of present-day
hymnography. Often, too, they create new stanza-forms which
would never have occurred to her. They are magnificent—but
they are not St. Teresa. They remind one rather of some early
Victorian "poetess"—Adelaide Ann Procter, for example, or
Felicia Hemans.

[1] *Minor Works of St. Teresa*, London, 1923.

Thus, the hymn on the Wise Virgins (XXV), written for the clothing of a nun, begins, in the simplest possible language, and in jingling octosyllables:

> Hermana, porque veléis,
> Os han dado hoy este velo,
> Y no os va menos que el cielo;
> Por eso no os descuidéis.

Which says, quite literally:

> Sister, they have given you this veil to-day: so that you may watch. Nothing less than Heaven is at stake. So do not be careless.

In the Stanbrook translation this simple, everyday language is given a literary flavour, while the octosyllabic quatrain is metamorphosed into a Sapphic stanza, the last line of which forms the refrain:

> To bid thee, sister, keep strict watch and ward,
> We, on this morn, bestowed this veil on thee,
> For heaven itself 'twill win thee in reward—
> Then watchful be!

Or, again, in the "love-talk" (IV) which P. Silverio, infected by a similar desire for eloquence, heads "Amorous Colloquy", St. Teresa uses the simplest metre and the simplest language imaginable. Stanbrook, on the other hand, invents a complicated pattern of short and long syllables which would undoubtedly have frightened the nun who was "no poet", and paraphrases her short, blunt sentences into terms of poetical gentility. Thus St. Teresa's "Soul, what wilt thou of Me?" (*Alma ¿qué quieres de mí?*) becomes "What cravest thou, O heart?"; "I beg Thee for a love. . . ." (*Un amor . . . os pido*) is changed to "Of love I'm fain"; "to love Thee afresh, wholly enkindled in love" (*Y en amor toda encendida Tornarte de nuevo a amar*) is transformed and expanded thus:

> And ever daily learn, with love afire,
> Love's deeper lore.

Now I am not in the least depreciating the value of the Stanbrook translations: on the contrary, to many, perhaps to most, of their twentieth-century English readers, they would appeal as strongly as did St. Teresa's rude verses to her daughters in sixteenth-century Spain. As I considered the question, however, it began to seem worth while attempting versions which might have only a minority appeal, but, if in the least successful, would certainly have a strong one. The translations which follow are the result of that attempt. What success, if any, they will have, I cannot say. But their aim is substantially the same as that of the translations of St. Teresa's prose—to get as close to their originals, both in spirit and in form, as is possible. No attempt has been made to smooth, soften or polish her: she has been left in the rough. Her simple, every-day language; her rhyme-patterns which change two or three times in quite a short poem; her stanzas which in the middle of a poem suddenly become longer or shorter; her many rhymes which are no rhymes at all but either assonances or the repetition of an identical syllable—all these and other characteristics of her verse are faithfully reproduced. St. Teresa's literary reputation will not be enhanced thereby—but then she never cared for literary reputation or claimed any. There is just a chance, on the other hand, that the straightforwardness of her "art"-less language may bring some reader a step nearer to the realities which meant everything to her. If it does, the experiment here made will be fully justified.

The largest manuscript collection of St. Teresa's poems is to be found in MS. 1400 of the National Library of Spain, which has already been referred to[1] as containing a transcript made by P. Andrés de la Encarnación of the Baeza version of the *Conceptions of the Love of God*. In the year 1759, while engaged on his Teresan researches at Toledo, he discovered, in the convent of Discalced Carmelites there, a manuscript entitled "Part of the Book of the Songs made by Mother Teresa of Jesus, foundress of the Discalced Carmelite nuns." At the end of this manuscript were sixteen of St. Teresa's poems, of which he made a copy and had it legally certified. This Toledo codex is followed in our text of all the poems which are to be found in it.

In the same codex P. Andrés transcribed five more poems found at Cuerva, Guadalajara and Madrid, four of which are by St. Teresa: these, too, are accompanied by the copy of a certificate from a public notary. He added some further transcriptions of less importance, some of them being repetitions of those already made.

Other manuscript sources in the National Library of Spain are MS. 12,764, which has twelve poems copied by P. Juan de Jesús María; MS. 12,763, containing three poems interspersed

[1] Vol. II, p. 355, above.

among St. Teresa's letters; MS. 5,492, in which are thirteen poems transcribed by two seventeenth-century Carmelites; the eighteenth-century MS. 7,741, which has four poems; MS. 12,977[3] (in which, under the date 1652, P. Antonio de la Madre de Dios certifies copies of three poems); and MS. 12,411, which prints in succession the poems by St. Teresa and that by St. John of the Cross[1] on the theme: "I live, yet no true life I know. . . ." These sources will be referred to further in the footnotes to the poems.

Besides the thirty-one poems believed by P. Silverio to be authentic, and translated below, there are others which may be, but are probably not, the work of St. Teresa, and others, again, which have been attributed to her but are certainly not genuine. Of the latter, the most famous is the "Sonnet to Christ Crucified" ("I am not mov'd, my God, to love of Thee. . . ."),[2] with which her admirers have credited her in a spirit of uncritical piety. The very considerable technical skill of this sonnet is quite beyond anything which she—or, for that matter, most of the Spanish mystics[3]—could have put into it, nor is there any evidence that she ever composed a sonnet, or knew what such a thing was. It would be strange if an author who had written one almost perfect sonnet never wrote another.

A second well-known poem of the time which has been incorrectly attributed to St. Teresa consists of four quatrains, on the subject of the transverberation of her heart, which begin:

> En las internas entrañas
> Sentí un golpe repentino.[4]

The author appears, in fact, to have been M. María de San José, Prioress successively of the convents at Seville and Lisbon and one of St. Teresa's frequent correspondents. In an eighteenth-century chronicle of the Discalced Carmelites in Portugal is printed a version of the poem which contains thirteen stanzas, the first four of which are substantially the same as those already mentioned but differ considerably from them in detail. The Portuguese chronicler seems to have used a manuscript left at Lisbon by M. María when she returned to Spain. In any case there are no solid grounds for attributing the poem to St. Teresa; it was no doubt originally ascribed to her because it refers to

---

[1] See *St. John of the Cross*, II, 450–1.
[2] Translated in *S.S.M.*, I. vi.
[3] I have referred briefly to the controversy on this question in *S.S.M.*, I, 202–3.
[4] [*Lit.*: "Within the entrails, I felt a sudden stab." The poem is translated by the Benedictines of Stanbrook, who consider it genuine. (*Op. cit.*, p. 18).]

a particularly intimate supernatural experience and one of which she was well known to have been the subject.

A number of other verse compositions which have been ascribed to St. Teresa by uncritical tradition are entirely unworthy of her and may be rejected without discussion. But there are some which may quite well be hers since they treat themes found in her authentic poems in a not dissimilar style. Most of them were transcribed by P. Andrés de la Encarnación from copies given him by the Discalced Carmelite nuns of Consuegra. One of them bears a close resemblance to "I live, yet no true life I know . . ." Another ("Di, Gil, ¿qué suena en el hato?") is a pastoral poem written for Christmas. Another, addressed to St. Joseph, is intrinsically about as likely to be authentic as those to St. Hilarion and St. Catherine. The trouble about all these poems of doubtful genuineness is the almost complete lack of reliable evidence in their favour. St. Teresa, holding the position she did in her Order, must have had many imitators. Her themes were popular; her technique was slight and highly flexible; and to reproduce her every-day language and her simple style could not have been difficult. Hence, in all that concerns the authorship of these verses, it seems well to adopt the conservative position of P. Silverio.

POEMS[1]

I[2]

("Vivo sin vivir en mí . . .")

I live, yet no true life I know,
And, living thus expectantly,[3]
I die because I do not die.[4]

Since this new death-in-life I've known,
Estrang'd from self my life has been,
For now I live a life unseen:
The Lord has claim'd me as His own.
My heart I gave Him for His throne,
Whereon He wrote indelibly:
"I die because I do not die."

Within this prison-house divine,
Prison of love whereby I live,
My God Himself to me doth give,
And liberate this heart of mine.
And, as with love I yearn and pine,
With God my prisoner, I sigh:
"I die because I do not die."

---

[1] [P. Silverio, "for the convenience of readers", supplies a title for each of the poems. As, however, their author gave them none, and they are generally referred to in Spanish by their first lines, I have omitted the editor's titles, adding the first lines of the originals to facilitate identification from any other edition than his.]

[2] This poem was written by St. Teresa when she came to herself after the ecstasy at Salamanca referred to in *Relations*, XV (Vol. I, pp. 340–2, above). The Toledo codex is followed throughout. [Technically, the poem is written with some care. I have conformed to the author's rhyme-scheme exactly.]

[3] Some MSS. read here: "And, living in expectation of so high a life."

[4] The theme-stanza (*tema*) of this poem is the same as that of one by St. John of the Cross [which will be found in translation in my edition of his works, II, 450–1]. The similarities between the two poems will be obvious and the question of possible plagiarism arises. Both poems are authentic and a MS. of St. John of the Cross's is extant with corrections in his hand. As St. Teresa's poem was written in 1571 and St. John of the Cross's in 1578, it would seem that he, if either, was the plagiarist. It may be, however, that the two wrote on the same theme quite independently, and that subsequent copyists have confused the poems, giving St. Teresa stanzas which she never wrote. Confusion has also arisen over two poems on this theme, both attributed to St. Teresa. [This question is too complicated to be discussed within the limits of a footnote, but P. Silverio's belief that St. Teresa only wrote one such poem, that it was subsequently divided into two and that stanzas were then added which she did not write, is supported by solid evidence.]

How tedious is this life below,
This exile, with its griefs and pains,
This dungeon and these cruel chains
In which the soul is forced to go!
Straining to leave this life of woe,
With anguish sharp and deep I cry:
"*I die because I do not die.*"

How bitter our existence ere
We come at last the Lord to meet!
For, though the soul finds loving sweet,
The waiting-time is hard to bear.
Oh, from this leaden weight of care,
My God, relieve me speedily,
Who die because I do not die.

I only live because I know
That death's approach is very sure,
And hope is all the more secure
Since death and life together go.
O death, thou life-creator, lo!
I wait upon thee, come thou nigh:
I die because I do not die.

Consider, life, love's potency,
And cease to cause me grief and pain.
Reflect, I beg, that, thee to gain,
I first must lose thee utterly.
Then, death, come pleasantly to me.
Come softly: undismay'd am I
Who die because I do not die.

That life, with life beyond recall,
Is truly life for evermore:
Until this present life be o'er
We cannot savour life at all.
So, death, retreat not at my call,
For life through death I can descry
Who die because I do not die.

O life, what service can I pay
Unto my God Who lives in me
Save if I first abandon thee
That I may merit thee for aye?[1]

[1] [*Lit.*, "That I may merit winning thee."] This is the reading of the Toledo codex.
The other manuscripts have: "That I may the better enjoy Him." They also read
"Him" for "thee" in the following line and "for Him alone" for "for my
Spouse".

I'd win thee dying day by day,
Such yearning for my Spouse have I,
Dying because I do not die.

II[1]

("Vuestra soy, para Vos nací. . . .")

I am Thine, and born for Thee :
What wilt Thou have done with me ?[2]

Sov'reign Lord upon Thy throne,
Endless Wisdom, One and Whole,
Goodness that dost feed my soul,
Good and great, One God alone:
Vile Thou seest me, yet Thine own,
As I sing my love for Thee.
What wilt Thou have done with me ?

Thine I am, for Thou didst make me;
Thine, for Thou alone didst save me;
Thine—Thou couldst endure to have me;
For Thine own didst deign to take me.
Never once didst Thou forsake me.[3]
Ruined were I but for Thee:
What wilt Thou have done with me ?

What, O good and loving Lord,
Wilt Thou have this creature do?
This Thy slave, a sinner too,
Waiting till she hears Thy word?
With Thy will in close accord,
Sweetest Love, I come to Thee:[4]
What wilt Thou have done with me ?

---

[1] These verses are said by Luis Vázquez, in his unpublished biography of Julián de Ávila (c. 1647–50), to have been often upon the latter's lips; he copies them with masculine pronouns and adjectives in place of feminines. There are many manuscript copies of the poem, with numerous variants, most of them attributable to copyists' errors. We follow here MS. 12,977[3] of the National Library of Spain, which seems the most trustworthy. Variants marked B. are those in MS. 12,763 of the same library.
[In the original, stanzas 6, 7, 10, 11 rhyme *ababbcc* instead of *abbaacc*; but, as there seems no particular point in this variation, it has not been reproduced.]

[2] B.: "My God, what wilt Thou have of me?" [This ending sometimes (cf., e.g., the beginning of Stanza 3) fits the context better than the corresponding line in the text. The difference consists only of *mi Dios* (B.) substituted for *hacer* and is thus slighter than appears from the English.]

[3] [*Lit.*: "Thine I am: Thou didst await me".] Thus the codices: the editions, however, have "preserve" for "await".]

[4] [The original has, for these two lines: "Thou seest me here, my sweet Love; sweet Love, Thou seest me here".]

Take, O Lord, my loving heart:
See, I yield it to Thee whole,
With my body, life and soul
And my nature's every part.
Sweetest Spouse,[1] my Life Thou art;
I have given myself to Thee:
What wilt Thou have done with me?

Let me live, or let me die;
Give me sickness, give me health;
Give me poverty or wealth;
Let me strive or peaceful lie.
Weakness give or strength supply—
I accept it all of Thee:
What wilt Thou have done with me?

Fame or shame may I be given;
Chasten me or make me glad;
Comfort me or make me sad;
Send me hell or grant me Heaven.
Sun, with veil for ever riven,
I have yielded all to Thee:[2]
What wilt Thou have done with me?

Teach me, if Thou wilt, to pray;
If Thou wilt not, make me dry.
Give me love abundantly
Or unfruitful let me stay.[3]
Sov'reign Master, I obey.
Peace I find not save with Thee:
What wilt Thou have done with me?

Give, I pray Thee, wisdom true,
Or remove it all from me;[4]
Plenteous years I fain would see;
Years of drought and leanness too.
Days of light and darkness through,
Send me where Thou'd'st have me be:
What wilt Thou have done with me?

[1] B.: "Light and Spouse".
[2] B.: "I was overthrown by Thee".
[3] B. has "in darkness" for "unfruitful".
[4] B.: "Give me truest constancy".

If in ease[1] Thou'lt have me lie,
I accept it for Thy love;
If my constancy Thou'lt prove,
May I suffer till I die.
Tell me, sweetest Love, I cry,
How and when to die for Thee:[2]
What wilt Thou have done with me?

Waste or fruitful land be mine,
Tabor's joy or Calvary's Cross.
Job be I, with pain and loss,
John, and on Thy breast recline.
Sterile stock or fruitful vine,[3]
As Thou will'st it, may I be:
What wilt Thou have done with me?

Joseph, captive once in chains,
Rules in Egypt over all.
David, held in cruel thrall,
Soon a crown and kingdom gains.
Jonas suffers direst pains;
Then is cast up from the sea:
What wilt Thou have done with me?

Let me speak or hold my peace,
Rich or barren as Thou wilt;
Let the Law proclaim my guilt
Or the Gospel give release.
Let my joys or pains increase.
All my life I live in Thee:
What wilt Thou have done with me?

I am Thine, and born for Thee:
What wilt Thou have done with me?

[1] B.: "If in rest".
[2] [*Lit.*: "Say: Where, how and when? Say, sweet Love, say".] B.: "Say: How, where and when? Since I was conquered by Thee."
[3] B. has "earth" for "vine".

III[1]

("Yo toda me entregué y dí. . . .")

I gave myself to Love Divine,
And lo ! my lot so changèd is
That my Beloved One is mine
And I at last am surely His.

When that sweet Huntsman from above
First wounded me and left me prone, [2]
Into the very arms of Love
My stricken soul forthwith was thrown.
Since then my life's no more my own
And all my lot so changèd is
That my Beloved One is mine
And I at last am surely His.

The dart wherewith He wounded me
Was all embarbèd round with love,
And thus my spirit came to be
One with its Maker, God above.
No love but this I need to prove:
My life to God surrender'd is
And my Beloved One is mine
And I at last am surely His.

IV[3]

("Si el amor que me tenéis. . . .")

God, if Thy love so great and high
Is like the love I have for Thee,
Why do I wait so doubtfully?
Why dost Thou wait to let me die?
"Soul, what is this thou dost desire?"
"Only, my God, to see Thy face."
"What dost thou fear so dread and dire?"
"That I may haply lose Thy grace."

[1] The Toledo codex and MSS. 12,764 and 5,492 of the National Library of Spain give as title to these lines: " On those words *Dilectus meus mihi*." [The reference is, of course, to Canticles vi, 2.] We use the Toledo text in both this and the next two poems. [The rhyme-scheme of the Spanish (*ababbcxc*) is followed exactly.]

[2] [*Lit.*: " exhausted ".] MS. 5,492 has " wounded " here, and below reads: " My soul remained exhausted in the arms of Love."

[3] [The Spanish has the rather complicated rhyme-scheme *abba cdcd effe eghgh*. The second and third *e*-rhymes are two identical words (*amar*). I have avoided this and altered the latter part of the poem to *affa fghgh*.]

Oh, when a soul is hid in Thee,
For what adventure can it yearn
Save love and still more love to learn,
And thus to love increasingly,
So deep does love within it burn?
My God, I pray Thee for a love
That yearns until I see Thy face,
And builds itself a nest above
Within its true abiding-place.

V[1]

("Dichoso el corazón enamorado. . . .")

Happy the heart where love has come to birth;
The thought that's centred upon God alone;
The man who tramples upon things of earth,
His joy and glory set upon the One.
His life he counts a thing of little worth;
His aim is that the will of God be done.
And so, rejoicing in life's stormy sea,
He breasts its waves as gaily as can be.

VI[2]

(" ¡ Oh Hermosura que ecedéis. . . . !")

O Loveliness, that dost exceed
All other loveliness we know,
Thou woundest not, yet pain'st indeed,
And painlessly the soul is freed
From love of creatures here below.

[1] [Except that the rhymes in Spanish are all feminine, the scheme of the original is exactly followed.]

[2] In a postscript to a letter addressed to her brother, Don Lorenzo de Cepeda, and dated January 2, 1577 (*Letters*, 158), St. Teresa writes: " I thought you would have sent us your carol: such things have neither feet nor head, yet everybody sings them. I have just remembered one which I once wrote when I was deeply absorbed in prayer and seemed to be enjoying more than my usual repose. They ran as follows (I am not sure if these were the exact words) and I am copying them because from where I am I want to give you pleasure." She then copies the three stanzas of this poem and adds: " I can't remember any more. What a head for a foundress! " On January 17, 1577, she wrote again to Don Lorenzo (*Letters*, 163), glossing part of the first stanza.

[Both the actual words of the poem and its figured, paradoxical style are so strongly suggestive of a number of profane poems to be found in the almost contemporary *Cancioneros* that there can be little doubt that St. Teresa had read these, or similar ones, and interpreted them *a lo divino*; perhaps in the state of absorption to which she refers in her letter she was unconsciously reproducing their turns of phrase. The student may compare the Spanish text of this poem with Pedro de Cartagena's "¡ O amor lleno de extremos!" (*Cancionero General de Hernando del Castillo*, Madrid,

O wondrous juncture, that dost bind
Two things that nature parts in twain,
I know not why thou com'st untwin'd,
Since thou canst strengthen mortal mind
And make it count its ills as gain.

Things being-less thou dost unite
With Being that can know no end.
Thou endest not, yet endest quite;[1]
Unforc'd to love, Thou lov'st at sight:
Thy nothingness Thou dost transcend.[2]

VII[3]

("¡ Cuán triste es, Dios mío. . . .!")

Ah, my God, without Thee
Life goes sadly by,
And my yearning for Thee
Makes me long to die.

What a tedious journey
Is our exile here!
Dreary is the sojourn,
Hard indeed to bear!
Oh, beloved Master,
Rescue me, I cry,
Since my yearning for Thee
Makes me long to die.

1882, I, 347: No. 143) in which even the rhyme-scheme is practically identical, and
with Tapia's " Hermosura tan hermosa " (*Op. cit.*, II, 53-4; No. 827).]
[I ought perhaps to add that my verses " O Heavenly Beauty ", published in
Songs of the Lover and the Beloved (London, 1931, p. 37) and reprinted in a number of
collections, were suggested by the first two lines of this poem, but owe nothing further
to it.]
[The rhymes in this version are as in the Spanish, *abaab*, except that St. Teresa
has three false rhymes (*hacéis: deshacéis; juntáis: desatáis; acaba: nada*) which are not
reproduced.]
[1] Here the author seems to transfer the apostrophe from the *ñudo* (knot, "juncture") to God Himself.
[2] [Without any authority, the *vuestra* (" Thy ") of this line is sometimes amended
to *nuestra* (" our ") as though this made the phrase more comprehensible. The
Benedictines of Stanbrook accordingly read: " *Our* naught grows precious by Thy
might." But I understand by *vuestra nada* " the creatures Thou hast made, who are
nothing ". Cf. St. John of the Cross, *Ascent of Mount Carmel*, Book I, Chapter IV:
" All the being of creation, then, compared with the infinite Being of God, is nothing."]
[3] Published in facsimile by Don Antonio Selfa in a booklet entitled *Varios autógrafos
de Santa Teresa de Jesús*. [Cf. P. Silverio, VI, 86, n.]
[The theme-stanza in the Spanish rhymes *xbxb*: the *b*-rhyme is imperfect, as it is
also in the other stanzas, the general scheme of which is *xcxcxbxb*, *c* being assonance
and not rhyme. The translation substitutes rhyme for assonance, but purposely
admits some loose rhymes, in order to convey something of the careless ease of the
original.]

Dark is this existence;
Bitter is its thrall:
Life that's lived without Thee
Is not life at all.
Oh, my sweetest Lover,
Miserable am I,
And my yearning for Thee
Makes me long to die.

Come, O death, come kindly;
Loose me from my pain.
Sweet the blows thou dealest:
Liberty they gain.
Blest are they, Beloved,
That have Thee ever by.
Thus my yearning for Thee
Makes me long to die.

Earthly love that's earthy
Clings to earth, its home;
Love divine sighs ever
For the life to come.
None can live, Redeemer,
Save when Thou art nigh,
So my yearning for Thee
Makes me long to die.

This our earthly desert
Is a vale of woe.
Life has no beginning
Till to Heaven we go.
Grant me, O my Saviour,
Thither soon to fly,
Since my yearning for Thee
Makes me long to die.

Who is he that shrinks from
Death, however keen,
Since the life it brings is
Boundless and serene?
Such it is to love Thee,
Lord, eternally,
And my yearning for Thee
Makes me long to die.

My afflicted spirit
Sighs and faints away.
Who from his Beloved
Absent long can stay?
Let my bitter suffering
Vanish speedily,
Since my yearning for Thee
Makes me long to die.

Soon the fish enmeshèd
By the crafty snare
Finds its torture ended:
Kindly death is there.
Like the fish I suffer
When Thou art not nigh;
And my yearning for Thee
Makes me long to die.

Vainly, Lord and Master,
Strive I after sight:
Thou, the Ever-Hidden,
Endest not my plight.
And my kindling passion
Drags from me the cry:
Oh, my yearning for Thee
Makes me long to die.

Hardly hast Thou enter'd
In my breast to stay
Than I fear, my Saviour,
Lest Thou flee away.
Then my deep affliction
Causes me to sigh:
How my yearning for Thee
Makes me long to die!

Oh, my Lord, I pray Thee,
End my agony:
Succour this Thy servant
As she sighs for Thee.
Rend apart these fetters:
Then how happy I,
Since my yearning for Thee
Makes me long to die!

Yet, Beloved Master,
Great has been my sin:
Meet it is I suffer,
Penitence to win.
May my weeping reach Thee;
Listen to my cry,
As my yearning for Thee
Makes me long to die.

VIII[1]

("Alma, buscarte has en Mí. . . .")

Soul, thou must seek thyself in Me
And thou must seek for Me in thee.

Such is the power of love's impress,
O soul, to grave thee on My heart,
That any craftsman must confess
He ne'er could have the like success,
Howe'er superlative his art.

It was by love that thou wert made
Lovely and beautiful to be;
So, if perchance thou shouldst have stray'd,
Upon My heart thou art portray'd.
Soul, thou must seek thyself in Me.

For well I know that thou wilt see
Thyself engraven on My breast—
An image vividly impressed—
And then thou wilt rejoice to be
So safely lodg'd, so highly blest.

And if perchance thou knowest not
Whither to go in quest of Me,
Go not abroad My face to see,
Roaming about from spot to spot,
For thou must seek for Me in thee.

[1] Found in the Toledo codex and in MSS. 12,764 and 5,492. The first-named is followed but the texts are practically identical. There is a close connection between this poem and the prose " Judgment " entitled " Seek thyself in Me " (p. 266, above). Cf. also *Relations*, XVIII (Vol. I, p. 343, above). The poem may not improbably have been written as a pendant to the " Judgment ".
[The stanza, a very common one in Spanish, rhymes, like that of VI, *abaab*. Stanzas 3 and 4, however—we neglect the theme and stanza in numbering— vary to *abbab*; there are several identical syllables instead of rhymes, and in Stanza 5 one very bad rhyme (*aposento: tiempo*). The variation is observed in the English and an eye-rhyme is admitted in Stanza 5. In the Spanish, as in the English, the refrain occurs only in alternate stanzas.]

For, soul, in thee I am confin'd,
Thou art My dwelling and My home;
And if one day I chance to find
Fast-clos'd the portals of thy mind
I ask for entrance when I come.

Oh, seek not for Me far away,
For, if thou wilt attain to Me,
Thou needest but My name to say
And I am there without delay,
For thou must seek for Me in thee.

IX[1]

("Nada te turbe. . . .")

Let nothing disturb thee;
Let nothing dismay thee:
All things pass;
God never changes.
Patience attains
All that it strives for.
He who has God
Finds he lacks nothing:
God alone suffices.

X[2]

("Caminemos para el cielo. . . .")

*Let us journey on to Heaven,
Nuns of Carmel.*[3]

Let us be most mortified,
Humble, though the world deride,

---

[1] [These rough unrhymed lines, generally known in English as "St. Teresa's Bookmark", have each, in the original, five syllables, and ll. 3, 6, 8, 9 assonance in *a—a*. I have substituted a stress-rendering which is practically a word-for-word translation.] The lines were found, after her death, in her breviary, in which P. Gracián wrote: "This breviary belonged to Mother Teresa of Jesus and she was using it for her prayers when Our Lord called her to Heaven from Alba. And because this is true I have signed it with my name: Fray Gerónimo Gracián de la Madre de Dios."

[2] The text followed is that of the Guadalajara MS. Variants are from that of Madrid (Md.).

[3] [In the original these lines rhyme and in the following stanzas each of the first couplets rhymes *aa*, while the third line rhymes with the refrain *bb*. As there are no suitable English rhymes for "Carmel", I have altered the rhyme-scheme to *aaax*.]

Setting happiness aside,[1]
Nuns of Carmel.

Let us, as we vow'd, obey,
Never from obedience stray,
For it is our aim and stay,
Nuns of Carmel.

We must walk in poverty:
'Twas the path of God Most High
When He journey'd from the sky,[2]
Nuns of Carmel.

He will love us all for aye;
And He calls us, day by day:
Tread we, fearless, in His way,
Nuns of Carmel.

He Who came a child to be,
Veil'd in our humanity,
Burns in love eternally,
Nuns of Carmel.

Riches we shall surely gain,
When that country we attain,
Free from poverty and pain,
Nuns of Carmel.

Like Elias we must go,
All his zeal and courage show,
Conquering nature here below,
Nuns of Carmel.

The double spirit that he gave
To Eliseus may we have;[3]
Pleasures may we never crave,
Nuns of Carmel.[4]

---

[1] Md. has [a picturesque metaphor, recalling many passages in the *Life*]: "Leaving honour on the ground."
[2] Md.: "When He came on earth to lie."
[3] [4 Kings (A.V., 2 Kings) ii, 9: "And Eliseus said: I beseech thee that in me may be thy double spirit."]
[4] This stanza is omitted from Md.

XI[1]

("¡ Ah, pastores que veláis. . . . !")

" Oh, shepherds, ye who watch your flocks
And keep them ever closely by,
Behold, to you is born to-day
A Lamb, the Son of God Most High.

" Poor and despis'd He comes to earth:
Begin to guard Him from this day
Or wolves will carry Him away
Ere we can celebrate His birth.
Gil, if my skill's of any worth,
He shall not 'scape while I am nigh.
Give me that crook: the Lamb is safe,
And, look you, He is God Most High."

" You may suppose that I am daz'd
With mingled joy and anguish fill'd.
This Babe is God? I am amaz'd:
How can He ever, then, be kill'd?"
" Ah, but this Sov'reign God has will'd
As Man to have the power to die
Behold and see this spotless Lamb
Who is the Son of God Most High.

" Oh, why do those who ask for Him
Resist Him when He deigns to come?"
" 'Twere better, Gil, upon my faith,
That He should take us to His home.
'Tis sin that makes us here to roam
And in His power all blessings lie,
So He will suffer now He's here,
This blessed Son of God Most High.

[1] This poem [a Christmas carol, like the three which follow it] is found only in
the Toledo codex, though the Carmelite convent at Florence has a pseudo-autograph,
composed of pasted letters, of the last two stanzas. The penultimate stanza is not
in the Toledo codex and has been taken from the Florence MS. [Both the Florence
stanzas have some bad rhymes (*tierra: destierra; hombre: asconde*) and the penultimate
has a masculine ending (*será*) in the middle of feminine endings.]
[The rhymes of the poem follow no single pattern. The theme-stanza rhymes
xrxr, r being the refrain rhyme, and the remaining stanzas thus: 1. *abbaarxr*; 2. *ababbrxr*;
3, 4 (Florence) *xaxaarxr.* I have observed this arrangement precisely and used two
imperfect rhymes in the Florence stanzas. About the assignment of the parts
to the two characters one can only conjecture.]

" Little thou carest for His woes,
How true it is, indeed, of men
That they forget each other's grief
When thinking on their selfish gain!
But glory cometh from His pain
Who for so vast a flock doth die,
Yet 'tis indeed an awful thing,
For, look you, He is God Most High."

XII[1]

("Hoy nos viene a redimir. . . .")

This day, to save our souls from death,
A shepherd-kinsman has been sent.
Gil, He is God Omnipotent.

So He has broken all our bars
To save us from the devil's thrall.
He is the kinsman of us all,
Of Bras and Menga and Laurent;
Yet he is God Omnipotent.

" If He is God, how was He sold
And crucified upon the Tree?"[2]
Why, sin was slain—dost thou not see?—
Because they slew the Innocent.
Gil, He is God Omnipotent.

" Upon my soul, I saw His birth:
His Mother was a comely maid.
But why does He remain on earth
If He is God and to us sent?"
Why, man, He is omnipotent!

So let us cease this foolish talk:
Rather to serve Him let us try,
And, since He comes for us to die,
Let us be true to Him, Laurent,
For He is God Omnipotent.[3]

---

[1] We follow the Toledo codex. The pseudo-autograph of Florence contains the refrain and the first two stanzas.

[2] [I have put what appear to be Gil's questions into quotation marks. The answers are presumably by the narrator, who is not named.]

[3] [The stanzas rhyme *abbrr*, except for Stanza 3, which has *abarr*. The English follows the Spanish here.]

XIII[1]

("Pues el amor . . .")

" Since love has given us
    God the Most High,
There's nothing more to fear:
Let us both die.

" See, 'tis our Father's gift,
    This Child His Son,
Born in a stable here,
    His work begun.
Now God and Man are one,
    Joyful we cry.
There's nothing more to fear:
Let us both die.

" Reflect, Laurent, upon
    Such wondrous love.
To this cold world the Child
    Comes from above,
Leaving His vast domain—
    This God Most High.
There's nothing more to fear:
Let us both die." [2]

" But, Pascual, how could He
    Make gifts like these,

[1] From the Toledo codex. [The rhymes of the theme-stanza follow the Spanish. The other stanzas rhyme *xaxaarxr* or (Stanzas 2 and 3) *ababbrxr*. This involves the translator in a new difficulty, which will be referred to here once and for all. In the Spanish ll. 4, 5 of each stanza are feminine, and thus the two halves of the stanza are effectively linked by the repetition of the rhyme. In English, however, there are so few feminine rhymes that it is customary to make the even lines masculine, and thus, as will be seen from Stanza 1, where the rhyme is repeated, the effect is lost. An attempt was made to preserve it by making the odd lines masculine also, but the alternative then presented itself of either shortening the even line or padding it verbally, which latter expedient, as has been said in the Introduction, I have tried to avoid throughout. The simplest solution, both here and in other similar poems, seemed to be to alter the rhymes to *xaxaxrxr* throughout, which increases the flexibility of the poems and in no way diminishes their charm.]

[2] This stanza is omitted in the Rivadeneyra edition and in later editions which follow it. [Its inclusion would mean the introduction of a third character, unless we assume the ubiquitous Gil to have disappeared and make the poem a dialogue between Pascual and Laurent. As this assumption alone gives meaning to the word " both " of the refrain, I have acted upon it and added quotation-marks accordingly, giving Pascual the major share in the dialogue. This allocation of parts, however, must be taken as a purely personal surmise of the author's intention and in the last stanza no such allocation seems quite satisfactory.]

And leave the wealth of Heav'n
For poorest frieze?"
"Why, He loves poverty;
So our reply
Must be to follow Him:
Let us both die."

"What will they give to Him
Who is so great?"
"Blows from the cruel lash
Must be His fate.
'How sad a thing is this!'
Will be our cry.
If this be really true,
Let us both die."

"How dare they torture Him,
God of all power?
Bad men shall cause His death
In evil hour."
"If this be so, Laurent,
With Him let's fly."
"Not so, for 'tis His will."
"*Then let us die.*"

XIV[1]

("Mi gallejo, mira quién llama . . .")

"*My shepherd-boy, go, see who's calling.*"
"*'Tis angels, and the day is dawning.*"[2]

"I heard a sound as of faintest music:
Seem'd they were singing a snatch of song.
Bras, let us visit the shepherd-maiden:[3]
Dawn is showing and night is gone."
"*My shepherd-boy, go, see who's calling.*"
"*'Tis angels, and the day is dawning.*"

[1] This poem is found only in a manuscript belonging to the Discalced Carmelite nuns at Cuerva. It bears the title: "Letrilla on the Nativity, composed by our holy Mother Teresa of Jesus". [A *letrilla* is a short poem with a refrain, generally written for music.]

[2] [The imperfect rhyme corresponds to the *llama: alba* of the original. The same is true of "song . . . gone" (*cantillana : zagala*). In other respects the rhymes follow the Spanish. The lines are very slightly lengthened, to bring out the rhythmical effect of the original. The quotation-marks are mine: I take the poem to be a dialogue between Bras and another shepherd—not the boy, who speaks only in the refrain.]

[3] [*Zagala*: it is a convention of pastoral poetry to make all the characters shepherdesses. The reference is, of course, to the Blessed Virgin.]

" Is she a kinswoman of the alcalde?[1]
If not, who is this damsel, say? "
" She is the daughter of God the Father,
Resplendent like to the star-of-day."
" *My shepherd-boy, go, see who's calling.*"
" *'Tis angels, and the day is dawning.*"

XV[2]

("Vertiendo está sangre . . .")

See, His blood He's shedding:
Dominguillo, why?[3]
I have no reply.

Why is it, I ask you,[4]
Why, in justice' name?
For the child is guiltless,
Free from sin and shame.
Wherefore does He love me?
I have no reply.
Yet He yearns to save me:
Dominguillo, why?

Must His cruel torments
At His birth begin?
Yes, for He is dying
To remove our sin.
What a mighty Shepherd
Have we, by my fay!
Dominguillo, eh!

---

[1] [The *alcalde* corresponds to the English mayor, or chairman of a district council—i.e. the chief citizen of his locality.]

[2] A carol for the Circumcision. The Cuerva MS. is followed: the Carmelite nuns of Santa Ana, Madrid, have also a manuscript copy of this poem, but it omits the last verse. A note prefaced to the poem in the Cuerva MS. says that on the eve of one Feast of the Circumcision, a festival to which she was most devoted, " the holy Mother came out of her cell, carried away by a marvellous spiritual impetus and fervour, dancing and singing, and made the community join her, which they did with a notable gaiety ". As they danced, the note continues, they clapped their hands, having no musical instrument to accompany them. It then concludes: " The villancicos [carols] which she made about the Circumcision are these."

[The original rhymes *xaxaar(x)r*, with feminine rhymes in ll. 4, 5 of stanzas 1, 3 and masculine rhymes in Stanza 2. I have modified the scheme for the reason explained in the first note to XIII. The Spanish, like the English, has an additional line in Stanza 1.]

[3] [For my " why ", the Spanish has *eh* throughout. I have kept this, however, only when the word has seemed to be an exclamation, substituting " why " when it is a question.]

[4] [The tone of these verses is so colloquial that I have used " you " for the Spanish " thou ".]

You have not yet seen Him:
Such an Innocent?
" No but I've been told by
Brasil and Laurent."[1]
We must surely love Him
From this very day,
Dominguillo, eh!

XVI[2]

("Este Niño viene llorando . . .")

Look, Gil, and see:
That Child is crying and He's calling thee.[3]

He came from highest Heaven to earth
To fight our foes and make us free.
The strife commences with His birth;
His blood flows down for thee and me.
Look, Gil, the Child is calling thee.

I count it naught that He should weep
When I survey His love for me.
He will be Shepherd of His sheep.
What power is in this Infant, see!
Look, Gil, the Child is calling thee.[4]

Already He is shedding blood.
Costly to Him His love will be.
So let my tears become a flood
Since He is suffering for me.
Look, Gil, the Child is calling thee.

He needed not to come and die:
Safe in His nest He still might be.
But, Gil, like lion roaring[5] high
This Infant comes: canst thou not see?
Look, Gil, the Child is calling thee.

[1] [These two lines alone I take to be Dominguillo's. The question in the preceding stanza seems to be a rhetorical one.]

[2] Another carol for the Circumcision, found in Madrid (Santa Ana), Cuerva and Guadalajara MSS: the first of these is followed.

[3] [The first line is shortened from nine syllables to four to avoid padding. In the body of the poem the refrain is two syllables longer than the other four lines of each stanza].

[4] The Cuerva MS. omits this stanza.

[5] " Clamouring ", amends the Cuerva MS.

" Pascual, what wouldst thou have me do?
Wherefore so loudly criest to me?"[1]
Why, as He loves thee, love Him too:
He's shivering in the cold for thee.
Look, Gil, the Child is calling thee.[2]

XVII[3]

("Pues que la estrella . . .")

See, it has stopped,
That star so high:
We will go with the Kings,
My flock and I.

To see the Monarch
Now go we all,
For the prophets foretold
That this would befall.
Their words are fulfill'd;
The star's on high:
We will go with the Kings,
My flock and I.

Let us take Him presents
Both rich and rare,
For the eager Kings
Are arriving there.
The Maid[4] will rejoice
As we all draw nigh:
We will go with the Kings,
My flock and I.

Don't stay to argue,
My good Laurent,
As to whether it's God
Whom God has sent.

[1] [These appear to be the only two lines spoken by Gil.]
[2] [The rhymes in this poem are all awry: each stanza has a different formula and in the last the first three lines do not rhyme at all. In the English, a single plan, *ararr*, which is that of Stanza 2 in the Spanish, is used.]
[3] An Epiphany carol, found only in the Toledo codex. [The rhyme-scheme is modified from *xaxaarxr*, ll. 4-5 in Stanzas 1 and 3 being feminine. In Stanza 2, as in the English, the rhymes are *xaxaxrxr*, with a bad rhyme (*Zagala: manada*) for *r*.]
[4] [*Lit: Zagala*, "shepherdess". Cf. p. 293, n. 3, above. This convention occurs frequently henceforward; it is disregarded in translation and will not normally be referred to.]

We'll give Him our hearts,
Not reason why;
We will go with the Kings,
My flock and I.

XVIII[1]

("Cruz, descanso sabroso de mi vida . . .")

O Cross, my joy and happiness!
O Cross of Christ, all hail!

O banner, thy protecting shade
Strengthens the feeblest for the strife,
For thou hast turn'd our death to life,
And life eternal thou hast made.
The lion cowers and is afraid:
Thou slay'st Thy foes and mak'st him quail.[2]
O Cross of Christ, all hail !

Who loves Thee not in bonds will stay
And far remov'd from liberty;
Who ever seeks to cling to thee
Will never falter on his way.
Oh, happy power and blessed sway
Which evil things can ne'er assail.
O Cross of Christ, all hail!

'Tis thou hast set us captives free
And brought our thraldom to an end.
Thou all our troubles didst amend,
Though costly was the remedy.
With God on high thou pled'st for me;
Thy intercession did avail.
O Cross of Christ, all hail!

---

[1] MS. 12,977[3], National Library of Spain, is followed here. The poem is also found in MSS. 12,763, 12,764 and 5,492 of the same library. [The first two stanzas rhyme *abbaarr*; the third has *ababbrr*; Stanza 2, ll. 1, 4, Stanza 3, ll. 1, 3 and 2, 4 are assonances. In the English, the former pattern is followed and full rhymes are used throughout.]

[2] [The exact sense here is doubtful. The original reads literally: " Thou hast tamed the lion, since through thee he lost his life."]

XIX[1]

("En la cruz está la vida . . .")

Through the Cross both happiness
And life are given,
For there is no other road
That leads to Heaven.

On the Cross there hangs the Lord
Of Heaven and earth
And amid the stress of war
Peace comes to birth.
All the evils of our life
Far off are driven;
And there is no other road
That leads to Heaven.

A precious palm-tree is the Cross,
So says the Bride,
Which her Beloved One has scal'd,
His arms stretch'd wide;
And its fruit a savour sweet
To God has given;
For there is no other road
That leads to Heaven

The Cross is like an olive-tree,
Fair to the sight,
Whereof the holy oil provides
Healing and light.
Wherefore, my soul, embrace the Cross,
Happy and shriven,
For there is no other road
That leads to Heaven.

[1] This poem is found in none of the early manuscripts. The Discalced Carmelite nuns of Soria, however, cherish a very old tradition that it was composed there by St. Teresa for Holy Cross Day (September 14), the date on which begins, for the Reform, the long period of fasting which lasts till Easter. As she was there from June 2 to August 16, 1581, this might very well have been so. An old manuscript belonging to the Soria community says that she wrote the poem " for the September Day of the Holy Cross, which was near at hand, and on Holy Cross Day the community sang it, walking in procession round the cloisters." In the eighteenth century there was a copy of the poem in the Madrid archives of San Hermenegildo. La Fuente published this and the next poem, as one, in his 1881 edition.

[In spirit and form it has every mark of genuineness. The rhyme-scheme (*xaxaarxr*) is constant but the rhymes are often faulty and three times identical words are used instead of rhymes. Several times the lines scan with difficulty. The metaphors and the way in which they are introduced are very Teresan.]

'Tis a tree all wondrous green,
Tree of desire;
In its shade the Bride sits down
With love afire,
Rejoicing in her Lover dear,
The King of Heaven,
For there is no other road
That leads to Heaven.[1]

When a soul unto its God
Submits indeed
And from every worldly thing
Is wholly freed,
To it as a tree of life
The Cross is given:
And a path delectable
That leads to Heaven.

Since the Lord embrac'd the Cross,
And for us died,
Honour has surrounded it:
'Tis glorified.
Life and happiness it brings
When we have striven:
'Tis the surest road to take
That leads to Heaven.

XX[2]

("Caminemos para el cielo . . .")

Let us journey on to Heaven,
Nuns of Carmel.

Let us take our cross each day,
Follow Jesus as we may;
Him our Light and Him our Way
Let us follow, glad and gay,
Nuns of Carmel.

[1] [The repetition of the end-word occurs in the Spanish.]

[2] According to the Sorian tradition (cf. XIX) St. Teresa wrote this at the same time as the last poem and for the same purpose. Some early copies are extant. For the form, see X. [The rhymes in the Spanish are *aaarr*, which, for the reason explained on p. 292, n. 1, are altered in the translation to *aaaar*. The additional lines in Stanzas 3 and 4 are found in the Spanish, which in Stanza 3 perpetrates the atrocious rhyme *ciencia*: *ofensa.*]

Your profession-vows are three:
Guard them all most jealously.
They will keep you ever free
From sadness and despondency,
Nuns of Carmel.

First, obedience did we swear:
Lofty science have we there,
But 'tis never hard to bear
Save when to rebel we dare:
God preserve us from that snare,
Nuns of Carmel.

Next, the vow of chastity:
Keep it most unfailingly;
Long for none save God Most High;
Live within Him till you die;
From all worldly pleasures fly,
Nuns of Carmel.

Last of all came poverty:
If we guard it honestly
Truest wealth it will supply
And ope the portals of the sky,
Nuns of Carmel.

When to keep these vows we've striven,
And our foes away have driven,
Rest we shall be surely given
With the Lord of earth and heaven,
Nuns of Carmel.

XXI[1]

("¿Si el padecer con amor. . . .?")

If suffering for the sake of love
Can be endured so joyfully,
What bliss 'twill be to gaze on Thee!

[1] Since the time of the foundation of Alba de Tormes (cf. *Foundations*, Chapter **XX**: p. 100, above) St. Teresa must have been greatly devoted to St. Andrew. This poem, found in the Toledo codex, was first published in 1768 by P. Antonio de San Joaquín (*Año Teresiano*, XI, 560). [The first stanza rhymes *xaxaarr*; the remainder rhyme *abbaarr*: in the last stanza *a* and *r* are identical. The translation conforms, as far as is possible, to this pattern.]

Saint Andrew, looking on the Cross,
Experienc'd joy at such a sight.
What then shall we when once we gaze
On Sov'reign greatness Infinite?
Oh, since this joy makes suffering light,
An ever-present help to me,
What bliss 'twill be to gaze on Thee!

Love fully grown will stay for none
And cannot fail to act aright,
Nor will the strong man fail to fight
For love of the Belovèd One;
And, when the battle's gain'd and done,
And love has won the victory,
What bliss 'twill be to gaze on Thee!

All men from death would gladly flee:
Dost thou, then, think thy dying sweet?
" Oh yes, for when my death I meet
'Twill bring a higher life to me."
O God, Whose dying agony
Strengthen'd the weak and made them free,
What bliss 'twill be to gaze on Thee!

O Cross, so full of majesty,
So precious and so fair to view
That, though espousèd by so few,
Wert wedded to the Lord Most High,
To Thee, all full of joy, come I,
Deserving naught, yet lovingly.
What bliss it is to gaze on Thee!

XXII[1]

("Hoy ha vencido un guerrero. . . .")

Since the world and all its friends
He has vanquishèd this day,
Come, my fellow-sinners, come;
Let us follow in his way.

---

[1] The subject of this poem is St. Hilarion, in whose honour (cf. *Life*, Chapter XXVII: Vol. I, p. 170, above) St. Teresa had a hermitage built in her first convent of St. Joseph. It is found only in the Toledo MS.

[The Spanish rhymes *abba* in the theme-stanza, and, in the other stanzas, *xaabbrxr* (1, 4); *abªbbrxr* (2) and *abbaarar* (3) I begin, for convenience, *xaxa*, but thereafter follow the pattern, except in Stanza 3, l. 7 (to preserve the refrain intact) and in Stanza 4, l. 1. (to strengthen the peroration of the poem).]

Let us live in solitude,
Never wishing we may die
Till to reach our life on high
Path of poverty we've trod.
Oh, what skill in strife for God,
Has our warrior, who can say?
Come, my fellow-sinners, come;
Let us follow in his way.

With the arms of penitence
He has conquered in the fight.
All our fear may vanish hence:
Patience quells the devil's might.
If we follow him aright
We can also win the day.
Come, my fellow-sinners, come;
Let us follow in his way.

Not a friend was by his side
When his cross he did embrace—
And to us came light and grace
Through Our Lord the Crucified.
Oh, what fervent love our guide
Show'd upon that fateful day!
Come, my fellow-sinners, come;
Let us follow in his way.

Now, at last, his suffering's done
And the victor's crown he's gain'd.
Sov'reign merit has attain'd
Glory that's surpass'd by none.
Blest the victory grandly won
By our warrior on this day.
Come, my fellow-sinners, come;
Let us follow in his way.

XXIII[1]

("O gran amadora. . . .")

O thou gentle lover
Of the Lord so fair,
Day-star all-resplendent,
Take us 'neath thy care.

[1] This poem is addressed to St. Catherine the Martyr, another saint in whose honour St. Teresa had a hermitage made in her convent at Ávila. Like the poem

As a tender maiden
Thou thy Spouse didst choose,
Full of loving fervour
Thy repose didst lose.
None whose courage fails him
Should approach to thee
If his life he prizes
And from death would flee.

Let the timorous coward
Gaze upon this maid,
Blind to wealth and beauty,
When he is afraid.
Persecutions met her,
War was everywhere,
But she suffered bravely
With a courage rare.

Absent from her Bridegroom,
Life her soul opprest,
But the fiercest tortures
Brought her peace and rest.
So, in this rejoicing,
How she long'd for death,
For she liv'd no longer
Though she still drew breath!

Friends, if we are eager
Like her to be blest,
Let us never struggle
For our peace and rest,
For there's not a lover
In this life of grief
Who by self-deception
Ever finds relief.

---

to St. Hilarion, it is found only in the Toledo codex. [It will be observed that, although it begins with a theme-stanza, it has no refrain. The theme-stanza in the Spanish rhymes *xaxa* and the following stanzas are on the pattern *xaxaabxb*, except the last, which has a halting penultimate line and a scheme *ababbcxc*. Five of the rhymes are imperfect. Owing to the difficulty, already referred to, of rhyming the fourth and fifth lines, the scheme has been modified throughout to *xaxaxbxb*.]

XXIV[1]

("¿Quién os trajo acá, doncella. . . .?")

"Maiden, who brought thee here
  Out of the valley of woe?"
"God and good fortune did so."

XXV[2]

("Hermana, porque veléis. . . .")

My sister, you are giv'n this veil
In token that your watch you take,[3]
And your reward in Heaven's at stake,
So you must watch and never fail.

This comely veil that you will wear
Reminds you of your Lord's command.
On sentry-duty you must stand
Until at last your Spouse draw near
And unexpectedly appear
Like to the robber in the tale,
So you must watch and never fail.

In the first watch He may appear
Or in the second or the third:
For that we have His royal word
And none can say when He'll be near.
So, sister, stay you ever here
And let no thief your house assail,
For you must watch and never fail.

[1] This refrain-like snatch of song, written for the clothing of Sister Jerórima de la Encarnación, niece of Cardinal Quiroga (January 13, 1573), has been preserved by P. José de Santa Teresa, who quotes it in his *Reforma de los Descalzos* (Book XIII, Chapter XXI) in this way: " The Saint, who was present and gave her the habit, celebrated the festive occasion by composing *coplas* and *villancicos* . . . and the refrain of one of these ran as follows . . ."

[2] Composed for the clothing of Sister Isabel de los Ángeles at Salamanca and found in six MSS. of the National Library of Spain. One of these copies has a note by P. Juan de San Antonio, dated 1694, and giving reasons for being "morally almost certain " that the poem is authentic. P. Andrés de la Encarnación stated that the autograph was preserved by the Discalced Carmelite nuns at San Sebastián, but this is no longer the case. We follow MS. 12,977[3].
[Unlike most of the poems, this attempts to keep the same rhyme-scheme (*abba*, followed by *abbaarr*) throughout. The fifth line, however, is unrhymed in Stanza 2 and imperfectly rhymed in Stanza 3. The translation follows the pattern exactly.]
[3] [There is word-play in the Spanish on *velar* (" watch ") and *velo* (" veil.")]

With ready-lighted lamp in hand,
Veilèd, your vigil you must keep
And look you never fall asleep,[1]
But with your loins well girded stand
At all times—such is the command.
Danger is near, and you are frail,
So you must watch and never fail.

See that the lamp that you will bear
Is fill'd with oil of virtuous deeds
And since the soul great merit needs
There must be this and more to spare.
For should your lamp go out while there
Your tears will be of no avail.
So you must watch and never fail.

For none will lend you from her store,
And if you go away to buy
Too soon the precious time will fly:
The Bridegroom will have clos'd the door.
And you will never see Him more,
Howe'er you knock, howe'er you wail,
So you must watch and never fail.

Be instant, then; your soul arouse;
Be full of courage to obey;
And ever, till your dying day,
Live steadfastly and keep your vows.
Then you will enter with your Spouse
All glorious in your nuptial veil,
So you must watch and never fail.

XXVI[2]

("Sea mi gozo en el llanto. . . .")

Let my rejoicing be in tears,
In troubles my tranquillity,
Let pain be true repose to me
And failures be a rest from fears.

---

[1] For *amodorrida* (" drowsy ") MS. 12,763 has *amortecida* (" in a swoon ").
[2] Composed for the profession of the nun referred to in XXV. The text follows MS. 12,764; the poem is also found in MS. 5,492. [The quatrains all rhyme *abba* and the English follows this pattern.]

My love shines on through fiercest gales;
My wounds their own relief have won;
My death will mean new life begun;
My help will come when all else fails.

I find my wealth in poverty;
I triumph even as I fight;
Labour is rest, and heavy, light;
Sorrows I bear contentedly.

In darkness I can find my sun:
When I am low, then am I high;
And trouble makes the goal seem nigh;
The Cross has all my glory won.

In suffering is all my pride;
I'm honour'd when I'm humbled low;
As others take from me I grow
And flourish as I'm vilified.

In hunger I can find my fill
And hope is born of every fear.
When perils threaten, joys appear,
And pleasure has its source in ill.

My memory in oblivion lives;
I'm highest when I'm brought most low;
Humbled, no greater fame I'd know;
The mere affront a victory gives.

My laurel wreath is wov'n of scorn;
In sorrows all my joys reside;
I'm noblest when I'm flung aside;
In solitude my joy is born.

In Christ I trust, whate'er I lack;
To Him alone I closely cling;
His trials comfort to me bring;
I love to follow in His track.

From Him I draw my constancy;
In Him for ever I'm secure;
He is Eternal Truth most sure;
His is the pattern-life for me.

XXVII[1]

("Oh, dichosa tal zagala. . . .")

Oh, blessèd is this happy maid,
For she has ta'en a Spouse to-day
Who reigns and Who shall reign for aye.

Oh, fortunate the happy maid
Who such a royal Spouse could win!
But, Gil, I tremble for my sin:
To look on her I am afraid,
Since such a Spouse she's ta'en to-day
Who reigns and Who shall reign for aye.

Ask her what dowry she could bring.
Her only dowry was her heart
And this she gladly set apart—
A modest prize for such a King!
How fair He is there's none can say
And He shall reign and reign for aye.

She'd give Him greater presents still,
But chide her not, for she has none.
With choice of gifts unto her run
And let her choose whate'er she will,
Since such a Spouse she's ta'en to-day
Who reigns and Who shall reign for aye.

But if she's giv'n Him all she had
What could He give her half so good?
Why, he redeemed her with His blood—
Oh, precious gift that makest glad!
And happy is this blessèd maid
To please Him Who that debt has paid.

---

[1] In the Toledo codex alone. Evidently written for a profession. [A pastoral poem, *a lo divino*: for " maid ", the Spanish has *zagala*, " shepherdess "; for " Spouse " *Zagal*, " Shepherd." The second stanza (" Ask her . . .") has seven lines in the Spanish but could not be lengthened in English without padding. The theme-stanza rhymes (imperfectly) *xaa*—followed above. The other stanzas rhyme wildly, and often badly (e.g. *tesoro: todo*; *amistad: reinar*), the refrain-rhyme predominating, thus: *abbrxr* (1, 3); *arxrxr* (4); *raarxr* (5); *axarxr* (6). The refrain varies slightly, and, in Stanza 4, is completely different from elsewhere. The translation stabilizes the rhymes as *abbarr*, thus harmonizing with the theme-stanza.]

How much He lov'd her none can tell,
But gifts He gave of worth unknown
And now He decks her as His own
With garments and with shoes as well,
Since such a Spouse she's ta'en to-day
Who reigns and Who shall reign for aye.

We shall do well to let her stay
Within this little flock of ours
And we shall try with all our powers
To make her love us as we may,
Since such a Spouse she's ta'en to-day
Who reigns and Who shall reign for aye.

XXVIII.[1]

("¡Oh qué bien tan sin segundo . . . !")

Oh, what unprecedented grace!
Oh, wedlock join'd in wondrous way!
A King in all His majesty
Has been the Bridegroom here to-day.

Oh, what a happy lot is this!
Accept it now with joy and pride,
For God desires you as His bride:
His death has brought you wondrous bliss!
So let your constant care be this:
To serve, as truly as you may,
This King, in all His majesty,
Who is your Bridegroom from to-day.

This King of Heaven, your Bridegroom He,
Will give you many jewels rare:
Wondrous the joys He will prepare
To comfort you eternally.
And greatest of His gifts will be
—Since He can give in royal way—
A spirit of humility:
And He's your willing Spouse to-day.

[1] Another profession-song. The Toledo codex is followed. The song is also found in MSS. 12,764 and 5,492; all three texts are almost identical.
[The rhyme-pattern in the Spanish is *xaxa*, followed by *abbaarxr*. Stanza 2 has penultimate *a*. The English conforms exactly, even to this last detail.]

This Lord will also give you here
A love for Him sincere and pure,
And this, you may be very sure,
Will take away your every fear.
The devil prowls no longer near
But bound and manacled will stay.
The King, in all His majesty,
Has been your Bridegroom here to-day.

XXIX.[1]

("Todos los que militáis. . . .")

All ye who with our Master fight,
And 'neath His banner take your stand,
Oh, sleep not, sleep not, 'tis not night:
There is no peace in all the land.

A Captain brave to do and dare,
Our God was pleased on earth to die,
So let us follow manfully,
Since it was we who slew Him there.
Who would have thought that life so fair
Could be to death so close at hand?
Oh, sleep not, sleep not, 'tis not night
And God is driven from the land.

To die for us upon the tree
A willing Host Himself He gave,
Our souls to enlighten and to save
By suffering so cruelly.
Oh, what a conquest this will be!
Oh, war how glorious and how grand!
Oh, sleep not, sleep not, 'tis not night
And God is driven from the land.

Let no one shrink but onward go
Unheedful if your lives be lost,
For they who never count the cost
Are they who true salvation know.

---

[1] This, also a profession-song, is found in the Toledo MS. only.
[Like XXVIII, the song has better rhymes than most of the poems. Its scheme is *abab*, followed by *abbaarxr*; this is varied in Stanza 3 by *ababbrxr*. I have conformed to the main type throughout.]

And He Who guides us here below
Will be our Prize if firm we stand.
Oh, sleep not, sleep not, 'tis not night:
There is no peace in all the land.

So let our solemn pledge be given
To die for Jesus every one,
And, when our life on earth is done,
We'll keep our wedding-day in Heaven.
Follow we Him Who thus has striven
And goes before our little band.
Oh, sleep not, sleep not, 'tis not night:
There is no peace in all the land.

XXX.[1]

("Pues que nuestro Esposo. . . .")

Since while still in prison
We to God are dear,
Sing we the religion
Which we practise here.

O what feasts supernal
Jesus makes to-day;
With His love eternal
Lights us on our way.
As the Cross we follow
We will never fear:
Sing we the religion
Which we practise here.

To this state He's brought us;
We are His elect,
Sinners, yet He sought us;
Weak, but He'll protect.
Priceless consolation
He will give us here:
Praise we His salvation
In this prison drear.

[1] A profession-song found in the Toledo codex and in MS. 5,492. We follow the former, but the two are almost identical.
[The rhyme "prison . . . religion" is St. Teresa's, though she alters the spelling of the second word, making it a perfect eye-rhyme. After an introductory *xaxa*, Stanzas 1 and 2 rhyme *ababbrxr*, Stanza 3 has *x* for *b* in l. 5, and Stanza 4 almost breaks down, with *xaxaxrxr*. I have tightened up the rhymes, using *abab*, followed by *ababcrxr*, but twice more introducing the imperfect rhyme with "religion" so characteristic of this poem.]

If a nun despises
Worldly scum and dross,
He will give her prizes
Greater than her loss.
For the world's perdition
And a prison drear:
Sing we the religion
Which we practise here.

This our strict enclosure,
This is freedom true,
Life of sweet composure,
Endless life in view.
This our life in prison
To my heart is dear:
Sing we the religion
Which we practise here.

XXXI.[1]

("Pues nos dais vestido nuevo . . .")

Since Thou giv'st us, King of Heaven,
New clothes like these,
Do Thou keep all nasty creatures[2]
Out of this frieze.

[1]At an early stage in the history of the Reform the Discalced nuns of St. Joseph's, Ávila, discarded their serge habits for rougher ones of frieze, which, it appears, they feared would become infested with vermin. The *Reforma de los Descalzos* (Book XVI, Chapter XXIII) tells how "one day, after Matins, which would be between ten and eleven at night, they resolved to organize a procession. Clad in their frieze habits, with an image of Christ (*Santo Cristo*) going before them, and with lighted candles in their hands, they went to the choir, where the Saint had remained in prayer. As they went, they sang hymns and psalms, among which was a verse, of greater simplicity than eloquence, running as follows:

Since Thou giv'st us, King of Heaven,
New clothes like these,
Do Thou keep all nasty creatures
Out of this frieze.

On reaching the choir, they prostrated themselves before the Most Holy Sacrament and remained thus for a time in prayer, before going to ask the Holy Mother for her benediction. Moved at witnessing her daughters' tender affection and fervour, she encouraged them to proceed with their song by . . . improvising some more verses, which ran . . ." [Here follows the song.]

St. Teresa's niece, Sister Teresa de Jesús, in her deposition for the Beatification, gives some further details, including the fact that "from that day to this" not a single "nasty creature" was ever found in any of the nuns' habits.

The song was first published in the *Reforma*. It can be found also in MS. 7,741 of the National Library of Spain.

[The English rhymes follow the Spanish except that in the Spanish ll. 4 and 5 rhyme.]

[2] [*Lit.*: "bad people". Perhaps "naughty people" would express the light-hearted tone of the song as well as "nasty creatures." The nuns were not taking their misgivings in the least tragically!]

ST. TERESA:

> Daughters, you've the Cross upon you;[1]
> Have courage too.
> Since salvation He has won you,
> He'll bring you through.
> He'll direct you, He'll defend you,
> If Him you please.

ALL:

> *Do thou keep all nasty creatures*
> *Out of this frieze.*

ST. TERESA:

> Drive away whate'er molests you
> With fervent prayer;
> Nothing else so surely tests you
> If love is there.[2]
> God will help you if within you
> Firm trust He sees.

ALL:

> *Do Thou keep all nasty creatures*
> *Out of this frieze.*

ST. TERESA:

> Since you came prepared to die here
> Be not dismay'd;
> Ne'er must things that creep and fly here
> Make you afraid.
> Help your God will always send you
> 'Gainst plagues like these.

ALL:

> *Do Thou keep all nasty creatures*
> *Out of this frieze.*

---

[1] [If, as Sister Teresa's deposition asserts, the *Santo Cristo* which the nuns carried was a crucifix, the reference may be to this: the present tense, *tomáis la cruz* (*lit.* " (since) you take the Cross "), rather suggests that it is. In that case, " among you " would be more appropriate than " upon you."]

[2] [The construction of these four lines in the Spanish is ungrammatical and their exact meaning can only be guessed at.]

APPENDIX

DOCUMENTS ILLUSTRATIVE OF THE LIFE, WORKS AND VIRTUES OF SAINT TERESA.[1]

I. Statement of P. Pedro Ibáñez on the Spirit of Saint Teresa.[2]

In the city of Ávila there is a house of Discalced nuns—newly founded in poverty and living on alms—belonging to the Order of Carmel. It was founded and established by order of a nun of the Convent of the Incarnation in the same city and of the same Order. This lady is now known as Teresa of Jesus: formerly she was Doña Teresa de Ahumada and she is a native of that city and born of parents of the same name. So many things are revealed to this lady and such marked signs does she give of the highest sanctity that they cause great wonder. And as, especially in our days, it is so rare to see spiritual edification and virtue so wonderfully displayed, there are not wanting those who say they are of the devil and likely to lead people astray. Others, who are more prudent, hesitate to condemn them, but are also doubtful whether they come from God or are illusions of the devil; others, again, take this lady to be a great servant of God, but this opinion is based more on the good will which they have for her than on reasons sufficiently strong to justify that belief. So, if there were no other end to be served by clearing up this matter than that of confirming the views of those who think rightly about it and undeceiving those who are unable to perceive the truth, this seems a fully sufficient reason for going to some pains in describing these things, the more so as, if they are true and come from God, it redounds to the great praise of His Majesty that He should work such heroic things in a woman and in one so weak and ill. It will also help those of us who are weak and imperfect to strive to serve God, since we can now see for ourselves what marvels God works in persons less strong

[1] On the inclusion of documentary material in this edition, see Translator's Preface (Vol. I, p. xxiii, above).

[2] This document, written between 1562 and 1564 and referred to and quoted from by Yepes in his biography of St. Teresa, was in the time of that writer in the possession of the nuns of St. Joseph's, Ávila, and later passed to the Archives of the Order. The original is now lost. It figures, however, in P. Jerónimo de San José's *Historia del Carmen Descalzo* (Bk. V, Chap. VII) and more recently a great part of it has been republished in Miguel Mir's *Santa Teresa de Jesús* (Madrid, 1912, I, 779) [It has never previously been translated into English].

than we. It will also refresh our memory concerning the wonderful things which His Majesty communicated in those good times before our own days when saints were so numerous. And, furthermore, if this nun is a saint,[1] it will be of great benefit to us to commend ourselves to her prayers and to take advantage of her help. These reasons alone are sufficient to justify us in trying to settle this problem; yet there is still another—namely, that it is very difficult, though for any prudent Christian very necessary, to learn to recognize those who do indeed have visions and revelations from God, and to know when, either in themselves or in others, such things are delusions.

This servant of God, Doña Teresa de Ahumada, began from childhood to show signs of great devotion and it became clear that His Majesty had destined her to leave the world, and all worldly intercourse, and to serve Him in the life of religion. For when she was still quite a child, she used to hear people talking of Heaven and of the great joy laid up for the good and of all the torment that awaits the bad; and as they used to speak, in her home, of the martyrs who had won such great blessings by suffering, she conceived a desire to go to the country of the Moors to die for Our Lord, and, as she saw that one of her tender years had no chance to accomplish this, she went to an orchard belonging to her house and made hermitages there for retirement from the world. . . . [2]

At the age of nineteen,[3] it pleased God, through the example of a holy nun, that she should go as a religious to the Convent of the Incarnation at Ávila. Here she experienced many good desires and also suffered much perturbation, which arose partly from her giving herself too little to prayer and partly from intercourse, which she did not then realize was bad, with certain people who hindered her from communion with God and from joy in Him. Eventually, however, she came to realize what was wrong with her, and through her infirmities and through the counsels of a Dominican friar, who became her confessor, grew wiser. This friar showed her what a great hindrance it was, not only to her spiritual profit, but also to her salvation, for her to be very friendly and familiar with people who enjoyed no true converse with God. Once she had got rid of these troubles she began to take great pains with her prayers, to practise a great deal of penance and many strict fasts, and to be strict about obedience to her confessor. And, as will be related

---

[1] [Or: " is holy ".]
[2] Cf. *Life*, Chap. I (Vol. I, p. 11, above).
[3] As we have seen (Vol. I, p. 20, n. 2, above), St. Teresa was actually twenty-one when she entered the Convent.

hereafter, this servant of God must have performed many and most excellent holy works, so often was His Majesty pleased to converse with her.

She enjoyed very special experiences: she believed, for example, in very truth, that Christ Our Lord was speaking to her, teaching her a great deal and revealing to her mysteries and most secret things, including future events, such as matters concerning the heretics in France and tasks which she herself was to perform. She also thought that God was commanding her to say certain things to her confessors and to other people. She also thought that she had Our Lord Jesus Christ beside her at her right hand as her Protector and Guide. As this servant of God knew herself for the weak and miserable person she was, she became most deeply distressed, thinking that, as she was not worthy to receive such gifts and favours from God, this must be a deception of the devil, and that God must be permitting her to be deceived and tormented because of her sins. She was confirmed in this suspicion by the unhappy events which were taking place at that time in these kingdoms, where women and other people who seemed very holy, and who continually frequented the Sacraments, were declared to be deceivers and heretics, and quite rightly so; it was also widely understood that some of these condemned women had experienced illusions and visions from the devil, which had contributed to their perdition. This nun was greatly troubled on this account and lamented what was happening. Her fears were further increased by what her confessors told her; for they assured her that it was the work of the devil, and not only did her confessors say this, but other most virtuous and really spiritual people insisted that she was being deceived, and warned her to avoid such things as far as she could. They all talked it over and then went to her and told her what they had decided, and, as soon as it got known in Ávila, she was roundly condemned.

This person was also greatly distressed because, although she tried to banish the visions and not to listen to what was said to her in prayer, she was unable to resist them, and so she became terribly distressed, for she could see no remedy, not venturing to doubt her confessors and these other people whom she considered persons of great learning and deeply versed in spiritual things and holding herself to be most ignorant and wretched. . . .

Whenever these visions and raptures actually came to her, she felt perfectly certain that they came, not from the devil, but from God; but, once they had gone, as she feared God and was mistrustful of herself, she believed what these people said to her and accepted the reasons which they gave her for thinking her to be deceived. For when the devil speaks he often says he is God or has been sent by God; indeed, this is the usual way in which he tempts imprudent souls, and although, when he sends counsels, advice or temptations, he does so under the guise of what is good, he takes even greater care to appear as a good angel when he comes in visions.

Now these servants of God, who said quite definitely that what was happening to Doña Teresa was deception, as well as others who had condemned her without being consulted in the matter, had many excellent reasons which would lead anyone not well-informed on the subject to condemn such a person and her devotions.

The first reason was that so many people have been known to be deluded about revelations and locutions from God, and not only so, but learned and religious men have mistakenly given these visions their approval . . . and later the world has clearly seen that they were wrong, despite the fact that they apparently came from God, and that God seemed to be confirming their truth by working miracles. These deceptions come principally to women, and very seldom to men. And as reason counsels us, when we are about to approve or condemn, to go by what commonly happens, it would seem as if this particular case merited condemnation, since such cases normally turn out to be mockery and deception.

The second reason was that, as revelations and visions are favours which God commonly grants to His servants and to holy men who enjoy great familiarity with Him, we must learn to understand them by following the doctrine and counsels of the saints. This is only like saying that in theology we must believe theologians, and in matters concerning war, captains; in every art we must give credence to those who have practice and experience in it. Now the saints have always taught that only very few revelations and visions can be accepted as true, and then only when it is impossible to do otherwise, and that not only do those who would make true progress in the love of God not desire them but they make a practice of fleeing from them as from something harmful. It is for this reason that many servants of God have refused to accept these apparitions, though outwardly, so far as they can judge, they represent angels and things of God. As Fray Juan Hurtado said when one of these apparitions came to him while he was at prayer: "I do not want this favour to be granted me, for I believe quite firmly without the aid of any of these miracles." A number of similar incidents, too, are described by Cassian. So if we follow the doctrine and experience of the saints, we shall condemn these visions and appearances, especially when they occur in such great numbers as they did to this nun.

The third reason was this. It is quite certain that, if these visions and appearances are genuine, they are miracles, and miracles are only performed in cases of great necessity, for so great a marvel cannot be wrought except when there is great need for it and there is no such need here. The principal reason for which miracles are ordained is the confirmation of the Faith and of the doctrine that is preached in the name of God, and this cannot apply to an enclosed nun, whose sole concern is with herself and God. . . .

The fourth reason, also of great weight, was that not only the saints, but all wise men, greatly resent the publication of the special favours granted them by God, especially when it is a question of appearances and visions. The saints experienced these again and again, but they were most careful to conceal them, and they considered it certain that, if they made them public, God would punish them and deprive them of these great favours. Further, it seems clear that humility is not compatible with the publication of these great and special mercies which God bestows on His servants, for the desire of the humble soul is that all men should regard it as evil. We have offended God; and miracles and wonders are a sign that we are intimate with God and enjoying His favour.

The last point was that this might be false and deceptive, and it does not seem right that men should be constrained to believe it to be otherwise; and so it should not be accepted as true; and even if for some reason it may seem to be so, this must not be taken as sufficient evidence. For the deceptions of the devil are of such a kind that they seem to be clothed with an appearance of truth and no detail seems to be lacking—indeed, he mixes a great deal of truth with his falsehood to make it the more credible. And if we add to this the fact that, as the Lord says, even the wicked can work miracles and possess the spirit of prophecy, there remains no reason for taking this to be true and authoritative; rather we must follow the experience and teaching of the ancients, who found it so difficult to believe such things were true and holy. . . .

But, for the surer attainment of this truth which we are seeking, it must be observed that there are many things which, considered by themselves, seem bad, but which, if some circumstance be taken into account, seem quite holy and virtuous. If anyone declared it to be lawful to take the property of another person, all would reply that it is wrong. But if it were added that the thing was taken from its owner so as to prevent him from killing himself, or someone else, it is evident that it would then become perfectly right. For the same reason, to believe revelations and visions is often not advisable or prudent, but in some particular cases and special circumstances it may be entirely justified.

We have also to consider that there has never been a time in the world when there have not been certain persons with whom Our Lord has been on very familiar terms and to whom His Majesty has expounded and revealed many secret things which He has determined to do. . . . In some ages there will be more of these than in others, but there will always be some, and as a rule they will be men given to prayer, contemplation and quiet. It must also be remembered that, although in times past, soon after the Passion of Our Lord, there may have been more saints, and people were holier and richer in spiritual blessings than they are in these miserable times of ours, yet there is no doubt that some such are to be found still. They are hidden from our sight and His Divine Majesty will not make them known to the world because of its sins, but they are as far advanced in virtue as some—as many, indeed—of those who lived in times past, for they are as much given to prayer and do all they can in the service of His Majesty. And God is no respecter of persons, but He gives His friendship to those who prepare themselves for it and not to those who will not do so. And to all who make the same degree of preparation, be they who they may and where they may and whatever be the age in which they live, God gives the same degree of grace. And there is also another point: just as for the good of His Church God gives it saints who by their prayers and intercession will benefit others and assuage the wrath of God which threatens the world, so, as these needs are still urgent to-day, and even more so than in the past, it is fitting that God's Providence should give to His Church a few persons so intimate with Him that they can placate Him at the time of their necessities.

These considerations suggest an important argument in the matter we are about to discuss. It is that, as God now has saints in the Church, it is not right that anyone should be offended if someone he knows and has had to do with should prove to be a saint. . . . Saints, after all, are those whose lives and habits show the greatest signs and marks of holiness. And if we doubt whether or no some revelation, or some marvel which we hear of about a person, is of God or no, the fact that such a person lives in great Christian perfection is a very relevant argument.

Many have laboured hard to discover signs by which it may be known if what seems to be a good spirit is so and if a revelation which appears to come from Heaven is really from God; yet, despite all their teaching on the subject, complete certainty is not possible, and even those who have known all the ways there are of deciding upon the matter have often fallen into error. . . . Although this teaching and our natural powers of reason are aids towards this end they are not sufficient to justify us in definitely disapproving and condemning such wonderful things. For, in the first place, there are many secrets in the sciences to which, however deeply we study them, we cannot attain, and the things of which we are ignorant, even in our every-day life, are much more numerous than those we know. In the second place, God works many things miraculously in His saints which transcend our natural reason. None the less, we shall set down some ways and means which are very sure, and through them we shall discover the truth we are seeking.

It must be understood, then, that, as we cannot read or see into the hearts of others, we have to find another way of telling if they are good or bad—namely, by observing the fruits which come from the heart. And just as the physician can diagnose a bodily infirmity from the effects it produces, such as the irregularity of the pulse, so the health and the true inward state of the soul can to some extent be told from the things which it does and from the way in which it does them. It must also be borne in mind that, as these revelations and visions are bound to be either true and good or false and bad, and as what is good and true comes from God and what is sinful and false from the devil, we must judge, in doubtful cases, from their relation to the nature of God, whether or no they come from God. Similarly we shall conclude that they come from the devil if they show signs of the wiles and subtleties used by the devil. We therefore set down the following rules by which this may be known.

First, when the person to whom these revelations are given is conscious, both during their communication and after they have passed, of a contempt for himself, and also realizes his faults, and owns himself to be weaker and more miserable than others, this is a clear sign that such a revelation is a genuine one and comes from God. This sign has been found in all the servants of God throughout the world and has been wanting in all the deceivers who have themselves been misled by the devil. True visions and revelations have always brought blessings to others and caused them edification, whereas those coming from the devil have been a source of pride and have produced wonder in those who have learned of them but nothing more. Just as a fire gives heat and burns wherever it goes, whereas ice reduces heat and makes things cool, just so, when God comes to a soul through a vision or a revelation, He leaves upon the soul some impression of what He causes and desires—namely, humility and love—whereas the devil produces pride and unrest. This we can clearly see in Our Lady and in Saint Elizabeth, when they had those revelations and the angel appeared to Our Lady. The Scripture says that Our Lady was perturbed by the salutation of the angel, realizing that that wonderful message and salutation far transcended her deserts and merits; and Saint Elizabeth, when she saw Our Lady and was filled with the spirit of prophecy, said that she was not worthy for the mother of her Lord to come to her. This is the exact contrary of what has been seen in people who have been deceived by the devil and have had these delusions.

The second rule for knowing if certain visions and revelations are from God or from the devil is whether or no their reception moves him to whom they are granted to recollection and to detachment from the things and affairs of the world. For if their effect is to make one flee from the world and not to have anything to do with it or to prize it, but to forget it and neglect it, most clearly they are then of God and are no deception. But when these visions and revelations lead a person to licence and to the desire to be seen and admired by the world and to proclaim how many favours God has shown him, or when something happens to him of the kind which men call marvellous, and he wants some people to see it and others not, or wants to be in a place where everyone can see him and at a time when a great many people are there, there is no doubt that this is deception. Let us mention a few examples, without referring to anyone by name. There have been certain people to whom visions and apparitions have come, and who, on seeing them, have changed their mode of life, and gone to the deserts, while others have left the world and become monks or friars. This is a clear sign that God has been concerned in the matter. There are other people, however, who have experienced visions and locutions which have seemed to be from God; but, after receiving them, they have abandoned the life of solitude which they had been living and begun to haunt public places, and to seek the company of crowds, and to desire to be seen in the courts of kings: it is perfectly clear that in cases like these the experiences have not been from God. We have also seen people who, after a few revelations and visions, have desired that these things should come to them in some place where they could be seen and admired—during Mass, for example, before an important and aristocratic congregation, so that it should be seen how they were raised above the ground and transported in ecstasy—

but have had no desire for them to be seen by poor and ordinary people. The reason for this is that the proud always wish to be thought much of and talked about and to have men marvelling at the great and extraordinary things that happen to them and not to others; and the world sets store by people like this, but love and humility and the spirit of God flee from all this and desire only to be generally despised. This effective manner and sign by which we may recognize genuine revelations and visions, and the true spirit of God, has high authority and is supported by texts from the Saints and has its basis in Scripture, but for the sake of brevity we will say no more about it. Let it suffice to quote those words from the prophet Isaias: "My secret for myself." This is as though he had said: "The gifts and favours which God grants me He grants me for myself and they are not to be published abroad nor do I desire them to be made known." It is true that certain saints who attained to great intimacy with God were commanded by God's Spirit to do things in the strength of Our Lord, by which they came to be known as great servants of God; but in these cases it was not their own wish to be proclaimed servants of God—it came about because they were forced to obey. Their aim was not to gain credit or author- ity from men; it was to seek the glory of God and to obey Him in this matter even though it conflicted with their own happiness.

The third way of knowing if these revelations and visions are of God, or are deceptions, is by considering if the person to whom they are granted is given to prayer, or if he has practised it but little and also if in his words and intercourse and behaviour he manifests a love for God which is not merely apparent, but genuine and recognizable as such. With regard to the first of these tests—namely, prayer—we find clear examples given us in Scripture. Rebecca, having no children, went to consult the Lord, Who revealed to her that she was to conceive and bring forth two sons, who would have such and such dispositions: in this case she consulted the Lord in prayer and the prophecy and revelation came true. Samuel, too, when in the house of God at Silo, often experienced such locutions. Of Anna the prophetess, who saw Our Lord as a child, when the Queen of the Angels presented Him in the Temple, Saint Luke tells us that she was a person of very great prayer and never absent from the Temple. In support of this it is enough to say that no one who is greatly given to prayer, and perseveres in it, has ever been deceived by the devil: on the contrary, the devil attacks him, to try to make him give up his prayer. True, some people who have been deceived, and have come to great harm in matters concerning the Faith, and have committed other vices, have seemed to be persons of prayer and quite faultless. But this has not been the case: what they have been given to is much speaking and they have been greatly attached to people who have given them no help towards progress in virtue. For it has often been proved that prayer, if practised as it should be, draws one near to God and makes one attached to Him, and weans one from those other friendships which are of no spiritual profit and are not ordered to that end. The devil, too, is to a great extent excluded by love for God, for there is nothing of which he has a greater hatred; when, therefore, a vision or a revelation leads one to love God, the devil cannot possibly have any share or operation in it; and, as this love of God is attained by means of earnest prayer, the devil's chief aim is to entice the soul away from prayer, for, once this is abandoned, we no longer have the favour and help of God but are left alone with our weakness.

The fourth sign is seen when a person to whom these revelations and visions are given is very diligent in seeking information from learned people whose opinion about this and similar things can be trusted—and in particular reports them to his confessors, telling them everything and keeping nothing back. I they do what such persons desire and counsel them it is a sure sign that there is no deception.

This is a very evident truth, as we can see both from experience and from reason. In the lives of the Fathers and of the Saints we read that some who at first were timorous in their intercourse with God were deceived thousands of times by visions and inventions from the devil, and thought they came from God; but those who made use of this means of grace and recounted to their superiors what befell them were enlightened by God through these servants of His and guided to a knowledge of how they had been deceived, if deception there was, whereas those who were guided by their own opinion and judgment fell into great error. . . . It must also be remembered that, when a person does not trust himself, but consults someone who understands these things and is willing to take such a person's advice, he is performing a great act of humility and merits that Our Lord should succour him and not allow him to be deceived. If it is great humility to wash people's feet and to serve them and put them before ourselves, it is much greater humility to make a surrender of our understanding, which is the chief of the faculties with which God has endowed the soul. So when a person has some vision or revelation and will not communicate it to one who understands such matters, his lack of humility and want of diligence in ascertaining the truth suggest that he is being deceived by the devil. . . .

The fifth means of discovering the truth concerning such cases is to ask the opinions of those who know most about them, including our own confessors, to whom we reveal ourselves so that we may be led in the way of truth. What I mean is this. A person sees certain visions and revelations, and, realizing what a miserable creature he is, becomes quite distressed, fearing that God is about to forsake him. But if this person is humble, and desires to know the truth, and goes to his confessor or to others who, according to general opinion, are qualified to advise him, then men may say what they will but he need not fear—he can be certain that the vision is genuine and free from any error. In all human affairs there are differences of opinion, just as there are differences in understanding and in desire, and, as all have not the same knowledge and experience, and truth is one, while opinions are many, truth can clearly not be in the possession of all, but only of a few, and these few are our confessors. . . . But there are two things to be noted. First, that in these matters scholastic theology is not sufficient, but some knowledge is necessary of spiritual things and of perfection: these are not studied in the Schools, but are of great intrinsic difficulty, so that in order to understand them one needs to have experienced or read about spiritual things—however deep one's studies, they cannot be properly understood without experience. This other science is affective, and so it is useless for theologians without experience of prayer to pronounce on such matters or to utter reproofs. The second point is that, if all such a person's confessors or advisers should declare his experience genuine, no further doubt about it should be entertained, especially if those consulted have been people of learning, of good lives and of great sanctity, and it will be explained that this is so in the case with which we are now dealing.

The sixth way to form a correct opinion on this subject is to ascertain whether the person concerned has suffered great annoyances and persecutions without having done anything to cause them, and also whether in the persecution which has come to him at the same time as these revelations he has suffered at the hands of good men, who have attacked him and found fault with him out of zeal and a desire to do right. This is a very good rule, for when a soul is zealous about serving the God of his salvation, and bears trials and tribulations patiently, God (as the Scripture says) dwells and has His throne in that heart. And if His Majesty is within our soul, it is not conceivable that the devil can have us in his power or for the time being can have any power to destroy us: it is more likely that our sufferings are a consolation granted us by God as a reward for the trials He has sent us, and Our Lord is not likely to reward our patience by sending us a delusion from the devil. Of this we have a clear example in the Book of Job. God permitted the devil to send Job tribulation and to afflict him in his possessions, in his sons and in his own body. This he bore with great patience. Then there came to him visions and revelations which were perfectly genuine and came from God Himself, the enemy having no part in them. As trial and persecution are means whereby God cleanses and purifies the soul and teaches it His doctrine so that it shall not be deceived, the severer are the temptations and the trials, the greater is the help which God sends so that the soul shall not be deceived And for those who are striving after their salvation, the worst kind of persecution is to find that good people and servants of God are opposing and humiliating and persecuting them. For this leads them to distrust God: because His servants are attacking and condemning them, they are afraid that God, Who guides these good people, has withdrawn His protection from themselves. This is especially so when confessors, preachers and those accounted holiest attack and persecute one who is really striving after his own salvation. When people not of this kind do us harm, it is a very great consolation to see that the ministers of the devil molest us, for it is then as if the devil himself were envious of our virtue and so came to attack us—not to condemn us but to tempt us.

There is a seventh way of distinguishing between revelations, which, though to some extent it can be discovered by all, can only be fully known to confessors and those who have to do with the soul's intimacy, and that is the purity of their conscience and the integrity of their virtue. In speaking of this, it must be pointed out that any man can deceive any other by making him believe he is good, either in confession or elsewhere, but as a rule it is hardly possible for all a person's confessors and directors to be deceived and for none of them to discover any of his weaknesses, for an evil disposition cannot be so completely concealed and hidden but that some of the more prudent will get some inkling of it, especially if among his spiritual advisers are many learned and prudent men or if within his own house there are persons averse from vice who do their utmost to understand and help them. This way of detecting any deception which there may be in revelations is a very safe and effective one. . . .

The eighth method of knowing this is to discover how much good people obtain from familiar converse with such a person. For, as the Saints teach, there is this difference between the grace which gives us the friendship of God and the graces which are spoken of as "freely given". The grace by which we become the friends of God is given for the good of our souls, which are justified and made divine; the other graces are imparted by God for the profit of our neighbours and in order that they may be brought to the love of God likewise. From this it follows that, as revelations and the spirit of prophecy are to be reckoned among the graces given us for the good of our neighbours, when those with whom we have to do are duly edified and led to God—not merely one of them, but all—any doubt as to whether our experiences have been genuine and come from God or no is completely removed. . . .

The ninth method of resolving this doubt with complete certainty is to find out of what such a person's visions and revelations consist. Here there are two things to be observed. First, it is a bad sign if that person tells some of what he has seen or heard, but conceals a part of it, and will not relate or explain it to learned men but avoids them and treats them like ignorant people—we refer here to a person who is himself welcomed: if he were a scholar, it would be a different matter. It is also a sign that the revelations are evil when there are things in them that are irrelevant, that gratify the curiosity, or that produce little edification. In these two cases there is no room for dispute or doubt but there is ample justification for stigmatizing the revelations as evil. When, on the other hand, the recipient describes and relates them quite frankly to all who are qualified to pronounce upon them, omitting and concealing nothing, and when they are all quite safe and certain and innocent of evil, and, above all, are in conformity with the teachings of Scripture, then there is no need for fear—the message can be received just as if it came openly from Heaven. . . .

Another way of satisfying oneself as to the truth about such things is this. If people who have been very diligent in their converse with the recipient of these favours have found nothing in him, during their intercourse, which is not of complete integrity and virtue, and if any doubts which they may have about him have been removed by such intercourse and they have found not a trace of vanity in his conversation, this is a clear sign that his experiences are genuine—that is, if the same impression is produced upon all. For if a preacher is a vain man, a single one of his sermons suffices to prove it, whereas a discreet and learned preacher at once touches hearts and makes his hearers conscious of their sins. . . .

The last way and method of ascertaining this is to study what the devil does with such a person. If he applauds him, or is pleased with him, it is a very bad sign, but if he persecutes him and attacks him and appears to him in a horrible form so as to terrify him and treat him ill, it is certain that he has not that soul in his power. For it is only the servant of God whom the devil tries to terrify and to deceive with his threats. There is this difference between the devil's appearances to the holy and to the wicked: to those who are good he appears in a horrible form; to his friends, whom he has deceived already, his appearances are pleasant.

If any one of these rules and arguments suffices to enable us to say and decide without presumption whether or no a person's revelations and experiences are genuine, how much more certain shall we not be if in that person all of them are present together?

A very long treatise could be written on the application of all the rules to this servant of God,[1] for there would be a great deal to be said about each of them: all I can do is to relate a small part of what there is to be said. First, with regard to her humility and self-contempt, all her conversations, her letters and the things she does are full of humility: her great desire is that everyone shall see her past faults and miseries and it is always a great trouble to her if people think her to be good. When first God began to multiply His favours upon her she would have died rather than that anyone should know about them lest they should suspect her goodness. Though highly intelligent, she has never believed in herself, but is always willing to be guided by others' opinions. She is very fond of engaging in the lowliest and humblest duties; and her companions assure me that, when it is her week to do the cooking, they never lack for anything in the house: it is most noteworthy how well Our Lord provides for them during that week.[2] She desires the greatest poverty and prefers to be seen by none, and her nuns never go out and nobody speaks to them save persons who treat of spiritual things: this argues great humility in her, especially as God so often speaks to her and she makes such progress. And although at first, when God begins to commune with her in this way, it may not be very clear if it is His Majesty Who is speaking to her or if she is being deceived, yet, as the revelations proceed, she begins to recognize certainly and distinctly that God is at work, though His Essence may not be perceptible. . . .

---

[1] [I.e. to St. Teresa.]

[2] When St. Joseph's, Ávila was founded, the Saint would have no lay sisters, so that the choir-nuns had to take their turns in the kitchen. The statement made in the text is one of the earliest traditions of the Discalced Carmelite nuns. The primitive kitchen of the Ávila convent is still preserved: it was here that St. Teresa once fell into a rapture while holding the frying-pan and all but poured away the only oil there was in the house, greatly to the distress of Isabel de Santo Domingo, who was there at the time.

In addition to all this, she experiences no revelation or locution without communicating it to her confessor or to some learned man whom she chooses so as to discuss these matters of conscience with the greater security. I will describe some incidents illustrating this person's deep humility.

Before her confessors became clearly aware how the Spirit of God was working in her, they decided, for certain reasons, to speak to her and tell her that, after mature and joint deliberation (for a great many of them had been discussing the matter), they had decided that she was being afflicted and deceived by the devil, and that, as she could not resist him, whenever he came and spoke to her she must make a great many gestures of contempt[1] and sign herself with the Cross, notwithstanding the interior profit that these locutions might bring her. She determined to obey: though believing them to be from God, she would not trust herself, grievous though it was to her to be compelled by obedience to treat her Master and Spouse in that way. So she began to weep and begged His Majesty not to allow her to be deceived by the devil, and besought Saint Peter and Saint Paul, whose festival it was on that day, to help her so that she should not be deceived. After that she often saw those Saints near her, on her left hand, and they assured her that they would not allow her to be deceived. Then there came to her another vision of Christ and she began to do as her confessors had told her but besought Christ to forgive her because it was in obedience to His ministers that she did it. And Our Lord told her that she was not to worry about it but to do as she was bidden and He would see that the truth was made plain. As her confessors were mistaken about her at that time, they made mistakes in the remedies they gave her and sometimes used to order her not to engage in prayer since it was when she was so occupied that these experiences came to her. Then He would show great displeasure and said she was to tell them that that was tyranny and He began to give her reasons to show that she was not being deceived. I wrote and told her that she might possibly receive a visit from a very important lady who was quite persuaded of the genuineness of her visions. This troubled her greatly, for she realized what an unimportant person she herself was and what a painful ordeal it would be for her to be visited by great people, especially if they came because they thought she was good. Our Lord then told her that she was not to let it trouble her, that it was well they should know of the favours she was receiving from His Majesty and that if any

---

[1] [*Que le diese muchas higas*. On this phrase, see *Life*, Chapter XXIX (Vol. I, p. 189), where St. Teresa herself records this experience.]

of these people who were great in the world should speak to her she must answer them freely and frankly, for she was in no way beholden to them—it was they who were beholden to her. . . . In short, her humility is quite incredible, as those who have most to do with her will bear witness.

The second test also shows that her visions are genuine, for, since His Majesty granted her the great favour of intimacy with Himself, she has had no aim but that of the highest degree of recollection possible in this life, as can be seen in her own little house. It has been a most wonderful thing to see how she undertook this business of founding the house of St. Joseph's and what success she has had with it. I am speaking from ocular testimony when I say that God has shown notable favour to the lady in this matter, and that all we can say in support of her sanctity is true. She did this through an express revelation of the Lord, which came to her many times, and this is well evidenced by the great sanctity that exists in that house, which I think will certainly achieve a great reputation for holiness. One day, after she had been reciting the hymn *Veni, Creator Spiritus*, and had spent almost two hours in prayer, there came to her a very sudden rapture, with such violence that it almost drew her out of herself, and she heard these words: "I will have thee now hold conversation, not with men, but with angels."[1] This was the first rapture that she experienced, and it terrified her, though it also made her very happy, since it came in such a way that she could not doubt that it was certainly of God. This servant of God bears witness that never since then has she been able to have any private friendship with another person—even with a relative—except with such as she believes to be endeavouring truly to serve God.

With regard to the third sign, important witness will be borne by her companions who live in the same house with her that her only interest is in prayer or in things connected with it. I asked her one day to tell me how she spent her time, thinking that she would spend some of it in prayer and the rest in other exercises. She answered that I was touching on a very difficult thing, and one that she felt very keenly about, for she could not imagine a person being in love with another and yet able to be for a single moment without her Beloved. So it was with her and Our Lord: in Him she found her happiness and she spoke of Him and to Him continually.

As to the fourth test, she has certainly taken the greatest pains to consult all the reliable learned men who have been in Ávila, or passing through it, without a single exception—more especially

[1] *Life*, Chapter XXIV (Vol. I, p. 155, above).

those who, as well as having other kinds of learning, are eminent in theology or have studied matters concerning prayer. This course she recommends to anyone else who has received the same revelation, even when it produces other and excellent effects, which lead such a person to believe that it is good and comes from God. Among others whom she consulted was a saintly Franciscan friar who was known to me, called Fray Peter of Alcántara, a man of great prayer and penitence and zeal for his profession. This saint had no great reason for coming to Ávila, but His Majesty sent him there for the comfort of this servant of His, who was meeting with great opposition on these matters. He assured her that her experiences came from God and that there was no deception about them, and with regard to the way in which she saw God and to the revelations and visions which were divinely bestowed upon her, he gave her great light and certainty.[1] And the fact that this holy man gave so much credence to her and showed her such great and special friendship caused all the rest to give way and leave her in complete peace. All, in fact, who have been consulted about this bear sure witness that her spirit is, without the slightest doubt, of God, and that there is no deception about this at all; and, whereas at first there were many who stubbornly opposed her and made her afraid, and persisted in that attitude, they all take her now for a great servant of God and honour her in every way they can. At that period she had also a great many trials to bear in her own house, which was a large one, for opinion of all kinds was against her, and this wounded her deeply, since she was not then as proficient as she became later. His Majesty has now given her great serenity of soul, so that she has complete certainty and no cause for fear. Her experiences seem to be, as indeed they are, a great work of the Lord and are themselves the greatest argument in favour of their own genuineness.

It is furthermore to be observed that the purity of conscience of this religious is such as to cause wonder in those of us who confess and communicate her, and also in her own companions. It may be said that the whole of her thoughts and intercourse are of God and that all she does is directed towards the honour of God and her own spiritual progress: nothing whatever will induce her to commit a venial sin, however slight, if she realizes it to be wrong. All she thinks about is how she can grow better every day and attain to greater perfection. And so she has founded this house of Saint Joseph and made it as perfect as anything in this world to do with women, or with men, can possibly be. This

[1] *Life*, Chapter XXVII (Vol. I, pp. 176-7, above).

will be borne out by those acquainted with the way of life observed in it.

If we would begin to describe the great spiritual fruit obtained by those who have to do with this servant of God, we should never come to an end, for what happens is one of God's great wonders. My shortcomings are such that I would not speak of myself, though I have a great deal of experience of this, for, since I have had to do with her, Our Lord has helped me in very many ways and I have seen clearly that this has been a special help from Him. In my own mind, therefore, I could no more refrain from thinking of her as a saint than I could tell myself that I was unacquainted with her. She has told me many things which could be known only to God, since they concern the future or have to do with the heart and with spiritual progress; they have seemed impossible, but I have found them all to be strictly true. There was one person who had not decided to seek intimacy with God, but whom I believed to have done so, because he and I had agreed to do so together. I did not want to go back to the place where this person was; but this saintly woman spoke to me and said that Christ, her Master, had told her that I was to go back to him and give him a brief message, from and on behalf of God. Doña Teresa told me that in the past she had tried to make excuses to the Lord and said: "Why dost Thou weary me with this task? Canst not Thou Thyself tell them? Why dost Thou order me to undertake it?" Our Lord answered her: "I do it because thou canst not undertake more for Me and so thou must help others to serve Me. He is not in a fit state for Me to speak to him in this way, and, if I were to do so, he has so little experience of prayer that he would not believe Me." Such Divine colloquies illustrate the spirit of this servant of His. Well, I went to this man and gave him the message, and so deeply was he moved by it that he began to weep—and he is not in the least a womanly or effeminate person, who weeps easily, but a most virile man, of the type that might rule the world.[1] There is also a lady living in Ávila—a widow, whose habits and character in no way suggested that she had much to do with holiness: indeed, she was greatly discredited by people for her wasteful habits and her lack of steadfastness. But God proposed to make her a great servant of His, and by what seemed mere chance the two ladies came to know each other, and she asked if she might have Doña Teresa for a time in her house. And now she has become a regular saint, has abandoned her way of life,

[1] It seems certain that the person referred to was a Dominican, possibly P. Vicente Barron.

has renounced her estate and is entering Saint Joseph's, and I can testify in writing that she feels the great improvement in herself to be due to the companionship of this servant of God.[1] And there are many cases, under this head, in which, through the prayers of this His servant, His Majesty has wrought wonders.

If we next turn to the ninth way of ascertaining the truth about this, there are convincing reasons for the belief that all the revelations which this saint has received are for the production of important spiritual results, for the great consolation of the afflicted and for the leading of men to progress in the love of God. It would be far too lengthy a task to relate all, or even any great part, of what has been revealed to her—all of it, as I have already said, against her will, for it caused her sore trials and she discoursed at great length about it with Our Lord. Once, in particular, when speaking to Him, she said: "Lord, are there no other people, especially men and persons of learning, who, if Thou didst speak to them, would do this that Thou commandest me, far better than I, who am so evil?" But His Majesty answered her, as one sad at heart: "Nay, the men and the persons of learning will not fit themselves to commune with Me, and so I come, in need, yet rejected by them, to seek feeble women to whom I can speak freely and with whom I can discuss My business." Those were the words of the Lord Himself. And with regard to these revelations she says that, though she has received numerous and important ones, things have always happened just as His Majesty has said and not a single part of them has failed. Clearly, had they come from the devil, it would have been realized that there was falsehood in them, for His Majesty, through Saint John, gave this test for recognizing the devil, that he is the father of lies.

Before we say anything of her experiences with the devil, I will relate in this connection what once happened to her with Christ, Whom she calls her Master. She was feeling very much wearied by these locutions and visions, seeing that, on the one hand, she could not escape them, and, while they were happening, was certain that they came from God and were not delusions, and yet that, on the other hand, she was being attacked by those servants of God, who told her that they were the work of the devil and even a matter for the Inquisition. Realizing also how wicked she was, in her own opinion, she was in the most acute distress, and besought His Majesty with tears not to lead her by that path. Then Our Lord came and spoke to

---

[1] Cf. *Life*, Chap. XXIV (Vol. I, p. 154, above). The lady was Doña Guiomar de Ulloa. She actually became a Discalced nun only in 1578 and had eventually to leave the Order on account of her health.

her, and comforted her, and explained to her how this could not be the work of the devil, because of the feelings which she had when she was with His Majesty, and finally told her to reflect that the devil could not give her that interior peace and spiritual consolation which she was experiencing, nor could his conversation produce the love and the increase of virtue which she had when He spoke to her. He assured her that He would make her realize that it was He, and not the devil, Who spoke to her and instructed her; and certainly the devil, with all his arts, has no power, nor does he claim, to give our souls and hearts interior peace or an increase of love and virtue such as are experienced by one to whom God gives these special favours.

With regard to the last point which we set down, this is very clearly explained by the occasions on which this servant of God has seen the devil, by the ways in which he has appeared to her and by what he has said. Once, when she was in an oratory, he appeared to her in abominable form: he had a particularly horrible mouth, out of which came a great flame of fire. He told her that she was safely out of his hands but that he would get her again, and she need not think that the Fathers of the Company would free her from him, for they would abandon her. These words terrified her and she made the sign of the Cross, but he came twice more; however, she had brought some holy water, which she sprinkled in his direction and that sent him away and for the time being he did not return.[1] On another occasion she was for five hours in great interior distress, and even with respect to outward things she felt helpless. So she asked His Majesty to let this state of things continue if it was of any service to Him. Our Lord was then pleased to explain to her what it meant and she saw at her side a hideous little negro, growling because he could not get what he wanted.[2] On many other occasions the devil has appeared to her to harm and terrify her; this he would not have done in such an open way if he had considered her his already and had been deceiving her.

It remains to make some reply to the reasons given for the assertion that this was all delusion.

First, in no victim of delusion have there ever been so many reasons or arguments why God should grant her those favours, nor have such reasons ever been as full as those set forth above, but quite the contrary. And there have always been saintly and learned people who, though aware of what was happening, have attacked such persons and got their own way.

[1] *Life*, Chap. XXXI (Vol. I, p. 204, above).
[2] *Ibid.* (p. 205).

Secondly, the Saints did not teach that we must never receive certain revelations or that we must never take any of them as being holy, for to do this would be very harmful to the Church and to Christians and quite contrary to the Saints' own experience. What they say is that we must not believe such things easily: where such great things are in question they cannot be lightly accepted.

Thirdly, for the comfort of His servants and for the salvation of others, His Majesty has always been wont to work these wonders for certain persons; and, as there are so many reasons why we should think this religious to be near to God, there is no reason for denying it and no foundation for so doing. Indeed, if what has been set down here is taken into account, there is no probability or likelihood of its falsity.

Fourthly, she revealed these things, in the first place, only to her confessors and to those who could enlighten her about them, and that only under strict vows and with the obligation to repeat them to no one. Since then they have been made public, but entirely against her will; she now endures these things being talked about, so that she may do as her confessors bid her and may consult them about what passes daily between herself and Our Lord.

Finally, I must say that this servant of God visited one of her kinsfolk, who was very ill of an incurable disease,[1] and was so sorry for him that she began to importune Our Lord to restore him to health. He at once recovered and has never suffered from that complaint again.

On another occasion, she was earnestly importuning Our Lord on behalf of a person to whom she was beholden and who had suddenly lost his sight. She was afraid that Our Lord would not hear her, but He appeared to her, and told her, among other things, that she would never ask His Majesty anything which He would not do for her. Then this person immediately recovered his sight. So this saint has worked miracles even in people's bodies. Glory be to His Majesty!

II. REPORT MADE BY THE MASTER FRAY DOMINGO BÁÑEZ ON THE SPIRIT OF SAINT TERESA AND ON THE AUTOGRAPH NARRATIVE OF HER LIFE

I have read with great attention this book in which Teresa of Jesus, a Carmelite nun and foundress of the Discalced Carmelite nuns, sets down a plain account of all that takes place in her

[1] *Life*, Chap. XXXIX (Vol. I, p. 280, below).

soul, so as to have the instruction and guidance of her confessors. In the whole of it I have found nothing which to my mind is erroneous teaching, while there is much good and edifying counsel for people who engage in prayer. For the great experience of this nun, and the discretion and humility which have always led her to seek enlightenment from her confessors and to profit from their learning, enable her to write well concerning prayer, as the most learned men are sometimes unable to do for lack of experience. There is only one thing in this book with which, after it has been fully examined, fault can fairly be found—namely, that it says a great deal about revelations and visions, which are always very much to be feared, especially in women, who are more apt to believe that they come from God and to attribute to them a sanctity which they may not possess. They are to be regarded rather as trials full of peril to those who are striving after perfection, for Satan is wont to transform himself into an angel of light and to delude souls that are curious and lacking in humility, as we have seen in our own times. Still we must not for this reason lay down a general rule that all these revelations and visions are of the devil. For, if this were so, and if angels of light did not sometimes illumine us, Saint Paul would not have said that Satan transfigures himself into an angel of light. Saints, both men and women, have had revelations, not only in the days of old, but also in modern times—such are Saint Dominic, Saint Francis, Saint Vincent Ferrer, Saint Catherine of Siena, Saint Gertrude, and many more who could be named. And as the Church of God is and will be holy even to the end, not only because it professes holiness but because there are in it those who are just and perfect in holiness, it is not right for us utterly to condemn and trample upon visions and revelations, for these are apt to be accompanied by great virtue and Christian living. Rather must we follow the Apostle's words in the fifth chapter of the first epistle to the Thessalonians: *Spiritum nolite extinguere. Prophetias nolite spernere. Omnia probate, quod bonum est tenete. Ab omni specie mala abstinete vos.* With regard to this passage, anyone who reads Saint Thomas will realize with what diligence one must examine those persons in the Church of God who reveal any special gift, which may be either useful or harmful to their neighbours, and with what care those who examine them must work, lest they extinguish the fervour of God's Spirit in those who are good and lest others become weak in the practice of the perfect Christian life.

This woman, to judge from her report, is not a deceiver, even though she might to some extent be herself deceived, for she speaks so plainly, both of what is good and of what is bad, and is so eager to write to good effect, that she leaves no doubt of the excellence of her intention. While there is ample reason for the examination of such persons, since in our own days there have been deceivers who have assumed a cloak of virtue, there is equal reason for defending those who appear, not only to be wearing the cloak of virtue, but to have the reality beneath it. For it is a strange thing how weak and worldly people delight to see those who seem to be virtuous, discredited. God, of old time, complained through the prophet Ezechiel (Chapter XIII) of the false prophets, who oppressed the just and flattered sinners, saying to them: *Moerere fecistis cor justi mendaciter, quem ego non contristavi: et confortastes manus impii.* This can in a sense be applied to those who frighten souls walking on the road of prayer and perfection by telling them that these are strange and perilous roads and that many who walk on them have fallen into error, and that a plain, ordinary high road is the safest.

Talk like this naturally distresses those who wish to follow counsels of perfection, with continual prayer, if this be possible, and to perform fasts and vigils and disciplines; and, on the other hand, those who are weak and vicious become bold and lose their fear of God, thinking their own road to be the safest. This is where deception lies—in ignorance and neglect of the precipices on our path and of the other dangers which we all meet in this world and in describing our road as a straightforward and safe one. Actually the only way to safety lies in the knowledge of our daily foes and the humble invocation of the mercy of God if we would not become their slaves. This is the truer since there are souls whom God afflicts so that they may enter upon the way of perfection, but who, if they lose their fervour, will be unable to avoid falling into fresh extremes of sin. Such as these have the greatest need of continual watchfulness and prayer. Lukewarmness, in short, has never failed to harm everybody. Let each enquire of his own conscience and he will find that this is the truth. I feel sure that, if God suffers the lukewarm for a time, it is by virtue of the prayers of the fervent, who continually cry: *Et ne nos inducas in tentationem.*

I have not said this so that we may suppose everyone who follows the path of contemplation to be a saint. To canonize all such people, as it were, without thinking, is another of the world's exaggerations and a covert form of persecution of virtue. To the people themselves it is an excuse for vainglory and virtue is not honoured thereby—indeed, it is placed in jeopardy, since if, after being so highly praised, such people fall, virtue loses more prestige than if they had never been esteemed at all. So

I look upon those exaggerated ideas about the sanctity of people living in this present life as temptations of the devil. It is quite right that we should think well of the servants of God, but, however good they are, we must always consider them as persons who are in danger and their goodness is never so outstanding that we can be sure about them even at the time.

Believing what I have said to be true, I have consistently observed caution in examining this nun's account of her prayer and her life, and no one has been more incredulous than I concerning her visions and revelations, though not in respect of her virtue and good desires, for of the reality of these I have had long experience—that is, of her obedience, penitence, patience and charity to her persecutors, and of her other virtues, which anyone who has to do with her will recognize. This is something which can be prized as a surer mark of a true love of God than visions and revelations. And yet I do not despise her revelations and visions and raptures—indeed, I suspect that they might be of God, as were those of other saints, but in dealing with this matter it is always safest to proceed with fear and caution. For, if we feel secure about it, the devil seizes the opportunity to attack us and what was God's will fall into the power of the devil.

I have decided that this book should not be shown to all and sundry, but only to men of learning and experience and Christian discretion. It very ably fulfils the purpose for which this nun wrote it—namely, to give an account of her soul to those who have to direct her so that she may not be deluded. Of one thing I am quite certain, as far as certainty is humanly possible—that she is not a deceiver; and it is only right, in view of the clarity with which she has written, that everyone should help her in her good purposes and good works. During the last thirteen years she has founded (I believe) a dozen convents of Discalced Carmelite nuns,[1] the life in which is of the greatest possible strictness and perfection. To this all who have visited them will bear definite witness: such are the Dominican Provincial, and Master in Sacred Theology, Fray Pedro Fernández, the Master Fray Hernando del Castillo, and many more. These are the present views which I have to express respecting this book; I submit my opinion to that of Holy Mother Church and her ministers. Done in the College of Saint Gregory in Valladolid on the seventh day of July in the year 1575: Fray Domingo Báñez.

---

[1] Actually there were eleven: Ávila, Medina, Malagón, Valladolid, Toledo, Pastrana, Salamanca, Alba de Tormes, Segovia, Beas and Seville. (Cf. Vol. I, pp. xxviii–xxxii, above).

III. Address given by Saint Teresa to the nuns of the Convent of the Incarnation, Ávila, when, in the year 1571, after having renounced the Mitigated Rule, she went to that Convent as Superior.[1]

My ladies, mothers and sisters: Our Lord has sent me to this house, by virtue of obedience, to hold this office, which I had never thought of and which I am far from deserving.

This election has greatly distressed me, both because it has laid upon me a task which I shall be unable to perform, and also because it has deprived you of the freedom of election which you used to enjoy and given you a prioress whom you have not chosen at your will and pleasure, and a prioress who would be accomplishing a great deal if she could succeed in learning from the least of you here all the good that is in her.

I come solely to serve and please you in every possible way that I can and I hope that the Lord will greatly assist me to do this—in other respects I could be instructed and improved by anybody. See, then, my ladies, what I can do for each of you; even if it be to give my life-blood, I shall do it with a right good will.

I am a daughter of this house and a sister of you all. I know the character and the needs of you all, or, at least, of the majority of you, so there will be no necessity for you to make a stranger of a person who is so eminently one of yourselves.

Have no misgivings as to how I shall govern you, for though I have thus far lived among, and governed, nuns who are Discalced, I know well, through the Lord's goodness, the way to govern those who are not. My desire is that we should all serve the Lord in quietness,[2] and do the little which our Rule and Constitutions command us for the love of that Lord to Whom we owe so much. I know well how very weak we are; but, if

---

[1] On making her profession as a Discalced Carmelite, St. Teresa had to render obedience to the Apostolic Commissary, Fray Pedro Fernández, who, after consulting the Definitor of the Calced, appointed her Prioress of the Convent of the Incarnation. She entered upon her new office, not without opposition on the part of some of the nuns, on October 15, 1571. The address which she gave to the community on this occasion is a perfect model of religious discretion and shows a rare ability for government [It should be added, for the benefit of the English reader, that the polite or courtly form of the personal pronoun " you "—*vuestras mercedes*— is used throughout]. Before long even the nuns who had been most opposed to the appointment recognized their mistake and eventually they all developed a deep affection for her. St. Teresa did not write this address, and we owe its reproduction, the form of which may be taken as approximately accurate, to the memories of nuns who heard it. It was published by Yepes in Book II, Chapter XXV of his *Life of Saint Teresa*. Some eighteenth-century editions give it as though it were a fragment of the Saint's works.

[2] [*Lit.*: " with gentleness " (*con suavidad*).]

we cannot attain in deed, let us attain in desire. For the Lord is compassionate and will see to it that gradually our deeds become commensurate with our desires and intentions.

IV. VIRTUES OF OUR MOTHER SAINT TERESA ACCORDING TO A REPORT MADE BY HER COUSIN THE VENERABLE MOTHER MARÍA DE SAN JERÓNIMO.[1]

I wish indeed that I had not such a bad memory now that I am setting out to perform what obedience demands of me—namely, to write down some of the things which I saw and heard concerning our holy Mother Teresa of Jesus during the time when we had her in the house. Were it not for this memory of mine, I could say a great deal, since for over twenty years (that is, since the early days of this house) she set those of us who had come to her such a continual good example; but at that time we took things so lightly that we never thought of writing anything down and so we allowed it all to be forgotten. All that can be said, then, about that period is of a general kind, such as the great humility and charity and affability which she observed in her dealings with every one of us.

In those early days there were no lay sisters, and we each took a week at a time in the kitchen. Despite all her numerous occupations, the holy Mother would take her week like the other sisters; and it gave us no small happiness to see her in the kitchen, for she worked very gaily and took great care to look after us all. It seemed to be His Majesty's will to send us more alms in her week than during any other, and she would say that Our Lord was falling in with her wishes, for what she wanted was to give us good meals and so He sent the wherewithal. It sometimes happened that there would be an egg or two, or something of that kind, to go round among the whole community and she would say that this must be given to the one who most needed it. We used to think that this was she herself, as she was so often ill, but she would never allow it to be given her, saying that she had no need of it, so that it might be given to her daughters: she would go to great extremes in sparing them trials and taking them upon herself.

---

[1] The reputation for sanctity which St. Teresa enjoyed in her lifetime grew rapidly after her death; and, long before the various processes of beatification and canonization began, the superiors of the Discalced Reform took great pains to collect testimony from responsible persons who had known her and had to do with her concerning the outstanding traits of her life and character. Among the most interesting of these reports is one by M. María de San Jerónimo, of which a manuscript copy,

She would go to exceptional lengths as regards the virtue of charity, especially with sick nuns, so that they should not lack anything that they needed, and we often found that Our Lord would help us by providing for our necessities and thus rewarding her great faith. She would often tell us that we could be sure that, if we did not fail in the service of Our Lord, He would never fail us. And this she would say as one who had had ample experience of beginning things with faith. One day, soon after the foundation of this house, I heard her say that it needed a little work done on it, but that she had not a farthing in hand and had no idea where to get the money; none the less, as she saw the work was necessary, she decided to arrange to have it done— it came to eighty ducats. No sooner had the arrangements been put in hand than someone came to see her, whom she told what she had done, whereupon he enquired why she had taken such a step without having any money. She answered that God would provide for her, and so it turned out; for on the very next day she received some letters from a brother of hers in the Indies, in which he sent her, I think, more than two hundred ducats.[1]

On another occasion a church had to be made in this house, the predecessor of the church which we now have: it had not to be specially built but a great deal of money needed to be spent on its construction. The holy Mother had not a farthing and did not know what could be done. She sent for the sister who acted as bursar and told her to give her anything she might have so as to get the work started. The sister replied that she had only one small coin. The holy Mother thought this reply very diverting but she did not allow it to discourage her from having the work begun, and it was finished quite quickly, as Our Lord provided alms, which paid for it.

If I were to write of the effect wrought in souls by her prayer, I should have a great deal to say. I knew of one important person in this country, who, she heard, was in difficulties, being anxious to escape from a certain occasion of sin, but unable to do so, because it was continually before his eyes and he was not strong enough to banish it. She besought Our Lord for him, with the result that, long though it had gone on, it was very soon entirely removed. . . .

---

over her own signature, is preserved by the Discalced Carmelite nuns of Ávila. The author, St. Teresa's cousin, was born at Ávila about the year 1541 and took the habit at St. Joseph's on September 30, 1563. Later, she was for many years prioress there. In 1591 she went as prioress to the Madrid Discalced and in 1595 founded a new community at Ocaña. She died at Ávila on April 6, 1602.

[1] Cf. Vol. I, p. 229, above.

I also heard about a priest in a certain village who for two years had been living in mortal sin. When the holy Mother learned about this, she wrote him a letter, which had such an effect upon him that they say it was enough of itself to save him from his sin and that he always carried it about with him. This must have cost her no little prayer. Whenever such things happened and she besought Our Lord for souls in this state, the prayer it cost her and the assaults made on her by the devils were such that we could often see, to our great distress, what inroads they made upon her strength of body. Although these assaults were interior ones, they were of such a kind as to leave many marks on the body; the devils were enraged at her work for these souls and they threatened her and said they would have their revenge. She told me about this several times after it was all over and said that, whenever she saw such a soul improving and making progress, she knew that she would have to pay for it. Many things of this kind happened to her, so great a yearning had she for others' good.

She had great desires for penance and was always looking for opportunities of doing more of it, though, as she had such poor health, they were not easy to find. One day she arranged with the sisters that we should all wear frieze, instead of serge, which we now wear next to the skin, and that our sheets and pillows should be made of the same material. But she said that she must be the first to try this, lest it should prove harmful, in which case only she, and not her sisters, would suffer. So she did so, and wore the frieze until the Superior ordered it to be discontinued, saying that it was very bad for the health. . . .

As to her habits of prayer, she took a great deal of trouble to conceal all that she did; yet, the more she hid it, the more determined Our Lord seemed to be to reveal it. She was greatly distressed when people spoke of her as a saint. I saw a paper written in her own hand containing a report to one of her confessors, from which I gathered that this was the opinion held about her. She wanted to go to a convent a long way from here, and enter it as a lay sister, so as to dissemble as much as she could and not to become known. She attempted to do this; but, as the Lord was keeping her for other and greater tasks, He would not allow the project to go any farther.[1] This happened before this house was founded.

I heard one of her confessors, a very learned and prudent man, say that she acted less like a human being than like an angel. The remark did not surprise me; for, besides what he knew of all the benefit that others had received through their

---

[1] Cf. *Life*, Chap. XXXI (Vol. I, p. 209, above).

relations with her, he had derived great profit from the same source himself. It was when she was commending this same Father to God one day that I heard her say to His Majesty: "Lord, this will be good for our friend." Such was the familiarity with which she spoke to God.

To return to what we were saying about the care which she took to conceal her experiences in prayer. It happened once that her body was raised above the ground. She was just going up to communicate at the time and as soon as she felt that this was happening she grasped the rails with both hands so as to control herself. She was greatly distressed when such outward manifestations took place and she used to say that she had striven long with the Lord in prayer for them to cease, as in time they did. She used also to be distressed when she was enraptured in our presence, though eventually she learned to endure that. But for it to happen before people from outside was a terrible trial to her and she would dissemble by saying that it was caused by heart weakness; so, whenever this happened in anyone's presence, she would ask for something to eat and drink in order to support the idea that it was due to illness.

While she was practising prayer and penance in this way, to the profit of souls, and, as always, setting us a great example of humility, the Father General came from Rome and gave her patents for the foundation of convents. The first of these[1] was founded five years after this house [Saint Joseph's, Ávila] had been established. We were all very sorry when the day came for her to leave us, for we were extremely fond of her, and any one of us would have counted it a great joy if she would have taken her for a companion. Before she went, she tried to leave us comfortably settled, with our own house and garden, so that we should not miss her so much. She had not a farthing to do this with and she ran into debt to the extent of nine thousand *reales*, showing faith, as in other things, that Our Lord would come to her aid. And, sure enough, He sent nuns here who brought all this with them as alms—and, what was more, they were as virtuous as anyone could wish. It was no small thing at this juncture that anyone else should come here to take the habit at all, for when it became known that the holy Mother was leaving the convent everyone thought that it was all up with us and that the house would go to pieces immediately. Those of us who were left behind, however, had no such misgivings, for the things that His Majesty had done since we entered the house had shown us very clearly that it was the work of God: our only trouble, therefore, was to find ourselves

[1] Medina del Campo (1567). Cf. pp. 1–15, above.

without our holy Mother. She herself felt the parting very keenly but tried to hide her feelings lest she should distress us. When the time came for her to leave, she went to a hermitage which we have in this convent, containing a representation of Christ bound to the Column, to entreat Him very earnestly that when she returned to this house she should find it as she left it. This, as events have proved, Our Lord granted her so truly that, not only in spiritual but in temporal things, it has become clear how much His Majesty has helped this house and that this has come to pass through her prayer. Despite the way she went about making foundations, she was always very much concerned about her first convent, and she remained its prioress, and the nun whom she left in charge had very little to do in the governing of it.

As she has left an account of all the time that she spent in founding convents I will say nothing further, though I am quite sure that what she has written is the smallest part of what happened, for, if all that I have heard about the persecutions and trials which she suffered were written down, that alone would make a book. I can speak here, however, of the patience which I observed in her during the two years she was here after founding the convent at Seville. She came here from Toledo when we had to render obedience to the Order.[1] To do this was a great happiness to her and she put up bravely with the trials and persecutions which then came upon her while attempts were being made to form a separate province. So many plots and intrigues did the devil contrive that she had great need of the perfection which God had given her for bearing them. For not only did he do his utmost to prevent the formation of a new province but he tried to bring about the dissolution of those that had already been founded; and to this end he invented things which were to the discredit of the friars and of our Mother and made up the most terrible stories accusing them of things so serious and so wicked that it was hard to bear even having to listen to them.

She often received letters telling her of all these things, as she did about every other kind of business, for nothing was done without her being consulted. All these things went on among people of importance and to the knowledge of the Nuncio. Let us now see how the holy Mother took it when she heard that some plot was being laid against her or that people were trying hard to belittle and destroy something that had cost her such great pains. She would call us all together and read us the letters in question and then she would be as peaceful and quiet

[1] In July 1577 [See Vol. I., p. xxxiii, above].

about it as can be imagined, and sometimes would even laugh at the things being said about her. I never saw her angry, or even perturbed, or in the very least upset, at any such thing that might be said—indeed, she would say that she was getting fond of these people and was commending them earnestly to God. Nor did she stop here, for I have heard her say that this often brought her great inward joy, and whenever these things took place she gave clear outward signs of the happiness and rejoicing that they caused her. She would say that they were acting very rightly because, although she was not to blame in the matters about which they were accusing her, there were other respects in which she had offended God, so the one would serve for the other. At other times news would come that all her affairs were going wrong and that things were getting worse daily. And through all this, so steadfast were her courage and confidence that not only was there no need to comfort her but, when she saw how distressed we were, it was she who would comfort us, telling us to commend it all to Our Lord, and not to be distressed, for everything would come right in the end. When everybody said that things were going wrong the news seemed to give her fresh confidence and she would say to such people: "You see all this that is happening? Well, it is all for the best." And it certainly seemed to be so for her: I used to hear her say what great spiritual benefit she had derived from the trials and annoyances that had come to her.

Not the least of these, but the greatest of all, were those which she had to endure from her friends, for she felt such things more keenly then and they were a greater trial to her. Seeing that her friends were zealous about what they did, and meant it for her good, she thought they must be right and that it was she who was wrong; being good people, they made her very much ashamed of herself, and, however much their actions oppressed her, I never heard her speak of any of them other than edifyingly —they were saintly people, she would say, and everything that they did was saintly. During the two years for which these persecutions raged in this way, she would use what time she had for such things in writing to the convents to comfort the nuns there, as indeed was necessary, for they were very much troubled at the attempts that were being made to dissolve their communities and it was a great happiness to them when they saw her writing.

Their happiness, however, was of short duration, for the devil did his utmost to interfere with it. And so one night she fell downstairs, in such a way that she must have been thrown down by the devil. For she was carrying a light in her hand, and, after having climbed the stairs, she was just about to enter the choir for Compline when suddenly her head began to swim and she staggered and fell backwards. She dislocated her arm so badly that she was never able to use it as before.[1] This gave her great pain: for years she could hardly move the arm at all. This was a great trial both to her and to us: for one thing, she was never again able to dress or undress without help or even to put a veil over her head; and for another, she was prevented from writing letters at a time when there was so much need for her to do so, and her communities, knowing that she was in this condition, were very much grieved. She bore it all, however, with great patience and joy. One of her sisters asked her if she had not great longings to communicate, as it was a month since she had done so. She replied that she had not, for she was so completely resigned to Our Lord's will that she felt it no more than if she were communicating daily.

During this illness she used often to feel very sick, and one day she said to the infirmarian that her mouth was so parched that she thought she would like some melon, but they were not to go out for one if there were none in the house. There were, in fact, none; and, as she had told them not to send for any, they dared not do so, though they saw the urgency. When they brought her a meal, she felt so ill that she could eat nothing, and so they had to take it away. At this moment, however, there was a knock at the turn, and, when they went to answer it, they found half a melon there. The person who had brought it had disappeared and to this day no one knows who it was: it can be taken that Our Lord moved someone to come to His servant's aid.

These two years of severe persecution were succeeded by a period of fifteen to twenty years during which persecution did not go to the same lengths. The Nuncio ordered these houses of ours to submit to the Provincial of the Calced, who at that time was Fray Ángel de Salazar, and he at once began to go round and visit them. When he reached the Salamanca convent he found that the holy Mother was urgently needed there in connection with some lawsuit concerning the purchase of a house. So he told her to go there under obedience and at the same

---

[1] This accident happened on Christmas night, 1577 [Cf. Vol. I, p. xxxiv, above]. Ribera (Book IV, Chap. XVII) describes it in almost the identical words of our text, adding that it was some time before anybody could be found who was able to set the arm, " a woman who came from Medina ", who did such things, being ill at the time. When she was able to come, the arm was so much worse that the rude operation, which Ribera describes in some detail, caused her " intolerable pain ". The idea that the fall was the devil's work seems to have found great favour with the nuns. St. Teresa, however, when it was put to her, did not commit herself, but proffered the cryptic remark: " He would do much worse things than that, if he were allowed to."

time ordered her to go to Valladolid, where a lady, Doña María de Mendoza (God rest her soul!) had been asking him to send her, as she was very much devoted to her. So she left this house to make these two visits. She took with her a sister from this house, who acted as her companion until she died, so all that will be said from here onwards is the account of an eye-witness, for she was always at her side, and she is a woman who can be believed since she is very virtuous and God has given her great skill.[1] I know that our holy Mother thought a great deal of her, and that, although she is a lay sister, she got more help from her counsel than from that of many choir-nuns. I have had to do with her for many years and I know a great deal about her conscience: it makes me give the greatest praise to God when I hear her and see what God has put into her soul. . . .[2]

When our holy Mother left this house of Saint Joseph at Ávila on the journey to which I have referred, they gave her as companion a priest who was one of the hardest to please that she had ever had, and who took the greatest trouble to scrutinize everything she did and opposed her continually. She accepted him for her escort as from the hand of God; seeing that he came with her under obedience, she treated him in a kindly and affectionate manner, which it made us praise God to observe, and not only did she humour him in every possible way but she gave him pictures and prints which she had brought with her for her own solace. "See, my Father," she would say, "if you would like anything else that I have brought, I shall be very glad to give it you." She gave him a picture representing the Holy Spirit, of which she was very fond and which she had not wanted to give to anyone else, saying that she was giving it to him because she was so much attached to him. There was a monastery a little way off their route, and, knowing that the inmates were opponents of hers, the holy Mother asked the priest who was escorting her to let them go there, though it meant making a detour of some leagues. He, knowing how much opposition she had encountered in that house, and observing the humility with which she made the request, acceded to it. When they reached the house, it looked as if the inmates were disturbed at our coming, for, although we walked about the place for a good time, not a soul appeared. ¡Then the holy Mother called them, and, when they came to receive her, she greeted each of them individually with such marks of affection that one would

[1] The Venerable Ana de San Bartolomé.
[2] At the end of this paragraph comes the autograph signature of M. María. The narrative which follows we owe jointly to V. Ana de San Bartolomé, and to M. María de San Jerónimo, who collected it.

have supposed they were her dearest friends. She stayed there from the hour of Mass until the evening and all the time she behaved kindly and cheerfully. When she had to go, they went with her until she was out of the village. They said they were really moved and felt quite deserted at her having to go so soon and they showed extreme confusion at the sanctity which they observed in her. And the Father who accompanied them was extremely sorry when he found that their journey was nearing its close, for he was so devoted and attached to the holy Mother that he asked her to consider if she would like to make use of him when she went on farther, and said that in that case he would be very pleased.

I found that there were many other people who did not share the good opinion of her activities which was generally held. When the holy Mother heard of such people she would go to see them if they were accessible and would discuss with them the things about which they seemed to be most obdurate, with the result that they seemed so pleased and happy that one could only praise God. Those who went with her on her journeys were very much amazed to see that, throughout the trials and misfortunes which we met and which caused them dismay, the holy Mother remained in good spirits and cheered them all as though she herself had suffered nothing whatever. She would go on for some days through rain and snow, without finding a village for leagues on end or having anything to keep off the wet, and at nightfall she would come to some inn where there was no fire, and no means of making one, and nothing to eat, and the sky was visible through the roof of her room and the rain would come through into the room, and sometimes even their clothes would suffer. It was in these and similar conditions that she made her journeys, so gaily and cheerfully that one would have thought she took a delight in suffering. This certainly appeared to be the case, for, however bad the weather and notwithstanding all her physical disabilities, she never desisted from the journeys she was making. To those who accompanied her she would say at such times: "You must have great courage, for these days are rich in opportunities for winning Heaven." To which one of her companions, who must have felt the trials very sorely, replied: "But I was winning Heaven just as much at home!"

On a night like those described, it chanced that we reached an inn greatly in need of shelter, for our clothes were wet through and this had brought on the holy Mother's liver trouble and palsy. I was with her at the time, and, seeing that she was shivering violently, went to look for a fire so that I could warm her a blanket. A good man who was in the inn and saw this began to say all kinds of hard things about her—things with which he must have been inspired by the devil, for he was a religious, and one would never believe that such a person would say such things, but God must have ordained it so that she should suffer the more. And, ill though she was, she bore it with great cheerfulness and resignation, thinking that she had not deserved to hear things of any other kind.

One day we came to a place in La Mancha, called La Puebla. It was Christmas Day and we alighted and went to the church to hear Mass and communicate. When the people in the church saw her, they exclaimed that she looked like a bad woman and ought to be arrested. When they saw her receiving the Most Holy Sacrament, they were greatly scandalized and went up to her and asked her how she had dared to communicate, and said that before she left she must make it clear who she was. The holy Mother was delighted to find what opinion they had of her and made them no answer at all.

There was such a tumult in the church, which I myself witnessed, that no description I could give of it would be adequate. A great festival was to take place that day, as it was the feast of the title of the church, but everything was held up because until they discovered what kind of people we could be they were all so much excited that they were in no fit state to take part in any festival at all. This excitement grew to such a pitch that the holy Mother and those of us who were with her had to retreat into our carriage so as not to be seen, although we had not had a mouthful to eat. If we had not had with us our Father Fray Antonio de Jesús, whom they knew in that part of the world, the disturbance would have gone farther. As it was, even after the assurances he gave them, they said they would send a man with them to see where they were going. To all these things the holy Mother answered not a word.

I saw her on many occasions like this, or when other trials presented themselves on her journeys, and suffering always inspired her with such spirit that, though she may have been ill, she seemed to recover immediately, as if it had restored her to health. Once, when going to Malagón, the journey had been a very trying one and she had had some bad nights, so that, when she arrived, she was so ill that she felt as if there were not a bone in her body that was not aching and she was unfit to move from her bed. The nuns were trying to arrange to move from the house they were in to a new one, but when she arrived the workmen said they would need to work on it for six months before it could be ready for them to go in. This distressed the holy Mother, and on the next day, at dawn (for we had arrived very

late on the day before), we went to see the house and found that
what the workmen had said was true. None the less she said that
they would be able to go in by the Feast of the Conception
[December 8], though it was already the Feast of Saint Catherine
the Martyr [November 25].

When the workmen heard this, they were amazed, for it
seemed to them impossible, and even I was surprised, when
I remembered how on the night before she had been so ill and
could hardly move her limbs, to see her with such spirit and
courage that one would never have thought she had been ill
at all. And she arranged things so well that she got the house
ready, as she intended it should be, for the day in question, and a
most solemn ceremony was held, attended by the people of the
town and the surrounding villages. The nuns walked in procession with the Most Holy Sacrament. During the whole of the
time they were getting the house ready, the holy Mother was with
the workmen every day from dawn to midnight. She was the
first each morning to take the brush and dustpan and she went to
bed every night at eleven o'clock after reciting the Divine Office.
Then the nuns and the prioress would come, and she would
entreat their pardon for her faults and for anything that she might
have done which they did not like, prostrating herself at their
feet as if she had been the least of them all. In everything she
did she set us a great example of humility. Sometimes she would
order certain things to be done, or at other times, when it was
necessary, would issue a reproof; and if she saw that the sister
concerned did not take it well or was cherishing a grievance
about it, she would go up to her, throw herself at her feet, tell
her that she had not reflected what she was saying, and beg her
forgiveness. She was very much given to asking everyone else's
opinion before doing anything whatever.

She was still in this house aforementioned, which she had got
ready for the Feast of the Conception, when on that very night
she was again seized with the same illness—a contraction of the
bones, so painful that she felt ill all over, precisely as she had
done on her arrival after her journey. It was very evident that
God had taken this illness from her because there was work for
her to do, and, once the work was done, had given it back to her
again. When Christmas arrived, her spirits were so high and
her joy was so great that they infected us all; and, as she was
now somewhat better, and up again, she went to choir. There
she made a mistake in reading one of the lessons of the Office
and atoned for it by prostrating herself in the middle of the choir;
and the sisters wept so much that some of them were unable to
speak.

As Our Lord had prepared another trial for her, He now began to give her better health. Shortly before Shrovetide Fray Antonio de Jesús and Fray Gabriel de la Asunción arrived to go with her to make the foundation at Villanueva de la Jara, and, as these Fathers were well known throughout La Mancha, so many people thronged to see her in all the villages they passed through that we could hardly move. We came to a place called Robledo, and, when the holy Mother had heard Mass and communicated, the Fathers took her to dine at the house of one of her devoted admirers. This was a very honourable lady, much attached to virtuous deeds, who gave the holy Mother and her companions a great welcome. So many people flocked to the house that two *alguaciles* had to be placed at the door to allow us to have our meal. It was so bad that the people swarmed over the walls so that nothing could stop them, and a few people had to be taken to prison before we could leave: their anxiety to see the Mother was tremendous, though there was no chance for them to speak to her. On the same occasion, in another place near this, the holy Mother saw to it that we left three hours before dawn so as to avoid the people. As we set out, the carriage broke down, and it was impossible to see in the dark what had happened; so we went on three leagues to the village, and, when it grew light and we saw what had happened, we were amazed that it had been possible to use it, and those who accompanied the holy Mother said that it seemed like a miracle.

In all these places there was very great devotion. In another place there lived a very wealthy farmer, who, when it became known that the holy Mother was to pass that way, arranged to give a large dinner for her in his house, and brought his children and their husbands and wives from various places so that she should give them her blessing. Nor did even this satisfy the devotion of these good people: they even brought their animals for her to bless. But, when the holy Mother arrived, she would not stop for all their entreaties; so the farmer brought all his people so that they could speak to her there and she could give them her blessing, and then we went straight on.

Before reaching Villanueva, we had to pass a place where there was a Discalced Carmelite monastery.[1] When the friars knew that the holy Mother was arriving, they came out to receive us in procession a long way from the monastery, and as it was open country and they must have come with great enthusiasm, they infected all who saw them. The holy Mother said that the sight had made her very happy, for it had reminded her of the saints of the desert of our Order. They all knelt down when they arrived

[1] La Roda, a house well known during the early years of the Reform.

and asked for her blessing, and then led her in procession to the church. A great many people came to see her while she was there as the news of her arrival had spread throughout the surrounding villages.

Thence we set out for Villanueva de la Jara, and a good while before we arrived there a great many children came out very devoutly to meet the holy Mother. When they met her carriage they knelt down and then went on in front of her, bareheaded, till they reached the church, where we alighted. As the holy Mother has left a written account of all that concerns this foundation I shall say no more here about the story of those devout ladies who lived in the house. When the convent was founded, our Mother took her share of its duties like all the rest; and, though she could use only one hand, did the sweeping and served in the refectory and did what she could in the kitchen. One day she was standing outside the refectory with a workman who was making a wheel for a well, which was a very large one, when he stumbled and fell against her and knocked her down. Instead of being quick about helping her up he stood there dumbfounded, but she got up by herself as quickly and briskly as if nothing had happened. They said it was a miracle that her fall had not killed her, for the part of her body which struck the wheel turned black and blue. This happened on the vigil of Saint Joseph and so we credited the Saint with having protected her.

From here we came on to Toledo and she was so cheerful as she travelled that everyone liked to go in her company. The order observed on these journeys was as follows. First, they heard Mass and communicated daily—and this, however hurried they were, was never omitted. Our Mother always took with her holy water and a little bell so that she could ring for silence; and this we did at the proper times, and everyone knew that as soon as the bell went they must be quiet. She also took her clock so as to keep the hours of prayer; and, when we rang the bell at the end of a period of prayer or silence, it was a great thing to see how pleased the drivers were and how glad at being able to talk again. At these times the holy Mother was always careful to give them something to eat because they had been so good at keeping silence.

She was very pleasant with all who had dealings with her. Sometimes there were people who would come and talk to her to see if they could catch her in any way, not believing what they heard about her to be true. She would speak to them in her usual way—namely, of things that profited the soul—and they benefited from this like any others. There were two youths who came with this intention, but, before she had finished with them,

Our Lord touched their hearts, and they confessed their guilt and told her why they had come. When they left her, therefore, they were completely changed.

She was very compassionate with those who were humble and subject to obedience and very severe with those who showed themselves too free. She had no love for gloomy people and she herself was certainly not gloomy nor did she desire those who accompanied her to be so. "God deliver me from frowning saints!" she would say. On her journeys she would give little talks about God, and those who were usually swearing and telling stories enjoyed hearing her more than all the pleasures of the world; and this I have myself heard them say. When on the road she was always the first to awaken the others, and, when night came, the last to betake herself to rest.

In one of the foundations to which she went, there was great need of water and those who accompanied her begged her earnestly to entreat Our Lord to give them some. So she made all the sisters who were entering this foundation say a litany, which was repeated by all the rest, and before they had finished it began to rain and it rained hard all that night. She then told them to sing a Te Deum to thank our Lord for the way He had helped them by giving them water. This aroused such devotion in the nuns who were entering the convent that they wept to see in how short a space of time the thing that the holy Mother had been asked to pray for had been granted them. But neither this nor many other such things that happened to them made her in the least vainglorious; so far, indeed, was she from this that I heard her say she had never had to confess this sin in her life.

And so as to show what extraordinary things happen in this world, I will add that on the next day, when she went to another village, some people came out and made cruel remarks about them, thinking that they had been arrested and were being taken before the Inquisition. They supposed this to be so because among the people who were accompanying the holy Mother on this road was an alguacil with his staff, but he had come from the Bishop of Osma, who had sent for the holy Mother to make a foundation at Soria. When she arrived, the Bishop was looking out for her at a window, whence he gave us his blessing. But as she has written about this Soria foundation I shall say no more of it here. From Soria she came to this convent of Saint Joseph at Ávila.

V. The last acts of the life of Saint Teresa. By the Venerable Ana de San Bartolomé.[1]

Our holy Mother Saint Teresa of Jesus arrived at this house of Saint Joseph's, Ávila, at the beginning of September in the year 1581. She came from Soria, where she had been founding a convent, and, as in this house of Saint Joseph's they had always wanted to have her as their superior, they effected this upon her arrival. The nun who was prioress at the time prevailed upon the Father Provincial to release her from that office so that our holy Mother might be elected immediately; and this was done.

This happened at a time when this house was in extreme temporal necessity. Ever since that day, God be praised, it has never lacked what it has needed, but has gained so much that, despite its numerous debts, the Lord has so helped it that not only have these all been paid but it has enough to live upon without any of the trouble and hardship which it had had to endure down to that time. If I were to speak of its spiritual life, there would be a great deal to say, but that must be left to the superiors, who know most about it: all I have to do myself is to make this report, as our Father Provincial has ordered me.

We were all very pleased to have our holy Mother here as our prioress. But Our Lord began to move someone[2] from the city of Burgos to take steps about the foundation of a convent there and she wrote to our Mother asking her to come there and make it. She answered that she would obtain a licence from the Archbishop[3] and when she had it would let her know. Her idea in doing this was not to go to make the foundation herself but to send nuns to do so. But after she had decided upon this, she learned that it was the Lord's will that she should go and do it in person. This was evidently true, to judge from the trials and worries which this foundation caused her: had she not gone, as will be seen later, it would have been impossible to make it at all.

---

[1] This is a continuation of the preceding document (see p. 338, n. 1, above) in the hand of the same copyist: P. Silverio was the first to publish it in Spanish. Ana de San Bartolomé, as has been said, accompanied St. Teresa on her foundations and acted as her personal attendant, and, when necessary, as her nurse. Born about 1550, at Almendral, in the province of Ávila, she professed as a lay sister at St. Joseph's, Ávila, on August 15, 1572. She was constantly with St. Teresa during her last days and was at her side when she died. In 1604, she went to France with some other nuns to make foundations there and subsequently, under obedience, became a choir-sister. She died at Antwerp on June 7, 1626.

[2] Doña Catalina de Tolosa.

[3] Don Cristóbal Vela: he was a distant relative of St. Teresa's. Cf. p. 184, above.

It was at this time that the Father Fray John of the Cross arrived—the first Discalced friar of our Order. He brought horses with him, for he was the bearer of a message asking our holy Mother to come and make a foundation at Granada, where they thought that, as it would be the first in that kingdom, it would be well if she were to go herself. The holy Mother saw that it would be impossible for her to do this as she had to go to Burgos, so she picked two nuns who she thought would be suitable for this task. One of them was the nun who had been prioress of this house when they elected our holy Mother; the other was a nun of great spirituality and perfection.[1] As the account of that foundation will contain all that there is to be said about these sisters, I will only remark here that their departure was greatly regretted and they were very much missed, such good company were they.

They left on the eve of Saint Andrew's Day and our holy Mother set out for Burgos on the day after New Year's Day, 1582. She took with her two nuns whom she had sent for from Alba for this purpose, and also her own companion. She was also accompanied by the Father Provincial, Fray Jerónimo de la Madre de Dios, and two other friars whom he had brought with him.[2] For most of the day on which they left it was raining and snowing, and this brought on her palsy again—a complaint which gave her a great deal of trouble. We had a very trying time getting to Medina, having to go all the way through the rain. She stayed in the Medina house for three days; thence we went to Valladolid, where her complaint gave her so much trouble that the doctors told her she would be very ill unless she left at once. It was hard to do this so quickly, but we went on to Palencia, where one of our houses had been founded a year since.[3] At that time they had become so devoted to our holy Mother in that city that, on hearing she was coming, so many people collected that, when she and her nuns alighted from their carriage, we could hardly get down for the press of people who had come to speak to her and ask for her blessing; those, however, who were disappointed of this were glad to have heard her speak.

When she got inside the convent, they received her, as her convents always did, with a Te Deum. The delight and joy of the nuns was very evident from the way they had arranged the courtyard: so full was it of altars and other things that it looked

---

[1] These were respectively María de Cristo and Antonia del Espíritu Santo, one of the first four nuns to take the habit at St. Joseph's.
[2] One was Fray Pedro de la Purificación: the name of the other is unknown.
[3] At the end of December, 1580.

like a regular paradise. For the whole time that we were in this house the holy Mother was very unwell, and the weather was still extremely rainy. But notwithstanding all this she would not desist from her intention of going on to Burgos. They told her she could not possibly set out in such weather, for it might kill her. Then they sent on a man to see what the roads were like and the report he brought back was a very bad one.

The holy Mother was so much distressed about this that she did not know what to do. Afterwards it was learned that Our Lord had told her to go on and said that He would help us; and by that time, after all the perils we had encountered, we were quite sure that, if His Majesty had not preserved us, we should have perished on the way. Once, when we were going along a river bank, the mud was so thick that the carriages stuck in it and we had to get down. After escaping from this danger we were climbing a hill when we saw before our eyes another and a worse one. For the holy Mother saw the carriage in which her nuns were travelling about to overturn and the hill we were climbing was so steep that even a large number of people could not have saved them by preventing the carriage from falling. But at the same moment one of the youths whom we had with us saw it and he seized the wheel and saved the carriage from overturning. He was really more like a guardian angel than a man, for he could certainly not have done this all alone had it not been God's will to save them.

On seeing this, our holy Mother was greatly troubled, for she thought her nuns would be drowned; and from that time forward she wanted to travel in the front carriage, so that if any further perils presented themselves she might be the first to meet them. As for resting after this trial that we had gone through, we arrived that night at an inn where they could not even make our holy Mother a bed; yet, poor as this lodging was, we thought it would be well to stay there for a few days, in view of the report which they gave us on the state of the road—the rivers were so swollen that the water had risen nearly two feet above the bridges. The innkeeper was à good fellow; and so sorry was he for us that he offered to go on ahead of us and pilot us through the water; for, with the river in such a state and the bridges submerged, it was impossible to see the road by which we were to travel. The bridges were wooden ones and so narrow that the carriage-wheels could hardly get on to them, and, if they had swerved only slightly, we should have fallen into the river. Faced with this peril, we made our confessions and asked our holy Mother to give us her blessing, as though we were going to die; and we also said the Creed. Seeing us so despondent, the holy Mother sympathized with us over some of these troubles, but, having more faith that Our Lord would deliver us safely out of this peril, she then cried out as gaily as could be: "Come, now, my daughters! What better end would you have than to become martyrs here for love of Our Lord?" And then she said that she would go on first, and, if she were drowned, they must not proceed any farther, but return to the inn. Eventually, however, God was pleased to free us from this peril.

Throughout these trials our holy Mother was so ill, and her tongue was so completely paralysed, because of the palsy, that it was pitiful to see her. Before midday we reached a village, where she got the Father Provincial to say Mass at once. He gave her Communion and at that very moment her tongue was loosened and she grew better. From there, on that same night, we went on to Burgos; and so heavy had the storms been that the streets were like rivers. But the lady who was awaiting us to put us up in her house is a most kindly person, and she had made a very good fire for us and looked after us very well.

As our Mother was so wet, she stayed longer by the fire that night than she should have done; and this did her such harm that on that same night she had an attack of dizziness and was terribly sick. Her throat was already badly inflamed and the sickness made it worse, so that she began to vomit blood, and so, on the next day, was unable to get up and go about her business. Instead, she lay on a couch which they put against a window opening into a passage and those who wanted to speak to her did so there. They sent to tell the Archbishop she had come but his reply was to ask why she had brought the nuns with her, for he had only told her to come and talk matters over with him. He was asked if the Most Holy Sacrament could be placed in the house where we were and Mass said there, since that was the house in which the convent was to be founded. To this His Lordship answered that we were not to worry about it and the matter would be attended to in due course. Several more people were then sent to him to speak about this, but it was all no use. Then our Father Provincial went, and the reply the Archbishop gave him was that we could go back where we came from as his city stood in no need of reformation, the monasteries and convents in it being quite reformed enough already. A few days later, yet another person went to see him about it and he said he had supposed that we should have gone by this time, and that we could return immediately.

By this time the holy Mother was really ill and her throat

trouble was so bad that she could only take liquid food. Being in this condition and hardly able to leave her bed, she found it a very great trial to have to go out on festivals to hear Mass; and for this reason they went to the Archbishop again to ask leave for Mass to be said in the house. They told him, too, that it distressed the nuns so much to find themselves in the church mixing with people from the world that they sometimes wept till the ground was watered with their tears; but the only help His Lordship gave them in their trouble was to tell them that it was of no importance and they were really setting a very good example. This, it must be understood, denoted no want of charity on His Lordship's part, for everyone knows what a saintly man he is: it happened because God was ordaining it so that the holy Mother and the sisters should suffer. This became very evident from the resignation and perfection with which the Mother endured it. A number of people came to speak to her about it, very cross and displeased at the lack of success they had had. But the holy Mother made so many excuses for the Archbishop, and spoke of him in such a way that the annoyance with which they had come entirely left them. Several weeks passed in this way, and, ill as she was, she still went out on festivals to hear Mass and communicate, despite the difficulty of making her way along the streets in such weather. Nor was this her greatest trial; it distressed her still more to witness the displeasure and grief of the Father Provincial and of the lady who had brought us here to found the convent. For when she went to make her confession she could not get absolution because she had us in her house and had been the cause of our coming.

When the holy Mother was a little better, she went to the Archbishop herself, to see if she could succeed where others had failed; and for the whole afternoon, while she was with the Archbishop, the sisters occupied themselves in taking the discipline. In the course of her conversation with him she said: "See, Your Lordship, my nuns are taking the discipline." To this he replied that they could discipline themselves as much as they liked but he had not decided to give her the licence. So the holy Mother went back without it. When we saw her coming, we went out to ask her what she had brought, for her expression denoted great happiness. On hearing that the news she had brought was not good we were very sad and began to grumble a little about the Archbishop. So she tried to comfort us and said that he was a saint and that he had given her very good reasons for what he was doing, which quite satisfied her, and that she had very much enjoyed her talk with him, and that we must not be distressed, but must trust in God, and He would not fail to help us.

It was now clear that there was no way of getting the licence for the convent or of having Mass said in the house we were in; so, as it distressed the holy Mother and all of us to have to go out to hear Mass, we were ordered to go and live in a house where we should not have to do so. The place where we now went was a hospital[1] and there they gave the Father Provincial a top room, which had a little platform, where Mass could be said. The room was unoccupied, for it was of such a kind that no one wanted to live in it: the story went that there were more hob-goblins there than anywhere else in Burgos. And there must have been something in this, for one thing or another kept on happening to us all the time we were there. Further, it was a room without proper protection from the elements, which in the holy Mother's weak state of health was a great trial to her. We commiserated with her about this, but she replied that it was far too good a place for her and she did not deserve it: all that was worrying her, she said, was our well-being; for herself she was not troubled at all and she was lucky that the hospital would take her. They made her up a very poor bed and she exclaimed: "Oh, my Lord, what a soft couch is this—and Thou didst hang on a cross!" Whenever she ate, blood would come from the place in her throat; but if anyone pitied her she would say: "Do not be sorry for me: my Lord suffered more than this when He drank the gall and vinegar."

One day she said that she felt very sick but that she could eat some oranges. On the same day a lady sent her some. She took a few very fine ones, put them in her pocket and said that she wanted to go downstairs to see a poor man who had been complaining a great deal of his illness. She went, and gave all the oranges to the poor. When she came back, we asked her why she had done this. "I wanted them more for the poor than for myself," was her reply. "I am very glad that they have given them so much pleasure." And her face showed clearly how pleased she was. On another occasion she was brought some limes, and, when she saw them, she exclaimed: "Blessed be God, Who has given me something to take to my friends the poor!"[2] One day a man was being treated for boils and was uttering such cries that it was torture for the others to hear him. The holy Mother was sorry for him, so she went down, and, as soon as the poor man saw her, he was silent. Then she said to him: "Son, why are you crying out like this? Will you not bear it

---

[1] The Hospital of the Conception. [Cf. p. 194, above.]
[2] [*Lit*: "to my little poor men"—the diminutive indicates affection.]

patiently for the love of God?" He answered: "I feel as if they are tearing the life out of me." But, after the holy Mother had been with him for a little while, he said that his pain had gone, and after that, although they continued to give him the same treatment, we never heard him utter a cry again.

These poor people in the hospital used to ask the nurse to bring that saintly woman to see them often, for the mere sight of her was a great comfort to them and she seemed to relieve their pain. It was the same nurse who told us that, after they had heard we were going to leave, she had found them in great distress and weeping about it. On Saint Joseph's eve, I remember, we were feeling sad about it ourselves, since the time was coming for us to be turned out of the hospital—for they had given us only till Easter and if we had no house by then we should have to go, and no house had yet been found. But, as I say, it was on the eve of the festival of our Father Saint Joseph, when Our Lord arranged things for us in a way that looked more like a miracle than anything else. But I understand that our holy Mother has written about this in her account of the foundation, so I shall say no more about it here.

Once we had arranged to have this house, we moved into it within two or three days, and we spent the time from then until Easter in getting it ready. After we had gone in, the Archbishop came two or three times to see our holy Mother, and to find out if the house was suitable for a convent, giving us hopes that he would grant her the licence by Easter. One day when His Lordship was with us he asked for a jug of water and when she gave it him the holy Mother brought out and offered him some little gift or other that she had had sent her. At this he exclaimed: "You have found great favour with me, Mother. I have never taken such a thing as this before from anyone in Burgos. But I am taking it now because it comes from you." To which the Mother replied: "I was also hoping for the favour of receiving the licence from the hand of Your Lordship." Even then he did not give it her, yet she was still very happy, and praised Our Lord as much as if he had, eulogizing his sanctity and remarking what a good thing it was that there were such prelates in the Church of God; and we never heard a word of a contrary nature.

We stayed there, waiting for the licence, until Easter. During Holy Week we went to a church to hear the Office. We were in this church on Maundy Thursday when some men, in trying to pass the holy Mother, pushed her out of the way and gave her a kick because she did not rise as quickly as they would have liked. When I went to help her up I found her all smiles and happiness and I gave praise to God.

Still we waited, in the hope that the licence would come in time for us to have Mass said in the house on Easter Sunday. Here God was pleased to test the holy Mother's patience still further—or, rather, the patience of the sisters, for she herself had enough and to spare. We waited for the three days of Easter but on none of these days did it come, so on each of them we had to go out to hear Mass. On the third day the sisters were feeling very much upset about it, and much more so was the lady who had brought us there—in fact, she was taking leave of the holy Mother and her nuns and saying that she would not come to see them again until she heard that the foundation had been made. The holy Mother was feeling very much grieved to see the distress of this lady and the sisters, when at that very moment there entered a gentleman, to whom we were very much beholden, bringing the licence from the Archbishop for the foundation of the convent. He was so pleased when he came in that, before saying a word to us, he ran to the little bell that we had there and began to ring it. From this we guessed that he had brought the licence. Thereupon we all rejoiced greatly: on the very next day[1] the Most Holy Sacrament was taken there, the first Mass was said, and at last we were able to have our enclosure, for which we all had no little longing. The first Mass was said, and the Most Holy Sacrament was reserved, by some Fathers of the Order of Saint Dominic, an Order whose Fathers have always been of great service to our holy Mother and helped her in her necessities.

A few days later, the habit was given to the daughter of that lady who arranged for our convent to be founded here. The Archbishop preached the sermon, with such tears and humility that we were all greatly embarrassed and the rest of the congregation were very much moved, for, among other things that he said, he showed that he now regretted having delayed about our business. He eulogized the lady who had brought us to the city and he evinced great affection for our holy Mother.

From that time forward the house got better and better known, and the holy Mother began to be visited by a number of important people. One of these was a lady who for years had been desiring that God would give her children, and she begged our Mother so trustfully to entreat His Majesty for this that her desire was granted. She was very grateful to God for this favour which He showed her.

Now just at this time, when our holy Mother and all of us were most happy in our house, and at finding ourselves at last enclosed, and everything turning out so well, Our Lord was

[1] April 18, 1582.

pleased to moderate our happiness and send us the trial which now came upon our house, and upon the city. This was that, on Ascension Day, the river rose and flooded the city, and all the monasteries and convents had to evacuate their inmates lest they should be drowned. When we found ourselves in danger of this, the Mother was advised to leave the convent. She would not do so, however, but had the Most Holy Sacrament removed to one of the top rooms of the house, and gathered us all together there, and we recited litanies. Eventually the flood reached such a height that dead bodies were washed out of their graves, and houses carried away. Our own was one of those in the greatest danger because it stood on level ground near the river. A great deal might be said about this, but lest I should be too lengthy I will merely end by adding that the opinion of many people, and in particular of the Archbishop, was that the fact of our holy Mother's being there had tied the hands of God so that the city should not perish.

One day, when this trial had passed (and it was much worse than I have here indicated), the holy Mother was with Our Lord and He said to her: "Lord, art Thou contented now?" And the answer which He gave her was: "Wait: there is another and a greater trial coming for thee." At the time she did not understand the meaning of this; but later it became very clear, as she had to endure many trials between then and the time she reached Alba—both ill-health and other grave trials that presented themselves.

While she was still in Burgos, rather worried at not knowing if she ought to leave at once or to stay, Our Lord told her to leave, for He had no more for her to do there, as everything was completed. So she left at once for Palencia, and thence went to Medina, with the intention of going straight on to Ávila. But at Medina she found the Father Vicar-Provincial, Fray Antonio de Jesús, who was awaiting her to tell her to go to Alba. Although God had granted her such help with respect to this virtue of obedience, she was so much distressed about it, thinking that they were sending her there at the request of the Duchess, that I never saw her so sad about anything which her superiors had ordered her to do as about this.

We left there in a carriage, which had such difficulty in doing the journey that, when we came to a little village near Peñaranda, the holy Mother was so weak and in such pain that she fainted. It made us all dreadfully sorry to see her like that, and we had nothing to give her but a few figs, which had to last her the night, for in the whole village we could not find so much as an egg. I was in anguish at seeing her in such straits and being unable to help her in any way, but she comforted me and told me not to be grieved—the figs were extremely good and there were many poor people who would have less. This she said to comfort me, but as I was aware of her great patience and of what she was enduring and what joy it gave her to suffer, I guessed that she was in greater straits than her remark suggested; and so, on the next day, we went on to another village to try to get her some relief. Here we got some cabbage, cooked with a great deal of onion, and she took some of this, although it was very bad for her complaint. On the same day we reached Alba, but our Mother was now so ill that she was unable to talk to the nuns. She said she felt so broken in health that she thought she had not a sound bone in her body. She went on with her work from that day, which was the eve of Saint Matthew, down to Michaelmas Day, when she went to Communion. But on her return she came straight back and lay down on her bed, and had a haemorrhage, which, it is understood, was the cause of her death.

Two days before she died she asked to be given the Most Holy Sacrament, for she knew now that she was dying. On seeing that they were bringing it to her she sat up in bed in such a spirited way that it looked as if she were going to get up, so they had to restrain her. Then she said, with great joy: "My Lord, it is time to set out; may the journey be a propitious one and may Thy will be done." She gave hearty thanks to God that she was a daughter of the Church and was dying as such, saying that through the merits of Christ she hoped to be saved, and she asked us all to beseech God to pardon her sins and to look, not at them, but only at His own mercy. With great humility she asked the pardon of all, telling them not to take into account the things she had done and the bad example she had set them.

When the sisters saw that she was dying, they begged her earnestly to say something to them which should be to their profit, and she said that she entreated them, for the love of God, to keep strictly to their Rule and Constitutions. There was nothing that she wished to add to this. Afterwards she said little more, save for repeating again and again that verse of David which says: *Sacrificium Deo spiritus contribulatus; cor contritum et humiliatum, Deus, non despicies.*[1] Especially the phrase beginning *cor contritum*: this she kept repeating till she could say no more. Before this, she had asked for Extreme Unction, which she received with great devotion.

On Saint Francis' Day, at nine o'clock in the evening, Our Lord took her to be with Him and left us all in such sorrow and grief that, if I had to describe it here, there would be a great

[1] Psalm l, 19 [A.V. li. 17].

deal to say. I heard a few things which the holy Mother said before she expired, but so wonderful are they that I shall not set them down here: my superiors can relate them if they think it well to do so.[1]

VI. Extracts from Depositions Taken from Sister Teresa de Jesús, the Saint's Niece. Ávila, 1596.[2]

1. Asked if she knew Mother Teresa of Jesus, the witness replied that she was her brother's daughter, and had known and had to do with her for the space of eight years. She had accompanied her from Seville to the house of Saint Joseph, Ávila, and some time later went with her thence to the Burgos foundation. In the last year of the holy Mother's life, she was constantly in her company. She knows that the holy Mother was a native of Ávila, her father being Alonso Sánchez de Cepeda and her mother Doña Beatriz de Ahumada. She has been told that she took the habit at the Incarnation on All Souls' Day, when twenty-one and a half years old,[3] and that she lived the religious life for forty-seven years, twenty-seven of them at the Incarnation and the last twenty in this Order of Discalced Nuns which she founded.

2. When asked if she knew the Mother Teresa of Jesus to have been a woman of great spirituality and much prayer and if she communed frequently in this way with God our Lord, she said that she could testify concerning the period when she had to do with her and also of what she had heard before and since, from religious both of this Order and of others. And she believed her to have been one of the most outstanding and most experienced souls in prayer that our age has seen, and through prayer to have received the greatest graces and favours from His Majesty, and to have been very conscious of His presence and communication of Himself and of an increase in the virtues. Thus in the last years of her life she had grown so near to God and was so much habituated to spiritual things that it seemed as though, save

---

[1] [Two paragraphs then describe the attentions paid to the Saint's dead body and a final paragraph sums up the entire narrative.]

[2] [As there is much repetition in these pages, brief extracts only are given here and the omissions are not indicated.] Teresa de Jesús was born at Quito (in present-day Ecuador) in 1566. She first met her aunt at Seville on her arrival in Spain in 1575: the foundation of Discalced nuns in that city was being made at the time. She began her novitiate at St. Joseph's, Avila, accompanied St. Teresa on the journey to Burgos (pp. 188 ff., above) and made her profession, shortly after the Saint's death, on November 5, 1582. She died, at the age of forty-three, in 1610.

[3] See p. 314, n. 3, above.

outwardly, she was not living this life at all, and the things which passed in her soul were so sublime that they could not be communicated to others, and so she used to say that she had not the leisure to speak of them. And thus she did not spend time in treating of them as she had done formerly, for her spirit now rejoiced in great tranquillity and quiet, which helped her to endure the sore trials that came to her at the time of the Burgos foundation.

She was unusually affable and gave proof of superhuman qualities and of a simplicity and dignity which recalled the days of our first innocence. She was very much devoted to the Saints and through their intercession received great favours from God. Sometimes they would appear to her: this witness found her one day all alone and greatly recollected, and when they began to talk she told her of the help being given her by Saint Clare, who had appeared to her and encouraged her to continue founding these convents, saying that she would help her and promising her that, wherever they were made, they should succeed. This prophecy has clearly been fulfilled, both in Burgos and in Palencia and also in this city; in their early stages these foundations were greatly helped by the nuns of the Order of Saint Clare.

3. She said that she knew it was the holy Mother Teresa of Jesus who had started the Order called that of the Discalced Carmelites and that she had been moved to do so by a desire for the glory of God Our Lord and for the good of souls. So she wished to try to live and to get others to live in the closest possible seclusion and to keep their vows by means of penance and poverty. She had no idea of founding a new Order, but desired to renew her own Order, which already existed in a mitigated form, and wished that she and those who followed her could spend their whole lives in prayer, beseeching God for the increase of the Catholic Church and the destruction of heresies, which, especially those in France, distressed her so much that she felt she would lay down a thousand lives to save one of the many souls that were being lost there. Being a woman, and prevented from benefiting them as she would have liked, she determined to undertake this work in order to make war on the heretics with her prayers and her life and with the prayers and lives of her nuns, and to help Catholics by means of spiritual exercises and continued prayer. She said it always caused her great joy to see one more church containing the Most Holy Sacrament.

This witness remembers having heard it said, both by the holy Mother and by others (particularly by a nun called Isabel de

San Pablo, formerly Sub-Prioress of this convent of Discalced nuns of Ávila and a contemporary of the holy Mother at the Incarnation, who must have been dead now about fifteen years), that Our Lord often ordered and commanded her in prayer to begin and proceed with these foundations, and gave her special favour and help, as can be seen from the way in which this Order of nuns and friars has prospered without human aid. Her establishment of the Reform for friars cost her numerous and fervent prayers. By means of her apt reasoning she obtained a licence from the Father General, but she was then greatly concerned because there seemed to be no friar in the Province of the Calced who could help her to carry her Reform into effect, nor anyone not a religious who would enter upon life in such an Order. So she did nothing but entreat Our Lord to provide such a person. Then she got into touch with a Father who was Prior of the Mitigated Carmelites of Medina, and with another Father. The name of the first was Fray Antonio de Heredia; that of the second, Fray John of the Cross. Both were desirous of joining the Carthusians and the holy Mother begged and urged them to abandon this idea and to enable her to carry into effect her desire that there should be Discalced Carmelite friars. She was able to bring forward such arguments that, with the help of God our Lord, they accepted her proposal willingly. This witness has heard that one of these two religious, Fray John of the Cross, died some years ago and that his body is in the city of Segovia, and that it is working miracles and is intact and uncorrupt. Mother Teresa had no idea what to do about a house in which these two religious might make a beginning but God our Lord ordained that a gentleman of Ávila should offer her one, though only a poor one, in a small village named Duruelo. The holy Mother went to see it and thus began the first foundation of Discalced Carmelite friars. She told her two friars about the kind of life which they would have to live, and both in this way and in the preparation of the things they needed for the foundation and with her continual prayers she did all she could to help them. The friars took up residence in the house, where the first Mass was said on a Sunday in Advent in the year 1568.

4. She said that she knew the holy Mother had great faith, hope and charity and was endowed with humility, patience, poverty, penitence and other virtues. As to faith, God had shown her such favour that not only had she a great deal of it but she was never tempted concerning it. So deeply rooted was it in her soul that she would feel she could face all the heretics everywhere and make them see the error of their ways.

Concerning the articles of the Faith she would say that, the less she understood them, the more she believed them and the greater was the devotion that they produced in her. And although she was continually with learned men she never asked them, nor even desired to know, how God did this or that, or how such a thing could be. For her it was sufficient to know that God did it; knowing that, she was never surprised at it but simply praised Him.

So full was she of the virtue of hope, and so great was her confidence in Our Lord and in His words, that, however badly the business of her foundations might go (and by human reckoning it often went irreparably badly), she never despaired but went on trustfully with her work in her great-souled way, for she believed that none of her hopes could be frustrated or fail. And it is a justification of her belief that a single woman, living an enclosed life, bound by obedience and having no money or human help in any other form but meeting with continual opposition, should have been able to found an Order of friars and nuns, as we see that she did.

As to charity, she had a most fervent love for God, which grew each day, together with her desire for His honour and glory and a vehement thirst to see Him and impulses so violent that they left her quite beside herself and led her to desire death with great yearnings and other feelings which are peculiar to love. She had made a vow always to do what was most perfect[1] and she would urge us not to say or do anything that was a venial sin. She was in the habit of going about praising God our Lord and this witness heard her utter most devout and moving words and repeat certain verses in Latin. So great were the impulses of love for God that came upon her that she could neither control herself nor resist the powerful raptures which visited her until she thought her life would come to an end. She used to say that she would rejoice to see others in Heaven with more glory than she, but that she would not bear it patiently if there were any who loved God more. All trials seemed slight to her if they were borne for love of Him and she would say that she thought she would suffer many deaths if only one more soul would serve Him. There was no harder or bitterer trial for her than to think that she might have offended Him.

She did all she could to conceal her ascetic practices and never indulged in outward signs of sanctity or in false modesty. Outwardly, indeed, she was so natural and so courteous that no one who looked at her would think there was anything of the saint about her at all. Yet there was always something funda-

[1] This vow she made about the year 1560, when living at the Incarnation. Five years later the Provincial gave his consent to its modification [P. Silverio, II, 128-9].

mental about her which forced even those who spoke ill of her to realize that she was a saint without making any attempt to be. She was never idle, and never at a loss for work to do right up to midnight or one o'clock in the morning. It distressed her greatly to find raptures coming upon her in public, or to have to speak, even to her confessors, of the favours which God was showing her, as much as, or even more than, if she were having to confess great sins. She desired that those who thought well of her should know how badly she had lived and tried to make them recognize her for a great sinner.

She detested hypocrisy, above all in herself, and also pride in her own achievements. She used to say in her lifetime—and it was manifestly true—that she had never had to confess to vainglory or had any cause for it. This witness remembers her once saying: "I do not know why they are calling me a foundress: it is God Who has founded these houses, not I." She was not afraid of poverty, but loved it, and all her early convents and monasteries were founded without any endowment, for she wanted them to live and maintain themselves on alms. Only when the number of her houses grew and they came to be founded in poor places, and only with the approval of grave and learned persons, did she permit endowments.

5. The witness said that she knew the holy Mother had to endure severe trials, which she bore with great courage and patience for the love of God our Lord. Persecutions and slander were particularly frequent during the years when her first houses were founded. There were times when hardly any priest would hear her confessions, for they all believed her to be deceived and deluded by the devil and were thus disinclined to have anything to do with her. All this she accepted with a deep resignation which it was very clear Our Lord was giving her supernaturally. There were times when such things distressed her, but she always practised the greatest recollection and prayer and took special care to say nothing against those who persecuted her; on the contrary, she would excuse them and speak well of them, for she loved them as her benefactors, attentive to the well-being of her soul, and she would reprove her nuns when they said anything about them but what was good.

On the journeys connected with her foundations she suffered great trials and inconveniences, and was often ill, but this never sufficed to deter her from what she had begun, nor would she postpone a journey by so much as a day in the hope that the next might be a better one. Never on her travels did she neglect her prayer or communion, nor even in the slightest degree did she lose her recollection and spiritual joy.

When she made her foundations at Seville and Burgos she suffered great trials and endured them with rare patience. She had a great thirst for them and her esteem of them grew proportionately to her spirituality till nothing could destroy it. A very ordinary expression with her was: "Either suffering or death." Though she had serious illnesses, she did in every respect as the community did, conformed to their practices as far as she possibly could and went to choir at the hours of prayer. Continual writing gave her constant headaches, yet she never neglected her business nor was deterred from making journeys which seemed to require more than human strength. Severe as were her penances, they were as nothing by comparison with the fervour of her desire for more after they were over. She practised many kinds of mortification, some of them imposed by her confessors with the aim of testing her spirituality. This witness heard her say that, when she was at the Incarnation, she tried to mortify herself by asking for the office of infirmarian. She had a great fellow-feeling for poor and sick people and did all she could for their comfort. She was always very particular about this in the houses she founded. While the licence for the Burgos foundation was being obtained, she lived in seclusion with her nuns in a room at the top of a hospital just above the room which was the infirmary for the poor. When she heard the sick people moaning she would have the greatest compassion on them and when she went down on her way to church she used to go in to cheer them and encourage them and take them anything she could, even robbing herself of necessaries, ill though she was, in order to give them to these sick people.

She had great strength of soul, which influenced her entire life and behaviour, together with a clarity of understanding and a discretion so sound that it made all who had to do with her marvel. There are clear indications that she was a virgin all her life long. One of these is that, in conversation with someone known to this witness, concerning certain carnal temptations, the holy Mother answered her: "I do not understand that, for the Lord has been so gracious to me that I have never in my whole life experienced such temptations." And although in her book she makes much of all the sins of her early years, this witness knows, from a Father of the Company of Jesus who went closely into the matter, that she never went so far as to lose that particular virtue. She had great courage, and she used to ask why, if she served God (as she did) to Whom all demons and all things else are subject, she should have any fear or fail to have strength enough to battle with all hell. She would, on occasion, defy the devils and tell them to come and see what they could do to her, saying that no trial or difficulty could dismay her or make her fail to do anything which she saw would be to the greater service of God our Lord.

6. The witness said she knew and remembered that Mother Teresa of Jesus died in her presence, at Alba, in the convent of Discalced Carmelites which she had founded, on Saint Francis' Day, October 4, 1582, at nine o'clock in the evening. The witness accompanied the holy Mother on the last journey which she made from Burgos to Alba, meaning to go on to Ávila, where at that time she was prioress. Her superior told her to go to Alba, so she postponed her own will and pleasure in order to obey his command. On her arrival at Alba, she was stricken with mortal illness: they got there on the eve of Saint Matthew in the said year 1582 and on the next morning she went to Mass and Communion. On Michaelmas Day, after communicating with the rest, she took to her bed, bearing her sufferings with great patience. When she drew near to death, all that she urged and begged her nuns to do was to keep their Rule and Constitutions perfectly; with great emotion and humility she asked pardon of all for the bad example which she felt she had set them; and she then said other similar things with great sincerity and contrition, such as that verse from the psalm of David which is in the Miserere, which she repeated a number of times: *Sacrificium Deo spiritus contribulatus*, etc. Several times she gave God hearty thanks because He had made her a daughter of the Catholic Church and permitted her to die as such; she trusted in the blood of her Spouse; and she had a sure hope of her salvation. She received the Sacraments with great spirituality and devotion and showed great devotion when she saw Our Lord in the Most Holy Sacrament of the Eucharist. With great fervour, her face all aglow, she rose from her bed as well as she could, uttering tender and moving words to this Lord, which showed that she knew and had had revealed to her that the hour of her death had come.

VII. LETTER FROM THE MASTER FRAY LUIS DE LEÓN TO THE MOTHER PRIORESS ANA DE JESÚS AND THE DISCALCED CARMELITE NUNS OF THE CONVENT AT MADRID.[1]

I never knew, or saw, Mother Teresa of Jesus while she lived on earth; but now that she lives in Heaven I do know her, and

[1] This letter appears in the first edition of the Works of St. Teresa, edited by Fray Luis de León and published in 1588.

I see her almost continuously in two living images of herself which she left us—her daughters and her books. These, in my judgment, are also exceptionally faithful witnesses to her great virtue. If I were to see her features, they would reveal her physical self, and if I were to hear her words, they would tell me something concerning the virtue of her soul. But the first of these things would be very commonplace and the second might be deceptive, whereas neither of these disadvantages attaches to the two ways in which I see her now. For, as the Wise Man says, a man is known by his children. It is the fruits which each of us leaves when he dies that are the true witness to his life, as Christ tells us in the Gospel when, to differentiate the evil from the good, He refers us to these alone. "By their fruits," He says, "ye shall know them." Just so, if I were to see Mother Teresa, I might be uncertain and doubtful about her virtue and sanctity, but now, when I cannot see her, but see her books and the works of her hands, which are her daughters, I consider this quite clear and certain. And the virtue resplendent in them unmistakeably reveals all the grace which God bestowed on her whom He made to be mother of this new miracle, as what God works in and through her daughters must needs be called. For what comes to pass outside the natural order of things is a miracle, and these things that have happened are so extraordinary and so new that it is a very small thing to call them a miracle—they are like a collection of many miracles all at once. For it is a miracle in itself that one woman alone should have restored perfection to a whole Order, both of men and of women; the perfection to which she restored it is another; while yet a third is the marvellous extent to which it has grown in so few years, after starting from such small beginnings: each of these things alone is well worthy of consideration. And again, as Saint Paul writes, it belongs to women not to teach, but to be taught, and so it is a fresh miracle to find a weak woman with courage enough for beginning so great a work and with wisdom and efficiency enough for succeeding in it, and for stealing away the hearts of those with whom she had to do and making them God's, and for attracting others to follow her in her abhorrence of sense. At a time like this, when the devil seems to be triumphing and a multitude of unbelievers follow him and so many nations are obstinate in their heresies and the many vices of the faithful debase and make a mock of religion, it seems, so far as I can judge, to have been God's will that they should be faced, not by a valiant man armed with learning, but by a poor woman who defied the devil and set up her standard against him and openly raised up people to conquer him and spurn him and trample him beneath their feet. Doubtless He was pleased to do this in order to demonstrate the greatness of His power in this present age when so many thousands of men, some with their deluded minds and others with their degraded habits, are attacking His kingdom, in that a woman should enlighten the understanding and reform the habits of many who daily increase in number and are repairing the harm wrought by the devil. And though the Church is now in her old age, He was pleased to show us that His grace never ages and that the power of His Spirit is no less than it was in her early and happy days. For He works the same things, or wellnigh the same things, as He did then, and with means that are weaker.

Now to come to the second miracle. This life which Your Reverences live and this perfection which your Mother instilled into you—what are these but a picture of the sanctity of the early Church? For the things of which we read in the histories of those times we can now see with our own eyes in your habits. Its life is manifested to us in your works—a life which had seemed to exist no longer save in writing and in speech: what we admire when we read of it, and what flesh can hardly believe, can now be seen in Your Reverence and in your companions. Detached from all that is not God, you offer yourselves to the arms of your Divine Spouse and are locked in His embrace. You have the limbs of weak and tender women, but the spirits of strong men, and you practise the loftiest and most generous philosophy that ever men have imagined. In your actual works you attain to heights of perfect life and heroic virtue to which the mind of man has hardly attained even in imagination. For you spurn wealth, hate freedom, despise honour and love humility and labour. Your whole efforts are directed towards proficiency in holy living and continual progress in virtue. And for this your Spouse rewards you by inspiring your souls with so powerful a joy that, although you have forsaken everything and are detached from everything that can bring you pleasure in this life, you have a treasure-house of true joy and a generous contempt of nature, being exempt from its laws and indeed superior to them. For you are not wearied by labour nor fatigued by enclosure, nor dismayed by infirmities, nor affrighted and terrified by death, but rather cheered and encouraged. And of all these things that which causes the greatest wonder is the pleasure —or perhaps we should say the ease—with which you do what is extremely difficult. For mortification to you is rejoicing; resignation, child's play; and the severest penance, a pastime. It seems to be affording you solace and pleasure when you practise things that cause nature dismay. You have turned the practice of heroic virtues into a pleasant diversion, and thus have illustrated the truth of the words of Christ, that His yoke is easy and His burden light. For there is no lady in the world who takes such pleasure in her own adornment as do Your Reverences in living like angels. And angels you certainly are, not only in perfection of life but also in the similarity and the unity that exists between you.

For there are no two things so similar as are Your Reverences among yourselves, each of you to any of the rest—in your language, your modesty, your humility, your discretion, your gentleness of spirit: indeed, in your whole manner of life and behaviour. As you are animated by one and the same virtue, so do you portray all the virtues in one and the same manner, for in all of you, as in a clear mirror, is reflected one face, which is that of the holy Mother, visible in her daughters. So that, as I said at the beginning, although I never saw her in her lifetime, I can see her more clearly now, since her daughters are not only the living images of her features but sure witnesses to her perfections, which are communicated to you all, and spread so rapidly from one of you to the rest that—and this is the third wonder—in the space of no more than the twenty years which must have gone by since the Mother made her first foundation, Spain is now full of her houses, in which God is served by more than a thousand religious, among whom Your Reverences her nuns shine like the brightest stars among the heavenly constellations. Just as it was one blessed woman who gave birth to this Reform, so it is women who take the lead in it throughout, and not only are they guiding lights to their Order but they are the honour of our nation, the glory of this age, fair flowers which beautify the barrenness of these present times, the choicest branches of the Church, living witnesses to the efficacy of Christ, clear proofs of His sovereign virtue and exact patterns in which we can almost experience what faith promises. All this has reference to her daughters, who are the first of the two images of herself which she has left us.

Nor is the second thing of which I spoke any the less clear or miraculous—namely, her writings and books, in which it was without any doubt the will of the Holy Spirit that Mother Teresa should become the rarest of examples. For in the sublimity of the subjects which she treats, and in the delicacy and charity with which she treats them, she surpasses many famous writers; while in the form of her writings, in the purity and ease of her style, in the gracefulness and skilful arrangement

of the words and in an unaffected elegance which is delightful
in the extreme, I doubt if there has been any writing of equal
merit in our language. Whenever I read her works I wonder
at them afresh, and in many parts of them I feel that I am
listening to no human voice at all. I do not doubt that in many
places it was the Holy Spirit Who spoke through her and Who
guided her pen and her hand. This is manifest from the light
which she sheds upon dark places and the fire which her words
kindle in the heart of him who reads them. Setting aside other
numerous and great benefits which come to those who read
these books, there are two, in my mind, which she chiefly con-
fers upon them. One is that she makes it easier for her readers
to follow the path of virtue; the other, that she enkindles them
in the love of her and of God. With regard to the first of these,
it is a marvellous thing to see how her readers keep God before
the eyes of the soul, and how they picture Him as easy to find
and as sweet and friendly to those who find Him; and as to the
second point, not only everything she says considered as a whole,
but each thing that she says considered separately, enkindles
the soul with heavenly flame, which sets it alight, as it were, and
consumes it. Her words remove all obstacles from the readers'
sight and sense—not that he no longer sees such obstacles, but
that he no longer attaches any importance or value to them;
not only does he become disillusioned with what a false imagination had set before him, but he becomes freed from his burden,
cured of his tepidity and so inspired and (if one may so say)
eager for what is good that he forthwith soars upward towards
it with a fervent desire. Such was the ardour that burned in
that saintly breast that it enkindled her words so that, wherever
they went, they burst into flame. Of this, I believe, Your
Reverences will be trusty witnesses, since you are the very
patterns of your Mother. I never remember having read these
works of hers without imagining that I am listening to Your
Reverences' voices, nor, on the other hand, have I ever heard
you speak without feeling that I was reading the words of the
Mother. Those who have experience of this will know that it
is the truth.

For they will find the same illumination and breadth of understanding in obscure and delicate spiritual matters, the same
easy and pleasant way of writing of them, the same skill and
the same discretion; they will feel within them the same Divine
fire; and they will conceive the same desires. They will find
the same kind of sanctity, neither ostentatious nor miraculous,
but so deeply infused and so solidly based that sometimes, though
the name of God be not mentioned, the reader's soul becomes

enamoured of Him. It is thus that (to return to what I said at first), if I never saw her when she lived on earth, I see her now in her books and in her daughters—or, to put it better, I see her now in Your Reverences alone, who of all her daughters follow her the most nearly and are a living picture of her books and her writings. These books, with the examination of which the Royal Council has entrusted me, are now to see the light, and I can very properly dedicate them to this holy convent of yours, as in fact I do. The labour which I have put into them has been far from slight. For not only have I laboured at reading and examining them, which was the task that the Council entrusted to me, but I have also collated them with their originals, which I had for a long time in my possession, and restored them to their original purity and the state in which they left the hands of the Mother. I have neither emended them verbally nor adopted the considerable changes which copies now in circulation have made in the text of them either through the copyists' own carelessness or out of presumption and error. For to make changes in the writings of one whose breast was the home of God, Who may be presumed to have moved her to write them, would be the utmost presumption and the grossest error. If her critics had a real understanding of Castilian, they would see that that of the Mother is elegance itself. For though she sometimes fails to carry her argument to its conclusion, but introduces other arguments which often break the thread of her sense, she inserts her digressions so skilfully and introduces her fresh thoughts with such grace that the bad habit only adds to the attractiveness of her work and is no real blemish at all. I have therefore restored the text of these works to their original purity.

But as there is nothing so good that evilly disposed men cannot construe it as a failure, it will be well here, while I am addressing Your Reverences, to reply briefly to ideas which some have brought forward. These books tell of revelations and discuss interior things which come to pass in prayer, and which are far removed from our ordinary experience. There may be those who will say that these revelations are open to doubt and that therefore it is not well that such things shall see the light. With regard to passages that touch upon the interior commerce of the soul with God, which is a very spiritual matter and concerns few, they say that to make these public to all would be an occasion of peril. Here they are quite wrong. First, with regard to revelations, it is certain that the devil sometimes transfigures himself into an angel of light, and mocks and deceives souls with false appearances, yet it is also a most sure thing, and a matter of faith, that the Holy Spirit talks with His own and reveals Himself to them in divers manners, either for their own good or for the good of others. And, though no heed should be paid to the first kind of revelation, nor should anything be written about it, since it is illusory, this second kind merits being known and written about as well. As the angel said to Tobias: "It is good to hide the secret of the king but the works of God it is a fitting and a holy thing to manifest or reveal."[1] What Saint is there who has not had some revelation? Or what Saint's life is ever written in which nothing is said of the revelations which he had? The histories of the Orders of Saint Dominic and Saint Francis can be seen and handled by anybody, and there is hardly a page in either of these which does not mention some revelation granted to the founders or to their disciples.

Without the slightest doubt God talks with His friends, and He does so, not so that no one shall know of it, but so that what He says to them shall come to light. For, being Himself Light, He loves light in everything, and, as He ever seeks men's salvation, He never bestows these special favours upon one soul save in order to bring profit by its means to many others. For so long as there was any doubt about the virtue of the holy Mother Teresa, and there were people who thought her the reverse of what she was, since the way in which God approved her works was not yet manifest, it was well that these histories should not see the light, nor circulate in public, in order to condone the temerity of others' judgments. But now that she is dead, and it is certain that these things are of God, and her body has been found miraculously uncorrupt, and this and other miracles taking place daily have set her sanctity beyond all doubt, to conceal the favours which God granted her in her lifetime and to be unwilling to publish abroad the means by which He perfected her to the good of so many souls would be in some sort to insult the Holy Spirit, to obscure His wonders and to veil His glory. No one of good judgment will think it well that these revelations should be hidden.

Some, again, say that the Mother should not have written about the revelations granted to herself, but this is not to the point and in no way reflects upon her humility and modesty, for she wrote them under orders and obligation. From our own point of view it is well that she wrote them: had anyone else done so, one might have suspected that he was being deceived or was himself trying to deceive; but this cannot be presumed of the Mother, who wrote of what actually happened to her and was so holy that on such grave matters she would never have

[1] Tobias, xii, 7.

departed from the truth. What I fear is that some will not find these writings acceptable, not because of any errors in the writings, but because of their own errors. They may find it impossible to believe that God can so far condescend to man; and yet if they thought about it they would not find it so. For, if they believe that God became man, why should they doubt that He talks with man? And if they believe that He was scourged and crucified for them, why should they be surprised that He takes delight in being with them? Which is the more wonderful thing—that God should appear to a servant of His and talk with her, or that He should become, as it were, our Servant and suffer death? Let men take courage and seek God by the road which He Himself shows us— namely, faith, charity and the strict observance of His law and counsels, and the least thing that He will do will be to show them such mercies.

Those, then, who criticize these revelations adversely are making the greatest mistake if they think they have not occurred; while if they do so because some of such revelations are illusory, they are in duty bound to judge favourably those of which the genuineness is guaranteed by their authors' proven sanctity. Such are the revelations described here; and thus not only is the account of them free from peril but it is beneficial and necessary for the recognition of genuineness in those who experience them. For these works do not merely give a bald account of the communications of God to Mother Teresa; they also tell of the pains she took to have them examined and show what were the effect of genuine revelations, and how we ought to judge such things, and if they should be desired or rejected. In the first place, these writings teach us that revelations which come from God always produce a great many virtues in the soul, both for the good of those who receive them and for the salvation of many more. In the second place, they warn us that we must not be ruled by them, for our rule of life must be the Church's teaching, and God's revelation of Himself in His Books, and the dictates of true and sound reason. They also tell us that we must not desire such things or think that in them consists spiritual perfection or that they are sure marks of grace, for the true welfare of souls consists in a greater love of God and in suffering more for Him, and in the greater mortification of the affections and a greater freedom and detachment from ourselves and from everything else. And what these works teach us in so many words is also demonstrated by the holy Mother's example, for we hear of the misgivings which she always had about all her revelations and of the way in which she examined them and of how she was never guided by them so much as by what her superiors and confessors ordered her, and of how their obvious genuineness was borne out by the good effects which they produced upon herself and upon her whole Order. The revelations described here, therefore, are neither to be doubted themselves nor do they open the door to others which are to be doubted; rather do they give light by which we may recognize others of the same kind and thus serve as a kind of touchstone.

Finally, something must be said to those who think these books perilous because of the delicacy of the matters treated in them, which, they say, are not meant for all. Now people are of three kinds: some practise prayer; others could do so if they would; and others cannot because of the kind of life they lead. For which of these classes, I ask, is there peril in these books? For spiritual folk? Nay, for it can do no harm to read of what one does and professes onself. For those who have the aptitude for spirituality? Still less so; for they have something here which will not only guide them in the practice of prayer, but will also encourage and enkindle them to pray, which is a very great advantage. Then it must be for the third class? But what peril is there here for them? Is it a peril to know of God's loving-kindness to men? That He who detaches himself from everything will find Him? That He brings souls comfort? That there is a great difference between the different kinds of favour that He gives? Is it perilous for them to know how He purifies and refines them? What is there here, in fact, a knowledge of which does not sanctify the reader, instil in him a wonder for God and enkindle in him a love of Him? If meditation upon God's outward works of creation and governance is a school from which all men generally may derive profit, how can the knowledge of His marvellous secrets be harmful to anyone? And even if anyone were evilly enough disposed to derive harm from them, would it be fair for that reason to shut out the great profit which they will bring to so many?

Ought there to be no preaching of the Gospel, since the Gospel, as Saint Paul said, is an occasion of greater perdition to him that receives it not? What writings are there, the sacred Scriptures among them, which the ill-disposed cannot interpret erroneously? One must judge things by whether or no they are good in themselves and likely to accomplish their proper ends—not by any possible ill use that may be made of them. If one acts on this last principle, there will be no writing so holy that it cannot be proscribed. What is there holier than the Sacraments? Yet how many people do themselves harm by their misuse of them! The devil, acute as he is and continually on the watch to harm us, appears in different lights. To the minds of some he reveals himself as cautious and solicitous about others' welfare, in order to blind men in general to what is good and profitable to all under cover of warning them against what may be harmful to a few: well does he know that he will lose more in those who through reading these books will become better and more perfect in spirituality than he will gain through the ignorance or malice of this or that person to whom they may prove a stumbling-block because he is insufficiently prepared for reading them. And so, in order not to lose those of the former class, he suggests and exaggerates the harm such reading will do to those of the latter class to whom he has already done harm in a thousand ways more. For that matter, as I said, I do not know anyone so ill prepared that he could derive harm from learning that God is gracious to His friends, and how gracious He is in Himself, and by what paths a soul may reach Him— matters of which the exposition is the aim of this whole work. My sole misgivings are about some who wish to guide everyone else by their own power and who disapprove of everything that is not done by themselves and try to see that nothing save what they judge to be good shall have any authority. I do not expect to satisfy these, because their error arises in their own will and thus they will refuse to be satisfied, but I will ask all others not to give them credit, because they do not merit it.

I will only mention one thing here, which must needs be remarked upon—namely that, in speaking of the prayer called the Prayer of Quiet and of other higher states, and in dealing with special favours which God shows to souls, the holy Mother is accustomed to say, in many parts of these books, that the soul is near God, and that each understands the other, and that souls know perfectly well when God is speaking to them, and other things of that kind. This must not be interpreted as meaning that she considers it certain that all who occupy themselves in these exercises, or any others, however holy they be, have grace and justification, in such a way that they are certain of themselves; this can only be said of those to whom God reveals it. The Mother herself, who enjoyed all the favours that she describes in these books, as well as many more that she does not describe, writes these words about herself in one of them: "And what I cannot bear, Lord, is not to know for certain if I love Thee and if my desires are acceptable in Thy sight." What she means, and what is true, is merely this—that in these exercises souls feel the presence of God through the effects which He works in them then, giving them delight and illumination and counsels and consolations. For, although these are great favours of God and are often accompanied by the grace of justification or lead the way to it, yet they are not themselves that grace, nor are they always born of it or united with it. As is seen in the prophecy, grace can exist in one who is in an evil state. Such a person is then certain that God is speaking to him, and does not know if He justifies him, and in fact God does not justify him at that time, though He speaks to him and teaches him. And this must be noted with respect to doctrine in general, for, as to that which touches the Mother in particular, it is possible that, after writing the words to which I referred, she had some revelation and certification of His grace of her own. It is not well that this should be affirmed as certain, and yet it is not right that it should be so pertinaciously denied, for the gifts which God gave her were very great ones, as were the favours which He showed her in her latter years, which are alluded to several times in what she writes in these books. But no general rule can be laid down as to what she may have received as a singular favour. So long as this is taken into account nothing that she has written can be a stumbling-block to anyone. I believe, and hope, that it will all be very profitable to souls, as can be seen in the souls of Your Reverences who were brought up and are nurtured in it, and whom I beg to make mention of me in your holy prayers. At Saint Philip's, Madrid, on the fifteenth of September, 1587.

SELECT BIBLIOGRAPHY

The total number of extant editions of the works of St. Teresa, in Spanish and in other languages, is very large, and anything like a complete list of their titles, and of the titles of books and articles dealing with her life and work, would fill several volumes. A tentative bibliography, still in manuscript, which the translator has compiled for the use of students should eventually supersede both the shorter list in his *Studies of the Spanish Mystics* (No. 169) and also Curzon's more ambitious monograph (No. 111), which, though useful and comprehensive, will in many places be found insufficiently detailed. It is, however, much too long to print here; and accordingly there follows a short list of books and articles comparatively easy of access which can be supplemented by the two bibliographies mentioned above.

Books of reference, purely ephemeral articles and translations into languages other than English are omitted. Of early editions, only a few which can be consulted in the British Museum or in the largest Spanish libraries are included; most of the modern editions, on the other hand, which are still in print, have been given a place. To economize space, certain details which can be found in Curzon, P. Silverio or *Studies of the Spanish Mystics* (abbreviated respectively C, P.S., S.S.M.) are omitted and references to those sources substituted. S.S.M. often states in what libraries the Spanish editions referred to can be found.

All the abbreviations are self-explanatory, with the exception of the following: B—Barcelona; Br—Brussels; L—London; M—Madrid; P—Paris. Short titles only are given, except where a work is of exceptional importance or of particular interest to English readers.

I. SPANISH EDITIONS OF COLLECTED WORKS
(In chronological order).

The following are well-known early editions:

1 *Los Libros de la Madre Teresa de Jesús,* Fundadora de los monesterios de monjas y frailes Carmelitas Descalzos de la primera regla. Salamanca, Guillelmo Foquel, 1588. [Details of this edition, P.S. I, lxxxv-lxxxvi. The edition was reprinted by Foquel in 1589, with the addition of some notes: P.S., I, xc.]

2 *Libros de la B. Madre Teresa.* Naples, 1604. 3 vols.

3 *Obras.* Br., Rogerio Velpio, 1610. [The first collected edition to contain the *Fundaciones:* C; P.S. I, xc.]

4 *Libros de la B. Madre Teresa de Jesús.* Lisbon, 1616.

5 *Obras.* Antwerp, Baltasar Moreto, 1630. 3 vols. [The completest edition at that date: C., P.S., I, xc.]

6 *Obras.* Antwerp, 1649-61. 4 vols.

7 *Obras.* Lisbon, 1654.

8 *Obras.* Corregidas según sus originales auténticos. M., José Fernández de Buendía, 1661. [P.S., I, xci.]

9 *Obras y cartas.* Br., 1674-75. 4 vols. in 2. [Contains 107 letters.]

10 *Obras.* M., Doblado, 1793. 2 vols. [Ed. Nicolás de Jesús María. P.S., I, xcvii.]

Of nineteenth- and twentieth-century editions the chief are:

11 *Obras completas.* B., 1844–7. 9 vols. (C).

12 *Obras escogidas de Santa Teresa de Jesús.* Ed. E. de Ochoa. M., 1847. [" Colección de los mejores autores españoles." Includes the life by Diego de Yepes: No. 194.]

13 *Escritos de Santa Teresa, añadidos e ilustrados por Don Vicente de la Fuente.* M., 1861. 2 vols. [" Biblioteca de Autores Españoles," Vols. 53, 55. On this edition, see C., pp. 12–13, P.S., I, xcviii–ci.]

14 *Obras y escritos de Santa Teresa.* Ed. P. García S. Juan. M., 1871-2. 4 vols.

15 *Obras de Santa Teresa.* M., 1876. [" Biblioteca Universal ", Vol. 31. Contains *Conceptos, Exclamaciones, Cartas, Poesías.*]

16 *Obras de Santa Teresa de Jesús.* Novísima edición, corregida y aumentada conforme a los originales y a las últimas revisiones, y con notas aclaratorias por D. Vicente de la Fuente, M., 1881. 6 vols.

17 *Obras escogidas de la Santa Madre Teresa de Jesús.* Libro de su vida. Las Moradas. Introducción por Rafael Mesa y López. L., P., n.d. [1913].

18 *Obras de Santa Teresa de Jesús.* Editadas y anotadas por el P. Silverio de Santa Teresa, C.D. Burgos, 1915–24. 9 vols.

19 *Obras de Santa Teresa de Jesús.* Pról. del Excmo. Sr. Marqués de San Juan de Piedras Albas. M., 1916. 4 vols.

20 *Obras de Santa Teresa de Jesús.* Ed. y notas del P. Silverio de Santa Teresa, C.D. Burgos, 1922.

21 *Obras de Santa Teresa de Jesús.* M., Apostolado de la Prensa, 1930, 2 vols.

22 *Obras completas de Santa Teresa de Jesús.* Con un estudio preliminar por L. Santullano. M., Aguilar, 1930.

23 *Obras de Santa Teresa de Jesús.* Ed. y notas del P. Silverio de Santa Teresa. 2a. ed. [of No. 20]. Burgos, 1931. Also (24) Burgos, 1939, 3a. ed.

25 *Libros de la Madre Teresa de Jesús,* etc. M., Biblioteca Nueva, 1935. 3 vols. [Facsimile of 1588 ed.]

II. SPANISH EDITIONS OF SINGLE WORKS
(In alphabetical order of titles).

26 *Avisos espirituales.* Comentados por el P. Alonso de Andrade. B., 1646, 2 vols.

Earlier than this, but in an abridged form, the *Avisos* were published in Tomás de Jesús' *Suma y compendio de los grados de oración,* etc., Rome, 1610 (See *S.S.M.,* II, 449). Abridgments of the *Exclamaciones* and *Relaciones,* too, are in this work. The *Avisos* were also published in Tomás de Jesús' *Reglas para examinar y discernir el interior aprovechamiento de un alma,* B., 1621 [See *S.S.M.,* II, 448].

27 *Avisos originales de Santa Teresa de Jesús,* etc. Reproducción por medio de la foto-litografía hecha por los artistas Selfa y Mateu. M., n.d. (? 1881).

28 *Avisos y Camino de Perfección.* Évora, 1583. (C).

29 *Camino de Perfección.* Salamanca, 1585. [P.S., III, xxxiv.]

30 *Camino de Perfección.* Ed. F. Herrero Bayona. Valladolid, 1883. [A facsimile of the Valladolid MS., together with that of *Modo de visitar los conventos,* etc.]

31 *Camino de Perfección.* Reproducción fidelísima del autógrafo de El Escorial, con las variantes del autógrafo vallisoletano. Ed. J. M. Aguado. M. 1929-30. 2 vols.

32 *Cartas.* Con notas de J. Palafox y Mendoça. Zaragoza, 1658.
  All the early editions of the *Cartas* contain so few letters that they have been entirely superseded by the twentieth-century editions of the *Obras completas.*

33 *Castillo interior (El), o las Moradas y el Camino de Perfección, obras de la Santa Madre Teresa de Jesús, seguidas de los Avisos que la misma da a sus religiosas,* etc. B., 1844.

34 *Castillo interior (El.), o Tratado de las moradas.* Ed. autobiografiada e impresa según el texto original. Sevilla, 1882. (C).

35 [*Castillo interior o*] *Las Moradas.* Ed. y notas de T. Navarro Tomás, M., 1916. ("Clásicos castellanos.")

36 *Castillo interior.* Ed. cotejada con el MS. original por Luis Carlos Viada y Lluch, y precedida del elogio de la Santa por Miguel S. Oliver. B., 1917. (In "Bibliotecas de Grandes Maestros.")

37 *Castillo interior (Las Moradas o el), y Conceptos del amor divino.* Buenos Aires, 1940.

38 *Conceptos del amor de Dios sobre algunas palabras de los Cantares de Salomón.* Valencia, 1613. [See also No. 37.]

39 *Exclamaciones de la Santa Madre Theresa de Jesús,* con la traducción que de ellas hizo en endechas endecasílabas. . . . (por) J. F. Escuoler. Zaragoza, 1725.

40 *Fundaciones de las Hermanas Descalzas Carmelitas,* Br., 1610. [P.S., I, xc.]

41 (*Libro de las*) *Fundaciones de Santa Teresa de Jesús.* Ed. autobiografiada conforme al original, etc. . . . y continuación del *Libro de su vida.* Ed V. de la Fuente. M., 1880.

42 *Libro de las Fundaciones.* Ed. J. M. Aguado. M., 1940. 2 vols. ("Clásicos Castellanos.")

43 *Modo de visitar los conventos de religiosas descalzas de Nuestra Señora del Carmen.* M., 1613. [See also No. 30.]

44 *Poesías.* See W. Storck: *Todas las poesías de San Juan de la Cruz y de Santa Teresa de Jesús,* recogidas y publicadas por . . . Monastero, 1854.

45 *Vida de Santa Teresa de Jesús,* escrita por ella misma. M., 1793.

46 *Vida de Santa Teresa de Jesús,* publicada por la Sociedad Fototipográfico-Católica, bajo la dirección del Dr. D. V. de la Fuente, conforme al original autógrafo. M., 1873.

47 *La Vida de la Santa Madre Teresa de Jesús.* Nueva ed. conforme al original autógrafo. Prol. V. de la Fuente. M., 1882.

48 Santa Teresa: *Su Vida.* M., 1927. 2 vols. [A popular pocket ed.]

III. SELECTIONS AND ANTHOLOGIES

(In chronological order).

49 *Ramillete de flores místicas y ascéticas sacadas de las obras de la inspirada y seráfica madre Santa Teresa de Jesús,* por Ramón Tavarés y Lozano. M., 1883.

50 *El Amor en la Mística española.* [Extracts from St. Teresa and other writers.] M., 1896.

51 *Santa Teresa y Felipe II.* [Chiefly selections from her writings.] Por D. H. Ciria y Nasarre. M., 1900.

52 Wasmer, M. de: *Huit mystiques espagnols.* P., 1940. [Contains translated extracts from St. Teresa and others.]

53 *Prosa escogida.* Selección, estudio y notas de A. González Palencia. Zaragoza, 1941.

IV. TRANSLATIONS INTO ENGLISH

Foundations

54 *The Second Part of the Life of the Holy Mother S. Teresa of Jesus, or the History of the Foundations.* Written by herself. N.p., 1669. [Cf. *S.S.M.*, I, 437.]
55 *Book of the Foundations.* Written by Saint Teresa. Tr. J. Dalton. L., 1853.
56 *The Book of the Foundations of S. Teresa of Jesus.* Written by herself. Tr. D. Lewis. L., 1871.
57 *Saint Theresa. The History of her Foundations.* Tr. Sister Agnes Mason, C.H.F., with a preface by the Rt. Hon. Sir E. M. Satow. Cambridge, 1909.
58 *The Book of the Foundations of St. Teresa of Jesus, with the Visitation of Nunneries, the Rule and Constitutions.* Written by herself. Tr. David Lewis. New and revised ed., with introd. by the Very Rev. Benedict Zimmerman, O.C.D. L., 1913.

Interior Castle

59 *The Interior Castle; or the Mansions.* Written by Saint Teresa. Tr. J. Dalton. L., 1852.
60 *The Interior Castle, or the Mansions,* and *Exclamations of the Soul to God.* By St. Teresa of Jesus. Tr from the autograph of St. Teresa by the Benedictines of Stanbrook. Revised with introd. and additional notes. by the Very Rev. Benedict Zimmerman, O.C.D. L., 1906. [2nd ed., 1912; 3rd ed., 1921.]

Letters

61 *The Letters of Saint Teresa.* Tr. from the Spanish by J. Dalton. [Vol. I, No more published.] L., 1853. [Reprinted, L., 1902.]
62 *The Letters of St. Teresa.* Tr. from the Spanish and annotated by the Benedictines of Stanbrook, with an introd. by Cardinal Gasquet. L., 1919-24. 4 vols. [Appendix to Vol. IV., L., 1927.]

Life

63 *The Flaming Hart, or the Life of the glorious S. Theresa,* etc. Antwerp, 1642.
64 *The Life of the Holy Mother S. Teresa.* N.p., 1671. 2 vols. [Cf. *S.S.M.* I, 437.]
65 *The Life of St. Teresa.* Written by herself. Tr. J. Dalton. L., 1851.
66 *The Life of St. Teresa of Jesus, of the Order of Our Lady of Carmel.* Tr. David Lewis. Notes and introd. by the Very Rev. Benedict Zimmerman, O.C.D. 4th ed. L., 1911. [Earlier editions, 1870, 1888, 1904.]

Minor Works

67 *Minor Works of St. Teresa: Conceptions of the Love of God, Exclamations, Maxims and Poems of St. Teresa of Jesus.* Tr. Benedictines of Stanbrook. Revised with notes and introd. by the Rev. Fr. Benedict Zimmerman, O.C.D. Also a short account of the Saint's death and canonization, etc., by the translator. L., 1913.

Way of Perfection

68 *The Way of Perfection and Conceptions of Divine Love.* Tr. J. Dalton. L., 1852. [2nd ed. L., 1901.]
69 *The Way of Perfection, by Saint Teresa.* Ed. A. R. Waller. L., 1901.
70 *The Way of Perfection, by St. Teresa of Jesus.* Tr. from the autograph of St. Teresa by the Benedictines of Stanbrook, including all the variants from both the Escorial and Valladolid editions. Revised, with notes and an introd. by the Very Rev. Fr. Benedict Zimmerman. L., 1911.

V. COMMENTARIES

71 " Acta Sanctorum ", Octobris, tom. vii (pars prior): *De Sancta Teresia Virgine.* Br., 1845.
72 Aguado, P. José María: " Relaciones entre Santa Teresa y Felipe II ", in *La Ciencia Tomista*, 1927, Año XIX, pp. 29–56.
73 Alet, P. V.,: *L'Esprit et l'oeuvre de sainte Thérèse à l'occasion de son 3e. centenaire.* Lille, 1883.
74 Alphonse de la Mère des Douleurs, P.: *Pratique de l'oraison mentale et de la perfection d'après Sainte Térèse et Saint Jean de la Croix*, P., 1909–11. 4 vols.
75 Altés y Alabart, J.B.: *Cuentos y cuadros teresianos.* B., 1884.
76 Altés y Alabart, J.B.: *Historietas teresianas.* B., 1884.
77 Alvarez, Fray Paulino: *Santa Teresa de Jesús y el P. Báñez.* M., 1882.
78 Antolín, P. Guillermo: *Los Autógrafos de Santa Teresa de Jesús como se conservan en el Real Monasterio del Escorial.* M., 1914.
79 Arintero, P. Juan G.: " Influencia de Santa Teresa en el progreso de la teología mística," in *Ciencia Tomista*, 1923, Vol. XXVIII, pp. 48–70.
80 Arintero, P. Juan G.: " Influencia de Santo Tomás en la mística de San Juan de la Cruz y Santa Teresa ". In *Vida sobrenatural*, 1924, Vol. VIII, pp. 21–42.
81 Arintero, P. Juan G.: " Santa Teresa y el P. Tomás de Jesús ". In *La Ciencia Tomista*, 1925, Vol. XXXI, pp. 54–73.
82 Arintero, P. Juan G.: " Unidad y grados de la vida espiritual según las *Moradas* de Santa Teresa ", in *Vida sobrenatural*, Mayo de 1923.
83 Artigas, Miguel: " Santa Teresa cantada por los grandes poetas españoles ", in *Basílica Teresiana*, 1922, pp. 75–90.
84 Back, A.: *Das mystische Erlebnis der Gottesnähe bei der heiligen Theresia von Jesus.* Eine religionspsychologische und religionsphilosophische Untersuchung. Würzburg, 1930.
85 Barine, A (*pseud. for* Cécile Vincens). *Portraits de femmes . . . Psychologie d'une Sainte (Sainte Thérèse)* P., 1887.
Also (86) P., 1917 [New ed.]
87 Barrès, Maurice: *Les Maîtres.* P., 1927. [Has a chapter on St. Teresa.]
88 *Basílica Teresiana.* Salamanca, 1914, ff. [V. note *S.S.M.*, I, 439 (No. 496).]
89 Bayle, C.: " El Espíritu de Santa Teresa y el de San Ignacio ". In *Razón y Fe*, 1922, Vol. LXII, pp. 294–304, 421–34; Vol. LXIII, pp. 5–21.
90 Bayle, C.: *Santa Teresa de Jesús.* M. 1932.
91 Bertrand, Louis: *Sainte Thérèse d'Ávila.* P., 1939.
92 Blot, P.; *Un pèlerinage en Espagne pour le 3e centenaire de Sainte Thérèse.* Etudes et récits. P., 1889–90. 2 vols.

93 Bonnard, Maryvonne: " Les influences réciproques entre Sainte Thérèse de Jésus et Saint Jean de la Croix ". In *Bulletin Hispanique*, 1935, Vol. XXXVII, pp. 129–48.
94 Bouix, P.M.: *Le XIXe Siècle et Sainte Térèse*. P. 1882.
95 Capefigue, J.B.H.R.: *Sainte Térèse de Jésus, fondatrice des Carmélites et des Carmes déchaussés*. P., 1865.
96 Carbonero y Sol, León: *Homenaje a Santa Teresa de Jesús en su centenario*. M., 1882. [Reprinted from *La Cruz*, II, 476–700.]
97 Cassidy, James F.: *A Queen of the Spirit*. Dublin and Cork, 1940.
98 Castro, Américo: *Santa Teresa y otros ensayos*. M., 1927.
99 Castro Albarrán, A. de: *Polvo de sus sandalias. Libro de hechos de Santa Teresa de Jesús*. Salamanca, 1939.
100 Cazal, Edmond: *Sainte Thérèse*. P., 1921. [With Bibliography. Cf. *S.S.M.*, I, 439.]
101 Cheix y Martínez, I.: *La Reformadora del Carmelo. Historia de Santa Teresa de Jesús*. M., 1893.
102 Chesterton, Ada E.: *St. Teresa*. L., 1928. [A popular biography.]
103 Ciadoncha, Marqués de: " Los Cepeda, linaje de Santa Teresa. Ensayo genealógico ". In *Boletín de la Academia de la Historia*, 1931, Vol. XCIX., pp. 607–52.
104 Coleridge, Henry James: *The Life and Letters of St. Theresa*. L., 1881–88. 3 vols.
105 Colvill, Helen Hester: *Saint Teresa of Spain*. L., 1909.
106 Condamin, J. *Sainte Thérèse d'après sa correspondance*. Lyon, 1885.
107 Crisógono de Jesús Sacramentado, P.: *Doctrina de Santa Teresa*. Avila, 1940. [By one of the leading modern commentators on St. John of the Cross.]
108 Crisógono de Jesús Sacramentado, P.: *Perfección y apostolado según Santa Teresa de Jesús*. M., n.d.
109 Crisógono de Jesús Sacramentado, P.: *Santa Teresa de Jesús. Su vida y su doctrina*. B., 1936.
110 Cuervo, P. Justo: " La edición valenciana, 1587, del *Camino de Perfección* de Santa Teresa ", in *Basílica Teresiana*, Vol. VIII, 1921, pp. 169–76.
111 Curzon, Henri Parent de: *Bibliographie Térésienne*. P., 1902.
112 Diego, Celia de: *Teresa de Jesús. Escenas de su vida*. Buenos Aires, 1939.
113 Domínguez Berrueta, Juan: *Sta. Teresa de Jesús y San Juan de la Cruz. Bocetos psicológicos*. M., 1915.
114 Domínguez Berrueta, J.: *Santa Teresa de Jesús*. M, 1934.
115 Domínguez Berrueta, J. and Chevalier, J.: *Sainte Thérèse et la vie mystique*. P., 1934.
116 Estienne d'Orves (Countess): *Sainte Thérèse*. P., 1890.
117 Etchegoyen, Gaston: *L'Amour divin. Essai sur les sources de sainte Thérèse*. Bordeaux, P., 1923.
118 Eulogio de San José, Fray: *Doctorado de Santa Teresa de Jesús y de San Juan de la Cruz*. Córdoba, 1896.
119 Farges, A.: *The Ordinary Ways of the spiritual life. A treatise on ascetic theology, according to the principles of S. Teresa*. L., 1927. [This and No. 120 are translations from the French.]
120 Farges, A.: *Mystical Phenomena. A treatise on mystical theology in agreement with the principles of St. Teresa*. L., 1926.
121 Fita, P. Fidel: *Elogio de Santa Teresa de Jesús*: M., 1915.
122 Forbes, F. A. M.: *The Life of St. Teresa*. L., 1917.
123 Froude, J. A.: " Saint Teresa ", in *The Spanish Story of the Armada*. L., 1892. Pp. 178–249.

124 Gabriel de Jesús, P.: *La Santa, o resumen de la vida de Santa Teresa.* M., 1915.
125 Gabriel de Jesús P.: *La Santa de la Raza. Vida gráfica de Santa Teresa de Jesús.* Pról. de P. Silverio de Santa Teresa. M., 1929-35. 4 vols.
126 Gabriel de Sainte Marie-Madeleine, P.: *Sainte Thérèse de Jésus.* Tr. de l'italien. P., 1938.
127 Galzy, J.: *Sainte Thérèse d'Ávila.* P., 1927.
128 Garate, Manuel: " Un Punto de Teología mística: Análisis de los capítulos XXVIII y XXIX del *Camino de Perfección.*" In *Razón y Fe,* Vols. XIX-XXI, 1907-8, *passim.*
129 García, F.: "El feminismo teresiano ", in *España y América,* 1927, Vol. XXV, pp. 25-36.
130 Gómez Centurión, José: *Relaciones biográficas inéditas de Santa Teresa de Jesús.* M., 1916.
131 Gracián, P. Jerónimo: *Declamación en que se trata de la perfecta vida y virtudes heroicas de la B. Madre Teresa de Jesús y de las fundaciones de sus monasterios.* Br., 1611.
132 Gracián, P. Jerónimo: *Dilucidario del verdadero espíritu . . . en que se declara la doctrina de la Santa Madre Teresa de Jesús.* M., 1604. 2nd ed. (133) Br., 1608, 2 vols. [Cf. *S.S.M.,* II, 422-3.]
134 Graciano Martínez, P.: "Santa Teresa de Jesús: la Enamorada." In *España y América,* 1924, Año XXII, pp. 241-52, 321-30.
135 Graciano Martínez, P.: "Santa Teresa ante los neurólogos." In *España y América,* 1925, Año XXIII, pp. 3-12, 161-71, 241-50.
136 Graham, Gabriela Cunninghame: *Santa Teresa, being some account of her life and times together with some pages from the history of the last great reform in the religious orders.* L., 1894, 2 vols. Single-vol. ed. (137) L., 1907.
138 Guerlin, Henri: *Sainte Thérèse.* P., 1918. [" L'Art et les Saints ".]
139 Hilda, Sister: *Saint Teresa: A Study of her life, character and influence.* L., 1939.
140 *Histoire de Sainte Thérèse d'après les Bollandistes, ses divers historiens et ses oeuvres complètes,* par une Carmélite de Caen (la M. Cornu). P., Nantes, 1883, 2 vols.
Also (141), 1886, 2 vols.
142 *Homenaje a Santa Teresa de Jesús. Documentos, discursos, poesías, artículos y pensamientos.* Pról. del Marqués de San Juan de Piedras Albas. Toledo, 1925.
143 Hoornaert, R.: *Sainte Térèse écrivain—son milieu, ses facultés, son oeuvre.* P., 1922.
144 Hoornaert, R.: *Saint Teresa in her writings.* Tr. J. Leonard. L., 1931. [Tr. of No. 143.]
145 Hough, Mary E.: *Santa Teresa in America.* New York, 1938.
146 Joly, H.: *Sainte Thérèse.* 1515-1582. P., 1902.
147 Joly, H.: *Saint Teresa.* Tr. E. M. Waller. L., 1903. [Tr. of No. 146.]
148 Juliá Martínez, E.: *La Cultura de Santa Teresa y su obra literaria.* Castellón, 1922.
149 Lagardère, J.: *Sainte Thérèse: l'enfant, la religieuse, la reformatrice.* Etude psychologique et mystique. Besançon, 1900.
150 Lamano y Beneite, J. de.: *Santa Teresa de Jesús en Alba de Tormes.* Salamanca, 1914.
151 Legendre, M.: *Sainte Thérèse d'Avila.* Marseilles, 1929.
152 León, Luis de: " De la Vida, Muerte y Virtudes y Milagros de la Santa Madre Teresa de Jesús " (Libro primero por el maestro Fray Luis de León) in *Revista Agustiniana,* Vol. V, 1883, pp. 63-6, 95-102, 195-203.
153 Léon, P.: *La Joie chez Sainte Thérèse d'Avila.* Br., 1930.

154 Marie-Joseph du Sacré-Coeur, P.: "La contemplation acquise est enseignée à leurs disciples par saint Jean de la Croix et sainte Thérèse: nouveaux témoignages qui le confirment." In *Etudes Carmélitaines*, 1925, Vol. X, pp. 109-32.

155 Marquina, E.: *Pasos y trabajos de Santa Teresa de Jesús.* I. La Alcaidesa de Pastrana. II. Las Cartas de la monja. B., 1941. 2 vols.

156 Martín, P. Felipe: *Santa Teresa de Jesús y la Orden de Predicadores.* Ávila, 1909.

157 Martínez, G.: "La mística española y Santa Teresa de Jesús" and "Santa Teresa de Jesús: la enamorada," in *España y América*, 1924, Vol. XXII, pp. 3-15, 81-92, 241-52, 321-30.

158 Maw, M. B.: *Buddhist Mysticism.* A study based upon a comparison with the mysticism of St. Theresa and Juliana of Norwich. Bordeaux, 1924.

159 Melgar y Abreu, Bernardino de: *Fray Jerónimo Gracián de la Madre de Dios, insigne coautor de la Reforma de Santa Teresa de Jesús.* Discurso leído ante la Real Academia de la Historia. M., 1918.

160 Miguel Angel, P.: "La Vie Franciscaine, etc." See *S.S.M.*, I. 433 (No. 390). [Osuna's influence upon St. Teresa's *Moradas.*]

161 Mir, Miguel: *Santa Teresa de Jesús.* Su vida, su espíritu, sus fundaciones. M., 1912. 2 vols.

162 Morel-Fatio, Alfred: "Les Lectures de Sainte Thérèse", in *Bulletin Hispanique*, 1908, pp. 17-67.

163 Morel-Fatio, Alfred: "Les deux premières éditions des oeuvres de Sainte Thérèse." In *Bulletin Hispanique*, 1908, pp. 87-94.

164 Morel-Fatio, Alfred: "Nouvelles études sur Sainte Thérèse". In *Journal des Savants*, 1911, pp. 97-104.

165 Mullany, Katherine Frances: *Teresa of Avila, the woman.* New York, 1929.

166 Norero, H.: *L'Union mystique chez Sainte Thérèse.* Macon, 1905.

167 Nóvoa Santos, R.: *Patografía de Santa Teresa de Jesús y el instinto de la muerte.* M., 1932.

168 Peers, E. Allison: *Spanish Mysticism, a Preliminary Survey.* L., 1924, pp. 23-6, 98-108, 211-9.

169 Peers, E. Allison: *Studies of the Spanish Mystics.* L., 1927, 1930. 2 vols. [Vol. I, pp. 133-225: Study of St. Teresa; Vol. I, pp. 433-42 and Vol. II, p. 399: Bibliography].

170 Pidal y Mon, A.: *Doña Isabel la Católica y Santa Teresa de Jesús.* Paralelo entre una reina y una santa. M., 1913. [A lecture].

171 Ribera, Francisco de: *Vida de Santa Teresa de Jesús*, Nueva edición aumentada con una introducción, copiosas notas y apéndices por el P. Jaime Pons. B., 1908.

172 Ríos de Lampérez, B. de los: *Influencia de la mística, de Santa Teresa singularmente, sobre nuestra grande arte nacional.* M., 1913.

173 Rodríguez Baños, P. Fr. Tomás: "Analogías entre San Agustín y Santa Teresa", in *Revista Agustiniana*, Vol. V, 1883, pp. 103-12, 204-16, 324-38, 435-43, 521-36; Vol. VI, 1883, pp. 17-24, 116-24, 231-8, 322-30, 433-8. Reprinted as a separate work (174) Valladolid, 1883.

175 Rousselot, P.: *Les Mystiques espagnols.* P., 1867. Pp. 308-78.

176 Salaverría, J. M.: *Santa Teresa de Jesús.* M., 1921.

177 Salaverría, J. M.: *Retrato de Santa Teresa.* M., 1939. [Revised edition of No. 176.]

178 Sánchez Moguel, A.: *El lenguaje de Santa Teresa de Jesús.* Juicio comparativo de sus escritos con los de San Juan de la Cruz y otros clásicos de su época. M., 1915.

179 Sánchez, Juan M.: *Las Cuatro Primeras Ediciones de los escritos de Santa Teresa.* Salamanca, 1916 [Reprint of an article].

180 *Santa Teresa de Jesús en el 4° centenario de su nacimiento*. Conferencias. B., 1916.
181 Sanvert, P. A.: *Sainte Thérèse. Etude d'âme*. P., 1902.
182 Savignol, M. J.: *Sainte Thérèse de Jésus, sa vie, son esprit, son oeuvre*. Toulouse, 1936.
183 Savignol, M. J.: *Sainte Thérèse de Jésus et l'Ordre de Saint-Dominique. Etude historique*. Toulouse, 1936.
184 Silverio de Santa Teresa, P.: *Santa Teresa de Jesús, síntesis suprema de la raza*. M., 1939.
185 Swainson, W. P.: *Christian Mystics. Theresa of Avila*. L., 1903.
186 Symons, Arthur: " The poetry of Santa Teresa and San Juan de la Cruz ", in *Contemporary Review*, 1899, Vol. LXXV, pp. 524–51.
187 Tamayo, J.: *Ideas pedagógicas de Santa Teresa. Notas para su estudio*. Jaén, 1930.
188 Truc, G.: *Les Mystiques espagnols: Sainte Thérèse et Jean de la Croix*. P., 1921.
189 Urbano, P. Luis: *Las analogías predilectas de Santa Teresa de Jesús*. M., 1925.
190 Virnich, M. R.: *Teresa von Avila*. Einsiedeln, 1934.
191 Whyte, Alexander: *Santa Teresa: an appreciation*. With some of the best passages of the Saint's writings. Edinburgh, L., 1897.
192 Wilkens, C. A.: " Zur Geschichte der Spanischen Mystik, Teresa de Jesus ". In *Zeitschrift fur wissenschaftliche Theologie*, 1862, pp. 113–80.
193 Wilson, James M.: *Three Lectures on St. Theresa*. L., 1912.
194 Yepes, Diego de: *Vida de Santa Teresa*. M., 1615.
195 Zimmerman, Fr. Benedict: *Carmel in England*. A history of the English Mission of the Discalced Carmelites, 1615 to 1849, drawn from documents preserved in the archives of their order. L., 1899.
196 Zöckler, O.: *Petrus von Alcantara, Theresa von Avila und Johannes vom Kreuze*. Ein Beitrag zur Geschichte der mönchisch-clerikalen Contra-Reformation Spaniens im 16 Jahrhundert. Leipzig, 1864–5.
197 Zugasti, J. A.: *Santa Teresa y la Compañía de Jesús*. Estudio histórico-crítico. M., 1914 [2nd ed., corrected].

INDICES

I. SUBJECT-INDEX TO THE WORKS OF ST. TERESA

(*Note.*—This index and those which follow have been made by the editor of the present edition and cover the whole of the text and introductions. In the subject-index anything approaching exhaustiveness is of course impossible to attain within small compass, since such themes as Love, Prayer, Rapture, Union occur on hundreds of pages. For this reason, the italicized cross-references should be consulted freely. References to the life and character of St. Teresa, and to related subjects, should be sought in Index IV, *sub* "Teresa of Jesus, St.", while further light on the Saint may be gained by consulting the appropriate headings of Index I.)

Abandonment of the soul to God, I, 101, 318; II, 299; III, 279–81
Absorption (*Quiet, Rapture, Suspension, Union*), III, 24, 26, 28, 32
Active and contemplative lives, II, 72–6, 129, 158, 344–50, 396; III, 22–3, 326, 338
Aridity (*Detachment, Temptations, Trials*), I, 57, 66–8, 70, 71, 93, 141, 160, 164, 182, 195, 306, 319, 333; II, 216, 217, 221, 223–9, 242, 273, 280, 341
Attachment, *v. Detachment, Relatives*
Awakening of the soul by God, II, 275–86, 340

Beginners in prayer (*Mansions (First), Meditation, Prayer, Waters (First)*), I, 65, 66, 69, 79–80, 81–2, 86, 94, 113, 143; II, 347
Betrothal, Spiritual (*Kiss, Mansions (Fifth), Marriage, Union, Waters (Fourth)*), II, 253–8, 264–8, 269, 331, 341, 387–90. Spiritual Betrothal and Spiritual Marriage, II, 264–5, 334–5

Cherubim, I, 192, 288
Communion, *v. Sacrament of the Altar*
Confessors, *v. Directors.* Trials of the soul with confessors, II, 272–5, 283, 298, 317–18
Consolations, Spiritual (*Devotions, Love, Rapture*), I, 52, 57, 58, 68, 70, 71, 93, 141, 142, 231, 261, 285, 346, 348; II, 51, 70, 72, 75, 80, 164, 165, 170, 171, 216, 320. Consolations and Prayer of Quiet, II, 236. Consolations and spiritual sweetness, II, 227–8, 230, 239
Constitutions of St. Teresa, III, 206–11, 219–38, 246
Contemplation, *v. Meditation, Mental Prayer*
Contemplatives and actives, *v. Active and contemplative lives*
Courage, I, 64, 166; II, 72, 86, 99, 159–60, 216, 294, 295, 297, 328; III, 3

Detachment, I, 121, 213, 269, 296, 315, 317; II, 37–9, 42–6, 56–7, 63, 166, 225, 254, 255; III, 17, 50, 258
Devil, Appearances of the (*Temptations, Visions*), I, 204–5, 207, 208–9, 275–6, 281; III, 332, 334. Methods of the Devil (*Pleasures*), II, 211–12, 262; III, 254, 259. Limitations of the Devil, II, 275, 278
Devotion (*Consolations, Meditation, Mental Prayer*), I, 68. Devotion and health, I, 76, 190–1, 314, 353; II, 46, 245–6, 286, 300; III, 27–8, 31–2, 39, 40, 166. Devotion stimulated by difficulties, I, 181. False devotion, I, 160–1. Unseemly devotions, I, 34
Dilation, *v. Enlargement*
Directors and confessors, I, 75, 79–83, 263, 293; II, 19–22, 313–14; III, 42, 250–1. Learning in directors, I, 80–3, 317; II, 22–6
Discernment of spirits, I, 283
Discipline, *v. Mortification, Penance, Religious*
Discursive reasoning, *v. Thought*
Dowries of nuns, II, 56, 59
Dryness, *v. Aridity*

Ecstasy, *v. Rapture*
Elevation of the spirit (*Rapture, Union*), I, 107, 119, 306
Emotion, Violence of, I, 191, 202–3, 306–7; II, 324, 336
Enlargement of the soul, II, 244
Etiquette *v. Honour, Punctiliousness*
Eucharist, *v. Sacrament*

Faculties of the soul (*Quiet, Rapture, Suspension, Union*), I, 89, 96–7, 109, 110, 126,
   140, 158, 172, 293, 294, 306, 327, 328; II, 104, 121, 127, 128, 130, 131, 211, 217,
   233, 237, 240, 252, 275, 301, 317, 336, 342, 389, 398, 418; III, 28. *V. also Memory,*
   Understanding, Will
Fasting, I, 75; III, 222–3
Favours, *v. Consolations, Locutions, Rapture, Sweetness, Visions*
Fear and love, II, 173, 174, 179. Fear of God, II, 177–82, 219, 244. Fears suggested
   by the Devil, II, 174–5
Flight of the spirit (*Rapture*), I, 330
Forgiveness, II, 154–60
Fortitude, *v. Courage*
Freedom of spirit, II, 39, 42; III, 32
Frenzy, I, 96–8, 128, 293; II, 244, 301
Friendship with God, I, 50–1, 139, 163, 263, 316, 357; II, 41, 71, 72, 100, 245, 363,
   367, 371, 372–7; III, 318. Human friendships, I, 46–7, 155, 236; II, 31–3, 87,
   106, 372. Friendships among religious, II, 17–19, 34–5; III, 244–5
Fruition of God (*Mansions (Seventh), Marriage, Union*), II, 340, 342, 415, 416; III,
   29, 260

Heaven, I, 58–9, 173–4, 261–2, 269; II, 114, 115, 124–5, 335, 337. Many mansions
   in Heaven, I, 79
Hell, Pains of, I, 215–17; II, 176, 316, 326, 411, 415. Fear of Hell, II, 244, 303,
   316
Heresy, I, 78, 217, 317, 349; II, xiii, 3, 4, 149, 152–3, 351; III, 12, 88, 364
Holy water, Virtues of, I, 205, 207; II, 373
Honour, I, 14, 63, 129, 165, 212, 213, 214, 352; II, 7, 50–7, 67, 155–8, 168, 225,
   374, 376
Humanity of Christ (*Life of Christ, Passion*), I, 24, 55, 71, 136–44, 152, 171, 179, 182,
   183, 187, 273, 332, 335; II, 304–9, 315, 321, 334
Humility, I, 59, 72, 73, 74, 87, 91, 95, 102, 140, 147, 148, 162, 182, 214, 234, 237,
   238, 283, 285, 328; II, 42–6, 51, 55, 60, 68, 70, 71, 73, 74, 91, 92, 95, 114–15,
   139, 143, 159, 164, 165, 167, 168, 169, 202, 208–10, 222–3, 226, 239, 262, 263,
   296, 319, 323, 347, 350, 379, 398; III, xxi, 34, 35, 42, 44, 258, 259, 317, 326,
   328. True and false humility, I, 197, 198, 210, 285–6; II, 169. Humility of Christ,
   II, 63, 74, 75, 95, 157

Illuminative Way (*Mansions, Waters*), I, 136
Immanence of God, I, 111, 136, 358; II, 114
Imprisonment of nuns, III, 37, 235, 236
Impulse (*Rapture, Union*), I, 330–1
Incarnation of Christ, III, 290–7
Inebriation, I, 110; II, 302, 384, 391, 397, 398; III, 157
Inquisition, I, 7, 226, 324; III, 266, 267, 331
Interior life, *v. Prayer, Life of*

Joys of prayer, I, 58–9
Jubilation, II, 301–2
Judgment, Day of, I, 182, 294; II, 415; III, 75

Kiss of God, II, 343, 359–82 *passim*

Life of Christ, I, 66, 138, 347; II, 76–7, 107–8, 115, 182, 258, 305, 307, 308, 318, 370
Locutions (*Raptures, Visions*), I, 155, 200, 219, 220, 229, 265, 273, 279, 280, 287–8,
   289, 291, 325, 333, 335, 338, 339, 340, 344, 345, 346, 347, 348, 349, 351–2, 353,
   357, 358, 360, 362, 364, 365, 366, 367; II, 279–86, 292, 294–5; III, 130, 167,

171, 185, 188, 194, 204, 215, 316, 327, 328, 330, 331, 360. Nature of locutions, I, 156–69, 172–3. Signs of their genuineness, II, 280–2, 284–6, 310–12. Three types of locution, II, 279. Locutions coming from the Devil, II, 283–4
Love (*Emotion, Fear, Will*), Nature of, I, 247; II, 233; III, 19–20, 23. Love and consolations, I, 68. Effects of love, I, 203. Wounds of love, I, 331–2; II, 277, 324–6, 417. Love of religious for each other (*Friendships*), II, 16–21, 158, 212. Spiritual love, II, 19–22, 26–37. Love and emotion, II, 33. Love given by God with trials, II, 135. Love for God a safeguard against temptations, II, 172–6. Love of one's neighbour, II, 202, 261–2, 263, 397, 399. Love more important than thought, II, 233; III, 19. Love and will, II, 392. Love a prison, III, 277
Lovers of God care little for life and honour, II, 49, 53
Lutherans, *v. Heresy*

Madness, *v. Frenzy*
Mansions, First, II, 190, 201–12, 330. Second, II, 190, 213–18. Third, II, 190, 219–29. Fourth, II, 191, 230–46, 293–4. Fifth, II, 191, 247–68. Sixth, II, 191, 269–328. Seventh, II, 192, 306, 329–50
Marriage, Spiritual (*Mansions, Seventh*), II, 264, 286, 306, 329–50. Comparison with Spiritual Betrothal, *v. Betrothal*. Effects of Spiritual Marriage, II, 339–43, 346
Meditation (*Beginners, Humanity, Life of Christ, Mental Prayer, Passion*), I, 24, 66, 292; II, 87, 257, 305–7, 369, 389–90; III, 28–9. Meditation and contemplation, II, 63–4, 81; III, 18. Meditation and prayer the gateway to the Mansions, II, 203–4, 218. Sweetness in meditation, II, 231, 237
Melancholy in religious persons, II, 234, 277, 278, 279–80, 302, 395; III, 16, 27, 36–40, 42, 143, 243, 244
Memory (*Faculties*), I, 84, 103, 159; II, 128
Mental Prayer (*Humanity, Meditation, Prayer*), I, 49–50; II, 64–7, 93–7, 101, 158, 161, 184, 398; III, 18. Fears and misgivings concerning mental prayer, I, 51–2; II, 94. All are not fitted for mental prayer, II, 68–72
Mortal Sin, II, 205–12, 330, 344, 372
Mortification (*Penance, Religious*), II, 46–8, 49, 75, 254, 348, 349, 370; III, 88–92, 370
Mystical Theology, I, 58, 64, 72, 106

Neighbour, Love of, *v. Love*
Novices, Reception and treatment of, III, 224–5, 230, 247, 251, 304–5

Obedience, I, 231, 299; II, 75, 199, 201, 220, 227, 357, 399; III, xxi, 1–2, 22, 24, 25, 26, 77, 91–2, 239, 257, 266, 337

Pain: physical and mental, I, 97–8, 216, 331–2, 340, 341; II, 271–2, 277–8, 303, 325–7; III, 166
Paradise, Earthly, I, 333
Passion of Christ, I, 79, 138, 152, 154, 320; II, 67, 77, 115, 258, 295, 304, 305, 307, 318, 381; III, 28, 318
Paternoster, I, xli; II, 89, 90, 93, 101, 104, 105, 110–86 *passim*
Peace, Inward, II, 235, 237, 256, 281, 296, 299, 338, 341, 343, 367, 371, 373, 377, 380; III, 144. False peace, II, 364–77
Penance, I, 307, 315, 317, 334, 366; II, 44–5, 60, 170, 211–12, 244, 255, 337, 370; III, 27, 37, 89, 231–8, 340, 370
Persecution, I, 353; II, 229, 339; III, 269
Pleasures bestowed by the Devil, I, 160–1
Poverty, Blessings of, II, 5–9, 167–8; III, 65–6, 289. Foundation of religious houses in poverty (*Detachment, Dowries, Novices*), I, 242, 243, 256–7, 314; II, 5–6; III, 45, 86, 103, 221, 239, 241–2. Poverty of spirit, II, 167–8
Prayer (*Beginners, Devotion, Mansions, Mental Prayer, Vocal Prayer, Waters*), Methods of, I, 24–5, 46, 79, 83, 202, 281–2, 306 ff. Effects of prayer, I, 284; II, 238, 244. Progress in prayer, I, 284–6; II, 50, 75, 217. Life of prayer, II, 16; III, 19
Preachers, I, 100; II, 3, 10, 11, 360–1, 397
Precedence (*Honour*), II, 50–3, 67, 112–13, 156
Presence of God, I, 58, 333, 362, 363; II, 311, 314–15, 332–3, 343

Probation of nuns (*Novices*), II, 55–9
Punctiliousness (*Honour*), I, 213; II, 55
Punishments given to nuns, II, 36; III, 224, 231–8, 243
Purgative Way (*Beginners, Mansions, Waters*), I, 136
Purification of the soul, I, 125, 200, 274, 288–9

Quiet, Prayer of (*Mansions, Fourth; Water, Second*), I, 23, 55, 80, 83–96, 101, 102, 104, 137, 144, 145, 170–1, 183, 306, 308; II, xxi, 115, 123–34, 161, 236, 263, 276, 283, 286, 290, 308, 383–7; III, 26, 268, 377

Rapture (*Suspension, Union*), I, 119–30, 154, 155, 158, 182, 193, 230–1, 233, 243, 258, 261, 270–1, 273, 288, 289, 290, 293, 294, 306, 307, 308, 309, 314, 328–9, 339, 340, 341, 354; II, 139, 246, 286–97, 299, 327, 340, 342; III, 18, 26, 27, 28, 159, 315, 328, 336, 366
Recollection, I, 66, 75, 83, 89, 137, 191, 206, 230, 269, 292, 327, 328, 354, 363; II, 90, 98, 115, 116, 233, 241, 281. Aids to recollection, II, 106–10. Prayer of Recollection, II, 119–23, 151, 240–6
Relatives, Religious and their, I, 359; II, 31, 39–42, 87, 261; III, 223–4
Relaxation (*Rest*), I, 74
Religious, Lives and behaviour of, I, 82, 175–8, 242, 266; II, 11–12, 44–5, 87, 140–1, 365, 375; III, 203, 219–38, 239–43
Reputation, *v. Honour*
Rest, I, 76, 78, 102, 108, 124; II, 342, 346, 347, 403, 416, 417
Resurrection Body of Christ, I, 138, 179, 188
Revelations, *v. Visions*
Riches, Obligations entailed by, II, 368–9; III, 50
Rights, *v. Honour, Precedence*
Rule, Importance of keeping the, II, 15–21

Sacrament of the Altar, I, 87, 138–9, 182, 188, 200, 230, 251, 252, 274, 275, 276, 312, 342, 343, 351, 360, 362; II, 14, 142, 143–50, 151–3, 154, 169, 251, 363–4, 382, 387; III, 12, 13, 33, 48, 88, 93, 133, 355
Scripture, Holy, I, xxiii, 92, 161, 290–1, 322; II, 90, 280, 361
Scruples, I, 200, 282, 356
Security, True and false, II, 170, 219, 298, 373; III, xxi
Self-examination, II, 171; III, 257
Self-indulgence, II, 44, 47, 49
Self-knowledge, I, 80; II, 208, 209, 258–9, 296, 319; III, 25
Silence, I, 83; II, 342
Sin, *v. Mortal Sin, Venial Sin*
Sleep of the faculties (*Faculties, Suspension, Swoon*), I, 96, 328; II, 248, 283; III, 26
Solitude, I, 66, 122, 124, 199, 307, 315, 331; II, 19, 102, 130, 151, 240, 255, 269, 274; III, 3, 24, 25
Suffering, *v. Pain*
Supernatural experiences (*Locutions, Mansions, Rapture, Suspension, Visions, Waters*) I, 70–3, 83, 86, 136, 146, 327; II, 132, 184, 230 ff.
Suspension (*Faculties, Rapture*), I, 328, 331, 346, 354; II, 104, 131, 248, 263, 288, 293, 299, 307, 321, 342, 390, 396, 398; III, 26, 32, 159
Sweetness in prayer, Spiritual sweetness, *v. Consolations*
Swoon (*Rapture, Suspension*), I, 108; II, 127, 328, 361, 384; III, 28

Temptations (*Devil, Love*), I, 74–83, 198–9, 201, 209, 210, 357, 358, 363; II, 1–2, 52, 163–76, 211–12, 280, 366; III, 35, 367
Tenderness in prayer, *v. Consolations*
Thought, Cessation from (in Prayer of Recollection), II, 241–3
Trance, *v. Rapture*
Transport, *v. Rapture*
Trials, Interior, II, 269–75, 346, 347
Trinity, Vision of the Holy, I, 350–1, 359, 361, 362; II, 331–2

Understanding (*Faculties*), I, 72, 84, 90, 91, 92, 101, 141, 145, 201, 328; II, 80, 128, 130, 132, 232, 233, 241, 242, 273, 305, 342; III, 266

Union[1] (*Betrothal, Marriage, Mansions (Fifth, Seventh), Waters (Fourth)*), I, 23, 96, 102, 103, 104, 105–35, 145, 149, 158, 161, 171, 172, 213, 293, 328, 348–9; II, 80, 127, 131, 159, 161, 248, 249, 252, 258–63, 301, 377, 383–7, 394, 420; III, 24, 28, 266. Prayer of Union, *v. Betrothal*

Venial Sin, II, 178–9, 222, 298, 344, 366, 372; III, 91
Vernacular, Books written in the, I, 168
Visions, I, 40, 58, 170, 178, 193, 195, 208, 209, 215–17, 219–20, 230–1, 240, 257, 258, 261, 262–3, 267, 271–9, 286–7, 288, 289, 290, 292, 294, 295, 308, 314, 315, 324, 332, 333, 335, 338, 341, 342, 343, 345, 346, 350, 352, 354, 358, 359, 361, 363, 364; II, 283, 288–90, 295–6, 309, 320, 321, 327, 331, 334; III, 28, 40, 44, 78, 159, 331, 334, 336, 373. Visions cannot be creations of the imagination, I, 183–4, 187–93, 358, 364; II, 296. Treatment of visions with contempt, I, 189; III, 41, 327. Effects of visions, I, 274; II, 310–11. Signs of the genuineness of visions, III, 315–26
Vocal Prayer, I, 333; II, 69, 100–5, 125–6, 185, 207, 278
Vocal and Mental Prayer, I, 92, 267, 282; II, 70, 71, 73, 91, 93, 94, 95, 97, 100–3, 104, 203–4, 274

Waters, Four, I, 65 (cf. II, 236–7). First, I, 70–83, 93. Second, I, 83–96, 158. Third, I, 96–104. Fourth, I, 105–35; II, 300
Will (*Faculties, Love*), I, 83, 91, 92, 100, 201, 328; II, 128, 129, 130, 132, 238, 243, 244, 252, 305, 389. Will given to God, II, 137; III, 24, 279–81. Will and love, II, 392
Women. Easily deluded, I, 73. Weak, I, 150; II, 245, 298; III, 16, 43. Ignorant, unlearned, I, 167; II, 117, 262, 359–60. Stupid, II, 360

---

[1] The reader should note that in her various uses of this word St. Teresa does not always mean the same thing. In this brief summary no attempt can be made to distinguish the separate meanings.

II. INDEX TO THE PRINCIPAL FIGURES OF SPEECH AND ILLUSTRATIONS USED BY ST. TERESA

(*Note.*—Scriptural figures are not included in this index where they are introduced merely as quotations.)

abyss, I, 292; II, 381. *V. also precipice*
alembic, II, 300
amber, II, 293
animal, *v. beast*
ant, I, 213; II, 166, 236; III, 7
ant-hill, I, 288
antidote, II, 217
apple, I, 128, 389, 395
apple-tree, II, 388, 389, 398
aqueduct, II, 191, 237, 239, 243
arms (weapons), I, 117; II, 8, 214, 412; III, 302
arms (of the body), II, 244, 298, 384, 386; III, 282
arrow, I, 191, 331; II, 277, 324, 336, 392, 417
ashes, I, 104, 289
ass, *v. donkey*
avenue, II, 266

ball, I, 199
banner(s), II, 8; III, 297, 309
basin, *v. fountain*
battle, I, 49, 286, 287, 295; II, 10, 12, 32, 37, 43, 48, 74, 84, 91, 99, 107, 163, 164, 210, 214, 216, 217, 219, 233, 245, 273, 343, 347, 365, 366, 380, 412, 413, 415, 417, 418; III, 177, 261, 301, 306, 309
bead, II, 86
beak, I, 284
beast, II, 65, 117, 204, 211, 218
beast of burden, II, 53
bed, II, 411
bed (of river), II, 303
bee, beehive, I, 91; II, 116, 208, 253; III, 42
betrothal, II, 96, 264-5, 286, 334
bird, I, 74, 108, 118, 122, 127, 284, 330, 358; II, 199, 228, 233, 234, 309
blind man, II, 173
blindness, II, 382, 404, 409, 413
blood, II, 164
blow, II, 92, 404, 418; III, 285
body, II, 338
bog, III, 32
bonds, II, 139, 191; III, 297
book, I, 168
bowels, II, 277
branch(es) of tree, I',
brand, II, 346
brazier, II, 238, 277

bread, I, 80, 118; II, 144, 145, 146, 224
breast, II, 336, 384, 389, 399
brick(s), II, 113
bride, II, 54, 55, 96, 97, 120, 254, 267, 290, 297, 316, 323, 336, 352, 360
bridegroom, *v. spouse*
brother, II, 115, 161, 415
bucket, *v. well*
building, I, 68, 153; II, 177, 207, 216, 217, 346; III, 18, 45
bull-fight, II, xxiv, 172
bullet, II, 296
butler, II, 206
butterfly, I, 110; II, 253, 255, 256, 264, 286, 297, 298, 323, 324, 336, 338, 342

camarín, II, 289
cambric, II, 315
candle, I, 96, 104; II, 130, 192, 335
cannon, II, 214
captain, I, 64, 127, 139; II, 10, 11, 30, 73; III, 120, 309
captive, *v. prisoner*
carnations, I, 86
castle(s), II, xvi, 10, 116, 173, 188-351 *passim*
castle, inhabitants of, II, 240
caterpillar, I, 213
cellar, II, 252, 257, 347, 388, 390-5 *passim*
chain(s), I, 213, 330, 419; III, 278. *V. also fetters*
chalice, II, 74; III, 266
chamber, I, 142; II, 222
chariot, III, 270
chess, II, xiv, xxiv, 63-4
child, III, 91
child at breast, I, 80; II, xv, 130-1, 245, 384-5
children, II, 86
citadel, fortress, I, 106, 127; II, 10, 219, 418; III, 236
city, I, 106; II, 10, 206
clay, I, 130; II, 113, 291, 411
cloak, II, 262
cloth, II, 206
cloud, I, 111, 119, 120, 180; II, 273, 311, 389
coal, II, 188
cobweb, I, 112, 129, 134
cocoon, II, 253, 254, 255
comet, II, 276

companion, II, 106, 120, 344
conduit, *v. aqueduct*
conflict, *v. battle*
contract, II, 264
country, II, 96, 176, 202, 296
court, I, 266; II, 114, 118, 203
crest, III, 51. *V. also summit*
crew, II, 294
crown, II, 379, 404; III, 302
crucible, I, 125; II, 238
crumb, III, 42
crystal, I, 180, 363; II, 180, 189, 201, 205, 206

darkness, I, 164, 171, 172, 180, 199, 216, 247, 287; II, 65, 205, 206, 240, 266, 322, 323, 332, 411, 412
dart, III, 282
daystar, *v. star*
debt, II, 139, 154, 183
demented creature, II, 244
desert, I, 142, 154; II, 267, 298; III, 285
dew, II, 389
diamond, I, 294; II, 189, 201, 202, 315
dice, II, 30
dirt, II, 296
donkey, I, 142, 202
door, I, 52, 112; II, 53, 203, 218, 219, 222, 247, 250, 252, 287, 290, 319, 334, 335; III, 143, 305
dove, I, 128, 271; II, 258, 259, 264, 275, 323–4, 343. *V. also turtle-dove*
dovecot, I, 84; III, 17
dowry, III, 307
dragon, I, 88
dream, II, 248, 249, 274, 283, 380, 396, 414
drug, I, 191
dung, dunghill, I, 88, 268; III, 50
dust, I, 129; II, 81, 210, 290, 398; III, 269
dwarf, II, 347
dwelling, III, 288

eagle, I, 120, 130, 284, 416
earth, soil, land, I, 112, 113, 134, 142, 203; II, 78, 79, 135, 227, 300, 338; III, 256, 281
edifice, *v. building*
Egypt, II, 44
emperor, II, 242, 294, 318
empress, II, 43
enamel, I, 125; II, 393, 394
enclosure, II, 267
engraving, III, 287
eyes, II, 107

farthings, II, 31, 90, 185
feast, III, 310
feathers, I, 127
fetters, II, 298, 419; III, 286, 309. *V. also chains*

field(s), I, 295, 309; III, 261
file, I, 213; II, 211
filth, *v. mud*
fire, I, 90, 91, 100, 104, 106, 107, 110, 111, 133, 191, 192, 199, 203, 214, 216, 217, 239, 245, 264, 265, 274, 288, 330; II, 10, 78, 79, 82, 117, 151, 153, 174, 178, 277, 287, 297, 300, 305–6, 324, 325, 327, 340, 349, 363, 389, 409, 410, 411, 412, 413, 417; III, 24
fish, III, 286
fist, I, 191
flame(s), *v. fire*
flies, I, 165
flight, I, 128, 260. 330; II, 228, 293, 296, 342
flock, III, 291
flood, III, 295
flour, II, 235
flower(s), I, 65, 66, 68, 86, 87, 88, 95, 97, 101, 108, 112, 134, 160, 309; II, 208, 366, 372, 395, 396, 397, 398, 404; III, 155
foam, II, 52
fog, II, 92
food, I, 102, 112, 143, 144, 173; II, 57, 66, 124, 144, 145, 146, 154, 254, 330, 348, 364; III, 258. *V. also meat*
foreign land, II, 176
fortress, *v. citadel*
foundation, I, 94, 153; II, 23, 123, 161, 175, 177, 217, 229, 346, 347, 350; III, 45
fountain, II, 77, 85, 91, 115, 127, 138, 185, 186, 236–7, 244, 351, 414
fragrance, *v. perfume*
friend(ship), II, 139, 152, 245, 372, 373, 375, 377, 410
fruit, II, 86, 101, 108, 112, 118, 130, 284, 293; III, 51, 135, 206, 300, 338, 387, 388, 389, 398, 403
fuel, I, 191. *V. also wood*
furnace, I, 215

gale, *v. storm*
garden, gardener, I, 65–8, 83, 86, 87, 88, 96, 100, 101, 102, 112, 113, 119, 127, 130, 134, 142; II, 351
garments, I, 334
garrison, II, 10
gate, *v. door*
giant, I, 120, 142; II, 293
gift, III, 307–8
glass-maker, II, 82
globe, II, 188
goal, II, 89
gold, I, 125; II, 29, 117, 159, 238, 314, 393, 394
gourd, *v. ivy*
governor, II, 206
grandee, II, 93
grass, II, 404

ground, v. earth, garden
guards, II, 95, 203
guide, II, 305
gun, II, 296

hair, II, 63
hand(s), I, 158; II, 176, 365
harbour, I, 49, 77
hart, II, 343
haven, I, 113, 298
heat, II, 254, 259, 277, 306, 324
hedgehog, II, 241
hens, I, 284
herald, II, 315
hive, v. beehive
hole, III, 177
honey, II, 116, 208; III, 42, 268
horse(s), II, 77
horseman, II, 77
house, I, 123; II, 36, 42, 71, 130, 254.
    V. also dwelling
hunter, III, 282
husband and wife, II, 96, 97, 98, 107,
    130

ice, I, 329
illumination, v. light
image, II, 337; III, 287.   V. also picture
inebriation, v. intoxication
inheritance, II, 75
inn, II, 176
interest (on a loan), II, 98
intoxication, II, 384, 391, 392, 397, 398
iron, I, 107; II, 48
ivy, II, 261

jewel(s), I, 59–60, 106, 184, 246, 358;
    II, 117, 138, 159, 297, 314, 315, 395,
    415; III, 308
journey, I, 68, 86, 89; II, 105, 108, 127,
    138, 226–7, 265, 294; III, 32, 284,
    287, 299
judge, II, 272, 314, 316, 411
junk, II, 118

key(s), I, 127, 128; II, 314; III, 35
king, I, 263, 265; II, 93, 114, 315, 319,
    338, 380, 410; III, 308
kingdom, I, 131; II, 107, 124, 125, 290,
    338
kiss, II, 343, 359–82 passim
knight(s), I, 93
knot, III, 284

ladder, II, 288
lake, II, 411
lamb, II, 14, 142
lamp, II, 367; III, 305
land, I, 63; III, 289. V. also earth
laurel, III, 306
lawsuit, I, 285
lead, II, 42

letter, II, 341
liegemen, v. vassal
light, I, 135, 164, 171, 180, 181, 268;
    II, 24, 25, 46, 59, 61, 77, 86, 92, 101,
    171, 174, 186, 188, 190, 210, 211, 238,
    243, 247, 250, 266, 267, 276, 281, 285,
    295, 305, 313, 315, 330, 331, 332, 335,
    337, 370, 375, 384, 409, 412, 413;
    III, 310
lightning, II, 276, 315
lion(s), I, 247; III, 295, 297
lizards, II, 249
load of wheat, III, 91
loan, v. interest
lodgings, II, 130, 176

madman, II, 130, 412; III, 29, 38
manna, II, 44, 144, 216, 388
mansion(s), II, 85, 128, 188–351 passim
march, III, 32
marriage, II, 47, 96, 97, 130, 190, 264,
    329–50 passim; III, 308, 310
marrow of the bones, II, 383
master (in a school), II, 90
master (of labour), II, 146
maze, II, 351
meat, I, 218
medicine, I, 114, 154, 192; II, 146, 254,
    274, 314, 410, 415
milk, II, 131, 336, 384, 399
mill, II, 235
mine, II, 29
mirror, I, 292, 294; II, 337
mist, II, 312
mite(s), I, 132
model, v. pattern
money, II, 124
mote, II, 290
moth, I, 104
mountain, II, 50, 244, 371; III, 17
mud, I, 130, 215; II, 80, 113, 206. V. also
    clay, slime
mulberry tree, II, 253
music, I, 309; II, 105, 271, 342

nausea, II, 57
needle, II, 416
needlework, I, 86
neighbour, II, 213
nest, I, 108, 118; III, 283, 295
net, III, 203, 286
night, v. darkness

ocean, I, 318; II, 96, 420
odour, II, 95, 188
oil, III, 305
ointment, I, 114; II, 65, 226, 383
olive-branch, II, 343
olive-tree, III, 298
orchard, I, 128. V. also garden
organ, I, 213

painter, II, 318; III, 41
painting, *v. picture*
palace, II, 115, 117, 118, 128, 188, 207, 208, 322, 338
palm-tree, III, 298
palmito, II, 207–8
paralysed people, II, 203
path, *v. road*
pattern, I, 95; II, 308
payment, II, 75
pearl, II, 205, 247, 394
peasant (-boy), II, 95, 319
peasant-girl, II, 380–1
peppercorn, II, 253
perfume, I, 309; II, 238, 278, 383, 396, 398
phoenix, I, 289; II, 287
physician, II, 226
picture, I, 292; II, 149, 182, 315, 316, 361
pillar, I, 116
pilot, II, 294
pin, II, 366
pit, II, 165
pitch, I, 363; II, 206
play, II, 87, 116
playthings, I, 165; II, 116
pledge, II, 125, 133
plot of ground, II, 208
plough, II, 68
poison, II, 164, 217, 360. *V. also reptiles*
pool, II, 85, 91, 206, 301
portals, III, 288, 300
portrait, I, 181
post, II, 330
pot, I, 191
preacher, II, 397
precipice, I, 247, 284
prince, II, 95
prison, I, 129, 217, 330; II, 139, 166, 330, 416, 419; III, 277, 291, 310, 311
prisoner, I, 133; II, 116, 125; III, 277, 297
prisoner of the Moors, II, 378–9
prize, II, 75; III, 310
pruning, I, 87, 88
pupil, II, 90

rain, I, 65, 108, 192, 335
ransom, II, 407, 414
refuse, II, 244
reins, I, 191, 284
reliquary, II, 314, 315
remedy, *v. medicine*
reptiles, I, 215; II, 190, 203, 208, 209, 211, 217, 231, 234, 249, 338, 344
revenue, I, 63; II, 75
rich man, II, 224
riches, I, 60, 63; II, 247, 248, 290, 291, 362, 367, 382, 394, 412, 414
rind, II, 132
ring, II, 98

river, I, 96, 150, 174, 215; II, 78, 192, 234, 303, 335, 336; III, 203, 270
road, I, 80, 89, 108, 117, 137, 139, 144, 169, 186, 217, 247, 289; II, 32, 67, 69, 72, 77, 84, 85, 86, 88, 89, 90, 91, 92, 93, 94, 95, 100, 105, 115, 116, 118, 157, 165, 171, 172, 180, 181, 185, 203, 209, 217, 226, 229, 233, 239, 248, 262, 270, 296, 298, 304, 308, 309, 313, 314, 319, 329, 348, 402; III, 16, 17, 19, 20, 21, 40, 51, 65, 89, 109, 114, 117, 172, 298–9, 302
robber, *v. thief*
room, *v. mansion*
root, II, 37, 262, 372
rope, I, 124
rosary, II, 86
rose, II, 366
rosemary, I, 316

salt, I, 284
sand, I, 202, 215, 216
scales, II, 331
scarecrows, I, 247
sea, I, 48, 108, 144; II, 12, 79, 115, 153, 175, 268, 294, 326, 335, 343, 376, 402; III, 283. *V. also ocean*
seal, II, 257
seed, II, 253, 259
serpent, II, 176, 226, 411
servant, II, 146
shade, II, 206
shadow, I, 53; II, 327, 387, 388, 389, 390; III, 297, 299
sheep, III, 295
shells, I, 271
shepherd-boy, II, 237, 240, 241, 362
ship, I, 202; II, 115, 294, 343
shutters, II, 332, 333
silkworm, II, 191, 253–6, 259, 260
sip, II, 184
sirens, II, 12
slave, I, 100, 104, 133; II, 116, 178, 204, 346, 347, 368, 420
sleep, I, 184; II, 245, 283, 385, 386, 391; III, 26
slime, I, 112
slough, II, 209
smoke, II, 238
snail, II, 226
snake, II, 210, 213
snare(s), II, 17, 43, 178
sobbing of children, I, 191
soil, *v. earth*
soldier(s), I, 64, 239; II, 11, 73, 99, 163
source, II, 80, 84, 207, 237, 238, 294. *V. also fountain, spring*
spark, I, 89, 90, 91, 192, 289; II, 117, 151, 274, 277, 282, 307
sparrow, I, 122
sparrow-hawk, II, 416
spear, I, 192, 288

spider, III, 42
sponge, I, 358
spouse, III, 307–9. *V. also bride*
spring, I, 96, 104, 202, 203; II, 84, 85,
  86, 100, 191, 206, 207, 244, 301, 335,
  336
square, II, 290, 418
staff, I, 116
standard, I, 127; II, 74, 159
standard-bearer, II, 74
star, III, 294, 302
step, II, 156, 181, 227
steward, II, 206, 368
stomach, II, 348
stone, I, 164; II, 23, 66; III, 18
stones, precious, *v. jewels*
storm(s), I, 48, 82; II, 102, 153, 175,
  229, 268, 273, 278, 317, 343, 402, 419;
  III, 305
strangling, I, 124
straw, I, 91, 142, 203, 214; II, 29, 155,
  293
stream, I, 65, 96, 114, 180; II, 85, 91,
  206, 209, 335, 336, 338; III, 203
street(s), II, 290, 418
suburbs, *v. streets*
suite, II, 315
summit, II, 50, 244, 371, 388
sun, sunlight, I, 109, 112, 126, 129, 130,
  171, 247, 268, 362; II, 65, 184, 205,
  206, 207, 208, 210, 273, 296, 315, 330,
  336, 394; III, 306
sundial, I, 126
swoon, I, 108; II, 127, 248, 384
sword, I, 295; II, 366

tabernacle, II, 343
table, I, 112; II, 66; III, 258
tabula rasa, I, 318
talents, I, 107
tar, II, 78
tares, II, 92
tempest, *v. storm*
temple, II, 240, 342
tenant, II, 96
thief, II, 42, 55, 90; III, 304
thirst, II, 78, 82, 86, 91, 100, 325, 409,
  414
thistles, III, 256
thorns, I, 113; II, 366, 404; III, 256
throne, II, 117
thunder, II, 276
toad, I, 41, 142; II, 188
tortoise, II, 241
touch, II, 341
tower, I, 132; II, 350
toys, *v. playthings*
track, III, 306
trappings, II, 51
treasure, I, 63, 64, 106, 112, 114, 274;

II, 56, 87, 90, 91, 122, 133, 166, 247,
  248, 290, 312, 382, 414, 415; III, 3, 24
tree, I, 213; II, 37, 205, 206, 207, 338,
  396, 398; III, 299, 309
turtle-dove, II, 233
twigs, I, 316

valley, I, 247; III, 285, 304
vapour, I, 119
vassal, II, 96, 178, 210, 222, 410
veil, III, 280, 305
venomous creatures, *v. reptiles*
vessel, I, 106; II, 82
vine, III, 281
vineyard, II, 66
viper, II, 188, 210, 214, 215
visitor, II, 118
voice, II, 396
voyage, II, 115, 117, 125

wall(s), II, 8, 113, 202
war, *v. battle*
wardens, II, 211. *V. also guards*
watch-tower, *v. tower*
water, I, 65–70, 83–4, 93, 96, 101, 103,
  104, 105, 108, 111, 112, 114, 119, 130,
  131, 164, 203, 205, 215, 309, 333, 358;
  II, 52, 72, 77, 78–82, 84, 85, 86, 91,
  115, 138, 145, 185, 186, 191, 205, 206,
  236–7, 239, 243, 244, 293, 294, 300,
  301, 325, 326, 335, 336, 338, 342, 343,
  409, 410, 414
water-wheel, I, 65, 83, 142
wave, II, 294; III, 283
wax, II, 257, 335
way, *v. road*
wealth, III, 300, 306
weapons, II, 274
web, I, 109. *V. also cobweb*
wedding, *v. marriage*
wedding garments, II, 405
weeding, weeds, I, 65, 87
weight, II, 42; III, 278
well, I, 65, 66, 67, 83–4, 114
wick, II, 335
wife, *v. husband*
wind, I, 202; II, 29, 31, 115, 411
window, II, 335
wine, I, 110; II, 72, 252, 255, 257, 347,
  382–7, 388, 390–5
wings, I, 61, 110, 120, 127, 128, 211, 271;
  II, 114, 209, 255
wood, I, 91, 203, 264, 329. *V. also fuel*
world of water, III, 190
worm, I, 121, 213; II, 175, 202, 215,
  261, 267, 289, 290, 363, 387, 407.
  V. also silkworm
wreath, III, 306
wrestler, II, 65

III. INDEX TO THE SCRIPTURAL QUOTATIONS AND REFERENCES MADE BY ST. TERESA

(*Note.*—The chapter and verse references are to the Vulgate.)

GENESIS

1, 26: II, 201
8, 8–9: II, 343
19, 26: II, 203
28, 12: II, 288
37: II, 17

EXODUS

3, 2: II, 288
14, 21–2: II, 298

NUMBERS

13, 18–24: II, 296

JOSUE

3, 13: II, 298
10, 12–13: II, 286

JUDGES

7, 5: II, 216

3 KINGS

11: II, 345
18, 30–9: II, 306
19, 10: II, 348

4 KINGS

2, 9: III, 289

TOBIAS

12, 7: III, 374

JOB

4, 17: I, 130
9, 10: II, 408

PSALMS

1, 3: II, 205, 338
4, 3: II, 404
8, 8: II, 79
17, 26: II, 347
29, 13: II, 420
30, 2: II, 420
33, 9: II, 415
33, 20–1: II, 120
36, 25: II, 120
41, 1: I, 192
41, 4: I, 123
41, 6, 12: II, 420
50, 19: III, 361
54, 7: I, 128
90, 1–4: II, 388

93, 20: I, 247
101, 8: I, 122
111, 1: II, 219, 221, 345
114, 3: II, 410
115, 11: II, 322
118, 32: II, 232, 237
118, 137: I, 115
121, 1: I, 177
126, 2: II, 206
142, 2: I, 130
147, 3: I, 355

PROVERBS

8, 31: I, 87; II, 201, 407

CANTICLE OF CANTICLES

1, 1: II, 352, 359, 377
1, 2: II, 383
1, 3: II, 252
2, 3–5: II, 352, 387, 388, 389
2, 4: II, 252, 257, 390
2, 5: II, 389, 395
2, 14, 16: II, 107
2, 16: II, 386, 387
3, 2: II, 252, 290, 418
3, 3: II, 306
4, 7: II, 393
5, 1: I, 345, 358
5, 2: II, 107
6, 2: III, 282
6, 2, 4: I, 174
6, 9: II, 394
6, 12: II, 107
7, 10: II, 386, 387
8, 1–4: II, 235
8, 5: II, 398
8, 6: II, 419

WISDOM

9, 14: II, 419

ECCLESIASTICUS

3, 27: II, 218

ISAIAS

24, 16: II, 61
30, 15: II, 420
64, 8: II, 409

JONAS

4: II, 282
4, 6–7: II, 261

Malachias

4, 2: I, 126

St. Matthew

3, 17: II, 407
5, 18: I, 290
7, 14: I, 247
7, 26–7: II, 216
8, 23–7: I, 164
8, 25: II, 153
10, 24: II, 218
10, 28: I, 165
11, 12: I, 90
11, 28: II, 408
14, 29: I, 75
14, 34, 38: II, 381
16, 16: I, 361
17, 4: I, 88; II, 128
19, 16-22: II, 221, 222
19, 26: I, 74
20, 10: I, 286
20, 16: I, 17; II, 247
20, 22: II, 216, 328
22, 11–12: II, 405
25, 41: II, 316
26, 41: II, 218

St. Mark

4, 35–40: I, 164
13, 31: II, 6

St. Luke

1, 34–5: II, 393
1, 35: II, 388
1, 46: I, 365; II, 408
1, 47: I, 348
2, 25, 29: II, 127
5, 8: I, 141
7, 37–9: II, 348
7, 44: II, 328
7, 50: II, 336
8, 22–5: I, 164
10, 16: III, 24
10, 40: II, 333, 406
10, 42: II, 348
11, 9: II, 100
12, 20: II, 368
12, 28: II, 294
15, 9: I, 97
15, 11–32: II, 301
15, 15–16: II, 215
17, 10: I, 141; II, 223
18, 13: II, 129, 343
22, 15: II, 257
23, 26, 28: I, 175
24, 36: II, 281

St. John

4: II, 397–8
4, 7-13: II, 326
4, 13: II, 77–8
4, 15: I, 203
6, 69: II, 408

7, 37: II, 85, 409
8, 44: I, 165
9, 1: II, 409
9, 2: II, 202
9, 6–7: II, 291
11, 16: II, 219
11, 35: II, 260, 410
11, 43: II, 410
14, 2: II, 85
14, 6: II, 218, 305
14, 9: II, 218, 305
14, 23: I, 336
16, 7: II, 308
16, 7–14: I, 136
16, 24: II, 406
17, 20, 21, 23: II, 337
17, 22: II, 261
18, 38: II, 322
20, 19: II, 252, 335, 336
20, 21: II, 217, 335, 336
21, 7: II, 376

Acts of the Apostles

9, 3–11: II, 388
9, 6: II, 341
9, 8, 18: II, 331
10, 34: I, 174

Romans

7, 24: I, 133; II, 83
8, 18: II, 385

1 Corinthians

6, 17: II, 335
10, 13: I, 151, 363
14, 34: II, 355

2 Corinthians

11, 14: I, 86
12, 9: I, 245

Galatians

2, 20: I, 36, 318, 362
6, 14: I, 123

Philippians

1, 21: II, 335
1, 23: II, 83
4, 13: I, 74; II, 183

Colossians

3, 3: II, 254

1 Thessalonians

2, 9: II, 345

Titus

2, 5: I, 344

1 St. Peter

4, 13: I, 360

2 St. Peter

1, 14: II, 420

Apocalypse

2, 23: I, 132
4, 6–8: I, 288
21, 3: II, 343

IV. INDEX TO THE PRINCIPAL PERSONS REFERRED TO IN THE INTRODUCTIONS, TEXT, AND NOTES OF THIS EDITION

(*Note.*—Contemporary writers are omitted, together with most persons later than the seventeenth century. Religious of the Carmelite Order and all saints are indexed under their Christian names; other persons, under their surnames. References are not given to the Bibliography.)

Abraham, III, 270

Acosta, P. Diego de, I, 332

Acuña (de Padilla), María de, III, 49–50

Agnes, St., III, 137

Aguiar, Antonio, III, xvii, 197, 198, 199

Águila, Juan del, I, 321

Águila, Mencía del, I, 147

Ahumada, *v. Cepeda, Dávila*

Alba, Duchess of, I, 190; II, 354; III, 360

Alba, Duke and Duchess of, I, xxxi; III, 97–103

Albert, St., III, 210, 211, 213, 219, 220

Alberta Bautista, III, 30

Alberto, Cardinal (Archbishop of Toledo), III, 209

Alfonso X, King, I, 232

Alfonso XII, King, III, 126

Alonso, (Canon) Juan, III, 185

Alonso, Martín, III, 157

Alonso de los Ángeles, P., III, 213

Alonso de Jesús María, P., III, 212

Álvarez, Alonso, *v. Ramírez*

Álvarez, P. Baltasar, I, xxviii, 155, 167, 185, 200, 220, 224, 228, 242, 245, 257, 272, 273, 276, 280, 288, 320, 336; III, 8, 13, 167, 207

Álvarez, García, III, 131, 133

Álvarez, P. Rodrigo, I, 302, 303, 319, 327; II, 196

Ambrosio de San Pedro, P., III, 142

Ana de los Ángeles, I, 77; III, 8, 45, 46

Ana de la Encarnación, III, 8, 10, 15, 93, 142

Ana de Jesús, Ven., II, 196; III, xix, 95, 133, 368

Ana de Jesús (Contreras), III, 75

Ana de Jesús (Jimena), III, 105

Ana de Jesús, III, 84, 93

Ana de la Madre de Dios (Palma), III, 76, 77, 155, 163

Ana de San Agustín, III, 155

Ana de San Alberto, III, 123, 142

Ana de San Bartolomé, I, xxxiv, xxxvi; III, xii, xv, 169, 179, 182, 191, 205, 345, 352

Ana de San José, II, 356

Ana de San Pedro, I, 304; II, xxi

Ana María de Jesús, III, 93

Andrés de la Encarnación P., I, xlii,

xlv, 5, 8, 304; II, 355; III, 208, 264, 270, 274, 276, 304

Andrew, St., III, 300, 301, 353

Ángel de San Gabriel, P., III, 120, 215

Ángela de la Trinidad, III, 163

Anna the Prophetess, III, 321

Anne, St., I, 303; III, 136, 152, 162, 163, 165, 213

Anthony of Padua, St., I, 139

Antiochus, III, 270

Antonia del Águila, III, 80, 214, 264

Antonia Brances, III, 80

Antonia del Espíritu Santo (Henao), I, 249, 250; III, 45, 62, 353

Antonio de Jesús (Heredia), P., I, xvi, xxix, xxxvi; III, 9, 10, 11–14, 15, 61, 63, 65, 66, 68, 84, 85, 121, 150, 153, 155, 163, 164, 205, 217, 347, 349, 360, 364

Antonio de la Madre de Dios, P., III, xix, 275

Antonio de San José, P., I, 302, 337; III, 213, 214, 262, 264

Aranda, Gonzalo de, I, 249, 256; III, 70

Araoz, P. Antonio, I, 320

Arias, Antonio, II, 197

Armentia, Prudencio de, III, 174

Augustine, St., I, 56, 75, 292, 293; II, 32, 114, 164, 241, 306, 386, 406

Avellaneda (de Cárdenas), Isabel de, I, xli

Ávila, Alonso de, III, 71, 72

Ávila, Isabel de, I, 253

Ávila, P. Juan de, I, 5, 6, 7, 299, 321, 351; III, 82

Ávila, P. Julián de, I, 229, 249; III, xii, xv, 8, 9, 11, 47, 62, 63, 70, 87, 95, 106, 123, 125, 126, 140, 141, 186, 215, 216, 217, 267, 268

Ávila, María de, I, 249

Baltasar de Jesús, P., III, 84, 120, 159

Báñez, P. Domingo, I, xxix, 2, 5, 6, 7, 61, 99, 111, 115, 127, 192, 206, 222, 238, 240, 272, 280, 298, 300, 302, 316, 322, 323, 336; II, xiii, xxvii, 1, 2, 8, 14, 127, 128, 138, 142, 164, 173, 186, 318, 353, 355, 357, 399; III, xviii, xix, 10, 23, 27, 31, 32, 41, 45, 54, 86, 97, 207, 215, 333, 336

Bárbara del Espíritu Santo, III, 118, 142

Barbatian, St., III, 162
Barrón, P. Vicente, I, 27, 45, 111, 117, 234, 322; III, 74, 80, 330
Bartholomew, St., II, 112, 183
Beamonte, v. Beatriz de Cristo
Beatriz de Cristo (Beamonte), III, 178, 180, 181
Beatriz de la Encarnación (Oñez), III, 57–61
Beatriz de Jesús, III, 169, 179
Beatriz de Jesús (Arceo), III, 205
Beatriz de la Madre de Dios (Chaves), III, 129, 135, 140
Beatriz del Sacramento, III, 80
Benedict XIII, Pope, I, xxxvi, 193
Benedict XV, Pope, III, 169
Bernarda de San José, III, 139
Bernardino, St., III, 150
Blázquez, Juan, I, 248
Braganza, Teutonio de (Archbishop of Évora), I, xxxiv, xliii; II, xvii, xix, xxviii; III, 212, 213
Buendía, Count of, III, 49
Buoncompagni, Cardinal, III, 150
Bustamante, P. Bartolomé, III, 115

Camarasa, Marquis of, III, 48
Cárdenas, P. Diego de, III, 150
Cárdenas, Iñigo de, I, xli
Cardona, Catalina de, I, 345; III, 153, 156–62
Carlos, Don (son of King Philip II), I, 345
Carranza, P. Bartolomé de, III, 70
Carrera, P. Francisco, III, 181
Cartagena, Pedro de, III, 283
Casilda Juliana de la Concepción, v. Padilla, Casilda de
Cassian, II, 84; III, 270, 316
Castillo, P. Hernando del, III, 86, 151, 336
Catalina de la Asunción, III, 142, 191
Catalina de Cristo, III, 179, 181
Catalina del Espíritu Santo, III, 169, 179, 186
Catalina de Jesús, III, 191
Catalina de San Alberto, III, 163
Catalina de San Ángelo, III, 163
Catherine, St., III, 271, 276, 302–3, 348
Catherine of Austria, Queen, III, 81
Catherine of Siena, St., I, 139; III, 334
Cepeda, Agustín de, I, 344
Cepeda, Alonso (Sánchez) de (father of St. Teresa), I, xxvii, xlii, 10, 13, 14, 15, 18, 20, 22, 27, 30, 31, 42–5, 77; III, xi, 262, 362
Cepeda, Diego de, I, 219
Cepeda, Francisco de, I, 13, 283
Cepeda de Ovalle, Juana de (also called Juana de Ahumada), I, 190, 212, 221, 228, 249, 358; III, 87
Cepeda, Lorenzo de, I, xxxii, xxxv, 7,

10, 42, 154, 212, 229, 336, 337, 358; III, xvii, 130, 131, 215, 216, 217, 218, 268, 283, 339
Cepeda de Barrientos, María de, I, xxvii, 14. 18, 22, 27, 77, 240, 258
Cepeda, Pedro de (uncle of St. Teresa), I, xxvii, 18, 23, 147
Cepeda, Pedro de (brother of St. Teresa), I, xxxii, 358
Cepeda, Rodrigo de, I, xlii, 10, 11, 12
Cepeda (y Ahumada), Teresa de, v. Teresa of Jesus, St.
Cepeda, Teresita de, v. Teresa (or Teresita) de Jesús
Cerda, Luisa de la, I, xxviii, xxix, xxx, 2, 5, 6, 232–4, 268, 282, 302, 314; II, 94; III, xv, 45, 46, 70, 73, 77, 115
Cerezo, Catalina, II, 196
Cerezo Pardo, Pedro, II, 196
Cervantes Saavedra, Miguel de, I, xxxviii
Cetina, P. Diego de, I, 321
Charles V, Emperor, I, 99; III, 48, 80
Chaves, Master, I, 322
Chrysostom, St., III, 269
Cimbrón, María, I, 253
Clare, St., I, 128; II, 8; III, 363
Clement XII, Pope, I, 193
Cobos, Francisco de los, III, 48
Constanza de la Cruz, III, 155
Cordobilla, Alonso de, II, 380
Covarrubias y Leiva, Diego de, III, 105
Cruz y Ocampo, Beatriz de la, I, 219
Cuevas, Francisco de, II, 195
Cuevas, P. Juan de las, III, 176, 210
Cyril, St., III, 176

David, King, II, 120, 345, 347, 359; III, 147, 169, 281, 368
Dávila, P. Gonzalo, I, 321
Dávila y Ahumada, Beatriz (mother of St. Teresa), I, 10, 12, 13, 14; III, 362
Daza, M. Gaspar, I, 5, 99, 147, 150, 223, 249, 256, 257; III, 207
Denia, Marquis of, III, 123
Díaz, María, I, 176
Diego, San, II, 377
Diego de San Matías, P., I, 278
Diego de la Trinidad, P., I, xxxiv
Dionysius, pseudo-, I, xxxviii
Domenech, P. Pedro, I, 233, 244, 321
Dominic, St., II, 266, 348; III, 334

Éboli, Prince of, I, 7; III, 79, 80, 153, 157, 159, 160
Éboli, Princess of, I, xxx, 6, 7; III, 79–87, 153, 159, 214
Elena de Jesús (Quiroga), v. Quiroga
Elena de Jesús (Tolosa), III, 204
Elias, II, 306, 348; III, 145, 156, 270, 289
Eliseo de la Madre de Dios, P., III, 179

Eliseus, III, 270, 289
Eliseus, St., III, 177, 180, 181
Elizabeth, St., III, 320
Elvira de San Ángelo, III, 155
Elvira de San José, III, 163
Ervias, Agustín de, III, 152, 153, 154, 162
Esteban, Alfonso, III, 9
Estefanía de los Apóstoles, III, 53
Estella, P. Diego de, III, 95
Eugenius, St., III, 148
Eugenius IV, Pope, I, 219; III, 209
Évora, Archbishop of, v. Braganza
Ezechiel, III, 335

Farfán, Inés, III, 136
Federico de San Antonio, P., I, 209
Ferdinand the Catholic, King, III, 188
Fernández, P. Gregorio, I, 220, 221, 224, 233, 245, 277
Fernández, P. Pedro, I, 343; III, 86, 94, 104, 105, 109, 131, 151, 176, 336, 337
Foligno, Ángela de, I, 128
Francis of Assisi, St., I, 139, 194; II, 79, 266, 301, 348; III, 258, 334, 361, 368
Francis Borgia, St., I, xxviii, 154, 227, 233, 320, 328; II, 129
Francis de Paula, St., III, 188
Francis Xavier, St., I, xxxvi
Francisca de la Madre de Dios, III, 143
Francisco de la Concepción, P., III, 23
Francisco de Santa María, P., I, xliv, 302; III, 23, 30, 71-2, 77, 114, 156
Francisco de Santo Tomás, P., II, 279
Franco, Manuel, III, 198
Françoise d'Amboise, B., I, 209
Fuente (de Gutiérrez), Ana de la, III, 93

Gabriel de la Asunción, P., III, 150, 153, 155, 349
García de Toledo, P., I, xxix, 2, 5, 61, 139, 206, 234, 240, 260, 261, 280, 298, 299, 300, 302, 316, 322; II, xvii, 9, 24, 112, 139, 383; III, xvi, xxi
Gaytán, Antonio (de), III, 106, 123, 140, 141
Gedeon, II, 216
Germán de Santo Matía, P., III, 150
Gertrude, St., III, 334
Godínez, Catalina, III, 109-16
Godínez, María, III, 114
Gómez, Ana, I, 258
Gómez de Chaves, Juana, III, 131
Gómez de Silva, Ruy, v. Éboli
González, P. Alonso, I, xxxi, 342; III, 5, 45, 63, 64, 83
González, P. Gil, I, 320; III, 8, 117
González de Mendoza, Pedro, III, 86
Gracián, v. Jerónimo de la Madre de Dios, P.

Granada, P. Luis de, II, 77; III, 164, 221
Gregorio Nacianceno, P., III, 123, 138
Gregory, St., I, 30; II, 1; III, 202, 228, 336
Gregory XIII, Pope, I, xxxv; III, 121, 210
Gregory XV, Pope, I, xxxvi
Guadalajara, P. Diego de, III, 165
Guevara, Antonio de, III, 221
Guiomar de Jesús, III, 103
Gutiérrez, P. Martín, I, 6, 340; III, 86
Gutiérrez, Nicolás, III, 93, 96
Gutiérrez de la Magdalena, P. Juan, III, 150
Guzmán, Aldonza de, I, 230
Guzmán y Barrientos, Martín de, I, 240

Henao, Alonso de, I, 278
Henríquez, P. Enrique, I, 321
Hermenegildo, St., III, 208, 209, 298
Hernández, P. Pablo, I, 320; III, 69, 70
Herrera, Licenciado, III, 107
Hilarion, St., I, 170; III, 271, 276, 301-2, 303
Hugo, Cardinal of Santa Sabina, I, 259
Hurtado, P. Juan, III, 316

Ibáñez, P. Pedro, I, 2, 3, 65, 99, 222, 225, 226, 235, 238, 243, 244, 258, 261, 271, 272, 279, 301, 302, 319, 322; III, 313
Ignatius of Loyola, St., I, xxxvi, 320; II, 198, 266
Inés de la Concepción, III, 30
Inés de la Cruz, III, 191
Inés de la Encarnación, III, 163
Inés de Jesús, III, 8, 10, 15, 169, 188
Innocent IV, Pope, I, 259
Isabel de los Ángeles, III, 31, 304
Isabel de la Cruz, III, 8, 9, 10, 47, 214
Isabel de Jesús, M., I, 340
Isabel de Jesús (Fontecha), III, 8
Isabel de Jesús (Gutiérrez), III, 46, 93
Isabel de Jesús (Jimena), II, 327, 353; III, 93, 106, 169
Isabel de Jesús (Tolosa), III, 204
Isabel de Santo Domingo, I, 283; II, xviii; III, 43, 70, 85, 118, 326
Isabel de San Francisco, III, 123
Isabel de San Jerónimo, III, 84, 123
Isabel de San José, III, 75
Isabel de San Pablo, I, 283; III, 70, 80
Isabel the Catholic, Queen of Spain, III, 178
Isabel of Portugal, Consort of Charles V, III, 80
Isaias, III, 321

Jacob, II, 288
Jerome, St., I, xvi, 19, 65, 267; II, 316; III, 184, 252

Jerónima de la Encarnación, III, 14, 304
Jerónima de Jesús, III, 93
Jerónima de San Agustín, III, 84, 93
Jerónimo de la Madre de Dios (Gracián),
  P., I, xxxii, xxxiii, xxxv, xxxix, xlii,
  xliii, 3, 5, 7, 61, 65, 77, 111, 200, 234,
  240, 253, 271, 272, 278, 295, 303, 305,
  320, 323, 337, 354, 355, 356, 357, 359,
  360, 361, 363, 364, 365; II, xxi, 188,
  189, 193, 194, 197, 198, 204, 205, 218,
  219, 220, 223, 225, 232, 234, 242, 249,
  251, 252, 253, 254, 268, 292, 330, 331,
  332, 336, 337, 354, 355, 356, 357, 359,
  367; III, xiii, xvi, xvii, xviii, xix, xx,
  2, 3, 17, 18, 19, 20, 21, 23, 26, 27, 31,
  32, 34, 38, 67, 84, 104, 117–23, 137,
  138, 142, 147, 148, 150, 161, 169, 170,
  176, 179, 188, 189, 191, 192, 193, 194,
  195, 196, 197, 203, 204, 207, 210, 211,
  212, 213, 214, 215, 217, 239, 241, 252,
  254, 255, 288, 353, 355, 356
Jerónimo de San José, P., I, xl, xli,
  258, 302; II, 353; III, 23, 208, 209,
  211, 219, 313
Jezabel, III, 146
Jimena, Ana de, v. Ana de Jesús
Jimena, Andrés de, III, 105, 106
Job, I, 339; II, 53; III, 281, 324
John Baptist, St., II, 369
John the Divine, St., I, 138, 336; III,
  281, 331
John of the Cross, St., I, xiii, xiv, xxii,
  xxiii, xxiv, xxix, xxx, xxxi, xxxiv, xl,
  xlii, xliii, xlv, 77, 109, 129, 130, 351;
  II, xxiv, 37, 204, 279; III, 9, 15, 47,
  61, 63, 65, 67, 105, 108, 120, 129, 149,
  150, 215, 216, 267–8, 275, 277, 284,
  353, 364
Jonas, II, 282; III, 281
José de Cristo, P., III, 67
José de Santa Teresa, P., III, 304
Joseph, III, 270, 281
Joseph, St., I, 197, 353; III, xxiii, 76, 105,
  109, 111, 114, 129; 130, 134, 148,
  153, 154, 157, 183, 197, 198, 214, 219,
  220, 259, 276, 301, 329, 331, 350, 358.
  V. also Ávila
Josue, II, 285
Juan de Arcediano, P., III, 202
Juan de la Cruz, San, v. John of the Cross,
  St.
Juan de Jesús (Roca), P., III, xxxiv,
  117, 150, 175
Juan de Jesús María, P., II, 65; III, 274
Juan de la Madre de Dios (Vega), P.,
  III, 170
Juan de la Magdalena, P., III, 73
Juan de la Miseria, P., III, 81, 115, 153
Juan de San Antonio, P., III, 304
Juana, Princess (sister of Philip II), III,
  160
Juana Bautista, III, 93, 179

Juana de la Cruz, III, 135
Juana del Espíritu Santo (Yera), III, 75,
  103
Juana de Jesús, III, 93
Juana de San Francisco, III, 169
Juana de San Jerónimo, III, 142
Juliana de la Magdalena, III, 93
Juliana de San José (sister of P. Gracián),
  II, 356

Laiz, v. Layz
Laredo, Bernardino de, I, 149
Layz, Teresa de, III, 98–103
Lazarus, II, 260, 410, 411
Ledesma, P. Francisco de, III, 87
León, Juan de, III, 161
León, P. Luis de, I, xxiv, xliii, xliv, 236,
  272, 301, 338; II, xix, xxi, xxii, 63,
  96, 118, 142, 144, 148, 158, 165, 172,
  178, 184, 187, 194, 195, 198, 199, 213,
  217, 221, 248, 249, 252, 260, 266, 268,
  275, 292, 331, 341, 342, 351, 353, 356,
  400, 401; III, xix, 105, 213, 368
Leonor de San Gabriel, III, 123
Loaysa, García de, III, xviii
Louis, St., III, xxiii
Lucía de Santa Ana, III, 163
Ludolph of Saxony, I, 270; III, 220
Luke, St., III, 198, 201, 321

Madrid, P. Alonso de, I, 71
Magdalena de la Cruz, I, 145; III, 12
Málaga, III, 188
Maldonado, P. Alonso, III, 3
Maldonado, P. Antonio, I, xxix
Mancio, P., I, 301–2, 319
Manrique, Luis, III, 151
Manrique, María, III, 187
Manrique, Pedro, III, xviii, 70, 74
Manso de Zúñiga, Pedro, III, 193, 200,
  201, 202
Manteca, Juan, III, 43
Manuel de Santa María, P., II, 355
María de la Asunción, III, 163
María Bautista (de Ocampo), I, 219,
  283; III, 2, 8, 54, 55, 57, 59, 166, 179,
  191
María de Cristo, II, 195; III, 93, 179,
  353
María del Espíritu Santo, III, 123
María de Jesús, I, 241, 259; III, 106, 163,
  179, 208
María de los Mártires, III, 155
María del Nacimiento, II, 196
María de la Paz, I, 249
María del Sacramento, I, xvi; III, 87,
  103
María de San Agustín (Victoria), III,
  169
María de San Bernardo, III, 169
María de San Francisco, III, 93, 103

María de San Jerónimo, I, 283; II, xviii; III, 338, 345
María de San José (sister of P. Julián de Ávila), III, 8
María de San José (sister of P. Gracián), I, 77, 111, 272, 337, 344, 364, 365; II, 354, 400; III, xiv
María de San José (Salazar), I, 303–4, 353, 360; II, 196; III, 131, 139, 142, 217, 275
María de San José (Tolosa), III, 204
María de San Pablo, I, 77
María de San Pedro, III, 93
María de la Visitación, I, 145
Mariana de los Ángeles, II, 196
Mariano de San Benito (Azaro), P., III, 67, 81–5, 126, 127, 128, 129, 132, 150, 153, 159, 160
Martha, St., II, 70, 71, 129, 333, 348, 396, 406
Martin, St., II, 79, 299, 416; III, 188
Martín de la Cruz, P., III, 71, 72
Mary Magdalen, St., I, 133, 142, 143; II, 109, 129, 147, 173, 304, 328, 333, 348–9, 396; III, 267
Mascareñas, Leonor de, I, xxix, xxx, 56, 241; III, 45, 81, 208
Matanzas, Hernando de, III, 195, 202
Mateo de la Fuente, P., III, 81–2
Matías, Pablo, III, 131, 139
Matthew, St., III, 361, 368
Matthias, St., III, 114, 163, 197
Mayllo, P. Juan, III, 87
Medina, P. Bartolomé de, I, 6, 322, 336
Medina, Blas de, III, 13
Medinaceli, Duke of, I, 232, 235; III, 45
Mejía, Rafael, I, xxx; III, 62
Mendoza, Álvaro de, Bishop of Ávila and of Palencia, I, xxviii, 139, 227, 232, 248, 256; II, 15, 23, 26; III, 2, 6, 9, 10, 64, 83, 165, 169, 170, 175, 184, 185, 186, 192, 201, 202, 204, 205, 216
Mendoza, Bernardino de, III, 45, 46
Mendoza, María de (sister of Álvaro de Mendoza), I, xxx; III, xv, 48, 64
Mendoza, María de (Princess of Éboli), v. Éboli
Meneses, P. Felipe de, I, 323
Mexía, Pedro, I, 280
Michael, St., I, 170
Molina, Juan de, I, 19
Monica, St., II, 32
Monterrey, Count and Countess of, I, xxxi; III, 96
Montesinos, Ambrosio de, I, 270
Moreto, Baltasar, I, xli, xliv, xlv, 302
Moses, II, 289, 331
Moya, Rodrigo de, III, 140, 141

Nicolás de Jesús María (Doria), P., I, xlii; III, xvii, 138, 175, 179, 182, 217

Nieto, P. Baltasar, III, 84
Noe, II, 343

Ocampo, María de, v. María Bautista
Ordóñez, P., I, 320
Ordóñez, María, I, 258
Ormaneto, P. Niccolo, I, xxix, xxxiii, 258; III, 121, 150, 160
Oropesa, Count of, I, 139
Orozco, Juan de, III, 107
Ortega de la Torre Frías, Juan, III, 198
Ortiz, Diego, III, 70, 76
Osorno, Countess of, I, 346
Osuna, P. Francisco de, I, xxiv, xxvii, 23; II, 240
Otálora, Catalina de, III, 140
Ovalle, Juan de, I, 212, 229, 249, 250, 358; III, 87, 97, 103

Padilla, Antonio de, III, 50, 51
Padilla, Casilda de, III, xix, 49, 51–7, 70
Padilla Manrique, Juan de, III, 49
Padilla, Luisa de, III, 49, 50, 51, 57
Padilla, María de, III, 49, 56, 57
Padilla, Martín de, III, 51–5, 57
Pantoja, P. Fernando, III, 132, 133
Pardo de Saavedra, Arias, I, 232; III, 115
Pardo Tavera, v. Tavera
Paul, St., I, xvi, 74, 123, 133, 139, 151, 179, 189, 267, 318, 344, 352, 353, 362, 363; II, 173, 183, 223, 260, 317, 331, 335, 341, 345, 355, 385, 388; III, 51, 103, 150, 191, 202, 221, 226, 267, 327, 334, 369, 376
Paul V, Pope, I, xxxvi
Paula, St., III, 252
Paulinus of Nola, St., II, 379
Pedro de la Purificación, P., III, 189, 199, 353
Pérez Nueros, P. Bartolomé, I, 321
Peter, St., I, 75, 88, 116, 141, 170, 189, 361; II, 112, 128, 222, 304, 345, 376; III, 51, 159, 327
Peter of Alcántara, St., I, xxviii, 1, 171, 176–7, 194, 195, 196, 197, 202, 221, 238, 243, 248, 249, 257, 279, 293, 301, 302, 321; II, 77, 242, 301, 380; III, 33, 102, 164, 221, 329
Peter Martyr, St., I, 235
Petronila de San Andrés, III, 78
Philip, St., III, 378
Philip II, King, I, xxx, xxxi, xxxii, xxxiv, xlii, 227, 322, 345; II, xvii; III, xvii, 5, 53, 81, 121, 122, 126, 142, 151, 160, 175, 176, 179
Philip III, King, III, 53
Pimentel, María, III, 96
Pinel, María, I, 258
Pino, Jerónimo del, III, 200
Piña, P., III, 157
Pius IV, Pope, I, 248; III, 207

Pius V, Pope, III, 5
Pizarro, Gonzalo, III, 184
Porras, P., III, 168
Prádanos, P. Juan de, I, 138, 151, 153, 321
Puente, P. Luis de la, I, 185

Quesada, Teresa de, III, 31
Quiroga, Elena de, III, 13, 14
Quiroga, Cardinal, III, 304

Ramírez, Alonso (Álvarez), III, 69, 70, 71-4
Ramírez, Martín, III, 69, 70, 76
Ramírez (de Ortiz), Francisca, III, 76
Rebecca, III, 321
Reinoso, (Canon) Jerónimo, III, 168, 169, 172, 174, 175
Ribera, Canon (of Palencia), III, 179, 182
Ribera, P. Francisco de, I, xlii, 11, 20, 30, 234, 295, 302, 303, 304, 305, 315, 338, 339, 340, 344, 349, 352, 359, 360, 362; II, 188, 193, 195, 196, 197, 199, 219, 220, 223, 400; III, xviii, xix, 13, 74, 123, 142, 170, 209, 344
Ripalda, P. Jerónimo, I, 6, 320, 336; III, xvi, xxii, 50, 148, 167
Rodríguez de Sandoval, Sancho, III, 109
Rodríguez de Santa Cruz, (Canon) Juan, III, 174
Rojas, Cristóbal de, III, 179
Rojas, Juan de, III, 152
Rojas y Sandoval, Cristóbal de, III, 123
Rossi, P. v. Rubeo
Rubeo, P. Juan Bautista (General of the Carmelite Order), I, xxix, xxxii, xxxiii, xxxiv; III, 5-7, 63, 83, 84-5, 104, 108, 121, 128, 146, 147, 149, 207, 208, 209, 210, 341, 364
Ruiz de Castro, Hernán, III, 187
Ruysbroeck, Jan van, I, xxxviii

Salazar, P. Ángel de, I, xxxiv, 220, 244, 251, 253, 255, 258, 277; III, 5, 63, 64, 83, 87, 147, 151, 153, 207, 344
Salazar, P. Gaspar de, I, xxviii, 227, 228, 233, 235, 238, 272, 320
Salcedo, Francisco de, I, 5, 99, 147, 150, 248, 249, 256, 257, 343; III, 215-16, 266-7
Salinas, P. Juan de, I, 323
Salinas, (Canon) Martín Alonso de, III, 169, 174, 191, 193
Samuel, III, 321
Sánchez de Cepeda, Alonso, v. Cepeda
Sandoval, María de, III, 109
Santander, P. Luis de, I, 320
Santotis, P. Cristóbal de, III, 200
Saul, II, 259, 319
Sebastian, St., III, 113, 114

Sebastián de Jesús, P., III, 186
Sega, P. Filippo, I, xxxiii, xxxiv; III, 150, 151, 153, 179, 344
Sigismund II of Poland, King, III, 81
Simeon, II, 127
Sobrino, Francisco, III, xvii, xviii
Solomon, II, 342, 345
Soto de Salazar, P. Francisco (Inquisitor, Bishop of Salamanca), I, 3, 5, 295
Suárez, P. Juan, I, 320
Suárez, Juana, I, 18
Suárez de Fuente, María, III, 9, 11

Tamayo, III, 170
Tapia, III, 284
Tavera, Cardinal Pardo de, III, 115
Tello Girón, Gómez, III, 71
Tendilla, Count of, III, 151
Teresa de la Columna, III, 8, 9
Teresa (or Teresita) de Jesús (niece of St. Teresa,) I, xxxvi, 221, 304, 337, 358; III, 191, 205, 311, 312, 362
TERESA OF JESUS, ST.
    LIFE. Childhood at Ávila, I, xlii, 10-17. Adolescence, I, 17-19. Enters the Convent of the Incarnation, I, 20, 355. Ill-health, I, 22, 26, 29-34, 42, 76, 268, 296; II, 199, 234; III, 87, 344, 352-61, passim. Ceases prayer, I, 42-3, 40-9. Second conversion, I, 54 ff., 116-17. Persecutions, I, 115, 198, 209, 221 ff. 287, 315, 316, 363; III, 344-7. Contact with the Society of Jesus, I, 145 ff., 185, 226-8, 245. Transverberation of her heart, I, 192-3. Contact with St. Peter of Alcántara, I, 194-7, 243, 248, 257. Foundation of St. Joseph's, Ávila, I, 219-20, 221-61; II, 3-5. Her life at St. Joseph's, I, 297-8; III, 1. Her penances, I, 307, 315, 317, 334, 366. Her subsequent foundations, III, 7, 15, 44-205 (v. also under places in Index V). Descriptions of her travels, III, xii-xvi, 190, 350-1, 366. Her last days, III, 352-61. Her method of prayer, I, 54-5; II, 69; III, 340-1
    WORKS. Writing of the Life, I, 1-7, 60-1, 298-300; of the Relations, I, 301-57; of the Way of perfection, I, 322; II, xiii-xix; of the Interior Castle, II, 187-96; of the Conceptions, II, 352-5; of the Exclamations, II, 400-1; of the Foundations, III, xvi-xvii; of the Constitutions, III 206-8; of the other minor works, III, 211-16. Style, I, xiv-xxii, 64; II, 68, 186, 189, 199, 207; III, xxii, 371-3. Conditions under which she wrote, II, 59, 189, 234, 236; III, xxiii, 266. Method in writing, II, 199, 207. Digressions, II, 9, 221, 291. Use of Scripture, I, 92, 161, 290-1, 322; II, 90, 280, 361. Verse, III, 271-4.

CHARACTER.[1] Affability, III, xv, 363. Charity, III, 338, 365. Courtesy, III, 365. Determination, III, xi. Dignity, III, 363. Faith, III, 364–5. Gloominess, Dislike of, III, 351. "Hardness of heart", II, 300. Hopefulness, III, 365. Humility, I, 57; III, 326–8, 341, 348. Impetuosity, I, 317. "Incompetence", I, 82. Industry, III, 366. "Ignorance", I, 181, 214. Laughter, I, 252, 263, 315; II, 369. Love for God, III, 365. Mortification, III, 367. Naturalness, III, 365. Obedience, III, 336. Patience, I, 30; III, 336, 359. Poverty, Love of, III, 366. Reading, Fondness for, I, 308. Sermons, Fondness for, I, 53. "Silly way" with God, I, 235. Simplicity, III, 363, 365. Stoutness of heart, I, 317. "Stupidity", I, 64, 79, 181, 264, 342; II, 199, 202, 362, 363; III, xxiii. "Unemotional", II, 300. "Weakness of memory", I, 91, 214; II, 199, 236; III, xxiii, 128, 132. Reflection of her character in her daughters, III, 369–71. St. Teresa and her detractors, I, 315, 316, 324, 336. St. Teresa and her relatives, I, 315, 359. St. Teresa and the poor, I, 314; III, 357. St. Teresa as a mystic, I, xxxvii–xl.

Thomas Aquinas, St., III, 334

Tobias, III, 374

Toledo, M. Ana de, I, xxxiii

Toledo, Luis de, III, 67

Tolosa (de Maláiz), Catalina de, III, 186, 187, 188, 189, 191, 193, 195, 200, 201, 202, 203, 204, 205, 352

Tomás de Aquino, P., II, 197, 198

Tomás de Jesús, P., I, 302

Tomasina Bautista, III, 103, 191

Torres, Francisco de, III, 157

Toscano, P. Sebastián, I, 56

Tostado, P. Jerónimo, I, xxxiii, xxxiv

Uceda, Count of, I, 248

Ulloa, Guiomar de, I, 99, 154, 194, 219, 230, 241, 243, 249; III, 331

Ulloa, P. Miguel de, III, 128, 147

Ursula, St., II, 266; III, 90

Ursula de los Santos (Revilla), I, 249, 250

Valdés, Fernando de, I, 168

Vargas, P. Francisco, III, 121

Vázquez, P. Dionisio, I, 185, 227

Vázquez, Luis, III, 279

Vázquez del Mármol, Juan, I, 305, 306

Vega, Juan de, III, 170

Vega, Suero de, III, 170

Vela, Cristóbal, Archbishop of Burgos, III, 184, 185, 187, 189, 191, 192, 193, 194, 195, 197, 200, 201, 202, 203, 204, 352, 355, 356, 358, 359, 360

Velázquez, Alonso, Bishop of Osma, I, 302, 334, 336, 365; II, 189; III, 152, 177, 178, 180, 181, 182, 205, 351

Velázquez, Francisco de, III, xvii, 97, 99, 103

Vergas, Ana de, III, 262

Villavicencio, P. Lorenzo de, III, 151

Villena, Marchioness of, I, xxx

Vincent Ferrer, St., I, 128; III, 334

Vitoria, Agustín de, III, 169

Yanguas, P. Diego de, I, xxxv, 323, 365; II, 193, 194, 353, 354

Yáñez de Ovalle, Beatriz, III, 87

Yepes, P. Diego de, I, 5, 11, 234, 295, 301, 302, 349, 365; II, 187, 251; III, xviii, 182, 313, 337

Zamora, III, 165

Zebedee, II, 328

[1] Words in quotation marks are from her own descriptions of herself.

V. INDEX TO THE PRINCIPAL PLACES REFERRED TO IN THE INTRODUCTIONS, TEXT, AND NOTES OF THIS EDITION

Alba de Tormes, I, xxxi, xxxiv, xxxvi, 212, 228, 249, 322, 340, 358; II, 353, 355, 356, 357, 373, 379, 393; III, xvii, 16, 87, 96, 97–103, 104, 106, 205, 288, 300, 336, 360, 361, 368
Albarracín, I, 321
Alcalá de Henares, I, xxix, xxxv, 241, 260, 277, 319, 338; III, 45, 46, 63, 67, 117, 118, 153, 157, 176, 197, 208, 209, 210, 215
Algiers, II, 380
Almendral, III, 352
Alminuete, III, 82
Almodóvar del Campo, I, xxxii, xxxiii, xxxiv; III, 63, 142
Antequera, III, 258, 260
Antwerp, I, xli, xliv, xlvi, 302; III, 352
Aranjuez, III, 81
Arévalo, II, 187; III, 9, 10
Ávila, I passim, notably xxvii, xxviii, xxix, xxx, xxxi, xxxii, xxxiii, xxxiv, xxxv, xxxvi, xlvii, 1, 2, 3, 4, 5, 11, 12, 13, 18, 20, 22, 30, 86, 120, 146, 147, 153, 154, 176, 212, 219, 221, 227, 229, 230, 234, 244, 248, 249, 270, 277, 290, 297, 300, 302, 303, 304, 305, 306, 316, 320, 321, 322, 323, 338, 339, 342, 343, 345, 346, 347, 348, 351, 352, 363, 367; II, xiii, xviii, xxvii, 12, 15, 23, 56, 187, 195, 197, 353; III, xi, xvi, xvii, xviii, xxi, 1, 4–7, 8, 9, 10, 15, 16, 44, 45, 46, 47, 62, 70, 75, 84, 86, 87, 93, 94, 96, 104, 105, 108, 132, 134, 140, 142, 149, 150, 166, 169, 179, 182, 184, 186, 187, 205–6, 207, 209, 210, 214, 215, 216, 217, 241, 302, 311, 313, 314, 315, 326, 328, 329, 330, 336, 337–8, 339, 341, 345, 351, 352, 360, 362, 363, 364, 365, 368

Baeza, II, 355, 364, 367, 369, 371, 373, 379, 388, 393, 398; III, 274
Barcelona, III, 5, 7, 181
Baza, III, 107
Beas de Segura, I, xxxii, 353, 354; III, xii, xiv, xv, 106, 108–16, 122, 123, 128, 140, 141, 145, 212, 336
Becedas, I, xxvii, 22
Béjar, I, 302
Brussels, I, xliv; III, xix
Burgo de Osma, I, xxxv, xxxvi, 302, 303, 334; III, 177, 180, 181, 182, 351
Burgos, I, xxxvi; III, xvii, 57, 166, 167, 183–205, 214, 352, 353, 355, 357, 358, 359, 360, 362, 363, 367, 368

Cádiz, II, 380
Calahorra, I, 339
Canary Islands, III, 184
Canillas, III, 193
Caravaca, I, xxxii, xxxiii; III, xviii, 116, 122, 123, 128, 140–8, 149; III, 212
Cartagena, III, 123
Castellanos de la Cañada, I, xxvii, 18, 22, 23, 240
Castellón de la Plana, III, 5
Cologne, III, 90
Consuegra, I, 354, 355; II, 356, 379, 381, 385, 386, 393; III, 276
Córdoba, I, 321; II, 197, 232, 292; III, xiv, 12, 123, 125–6, 127
Cordobilla, II, 380
Cuerva, III, 77, 274, 293, 294, 295
Cuevas, Las, III, 132, 133

Duruelo, I, xvi, xxx, 62, 63, 64, 68, 214, 364

Ecija, I, xxxii, 355, 356
Escalona, I, xxx
Escorial, El, I, xxxiv, xlii, 7; II passim; III, xviii, 211
Estremera, III, 157
Évora, I, xxxiv, xliii; II, xvii, xxi, xxviii, 17, 36, 118, 126, 134, 157, 212, 213, 257

Florence, III, 290

Gallegos, III, 67
Genoa, III, 5, 177
Granada, I, xxxvi, 241; II, 400, 401; III, 63, 353
Guadalajara, III, 214, 218, 274, 288, 295
Guadix, III, 107

Hortigosa, I, xxvii, 23

Jaén, III, 108
Jupille, I, 340

Lisbon, I, 145; III, 5, 131, 275
London, I, xlvi

Madrid, I, xxix, xxx, xxxv, xliv, xlv, 185, 257, 303, 324, 334; II, 195; III, 80, 81, 93, 114, 118, 122, 128, 150, 179, 208, 209, 212, 213, 274, 288, 294, 295, 298, 339, 368, 378
Malagón, I, xxix, xxx, xxxii, xxxiii, xxxiv, xxxv, 338; III, xv, 44–6, 62,

69, 70, 75, 87, 91, 97, 131, 134, 142, 145, 153, 154, 155, 208, 336, 347
Mancera, III, 63, 68, 84, 159
Medina, I, xvi, xxix, xxx, xxxi, xxxiv, xxxv, xxxvi, 155, 185, 337, 339, 343, 344; II, 187, 353; III, xvi, 8, 9, 11, 12, 14, 30, 31, 44, 46, 47, 61, 62, 63, 66, 67, 84, 86, 87, 93, 167, 205, 214, 269, 336, 341, 344, 353, 360
Montalvo. III, 67
Moraleja, La, I, xxxiii, xxxiv; III, 45, 150

Nájera, III, 193
Naples, I, xliv, 345
Nieves, Las, II, 379, 381, 385, 386, 393
Noharros, III, 67

Ocaña. III, 262, 339
Olmedo, III, 10, 31, 46
Onda, III, 5
Osma, v. Burgo de Osma
Oviedo, III, 123

Padua, III, 5
Palencia, I, xxxv, xxxvi, 303, 334, 335; III, 165–77, 179, 182, 184, 185, 186, 187, 188, 190, 191, 204, 353, 360, 363
Paris, I, 346; II, 112, 353, 401; III, 181
Pastrana, I, xxx, xxxi, xxxii, 7, 229, 345; III, 63, 79–86, 117, 118, 119, 120, 153, 159, 160, 214, 215, 336
Paterna, I, 360
Paular, El, III, 15
Pedroso, El, III, 102
Peñaranda, I, xxxvi; III, 360
Peñuela, La, III, 63
Piacenza, I, xxxii; III, 146
Plasencia, I, 365
Puebla, La, III, 347

Quito, III, 362

Ravenna, III, 5
Río de Olmos, III, 45
Robledo, III, 349
Roda, La, I, xxxv; III, 23, 63, 150, 153, 156, 160, 349
Rome, I, xxxiv, 3, 4, 227, 241, 242, 248, 340, 345; III, 5, 6, 150, 153, 165, 175, 176, 341

Salamanca, I, xvi, xxxi, xxxiv, xliii, 2, 7, 272, 295, 304, 319, 320, 321, 322, 340, 346; II, xviii, xxi, 1, 195, 197, 353, 400, 401; III, xvi, xxi, 5, 8, 36, 82, 86–97, 99, 104, 108, 148, 169, 186, 208, 213, 277, 304, 336, 344
Salmoral, III, 67

San Miguel, III, 67
San Sebastián, III, 304
Sanahuja, III, 117
Sanlucar de Barrameda, I, 358
Santa Gadea del Cid, III, 57
Santiago de Compostela, I, 334; III, 81, 182
Saragossa, I, xliv, 353; III, 218
Segorbe, I, 321
Segovia, I, xxxii, xxxv, xxxvi, 7, 320, 323; II, 194, 196, 353; III, xvi, 16, 85, 86, 104–7, 118, 183, 212, 336, 364
Seville, I, xxxii, xxxiii, xlii, 71, 149, 302, 319, 321, 327, 353, 355, 357, 358, 359, 360, 361, 362, 363, 364, 365; II, 196, 198, 356; III, xii, xiv, xix, 5, 63, 82, 106, 116–39, 140, 142, 143, 146, 147, 149, 152, 212, 213, 217, 275, 336, 342, 362, 367
Siena, III, 5
Soria, I, xxxv, xxxvi; III, 175, 177–83, 185, 186, 188, 190, 298, 299, 351

Talavera de la Reina, III, 176
Tarazona, I, 365
Tardón, El, III, 82
Toledo, I, xxviii, xxix, xxx, xxxii, xxxiii, xxxiv, xxxv, 2, 227, 233, 244, 249, 302, 303, 304, 314, 320, 321, 322, 323, 332, 334, 336, 337, 338, 339, 349, 363, 365, 366; II passim, notably xvii, xxi, xxii, xxiv, xxv, 188, 193, 195, 196, 197, 200, 351; III, xvi, xviii, 9, 14, 23, 45, 47, 62, 66, 69–79, 80, 85, 86, 93, 104, 108, 148, 150, 152, 154, 155, 157, 160, 166, 167, 177, 188, 205, 212, 216, 274, 278, 282, 287, 290, 291, 292, 296, 300, 301, 307, 308, 309, 310, 336, 342, 350
Tordillos, III, 98
Toro, I, 249
Triana, III, 132, 137, 138
Trianos, I, 226, 243, 272

Úbeda, III, xiv, 46

Vala de Rey, III, 156
Valencia, I, xliv, 19; II, xxi; III, 5, 7
Valladolid, I, xxx, xxxii, xxxiv, xxxv, xxxvi, xlii, 99, 151, 190, 293, 320, 322, 323, 336; II passim, notably 195, 399; III, xvi, xvii, xviii, 2, 45, 46–9, 54, 56, 58, 61, 62, 63, 65, 70, 93, 104, 117, 165, 166, 167, 168, 175, 184, 187, 191, 192, 196, 202, 214, 336, 345, 353
Villacastín, I, xxxvi
Villanueva de la Jara, I, xvi, xxxv; III, xv, 149, 152–5, 160, 162–5, 349, 350
Viterbo, I, 303

Zaragoza, v. Saragossa